A Genealogy of the Family
of
RICHARD HOWELL
OF MATTITUCK, SOUTHOLD TOWN
LONG ISLAND, NEW YORK
TO
SEVEN GENERATIONS

I0084390

Dedicated to the Memory of
Sarah Ann (Howell) Booth Pedrick

Compiled by
Thomas H. Donnelly

HERITAGE BOOKS
2008

HERITAGE BOOKS
AN IMPRINT OF HERITAGE BOOKS, INC.

Books, CDs, and more—Worldwide

For our listing of thousands of titles see our website
at
www.HeritageBooks.com

Published 2008 by
HERITAGE BOOKS, INC.
Publishing Division
100 Railroad Ave. #104
Westminster, Maryland 21157

International Standard Book Numbers
Paperbound: 978-0-7884-1653-8
Clothbound: 978-0-7884-7288-6

- TABLE OF CONTENTS -

- INTRODUCTION-

While the origins of the family of Richard Howell, of Mattituck, Southold Town, Long Island, New York, are shrouded in uncertainty, legend and myth, the family itself was of some significance in the Colonial United States and later. Since the principal genealogy of this family, that developed by Wilbur Franklin Howell {1}, is not available in printed form, but as a set of several notebooks which may be found at only a few locations, and which contains certain discrepancies and errors, it seems appropriate to develop a new genealogy of this family. This is our attempt to do that.

Legend has it that Richard Howell was the son of the "Widow Howell", who was wooed by "Peter Hallock" into becoming his wife, and returning to the New World with him, by his promise to treat her son, Richard, as his own in matters of inheritance and so forth. As may be seen from the sources used to develop this genealogy, it is more likely that it was William Hallock who married the "Widow Howell", since it was he who deeded land to Richard Howell. It is also likely that Richard Howell was his stepson, and not his son-in-law, as usually reported, since the expression, "son-in-law", was used in those days to mean what is now meant by the word, "stepson", as may be seen by inspection of the early records of the Town of Southold, especially the documents referring to the relationship of John Conkling to his Salmon stepchildren {2}.

In another version of this legend, the "Widow Howell" is said to have returned to the New World with "Peter Hallock" and her two daughters {3}. From all this, we believe that Richard Howell was the son of the "Widow Howell", Margaret Howell, and that she later became the wife of William Hallock, and the mother of his children, an interpretation of the available information which would seem to be most compatible with the legends of both the Howell and the Hallock families.

The Howells are thought to have descended from, or to have been otherwise related to, King Howel the Good. "..Howel Dda, or Howel the Good, stands out as the most famous of the early Welsh kings, and he is described in William of Malmesbury's Chronicle as "King of all the Welsh". The son of Cadell, the son of Rhodi the Great, his pedigree was traced by a tenth century genealogist to Cunedda, thence to Ann, cousin of the Blessed Virgin. Howell succeeded his father circa 909, and, although subject to the lady of the Mercians, Æthelflæd, and her husband, Æthelred, as well as their successor, Edward the elder, became Lord of the North Welsh in 922, and King of the West Welsh in 926. He attested charters drawn in the reign of Athelstan as "Howel subregulus", in the reign of Eadred as "Howel regulus", and in 949 as "Howel rex". He is styled by Simeon of Durham,

---

1. Wilbur Franklin Howell, RICHARD HOWELL OF SOUTHOLD, L.I., N.Y., AND SOME OF HIS DESCENDANTS.
2. SOUTHOLD TOWN RECORDS (STR), Liber A, 78, 103-104; (Printed records, I, 163-165, 215-216).
3. Augustus Griffin, GRIFFIN'S JOURNAL, 1857, Reprinted by the Oysterponds Historical Society, Inc., 1983, 17-19.

a cotemporary, "rex Brittonum". Stripped of legendary lineage and..interesting fictions.., Howel's best claim to remembrance is as a lawgiver, though the vast code of Welsh laws, which is known as the Laws of Howel the Good, survives only in..Two Latin manuscripts, one of the twelfth century at Peniarth, the other of the thirteenth century at the British Museum, and á Welsh manuscript of the North Welsh Code, also at Peniarth..These set forth that Howel, observing that "the Welsh were perverting the laws", summoned a kind of parliament to meet with him..and that the members thereof critically examined the old laws, abrogated some, amended others, and enacted new ones. The altered code was then promulgated by Howel..after which he..made a pilgrimage to Rome, where the laws were laid before the pope, who also gave them his sanction. And from that time until the reign of Edward I, the laws of Howel the Good remained in force.

The Welsh traditional judgement of Howel, who died A.D. 950, was that he was "the chief and glory of the Britons", that he loved peace, feared God, and governed conscientiously. He married Ellen, the daughter of Loumarc..They had four sons, the eldest of whom, Owain, succeeded his father..The other sons were Dyvnwal, Rhodi, and Gwyn, sometimes called Etwin." {4}.

King Hywel, the father of Prince Owen (Owain), was the grandfather of Prince Roderic, who became known as Roderic the Great. An extension of the family legends tells us that Roderic gave his son, Prince Tewdur, a cane which had come down to him from his ancestors, and which was to be passed down to their descendants. A "John Howel", said to have been born in about 1600, and to have come to Connecticut in about 1640, is said to have descended from Prince Tewdur through his son, Prince Rhys, his grandson, Prince Gruffedd, and his great-grandson, Prince Maradudd, from whom the ancestral estate was said to have been confiscated, by the English, in 1246 A.D. This "John Howel" is said to have brought with him, to the New World, the ancestral cane, as well as a "Welsh Bible", which contained the family records from Prince Maradudd to James Howell, said to have been born in 1790. Further, the "Welsh Bible" was said to have contained a sheet of parchment on which was written a contract between John Howel and Charles Stuart, King Charles I of Great Britain, by which Charles Stewart agreed to pay, to John Howel's heirs after the third generation, one million pounds sterling at $2^1/_2$% interest, in consideration for the Howell estate. The legend further states that, although several of the Welsh estates were restored to their owners between 1600 and 1640, the Howel estate was never settled. The legend goes on to say that this John Howell left a widow and three sons, of whom Richard was the eldest. While Richard went to Long Island with his mother, one of his brothers went to New Jersey, and the other took to the sea, and was never heard from again {5}. As with most family lore, there is a definite element of truth in some of these stories, and probable elements in some of the others, which may be

---

4. Josiah Granville Leach, GENEALOGICAL AND BIOGRAPHICAL MEMORIALS OF THE READING, HOWELL,..FAMILIES.., 129-130.
5. James Peter Howell, from his manuscript, A BRIEF ACCOUNT OF THE ANCESTORS AND DESCENDANTS OF RICHARD HOWELL..., in the possession of Mr. and Mrs. Arthur Howell, Salt Lake City, 1990.

given credence in part by what follows.

In any case, we will begin this genealogy with Richard Howell, who was certainly a historical person. In developing this genealogy, which is in many ways an amalgamation of several previously developed genealogies of parts of this family, we have placed our confidence in the prior workers we have cited, accepting as fact the genealogies they have left for us, unless we have found good reason not to accept some of their information. Also, we have had assistance from many co-workers in the genealogy of this family, most of whom have been cited in the text. However, we should especially mention some, such as Doris Loomis, who had compiled all the Howell entries from the United States Censuses of Suffolk County (NY), and who generously made copies of her compilations available to us, Ruth Lucas, who provided us with other relevant information which we have cited, and Nate Carter, who loaned me his copy of Caroline Grendler's JAMES HOWELL manuscript for copying. Further, we would be remiss if we did not acknowledge the many librarians and historians who have been of assistance. Thus, we especially thank Dorothy T. King, the Librarian of the Long Island Collection at the East Hampton Library, the several Librarians at the Suffolk County Historical Society, including Joanne Brooks, Lois DeWall, Eileen Earl, and David Kerkhof, and the Town Historians, David A. Overton and his assistant, Mallory Leoniak, of Brookhaven, Rufus Langhans, of Huntington, and Antonia Booth, of Southold. Further, we could not have done this without using the considerable resources of Chicago's Newberry Library, the Federal Records Center at Chicago and, especially, the Family History Center at the Church of Jesus Christ of Latter Day Saints in Naperville.

Many details concerning the first three generations of this family can be found in our study, "RICHARD[1] HOWELL OF MATTITUCK IN THE TOWN OF SOUTHOLD, LONG ISLAND, NEW YORK", published in *The Genealogist*, Vol. 13, #2, 131-179, Fall 1999. Regarding that publication, we are indebted to Dr. Gale I. Harris for his excellent editing of the manuscript, so much so that it would be helpful for any student of this family to consult that publication for added information.

A reader may note that we have frequently used U.S. Census data, especially where an index was available. When using the Soundex for the 1880, and later, Censuses, we have frequently not been able to be sure that the entry we found actually represented the person we expected it to. Thus, we have infrequently used later Censuses, hoping that readers might bring to our attention more information on those we had little of.

In offering this treatise, we would observe that it likely contains errors, both of commission and of omission, and that we are responsible for these errors. From our observations of the fates of other genealogies, we would expect that this one will be somewhat suspect until it appears in about its Third Edition. Nonetheless, we offer it, realizing that, if we do not, it will never get to the point where the information it contains is as good as it can be. We hope any and all readers spotting errors will bring them to our attention.

- FIRST GENERATION -

1. RICHARD[1] HOWELL, the progenitor of the Howell family which arose, in the New World, on the North Fork of eastern Long Island, is first mentioned historically in the Southold Town Records, in a deed dated 26 Apr 1675, by which "..William Hallieke..for divers considerations me hereunto moving..doe hereby give grant and confirm unto my son in law Richard Howell of Southold, twenty roods wide of land from North to South Sea, lying and being next unto y[e] lands of William Halliock, on y[e] east side and John Conklin Jun on y[e] west side--and y[e] s[d] Richard Howell doth obledge himself unto the s[d] William Hallock that what land he shall from time to time take in from y[e] comon, he shall sett up and maintaine a sufficient fence and shall not lett said land to any person but shall be approved by y[e] neighborhood-and in case s[d] Richard Howell die without issue, then y[e] s[d] land to fall to John Hallocke he paying for the houseing and fencing." {6}.

Elizabeth Hallock, the daughter of William Hallock, is said to have been the first wife of Richard Howell {7}. While this may be true, it cannot be accepted as proven, since it appears to have been derived from the wording, "son-in-law", in the deed cited above, the will of Richard Howell, naming his wife, Elizabeth, and the record of her death. As will be seen, these last two points refer to his last wife, Elizabeth, who may have been the former wife of John Harrud, who could not have been the wife of Richard Howell in 1675, since John Harrud died on 24 Nov 1684 {8}, or an unidentified third wife {9}.

In the Southold Estimate of 16 Sep 1675, Richard Howell was listed as possessing -

"

1 heade 6 acors land	£24	___	___
2 oxen 1 cow	17	___	___
1:3 yr old	04	___	___
2:2 yr 2 yerlings	08	___	___
1 horse 1 yrling	15	___	___
5 Gotes 7 swine	09	___	___
	£77	___	___ "

{10}.

"An account of what I paid John Salmon for fframing my house, and helping to shingle it.." was dated 12 Nov 1678 by Richard Howell {11}. Among the items listed are "1 qt of boof paid to Rich[d] Clark-- 18s", "Also paid him

---

6. STR, Liber A, 160; (Printed records, I, 317-318); Id., Liber C, 110; (II, 222-223).
7. Charles B. Moore, AN INDEX OF SOUTHOLD, 92.
8. Gale I. Harris, THE STORY OF JOHN HARWOOD/HARRUD, *The Genealogist*, Fall 1999, 13, 178-188.
9. Thomas H. Donnelly, RICHARD[1] HOWELL OF MATTITUCK IN THE TOWN OF SOUTHOLD, LONG ISLAND, NEW YORK, *The Genealogist*, Fall 1999, 13, 131-177.
10. Edmund Bailey O'Callaghan, LISTS OF INHABITANTS OF COLONIAL NEW YORK, 75, Excerpted from THE DOCUMENTARY HISTORY OF THE STATE OF NEW YORK, Albany, N.Y., 1849-1851.
11. Virginia Wines, PIONEERS OF RIVERHEAD TOWN, 42, 44.

408 pounds of porke-- £5 2s 0d", and "by what I paid my father for his horse..-- 3s". This first Howell house stood somewhat to the northeast of the second Howell house currently (1999) standing in West Mattituck. When the boundary line was run south of the swamp, it was found to pass through this first house, so that Richard Howell an additional four acres jogging to the east four rods, and running to the highway {12}. The western boundary of the farm of Richard Howell became the dividing line between the towns of Riverhead and Southold when the former was established in 1792.

On the "Estemation of Southold for Yᵉ Year 1683", Richard Howell was listed as having assets worth £098-00-00 {13}.

On 7 June 1683, John Conklin, of the Town of Southold, sold "..unto Richard Howell of yᵉ same Town, Twenty acres of woodland lying in the first division of Accabauke, and adjoyneth to the said Howels own land;-the said twenty acres is to ly twenty poles in breadth and is to begin (southward) at the highway that leadeth to Sataucutt and to run Northward the sᵈ breadth till the said twenty acres be fully compleated.." {14}.

In about 1685, Richard Howell married Elizabeth (Cooke) Harrud, the widow of John Harrud, as his second wife. She was the daughter of John and Mary Cooke, of Warwick, Rhode Island, was born in about 1649, married John Harwood on 24 Dec 1666, and was the mother of his eight children {15}.

A receipt dated 26 Sep 1685, for £14 11s 9d, "..of her former husband's estate..", from Elizabeth Howell, indicates that Richard Howell had married the widow, Elizabeth Harrud, by that date. A second receipt, also dated 26 Sep 1685, and signed by Benjamin Moore, indicates that Richard Howell had received goods to the value of 3s 3d "..of his wife's estate..". Another receipt, dated 16 Feb 1686/7, indicates that Stephen Bailey had received 40s from Elizabeth Howell, "..yᵉ widow and relique of John Harrud..", for the account of Josiah Bartholomew {16}.

Elizabeth, the daughter of William Hallock, was mentioned in his will, written on 10 Feb 1684 and proved on 21 Oct 1684 {17}.

Richard Howell was listed as the head of a family consisting of six white males and three white females residing in the Town of Southold in 1686 {18}.

---

12. Personal communication, Chauncey Perkins Howell to Halsey W. Hallock, 9 Feb 1920, passed on to Bessie L. Hallock, thence to the Riverhead Town Historian's office. Generously provided by Justine Warner Wells, Historian, Town of Riverhead.
13. O'Callaghan, op. cit., 156.
14. STR, Liber B, 74; (I, 411-412).
15. Harris, op. cit.
16. Documents, CHAUNCEY PERKINS HOWELL COLLECTION, Suffolk County Historical Society (SCHS), cited by Wilbur Franklin Howell, op. cit., xxii.
17. WILLS ON FILE IN THE SURROGATE'S OFFICE, CITY OF NEW YORK (WNYSO), Liber 3-4, 2-7; From Printed ABSTRACTS OF WILLS ON FILE IN THE SURROGATE'S OFFICE, CITY OF NEW YORK, 1665-1800, From COLLECTIONS, NEW YORK HISTORICAL SOCIETY, XXV (WILLS, Vol. I) - XLI (WILLS, Vol. XVII), 1892 - 1908, I, 128-129 (NOTE: *A copy is also available in the Historical Documents Collection at the Office of the Suffolk County Clerk*).
18. NEW YORK GENEALOGICAL & BIOGRAPHICAL RECORD (NYG&BR), XXX, 121 (1899).

An undated document indicates that Elizabeth Howell apprenticed her son, Job Harrud, to Jonathan Horton for a period of three years {19}.

On 15 Jan 1686/7, "..Elizabeth Howell (wife of Richard Howell) of Southold and George Harrud, of the one partie, and Joshua Horton of yᵉ same Towne, of yᵉ other partie..", made an indenture by which "..Elizabeth Howell, doth put out her said son George Harrud, with his full consent, an apprentice unto..Joshua Horton, for the term of foure years and three months..to learn him to read and write, and to teach him the tread of house carpenter.." {20}.

By a deed of 4 Feb 1691, John Curwin, Senʳ of Southold, conveyed, to Richard Howell, "..a second lott of meadow..on the other side of Peheconock river bounded West by John Swazy Senʳ--East by John Curwin Junʳ--North by the River and South by the upland." {21}.

Richard Howell purchased, from Thomas Moore, Sr., of Southold, "..one first lott of woodland..at Ocquabauke, bounded on the West by the land of Isaac Osman-east by Wᵐ Coleman-North by the Sound and South by the Bay:-Also one second lott of salt meadow, in Ocquabauk on the North side the deep kreek, bounded East by William Mapes-West by Samuel Wines..", on 15 Apr 1691 {22}.

On 3 Jly 1691, Richard Howell purchased, from Jabish Mapes, "..two lotts of meadow on the South side Peheconick River bounded West by the meadow of Thomas Terrill-East by Thomas Mapes-North by the River and South by the upland." {23}.

Richard Howell purchased, from John Tuthill, Sr., of Southold, "..three lotts of Salt Meadow..on the South Side of the river at Ocquabauk..bounded..by John Curwin on the West, and on the East by William Reevs, originally Stephen Bailys.." {24}.

In about 1692, Richard Howell made out an "Account of what tobacco hath been sould at home & at the town". Among the entries listed was "Mother Hallock 5 pounds" for £0 2s 6d {25}.

Richard Howell's house was apparently used as a tavern by him, since it was agreed "..for yᵉ exise of all such strong drink that he shall sell in his now dwelling house from the date hereof until the 17ᵗʰ day of may next ensuing.." by James Brading on 27 Sep 1692 {26}.

On 4 Aug 1694, Richard Howell purchased, from Thomas and Mary Mapes, of Southold, "..a third lott of meadow or Marsh ground containing about three acres..on the South side of Peheconuck River bounded by sᵈ River Northward-East by a small brook running into sᵈ River and South by the upland, and West by

19. Document, CHAUNCEY PERKINS HOWELL COLLECTION, SCHS.
20. STR, Liber B, 76; (I, 413-414).
21. Id., Liber C, 111; (II, 224).
22. Id., 111; (II, 223-224).
23. Id.; (II, 223).
24. Id., 112; (II, 224-225).
25. Document, CHAUNCEY PERKINS HOWELL COLLECTION, SCHS.
26. Document, CHAUNCEY PERKINS HOWELL COLLECTION, SCHS.

ye meadow of s^d Richard Howell, which he purchased of Jabez Mapes.." {27}.

In the Census of 1698 for the Township of Southold, the Howell family was listed as consisting of Richard, David, Jonathan, Richard Junjr., Isaac, Jacob, Eliza and Dorathy {28}. "Jno. Howel" was listed separately {29}, while Ruth Howell was listed with the family of William Hallock {30}.

John Hallock, of the Town of Brookhaven, sold Richard Howell "..a second lot of upland in ye second Division at Occabogue..bounded by ye land of Benjamin Concklin East and Isaac Arnold on ye West which..land formerly did belong to William Hallucke late of Southold..Deceased and did Discend to ye said John Hallucke by way of inheritance..", on 4 Feb 1698/9 {31}.

Richard Howell was chosen Collector for the ensuing year for the Town of Southold on 4 Apr 1699 {32}. It was probably during that year that he made out the following account:

"On account of ye several parsells of money collected for ye Governors Levey (sic) by Mr. Richard Howell for Southold:

	£	s	d
60: 17 peny weight	20	05	00
78: Dollars at 5s 6d per dollar, ie.	21	09	00
56: Double bitts,	04	04	06
150: Single Bitts, ie.	05	12	06
20: Halfe Pieces of eight, ie.	03	00	00
YE TOTAL	54	10	06(sic)
y^e remainder is	17	12	02
	70	02	08 " {33}.

Near the end of his term, he was given the following receipt:

"Received of Richard Howell of Southold collection of the said Town for the year 1699. Twelve pounds cash four shilling and eight pence $^1/_2$ of which is the balance of the whole county rate and from y^e town.
This 27th March 1700. In Southampton
Samuel Cooper, Treasurer" {34}.

Richard Howell was paid a bounty of two shillings for the destruction of three foxes in 1700 {35}.

On 2 Nov 1700, Richard Howell purchased, from Joseph Ackerly and Zipporah, his wife, of the Town of Brookhaven, "..a three acre lot of land..at a

27. STR, Liber C, 110; (II, 221-222).
28. O'Callaghan, op. cit., 48.
29. Id., 49.
30. Id., 51.
31. ACKERLY RECORD BOOKS, Book 5, 115-117, in the possession of the Suffolk County Historical Society, 1991.
32. STR, Liber D, 112 right; (III, 163).
33. Receipt, CHAUNCEY PERKINS HOWELL COLLECTION, SCHS, cited by Wilbur Franklin Howell, op. cit., x.
34. Document, CHAUNCEY PERKINS HOWELL COLLECTION, SCHS, cited by Wilbur Franklin Howell, op. cit., xi.
35. STR, Liber D, 8 left; (III, 16).

place called Crane's Neck within y^e..towne of Brookhaven..joyning to ye land..of Robert Ackerly on ye East and ye land of Zachary Hawkings on ye West and South and ye clefts on ye North.." {36}.

Richard Howell purchased, from Samuel Ackerly, husbandman, and his wife, Hannah, of the Town of Brookhaven, by a deed dated 10 Nov 1700, "..a certain three acre lot..being at ye utmost point of a place..called Crane's Neck joyning to ye land..of Zachary Hawkings on ye south.." {37}.

Jonathan Mapes sold Richard Howell "..a certain parcell of meadow being a second lott containing two acres more or less scituat lying & being on ye South side of Peaconneck river.. bounded on ye North by ye said River on ye East by ye meadow of ye said Richard Howell on ye south by ye upland and on the West by the meadow of Thomas Terrill.." by a deed dated 24 Dec 1701 {38}.

On 9 Nov 1702, Richard Howell purchased, from William Whitier, of the Town of Brookhaven, "All that land and meadow next adjoyning to ye highway near ye house lot of Zachary Hawkings..in a place called Crane's Neck within ye bounds of Brookhaven..part of which meadow lyeth within ye ffence belonging to ye said necke & part thereof without ye s^d ffence adjoyning to ye fresh pond on ye Westward side..which..was given to me by my honored father Peter Whitier.." {39}. He purchased another such meadow, containing about ten acres, at the same location, from William Whitier on 15 Jan 1703 {40}.

On 6 Sep 1703/4, Richard Howell did "..let out and lett to farm unto..John Cleves a certain lot of land with one dwelling house..purchased of John halliock..and two lotts of meadow in ye broad meadows and half my meadow near the head of s^d river which I purchased of Thomas Mapes..and..four to six cows..one or two breeding swine..and..a pair of working oxen.." {41}.

Richard Howell was one of "..the men that wrought at the clearing(?) of the high way from the Town East ward to the horne Taverne on the 28th day of July 1704.." {42}.

On "May:y^e2:1705Delivered to Richard Howell upon acc^t of ye town in cash:£1 - 10s for a Barrill of beefe deliver^d to Isaac Osman" {43}.

As "brother howell", Richard Howell was informed by Jasper Griffing that Griffing's Indian, Jobe, had run away, and Howell was asked to apprehend him, if possible {44}.

By his will of 24 Aug 1709, proved on 1 Jan 1709/10, Richard Howell left, to his wife, Elizabeth, one third of his estate. He also left land and the remainder of his estate after all other bequests to his sons, John, David, Jonathan, Richard, Isaac and Jacob. He left his daughters, "Hannah Haughins"(Hawkins) and

36. ACKERLY RECORD BOOKS, Book 5, 117.
37. Id., 118.
38. Id.
39. Id., 119.
40. Id.
41. Document, SCHS Collections, cited by Wines, op. cit., 63-64.
42. BROOKHAVEN TOWN RECORDS, (BTR), Book C, 293ff.; (Printed records, C, 434).
43. STR, Liber D, 9 left; (III, 19).
44. Documents, CHAUNCEY PERKINS HOWELL COLLECTION, SCHS.

Dorothy Reeve, each £20 {45}.

Richard Howell died on 9 Nov 1709 {46}.

Elizabeth (Cooke) Harrud Howell may have died on 4 Mch 1724/5 at the age of 70 (sic) {47}.

Richard Howell and his first wife were probably the parents of six children.

+ 2. i. JOHN² HOWELL, born on 24 May 1670 {48}.

+ 3. ii. HANNAH² HOWELL.

+ 4. iii. DAVID² HOWELL, born in about Nov 1676.

+ 5. iv. JONATHAN² HOWELL.

+ 6. v. RICHARD² HOWELL, born in about 1684.

Richard and Elizabeth (Cooke) Harrud Howell may have been the parents of three children.

+ 7. vi. ISAAC² HOWELL.

+ 8. vii. JACOB² HOWELL.

+ 9. viii. DOROTHY² HOWELL.

Richard Howell may also have been the father of two other children.

10. ix. RUTH² HOWELL, listed with the household of William Hallock in the Census of 1698. Possibly a sister of Richard Howell.

11. x. ELIZABETH² HOWELL, listed by Moore {49} and Craven {50}, as a daughter of Richard Howell, since an "Eliza Howell" was listed with the household of Richard Howell in the Census of 1698 in a position usually given to a child, but who may have been his wife, Elizabeth. If this "Eliza Howell" was a child, of whom no more is known, and not his wife, then this would imply that he married a third time to another woman named Elizabeth.

- END OF FIRST GENERATION -

---

45. WNYSO, Liber 7, 568; (II, 36-37). NOTE: *The original will must be consulted, since W. S. Pelletreau did not give a surname for Hannah.*

46. The Salmon Records (SR), Vol. I, ANCESTRAL FOOTPRINTS, Series I - Suffolk County, N.Y., Published by Albert G. Overton, 8; NYG&BR, XLVII, 351 (Oct 1916).

47. Id., 13; NYG&BR, XLVII, 356 (Oct 1916).

48. Wilbur Franklin Howell, op. cit., 1.

49. Moore, op. cit., 93.

50. Charles E. Craven, A HISTORY OF MATTITUCK, LONG ISLAND, N.Y., 75.

- SECOND GENERATION -

2. JOHN[2] HOWELL (Richard[1]), the son of Richard[1] Howell, was born on 24 May 1670 {51} in the vicinity of Mattituck.

"Jno. Howel" was listed separately from the household of Richard Howell in the Census of 1698 {52}.

John Howell was paid a bounty of eight pence for the destruction of one fox in 1707 {53}.

"John Howels wife Margarit" died on 2 Feb 1707/8 {54}.

By his will of 24 Aug 1709, Richard Howell gave "..unto my son John Howell and to his Heirs for ever all my messuage or farme where I now live and bounded on y° north by y° Sound and on y° South by y° road Lately laid out that leads to Brookhaven by y° way of y° beach and also one Equall fourth part of all my meadow on y° South Side of peaconnek river:" {55}.

With his brothers, David and Jonathan, John Howell was an executor of his father's will {56}. As such, he may have written a memorandum, dated 28 Dec 1709, which stated -

"-Then put aside for Brother Jonathan	£8	7s	3p
Paid to Richard	7	13	11
Paid to Isaac	7	13	11
Paid to Jacob	7	13	11
also paid January 12 1709/10			
Then put aside for Brother Jonathan	6	0	9
Paid to Richard	6	0	9
Paid to Isaac	6	4	1
Paid to Jacob	6	4	1"

{57}.

One of the "..lotts in y° land laid out Decem' 1711 betweene the fresh pond & y° wading river at acquabauk which is called y° fourth dividend of acquabauk lands.." was assigned to John Howell {58}.

John Howell was a member of the Southold Company Number Two of the Suffolk County militia in 1715 {59}.

On 13 Sep 1716, John Howell was witness to a deed by which "..Peter Halyocke.." sold, to his "..brother, William Halyock, a certain tract of land situate

51. Wilbur Franklin Howell op. cit., 1.
52. O'Callaghan, op. cit., 49.
53. STR, Liber D, 10 left; (III, 21).
54. SR, 7; NYG&BR, XLVII, 350 (Oct 1916).
55. WNYSO, Liber 7, 568; (II, 36-37).
56. Id.
57. Memorandum, CHAUNCEY PERKINS HOWELL COLLECTION, SCHS, cited by Wilbur Franklin Howell, op. cit., xii.
58. STR, Liber C, 241; (II, 400).
59. THE REGISTER, SUFFOLK COUNTY HISTORICAL SOCIETY (SCHS), XXIII, #4, 121 (Spring 1998), taken from Second Annual Report of the State Historian of the State of New York (Albany and New York; 1987) Vol. I, 508-521.

in ye first division of land at hockquaboge containing by estimation one hundred and sixty acres.." {60}.

Jonathan Howell instructed his brother, John, to deliver, to Mr. Joseph Hawkins, six sheep which had been in his custody, by a letter from Southampton dated 30 Mch 1720 {61}.

"May th 23/1726 the highway that Leads from John Howells to the beach was Discontinued so far as within two rods of ye west side of Theophilus Corwin his land, and att ye same time a highway was Layd out foor rods wide from ye said John Howells Lands Westward Cross ye North End of the Lotts to the Highway that parts ye pottin Land and ye sd Lotte which Rhoads meet about 2 miles from ye Head of Waideing River.." {62}.

John Howell was a witness to the will of James Reeve, written on 15 Jan 1731/2, and proved on 24 Aug 1732 {63}.

"Att a Town meeting held april ye 4th 1732 - - John Howel, at Mattituck..was chosen.." Constable "..for ye Year Ensuing.." {64}.

By his will of 14 Dec 1733, John Howell left all his lands to his son, Jonathan. He left his son, John, "..two steers and a heifer..", and his daughters, Eunice, Jemima and Esther, "..one good cow.." each. He left his wife, Hannah, "..all my movable estate..", the use of his lands for four years, and one third of his lands during her widowhood. This will, of which he made his wife the sole executor, was proved on 12 Feb 1733/4 {65}.

"J^n Howel" died on 20 Jan 1733/4 {66}.

Hannah Howell was a witness to the will of Zachariah Hawkins, written on 11 May 1737, and proved on 6 Jan 1749/50 {67}.

"J^n Swesey & Wi^d Hannah Howel" were married in about Mch 1745 {68}.

"Hann Howel widow to John" died on 15 Mch 1768 {69}.

John^2 and Margaret Howell were the parents of at least one son.

+ 12.   i.   JOHN^3 HOWELL.

John^2 and Hannah Howell were the parents of at least four children.

+ 13.   ii.   EUNICE^3 HOWELL, born on 11 Dec 1713 {70}.

---

60. Id., 300; (II, 470).
61. Letter, CHAUNCEY PERKINS HOWELL COLLECTION, SCHS, cited by Wilbur Franklin Howell, op. cit., xi.
62. STR, Liber D, 219 right; (III, 378).
63. WNYSO, Liber 11, 392-395; (III, 79-80).
64. STR, Liber D, 121 right; (III, 188).
65. WNYSO, Liber 12, 142; (III, 139).
66. SR, 20; NYG&BR, XLVIII, 22 (Jan 1917).
67. WNYSO, Liber 17, 58; (IV, 253).
68. SR, 86; NYG&BR, XLIX, 154 (Apr 1918).
69. Id., 41; NYG&BR, XLVIII, 174 (Apr 1917).
70. Caroline Howell Grendler, THE RECORD OF JAMES HOWELL AND SOME OF HIS DESCENDANTS, 1.

+ 14. iii. JEMIMA[3] HOWELL.

+ 15. iv. JONATHAN[3] HOWELL, born in about 1720 {71}.

+ 16. v. ESTHER[3] HOWELL.

3. HANNAH[2] HOWELL (Richard[1]), the daughter of Richard[1] Howell, was born in the vicinity of Mattituck.

Hannah Howell married Zachariah Hawkins before 1698 {72}. He was the son of Zachariah and Mary (Biggs) Hawkins, and was born in Setauket in about 1675 {73}.

Zachariah and Hannah (Howell) Hawkins lived at Crane Neck in the Town of Brookhaven on a farm which he had received by the will of his father {74}. Their farm bordered on several properties which were purchased by her father, Richard Howell.

By his will of 24 Aug 1709, proved on 1 Jan 1709/10, Richard Howell gave "..unto my Daugh ter Hannah Haughins and to her Heirs for ever twenty pounds as mony of the Collony to be paid her by Execut[t].." {75}.

On 6 June 1715, Selah Strong and Daniel Brewster reported that they had "..Allso Layde oute on y[e] West side of y[e] Towne for a shepe past(er) begining at the path that goes to Eleazors Hawkins house & so Ex(tend)ing norwesterly to Zachariah Hawins Land.." {76}.

In 1721, it was reported that there was "..Layd out to Zackriah howkins 20 akers of Land In & ny his home land and 35 akers more on y[e] playns aJoyning to Edward Biggs Land which is all his dew.." {77}.

In 1730, it was recorded that there was taken up "..By Zachariah Hawkins a stere come: 2: yere old mark with a crop on y[e] Rite Eare & a hapeny on y[e] uper side of y[e] same & 2 Nicks under side y[e] Ny: Eare.." {78}.

On 4 Mch 1734/5, there was "..Layd oute to Zachariah Hawkins: thr(missing) kers of Land bounded Westward by William Jeane Land in y[e] hills Eastward to y[e] Comans Norward to y[e] Rode Leadeing to John woods Landes southward to Lande of thomas Hulc: i(n) lew of land Sould by the Trustees {79}.

Zachariah Hawkins signed a protest against laying out lands that were set apart as sheep pastures on 14 Feb 1737/8 {80}.

---

71. Wines, op. cit., 43.
72. Thomas H. Donnelly, The Hawkins Association Newsletter, 11, #2, 125 (Summer 1989).
73. Ralph Clymer Hawkins, A HAWKINS GENEALOGY, 11.
74. Id.
75. WNYSO, Liber 7, 568; (II, 36-37).
76. BTR, Book C, 57; (C, 66).
77. Id., 86; (C, 109).
78. Id., 1; (C, 6).
79. Id., 120; (C, 164).
80. Id., 132; (C, 187-188).

At a meeting of the Trustees of the Town of Brookhaven on 27 Feb 1737/8, it was "..Voted that Zachariah Hawkins shall haue a Rode to his meddow tow Rod wide Runing by ye End of ye land that was John Satterlys & by ye lande that was Mr Nickalls & soe to ye foot of ye west meddow Beach & from ye Sd Beach to Consienc meddow.." {81}.

The first lot laid out at west Meadow Neck was bounded by the land of "Zachariah Hawins" on the west. Six lots were bounded on the west by "ye west medow or apon a nother line Run from Zacariah Hakeins lodg fenc nere his Bound tree by ye High way that goes to Craneneck..". These lots were "..not to hinder High wayes or Rodes..", including the "..high way that leads to Zacharish Hawkans..", which was to "..run by the old field fence to the Said Hawkins land..", as recorded on 4 Apr 1738 {82}.

At a meeting of the Trustees of the Town of Brookhaven on 7 Jan 1739/40, it was decided that Eleazer Hawkins was to leave a "..highway Twenty foot wide..between his fifty acres that was formerly JoSeph Smiths and his Twenty acre lot laid out on Zachariah Hawkins Righ(t).." {83}.

By his will of 11 May 1737, proved on 6 Jan 1749/50, Zachariah Hawkins left to his "..wife Hannah the use of.." his "..dwelling house, barn, and orchard, and all lands and meadows, till my grandson Zachariah is of age.." This grandson was then "..strictly obliged, carefully and respectfully to provide for and maintain his grand mother, or if she thinks fit, to let her have the use of $^1/_2$.." of his farm and lands in Crane Neck, Wood island, with the meadow adjoining "..and the use of.." his "..house and barn, and all.." his "..equalizing lands and meadows, and $^1/_2$ of $^2/_3$ of a right of commonage..". She also received all his movable estate and all his division lands with the power to sell, and was named executor of this will {84}.

Zachariah and Hannah (Howell) Hawkins were the parents of at least one son.

     i.   ZACHARIAH HAWKINS, born in about 1695 {85}.

4. DAVID^2 HOWELL (Richard^1), the son of Richard^1 Howell, was born in about Nov 1676 in the vicinity of Mattituck.

David Howell was listed among the members of his father's household in the Census of 1698 {86}.

By his will of 24 Aug 1709, proved on 1 Jan 1709/10, Richard Howell gave "..unto my Son David Howell and to his Heirs and assignes for ever one equal

81. Id., 133; (C, 189).
82. Id., 134-135; (C, 191-194).
83. Id., 148; (C, 217).
84. WNYSO, Liber 17, 58; (IV, 253).
85. Hawkins, op. cit., 11.
86. O'Callaghan, op. cit., 48.

fourth part of all my meadows on y⁰ South Side of Said peaconneke river.." {87}.

David Howell was an executor of his father's will {88}.

David Howell was paid a bounty of 11s 3d for "..1 catt & 1 young fox.." on 6 May 1718 {89}.

A "David Howell" was a member of the Calvalry Troop of the Suffolk County militia in 1715 {90}.

David Howell married Abigail Conkling in about 1718 {91}. She was the widow of Jacob Conkling {92}, who died on 20 Aug 1715 {93}.

On 7 Apr 1724, "..David Howel was chosen Collector..Att a Town meeting.." {94}.

"David Howel wife Abigail" died on 7 Apr 1726 {95}.

"At a Town meeting held april y⁰ 1ᵗ:1729..David Howell.." was chosen as one of the "..vewers of fence and prisers of Damage.." {96}.

On 9 Mch 1732, letters of administration on the estate of Jacob Howell were granted to his brother, David Howell, and his widow, Margaret Howell {97}.

"David Howels wife Mary" died on 22 Dec 1742 {98}, "..in her 66th year..", and is buried in the cemetery at the Mattituck Presbyterian Church {99}.

"David Howels Jack Dround" on 8 Jly 1747 {100}.

By his will of 12 Feb 1756, proved on 25 Aug 1756, David Howell left property, both real and personal, to his sons, David, Aaron, Israel, Richard and James. He left his daughter, Mary Longbotham, £50. He named his "..sons, Aaron and Richard..", and his friend, Daniel Welles, executors of this will {101}.

"David Howel aged 79" died on 18 Aug 1756 {102}. He is buried beside his wife, Mary, at Mattituck, where his gravestone indicates that he died "..at the age of 79 years and 9 months.." {103}.

David Howell was the father of at least eight children.

+ 17.   i.   DAVID³ HOWELL.

87. WNYSO, Liber 7, 568; (II, 36-37).
88. Id.
89. STR, Liber D, 139; (I, 477-478).
90. THE REGISTER, SCHS, XXIII, #4, 116 (Spring 1998).
91. SR, 75; NYG&BR, XLIX, 65 (Jan 1918).
92. Conklin Mann, THE AMERICAN GENEALOGIST (TAG), 22, 232 (1946).
93. SR, 8; NYG&BR, XLVII, 351 (Oct 1916).
94. STR, Liber D, 119 left; (III, 184-185).
95. SR, 15; NYG&BR, XLVII, 358 (Oct 1916).
96. STR, Liber D, 120 left; (III, 187).
97. WNYSO, Liber 12, 3; (III, 104).
98. SR, 26; NYG&BR, XLVIII, 28 (Jan 1917).
99. Craven, op. cit., 373.
100. SR, 29; NYG&BR, XLVIII, 31 (Jan 1917).
101. WNYSO, Liber 20, 97-99; (V, 132-133).
102. SR, 40; NYG&BR, XLVIII, 173 (Apr 1917).
103. Craven, op. cit., 373.

+ 18. ii. MARY³ HOWELL.

+ 19. iii. AARON³ HOWELL, born in about 1707.

+ 20. iv. ISRAEL³ HOWELL.

+ 21. v. RICHARD³ HOWELL, born in about 1712.

+ 22. vi. JAMES³ HOWELL.

23. vii. Daughter³, "David Howels child Dau." died on 8 Dec 1719 {104}.

24. viii. Daughter³, "David Howils child Dau." died on 10 Dec 1720 {105}.

NOTE: *By his will of 25 Jan 1724/5, proved on 2 Apr 1725, "..Richard Clark, of ye Manor of St. George in the County of Suffolk, Yeoman.." left, to his grandson, Aaron Howell, a colt, and, to his grand-daughter, Hannah Howell, a heifer {106}. It is possible that this "Aaron Howell" was the son of David Howell. If so, then David Howell might have been the father of another daughter, Hannah, and his first wife, and the mother of most, if not all, of his children, might have been a daughter of Richard Clark. She has been entered into the International Genealogical Index as "Hannah Clark", but we have not determined the basis for this entry.*

Although it was recorded that "David Howel & W^d Li^d Hilderidg" were married on 2 Nov 1726 {107}, it is unlikely that this David Howell was the one concerned. Rather, it is likely that David Howell, the son of David and Mary (Herrick) Howell, who married Lydia (Norris) Hildreth, was the subject of this record {108}.

It has been reported that the second wife of David Howell was born "Abigail Case" {109}. It is believed that this is unlikely, and that it is the result of confusion with the record of the marriage of "David Howell" and "Abigail Case" on 15 Jly 1797 {110}.

5. JONATHAN² HOWELL (Richard¹), the son of Richard¹ Howell, was born in the

104. SR, 10; NYG&BR, XLVII, 353 (Oct 1916).
105. Id., 11; NYG&BR, XLVII, 354 (Oct 1916).
106. WNYSO, Liber 10, 236-238; (II, 359).
107. SR, 78; NYG&BR, XLIX, 68 (Jan 1918).
108. David Faris, in Emma Howell Ross's DESCENDANTS OF EDWARD HOWELL (1584-1655).., Second Edition, 109.
109. Wilbur Franklin Howell, op. cit., 2.
110. SR, 108; NYG&BR, XLIX, 275 (Jly 1918).

vicinity of Mattituck.

Jonathan Howell was listed among the members of his father's household in the Census of 1698 {111}.

By a deed acknowledged on 21 May 1708, Jonathan Howell purchased, from Christopher Youngs, all his "..right, title and interest in the fresh meadows lying..neare Peaconneck, on ye North side ye River, which is one halfe of all ye fresh meadows lying Eastward from ye fresh meadow belonging to Josiah Youngs, to extend westward by ye River side soe far as ye former right of Mr John Budd dec^d did claime." {112}.

By his will of 24 Aug 1709, proved on 1 Jan 1709/10, Richard Howell gave "..unto my Son Richard Howell & my Son Jonathan Howell all my lands neare the head of ye Said peaconnek river with ye appurtenances thereunto belonging and also one Equall halfe part of all my meadow on ye South Side of Said river, to be equally divided between them and to ye proper use & behalfe of them my Said Sons Richard & Jonathan Howell their Heirs and assignes for Ever, also I give Equally between my Sd. Sons, Richard and Jonathan and to their Heirs and assignes for Ever all my land & meadow at Brookhaven freely to be possessed & enjoyed.." {113}.

Jonathan Howell was an executor of his father's will {114}.

Jonathan Howell sold land bounded south and west by the land of his brother, Richard Howell, north by the Sound, and east by James Fanning, to his brother, David Howell, as well as a "..fresh meadow on the south side of the Peconic river.." {115}.

Jonathan Howell apparently moved to Southampton where he wrote the note -

"Brother J. Howell bee pleased to deliver to Mr. Joseph Hawkins the six sheep (?) that you have of mine in your custody if any bee wanting of ye number what is remaining please to deliver to ye s^d Hawkins and in so doing you will much oblige Y^r. very loving Brother

Jonathan Howell

Southampton
30th March 1720" {116}.

No further information on this Jonathan Howell has been found.

6. RICHARD^2 HOWELL (Richard^1), the son of Richard^1 Howell, was born in the vicinity of Mattituck in about 1684.

"Richard Howell Junjr." was listed among the members of his father's

---

111. O'Callaghan, op. cit., 48.
112. STR, Liber C, 266; (II, 425).
113. WNYSO, Liber 7, 568; (II, 36-37).
114. Id.
115. Id., Liber 20, 97-99; (V, 132-133).
116. Letter, CHAUNCEY PERKINS HOWELL COLLECTION, SCHS, cited by Wilbur Franklin Howell, op. cit., xi.

household in the Township of Southold in the Census of 1698 {117}.

By his will of 24 Aug 1709, proved on 1 Jan 1709/10, Richard Howell gave "..unto my Son Richard Howell & my Son Jonathan Howell all my lands neare ye head of ye Said peaconnek river with ye appurtenances thereunto belonging and also one Equall halfe part of all my meadow on·ye South Side of Said river, to be equally divided between them and to ye proper use & behalfe of them my Said Sons Richard & Jonathan Howell their Heirs and assignes for Ever, also I give Equally between my Sd. Sons, Richard and Jonathan and to their Heirs and assignes for Ever all my land & meadow at Brookhaven freely to be possessed and enjoyed." {118}.

On 2 Mch 1709/10, Richard Howell purchased, from Abraham and Rebecka Osman, "..a certaine percell of woodland situate at Ockebog-bounded West by John Swazey-East by ye said Abraham Osman-South by ye baye or ye beach and North butting to ye fresh pond known by ye name of Swazeys pond:-and in breadth from ye land of John Swazey to ye land of ye said land of Abraham Osman twenty four rods wide the whole length from ye bay South, to ye pond on ye north end (NOTE:"This lot was the west part of the farm of..Merrit Howell, lying next east of the M.E. Church and cemetery at Riverhead."). {119}.

On 9 Jan 1712/3, Richard Howell sold, to "..Archable Tomson..", a tract of land "..situate at Acquabauke, by estimation fifty acres, bounded on ye North by a fresh pond-East by Walter Brown-South by ye baye and West by John Swazey." {120}.

Richard Howell was a member of Southold Company Number Two of the Suffolk County militia in 1715 {121}.

"Richd Howels wife Debrah" died on 21 Feb 1724/5 at the age of 35 {122}.

"Richd Howel & Wid^w Prudence Griffing" were married in 1725 {123}.

"J^n Griffing & Prudence Hallock" were married on 24 Nov 1715 {124}. "John Griffing" died on 8 Jan 1722/3 {125}. Prudence Hallock was listed with the household of William and Mary Hallock in the Census of 1698 for the Township of Southold {126}.

Richard Howell was a witness to a memorandum stating that Jonathan Horton had taken possession of a tract of land in the Second Division of Aquebogue sold to him by James Terry by a deed dated 4 Mch 1734/5 {127}.

On 29 Apr 1748, Samuel Terry and John Goldsmith, two of the

117. O'Callaghan, op. cit., 48.
118. WNYSO, Liber 7, 568; (II, 36-37).
119. STR, Liber C, 284; (II, 448-449).
120. Id., 283; (II, 446).
121. THE REGISTER, SCHS, XXIII, #4, 122 (Spring 1998).
122. SR, 13; NYG&BR, XLVII, 356 (Oct 1916).
123. Id., 78; NYG&BR, XLIX, 68 (Jan 1918).
124. Id., 75; NYG&BR, XLIX, 75 (Jan 1918).
125. Id., 12; NYG&BR, XLVII, 355 (Oct 1916).
126. O'Callaghan, op. cit., 51.
127. ACKERLY RECORD BOOKS, Book 2, 133-136.

Commissioners of Highways for the Town of Southold, did "..assert the kings high way near the head of peconet River as followeth first a stake sett by the east side of the path att the Comon going over begining at the River & so Run Northward toward ye County house to a stake within aboute a rod & half of said house the way to be four pole wide & extend itts bredth westerly from sd stakes & from the stake by sd County house Run west to apople tree before Capt ffanings house & so runing west Aboute Twentie pole to a stake the south part Giving way four poles in bredth -- -- -- - - We allso staked ye way easterly from ye aforementioned stake By sd County house unto a saplying aboute one rod Northerly from ye Common Road near Richard Howells Corner ye south side Giving way four poles in bredth allso we asert a four pole way between the Two Rivers that is between ye County house & William Albersons as followeth. the East side of said way is near where the old fence formerly Run & so According as sd fence Did run & to extend its bredth west from sd Line." {128}.

On 7 Jly 1760, Nathaniel Wells testified that several papers which he had been keeping for "..Mr Richard Howell, then a dweller near the Riverhead.." were destroyed when his house burned on 18 May 1760. Included was a "..deed..from Richard Howells brother John Howell for one lott of land in the second division of..Aquabague on which he..Richard then and now dwelleth.." {129}.

On 11 Oct 1760, Richard Howell attested that the papers destroyed in the fire at the house of Nathaniel Wells also included deeds to "..two lotts and half of meadow att the broad meadows adjoyning to his own meadow on the further side of the River.", bought from David Horton, "..one parcle of meadow purchased of Daniel Terry lying north of Peconnick River..", "..one piece of land purchased of my brother David Howell..on the South side of ye kings highway and North of Peconeck River against wheer I now live." {130}.

On 7 Apr 1761, Richard Howell was one of several men selected to serve as Fence Viewers by the Annual Meeting of the Town of Southold {131}.

By his will of 10 Jan 1758, proved on 7 Apr 1769, Richard Howell left, to his "..beloved wife Prudence such a part of my estate as the Law directs or allows her, and no more..". Except for this, he left his entire estate to his "..only son Richard..", whom he directed to pay all his debts and legacies. Of his daughters, Dorothy Conkling was to receive £7, Hannah Ketchum, £10, and Abigail Horton, 5s. The children of his deceased daughters, Deborah Doddy and Sarah Penny, were to receive £5 each when of age {132}.

"Richard Howel 85" died on 15 Mch 1769 {133}.

Richard and Deborah (Reeve?) Howell were the parents of at least seven children.

+ 25. i. DEBORAH³ HOWELL.

---

128. STR, Liber D, 223 left; (III, 387-388).
129. Id., Liber C, 283; (II, 447-448).
130. Id.
131. Id., Liber D, 129 right; (III, 209).
132. WNYSO, Liber 27, 61-62; (7, 264).
133. SR, 42; NYG&BR, XLVIII, 175 (1917).

+ 26. ii. SARAH³ HOWELL.

+ 27. iii. RICHARD³ HOWELL, born in about 1719.

+ 28. iv. DOROTHY³ HOWELL.

+ 29. v. HANNAH³ HOWELL.

+ 30. vi. ABIGAIL³ HOWELL.

   31. vii. Child³, "Richard Howels child" died on 27 Feb 1724/5 {134}.

7. ISAAC² HOWELL (Richard¹), the likely son of Richard¹ and Elizabeth (Cooke) Harrud Howell, was born in the vicinity of Mattituck.

Isaac Howell was listed among the members of his father's household in the Township of Southold in the Census of 1698 {135}.

By his will of 24 Aug 1709, proved on 1 Jan 1709/10, Richard Howell gave "..unto my Son Isaac and to his Heirs and assignes for Ever all that messuage or Tenament where my Son John now lives and bounded north by my Son Davids land & South by the bay and also one Equall halfe part of all my meadow at Deep creeke to him my Said Son Isaac Howell his Heirs & assignes freely to be possessed & enjoyed.." {136}.

On 7 Feb 1714/5, Isaac Howell purchased, with his brother, Jacob Howell, "..two lotts containing three acres and a halfe, bounded on yᵉ North by Mathias Curwin-on yᵉ East by John Youngs-on the South by William Coleman and on the west by a Creek-said meadow..being on the South side of Peaconneck river.." from Thomas Shaw, yeoman, of Southold {137}.

On 7 Mch 1714/5, Isaac Howell purchased, again with his brother, Jacob Howell, "..one piece and percell of meadow lying at Ackabauck-bounded South by yᵉ deep Creek-north by a Stake in the narrows-East by yᵉ meadow of John Youngs, and West by yᵉ meadows of yᵉ said Howells, containing by Estimation three acres.." from William Mapes, Yeoman, of Southold {138}.

Isaac Howell was a member of Southold Company Number Two of the Suffolk County militia in 1715 {139}.

On 17 Feb 1717/8, and again on 28 Apr 1718, Isaac Howell received a bounty of 5s 6d for destroying one fox {140}.

---

134. Id., 13; NYG&BR, XLVII, 356 (Oct 1916).
135. O'Callaghan, op. cit., 48.
136. WNYSO, Liber 7, 568; (II, 36-37).
137. STR, Liber C, 58; (II, 133).
138. Id., 80; (II, 173).
139. THE REGISTER, SCHS, XXIII, #4, 122 (Spring 1998).
140. STR, Liber B, 139; (I, 477-478).

On 4 Apr 1730, Isaac Howell was selected as one of several "..vewers of fences and prisers of damage.." at the Annual Meeting of the Town of Southold {141}. He was again selected to this office on 7 Apr 1752 {142}.

Isaac Howell was elected an Overseer of the Poor on 4 Apr 1738, on 2 Apr 1745, and on 5 Apr 1748 {143}.

Isaac Howell was selected to be an Assessor for the ensuing year at the 5 Apr 1748 meeting of the Town of Southold, and again on 3 Apr 1753 {144}.

In addition, Isaac Howell served as a Commissioner of Highways. He was selected for that office on 1 Apr 1740, and again on 7 Apr 1743 {145}. As such, he was responsible, with Benjamin Hutchinson, for several roads described in a record of 6 Apr 1743 {146}, and for a "..two pole way..going out of the Kings Road between William Penny & Daniel Pike running down to ye Mill at the head of Peter Halliocks meadows & from thence to Peconick Medows..", as described on 23 Mch 1743/4 {147}.

Isaac Howell was an executor of the will of Nathaniel Mather, written on 26 Nov 1747, and proved on 28 Mch 1748 {148}.

Isaac Howell joined the United Parishes of Mattituck and Aquebogue during the pastorate of the Rev. Joseph Park, 1751-1756 {149}.

By his will of 30 Sep 1757, Isaac Howell left, to his wife, Phebe, his house, some furniture, and livestock. He left land to his sons, Daniel and Micah, and to his grandson, Nathan Howell. To his daughter, Hannah, he left "..1 bed, 1 cow and 6 sheep..". He left his wearing apparel to his two sons. The rest of his estate was to be divided among his children, Micah, Daniel, Hannah, Phebe Corwin and Rachel Corwin. This will, of which his sons, Micah and Daniel, were named executors, was proved on 28 Nov 1759 {150}.

"Phebe Howell, widow of Isaac, son of 1st Richard" was received into the communion of the United Parishes of Mattituck and Aquebogue during the pastorate of the Rev. Nehemiah Barker, 1756-1772 {151}.

"Phebe Howel widow to Isaac" died on 29 Feb 1772 {152}.

Isaac and Phebe Howell were probably the parents of at least seven children.

+ 32.   i.   ISAAC[3] HOWELL.

+ 33.   ii.   PHEBE[3] HOWELL.

---

141. Id., Liber D, 120 left; (III, 187).
142. Id., Liber D, 126 left; (III., 202).
143. Id., 122 left, 124 left, 125 left; (III, 191, 196, 199).
144. Id., 125 left, 127 right; (III, 199, 203-204).
145. Id., 123 left; (III, 193), 124 left; (III, 195).
146. Id., 222 left; (III, 384-385).
147. Id., 223 left; (III, 387-388).
148. WNYSO, Liber 16, 265; (4, 169).
149. Craven, op. cit., 107.
150. WNYSO, Liber 21, 465-467; (5, 350-351).
151. Craven, op. cit., 113.
152. SR, 44; NYG&BR, XLVIII, 177 (1917).

34. iii. Child[3], "Isaac Howils child" died on 6 Apr 1720 {153}.

+ 35. iv. MICAH[3] HOWELL, born in about 1720.

+ 36. v. DANIEL[3] HOWELL, born in about 1726.

+ 37. vi. RACHEL[3] HOWELL, born in about 1730.

38. vii. HANNAH[3] HOWELL.

8. JACOB[2] HOWELL (Richard[1]), the son of Richard[1] Howell, was born in the vicinity of Mattituck.

Jacob Howell was listed among the members of his father's household in the Township of Southold in the Census of 1698 {154}.

By his will of 24 Aug 1709, proved on 1 Jan 1709/10, Richard Howell gave "unto my Son Jacob Howell and to his Heirs & assignes for ever all that land lying between ye baye and the highwaye leading to Brookhaven by the waye of ye beach, which is the remaining part of the alotment where my messuage is herein given unto my Son John, also I give unto my Said Son Jacob Howell and to his Heirs & assignes for Ever one equall halfe part of all my meadow at Deep Creek freely to be possessed and enjoyed.." {155}.

"....b Howil & Maregit Parshal" were married in 1710 {156}.

"Margaret Pershall Junjr" was listed among the members of the household of James and Margaret Parshall in the Township of Southold in the Census of 1698 {157}. She was born in about 1694.

The land of Jacob Howell was the eastern bound of two lots of land in the First Division of Aquebogue, received by Joseph Conkling from the estate of his grandfather, John Conkling, by 10 Nov 1712 {158}.

Jacob Howell, with his brother, Isaac Howell, bought two lots on the south side of the Peconic River from Thomas Shaw, yeoman, of Southold, on 7 Feb 1714/5 {159}.

On 7 Mch 1714/5, Jacob Howell bought, again with his brother, Isaac Howell, a parcel of meadow at Aquebogue from William Mapes, yeoman, of Southold {160}.

Jacob Howell was a member of Capt. Reeves Southold Company Number Two of the Suffolk County militia in 1715 {161}.

153. Id., 10; NYG&BR, XLVII, 353 (Oct 1916).
154. O'Callaghan, op. cit., 48.
155. WNYSO, Liber 7, 568; (II, 36-37).
156. SR, 74; NYG&BR, XLIX, 69 (Jan 1918).
157. O'Callaghan, op. cit., 50.
158. STR, Liber C, 68; (II, 152-155).
159. Id., 58; (II, 133).
160. Id., 80; (II, 173).
161. Wines, op. cit., 46; THE REGISTER, SCHS, XXIII, #4, 122 (Spring 1998).

On 30 Mch 1718, Jacob Howell was paid a bounty of 9s for the destruction of "1 catt" {162}.

"Jacub hoel..Workt upon the meting hous tember.." one day in 1731 {163}.

"Jacob Howel died" on 24 May 1732 {164}.

Letters of administration on the estate of Jacob Howell, of Southold, were issued to his widow, Margaret Howell, and his brother, David Howell, on 9 Mch 1732/3 {165}.

"Richd Swesey & Wi^d Marga^t Howel" were married on 10 Aug 1739 {166}. His first wife, Elizabeth, probably Parshall, had died on 12 Mch 1739, at the age of 38, and is buried at Mattituck {167}.

"Richard Swasey" was selected as one of several "..fence vewers.." at the Annual Meeting of the Town of Southold on 6 Apr 1731 {168}. He was again selected for one of these positions on 6 Apr 1742, on 3 Apr 1744, on 7 Apr 1747, and on 4 Apr 1749. He was apparently again so selected on 7 Apr 1772 {169}.

"Richard Sweseys wife Margret" died on 6 Jly 1769 {170}. She is buried in the cemetery at the Mattituck Presbyterian Church, where her tombstone indicates that she died at the age of 75 {171}.

"Richard Swesy, 92" died on 26 Dec 1782 {172}.

Jacob and Margaret (Parshall) Howell were probably the parents of at least two children.

+ 39.   i.   MARGARET³ HOWELL.

+ 40.   ii.   JACOB³ HOWELL.

9. DOROTHY² HOWELL (Richard¹), the daughter of Richard¹ Howell, was born in the vicinity of Mattituck.

"Dorathy Howell" was listed among the members of her father's household in the Township of Southold in the Census of 1698 {173}.

By his will of 24 Aug 1709, proved on 1 Jan 1709/10, Richard Howell gave "..unto my Daughter Dorithy Reeve for ever twenty pounds as mony of this

162. STR, Liber B, 139; (I, 477-478).
163. Wines, op. cit., 46.
164. SR, 19; NYG&BR, XLVIII, 21 (Jan 1917).
165. WNYSO, Liber 12, 3; (III, 104).
166. SR, 83; NYG&BR, XLIX, 73 (Jan 1918).
167. Craven, op. cit., 389.
168. STR, Liber D, 121 right; (III, 188).
169. Id., 124 right, 124 left, 125 left, 126 right, 133 right; (III, 194, 196, 198, 200, 220).
170. SR, 43; NYG&BR, XLVIII, 176 (Apr 1917).
171. Craven, op. cit., 388.
172. SR, 53; NYG&BR, XLVIII, 281 (Jly 1917).
173. O'Callaghan, op. cit., 48.

Collony to be paid her by my Execut'.." {174}.

Dorothy Howell married John Reeve. On 27 Dec 1709, John and "Dorraty" Reeve signed a receipt for the £20 left to her by her father's will {175}.

John Reeve, the son of John and Hannah (Brown) Reeve {176}, was born in about 1682. He was listed among the members of his father's household in the Township of Southold in the Census of 1698 {177}.

John Reeve was a member of Southold Company Number Two of the Suffolk County militia in 1715 {178}.

On 10 Aug 1727, "John Reeve died aged 45 years" {179}.

"Wid Dority Reeve Relect to John" died on 23 Sep 1752 {180}.

John and Dorothy (Howell) Reeve may have been the parents of at least two sons {181}.

    i.   WALTER REEVE, married Mary Burt on 2 Aug 1765, died on 3 Feb 1791.

    ii.   DAVID REEVE.

- END OF SECOND GENERATION -

174. WNYSO, Liber 7, 568; (II, 36-37).
175. Receipt, CHAUNCEY PERKINS HOWELL COLLECTION, SCHS.
176. Wesley L. Baker, GENEALOGY..OF REEVE FAMILY.., 349.
177. O'Callaghan, op. cit., 48.
178. THE REGISTER, SCHS, XXIII, #4, 122 (Spring 1998).
179. SR, 16; NYG&BR, XLVII, 359 (Oct 1916).
180. Id., 33; NYG&BR, XLVIII, 166 (Apr 1917).
181. Baker, op. cit., 350.

12. JOHN[3] HOWELL (John[2], Richard[1]), the son of John[2] and Margaret (Reeve?) Howell {182}, was born in about 1708 in the vicinity of Mattituck.

By his father's will of 14 Dec 1733, proved on 12 Feb 1733/4, John Howell inherited "..two steers and a heifer.." {183}.

John Howell was a witness to the will of Joseph Goldsmith, of Southold, written on 22 May 1734 {184}.

Earmarks for the livestock of John Howell were registered with the Town of Brookhaven, on 2 Jan 1734/5, as "..a hapeny under Each (Each) Eare and a crop of the top of the Left Eare." {185}.

"John Howel" was a Freeholder in Suffolk County on 27 Feb 1737/8 {186}. Since he was listed with Southold men, he was probably then a resident of that town.

John Howell was a resident of the Town of Brookhaven on 17 Mch 1740, when "William Smith of Brook haven in the County of Suffolk and Province of New York Farmer of the one part and Barnabas Rider of the Town County and Province afore Said Farmer of the other part.." mutually chose "..Richard Woodhul Esqr Mr James Tuttell Mr Iohn Howell of the Town afore s[d] to Divide Lay off and preportion unto each of us our parts.." following the sale of one-quarter of his property at Accombomack Neck by William Smith to Barnabas Rider {187}. This division was completed by 22 Apr 1740 {188}.

The Howell family in the Town of Brookhaven owned Lots 49 and 50 of the lots on the south side of the Country Road, as reported to have been laid out by Nathaniel Brewster and Richard Woodhull on 4 May 1731. Of these, Lot 49 was originally drawn by Joseph Mapes, of Southold, while Lot 50 was drawn by Richard Woolley, of Southampton. All these lots were "..on the south side of the Cuontry Rode that Leades from Whelers tto the townes Eastward betwene Smithtowne line and the head of Conettecut Hollow..". Lots 49 and 50 were among the nineteen easternmost lots, which were "..fifty fowe Rods in Width Mesuering by the saide Rode And Every Lot to Runn from: th Said Cuntry Rod a Due: South Line to the Midel of the Island or to the Land belonging to mr wintrup.." {189}.

The house built by John Howell was still standing on the north side of New York State Route 25 in Middle Island, somewhat to the west of its intersection with Route 21, and somewhat to the east of the Middle Island Presbyterian Church, until 14 Jan 1989, when it was destroyed by fire. This part of Route 25 more or less

---

182. Craven, op. cit., 205.

183. WNYSO, Liber 12, 142; (III, 139).

184. Id., Liber 13, 7; (3, 209).

185. BTR, Book B, p. XIV; (Printed records, B, 524).

186. O'Callaghan, op. cit., 249.

187. BTR, Book B, 335; (B, 449).

188. Id., 336-337; (B, 450-452).

189. Id., Book C, 113-114; (C, 150-153).

follows the path of the Country Road, however, the path of that road was changed so that it passed on the south side of John Howell's house, rather than on the north side, by 5 Feb 1755, at John Howell's request {190}.

"John Howel" was assessed 1s 3d on the Brookhaven Town Assessment, 1741 {191}.

John Howell was chosen to be a Fence Viewer for the ensuing year at the Annual Meeting of the Town of Brookhaven on 1 May 1744 {192}.

John Howell was assessed 6s 8d on the Brookhaven Town Assessment, 1749 {193}.

John Howell was one of several men chosen as "Comisinors" at the Annual Meeting of the Town of Brookhaven on 1 May 1750 {194}.

At a meeting of the Trustees of the Town of Brookhaven on 5 May 1755, "..it was..voted and agreed upon by ye Trustees that yᵉ Land formerly laid to upon yᵉ right of John Thomas: and now in yᵉ possession of John Howell by yᵉ Country road; Does and aught to enclude all yᵉ Swampy Land, Eastward to a Straight line throw yᵉ Swamp; and we Do hereby for us and our Successors Remise release and forever quit our Claim and all right property and Demand to yᵉ Same unto yᵉ Said John Howell and to his Heirs and Assigns forever.." {195}.

"John Howel" was assessed 2s 6d on the Brookhaven Town Assessment, 1758 {196}.

By 15 Apr 1762, the Commissioners of Highways for the Town of Brookhaven had "..Laid out a highway Turning out of yᵉ Country road on yᵉ East side of yᵉ Swamp near John Howells.." {197}.

The identity of the wife of John Howell has not been established. She may have been the "Hann Howel widow to John" who died on 15 Mch 1768 {198}.

John Howell was not listed on the Brookhaven Town Assessment, 1775, nor in the Census of 1776, so it is likely that he died before the times at which these were taken.

John Howell was the father of at least two children.

+ 41.   i.   JOHN⁴ HOWELL, born in about 1734.

+ 42.   ii.   REEVE⁴ HOWELL, born in about 1738.

NOTE: *In accepting John³ Howell, of Middle Island in the Town of Brookhaven, as a son of John² Howell, of West Mattituck in the Town of Southold, we follow*

---

190. Id., 381-382; (C, 494-495).
191. Benjamin Hutchinson, RECORDS, TOWN OF BROOKHAVEN, UP TO 1800, 153.
192. BTR, Book C, 162; (C, 238-239).
193. Hutchinson, op. cit., 162.
194. BTR, Book C, 191; (C, 279).
195. Id., 181; (C, 264).
196. Town of Brookhaven Tax Assessment, 1758, from a copy in the possession of David A. Overton, Historian, Town of Brookhaven, 1991.
197. BTR, Book C, 205; (C, 303).
198. SR, 41; NYG&BR, XLVIII, 174 (Apr 1917).

Charles E. Craven, who was probably following Richard M. Baylis, who stated that "..we are fairly supported in the supposition that the John Howell whom tradition says was born about 1718 was the son of John, who was the son of the first Richard and that he was the first Howell of Brookhaven who settled here about 1739, he being then about 21 years old." {199}. On the other hand, this leaves unaccounted for the John Howell, weaver, of Southold, who died on 19 Mch 1741 {200}, and whose will of 11 Nov 1740, by which he left the use of his dwelling house and furnishings to his wife, Alethea, was proved on 26 Mch 1740/1 {201}. She died on 7 May 1751 {202}. By her will of 13 Nov 1746, proved on 7 June 1751, she left her estate to her near kinsman, John Benjamin, of Southold, and named her kinsman, James Reeve, executor {203}. This would all seem to indicate that John and Alathea Howell had no children, however, since the name of Althea was frequently used among the descendants of John Howell, of Middle Island, it would seem that there must have been some relationship. Further, since Richard[1] Howell left his lands in Brookhaven to his sons, Jonathan and Richard, and Richard[2] had but one son, Richard[3], it would seem possible that John[3] Howell, of Middle Island, might have been a son of Jonathan[2] Howell, who apparently removed to Southampton, and regarding whom no further information has been found.

13. EUNICE[3] HOWELL (John[2], Richard[1]), the daughter of John[2] and Hannah Howell, was born on 11 Dec 1713 {204}, in the vicinity of Mattituck.

"Jacob Brown & Eunice Howell" were married in about Dec 1735 {205}.

Eunice Brown was a witness to the signing of the will of Thomas Reed, of Southold, on 11 June 1740 {206}.

"Jacob Browns wife Unise" died on 26 Nov 1755 {207}.

No record of the family of Jacob and Eunice (Howell) Brown has been found or developed.

14. JEMIMA[3] HOWELL (John[2], Richard[1]), the daughter of John[2] and Hannah Howell, was born in the vicinity of Mattituck.

"Adonijah osman & Jemimah Howel" were married in about Feb 1732/3

199. Richard M. Baylis, Manuscript, HOWELL FAMILY, BROOKHAVEN TOWN, in the possession of David A. Overton, 1993.
200. SR, 26; NYG&BR, XLVIII, 28 (Jan 1917).
201. WNYSO, Liber 14, 40-41; (III, 322).
202. SR, 32; NYG&BR, XLVIII, 165 (Apr 1917).
203. WNYSO, Liber 17, 387-388; (IV, 341).
204. Grendler, op. cit., 1.
205. SR, 82; NYG&BR, XLIX, 72 (Jan 1918).
206. WNYSO, Liber 15, 56-57; III, 393).
207. SR, 39; NYG&BR, XLVIII, 172 (Apr 1917).

{208}. He was born on 21 June 1710.

By her father's will of 14 Dec 1733, proved on 12 Feb 1733/4, Jemima Osman received "..one good cow.." {209}, for which she and her husband, Adonijah Osman, signed a receipt dated 22 Feb 1733/4 {210}.

Adonijah Osman moved his family to Baiting Hollow in Apr 1749, "..and probably lived on the John Parker lot, the old house stood on the north side of the road, just east of Roanoke Avenue. He lived there almost 48 years, dying in March 1797, aet. nearly 86 years. His wife died earlier, and in 1799 an unmarried daughter died. Their graves are lost. They did not live in the Wickham house (Parker's grandson) after 1748, but further west." {211}.

"adonijah Osman" was selected to be a Fence Viewer for the ensuing year at the Annual Meeting of the Town of Southold on 2 Apr 1751 {212}.

Adonijah Osman was listed as the head of a family consisting of one male of above 50 years of age, one of 16 and under 50, one of under 16, and four females of above 16, residing in Southold Township, Suffolk County, in the Census of 1776 {213}.

It is possible that Jemima (Howell) Osman died on 11 Sep 1777, since it was recorded that "Adonijah osborn" died on that date {214}.

"Adonijah Osbond" was listed, by Josiah Woodhull, as the head of a family of six residing in the Wading River district of the Southold Township on 22 Aug 1778 {215}.

Adonijah Osman was a signator to a set of Articles of Agreement by which the owners of the "..great lots in Aquebogue in the Second Division as far as from Ambrose Horton East bounds to Daniel Edwards west bounds.." agreed to "..abide by their bounds which they have peaceably enjoyed for a number of years.." {216}.

"Adonijah Osburn" was listed as the head of a family consisting of one free white male of 16 years of age and upwards, and two free white females, residing in Southold Town, Suffolk County, New York, in the First Census of the United States, 1790 {217}.

"An old record reads "1796, March 25, died Adonijah Osborn, aet. 85 years, 9 months, 4 days, removed to this place in April 1749. He lived then on the

---

208. Id., 81; NYG&BR, XLIX, 71 (Jan 1918).

209. WNYSO, Liber 12, 142; (III, 139).

210. Receipt, CHAUNCEY PERKINS HOWELL COLLECTION, SCHS; See also Wines (41).

211. James Franklin Young, from a manuscript written in 1906, THE REGISTER, SCHS, VII, 105 (Mch 1982).

212. STR, Liber D, 126 left; (III, 201).

213. CENSUS OF SUFFOLK COUNTY, NEW YORK, 1776, Excerpted from *Calendar of Historical Manuscripts Relating to the War of the Revolution*, New York Secretary of State (Albany, 1868) Volume 1, 21.

214. SR, 49; NYG&BR, XLVIII, 277 (Jly 1917).

215. NATIONAL GENEALOGICAL SOCIETY QUARTERLY (NGSQ), 63, 283 (1975).

216. RIVERHEAD TOWN RECORDS (RTR), Liber B, 26; (Printed records, I, 274).

217. HEADS OF FAMILIES AT THE FIRST CENSUS OF THE UNITED STATES TAKEN IN THE YEAR, 1790, NEW YORK, 170.

kham property, probably in the old house that used to stand a little east of anoke Avenue, and was demolished about 1870." " {218}.

Adonijah and Jemima (Howell) Osman were the parents of at least four children.

    i.   JEMIMA OSMAN, died 2 Apr 1799 {219}.

    ii.   ADONIJAH OSMAN.

    iii.   JACOB OSMAN.

    iv.   Child, "Adonijah Osbons child" died on 15 Jan 1755 {220}.

15. JONATHAN[3] HOWELL (John[2], Richard[1]), the son of John[2] and Hannah Howell, was born in about 1720 in the vicinity of Mattituck {221}.

By his will of 14 Dec 1733, proved on 12 Feb 1733/4, John Howell left, to his "..son, Jonathan Howell (the son of Hannah Howell, my present wife), all my lands and tenements whatsoever, after my wife's decease, also 2 steers and 1 heifer." {222}.

"Jonath[n] Howel & Elesab[th] Sherry" were married on 26 Jan 1737/8 {223}. She was the daughter of Recompence and Margaret (Cady) (or Sarah (Parsons)) {224} Sherrill, and was baptized at East Hampton, with several of her siblings, on 5 Apr 1719 {225}.

Jonathan Howell was selected to be one of several "..Viewers of fence & Damage.." at the Annual Meeting of the Town of Southold on 6 Apr 1742 {226}. He was selected as a Constable on 4 Apr 1749 {227}, and again on 9 Apr 1750 {228}. He was again selected as a "Viewer of fences" on 2 Apr 1751, on 3 Apr 1753, on 1 Apr 1755, on 3 Apr 1757, on 3 Apr 1759, on 6 Apr 1762, on 5 Apr 1763, on 5 Apr 1769, on 7 Apr 1772, and on 4 Apr 1775 {229}.

On 11 Apr 1753, Jonathan Howell was a witness to the signing of the will of Peter Halliock of Southold {230}.

---

218. James Franklin Young, op. cit., VII, 90 (Mch 1982).
219. RTR, Liber A, 45; (I, 28).
220. SR, 38; NYG&BR, XLVIII, 171 (Apr 1917)
221. Wines, op. cit., 43.
222. WNYSO, Liber 12, 142; (III, 139).
223. SR, 83; NYG&BR, XLIX, 73 (Jan 1918).
224. Jeannette Edwards Rattray, EAST HAMPTON HISTORY.., 545.
225. EAST HAMPTON TOWN RECORDS (EHTR), 5, 460-461.
226. STR, Liber D, 124 right; (III, 194).
227. Id., 126 right; (III, 199).
228. Id., 126 right; (III, 200).
229. Id., 126 left, 127 right, 127 left, 128 right, 128 left, 129 left, 129 left, 131 left, 133 right, 134 right; (III, 201, 203-204, 204, 205-206, 207-208, 209-210, 211, 216-217, 220, 223-224).
230. WNYSO, Liber 20, 149-150; (V, 143).

Jonathan Howell was a witness to the signing of the will of David Howe written on 12 Feb 1756, and proved on 25 Aug 1756 {231}.

Mary Halliock made her "..friend Jonathan Howell executor.." of her will of 26 Feb 1761 {232}.

Jonathan Howell was listed as the head of a family consisting of one male of above 50 years of age, one of 16 and under 50, one of under 16, and three females of above 16, residing in Southold Township, Suffolk County, New York, in the Census of 1776 {233}.

"About this same time, there was a Mr. Jonathan Howell, a peaceable farmer, residing in the neighborhood of Mattituck. He being a staunch friend of American liberty, had unguardedly spoken a word against the proceedings at Oysterpond. They heard of his just remarks - sent a guard of soldiers, took him and bound him to a tree, and with the hearts of Demons, gave him between three and four hundred lashes on his naked back. He hardly survived this awful scourge. His friends offered three hundred dollars to save him from this calamity." {234}. (NOTE: *This story may actually apply to Jonathan[4] Howell, #43*).

"Jonath[n] Howels Wife Elis[th]" died on 12 Nov 1779 {235}.

"Jon[n] Howell, Sen[r]" was listed as the head of a family consisting of two free white males of 16 years of age and upwards, one of under 16, and two free white females, residing in Southold Town, Suffolk County, New York, in the First Census of the United States, 1790 {236}.

By his will of 24 Jly 1793, proved on 13 May 1805, Jonathan Howell left his entire estate to his son, John, with instructions that legacies be paid to his other sons, Recompense, Jeremiah and Eli. His daughters, Elisabeth, Margaret and Hannah, were each to receive household furniture {237}.

Jonathan Howell died on 26 Mch 1804 {238}.

Jonathan and Elizabeth (Sherrill) Howell were the parents of at least eight children.

+ 43. i. JONATHAN[4] HOWELL, born in about 1739.

+ 44. ii. ELIZABETH[4] HOWELL, born in about 1742.

+ 45. iii. RECOMPENSE[4] HOWELL, born in about 1745.

+ 46. iv. JEREMIAH[4] HOWELL.

+ 47. v. MARGARET[4] HOWELL, born in about 1751.

---

231. Id., 97-99; (V, 132-133).
232. Id., Liber 24, 161; (VI, 263).
233. CENSUS OF SUFFOLK COUNTY, 1776, 21.
234. Griffin, op. cit., 157.
235. SR, 51; NYG&BR, XLVIII, 279 (Jly 1917).
236. HEADS OF FAMILIES.., 1790, NEW YORK, 170.
237. Suffolk County Wills, Liber B, 358-359.
238. Craven, op. cit., 354.

48. vi. HANNAH⁴ HOWELL.

+ 49. vii. JOHN⁴ HOWELL, born in about 1759.

+ 50. viii. ELI⁴ HOWELL, born in about 1761.

16. ESTHER³ HOWELL (John², Richard¹), the daughter of John² and Hannah Howell, was born in the vicinity of Mattituck.
"Benajah Huntly & Esther Howel" were married in about 1740/1 {239}.
Benajah and Esther (Howell) Huntly were the parents of at least one child.
    i.   Child, "Benajah Huntlies child" died on 3 Nov 1743 {240}.

17. DAVID³ HOWELL (David² , Richard¹), the son of David² Howell, was born in the vicinity of Mattituck.
"David Howel & Deb Saterly" were married on 27 Nov 1728 {241}.
"David hoel..Workt upon the meting hous tember.." in 1731 in the construction of the Aquebogue Meeting House, now the Jamesport Church {242}.
    James Reeve left, to his "..kinswoman Deborah, wife of David Howell, Jr., one cow.." by his will of 15 Jan 1731/2, proved on 24 Aug 1732 {243}.
    "David Howel juʳ" was selected to be a Fence Viewer for the ensuing year at the Annual Meeting of the Town of Southold held on 4 Apr 1732 {244}. He was again selected to be a Fence Viewer on 6 Apr 1736, and on 7 Apr 1741 {245}.
    "David Howel" was a Freeholder of Suffolk County on 27 Feb 1737/8 {246}. Since he appeared "..to be living near Riverhead..it can be assumed he was at Indian Island." {247}.
    "David Howels wife Deborah" died on 29 Dec 1746 {248}.
    "David Howel & Lydia Case" were married on 18 Sep 1748 at Southold {249}{250}.
    "David Howell, Sr." and Mary Murrow were married on 13 Nov 1764 at

239. SR, 84; NYG&BR, XLIX, 74 (Jan 1918).
240. Id., 27; NYG&BR, XLVIII, 29 (Jan 1917).
241. Id., 79; NYG&BR, XLIX, 69 (Jan 1918).
242. Wines, op. cit., 10.
243. WNYSO, Liber 11, 392-395; (III, 79-80).
244. STR, Liber D, 121 right; (III, 188).
245. Id., 122 right, 124 right; (III, 190, 193-194).
246. O'Callaghan, op. cit., 248.
247. Wines, op. cit., 46.
248. SR, 28; NYG&BR, XLVIII, 30 (Jan 1917).
249. Id., 87; NYG&BR, XLIX, 155 (Apr 1918).
250. RECORDS OF THE FIRST CHURCH OF SOUTHOLD, Vol. II, ANCESTRAL FOOTPRINTS, Series I, Suffolk County, N.Y., Published by Albert G. Overton, 1; NYG&BR, LXIV, 217 (Jly 1933).

Mattituck {251}.

David Howell purchased land near Sugar Loaf in the Town of Warwick in Orange County, New York, on 2 Mch 1774 {252}. He was "..of the Precinct of Goshen .." when he wrote his will on 16 June 1775. By this will, he gave his "..well beloved wife Mary Howell all my land and buildings..all my personal estate (Excepting what I have given away before) out of which I mean that my just Debts shall be paid. Also..all my bog-meadow and the land adjoining thereto." He appointed his wife an executor of this will, along with Barnabas Horton, Jr., and Capt. Henry Wisner. He left each of his children 5s, naming them as David, Ruth, ?opping (first letter not clear), John, George, Mehitable, Jemima, Benjamin, Ezra, Mary, Lydia, Noble, Deborah and Frances. He provided that his "..Son Noble should have all my land and buildings..if my wife should die before me.." {253}.

David Howell refused to sign the Articles of Association {255}.

David Howell, residing in District #6, in the Town of Warwick, Orange County, New York, was assessed £2 9s 9d by John Wood, Assessor, in Sep 1775 {256}.

It is said of David Howell that he became blind when he reached an advanced age, and that it was his custom to sit beneath a chestnut tree beside his house on the street in Sugar Loaf. There he could distinguish each passerby by the sound of their footsteps as well as the tone of their voice {257}.

It is believed that David Howell died at Sugar Loaf in Orange County {258}, although letters written by Thomas Howell and by Coe S. Howell after their father, Ezra Howell, died, state that their grandfather, David Howell, lived and died in Mattituck {259}. However, since he was not listed in the Census of 1776 for Suffolk County, nor did he sign the Oath of Allegiance and Peaceable Behaviour there in 1778, it is likely that he did die at Sugar Loaf. In fact, data from the First Census of the United States, 1790, suggest that he was still living then, and that his wife, and others, were living in his household. Thus, David Howell was listed as the head of a family consisting of one free white male of 16 years of age and upwards, one of under 16, and four free white females, residing in the Town of Warwick, Orange County, New York {260}.

---

251. Craven, op. cit., 319; SR, 97; NYG&BR, XLIX, 165 (Apr 1918).
252. Jessie Howell Finch, THE ANCESTRAL LINES OF CHESTER EVARTS HOWELL, 1867-1949.., 3.
253. Will, David Howell, from a copy at the Orange County Genealogical Society (OCGS). The original of this will, which was never probated, was in the possession of Mrs. Jesse Holbert, of Lake, N.Y., in 1914 {254}.
254. Charles E. Stickney, THE HOWELL FAMILY (HOWELL), #154, from a copy in the possession of the Sussex County (NJ) Historical Society, 1988.
255. Edward Manning Ruttenber and L. H. Clark, A HISTORY OF ORANGE COUNTY, 67.
256. Id., 566.
257. Helen R. Predmore, NOTES, in the possession of the OCGS, 1996.
258. Finch, op. cit., 3.
259. Id., 1-2, 3.
260. HEADS OF FAMILIES.., 1790, NEW YORK, 147.

David and Deborah (Satterly) Howell were probably the parents of at least eight children {261}.

    51.   i.   DEBORAH[4] HOWELL, born in about 1729, died on 10 Sep 1735 "..in y[e] 7th.." year of her age, and is buried in the cemetery at the Jamesport Church.

    52.   ii.   DAVID[4] HOWELL, born in about 1731, "..Died July the 19th 1736, in y[e] 6th Year of his Age..", and is buried at Jamesport.

+ 53. iii.   RUTH[4] HOWELL, born on 22 June 1733 {262}.

    54.   iv.   REUBEN[4] HOWELL, born in about 1736, "..Died March y[e] 2[th]4 1737/8 in y[e] 2nd Year of his age..", and is buried at Jamesport.

+ 55. v.   DAVID[4] HOWELL, born in about 1740.

    56.   vi.   TOPPING (or HOPPING)[4] (or "HUNTING" {263}) HOWELL.

+ 57. vii.   JOHN[4] HOWELL, born in about 1744.

    58. viii.   Child[4], "David Howels Jun[r] wifes child Infant" died on 22 Jan 1748/9 {264}.

David and Lydia (Case) Howell were probably the parents of five children.

+ 59. ix.   GEORGE[4] HOWELL, born in about 1749 {265}.

+ 60. x.   MEHETABLE[4] HOWELL.

+ 61. xi.   JEMIMA[4] HOWELL, born on 10 Jly 1755 {266}.

+ 62. xii.   BENJAMIN[4] HOWELL, born in about 1759.

+ 63. xiii.   EZRA[4] HOWELL, born on 12 Oct 1762 {267}.

David and Mary (Murrow) Howell were probably the parents of at least five children.

    64. xiv.   MARY[4] HOWELL.

---

261. Wines, op. cit., 47.
262. James Clark Parshall, THE HISTORY OF THE PARSHALL FAMILY.., 32.
263. Stickney, op. cit., #B58$^1/_2$.
264. SR, 30; NYG&BR, XLVIII, 32 (Jan 1917).
265. Finch, op. cit., 6.
266. Id., 4.
267. Stickney, op. cit., #B58.

+ 65. xv.   LYDIA[4] HOWELL, born on 22 Feb 1767 {268}.

+ 66. xvi.   NOBLE[4] HOWELL, born on 23 Mch 1769 {269}.

+ 67. xvii.   DEBORAH[4] HOWELL, born on 6 Mch 1771 {270}.

  68. xviii.   FRANCES[4] HOWELL.

18. MARY[3] HOWELL (David[2], Richard[1]), the daughter of David[2] Howell, was born in the vicinity of Mattituck.

"Joseph Longbottom & Mary Howel" were married on about 10 Nov 1724 {271}.

On 24 Apr 1738, "Joseph Longbothem" joined in signing an agreement to give Mr. George Phillips the "..right and title to y[e] acre& a half of land he desires, y[t] is joining to his now dwelling house.." {272}.

Joseph Longbottom was listed for 1s 8d on the Brookhaven Town Assessment for 1741 {273}.

"Joseph Longbotum" signed the "Subscription Concerning the Meeting House" in support of the appointment of Rev. George McNish and dated 30 Jan 1742 {274}.

"Joseph Longbotom" was listed for 6s 7d on the Brookhaven Town Assessment for 1749 {275}.

No listing of the family of Joseph and Mary (Howell) Longbottom has been found or developed.

19. AARON[3] HOWELL (David[2], Richard[1]), the son of David[2] Howell, was born in about 1707 in the vicinity of Mattituck.

"Aaron Howel & Sarah Hallock" were married on 24 Nov 1726 {276}.

"Aaron Howel" was a Freeholder in Suffolk County on 27 Feb 1737/8 {277}.

Aaron Howell was an executor of his father's will, written on 12 Feb 1756 and proved on 25 Aug 1756, by which will David Howell left, to his "..second son Aaron all the land I bought of Jacob Osman, which he now has in his possession; and also my right in the manor of St. George, and $1/2$ of my meadow at Saw mill

---

268. Id., #B61$^{1}/_{2}$.
269. Id., #B63.
270. Id., #B62$^{1}/_{2}$.
271. SR, 78; NYB&BR, XLIX, 68 (Jan 1918).
272. Hutchinson, op. cit., 141-143.
273. Id., 154.
274. Belle Barstow, SETAUKET'S RELIGIOUS BEGINNINGS, 60-61.
275. Hutchinson, op. cit., 153.
276. SR, 78; NYG&BR, XLIX, 68 (Jan 1918).
277. O'Callaghan, op. cit., 249.

brook, which I bought of William Mapes, Also $^1/_3$ of my right in the Parsonage, and $^1/_4$ of my movables." {278}.

In his will of 14 Feb 1774, Henry Brown left to his son, Henry, "..all that land (which I bought of Aaron Howell, which he bought of Jehobod Hallock).." {279}.

On 20 Jly 1774, Aaron Howell married (2) Abigail Crane, the widow of Josiah Crane {280}.

Aaron Howell signed the Articles of Association in the Precinct of Cornwall {281}.

Aaron Howell, AE. 93, died on 23 May 1800 {282}.

Aaron and Sarah (Hallock) Howell were probably the parents of at least five children.

69.	i.	Child[4], "Aaron Howels child" died about Sep 1736 {283}.
70.	ii.	Child[4], "Aaron Howell Infant" died on 7 Jan 1739/40 {284}.
+ 71.	iii.	ISAIAH[4] HOWELL, born in about 1743.
72.	iv.	Child[4], "Aaron Howels child" died in about Oct 1754 {285}.
+ 73.	v.	AARON[4] HOWELL.

NOTE: *While it has not been definitely established that this Aaron Howell was the one who married the widow, Abigail Crane, his age at death suggests that this is a correct identification. Further, the Aaron Howell who married and died at Morristown has not, as far as we know, been claimed by any other Howell family branch.*

20. ISRAEL[3] HOWELL (David[2], Richard[1]), the son of David[2] Howell, was born in the vicinity of Mattituck.

"Israel Howel & Hannah Smith" were married in about Feb 1734/5 {286}.

By his will of 12 Feb 1756, proved on 29 Oct 1756, David Howell gave to his "..third son Israel Howell one equal fourth part of all my moveable estate of every kind excepting £100 - which I gave to my son David and my daughter Mary

---

278. WNYSO, Liber 20, 97-99; (V, 132-133).
279. Id., Liber 34, 376; (X, 168).
280. HISTORY OF THE FIRST PRESBYTERIAN CHURCH OF MORRISTOWN, N.J., II, THE COMBINED REGISTERS, 1742-1885, 111.
281. Russel Headley, THE HISTORY OF ORANGE COUNTY, NEW YORK, 78.
282. HISTORY..FIRST PRESBYTERIAN CHURCH..MORRISTOWN, N.J., II, 111.
283. SR, 21; NYG&BR, XLVIII, 23 (Jan 1917).
284. Id., 23; NYG&BR, XLVIII, 25 (Jan 1917).
285. Id., 37; NYG&BR, XLVIII, 170 (Apr 1917).
286. Id., 81; NYG&BR, XLIX, 71 (Jan 1918).

and also all that land which I bought of my brother, Jonathan Howell, bounded on the south and west by my brother, Richard Howell, on the North by the sound and on the East by the land of James Fanning and also two lots of salt meadow upon the South side of Peconac river which my honored father gave me and also all that fresh meadow upon the South Side of Peconac river which I bought of my brother, Jonathan Howell, all which I give to him and to his heirs and assigns forever." {287}.

Israel Howell was an early settler of Baiting Hollow, to which he moved probably "..soon after 1740, and sold to Calvin Cook before the Revolution. He did not move immediately, and Cook built himself a house nearby - that was the fourth house (in Baiting Hollow) of a certainty just by what was called the Clay Pit, a little pond southwest of Jerich Hill. The two original houses were nearly north of the Pond, one farther north than the other. Howell's was nearby, W. Cook's was directly south. Tradition says that Terry built before Howell, and the one before him has been lost." {288}.

Israel Howell was elected as one of several "fence views" at the Annual Meeting of the Town of Southold on 7 Apr 1761 {289}.

On 12 Mch 1765, Freegift Wells and William Benjamin, two of the Commissioners of Highways for the Town of Southold, established a roadway "..a Cross a number of Lotts In the Second Devision att aquabague..so Runing Westerly along by the Southside of Abner Lows house and thence Westerly to the Southside of the house of Israel Howells and thence Westerly along by the Southside of the house of Joshua Wells.." {290}.

"Isrel Howell" was listed as the head of a family consisting of one male of above 50 years of age, one of under 16, and one female of above 16, residing in Southold Township, Suffolk County, New York, in the Census of 1776 {291}.

Israel and Hannah (Smith) Howell "..lived and died one fourth of a mile north of the North Road, opposite Israel Howell's, Baiting Hollow." {292}.

Israel and Hannah (Smith) Howell "..are probably buried in the cemetery (at Baiting Hollow), but their graves are unmarked." {293}.

Israel and Hannah (Smith) Howell were the parents of at least five children {294}.

+ 74. i. SILAS⁴ HOWELL, born in about 1743.

+ 75. ii. ISRAEL⁴ HOWELL, born in about 1744.

  76. iii. MARY⁴ HOWELL.

287. WNYSO, Liber 20, 97-99; (V, 132-133).
288. James Franklin Young, op. cit., VIII, 10-11, (June 1982).
289. STR, Liber D, 129 right; (III, 209).
290. Id., 225 left; (III, 393).
291. CENSUS OF SUFFOLK COUNTY, NEW YORK, 1776, 23.
292. George H. Tuthill, Personal communication, in the possession of the SCHS, 1996.
293. Young, op. cit.
294. Id.

+ 77. iv.   SAMUEL[4] HOWELL, born in about 1748.

   78. v.   ANNA[4] HOWELL.

21. RICHARD[3] HOWELL (David[2], Richard[1]), the son of David[2] Howell, was born in the vicinity of Mattituck in about 1712.

Richard Howell and Elizabeth Tuthill were married in about 1732 {295}, although the marriage of "Rich[d] Howel & Mehete[bl] Howel" was recorded in about Sep 1732 {296}.

"Richard Howel" was a Freeholder in Suffolk County on 27 Feb 1737/8 {297}.

"Lei[t] Richard Howell" was elected as one of several "fence viewers & prisors" at the Annual Meeting of the Town of Southold on 7 Apr 1752. He was again elected to this office on 5 Apr 1769, and on 7 Apr 1772 {298}.

By his will of 12 Feb 1756, proved on 25 Aug 1756, David Howell left to his "..fourth son Richard all my land and meadow not herein disposed of, and all the rest of my movable estate.". Richard Howell was also named as an executor of this will {299}.

James Halliock left, to his son, James, "..the house and land whereon I now live, bounded easterly on Richard Howell and Micah Howell, containing about one hundred and twelve acres. Also, another piece of land containing thirty acres, bounded easterly by Capt. Richard Howell.." by his will of 22 Sep 1774 {300}.

Richard Howell signed as "Not agreeing to y[e] Association" in 1775 {301}.

Richard Howell was listed as the head of a household consisting of one male of above 50 years of age, three of above 16 and under 50, three females of above 16, three of under 16, three negroes of above 16, and six of under 16, all residing in Southold Township, Suffolk County, New York, in the Census of 1776 {302}.

"Capt. Richard Howell" was listed as the head of a household consisting of thirteen persons in Mattituck parish by Lt. Isaac Reeve on 15 Jan 1778 and again on 25 Aug 1778 for Andrew Eliot, lieutenant governor {303}.

Richard Howell, farmer, of the Township of Southold, gave his age as 67 when he signed the Oath of Allegiance and Peaceable Behaviour required by

---

295. Wilbur Franklin Howell, op. cit., 74.
296. SR, 80; NYG&BR, XLIX, 70 (Jan 1918).
297. O'Callaghan, op. cit., 249.
298. STR, Liber D, 126 left, 131 left, 133 right; (III, 202, 216-217, 220).
299. WNYSO, Liber 20, 97-99; (V, 132-133).
300. Id., Liber 34, 395-396 (X, 177).
301. Frederic Gregory Mather, THE REFUGEES OF 1776 FROM LONG ISLAND TO CONNECTICUT, 1057.
302. CENSUS OF SUFFOLK COUNTY, NEW YORK, 1776, 20.
303. NGSQ, 63, 280 (1975).

Governor William Tryon in 1778 {304}.

By his will of 14 Mch 1783, proved on 17 Mch 1784, Richard Howell left household furniture and livestock to his wife, Elizabeth, land to his sons, Edmund, Phineas and Parshall, £30 to his son, Richard, 30s each to his daughters, Elizabeth Brown, Joanna Terry, Keziah Soper and Mary Benjamin, and directed that all his negroes be sold, and that his son, Abram, be supported by his son, Parshall, who was his principal heir. His sons, Edmund and Parshall, along with Daniel Wells, were named as executors of this will {305}.

"Capt. Richard Howell" died on 13 Nov 1783, in his 72nd year, and is buried in the cemetery at the Mattituck Presbyterian Church {306}.

Richard and Elizabeth (Tuthill) Howell were the parents of at least ten children.

+ 79. i.   ELIZABETH[4] HOWELL, born in about 1733.

  80. ii.   Son[4], "Richard Howell Juner son" died on 21 Mch 1737/8 {307}.

+ 81. iii. EDMUND[4] HOWELL, born in about 1739.

+ 82. iv. JOANNA[4] HOWELL.

+ 83. v.   MARY[4] HOWELL, born in 1744 {308}.

+ 84. vi. PHINEAS[4] HOWELL, born in about 1746.

+ 85. vii. KEZIAH[4] HOWELL.

  86. viii. ABRAHAM[4] HOWELL, was apparently physically or mentally retarded, died on 26 June 1802 {309} {310}. James Peter Howell stated that "Richard Howell was idiotic" {311}, suggesting that, perhaps, the family legends had confused him with Abraham.

+ 87. ix. RICHARD[4] HOWELL, born in about 1756.

+ 88. x.   PARSHALL[4] HOWELL, born in about 1760.

---

304. P.R.O. Colonial Office, Class 5, Vol. 1109, 87, from a copy in the possession of the East Hampton Library, generously made available through the assistance of Dorothy King, Librarian, THE PENNYPACKER COLLECTION.
305. WNYSO, Liber 36, 428-429; (XII, 255-256).
306. Craven, op. cit., 373.
307. SR, 22; NYG&BR, XLVIII, 24 (Jan 1917).
308. Gloria Wall Bicha and Helen Benjamin Brown, THE BENJAMIN FAMILY IN AMERICA, 694.
309. Craven, op. cit., 353.
310. SR, 66; NYG&BR, XLVIII, 344 (Oct 1917).
311. James Peter Howell, op. cit.

22. JAMES³ HOWELL (David², Richard¹), the son of David² Howell, was born in the vicinity of Mattituck.

"(J)ames Howel & Mary Holloway" were married on 26 Nov 1741 {312}.

By his will of 12 Feb 1756, proved on 25 Aug 1756, David Howell left to his "..fifth son James ¹/₄ of all movables, and all that part of my land where he now lives, which he now has in possession, with the meadow belonging thereto, Also ¹/₃ of my two lots of meadow on the Broad meadow, on the south side of Peconic river, which I bought of John Howell, Also ¹/₃ of my right in the Parsonage." {313}.

On 26 Mch 1759, James Howell, "Tayler", of the Precinct of Goshen, sold his share in a "..Lot of Land and Lot of Meadow Situate in the Patent of Wawayanda in the County of Orange within the Province of New York being part of a Tract of Land called by the Name of Cromelins Tract and known by the Lots Number five and Eight..", purchased from "..Ezekiel Roe of Flushing in Queens County on long Island and Province af᷈. by a Certain Deed bearing date the third day of April 1756.." to his "..Tennant in Common..", Joseph Drake, by a deed recorded on 28 Oct 1765 {314}.

James Howell, of District #5 of the Town of Warwick, was assessed for £3 7s in Sep 1775 by John Wood, Assessor {315}.

James Howell signed the Articles of Association as an "Exempt" at Goshen on 8 June 1775 {316}.

A James Howell earned bounty rights for his service in the Fourth Regiment of Orange County militia {317}.

James and Mary (Holloway) Howell were the parents of at least one child.

89.   i.   DAVID⁴ HOWELL, baptized at Mattituck on 26 Oct 1755 {318}.

NOTE: *It now appears that we were in error when we took the James Howell who was of Warwick in 1775 to be the same person as the James Howell who was of Walkill in 1790 ff {319}. However, we still believe that James Howell of Warwick was in fact the son of DAVID HOWELL (#4), since we believe that he and DAVID HOWELL (#17), both residents of the Town of Warwick in 1775, were brothers, and he had a son, David, as mentioned by Craven {320}.*

25. DEBORAH³ HOWELL (Richard², Richard¹), the daughter of Richard² and

---

312. SR, 84; NYG&BR, XLIX, 74 (Jan 1918).
313. WNYSO, Liber 20, 97-99; (V, 132-133).
314. Orange County Deeds, Liber C, 217-219.
315. Ruttenber & Clark, op. cit., 567.
316. Samuel W. Eager, AN OUTLINE HISTORY OF ORANGE COUNTY.., 502.
317. James A. Roberts, NEW YORK IN THE REVOLUTION, Vol. I, 256.
318. Craven, op. cit., 256.
319. Donnelly, *The Genealogist*, Fall 1999, 13, 170-171.
320. Id.

Deborah Howell, was born in the vicinity of Mattituck.

"_____ Singletery & Deb Howel" were married in about Dec 1730 {321}.

Richard Howell left "..to the children of my deceased daughter, Deborah Doddy, £5 each when of age.." by his will of 10 Jan 1758, proved on 7 Apr 1769 {322}.

No listing of the children of Deborah (Howell) Doddy has been found or developed.

26. SARAH[3] HOWELL (Richard[2], Richard[1]), the daughter of Richard[2] and Deborah Howell, was born in the vicinity of Mattituck.

"Willi Pene..Workt upon the meting hous tember..1.." day in 1731, in the construction of the Aquebogue Meeting House {323}.

"W[m] Penny & Sarah Howel" were married on about 13 Jan 1731/2 {324}.

On 23 Mch 1743/4, "The Commiss[rs] of the highways have layed out a two pole way through Gates or barrs going out of the Kings Road between William Penny & Daniel Pike running down to y[e] Mill at the head of Peter Halliocks meadows & from thence to Peconick Medows with privileges to each one medow" {325}.

In June 1749, there died "W[m] Penneys wife Sarah about y[e] 15th" {326}.

By his will of 10 Jan 1758, proved on 7 Apr 1769, Richard Howell directed his son, Richard, to pay the children of his deceased daughter, Sarah Penny, £5 each when they became of age {327}.

"William Pennie" was listed as the head of a family consisting of one male of above 50 years of age, one of under 16, and one female of over 16, residing in Southold Township, Suffolk County, New York, in the Census of 1776 {328}.

William Penny was listed as the head of a family of three persons residing in the Aquebogue district of Southold on 22 Aug 1778 by Daniel and Jeremiah Wells {329}.

William Penny died on 19 Mch 1781 {330}.

William and Sarah (Howell) Penny were the parents of at least four children {331}.

---

321. SR, 80; NYG&BR, XLIX, 70 (Jan 1918).
322. WNYSO, Liber 27, 61-62; (VII, 264).
323. Wines, op. cit., 10.
324. SR, 80; NYG&BR, XLIX, 70 (Jan 1918).
325. STR, Liber D, 223 left; (III, 387-388).
326. SR, 30; NYG&BR, XLVIII, 32 (Jan 1917).
327. WNYSO, Liber 27, 61-62; (VII, 264).
328. CENSUS OF SUFFOLK COUNTY, 1776, 21.
329. NGSQ, 63, 277 (1975).
330. SR, 52; NYG&BR, XLVIII, 280 (Jly 1917).
331. Wines, op. cit., 27.

i.   Son, "Wᵐ Penneys son" died about Aug 1738 {332}.

ii. WILLIAM PENNY, born in about 1740.

iii. JOHN PENNY, born in about 1744.

iv. Daughter, "Wᵐ Pennys daughter" died on 24 Dec 1748 {333}.

27. RICHARD³ HOWELL (Richard², Richard¹), the son of Richard² and Deborah (Reeve?) Howell, was born in about 1719, probably in the vicinity of Riverhead.
   "Richᵈ Howel & Patience Welse" were married on 21 Aug 1740 {334}. She was the daughter of Henry and Patience Wells, and was born in about 1719 {335}.
   "Richard Howell juʳ" was one of several Fence Viewers elected at the Annual Meeting of the Town of Southold on 3 Apr 1754 {336}.
   Richard Howell was bequeathed "..all my personal estate..", except what was left to his stepmother, by his father's will of 10 Jan 1758, proved on 7 Apr 1769. He was also instructed to pay all his father's debts and legacies {337}.
   Richard Howell was listed as the head of a household consisting of one male of above 50 years of age, one of above 16 and under 50, four females of above 16, and one other free person, residing in Southold Township, Suffolk County, New York, in the Census of 1776 {338}.
   "Richᵈ Howel Junʳ", farmer, of the Township of Southold, gave his age as 59 when he signed the Oath of Allegiance and Peaceable Behaviour required by Governor William Tryon in 1778 {339}.
   "Richard Howell, Jr." was the enumerated as the head of a household of six persons residing in the Aquebogue District of Southold on 22 Aug 1778 by Daniel and Jeremiah Wells {340}.
   "Richard Howel Riverhead" died on 30 Dec 1779 {341}.
   Richard and Patience (Wells) Howell were the parents of at least three children.

+ 90. i.   RICHARD⁴ HOWELL, born in about 1746.

332. SR, 23; NYG&BR, XLVIII, 25 (Jan 1917).
333. Id., 30; NYG&BR, XLVIII, 32 (Jan 1917).
334. Id., 84; NYG&BR, XLIX, 74 (Jan 1918).
335. Walter M. Wells, Jr., WILLIAM WELLS OF SOUTHOLD, D3014.
336. STR, Liber D, 127 right; (III, 203-204).
337. WNYSO, Liber 27, 61-62; (VII, 264).
338. CENSUS OF SUFFOLK COUNTY, NEW YORK, 1776, 24.
339. P.R.O. Colonial Office, Class 5, Vol. 1109, 89.
340. NGSQ, 63, 276 (1975).
341. SR, 51: NYG&BR, XLVIII, 279 (Jly 1917).

91.   ii.   Son[4], "Rich[d] Howel[s] Ju[r] son" died on 21 Apr 1750 {342}.

+ 92.   iii.   MERRITT[4] HOWELL, born in about 1750.

28. DOROTHY[3] HOWELL (Richard[2], Richard[1]), the daughter of Richard[2] and Deborah Howell, was born in the vicinity of Mattituck.

"David Conkline and Dorothy Howel" were married at Huntington on 29 Jan 1735/6 by the Rev. Ebenezer Prime {343}. He was the son of Timothy Conklin and was born on 29 Mch 1714. He had a twin sister, Mary {344}.

By the will of his father, Timothy Conklin, written on 30 Dec 1734, and proved on 14 Dec 1743, David Conklin was given "..my team and tackling..my home lot on the west side of the road, over against my now dwelling-house..". With his brother, Thomas, he was instructed to pay £12 to his borther, Stephen, and to contribute his "..equal proportion for the support.." of his mother, Abigail. He and Thomas also inherited all the remainder of their father's lands and meadows not otherwise bequeathed {345}.

Daniel Turner left, to his "..sister, Mercy Smith..the assignment of a bond due..from William Ferguson and David Conklin, of Bedford, for £10.." by his will of 15 Mch 1742, proved on 18 Mch 1746 {346}.

The earmark for the livestock of David Conkling was recorded as "..a step afore side of the off ear and halfpenney under same ear Recorded December 11th 1747 p Reuben Holms clak" {347}.

On 27 Dec 1751, David Conkling, of Bedford, Westchester County, New York, sold, to Joseph Clark, II, "Nine or ten lots of land in..Bedford New Purchase called the Rough Lotts being two hundred and twenty of fifty acres and bounded..easterly by a high way that leads from the above sd David Conklins by Benjamin Griffins southerly by a lot being John Holmes Es[qr] - westerly the Woseas land and northerly by Moses Crisseas land and a highway.." for "..£80 currant lawfull money of New York" {348}.

Nehemiah Lounsberry and Joseph Clark, friends of David Conklin, and his principal creditors, were issued letters of administration on his estate on 5 Mch 1756, after his widow, Dorothy, declined {349}.

No listing of the children of David and Dorothy (Howell) Conklin has been found or developed.

---

342. Id., 31; NYG&BR, XLVIII, 164 (Apr 1917).
343. RECORDS, FIRST CHURCH IN HUNTINGTON, 70.
344. HUNTINGTON TOWN RECORDS, Printed Records, (HTR), 2, 320.
345. WNYSO, Liber 15, 152-154; (III, 415-416).
346. Id., Liber 16, 111; (IV, 119-120).
347. BEDFORD TOWN RECORDS (BdTR), (Printed records, 4, 2).
348. Id., (Printed records, 4, 45).
349. Dr. Kenneth Scott, GENEALOGICAL DATA FROM ADMINISTRATION PAPERS.., 66.

29. HANNAH[3] HOWELL (Richard[2], Richard[1]), the daughter of Richard[2] and Deborah Howell, was born in the vicinity of Mattituck.

Hannah Howell may have married Phillip Ketcham. Philip Ketcham was born on 26 Feb 1716/7, the son of Philip Ketcham {350}.

On 20 Jan 1748/9, Nathan Clark, yeoman, and Abigail his wife, of Bedford, Westchester County, New York, sold to Zerubbabel Hayt of Canaan Parish, Fairfield County, Connecticut, for "..£300 corrant money of New York.." a "..House and hum lot which is in Bedford New Purchase contain one hundred acres..bounded..northerly by a highway westerly by Nehemiah Lounsbury land southerly by Philip Cetchums farm and easterly by Jonathan Taylors land" {351}.

On 27 Dec 1751, Philip Ketcham was a witness to a bill of sale by which David Conkling sold land in Bedford New Purchase to Joseph Clark {352}. On 11 Jan 1757, he swore, before Gilbert Bloomer, Esq., one of the judges of the Inferior Court of Common Pleas, that he saw David Conkling execute this deed {353}.

By her father's will of 10 Jan 1758, proved on 7 Apr 1769, "Hannah Ketchum" was to receive £10 from her brother, Richard {354}.

Philip Ketcham moved to Orange County, where he "..located about half-way between Warwick & Belvale." {355}.

"Philip Ketcham", and a "Hannah Ketcham", were members of the Warwick Baptist Church in 1765 {356}.

Philip and Hannah (Howell) Ketcham were probably the parents of at least three children {357}.

    i.   NATHANIEL KETCHAM, born in 1750.

    ii.   PHILLIP KETCHAM.

    iii.   SAMUEL KETCHAM, born on 13 Nov 1757.

30. ABIGAIL[3] HOWELL (Richard[2], Richard[1]), the daughter of Richard[2] and Deborah Howell, was born in the vicinity of Mattituck.

By her father's will of 10 Jan 1758, proved on 7 Apr 1769, "Abigail Horton" was to receive 5s from her brother, Richard {358}.

The husband of Abigail (Howell) Horton has not been identified, nor has

---

350. HTR, 2, 371.
351. BdTR, (Printed records, 4, 46).
352. Id.; (4, 2).
353. Id.; (4, 46).
354. WNYSO, Liber 27, 61-62; (VII, 264).
355. Ruttenber & Clark, op. cit., 569.
356. Id., 582.
357. Hester Halstead Pier, Personal communication.
358. WNYSO, Liber 27, 61-62; (VII, 264).

a listing of their family been found. It has been established that she was not the wife of Simon Grover Horton {359}, as speculated by Charles B. Moore {360}.

32. ISAAC[3] HOWELL (Isaac[2], Richard[1]), the son of Isaac[2] and Phebe Howell, was born in the vicinity of Mattituck.

"Isaac Howel & Mary Curtice" were married on 6 May 1731 {361}.

"Isaac Howel" was a Freeholder in Suffolk County on 27 Feb 1737/8 {362}.

"Isaac Howel Juner.." was "..kild" on 26 Apr 1746 {363}.

Isaac and Mary (Curtice) Howell may have been the parents of at least three children.

+   93.   i.   NATHAN[4] HOWELL.

    94.   ii.   Child[4], "Isaac Howel Juner child" died in about Dec 1739 {364}.

+   95.   iii.   ISAAC[4] HOWELL, born in about 1746.

NOTE: *Family tradition says that Isaac[4] Howell had a half-sister, Lois, who married a Schellinger {365}, indicating that Mary (Curtiss) Howell remarried after Isaac's death. No confirmation of this has been found.*

33. PHEBE[3] HOWELL (Isaac[2], Richard[1]), the daughter of Isaac[2] and Phebe Howell, was born in the vicinity of Mattituck.

"Nath[n] Curwin & Phebe Howel" were married in Feb 1736/7 {366}. Nathan Corwin, the son of Daniel Corwin and his first wife, Mary Ramsey {367}, was born in 1714 {368}.

By the will of his father, written on 4 Sep 1747, and proved on 6 Oct 1747, Nathan Corwin, who was an executor of this will, received "..all my land north of the North Country road, called the new road..", and he was instructed to

359. Hester Halstead Pier, op. cit.
360. Moore, op. cit., 93.
361. SR, 80; NYG&BR, XLIX, 70 (Jan 1918).
362. O'Callaghan, op. cit., 249.
363. SR, 28; NYG&BR, XLVIII, 30 (Jan 1917).
364. Id., 24; NYG&BR, XLVIII, 26 (Jan 1917).
365. James Barnaby Howell, HOWELL GENEALOGY, Supplemented by Ella Elizabeth (Howell) Pyle and Amanda N. (Frink) Hawkes, 3, from a copy in the possession of the library of the Society of the Daughters of the American Revolution, 1992.
366. SR, 82; NYG&BR, XLIX, 72 (Jan 1918).
367. Mather, op. cit., 315; Wines, op. cit., 55, 56.
368. Craven, op. cit., 317.

"..pay to my two grand-sons, Edward and Separate Corwin, each £5 when of age.."
{369}.

On 3 Apr 1754, Nathan Corwin was selected to be a Fence Viewer for the ensuing year at the Annual Meeting of the Town of Southold {370}.

It is likely that Nathan Corwin died near the end of Apr 1774, since it was recorded that "Widow Phebe Corwin Ralect to Nathen" died on 31(sic) Apr 1774 {371}.

"Wid Corwin" was listed as the head of a family consisting of one male of 16 and under 50 years of age, and three females of over 16, residing in Southold Township, Suffolk County, New York, in the Census of 1776 {372}.

On 22 Aug 1778, the widow, Phebe Corwin, was enumerated by Daniel and Jeremiah Wells as the head of a family of two persons in the Aquebogue district of Southold {373}.

Phebe Corwin, widow, died on 4 May 1783 {374}, although it was recorded that "Wid Phebe C(orwin) Relect Nath." died on 1 June 1783 {375}.

Nathan and Phebe (Howell) Corwin were the parents of at least one child.

    i.   NATHAN CORWIN, born about 1749 {376}.

35. MICAH³ HOWELL (Isaac², Richard¹), the son of Isaac² and Phebe Howell, was born in the vicinity of Mattituck in about 1720.

"Micah Howel & Bethia Reeve" were married on 10 June 1741 {377}. She was the daughter of Thomas and Mary (Salmon) Reeve {378}.

Micah Howell was an executor of the will of Peter Halliock, of Southold, written on 11 Apr 1753, and proved on 7 Oct 1756 {379}.

"Mica Howell" was selected to be a Constable for the ensuing year at the Annual Meeting of the Town of Southold on 3 Apr 1754 {380}.

By the will of his father, Isaac Howell, written on 30 Sep 1757, and proved on 28 Nov 1759, Micah Howell received "..all my lands and meadow and buildings not disposed of, and also my now dwelling house, which I gave to my wife, after her interest in the same shall expire, also my farming tackling, and he is to provide for his mother a good garden, and 6 bushels of wheat, 6 bushels of corn, 30 pounds of flax, a cow, and ²/₃ of her firewood." Micah and Daniel Howell

369. WNYSO, Liber 16, 261; (IV, 167)
370. STR, Liber D, 127 right; (III, 203-204).
371. SR, 45; NYG&BR, XLVIII, 178 (Apr 1917).
372. CENSUS OF SUFFOLK COUNTY, NEW YORK, 1776, 17.
373. NGSQ, 63, 276 (1975).
374. Craven, op. cit., 345.
375. SR, 54; NYG&BR, XLVIII, 282 (Jly 1917).
376. Mather, op. cit., 318.
377. SR, 84; NYG&BR, XLIX, 74 (Jan 1918).
378. Craven, op. cit., 72.
379. WNYSO, Liber 20, 149-150; (V, 143).
380. STR, Liber D, 127 right; (III, 203-204).

were to serve as executors of their father's will, and to divide his wearing apparel, and to share the rest of his estate not disposed of with their sisters, Phebe Corwin, Rachel Corwin and Hannah Howell {381}.

"Mica Howell" was one of three voted to have to assist the assessors by the Annual Meeting of the Town of Southold on 6 Apr 1757 {382}.

Micah Howell was an executor of the will of his father-in-law, Thomas Reeve, written on 24 Sep 1760, and proved on 10 Nov 1761 {383}.

Micah Howell was a witness to the will of Zerubabel Halliock, written on 3 Mch 1761, and proved 15 May 1761 {384}.

On 2 Apr 1765, Micah Howell was selected to be one of several "..fence Viewers & prisors of Damage.." {385}.

On 9 Feb 1769, Micah Howell signed a document which stated that "We whose Names are underwritten Inhabitants of Southold in Mattituk Society, having Rights in the Personage belonging to Mattituk, considering the Difficult Circumstances in which it lies at present, Do consent and agree that the same shall be sold, upon the Terms following (viz) that the Money arising from said Sale shall be converted to the Support of the Gospel in Mattituk, and we also bind not only ourselves but our Heirs, Executors, Administrators and Assigns to the performance of the above Terms or Premises.." {386}.

"The next month, March 24th, 1769, a more explicit agreement was signed, providing that the proceeds of the sale of the parsonage "shall be devoted as a bank for the support of the gospel ministry according to ye presbyterian order in Mattituk", and that a committee, consisting of Thomas Reeve, Micah Howell and John Gardiner, and their successors, "shall have full power to hire out the sd money and dispose of the Interest for the support of the gospel ministry yearly and not to have any liberty to dispose of any of the principal otherways unless it be to pay out of ye principal their parts that do not live in ye parish"" {387}.

"The parsonage was sold and was probably bought by Micah Howell, whose descendants afterwards owned it, but the deed is not on record" {388}.

In about 1772, Deacon Micah Howell reported that the Mattituck Church had invited Rev. Jesse Ives, a member of the Eastern Association of New London District, to come and preach among them {389}.

"Mica Howell, yeoman" was a witness to the 22 Sep 1774 will of James Halliock, of Southold, which was proved on 14 Dec 1775 {390}.

Micah Howell signed the Articles of Association in 1775 {391}.

---

381. WNYSO, Liber 21, 465-467; (V, 350-351).
382. STR, Liber D, 128 right; (III, 206).
383. WNYSO, Liber 23, 215-216; (VI, 129).
384. Id., 73-74; (VI, 95).
385. STR, Liber D, 131 left; (III, 213).
386. Craven, op. cit., 95.
387. Id.
388. Id., 96.
389. Id., 117.
390. WNYSO, Liber 34, 395-396; (X, 177).
391. Mather, op. cit., 1057.

Micah Howell was listed as the head of a household consisting of one male of above 50 years of age, one female of above 16, and two Negroes of above 16, residing in Southold Township, Suffolk County, New York, in the Census of 1776 {392}.

Micah Howell was selected to be an "overseer" for the ensuing year at the Annual Meeting of the Town of Southold held on 7 Apr 1778 {393}.

Micah Howell, farmer, of the Township of Southold, gave his age as 58 when he signed the Oath of Allegiance and Peaceable Behaviour required by Governor William Tryon in 1778 {394}.

Micah Howell was listed as the head of a household consisting of five persons in Mattituck parish on 25 Aug 1778 {395}.

"Micah Howell and Abner Wells.." were "..chosen to make return of votes" at the Annual Meeting of the Town of Southold on 6 Apr 1779 {396}.

"Micah Howels Wife" died on 21 Sep 1782 {397}.

On 1 Apr 1783, "Micah Howel" was chosen as an "Overseer of the Poor", for the ensuing year, by the Annual Meeting of the "Freeholders of Southold" {398}.

Micah Howell and Deborah Hubbard were married at Mattituck on 3 June 1788 {399}. She was the widow of Isaac Hubbard, whom she had married on 10 Jly 1760 {400}, was the daughter of Henry and Temperance (Bayley) Conkling {401}, and was born on 1 Nov 1732 {402}.

"Mecah Howell Senr" was listed as the head of a household consisting of one free white male of 16 years of age and upwards, one free white male of under 16, one free white female, and two slaves, residing in Southold Town, Suffolk County, New York, in the First Census of the United States, 1790 {403}.

"In 1796 Deacon Micah Howell provided in his will for the economical use of his farm as follows: "Ordering my farm to be used in the most prudent manner, with but little plowing, and to cut no more timber than what is nesessary for ye use of the farm." {404}. This will, which was written on 14 Apr 1796, and proved on 1 Oct 1799, included bequests to his wife, Deborah, his son, Micah, and his grand-daughters, "Sinthy" and "Christian" Howell. His estate was to be divided between his son, Micah, and his grand-son, Daniel Howell {405}.

392. CENSUS OF SUFFOLK COUNTY, 1776, 20.
393. STR, Liber D, 136 right; (III, 228).
394. P.R.O. Colonial Office, Class 5, Vol. 1109, 87.
395. NGSQ, 63, 280 (1975).
396. STR, Liber D, 137 left; (III, 229).
397. SR, 53; NYG&BR, XLVIII, 281 (Jly 1917).
398. STR, Liber D, 139 right; (III, 232).
399. Craven, op. cit., 331.
400. SR, 94; NYG&BR, XLIX, 162 (Apr 1918).
401. Leigh Mark Young, THE REGISTER, SCHS, XXII, #1, 23 (Summer 1996).
402. NYG&BR, XXXIX, 132-133 (Apr 1908).
403. HEADS OF FAMILIES.., 1790, NEW YORK, 170.
404. Craven, op. cit., 226.
405. Suffolk County Wills, Liber B, 77-79; Suffolk County Estates, File 430.

Retus, the servant of Micah Howell, was baptized at Mattituck on 28 Feb 1798 {406}. He died on 1 May 1802 {407}.

Micah Howell died on 24 Aug 1799 {408}.

Deborah (Conkling) Hubbard Howell died on 26 Dec 1806 {409}, and is buried in the cemetery at the Mattituck Presbyterian Church, where her gravestone indicates that she was 73 years of age when she died {410}.

Micah and Bethia (Reeve) Howell were probably the parents of two childen {411}.

+ 96. i. MICAH^4 HOWELL, born in about 1742.

+ 97. ii. BETHIA^4 HOWELL.

36. DANIEL^3 HOWELL (Isaac^2, Richard^1), the son of Isaac^2 and Phebe Howell, was born in the vicinity of Mattituck in about 1726.

"Dan^{ll} Howel & Sarah Swesey" were married in about Apr 1747 {412}. She was born in about 1726.

On 6 Apr 1757, Daniel Howell was chosen to serve as a "Fence Viewer" for the ensuing year by the Annual Meeting of the Town of Southold, an office for which he was again selected on 5 Apr 1769 {413}. He was selected to serve as one of several Commissioners for the Highways on 7 Apr 1767 {414}.

On 3 Apr 1770, Daniel Howell was selected to be one of three "Overseers" {415}.

At the Annual "..publick Town meeting.." on 5 Apr 1774, it was "..Voted to Devide the Town into Eight Distrects for mending & Repairing High ways..". Of these, the Sixth District extended "..from Sd John Terrys Westerly as far as the River head & to ye manner Loin..". It had "..Daniel Howell Commisiner or overseer.." {416}.

Daniel Howell was listed as the head of a household consisting of one male of above 50 years of age, two of above 16 and under 50, two of under 16, three females of above 16, one of under 16, and two Negroes of under 16, residing in Southold Township, Suffolk County, New York, in the Census of 1776 {417}.

On 1 Apr 1777, Daniel Howell was selected to be one of several

---

406. Craven, op. cit., 307.
407. Id., 353.
408. Id., 352; SR, 65; NYG&BR, XLVIII, 343 (Oct 1917).
409. Craven, op. cit., 355.
410. Id., 374.
411. Thomas H. Donnelly, THE REGISTER, SCHS, XVI, 93-96 (Spring 1991).
412. SR, 86; NYG&BR, XLIX, 154 (Apr 1918).
413. STR, Liber D, 128 right, 131 left; (III, 205-206, 216-217).
414. Id., 131 right; (III, 214).
415. Id., 132 right; (III, 217-218).
416. Id., 134 left; (III, 221-222).
417. CENSUS OF SUFFOLK COUNTY, NEW YORK, 1776, 22.

"Overseers for the poor" {418}. He was selected as one of seven men "..Chosen to adjust the Representatives Accompts.." on 4 Apr 1780 {419}.

On 14 Apr 1778, it was recorded "To payd Daniel Howell Browne Children..£9 10s 0d" {420}.

On 21 Apr 1779, it was recorded that there was paid "to Daniel Howell Overseer - -£1 0s 0d" {421}, on 11 Apr 1780, "To Daniel Howell for a Child of Elizabeth Teleball - - £1 12s 0d", and, on 10 Apr 1781, "to Daniel Howell for Elias White and Frederick White £19 1s 4d" {422}.

On 22 Aug 1778, Daniel Howell was listed as the head of a family of seven persons living in the Aquebogue district of Southold by Daniel and Jeremiah Wells {423}.

Daniel Howell, farmer, of the Township of Southold, gave his age as 52 when he signed the Oath of Allegiance and Peaceable Behaviour required by Governor William Tryon in 1778 {424}.

Deacon Daniel Howell died on 28 Jan 1782 {425} at the age of 56, and is buried in the Aquebogue Cemetery {426}.

Sarah (Swesey) Howell died on 13 Jan 1803, at the age of 78, and is buried beside her husband at Aquebogue {427}.

Daniel and Sarah (Swesey) Howell were the parents of at least four children.

+ 98. i. SILAS[4] HOWELL, born in about 1751.

99. ii. Child[4], "Daniel Howels child" died on 13 Oct 1754 {428}.

+ 100. iii. JOSEPH[4] HOWELL, born in about 1757.

101. iv. SARAH[4] HOWELL, born in about 1762, died on 6 Nov 1798 at the age of 36, and is buried beside her parents at Aquebogue {429}.

37. RACHEL[3] HOWELL (Isaac[2], Richard[1]), the daughter of Isaac[2] and Phebe Howell, was born in the vicinity of Mattituck in about 1730.

---

418. STR, Liber D, 30 right, 136 left; (III, 57, 227).
419. Id., 137 left; (III, 230).
420. Id., 30 left; (III, 59).
421. Id., 31 right; (III, 59-60).
422. Id., 32 left; (III, 61).
423. NGSQ, 63, 276 (1975).
424. P.R.O. Colonial Office, Class 5, Vol.1109, 81.
425. SR, 52; NYG&BR, XLVIII, 280 (Jly 1917)
426. Gravestone, Aquebogue Cemetery, from the collection of gravestone markings at the SCHS, with those for Aquebogue and Jamesport probably being the work of Orville B. Ackerly.
427. Gravestone, Aquebogue Cemetery.
428. SR, 37; NYG&BR, XLVIII, 170 (Apr 1917).
429. Gravestone, Aquebogue Cemetery.

"Johath[n] Curwin & Rechel Howel" were married on 15 Dec 1748 {430}. Jonathan, the son of Theophilus and Hannah (Ramsay) Corwin {431}, was born on 13 Dec 1721.

Jonathan Corwin was selected to be a "..fence viewer.." for the ensuing year by the Annual Meeting of the Town of Southold on 3 Apr 1754, an office for which he was again selected on 7 Apr 1789 {432}.

In his will of 4 Feb 1762, proved on 1 Apr 1762, Theophilus Corwin left, to his "..son Jonathan all my farm and meadow at Long Swamp, and 2 lots of meadow on the south side of the Peconic river, And he shall pay to my eldest grandson, Theophilus Corwin, £10. "Theophilus Corwin also named his "..son Jonathan and..daughter Hannah executors." {433}.

Jonathan Corwin was listed as the head of a family consisting of one male of 50 years of age and above, two males of 16 and under 50, two females of 16 and above, and one of under 16, residing in Southold Township, Suffolk County, New York, in the Census of 1776 {434}.

On 22 Aug 1778, Jonathan Corwin was enumerated by Daniel and Jeremiah Wells as the head of a family consisting of four persons in the Aquebogue district of Southold {435}.

Jonathan Corwin, farmer, of the Township of Southold, gave his age as 57 when he signed the Oath of Allegiance and Peaceable Behaviour required by Governor William Tryon in 1778 {436}.

Jonathan Corwin was selected to be one of several "Overseers of the high way" for the ensuing year on 6 Apr 1779 {437}.

Rachel Corwin died on 10 May 1785 {438}, although it was recorded that "Jonath[n] Curwin Wife Rach[l]" died on 14 May 1785 {439}, and is buried in the cemetery at the Mattituck Presbyterian Church, where her gravestone indicates that she died on 17 May 1785 in the 56th year of her age {440}.

"Jon[n] Currie" was listed as the head of a family consisting of one free white male of 16 years of age and upwards, and one free white female, residing in Southold Town, Suffolk County, New York, in the First Census of the United States, 1790 {441}.

Jonathan Corwin died on 11 Apr 1798 {442}, and is buried beside his wife at Mattituck, where his gravestone indicates that he was 79 years, 3 months

430. SR, 87; NYG&BR, XLIX, 155 (Apr 1918).
431. Craven, op. cit., 75.
432. STR, Liber D, 127 right, 142 right; (III, 203-204, 239-240).
433. WNYSO, Liber 23, 391-393; (6, 163-164).
434. CENSUS OF SUFFOLK COUNTY, 1776, 21.
435. NGSQ, 63, 276 (1975).
436. P.R.O. Colonial Office, Class 5, Vol. 1109, 91.
437. STR, Liber D, 137 left; (III, 229).
438. Craven, op. cit., 346.
439. SR, 56; NYG&BR, XLVIII, 284 (Jly 1917).
440. Craven, op. cit., 363.
441. HEADS OF FAMILIES.., 1776, NEW YORK, 170.
442. Craven, op. cit., 351.

and 29 days of age when he died {443}.

Jonathan and Rachel (Howell) Corwin were the parents of ten children.

    i.   RACHEL CORWIN, died on 10 Dec 1771 {444}.

    ii.   JONATHAN CORWIN, baptized at Mattituck on 28 Jly 1754 {445}, married (1) Elizabeth Corwin on 26 May 1774 {446}, married (2) Hannah Kasar, the daughter of Samuel and Hannah (Wedge) Keizer, on 4 Feb 1778 {447}, three children, died on 4 Jan 1785 {448}.

    iii.   SELAH CORWIN, baptized at Mattituck on 16 Jan 1757 {449}, married Joanna Hallock, who was probably the daughter of William and Miriam Hallock, nine children {450}. Joanna Corwin died on 11 May 1846, at the age of 89, and is buried in the cemetery at the Mattituck Presbyterian Church {451}.

    iv.   ISAAC CORWIN, baptized at Mattituck in 1759 {452}, died on 10 Sep 1777 {453}.

    v.   ASA CORWIN, born in about 1762.

    vi.   HANNAH CORWIN, baptized at Mattituck on 22 Jly 1764 {454}, married Josiah Goodale on 27 Feb 1784 {455}.

    vii.   Infant, died on 21 Nov 1767 {456}.

    viii.   RICHARD CORWIN, died on 7 Oct 1777 {457}.

    ix.   JASON CORWIN, born on 2 May 1773 {458}, died on 12

---

443. Id., 363
444. Id., 341.
445. Id., 255.
446. Id., 322.
447. Bessie L. Hallock, Notes, from a copy generously provided by Justine Warner Wells, Historian, Town of Riverhead (1999).
448. Craven, op. cit., 346.
449. Id., 258.
450. Lucius H. Hallock, A HALLOCK GENEALOGY, 408.
451. Craven, op. cit., 363.
452. Id., 260.
453. Craven, op. cit., 343; SR, 49; NYG&BR, XLVIII, 277 (Jly 1917).
454. Id., 269.
455. Id., 329.
456. Id., 340.
457. Id., 343.
458. Mather, op. cit., 317.

Apr 1775 {459}.

x.   ELIZABETH CORWIN, died on 10 Mch 1783 {460}.

39. MARGARET[3] HOWELL (Jacob[2], Richard[1]), the daughter of Jacob[2] and Margaret (Parshall) Howell, was born in the vicinity of Mattituck.

On 16 May 1728, "John Downs & Maraget Howell" were married {461}. He was the son of William and Abigail (Ryder) Downs, and was born in 1704 {462}.

John Downs died on 18 Jly 1745 {463}, and is buried in the Jamesport Cemetery {464}.

"Isaac Penney & w[d] Margarit Downs" were married, probably in Oct 1748 {465}.

Isaac Penny was enlisted on 3 Apr 1758 by Capt. Thomas Terry {466}. He gave his age as 32, and his occupation as a carpenter, when he re-enlisted on 28 Apr 1760 {467}. He was a Corporal in the company of Capt. Israel Horton {468}.

Isaac Penney was listed as the head of a family consisting of one white male of above 16 and under 50 years of age, one of under 16, and one female of above 16, residing in Southampton Town, West, in the Census of 1776 {469}.

Isaac Penny, farmer, gave his age as 50 when he signed the Oath of Allegiance and Peaceable Behaviour required by Governor William Tryon in 1778 {470}.

"Widdow Marg Penney" died on 19 Dec 1789 {471}.

John and Margaret (Howell) Downs were the parents of at least five children {472}.

i.   JOHN DOWNS, born in about 1729.

ii.   MARGARET DOWNS, born in about 1731, married Ebenezer Mather on 16 Apr 1752 {473}.

---

459. Craven, op. cit., 342.
460. Id., 345.
461. SR, 79; NYG&BR, XLIX, 69 (Jan 1918).
462. Wines, op. cit., 24-25.
463. SR, 27; NYG&BR, XLVIII, 29 (Jan 1917).
464. Wines, op. cit., 26.
465. SR, 87; NYG&BR, XLIX, 155 (Apr 1918).
466. MUSTER ROLLS OF NEW YORK PROVINCIAL TROOPS, 1755-1764, Volume XXIV, COLLECTIONS, NEW YORK HISTORICAL SOCIETY, 1891, 128.
467. Id., 234-235.
468. Id., 524.
469. CENSUS OF SUFFOLK COUNTY, NEW YORK, 1776, 35.
470. P.R.O. Colonial Office, Class 5, Volume 1109, 22.
471. SR, 59; NYG&BR, XLVIII, 287 (Jly 1917).
472. Wines, op. cit., 26.
473. SR, 90; NYG&BR, XLIX, 158 (Apr 1918).

iii. DANIEL DOWNS, born on 12 Oct 1737, married Desire Parshall on 19 Jan 1755 {474}, died on 16 Apr 1782.

iv. Child, "J^n Downs child" died about Jan 1739 {475}.

v. JAMES DOWNS, born on 3 May 1740, married Mehetabel Wells on 23 Oct 1764 {476}, died on 23 May 1791 {477}.

40. JACOB^3 HOWELL (Jacob^2, Richard^1), the son of Jacob^2 and Margaret (Parshall) Howell, was born in the vicinity of Mattituck.

"Jacob Howel & Elesabeth Dimond were married on 7 Nov 1734 {478}.

Jacob Howell was one of several men selected to be "Viewers of fence & Damage --" for the ensuing at the Annual Meeting of the Town of Southold on 6 Apr 1742 {479}. He was again selected for this office on 2 Apr 1745, on 7 Apr 1761, and on 5 Apr 1763 {480}.

On 9 Jly 1745, Jacob Howell was a witness to the signing of the will of John Downs, proved on 5 Aug 1745 {481}.

Jacob and Elizabeth (Dimon) Howell may have been the parents of at least two children.

+ 102. i. JACOB^4 HOWELL.

103. ii. JONATHAN^4 HOWELL, "Jacub Howels son Jonathan" died on 16 Jan 1748/9 {482}.

- END OF THIRD GENERATION -

474. Id., 91; NYG&BR, XLIX, 159 (Apr 1918).
475. Id., 22; NYG&BR, XLVIII, 24 (Jan 1917).
476. Id., 97; NYG&BR, XLIX, 165 (Apr 1918).
477. Id., 60; NYG&BR, XLVIII, 288 (Jly 1917).
478. Id., 81; NYG&BR, XLIX, 71 (Jan 1918).
479. STR, Liber D, 124 right; (III, 194).
480. Id., 125 right, 129 right, 130 right; (III, 196-197, 209, 211).
481. WNYSO, Liber 15, 421-423; (IV, 49-50).
482. SR, 30; NYG&BR, XLVIII, 32 (Jan 1917).

41. JOHN[4] HOWELL (John[3], John[2], Richard[1]), the son of John[3] Howell, was born in about 1734, probably in the vicinity of Mattituck.

"John Howel, Jur" was listed for 6d on the 1758 Tax List for the Town of Brookhaven {483}.

"John Howel" was listed for 8s 9d on the 1775 Tax List for the Town of Brookhaven {484}.

"Jno. Howel" was paid 12s 2d for service in Lt. Isaac Davis' company {485}.

"John Howell Serjt" signed the Articles of Association on 16 May 1775 {486} and, as "John Howell", on 8 June 1775 in Brookhaven {487}.

"John howel" was listed as the head of family consisting of two males of 16 and under 50 years of age, one of under 16, one female of 16 and above, and one of under 16, residing in Brookhaven Township, Suffolk County, New York, in the Census of 1776 {488}.

John Howell, farmer, of the Township of Brookhaven, gave his age as 44 when he signed the Oath of Allegiance and Peaceable Behaviour required by Governor William Tryon in 1778 {489}.

"Iohn Hoel" was chosen as one of several "Comisin(ers)" for the Town of Brookhaven at the Annual Meeting on 4 May 1779 {490}.

In the First Census of the United States, 1790, John Howell was listed as the head of a household consisting of one free white male of 16 years of age and upwards, one free white female, and one other free person, residing in Brookhaven Town, Suffolk County, New York {491}.

On 7 Dec 1791, Isaac Overton, Jonas Hawkins and Gershom Brown, Commissioners of Highways for the Township of Brookhaven, reported that they had laid out "..a Publick; Rode, South Side of all the Cleared Land South Side of the Bald Hills. which Road We Laid Out Begining at Patch Ogue Road'..untill it Comes to the Road that Goes from Isaac Ketcham,s mill to Corum; west of John Howells Barn." {492}.

It is likely that John Howell died before 1795, since his name has not been found on the Town of Brookhaven Tax Estimate for that year {493}.

483. Town of Brookhaven Tax Assessment, 1758.
484. THE REGISTER, SCHS, II, 31 (Dec 1976).
485. Mather, op. cit., 992.
486. Id., 1060.
487. Id., 1061.
488. CENSUS OF SUFFOLK COUNTY, NEW YORK, 1776, 9.
489. P.R.O. Colonial Office, Class 5, Vol. 1109, 9.
490. BTR, Book C, 264; (C, 387).
491. HEADS OF FAMILIES.., 1790, NEW YORK, 161.
492. BTR, Book A, Part III, 236; (A, 102).
493. Town of Brookhaven Tax Estimate for 1795, from a copy in the possession of David A. Overton, 1990.

The name of the wife of John Howell has not been established, although it has been speculated that her maiden name was "Norton" {494}.

John Howell was the father of at least four children.

+ 104. i.   JONATHAN[5] HOWELL, born on 22 Mch 1758 {495}.

+ 105. ii.   JOHN[5] HOWELL, born in about 1763.

+ 106. iii. CHARITY[5] HOWELL, born in about 1764 {496}.

   107. iv. HANNAH[5] HOWELL {497}.

42. REEVES[4] HOWELL (John[3], John[2], Richard[1]), the son of John[3] Howell {498}, was born in about 1738. In 1763 {499}, he married Bathsheba Clark, who was born on 8 Dec 1744, the daughter of William and Mary (Reeve) Benjamin Clark {500}.

Ear marks for the livestock of Reeve Howell were recorded for the Town of Brookhaven on 31 Mch 1763 {501}.

Reeves Howell asked for more time to consider signing the Articles of Association in 1775 {502}. He signed in Brookhaven in May 1775 {503}, and again on 8 June 1775 {504}.

"Reves Howel" was listed for 8s 9d on the 1775 Tax List for the Town of Brookhaven {505}.

"Reivs Hoel" was listed as the head of a family consisting of two males of 16 and under 50 years of age, three of under 16, one female of 16 and over, and two of under 16, residing in Brookhaven Township, Suffolk County, New York, in the Census of 1776 {506}.

---

494. Grendler, op. cit., 2.

495. Bible record, Mordecai Homan's New Testament, from a copy in the possession of David A. Overton, 1992.

496. Id.

497. George Rogers Howell, THE EARLY HISTORY OF SOUTHAMPTON, L.I., NEW YORK.., Second Edition, 321.

498. Craven, op. cit., 205.

499. Sarah (Vail) Howell Terry, "Record of Near Relatives of Elias Willis Howell. Given by his Mother" from the ELIAS W. HOWELL FAMILY TEMPLE RECORDS, 80, in the possession of Eldon Willis Howell, Fairview, UT, 1990.

500. Clark Family Bible, formerly owned by Julia Clark, and given by Harriet Rose, her niece, of Fire Place, to Mr. William Rose, of the same place, and from the family Bible of Jehiel H. Woodruff, owned by his grandson, Chas. A. Glover, of Bellport, 1933. Data compiled by Osborn Shaw, and in the possession of David A. Overton, 1992.

501. BTR, Book C, 293ff; (C, 419).

502. N.Y. State Calendar of Historical Manuscripts, War of the Revolution, I, 1868, cited by Wilbur Franklin Howell, op. cit., 338 (reverse).

503. Mather, op. cit., 1057.

504. Id., 1061.

505. THE REGISTER, II, 31 (Dec 1976).

506. CENSUS OF SUFFOLK COUNTY, NEW YORK, 1776, 12.

Reeve Howell, farmer, of the Township of Brookhaven, gave his age as 40 when he signed the Oath of Allegiance and Peaceable Behaviour required by Governor William Tryon in 1778 {507}.

Reeve Howell was selected to be a Fence Viewer for the ensuing year at the Annual Meeting of the Town of Brookhaven on 1 May 1781, and again on 6 May 1783, on 3 Apr 1787, on 1 Apr 1788, on 7 Apr 1789, on 6 Apr 1790, on 5 Apr 1791, and on 3 Apr 1792 {508}.

William Turner, of the Town of Brookhaven, named his friend, Reeve Howell, to be one of three executors of his will of 2 Jan 1782, proved on 10 Aug 1787 {509}.

Reeves Howell was listed as the head of a family consisting of two free white males of 16 years of age and upwards, two of under 16, and four free white females, residing in Brookhaven Town, Suffolk County, New York, in the First Census of the United States, 1790 {510}.

Ear marks for the livestock of Reeves Howell were recorded in a book presented to Captain Thomas S. Strong by his brother, Benjamin Strong, of Mount Mercy, on 4 Feb 1790 {511}.

"Reeves Hoel" was assessed as possessing real estate worth £350, and a personal estate worth £60, on the Town of Brookhaven Tax Estimate for 1795 {512}.

By his will, dated 16 Dec 1797, and proved on 6 Sep 1802, Reeve Howell bequeathed to his "..wife Bassheba one cow to be kept by my son Daniel..", to his daughters, Deborah Clark, Bathsheba Howell and Mary Howell, one cow and six sheep each, to his son, William, six sheep and "..the remaining part of my stock and moveable estate after paying my debts out of the same and furnishing my son Daniel Howell with a team and farming Tackling my will is that should be divided equally amongst my children and further my will is that my son Daniel Howell should provide household furniture for all his sisters that is not married to make them equal in household furniture to those that is married and also to provide a home at my now dwelling place for my son William Howell and Bassheba Howell and Mary Howell so long as they remain single and further my will is that my son Isaac Howell should pay unto my son James Howell or give an obligation for the same at the delivery of the deed for his place the sum of £60 current money of New York and my will is that my son Daniel Howell should pay my son William Howell £60 current money of New York at the delivery of a deed for my place or give an obligation for the same and lastly I do hereby appoint my wife Bassheba Howell executrix and Isaac Hulse and my son Isaac Howell executors.." {513}.

---

507. P.R.O. Colonial Office, Class 5, Vol. 1109, 10.
508. BTR, Book C, 267, 272, 281, 283, 286, Book A, Part III, 211, 220, 238; (C, 390, 400, 406, 406, 411, A, 83-84, 91, 103).
509. Suffolk County Wills, Liber A, 13-15.
510. HEADS OF FAMILIES.., 1790, NEW YORK, 161.
511. THE REGISTER, SCHS, VI, 10, 13 (June 1980).
512. Town of Brookhaven Tax Estimate for 1795.
513. Suffolk County Wills, Liber B, 205-208; Suffolk County Estates, File #554.

"Reve Howell" was listed as having having a house and land valued at $1,470, and personal property worth $48, in the Town of Brookhaven Estimate for 1799 {514}.

On 2 Dec 1799, John Bayles and Daniel Saxton, Commissioners of Highways, Brookhaven Town, ordered that "..a Road..be Opened thirty feet wide Begining at Reve Howells so Runing southerly as the Lane Now Leads until it comes to the Bars Turning into Nathaniel Homans Lot from thence Going threw the Lot Nearly where the Road Now Runs until it Comes to the Granny Road from thence Runing Westerly until it Comes to the West Line of John Howells Land from thence Southerly On the Line Between John Howells an Reve Howells Land until it Comes to the Top of the hill.." {515}.

Reeve Howel" was listed as the head of a family consisting of one free white male of 45 years of age and over, two of 16 and under 26, one of 10 and under, one free white female of 45 and over, and one of 10 and under 16, residing in the Town of Brookhaven, Suffolk County, New York, in the Second Census of the United States, 1800 {516}.

In a codicil, dated 1 Sep 1802, to his will of 16 Dec 1797, Reeve Howell ordered his son, Isaac Howell, to "..give unto my son William Howell and to his heirs and assigns forever..part of the land which I have heretofore given to my son Isaac..all the land and timber that shall be between the Granny Road and a certain line to be drawn east and west 10 rods South of S^d Granny Road and I also order my son Danniel to give allow and acquit unto my son William Howell part of the land I have heretofore given to my son Daniel, that is to say, I order my S^d son Danniel to give my S^d son William Howell to his heirs and assigns forever the land and timber that shall be or lye between the Granny Road and a certain line to be drawn east and west 10 rods north of S^d Granny Road and also one other certain piece or lot of land called second lot bounded on the east by the lane that leads southward from my dwelling house on the south by John Turners land on the west by a line that runs to the Middle Island on the north by a hedge fence as the fence now stands and also one other certain piece of land lying east of the road opposite my dwelling with the priviledge of the lane to pass across to the lot called second lot also one piece of land lying on the west side of the pond which I had of William Swezeys estate south bound to be a chesnut tree with a priviledge of going to the same in some convenient place..". At the same time, William Howell was ordered to pay Daniel Homan what the estate of Reeve Howell owed him, and Daniel Howell was acquited from his obligation to pay William Howell $150 (£60). Further, the witnesses to this codicil, namely, Apollos Whitmore, David Woodhull and Patty Davis, testified that Reeve Howell did order his son, Daniel Howell, to pay his grandson, Reeve Davis, $25 when he reached the age of 21 {517}.

Reeves Howell died on 3 Sep 1802, and is buried in the Union Cemetery

514. Town of Brookhaven Tax Estimate for 1799, from a copy in the possession of David A. Overton, 1990.
515. BTR, Book A, Part III, 334; (D, 22-23).
516. NYG&BR, LVI, 328 (Oct 1925).
517. Suffolk County Wills, Liber B, 205-208; Suffolk County Estates, File #554.

at Middle Island, where his epitaph reads, "REEVES HOWELL, Died Sept. 3, 1802, AE 64" {518}.

"Bashaby Howell" was a witness to the will of her son, Daniel Howell, written on 28 Jan 1808, and proved on 23 Feb 1808 {519}.

"Mrs. Bathsheba Howell, aged 66, died at Middle Island.." on 3 Dec 1809 {520}. She is buried beside her husband at Middle Island, where her epitaph reads, "BATHSHEBA, Relict of Reeves Howell, Died Dec 3, 1809, AE 66" {521}.

Reeves and Bathsheba (Clark) Howell were the parents of at least nine children.

+ 108. i. ELIZABETH, "BETSEY", [5] HOWELL, born on 23 Nov 1763.

+ 109. ii. ALTHEA[5] HOWELL, born on 22 Jly 1766 {522}.

+ 110. iii. ISAAC REEVES[5] HOWELL, born on 19 Feb 1769 {523}.

+ 111. iv. JAMES[5] HOWELL, born in about 1771 {524}.

+ 112. v. DANIEL[5] HOWELL, born in about 1773.

+ 113. vi. DEBORAH[5] HOWELL, born in about 1775.

+ 114. vii. WILLIAM[5] HOWELL, born in about 1783.

  115. viii. BATHSHEBA[5] HOWELL, born in about 1785, died on 31 Mch 1807 at the age of 22, and is buried in the family plot in the Union Cemetery at Middle Island {525}.

+ 116. ix. MARY[5], "POLLY", HOWELL, born on 28 Nov 1788.

NOTE: *Grace Lillian (Hammond) Sherwood, the daughter of Samuel Mowbray and Frances Amanda (Howell) Hammond, and great-great-grand-daughter of Reeves Howell, was, along with her mother, an early historian of this family. She left notes {526}, which indicate that "..John (sic) married Bathsheba Clark..", and that they had twelve children, "..as given by Gershom Howell..". In addition to the nine listed above, she gave "..Jonathan, eleventh child of John and*

---

518. Gravestone, Union Cemetery, Middle Island.
519. Suffolk County Wills, Liber B, 490-491; Suffolk County Estates, File #795.
520. SUFFOLK GAZETTE, 9 Dec 1809; NYG&BR, XXV, 164 (Oct 1894).
521. Gravestone, Union Cemetery, Middle Island.
522. Sarah (Vail) Howell Terry, op. cit.
523. Grace (Hammond) Sherwood, Notes, transcribed by Thomas B. Cornell, in the possession of Thomas H. Donnelly, 1999.
524. Grendler, op. cit., 2.
525. Gravestone, Union Cemetery, Middle Island.
526. Sherwood, op. cit.

Bathsheba..", and "..John, twelfth child of John and Bathsheba..". These were probably the sons of John Howell, brother of Reeves. Further, she listed "..Reeve, the fifth child of John and Bathsheba, died without issue..", and "..Five daughters of John and Bathsheba, Betsey, Althea, Polly, Bersheba (all listed above), and Polly (sic)..", as well as "..Lucinda, married John Ruland..". Of these, Lucinda was probably the daughter of William[5] Howell.

Another source of information on this family is found in the Family Records of the Howell family in Utah {527}, descendants of Edmund Wheeler Howell, the grandson of Reeves Howell. In these, Sarah Terry, the mother of Elias Willis Howell, indicated the he was the "Gt.Gd son" of Reeves Howell and Bathsheba Clark, whose family included Isaac, Daniel, William, James, Deborah (who married Ludlow Clark), Mary and Bathsheba (unmarried). She also indicated that he was the "Gd son" of James and <u>Catherine</u> Howell. She went on to indicate that he was the nephew of James, Youngs, Daniel, Nancy, Phebe, Mehitable, Elizabeth, Mary, Elthea and Deborah Howell, the cousin of Shepard Howell, and the "Neph,in Law" of Daniel Youngs, Nathan Davis, Isaac Tucker, Ludlow Clark and Daniel Tucker. Since he was not a nephew to all of these, it would seem that he might have been a grand-nephew to some, which would give further clues to the family of Reeves and Bathsheba (Clark) Howell. For example, it would seem that the "Reeve Davis" mentioned by Reeve Howell in the codicil to his will, was the son of Nathan Davis and his wife, Betsey, who would have been a daughter of Reeves and Bathsheba Howell, as mentioned by Grace Hammond Sherwood, corresponding to the "Elizabeth" mentioned by Sarah Terry. Further, since Sarah Terry mentioned "Elthea", and Daniel Tucker, Grace Hammond Sherwood mentioned "Althea", and Daniel and Althea (Howell) Tooker had a son, William Clark Tooker, it would seem to be established that Althea was a daughter of Reeves and Bathsheba Howell. In addition, it would seem to be firmly established that Deborah Howell, the daughter of Reeves and Bathsheba, married Ludlow Clark.

It is also true that Isaac Tooker married Mary Howell, but it has not yet been well established that she was the "Polly" mentioned by Grace Hammond Sherwood, or the "Mary" mentioned by Sarah Terry, even though she did note that Elias Willis Howell was the "Neph, in Law" of Isaac Tucker. It should be noted that the 1800 Census data for the family of Reeves Howell do not support the dates recorded for Mary, the wife of Isaac Tooker.

With this in mind, however, it is possible that Reeves and Bathsheba (Clark) Howell were also the parents of Reeve, Phebe and Mehitable Howell, or that they had two daughters named Mary, one of whom died young, thus indeed having been the parents of twelve children, as stated by Grace Hammond Sherwood, on the authority of Gershom Howell.

43. JONATHAN[4] HOWELL (Jonathan[3], John[2], Richard[1]), the son of Jonathan[3] and Elizabeth (Sherrill) Howell, was born in the vicinity of Mattituck in about 1739.

---

527. Sarah (Vail) Howell Terry, op. cit.

Jonathan Howell was enlisted in the New York provincial troops by Capt. Thomas Terry on 15 Apr 1758 {528}.

Jonathan Howell signed the Articles of Association on Shelter Island in May 1775 {529}.

Jonathan Howell, farmer, of the Township of Southold, gave his age as 39 when he signed the Oath of Allegiance and Peaceable Behaviour required by Governor William Tryon in 1778 {530}.

"Bethiah Howel, Wife of Jonathan, Jr.", died on 24 Nov 1786 {531}, "Jonathan Howils Wife Jun[r]." {532}. She was the daughter of Micah[3] and Bethia (Reeve) Howell {533}.

By his will of 25 Aug 1791, proved on 27 Mch 1793, Jonathan Howell gave the balance of his estate, after legacies and bequests to his son, Daniel, and his daughter, Cynthia, to his son, Jonathan. His brother, John Howell, was named Executor of this will {534}.

Jonathan Howell, Jr., died on 11 Sep 1791 {535}.

Jonathan and Bethiah (Howell) Howell were the parents of three children, all baptized at Mattituck.

+ 117.   i.   JONATHAN[5] HOWELL, baptized on 7 Oct 1770 {536}.

+ 118.   ii.   DANIEL[5] HOWELL, baptized on 7 Jly 1782 {537}.

+ 119.   iii.   SYNTHA (CYNTHIA)[5] HOWELL, baptized on 18 Mch 1787 {538}.

44. ELIZABETH[4] HOWELL (Jonathan[3], John[2], Richard[1]), the daughter of Jonathan[3] and Elizabeth (Sherrill) Howell, was born in the vicinity of Mattituck in about 1742.

On 19 June 1794, Elizabeth Howell married Isaac Davis {539}, probably as his second wife, since Isaac Davis was listed as the head of a family consisting on one male of above 16 and under 50 years of age, and one female of above 16, residing in Southold Township in the Census of 1776 {540}. An

---

528. MUSTER ROLLS OF NEW YORK PROVINCIAL TROOPS, 126.

529. Mather, op. cit., 1064.

530. P.R.O. Colonial Office, Class 5, Vol. 1109, 89.

531. Craven, op. cit., 347.

532. SR, 57; NYG&BR, XLVIII, 288 (Jly 1917).

533. Donnelly, THE REGISTER, SCHS, XVI, 93-96 (Spring 1991).

534. Suffolk County Wills, Liber A, 281-282; Suffolk County Estates, File #203.

535. Craven, op. cit., 349.

536. Id., 276.

537. Id., 288.

538. Id., 293.

539. Sidney C. Howell, Notes, copied by Bessie L. Hallock, from a copy generously provided by Justine Warner Wells, Historian, Town of Riverhead.

540. CENSUS OF SUFFOLK COUNTY, 1776, 22.

Isaac Davis was also listed in the First Census of the United States, 1790, as the head of a household consisting of one free white male of 16 years and upwards, one free white female, and one other free person, residing in Southold Town, Suffolk County, New York {541}.

Isaac Davis was listed as the head of a household consisting of one free white male of 45 years of age and older, one of 16 and under 26, one free white female of 26 and under 45, and one of 10 and under 16, residing in the Town of Southold, Suffolk County, New York, in the Second Census of the United States, 1800 {542}.

Isaac Davis was selected to serve as an Overseer of the Highways for the ensuing year at the annual meeting of the Town of Southold held on 2 Apr 1793. He was again selected to serve as an Overseer of Roads on 3 Apr 1804 {543}.

Elizabeth Davis died on 24 Mch 1826 at the age of 84, and is buried in the cemetery at the Mattituck Presbyterian Church {544}.

Isaac Davis died on 15 Nov 1830 at the age of 86, and is buried beside his wife at Mattituck {545}.

Isaac and Elizabeth (Howell) Davis had no children {546}.

45. RECOMPENCE[4] HOWELL (Jonathan[3], John[2], Richard[1]), the son of Jonathan[3] and Elizabeth (Sherrill) Howell, was born in the vicinity of Mattituck in about 1745.

"Recompence Howel & Marther Horton" were married on 19 Feb 1769 {547}.

Recompence Howell signed the Articles of Association in 1775 as a member of Capt. Hallock's company {548}.

"Roke Howell" was listed as the head of a household consisting of two males of 16 and under 50 years of age, one female of 16 and over, and one of under 16, residing in Southold Township, Suffolk County, New York, in the Census of 1776 {549}.

Four persons from the family of "Recomp[ce] Howell" were transported to Guildford, Connecticut, by Captain David Landon, in the sloop, POLLEY, 55 tons burthen, belonging to Samuel Brown, of Guildford, in Sep or Oct 1776 {550}.

---

541. HEADS OF FAMILIES.., 1790, NEW YORK, 169.
542. NYB&GR, LVII, 57 (Jan 1926).
543. STR, Liber D, 144 right, 152 right; (III, 244, 266).
544. Craven, op. cit., 365.
545. Id.
546. Sidney C. Howell, op. cit.
547. SR, 99; NYG&BR, XLIX, 266 (Jly 1918).
548. Mather, op. cit., 1057.
549. CENSUS OF SUFFOLK COUNTY, 1776, 22.
550. Mather, op. cit., 834-835.

On 25 Dec 1776, Recompence Howell paid Captain Jonathan Vail £1 2s 8d "......for transporting from Long Island to Guilford

for one Cow and Calf £0	7s	6d
to one hog 0	0	9
to 11¹/₂ of wheat 0	4	4
to 12 Bushel of Salt 0	3	0
to 1 Side of Leather 0	0	4
to household Goods 0	3	0
to 2 passengers 0	6	0

	£1	4s	11d
By an overcharge of hog and passage		2	3

	£1	2s	8d
Pr me (Capt.) Jonathan Vaill			

Guilford Febry 17, 1777 Personally appeared Recompense Howell & made oath to the Truth of the above acct - before me

Sam¹ Brown Justᵉ Peace "

This was reviewed by the Committee of Examiners, Thomas Dering, John Foster and Thomas Wickham, who concluded that there was "..justly due to R. Howell the sum of one pound 2 shillings 8d Lawfull money of Connecticut.." on 21 Feb 1777 {551}.

Recompence Howell, cordwainer, of the Township of Southold, gave his age as 33 when he signed the Oath of Allegiance and Peaceable Behaviour required by Governor William Tryon in 1778 {552}.

Recompense Howell was listed as the head of a household of three persons in Mattituck parish on 15 Jan 1778 by Lt. Isaac Reeve, and again on 25 Aug 1778, for Andrew Eliot, lieutenant governor {553}.

In the First Census of the United States, 1790, Recompence Howell was listed as the head of a household consisting of one free white male of 16 years of age and upwards, two free white females, and one other free person, residing in Southold Town, Suffolk County, New York {554}.

"In Southold at a General Town Meeting held the third day of April 1792..", it was "..Voted to have three pounds to be built in the Town..One at the Old parish where the Old pound used to be..And that the Overseers of the Poor to take the Charge of the building the pounds - - And that the pounds to be built two Rods Square and five feet Six Inches high..Recompence Howell pound Master for the pound in the old parish.." {555}.

Recompence Howell was selected as one of the Pound Masters at the Annual Meeting of the Town of Southold on 4 Apr 1797, and again on 3 Apr 1798,

---

551. Id., 783-784.
552. P.R.O. Colonial Office, Class 5, Vol. 1109, 93.
553. NGSQ, 63, 280 (1975).
554. HEADS OF FAMILIES.., 1790, NEW YORK, 169.
555. STR, Liber D, 201 left; (III, 340).

2 Apr 1799, 7 Apr 1801, 6 Apr 1802, 5 Apr 1803, 3 Apr 1804, 2 Apr 1805, 1 Apr 1806, 7 Apr 1807, 5 Apr 1808, 4 Apr 1809, 3 Apr 1810, 2 Apr 1811, 7 Apr 1812, 6 Apr 1813, and on 4 Apr 1814 {556}.

In the Second Census of the United States, 1800, Recompence Howell was listed as the head of a family consisting of one free white male of 45 years of age and older, one free white female of 45 and over, and one free white female of 26 and under 45, residing in the Town of Southold, Suffolk County, New York {557}.

"Recompence howels wife Martha" died on 27 June 1801 {558}.

"Gany Recompence Howell" married "Elizabeth Taylor, widow of Sagg Harbor" on 31 Jan 1803 at Southold. Elizabeth (Brown) Taylor was the widow of Schoolmaster George Taylor of Edinburgh {559} {560}.

One right of James Overton as a "..Subscriber having associated for the purpose of Supporting a School in the first parish in Southold.." was transfered to "Recompence Howel" in Aug 1803 {561}.

"Recompence Howel" was selected to be one of several "Fence Viewers" at the Annual Meeting of the Town of Southold on 3 Apr 1804 {562}.

Recompence Howell was listed as the head of a family consisting of one free white male of 45 years of age and older, one free white female of 45 years of age and older, one of 26 and under 45, and one of 16 and under 26, residing in the Town of Southold, Suffolk County, New York, in the Third Census of the United States, 1810 {563}.

By his will of 28 Sep 1814, signed on 2 Dec 1814, and proved on 11 Apr 1815, Recompense Howell left his estate to his daughter, Bethiah, the wife of Wines Osborn, for life, then to her son, Joseph Osborn, with bequests to his own wife, with all that she brought {564}.

Recompence Howell died on 29 Mch 1815 {565}.

Elizabeth (Brown) Taylor Howell died on 10 Nov 1841, and is buried in the Southold Cemetery {566}.

Recompence and Martha (Horton) Howell were the parents of one daughter.

+ 120.   i.   BETHIAH[5] HOWELL, baptized on 6 Nov 1774 at Mattituck by

556. Id., 147 left, 148 right, 148 left, 150 left, 150 right, 151 right, 152 right, 153 left, 153 right, 154 left, 154 right, 155 right, 156 right, 158 left, 158 right, 159 right, 162 left; (III, 251, 253, 255, 260, 262, 264, 266, 267, 268, 268, 271, 273, 275, 279, 281, 283, 288).
557. NYG&BR, LVII, 60 (Jan 1926).
558. SR, 66; NYG&BR, XLVIII, 24 (Jan 1917).
559. RECORDS OF THE FIRST CHURCH OF SOUTHOLD, 33; NYG&BR, LXV, 157 (Apr 1918).
560. SR, 110; NYG&BR, XLIX, 277 (Jly 1918).
561. STR, Liber D, 37 right-38 right; (III, 66-69).
562. Id., 152 right; (III, 266).
563. U.S. Census, Southold, Suffolk County, New York, 1810, Page 260.
564. Suffolk County Wills, Liber C, 512-514; Suffolk County Estates, File #1199.
565. RECORDS OF THE FIRST CHURCH OF SOUTHOLD, 71.
566. Wilbur Franklin Howell, op. cit., 407.

the Rev. Joseph Lee {567}.

46. JEREMIAH[4] HOWELL (Jonathan[3], John[2], Richard[1]), the son of Jonathan[3] and Elizabeth (Sherrill) Howell, was born in the vicinity of Mattituck.

Jeremiah Howell "..went to Goshen" {568}.

"James (sic) Howell came from Long Island before the Revolution, located first in the Town of Marlborough, then at Modena, in the Town of Plattekill.." {569}. "Jonathan (sic) Howell came from Long Island about 1750" {570}.

Jeremiah Howell was an early settler in the central part of the Town of Plattekill {571}.

On 10 Nov 1774, Jeremiah Howell married Elthena Harris before the Rev. John Close at the New Windsor Presbyterian Church {572}.

Jeremiah Howell signed the Articles of Association in the Precinct of Cornwall in 1775 {573}.

Jeremiah Howell was an enlisted man in the Fourth Regiment of the Ulster County militia {574}.

Jeremiah Howell worked for Pathmaster John Polhemols in District #2 in 1788 {575}. He worked six days in District #37 in 1797 {576}, and two days for the Overseer of Highways in District #22 in 1799 {577}.

Jeremiah Howell was listed as the head of a family consisting of two free white males of 16 years of age and upwards, five of under 16, and two free white females, residing in the Town of Marlborough, Ulster County, New York, in the First Census of the United States, 1790 {578}.

Jeremiah Howell was listed as the head of a family consisting of one free white male of 45 years of age and over, two of 16 and under 26, two of 10 and under 16, one of under 10, one free white female of 26 and under 45, and one of under 10, residing in the Town of Plattekill, Ulster County, New York, in the Second Census of the United States, 1800 {579}.

---

567. Craven, op. cit., 268.
568. Sidney C. Howell, op. cit.
569. Nathaniel Bartlett Sylvester, HISTORY OF ULSTER COUNTY, Part II, 125.
570. Id., 136.
571. Id., 171.
572. NEW WINDSOR PRESBYTERIAN CHURCH MARRIAGES, from a RECORD OF BAPTISMS, MARRIAGES AND BIRTHS, by Rev. John Close, published in Publication #2 of the Historical Society of Newport Bay and the Highlands, reprinted in THE QUARTERLY, OCGS, 17, #4, 31 (Feb 1988), and in RECORDS FROM NEWBURGH, NEW WINDSOR, AND OTHER NEARBY TOWNS, OCGS, 1997, 4.
573. Headley, op. cit., 77.
574. James A. Roberts, NEW YORK IN THE REVOLUTION, Second Edition, Vol. I, 264.
575. Sylvester, op. cit., 79.
576. Id., 81.
577. Id., 80.
578. HEADS OF FAMILIES.., 1790, NEW YORK, 178.
579. U.S. Census, Platekill, Ulster County, NY, 1800.

Jeremiah Howell was listed as the head of a family consisting of one free white male of 45 years of age and older, one of 16 and under 26, one of 10 and under 16, one free white female of 45 and older, and one of 16 and under 26, residing in the Town of Plattekill, Ulster County, New York, in the Third Census of the United States, 1810 {580}.

By a deed dated 14 Oct 1820, John Howell, the son of Jeremiah Howell, and his wife, Esther, of New Paltz, sold, to John C. Brodhead and Richard C. Brodhead, "..All that farm Piece or Parcel of land Situate lying or being in the Town of Plattkill in the County of Ulster aforesaid and bounded and described in a Deed given by Hezekiah Smith and Rhoda his wife..bearing date on the first day of February one thousand eight hundred and three..which Premifes above described is the Same which Jeremiah Howell Occupied and Pofsefsed in his life time.." {581}.

Jeremiah and Elthena (Harris) Howell were probably the parents of five sons and two daughters {582}.

+ 121.   i.   JEREMIAH[5] HOWELL, born in about Jly 1775.

+ 122.   ii.   JOHN[5] HOWELL, born in about 1780.

   123.   iii.   JAMES[5] HOWELL.

   124.   iv.   Son[5].

   125.   v.   Son[5].

   126.   vi.   Daughter[5].

   127.   vii.   Daughter[5].

47. MARGARET[4] HOWELL (Jonathan[3], John[2], Richard[1]), the daughter of Jonathan[3] and Elizabeth (Sherrill) Howell, was born in the vicinity of Mattituck in about 1751.

Margaret Howell married Henry Terry as his second wife. He was the son of James and Mary (Corwin) Terry {583}, and was born in about 1738. His first wife was Abigail, the daughter of Daniel and Mary (Penny) Youngs, who was born in about 1742. She died in Aug 1791, at the age of 49, and is buried in the Aquebogue Cemetery {584}.

Henry Terry signed the Articles of Association in Brookhaven during the

580. Id., 1810, Page 119.
581. Ulster County Deeds, Liber 24, 380-383.
582. Sylvester, op. cit., 125.
583. Wines, op. cit., 54.
584. Gravestone, Aquebogue Cemetery.

summer of 1775 {585}.

"Hennery Terry" was listed as the head of a family consisting of one male of 16 and under 50 years of age, three of under 16, one female of above 16, and one of under 16, residing in Southold Township, Suffolk County, New York, in the Census of 1776 {586}.

Henry Terry was enumerated as the head of a family of six, residing in the Aquabogue District of Southold, on 22 Aug 1778, by Daniel and Jeremiah Wells {587}.

Henry Terry, carpenter, of the Township of Southold, gave his age as 38 when he signed the Oath of Allegiance and Peaceable Behaviour required by Governor William Tryon in 1778 {588}.

"Henry Terry" was listed as the head of a family consisting of two free white males of 16 years of age and upwards, and two free white females, residing in Southold Town, Suffolk County, New York, in the First Census of the United States, 1790 {589}.

"Hen^y Terry" was listed as the head of a household consisting of one free white male of 45 years of age and over, two of 16 and under 26, one free white female of 45 and over, two of 16 and under 26, and one slave, residing in the Town of Riverhead, Suffolk County, New York, in the Second Census of the United States, 1800 {590}.

Margaret (Howell) Terry died on 1 Sep 1803, at the age of 52 {591}, and is buried in the Aquebogue Cemetery {592}.

As his third wife, Deacon Henry Terry married Jane Sandford {593}. She was the daughter of David and Abigail (Jessup) Sandford, and was born in about 1754 {594}. She died on 12 Feb 1824, at the age of 70, and is buried in the Aquebogue Cemetery {595}.

Deacon Henry Terry died on 14 Dec 1812, at the age of 74, and is buried beside his wives in the Aquebogue Cemetery {596}.

On 17 Dec 1812, letters of administration on the estate of Henry Terry, farmer, of the Town of Riverhead, were issued to his daughter, Abigail, and his son-in-law, Daniel Wells, Jr., after his wife, Jane, resigned. His son, Joshua Terry,

585. Mather, op. cit., 1059.
586. CENSUS OF SUFFOLK COUNTY, 1776, 21.
587. NGSQ, 63, 276 (1975).
588. P.R.O. Colonial Office, Class 5, Vol. 1109, 83.
589. HEADS OF FAMILIES.., 1790, NEW YORK, 170.
590. NYG&BR, LVII, 55 (Jan 1926).
591. Wines, op. cit., 54.
592. Gravestone, Aquebogue Cemetery.
593. Wines, op. cit.
594. G. Merle Sanford, THE SANDFORD/SANFORD FAMILIES OF LONG ISLAND.., 18.
595. Id.
596. Gravestone, Aquebogue Cemetery.

was later appointed to administer in conjunction with the other named administrators {597}.

Henry and Abigail (Youngs) Terry were the parents of at least three children.

i.   HENRY TERRY, born in about 1764, died on 25 Sep 1781 at the age of 17, and is buried in the Aquebogue Cemetery {598}.

ii. ABIGAIL TERRY.

iii. JOSHUA TERRY.

48. HANNAH[4] HOWELL (Jonathan[3], John[2], Richard[1]), the daughter of Jonathan[3] and Elizabeth (Sherrill) Howell, was born in the vicinity of Mattituck.

Hannah Howell married Watson Aldrich. They lived on Aldrich Lane {599}.

Watson and Hannah (Howell) Aldrich were the parents of two children {600}.

i.   WATSON ALDRICH.

ii. JANE ALDRICH, married Thomas Penny.

49. JOHN[4] HOWELL (Jonathan[3], John[2], Richard[1]), the son of Jonathan[3] and Elizabeth (Sherrill) Howell, was born in the vicinity of Mattituck in about 1759.

"John Howel" was a private in Captain Paul Reeves' Ninth Company of Colonel Josiah Smith's First Regiment of Minute Men of Suffolk County from 21 Mch 1776 to 21 Jly 1776 {601}.

John Howell, farmer, of the Township of Southold, gave his age as 19 when he signed the Oath of Allegiance and Peaceable Behaviour required by Governor William Tryon in 1778 {602}.

John Howell was the executor of the will of his brother, Jonathan Howell (#43), written on 25 Aug 1791, and proved on 27 Mch 1793 {603}.

John Howell was an executor of the will of his father, Jonathan Howell, written on 24 Jly 1793, and proved on 13 May 1805. By this will, he was the principal heir to his father's estate {604}.

John Howell married Hannah Corwin, widow, on 19 June 1794, at

597. Suffolk County Letters of Administration, Liber D, 19, 23 and 26; Suffolk County Estates, File #966.
598. Gravestone, Aquebogue Cemetery.
599. Sidney C. Howell, op. cit.
600. Id.
601. Mather, op. cit., 1008.
602. P.R.O. Colonial Office, Class 5, Vol. 1109, 90.
603. Suffolk County Wills, Liber A, 281-282; Suffolk County Estates, File #203.
604. Suffolk County Wills, Liber B, 358-359, Suffolk County Estates, File #699.

Mattituck {605}. She was the widow of Jonathan Corwin, who was the son of Jonathan and Rachel (Howell) (#37), Corwin {606}, and who died on 4 Jan 1785 {607}. He married Hannah Kasar, of Norwich, Connecticut, on 4 Feb 1778 {608}. She was the daughter of Samuel and Hannah (Wedge) Keizer, and was born on 23 Feb 1753 {609}.

The widow, Hannah Corwin, was baptized as an adult, with her children, on 30 Oct 1785, at Mattituck {610}.

"John Howel" was baptized, as an adult, on 4 Jan 1798 at Mattituck {611}.

In the Second Census of the United States, 1800, John Howell was listed as the head of a family consisting of one free white male of 26 and under 45 years of age, one of under 10, one free white female of 45 and over, one of 26 and under 45, one of 16 and under 26, and one of under 10, residing in the Town of Southold, Suffolk County, New York {612}.

On 17 Apr 1809, John Howell was a subscriber toward meeting the estimated expense of making a board fence around the burying ground at the Mattituck Parish Burying Ground {613} {614}.

John Howell was listed as the head of a family consisting of one free white male of 45 years of age and older, one of 10 and under 16, one free white female of 45 and older, one of 16 and under 26, one of 10 and under 16, and one of under 10, residing in the Town of Southold, Suffolk County, New York, in the Third Census of the United States, 1810 {615}.

In the Fourth Census of the United States, 1820, John Howell was listed as the head of a family consisting of one free white male of 45 years of age and older, one of 10 and under 16, and one free white female of 45 and older, residing in the Town of Southold, Suffolk County, New York {616}.

Hannah (Kasar) Corwin Howell died on 25 Dec 1831, at the age of 78, and is buried in churchyard cemetery at Mattituck {617}.

John Howell died on 11 Mch 1837 at age of 78, and is buried beside his wife at Mattituck {618}.

John and Hannah (Kasar) Corwin Howell were the parents of at least five

605. Craven, op. cit., 333.
606. Sidney C. Howell, op. cit.
607. Craven, op. cit., 363.
608. Mather, op. cit., 317.
609. Stonington, CT, Vital Records, 3-115, taken by Mrs. Albert H. Chase, obtained by Bessie L. Hallock, and passed on to the Riverhead Town Historian's office. Generously provided to me by Justine Warner Wells.
610. Craven, op. cit., 292.
611. Id., 306.
612. NYG&BR, LVII, 57 (Jan 1926).
613. Craven, op. cit., 154.
614. Id., 156.
615. U.S. Census, Southold, Suffolk County, NY, 1810, Page 256.
616. Id., 1820, Page 352.
617. Craven, op. cit., 374.
618. Id.

children.

128. i. JOHN[5] HOWELL, baptized on 4 Jan 1798 at Mattituck {619}, died on 6 Jan 1798 {620}.

+ 129. ii. HARMONY[5] HOWELL, baptized at Mattituck on 29 Apr 1798 {621}.

+ 130. iii. SYLVESTER[5] HOWELL, baptized at Mattituck on 1 June 1800 {622}.

131. iv. ELISHA[5] HOWELL, twin of "Elijah", died young {623}.

132. v. ELIJAH[5] HOWELL, twin of "Elisha", died young {624}.

Jonathan and Hannah (Kasar) Corwin were the parents of at least three children {625}.

(i.) HANNAH CORWIN, baptized at Mattituck on 30 Oct 1785, married Josiah Buel, no children {626}.

(ii.) JASON CORWIN, baptized at Mattituck on 30 Oct 1785.

(iii.) REBECCA CORWIN, baptized at Mattituck on 30 Oct 1785, married Jeremiah Randall, six children {627}.

50. ELI[4] HOWELL (Jonathan[3], John[2], Richard[1]), the son of Jonathan[3] and Elizabeth (Sherrill) Howell, was born in the vicinity of Mattituck in about 1761.

"Ely Howell", cordwainer, of the Township of Southold, gave his age as 17 when he signed the Oath of Allegiance and Peaceable Behaviour required by Governor William Tryon in 1778 {628}.

Eli Howell "..went to Goshen" {629}.

Eli Howell was listed as the head of a family consisting of one free white male of 16 years of age and upwards, one of under 16, and one free white female, residing in Shawangunk Town, Ulster County, New York, in the First Census of

619. Id., 306.
620. Id., 351.
621. Id., 306.
622. Id., 307.
623. #271306, Daughters of the American Revolution.
624. Id.
625. Craven, op. cit., 292.
626. Sidney C. Howell, op. cit.
627. Id.
628. P.R.O. Colonial Office, Class 5, Vol. 1109, 85.
629. Sidney C. Howell, op. cit.

the United States, 1790 {630}.

In the Second Census of the United States, 1800, Eli Howell was listed as the head of a family consisting of one free white male of 26 and under 45 years of age, one of 10 and under 16, one of under 10, one free white female of 45 and over, and one of 26 and under 45, residing in the Town of Montgomery, Orange County, New York {631}.

Eli Howell married Mary McKalyon at the Shawangunk Reformed Dutch Church on 16 May 1802 {632}.

Eli Howell was listed as the head of a family consisting of one free white male of 45 years of age and over, one of 16 and under 26, two of under 10, one free female of 26 and under 45, and two of under 10, residing in the Town of Mount Pleasant, Wayne County, Pennsylvania, in the Third Census of the United States, 1810 {633}.

Eli Howell was the father of at least three children {634}.

+ 133. i.   JOHN[5] HOWELL, born in about 1792.

+ 134. ii.   DAVID[5] HOWELL, born on 27 Nov 1795 {635}.

+ 135. iii. ELI[5] HOWELL, born in Jly 1814.

NOTE: *The data from the 1790 and 1800 Censuses suggest that we may have missed one generation of "Eli Howell", and that the Eli Howell who married Mary McKalyon may have been the son of our #50, and the father of our #135. This remains unresolved.*

53. RUTH[4] HOWELL (David[3], David[2], Richard[1]), the daughter of David[3] and Deborah (Satterly) Howell, was born on 22 June 1733 {636}, probably in the vicinity of Indian Island.

In about 1753, Ruth Howell married Israel Parshall, who was born on 7 Oct 1736, the son of Israel Parshall {637}.

Israel Parshall signed the Association on 24 Jan 1776 as a Second Lieutenant in the 3rd Company of the 2nd Battalion of the Northumberland County, Pennsylvania, militia {638}.

Israel Parshall was a taxpayer in Muncy Township, Northumberland County, from 1783 to 1787. He was among the earliest settlers of Chemung, New York, arriving there in about 1790, and he was present, with his son, Asa, at the

630. HEADS OF FAMILIES.., 1790, NEW YORK, 183.
631. NYG&BR, LXXXVII, 98 (Jan 1956).
632. Id., LXII, 314 (Oct 1931).
633. U.S. Census, Mount Pleasant, Wayne County, PA, 1810, Page 114.
634. Scott Sliker, Personal communication.
635. Craig Robert Howell, Personal communication.
636. James Clark Parshall, op. cit., 32.
637. Id.
638. Id., 34.

signing of the Newtown treaty in 1790. He received a deed signed by Governor Clinton to Lot 10 in the Town of Chemung {639}.

Ruth Parshall died on 20 Feb 1802 at Chemung, N.Y., and is buried in the Riverside Cemetery there {640}.

Israel Parshall died on 18 Feb 1827 at Chemung, probably as a result of being thrown from a colt he was riding to a sugar camp, and the resulting exposure to wintry weather. He is buried beside his wife in the Riverside Cemetery {641}.

Israel and Ruth (Howell) Parshall were the parents of eleven children {642}.

    i.   JOANNA PARSHALL, born on 16 Feb 1754, married Benjamin Burt, who was born on 9 Mch 1750, the son of Benjamin and Anna (Blaine) Burt, eight children, died on 19 Mch 1850 at Chemung, while he died on 10 May 1826.

    ii.   JERUSHA PARSHALL, married Joseph Shoemaker.

    iii.   ISRAEL PARSHALL, born in about 1760, married Deliverance Terry, who was born in about 1765, ten children, removed to Michigan where he died in 1840 {643}.

    iv.   DAVID PARSHALL, born on 20 Aug 1762, married Sarah Cronover, who was born on 3 Sep 1769, thirteen children, died on 25 June 1836, while she died on Mch 1856 {644}.

    v.   DEBORAH PARSHALL, born in about 1765, married Joseph Scott.

    vi.   LYDIA PARSHALL, married (1) Mr. Annis, married (2) Mr. Cooley.

    vii.   KEZIAH PARSHALL, married Benjamin Hulse on 10 Mch 1783 {645}.

    viii.   ASA PARSHALL, born on 26 Mch 1770, married Susannah Keeney, who was born on 5 Mch 1781, the daughter of Thomas and Mercy (Lamb) Keeney, of Hartford, CT, seventeen children,

639. Id.
640. Id., 32.
641. Id., 35.
642. Id.
643. Id., 57-58.
644. Id., 59-60.
645. Charles C. Coleman, THE EARLY RECORDS OF THE FIRST PRESBYTERIAN CHURCH OF GOSHEN NEW YORK.., 15.

died on 23 Mch 1848, while she died on 19 Oct 1871 {646}.

ix.   RUTH PARSHALL, married Jonathan Kenny.

x.   ANNA PARSHALL, born on 2 Apr 1778, married Thomas
      Keeney, who was born on 28 Sep 1776, the son of Thomas and
      Mercy (Lamb) Keeney, died 28 Feb 1827, while he died on 1 Sep
      1853.

xi.   JESSE PARSHALL, born in about 1779, married Mary Van
      Gorder, ten children, died in 1856 {647}.

55. DAVID⁴ HOWELL (David³, David², Richard¹), the son of David³ and Deborah
(Satterly) Howell, was born in about 1740, probably in the vicinity of Indian Island.
      "David Howel", farmer, 5'6" tall, 22 years of age, born in Suffolk County,
New York, enlisted in Captain Daniel Griffin's company of provincial troops on 14
May 1762 {648}.
      "Davᵈ Howil & Juruse Smith" were married on 16 Feb 1764 {649}.
      "David Howell, jr." signed the Articles of Association in the Blooming
Grove district of the Precinct of Goshen on 8 June 1775 {650} {651}.
      "David Howell, Jr.", of District #5 in the Town of Warwick, Orange
County, New York, was assessed £2 15s in Sep 1775 by John Wood, Assessor
{652}.
      David Howell was an enlisted man in the Fourth Regiment of Orange
County militia {653}.
      "A 1783 petition endorsement mentions "David Howell, Jun., of the
precinct of Goshen in the County of Orange", wherein "..the petitioners describe
themselves as men but in low circumstances who have been most zealously engaged
in the American cause.." " {654}.
      "On April 24, 1784, there was a petition of David Howell and others of
Goshen, Orange County, New York, for a mitigation of the costs accrued in a
prosecution against them under the act "to prevent Private Lotteries." " {655}
{656} {657}.

---

646. Parshall, op. cit., 60-64.
647. Id., 64-65.
648. MUSTER ROLLS OF NEW YORK PROVINCIAL TROOPS, 1755-1764, 470-471.
649. SR, 97; NYG&BR, XLIX, 165 (Apr 1918).
650. Eager, op. cit., 502.
651. Headley, op.cit., 76.
652. Ruttenber & Clark, op. cit., 566.
653. Roberts, op. cit., 164.
654. Wines, op. cit., 46.
655. Id.
656. Id., 47.
657. Mather, op. cit., 715-716.

On 18 May 1787, "..David Howell Jun[r] of the Precinct of Goshen in the County of Orange aforesaid Yeoman.." purchased land from the estate of Joshua Welles, said land in the Precinct of Goshen having been conveyed to Joshua Wells by Jacob Swarthout by an indenture dated 6-7 Jly 1771 {658}.

"David Howell, Jun[r]" was listed as the head of a family consisting of two free white males of 16 years of age and upwards, two of under 16, and three free white females, residing in Warwick Town, Orange County, New York, in the First Census of the United States, 1790 {659}.

David Howell was listed as the head of a family consisting of one free white male of 45 years of age and over, two of 10 and under 16, one of under 10, one free white female of 26 and under 45, and three of under 10, residing in the Town of Warwick, Orange County, New York, in the Second Census of the United States, 1800 {660}.

David Howell married Eleanor McLaughlin at Monroe on 1 Nov 1808 {661}.

David Howell was listed as the head of a household consisting of one free white male of 45 years of age and older, one of 16 and under 26, one free white female of 45 and older, two of 10 and under 16, and one slave, residing in the Town of Warwick, Orange County, New York, in the Third Census of the United States, 1810 {662}.

David Howell was listed as the head of a family consisting of one free white male of 45 years of age and older, one free white female of 45 and older, and one of 10 and under 16, residing in the Town of Warwick, Orange County, New York, with one person engaged in agriculture, in the Fourth Census of the United States, 1820 {663}.

By his will of 26 Nov 1816, proved on 31 Mch 1830, David Howell, of the Town of Warwick, left legacies to his wife, "Nelly", his sons, Josiah and Joseph, his daughters, Lois, Joanna, Mary, Boadicea and Permelia, and his two grand-daughters, the daughters of his deceased son, James. Josiah Howell and Jesse Wood, Jr., were the executors of this will {664}.

David Howell was probably the father of at least nine children.

+ 136.　　i.　　DAVID[5] HOWELL {665}, born in 1776 {666}.

+ 137.　　ii.　　LOIS[5] HOWELL, born on 17 Apr 1781 {667}.

658. Orange County Deeds, Liber D, 366-369.
659. HEADS OF FAMILIES.., 1790, NEW YORK, 147.
660. NYG&BR, LXIV, 61 (Jan 1933).
661. Gertrude A. Barber, BLOOMING GROVE MARRIAGES, 2, from LDS microfilm #0017833.
662. U.S. Census, Warwick, Orange County, NY, 1810, Page 363.
663. Id., 1820, Page 264.
664. Orange County Wills, Liber I, 97; Abstracted in EARLY ORANGE COUNTY WILLS, II, 272.
665. George Rogers Howell, op. cit., 322.
666. THE FAMILY RECORD, Devoted for 1897 to the Sackett, the Weygant, and the Mapes families and to ancestors of their intersecting lines. Published by C.H Weygant, Newburgh, N.Y., 146.
667. Ward Family Bible, cited in THE QUARTERLY, OCGS, 6, #3, 17 (Nov 1976).

+ 138. iii.   JOANNA[5] HOWELL, born on 29 Mch 1783 {668}.

+ 139. iv.   JAMES[5] HOWELL, born on 4 Nov 1785 {669}.

+ 140. v.   JOSIAH[5] HOWELL, born on 17 Apr 1787 {670}.

  141. vii.   MARY[5] HOWELL.

+ 142. vi.   JOSEPH[5] HOWELL, born on 28 May 1794 {671}.

+ 143. viii.   BOADICEA[5] HOWELL, born on 28 Nov 1796 {672}.

  144. ix.   PERMELIA[5] HOWELL.

57. JOHN[4] HOWELL (David[3], David[2], Richard[1]), the son of David[3] and Deborah (Satterly) Howell, was born in about 1745, probably in the vicinity of Indian Island.

"John Howel", farmer, of Suffolk County, 5'5" tall, 17 years of age, enlisted in Capt. Daniel Griffin's company of provincial troops on 3 May 1762 {673}.

John Howell "..was an old sailor - had been on one or two whaling voyages to the Artic regions, besides numerous trips to other shores "before the mast" of a merchantman." {674}.

John Howell married Sarah, "Sally", Dougherty {675}. She was the adopted daughter of David McCamley, of New Milford, Orange County, NY, and was born in about 1752 {676}.

John Howell signed the Articles of Association in the Blooming Grove district of the Precinct of Goshen on 8 June 1775 {677} {678}.

John Howell, of District #5, in the Town of Warwick, was assessed for £2 5s 9d by John Wood, Assessor, in Sep 1775 {679}.

John Howell "..resided at Sugar Loaf, in the Town of Warwick."

---

668. Stickney, HOWELL, Last page.
669. CEMETERIES OF CHESTER, NEW YORK (OCGS, 1977), 84.
670. Mrs. Mary E. (Grunendike) Haworth, Personal communication, from a copy in the possession of Linda S. Flesch, 1998.
671. Stickney, HOWELL, #675.
672. Ward Family Bible, op. cit.
673. MUSTER ROLLS OF NEW YORK PROVINCIAL TROOPS, 1755-1764, 470-471.
674. Charles E. Stickney, A HISTORY OF THE MINISINK REGION (MINISINK), 169.
675. Finch, op. cit., 4.
676. Stickney, HOWELL, #B62.
677. Eager, op. cit., 502.
678. Headley, op. cit., 76.
679. Ruttenber & Clark, op. cit., 566.

{680}. He moved to the Town of Wawayanda in "..about the year 1778." {681}.

John Howell was a Lieutenant in the Fourth Regiment of Orange County militia {682}.

John Howell fought in the Battle of Minisink, which was "..fought on 22 Jul 1779, in Sullivan County, New York, on the Delaware River, opposite Lackwaxen, Pennsylvania, between Joseph Brandt at the head of about 300 Indians and Tories and about 90 Americans, mostly militia of Orange County, New York, and Sussex County, New Jersey..when the Americans broke and fled, (he) stepped behind a tree and pulled off his shoes. Just then a tall Indian came along and stopped close by him, resting the butt of his gun on the ground and gazing after the fugitives, glimpses of whom could frequently be seen among the brush on the hill sides. Mr. Howel saw that the Indian would soon become aware of his presence, and determined to be beforehand with him; so he took good aim at his head and fired. He said he never knew whether he killed the Indian or not, for he ran as fast as possible and did not look back to see. He was not pursued however, and escaped." {683}.

By his will of 27 Mch 1789, proved on 11 Feb 1790, John Howell left his property to his wife, Sarah, for the bringing up of their children. He willed that she divide half the household furniture among their daughters, "Meale, Salle, Phebah and Hepsebe". His farm was ultimately to be divided between his sons, John and "Jeffree", who were to pay each of their sisters £10 one year later. His youngest son, Benjamin, was to be "learned a trade", and to receive £10 each from his brothers when he reached the age of 21. Sarah Howell, David Mc Cambly and Joshua Davis were appointed executors of this will {684}.

John Howell "..died at Stewarttown near Ridgebury 25 Dec 1790 (sic).." {685}, "..and was buried at the corners, about two miles below Ridgebury, where for years his grave, solitary and alone among the bushes, was a sort of sacred spot to the passer by. Since then others of his connection have gone to their long rest near him, and the whole, ornamented with tasteful monuments and enclosed with a substantial iron fence, now forms one of the most beautiful cemeteries in the town." {686}. He was "..aged 45 years.." at the time of his death {687}.

"Sally Howell" was listed as the head of a family consisting of two free white males of 16 and over, one of under 16 years of age, and five free white females, residing in Minisink Town, Orange County, New York, in the First

680. Stickney, MINISINK, 170.
681. Id., 169.
682. Roberts, op. cit., 161.
683. Id., 105-106.
684. Orange County Wills, Liber A, 82; Abstracted in EARLY ORANGE COUNTY WILLS, II, 7.
685. Finch, op. cit., 4.
686. Stickney, MINISINK, 170.
687. William J. Coulter, Mary Flynn and Helen M. Benjamin, RECORDS OF THE RIDGEBURY PRESBYTERIAN CHURCH.., Published by the OCGS (1993), 65.

Census of the United States, 1790 {688}.

"Sarah Howel" was listed as the head of a family consisting of one free white female of 45 years of age and over, two of 16 and under 26, one free white male of 16 and under 26, and one of ten and under 16, residing in the Town of Minisink, Orange County, New York, in the Second Census of the United States, 1800 {689}.

"Widow Sarah Howell and sons" were included in the original School District #7 in old Minisink Town in 1813 when school districts were first established {690}.

Sarah (Dougherty) Howell died on 24 June 1834 in the 83rd year of her age, and is buried beside her husband at Stewartstown {691}.

John and Sarah (Dougherty) Howell were the parents of at least seven children {692}.

+ 145.   i.   MELLICENT[5] HOWELL, born on 10 Jan 1775.

+ 146.   ii.   SARAH[5] HOWELL, born in about 1778.

+ 147.   iii.   JEFFREY[5] HOWEL, born on 23 Aug 1780.

+ 148.   iv.   PHEBE[5] HOWELL, born in about 1782.

+ 149.   v.   JOHN[5] HOWELL, born in about 1784.

+ 150.   vi.   BENJAMIN[5] HOWELL.

  151. vii.   HEPZIBAH[5] HOWELL, born in about 1788, "..died Sept. 24, 1857 in the 70th year of her age." {693}.

59. GEORGE[4] HOWELL (David[3], David[2], Richard[1]), the son of David[3] and Lydia (Case) Howell, was born near Indian Island in about 1749.

George Howell married Eunice Horton in Orange County {694}. She was the daughter of Israel and Sarah (Lee) Horton, and was born in about Nov 1760 {695}.

George Howell signed the Articles of Association in the Blooming Grove district of the Precinct of Goshen on 8 June 1775 {696} {697}.

---

688. HEADS OF FAMILIES.., 1790, NEW YORK, 143.
689. NYG&BR, LXIII, 84 (Jan 1932).
690. Ruttenber and Clark, op. cit., 662.
691. Coulter, et al., 65.
692. ANCESTORS OF DR. JAMES CASH COLEMAN.., from a copy in the possession of the OCGS, 1995, 14.
693. Coulter, et al., op. cit.
694. Finch, op. cit., 4.
695. Id., 16.
696. Eager, op. cit., 501.

George Howell was assessed for £1 3s in District #5, Town of Warwick, by John Wood in Sep 1775 {698}.

"At the time of the War of the Revolution, George Howell was living in Warwick, Orange County. He served in the 4th Orange Co. Militia under Major John Hathorn. After the close of the War he removed with his family probably first to Newburgh, then to Delaware County where some of his children were born. By 1802 he was in Genoa, Cayuga County and from that place he shortly moved to Hector, Seneca Co, N.Y. where he settled near the Presbyterian Church formed in 1809.

The locality around this Church was called Peach Orchard a translation of the Indian name of the place. George and Eunice Howell were early members of this congregation..The house which George Howell built was about two miles from the Church toward the east and up a steep hill. It was just north (on the west side of the road) of the corners now called Logan. When this house burned in 1930, the family Bible was destroyed." {699}.

"George Howel" was listed as the head of a family consisting of two free white males of 16 years of age and upwards, two of under 16, and eight free white females, residing in Warwick Town, Orange County, New York, in the First Census of the United States, 1790 {700}.

George Howell died on 29 Apr 1829, at the age of 79 years, and is buried in the cemetery at the Hector Presbyterian Church {701}.

Eunice (Horton) Howell died on 9 Mch 1835, at the age of 74 years and 4 months, and is buried beside her husband at Hector {702}.

George and Eunice (Horton) Howell were the parents of thirteen children {703}.

+ 152. i. BENJAMIN[5] HOWELL, born on 1 Oct 1776.

+ 153. ii. LUCINDA[5] HOWELL, born on 11 Dec 1778.

+ 154. iii. SALLY[5] HOWELL, born on 27 Sep 1781.

+ 155. iv. MEHITABLE[5] HOWELL, born on 24 Aug 1783.

156. v. WILLIAM[5] HOWELL, born on 21 Sep 1785, died unmarried at Hector at the age of 53 years, 6 months and 26 days in 1839 {704}.

---

697. Headley, op.cit., 75.
698. Ruttenber & Clark, op. cit., 566.
699. Finch, op. cit., 6.
700. NYG&BR, LXIV, 61 (Jan 1933).
701. Finch, op. cit., 6.
702. Id.
703. Id.
704. Id., 8.

+ 157. vi.   ANNA[5] HOWELL, born on 21 Sep 1787.

+ 158. vii.   JEMIMA[5] HOWELL, born on 6 Apr 1790.

   159.viii.   FANNY[5] HOWELL, born on 9 Jly 1792, died young.

+ 160. ix.   JEREMIAH[5] HOWELL, born on 4 Dec 1793.

+ 161. x.   HANNAH[5] HOWELL, born on 31 Aug 1796.

+ 162. xi.   GEORGE[5] HOWELL, born on 7 Feb 1802.

   163. xii.   ELIZA[5] HOWELL, born on 27 Aug 1807, died unmarried at
                 Hector on 18 Sep 1844, at the age of 37 years and 27 days, and
                 is buried in the cemetery at the Hector Presbyterian Church
                 {705}.

+ 164. xiii.   SAMUEL[5] HOWELL, born on 7 Jly 1810.

60. MEHITABLE[4] HOWELL (David[3], David[2], Richard[1]), the daughter of David[3]
and Lydia (Case) Howell, was born in the vicinity of Indian Island in Southold
Township, Suffolk County, New York.
     Mehitable Howell married Joshua Reeves of Southold {706} before
1772 {707}. He was the son of Daniel and Experience (Parshall) Reeve, and
was born in about 1746 {708}.
     "Joshua Reeve", shoemaker, of Suffolk County, 5'6" tall, 16 years of age,
enlisted in Captain Daniel Griffin's company of provincial troops on 3 Apr 1762
{709}.
     Joshua and Mehitable (Howell) Reeves moved to Orange County and
settled in the Town of Minisink, about two miles south of Johnson, on a farm on
which their son, Howell Reeves, lived and died, and which was owned by Miss
Jennie Reeve in 1914 {710}.
     Mehitable (Howell) Reeve "..died at Westtown, Orange Co. between 1782
& 86." {711}.
     On 27 Apr 1786, Joshua Reeves married (2) Abigail Haff {712}. He

---

705. Id., 7.
706. Wines, op. cit., 48.
707. Finch, op. cit., 4.
708. Baker, op. cit., 384-385.
709. MUSTER ROLLS OF NEW YORK PROVINCIAL TROOPS, 1755-1764, 470-471.
710. Stickney, HOWELL, #B59.
711. Finch, op. cit., 4.
712. Coleman, op. cit., 16.

subsequently moved to Seneca County, where he died at Romulus before 1812 {713}.

Joshua and Mehitable (Howell) Reeves were the parents of three children {714}.

    i.   JOSHUA REEVES, born on 10 Apr 1772, married (1) Sarah Simmons, (2) Mary Bailey, buried in the family cemetery {715} {716}.

    ii.   LYDIA REEVES, born on 11 May 1775, married Phineas Terry, eight children, died 29 May 1841.

    iii.   HOWELL REEVES, born on 11 Oct 1777, married (1) Elizabeth Wood, who was born on 11 Oct 1783, the daughter of Jonathan Wood, and died on 11 Jly 1816, and is buried in the family cemetery. He married (2) Mary (Corwin) Pellet, who was born on 4 Mch 1780, and died on 3 Mch 1873 {717}.

Joshua and Abigail (Huff) Reeves were the parents of one child.

    iv.   KITSEY REEVES, born on 11 Jan 1787, baptized on 4 Feb 1794 {718}.

61. JEMIMA[4] HOWELL (David[3], David[2], Richard[1]), the daughter of David[3] and Lydia (Case) Howell, was born on 10 Jly 1755 in the vicinity of Indian Island.

"Silus Howel & Jemime Howel" were married in about Apr 1775 {719}. Silas Howell (#98) was the son of Daniel[3] (#36) and Sarah (Swesey) Howell, and was born on 22 Feb 1750/1 in the vicinity of Mattituck {720}.

Jemima (Howell) Howell died on 25 June 1811 in her 57th year {721}.

Silas and Jemima (Howell) Howell were the parents of nine children {722}, as listed under #98, Silas[4] Howell.

62. BENJAMIN[4] HOWELL (David[3], David[2], Richard[1]), the son of David[3] and Lydia (Case) Howell, was born in the vicinity of Indian Island in 1759. He served in the Revolutionary War as a member of the First Regiment of Orange County

713. Finch, op. cit., 4.
714. Stickney, HOWELL, #B59.
715. CEMETERIES OF THE TOWN OF MINISINK (OCGS, 1988), 127.
716. Coulter, et. al, op. cit., 61-62.
717. CEMETERIES OF THE TOWN OF MINISINK, 127.
718. Coleman, op. cit., 115.
719. SR, 102; NYG&BR, XLIX, 269 (Jly 1918).
720. Wilbur Franklin Howell, op. cit., 118.
721. Id.
722. Id.

militia {723}, and received a pension after 1832 {724}.

Benjamin Howell married Sarah Webster at the Goshen Presbyterian Church on 30 Mch 1784 {725}.

Benjamin Howell was listed as the head of a family consisting of one free white male of 16 years of age and upwards, four of under 16, and two white females, residing in Goshen Town, Orange County, New York, in the First Census of the United States, 1790 {726}.

"Sarah Howell, wife of Benj. Howell" joined the communion of the First Presbyterian Church of Goshen on 14 June 1795 {727}.

The house of Benjamin Howell was adjoining the property of Isaac Sargent in the Town of Minisink in 1798 {728}.

Benjamin Howell and Eleanor Webb were married on 10 Nov 1798 {729}.

Benjamin Howell was listed as the head of a family consisting of one free white male of 26 and under 45 years of age, one of 16 and under 26, two of under 10, one free white female of 26 and under 45, and one of under 10, residing in the Town of Minisink, Orange County, New York, in the Second Census of the United States, 1800 {730}.

Benjamin Howell contributed £6 to the Ridgebury Presbyterian Church in 1805-1806 {731}.

In 1813, Benjamin Howell was a resident of School District 4, the Ridgebury District, in the Town of Wawayanda {732}.

"Eleanor wife of Benjamin Howell..died Jan. 27, 1814 48 years", and is buried in the Ridgebury Cemetery {733}.

Benjamin Howell was elected as a Ruling Elder of the Ridgebury Presbyterian Church on 19 Jly 1817 {734}.

Benjamin Howell was listed as the head of a family consisting of one free white male of 45 years of age and older, two of 10 and under 16, one free white female of 45 and older, and one of 16 and under 26, residing in the Town of Minisink, Orange County, New York, and having two persons engaged in agriculture, in the Fourth Census of the United States, 1820 {735}.

Benjamin Howell lived near Ridgebury, but is said to have moved to

723. Roberts, op. cit., 253.
724. Finch, op. cit., 4.
725. Coleman, op. cit., 14.
726. HEADS OF FAMILIES.., 1790, NEW YORK, 139.
727. Coleman, op. cit., 52.
728. Town of Minisink House Assessment Roll, 1798, cited in THE QUARTERLY, OCGS, 4, #2, 12 (Aug 1974).
729. Coleman, op. cit., 22.
730. NYG&BR, LXIII, 85 (Jan 1932).
731. Coulter, et. al., op. cit., 2.
732. Ruttenber and Clark, op. cit., 682.
733. Coulter, et. al., op. cit., 40.
734. Id., 3, 75, 76.
735. U.S. Census, Minisink, Orange County, NY, 1820, Page 239.

Blooming Grove late in his life {736}. However, he died at Ridgebury on 13 May 1840, at the age of 81 years {737}, and is buried in the Ridgebury Cemetery {738}.

Benjamin Howell apparently married a third time, since he left to his wife, "..Mirian Howell all the moovable property that she brought to my house that shall remain after my decease.." by his will of 17 Nov 1828. He also ordered his son, Preston W. Howell, who was his principal heir, and who was bequeathed all his real estate, to support her as long as she should remain his widow. Preston W. Howell was also directed to pay all of Benjamin Howell's debts and funeral expenses out of his movable property. If any surplus was left, it was to be divided in equal shares among his eight sons, James, George W., Benjamin, John, Daniel, Chauncy G., Horace, and Henry. George W. Howell and Preston W. Howell were named as executors of this will, but George W. Howell withdrew. This will was proved on 24 Jly 1840 {739}.

"Miriam, wife of Benjn. Howell, Ridgebury" apparently joined the First Presbyterian Church at Goshen on 27 May 1787, and was a member on 27 Apr 1818 {740}.

Benjamin and Sarah (Webster) Howell may have been the parents of eight children.

+ 165. i. JAMES[5] HOWELL.

+ 166. ii. GEORGE W.[5] HOWELL, born in 1786.

+ 167. iii. BENJAMIN[5] HOWELL.

+ 168. iv. JOHN[5] HOWELL, born in about 1794.

+ 169. v. DANIEL[5] HOWELL.

+ 170. vi. CHAUNCEY[5] HOWELL.

171.viii. HORACE[5] HOWELL.

+ 172. vii. HENRY[5] HOWELL.

Benjamin and Eleanor (Webb) Howell were the parents of at least one child.
+ 173. ix. PRESTON W.[5] HOWELL, born in 1811.

63. EZRA[4] HOWELL (David[3], David[2], Richard[1]), the son of David[3] and Lydia

736. Stickney, HOWELL, #B60.
737. Coulter, et. al., op. cit., 33.
738. Id., 40.
739. Orange County Wills, Liber L, 35-39.
740. Coleman, op. cit., 54.

(Case) Howell, was born in the vicinity of Indian Island on 12 Oct 1762 {741}.

Ezra Howell came from Sugar Loaf to Ridgebury, and later moved to Blooming Grove. He married Jane Chatfield, the daughter of Thomas Chatfield, and they lived on the farm he bought from his father-in-law {742}.

Ezra Howell, "..of Blooming Grove,..was..a Revolutionary soldier, and (was) noted for having refused a pension from the government." {743}. He was a member of the Fourth Regiment of Orange County militia {744}.

Ezra Howell was baptized at Goshen on 20 Aug 1785 {745}. He became a member of the First Presbyterian Church of Goshen on 21 Jan 1787 {746}.

Ezra Howell was listed as the head of a family consisting of one free white male of 16 years of age and upwards, one of under 16, and two free white females, residing in New Cornwall Town, Orange County, New York, in the First Census of the United States, 1790 {747}.

Ezra Howell was listed as the head of a family consisting of one free white male of 26 and under 45 years of age, one of 10 and under 16, three of under 10, one free white female of 26 and under 45, one of 10 and under 16, and two of under 10, residing in the Town of Blooming Grove, Orange County, New York, in the Second Census of the United States, 1800 {748}.

Ezra Howell was listed as the head of a family consisting of one free white male of 45 years of age and older, three of 16 and under 26, two of under 10, one free white female of 26 and under 45, one of 16 and under 26, two of 10 and under 16, and two of under 10, residing in the Town of Blooming Grove, Orange County, New York, in the Third Census of the United States, 1810 {749}.

Ezra Howell was listed as the head of a family consisting of one free white male of 45 years of age and older, one of 18 and under 26, one of 10 and under 16, one of under 10, one free white female of 45 and older, one of 26 and under 45, one of 16 and under 26, one of 10 and under 16, and one of under 10, residing in the Town of Blooming Grove, and having three persons engaged in agriculture, in the Fourth Census of the United States, 1820 {750}.

On 15 Aug 1850, Ezra Howell, 90, farmer, was listed as the head of a household consisting of himself, his daughter, Eunice, 40, and two hired hands, residing in the Town of Blooming Grove, Orange County, New York, in the Seventh Census of the United States, 1850 {751}.

741. Stickney, HOWELL, #B58.
742. Id.
743. Ruttenber and Clark, op.cit., 680.
744. Roberts, op. cit., 164.
745. Coleman, op. cit., 111.
746. Id., 50.
747. HEADS OF FAMILIES.., 1790, NEW YORK, 146.
748. NYG&BR, LXIII, 404 (Oct 1932).
749. U.S. Census, Blooming Grove, Orange County, NY, 1820, Page 392.
750. Id., 1830, Page 305.
751. Id., 1850, Dwelling House 25, Family Number 25, Page 320.

Ezra Howell died on 21 June 1851 at Blooming Grove {752}, although Stickney gives a date of 20 Jan 1852 {753}.

Ezra and Jane (Chatfield) Howell were the parents of thirteen children {754}.

174.   i.   LUCRETIA[5] HOWELL, born on 17 Jan 1788.

175. ii.   THOMAS C.[5] HOWELL, born on 3 Feb 1790, contacted ship fever, from which he died, on 23 Dec 1811, on a second voyage to China {755}.

+ 176. iii. JOHN[5] HOWELL, born on 14 Feb 1792.

+ 177. iv. HUNTTING[5] HOWELL, born on 6 June 1794.

+ 178. v.   HANNAH[5] HOWELL, born on 30 Sep 1796.

179. vi.   EUNICE[5] HOWELL, born on 3 Feb 1799, died unmarried in 1870 {756}.

+ 180. vii. COE SAYER[5] HOWELL, born on 24 Mch 1801.

181. viii. ELIOT[5] HOWELL, born on 15 Apr 1803, burned to death on 10 Nov 1804 {757}.

+ 182. ix. ASA R.[5] HOWELL, born on 8 Mch 1805.

+ 183. x.   JULIET[5] HOWELL, born on 7 May 1807.

184. xi.   JANE C.[5] HOWELL, born on 29 May 1809, died unmarried {758} on 20 May 1844 at Blooming Grove {759}.

185. xii. SUSAN[5] HOWELL, born on 4 June 1811, died on 29 Sep 1827 {760}.

---

752. GOSHEN DEMOCRAT, 11 Jly 1851, from ORANGE COUNTY DEATHS, by Caroline Still Weller.
753. Stickney, op. cit., #B58.
754. Id.
755. Id., #B68.
756. Id., #B68$^1/_2$.
757. Id., #B65$^3/_4$.
756. Id., #B67$^1/_4$.
759. GOSHEN INDEPENDENT REPUBLICAN, 31 May 1844, from Weller, op. cit.
760. Stickney, HOWELL, #B67$^3/_4$.

+ 186. xiii.   THOMAS CHATFIELD[5] HOWELL, born on 18 Jly 1818
                 {761}.

65. LYDIA[4] HOWELL (David[3], David[2], Richard[1]), the daughter of David[3] and
Mary (Murrow) Howell, was born in the vicinity of Indian Island on 22 Feb 1767
{762}.
    Lydia Howell and Constantine Fuller, the son of Amariah Fuller, of
Chester, were married on 18 Mch 1794. They lived at Wantage, in Sussex County,
New Jersey {763}.
    Constant Fuller died on 2 Apr 1813 {764}.
    By her will of 28 Feb 1837, proved on 23 Dec 1854, Lydia Fuller left all
her real property to her son, Beach Fuller, who was named an executor of her will
with Henry Shepherd, her son-in-law. Her personal property was divided between
her daughters, Sarah Shephard and Phebe DeWitt {765}.
    Lydia Fuller died of dysentery on 16 Sep 1854, at the age of 87
{766}.
    Constantine and Lydia Ann (Howell) Fuller were probably the parents of
six children {767}.

    i.   SARAH FULLER, born on 20 Apr 1795, married Henry Sheperd,
            who was born on 20 Apr 1788, on 16 Mch 1812.

    ii.   FANNY FULLER, born on 6 Apr 1796, died on 4 Apr 1814, at
            the age of 17 years, 11 months, and 28 days, and is buried in the
            Slawson cemetery at Wantage.

    iii.   BEACH FULLER, born in about 1799, died of a liver ailment on
            16 Dec 1876 {768}.

    iv.   PHEBE FULLER, married Jacob W. DeWitt on 3 Feb 1830,
            seven children, died on 4 Sep 1857 {769}.

    v.   JESSE FULLER, born in about 1803, died on 3 June 1816, and
            is buried in the Slawson cemetery.

    vi.   JOHN FULLER, born on 3 Jan 1805, married Mary, the daughter
            of Abiah and Mary (Lobden) Wilson, died on 25 Oct 1865. She

761. Finch, op. cit., 5.
762. Id.
763. Id.
764. Roger F. Hutson, Personal communication.
765. Sussex County (N.J.) Wills, Liber , 544-556 (sic).
766. New Jersey Returns of Deaths, Vol. AF, 637.
767. Hutson, op. cit.
768. New Jersey Returns of Deaths, Vol. BD, 301.
769. Charles E. Stickney, OLD SUSSEX COUNTY FAMILIES (SUSSEX), 102.

was born on 18 May 1812, and died on 16 Aug 1844 {770}.

66. NOBLE[4] HOWELL (David[3], David[2], Richard[1]), the son of David[3] and Mary (Murrow) Howell, was born in the vicinity of Indian Island on 23 Mch 1769 {771}.

Noble Howell married Tabitha Mapes. They had a residence on the road leading from Sugar Loaf to Bellvale {772}.

Noble Howell was listed as the head of a family consisting of one free white male of 26 and under 45 years of age, two of 10 and under, one free white female of 26 and under 45, and three of under 10, residing in the Town of Warwick, Orange County, New York, in the Second Census of the United States, 1800 {773}.

Noble Howell was listed as the head of a household consisting of one free white male of 26 and under 45 years of age, one of 16 and under 26, one of 10 and under 16, three of under 10, one free white female of 26 and under 45, one of 16 and under 26, one of 10 and under 16, and two of under 10, residing in the Town of Warwick, Orange County, New York, in the Third Census of the United States, 1810 {774}.

In the Fourth Census of the United States, 1820, Noble Howell was listed as the head of a family consisting of one free white male of 45 years of age and older, one of 18 and under 26, two of 10 and under 16, one of under 10, one free white female of 45 and older, two of 10 and under 16, and one of under 10, residing in the Town of Warwick, Orange County, New York, with two persons engaged in agriculture {775}.

Noble Howell died on 31 Mch 1829 {776}, at the age of 59 years, 10 months and 8 days, and is buried in the family burying ground on the west side of Sugar Loaf Mountain Road {777}.

On 24 Apr 1841, Tabitha Howell, and her children, deeded, to Coe Howell, 15 acres of land on the road from Sugar Loaf to Bellvale {778}.

Tabitha (Mapes) Howell died on 20 Oct 1857, at the age of 88 years, 7 months, and 19 days. She was blind for some of the later years of her life {779}. She is buried beside her husband {780}.

770. Stickney, SUSSEX, 58.
771. Stickney, HOWELL, #B63.
772. Id.
773. NYG&BR, LXIV, 61 (Jan 1933).
774. U.S. Census, Warwick, Orange County, NY, 1810, 363.
775. Id., 1820, Page 264.
776. Finch, op. cit., 5.
777. CEMETERIES OF CHESTER,.., 86.
778. Stickney, op. cit.
779. Id.
780. CEMETERIES OF CHESTER,.., 86.

Noble and Tabitha (Mapes) Howell were the parents of ten children {781}.

+ 187. i.   CADWALADER⁵ HOWELL, born on 20 Jly 1793.

+ 188. ii.   HANNAH⁵ HOWELL, born on 2 Jan 1795.

+ 189. iii.   MARY⁵ HOWELL, born on 10 Feb 1797.

+ 190. iv.   ELBERT (or ALBERT)⁵ HOWELL, born on 8 Oct 1798.

+ 191. v.   FANNY⁵ HOWELL, born on 6 Dec 1800.

+ 192. vi.   COE⁵ HOWELL, born in 1803.

+ 193. vii.   PETER⁵ HOWELL, born on 26 Nov 1807.

+ 194. viii.   JANE⁵ HOWELL, born on 25 Feb 1809.

+ 195. ix.   JOHN⁵ HOWELL, born on 21 Oct 1813.

+ 196. x.   LYDIA⁵ HOWELL, born on 14 Aug 1817.

67. DEBORAH⁴ HOWELL (David³, David², Richard¹), the daughter of David³ and Mary (Murrow) Howell, was born on 6 Mch 1771 {782}, probably in the vicinity of Indian Island.

Deborah Howell married Peter Mills, Jr. {783}, who was born on 16 Oct 1768.

Peter Mills was a resident of District No. 9, the Slate Hill District, in 1813 {784}.

Peter Mills was a witness to the will of James Dolsen, written on 5 May 1824, and proved on 2 Apr 1825 {785}.

Peter Mills, Jr. died on 7 Mch 1831, "..aged 62 yrs. 5 mo. 19 ds..", and is buried in the "Old Mills Farm Cemetery" {786}.

Deborah (Howell) Mills died on 21 Jly 1864, at the age of "..93 yrs. 4 mo. 15 ds..", and is buried beside her husband {787}.

---

781. Stickney, op. cit.
782. Finch, op. cit., 5.
783. Id.
784. Ruttenber and Clark, op. cit., 683.
785. Orange County Wills, Liber G, 278-279; Abstracted in EARLY ORANGE COUNTY WILLS, II, 225.
786. Coulter, et. al., op. cit., 63.
787. Id.

Peter and Deborah (Howell) Mills were the parents of at least one child {788}.

     i.   ARCHIBALD MILLS, born in 1793.

71. ISAIAH[4] HOWELL (Aaron[3], David[2], Richard[1]), the likely son of Aaron[3] and Sarah (Hallock) Howell, was born in about 1743 in the vicinity of Mattituck.

Isaiah Howell, joyner, 5'3" in stature, of the Town of Southold, was enlisted in the company of Capt. Daniel Griffen on 14 May 1761, at the age of 18, by Capt. Griffen {789}.

Isaiah Howell signed the Articles of Association in the Precinct of Cornwall {790}.

"Isiah Howell" was an enlisted man in the Orange County levies at the time of the Revolution {791}.

"Isaiah Howel" was listed as the head of a family consisting of one free white male of 16 years of age and upwards, three of under 16, and three free white females, residing in Minisink Town, Orange County, New York, in the First Census of the United States, 1790 {792}.

Isaiah Howell was listed as the head of a family consisting of one free white male of 45 years of age and over, two of 16 and under 26, one of under 10, one free white female of 45 and over, and one of 10 and under 16, residing in the Town of Minisink, Orange County, New York, in the Second Census of the United States, 1800 {793}.

On 20 Jan 1802, "..Isaiah Hoell of the Town of Minisink County of Orange and State of New York Yeoman and Sarah his Wife.." sold to "..Ifsac Vandeuzer of the same place..All that certain Lot.. Containing twelve Acres of Land.." {794}.

"Isiah Howell" was a witness to the will of Kezia Hait, of the Town of Wallkill, Orange County, New York, written on 21 May 1823, and proved on 6 Sep 1823 {795}.

Isaiah and Sarah Howell were probably the parents of at least four children {796}.

  197.   i.   MOSES[5] HOWELL.

+ 198. ii.   AARON[5] HOWELL, born in 1769.

---

788. Betsy Mills Del Santo, Personal communication, cited in THE QUARTERLY, OCGS, 8, #1, 2 (May 1978).

789. MUSTER ROLLS OF NEW YORK PROVINCIAL TROOPS.., 406-407.

790. Headley, op. cit., 77.

791. Roberts, op. cit., 84.

792. HEADS OF FAMILIES.., 1790, NEW YORK, 143.

793. NYG&BR, LXIII, 81 (Jan 1932).

794. Deed, from a copy in the possession of Mrs. Hester Halstead Pier, 1992.

795. Orange County Wills, Liber G, 129; Abstracted in EARLY ORANGE COUNTY WILLS, II, 209.

796. Marjorie (Mrs. William W.) Sederlund, Personal communication, cited in THE QUARTERLY, OCGS, 3, #4, 26 (Feb 1974).

199. iii.   ABIGAIL⁵ HOWELL, married Isaac Manning.

200. iv.   JULIA⁵ HOWELL, married Mr. Cornell.

73. AARON⁴ HOWELL (Aaron³, David², Richard¹) may have been the son Aaron³ and Sarah (Hallock) Howell.

   Aaron Howell, Jr., signed the Articles of Association in the Precinct Cornwall {797}.

   Aaron Howell was a member of the First New York Regiment of the Lii {798} and, at another time, of the Third New York Regiment of the Lii {799}.

   Aaron, Jr., and Phebe Howell renewed covenant in the First Church (Morristown, N.J. on 8 Jly 1783 {800}.

   Aaron and Phebe Howell were the parents of at least two childre. {801}.

   201. i.   CATHERINE⁵ HOWELL, born on 22 Mch 1783, baptized on ¡ Jly 1783.

   202. ii.   MARY⁵ HOWELL, born on 18 Dec 1790, baptized on 5 Jly 1791.

74. SILAS⁴ HOWELL (Israel³, David², Richard¹), the son of Israel³ and Hannah (Smith) Howell, was born in about 1743, possibly at Baiting Hollow.

   "Silas Howell, Jr.", labourer, 16, enlisted in Captain Jonathan Baker's company of New York provincial troops on 2 May 1760 {802}.

   "..us Howels & mary Benjaman" were married in Oct 1764 {803}. She was the daughter of Nathan Benjamin {804}, and his second wife, Sarah Conkling, whom he married on 11 Jan 1736/7 {805}.

   Silas and Mary Howell "..lived first at Upper Mills, moved to Rabbit Swamp, moved to North Road west of Micah Howell's, moved to Wading River, moved to Long Pond.." {806}.

   Silas Howell was a member of Captain Josiah Lupton's company of militiamen in 1775 {807}. As such, he signed the Articles of Association in

797. Headley, op. cit., 78.
798. Roberts, op. cit., 22.
799. Id., 43.
800. HISTORY..FIRST PRESBYTERIAN CHURCH OF MORRISTOWN, N.J., II, 111.
801. Id.
802. MUSTER ROLLS OF NEW YORK PROVINCIAL TROOPS, 284-285.
803. SR, 97; (NYG&BR, XLIX, 165 (Apr 1918)).
804. George H. Tuthill, op. cit.
805. SR, 82; (NYG&BR, XLIX, 72 (Jan 1918)).
806. George H. Tuthill, op. cit.
807. THE REGISTER, SCHS, VIII, #1, 23-24 (June 1982).

1775 {808}.

Silas Howell, farmer, of the Township of Southold, gave his age as 35 when he signed the Oath of Allegiance and Peaceable Behaviour required by Governor William Tryon in 1778 {809}.

"Silas Howel" was listed by Josiah Woodhull as the head of a family of nine residing in the Wading River district on 22 Aug 1778 {810}.

At the Annual Meeting of the Town of Southold held on 3 Apr 1781, Silas Howell was selected to be an "Overseer of Highways" for the ensuing year {811}.

"Silass Howell" was listed as the head of a family consisting of three free white males of 16 years of age and upwards, two of under 16, and three free white females, residing in Southold Town, Suffolk County, New York, in the First Census of the United States, 1790 {812}.

Silas Howell died of smallpox in 1792 {813}, at Long Pond, and is buried there {814}. Letters of administration on the estate of Silas Howell, taylor, of the Town of Riverhead, were issued to his son, Silas Howell, mariner, on 18 Dec 1792, after his widow, Mary Howell, declined {815}.

Mary (Benjamin) Howell moved to Setauket with her family shortly after the death of her husband, Silas Howell. On 3 June 1798, she married Joseph Brewster there {816}, and died shortly thereafter.

Joseph Brewster, Sr., was listed as the head of a household consisting of one free white male of 45 years of age and older, two of 16 and under 26, one free white female of 45 and older, two of 16 and under 26, one of 10 and under 16, one other free person, and 4 slaves, residing in the Town of Brookhaven, Suffolk County, New York, in the Second Census of the United States, 1800 {817}.

Silas and Mary (Benjamin) Howell were the parents of at least ten children.

+ 203.   i.   MARY[5] HOWELL, born on 25 Jly 1765.

+ 204.   ii.   SILAS[5] HOWELL, born in about 1766.

+ 205. iii.   HENRY[5] HOWELL.

+ 206. iv.   SARAH[5] HOWELL.

808. Mather, op. cit., 1056.
809. P.R.O. Colonial Office, Class 5, Vol. 1109, 91.
810. NGSQ, 63, 283 (1975).
811. STR, Liber D, 188 left; (III, 231).
812. HEADS OF FAMILIES.., 1790, NEW YORK, 170.
813. James Franklin Young, op. cit., VIII, 10-11, (June 1982).
814. George H. Tuthill, op. cit.
815. Suffolk County Letters of Administration, Liber AB, 69; Suffolk County Estates, File #194.
816. RECORD OF MARRIAGES PERFORMED BY REV. ZACHARIAH GREENE, 6, from a copy in the LONG ISLAND COLLECTION, East Hampton Library, generously made available by Dorothy T. King, Librarian.
817. NYG&BR, LVI, 324 (Oct 1925).

+ 207. v. JOSEPH[5] HOWELL, born on 19 Dec 1770 {818}.

+ 208. vi. MICAH[5] HOWELL, born on 20 Jan 1773 {819}.

+ 209. vii. SMITH[5] HOWELL, born on 19 Dec 1779 {820}.

+ 210. viii. BENJAMIN[5] HOWELL.

+ 211. ix. CHARITY[5] HOWELL, born on 22 June 1779 {821}.

+ 212. x. AZUBA[5] HOWELL.

75. ISRAEL[4] HOWELL (Israel[3], David[2], Richard[1]), the son of Israel[3] and Hannah (Smith) Howell, was born in about 1744, probably at Baiting Hollow.

Israel Howell married Tabitha Hulse, who was born on 15 May 1751 {822}, the daughter of Deacon Paul and Esther (Mapes) Hulse.

"Israel Howell Ju[r]" was a member of Captain Josiah Lupton's company of militiamen in 1775 {823}. As such, he signed the Articles of Association in 1775 {824}.

Israel Howell was paid £12 16s 7d on 4 Apr 1778 by the Town of Southold {825}.

Israel Howell, farmer, of the Township of Southold, gave his age as 34 when he signed the Oath of Allegiance and Peaceable Behaviour required by Governor William Tryon in 1778 {826}.

"Israel Howel" was listed, by Josiah Woodhull, as the head of a family of three persons living in the Wading River district on 22 Aug 1778 {827}.

Israel Howell, Jr., along with other property owners in Baiting Hollow, signed an "..agreement..to agree to lines as they had found them - from Ambrose Horton's east line to Daniel Edwards west line, which was the Creek." {828}.

"Mr. Cook purchased his farm of 2nd Israel Howell, who was a great-grandson of 1st Richard Howell. Their buildings were not on the road, but three-eighths of a mile north, where there was light land for easy tillage, and a bed of clay near the surface to furnish water. Three generations of Howells had lived there,

818. Wilbur Franklin Howell, op. cit., 8
819. Id., 9.
820. Id., 48.
821. Id., 53.
822. Ida A. Maddrah, Personal communication, from a copy in the possession of David A. Overton, Historian, Town of Brookhaven, 1992.
823. THE REGISTER, SCHS, VIII, #1, 23-24 (June 1982).
824. Mather, op. cit., 1056.
825. STR, Liber D, 30 left; (III, 59).
826. P.R.O. Colonial Office, Class 5, Vol. 1109, 94.
827. NGSQ, 63, 283 (1975).
828. James Franklin Young, op. cit., VIII, 11 (June 1982).

but Cook did not occupy the Howell house, but built his own. He probably bought but a small piece at first, as both lived there near together, for several years. Like the rest of his neighbors, his principal farming consisted in cutting and carting cordwood, and burning charcoal..It might interest the present owners to know that when the Howells sold to Cook, neither of the lanes on that farm existed..The old lane of the Howells was a northerly and northeasterly route from the late John R. Smith's lane by way of the Howell house to Jericho Landing..They generally brought water from the Howell well, but in very dry times it failed, then the Hollow well, or spring at the creek, about equally distant, was used. The Howells had no cleared land on the road.." {829}.

"When Israel Howell left the north house, he went to Deep Hole, built there on the west side of the Hollow - died there and his son David also lived out his days and died there nearly 80 years old. Then the old house was neglected. A fire in the woods landed sparks on the roof about 1860, and then its finish came quickly.." {830}.

"Irael Howell" was listed as the head of a family consisting of two free white males of 16 years of age and upwards, and three free white females, residing in Southold Town, Suffolk County, New York, in the First Census of the United States, 1790 {831}.

Israel Howell was listed as the head of a family consisting of one free white male of 45 years of age and older, two of 16 and under 26, one free white female of 45 and older, one of 16 and under 26, one of 10 and under 16, and two of under 10, residing in the Town of Riverhead, Suffolk County, New York, in the Second Census of the United States, 1800 {832}.

By his will of 4 Nov 1805, proved on 2 Jly 1811, Israel Howell, of the Town of Riverhead, left his estate, with bequests to his wife, Tabitha, to his son, David, who was instructed to pay legacies to Esther and Hannah, the surviving daughters of Israel Howell, and to maintain Hannah while she was still single {833}.

Israel Howell died on 24 Nov 1805, at the age of 64, and is buried in the Baiting Hollow Cemetery {834}.

Tabitha Howell was listed as the head of a family consisting of one free white female, residing in the Town of Riverhead, Suffolk County, New York, in the Fourth Census of the United States, 1820 {835}.

"Tabitha, Relict of Israel Howell" died on 28 Sep 1829, and is buried beside her husband in the Baiting Hollow Cemetery {836}.

829. Id., 12-13.
830. Id., 11 (June 1982).
831. HEADS OF FAMILIES.., 1790, NEW YORK, 168.
832. NYG&BR, LVI, 330 (Oct 1925).
833. Suffolk County Wills, Liber C, 150-151.
834. Gravestone, Baiting Hollow Cemetery.
835. U.S. Census, Riverhead, Suffolk County, NY, 1820, Page 354.
836. Gravestone, Baiting Hollow Cemetery.

Israel and Tabitha (Hulse) Howell were the parents of at least three children {837}.

+ 213.   i.   ESTHER[5] HOWELL, born on 10 Oct 1770, baptized at Mattituck on 6 Mch 1771 {838}.

+ 214.   ii.   DAVID[5] HOWELL, born on 31 Aug 1773, baptized at Mattituck on 24 Nov 1773 {839}.

+ 215.   iii.   HANNAH[5] HOWELL, born on 25 Jan 1779, baptized at Mattituck on 28 June 1780 {840}.

NOTE: *An orphan child, David, under the care of Israel and Tabitha Howell, was baptized on 5 Nov 1788 at Mattituck* {841}.

77. SAMUEL[4] HOWELL (Israel[3], David[2], Richard[1]), the son of Israel[3] and Hannah (Smith) Howell, was born in about 1748, probably at Baiting Hollow.

Samuel Howell and Elizabeth Tuthill were married at Mattituck on 30 Nov 1773 {842} {843}. She was the daughter of James Tuthill, and was born in about 1755 {844}.

Samuel Howell was a Corporal in Captain Josiah Lupton's company of militiamen in 1775 {845}. As such, he signed the Articles of Association in 1775 {846}.

"Sm[l] Howell" was listed as the head of a household consisting of one male of above 16 and under 50 years of age, one female of above 16, one of under 16, and one Negro of above 16, residing in Southold Township, Suffolk County, New York, in the Census of 1776 {847}.

Samuel Howell, farmer, of the Township of Southold, gave his age as 30 when he signed the Oath of Allegiance and Peaceable Behaviour required by Governor William Tryon in 1778 {848}.

Samuel Howell was listed, by Josiah Woodhull, as the head of a family of four residing in the Wading River district on 22 Aug 1778 {849}.

On 11 Apr 1780, Samuel Howell was paid £10 11s, by the Town of

---

837. Ida A. Maddrah, op. cit.
838. Craven, op. cit., 277.
839. Id., 281.
840. Id., 286.
841. Id., 295.
842. Id., 322.
843. SR, 101; NYG&BR, XLIX, 268 (Jly 1918).
844. Alva M. Tuttle, TUTTLE*TUTHILL LINES IN AMERICA, 153.
845. THE REGISTER, SCHS, VIII, #1, 23-24 (June 1982).
846. Mather, op. cit., 1056.
847. CENSUS OF SUFFOLK COUNTY, 1776, 23.
848. P.R.O. Colonial Office, Class 5, Vol. 1109, 94.
849. NGSQ, 63, 283 (1975).

Southold, for keeping James Berry {850}. He received a payment of £20 16s, on 10 Apr 1781, for providing the same service during the following year {851}.

Samuel Howell was selected to be a Fence Viewer for the ensuing year by the Annual Meeting of the Town of Southold on 6 Apr 1790 {852}.

"Sam¹ Howell" was listed as the head of a household consisting of one free white male of 16 years of age and upwards, four of under 16, three free white females, and one other free person, residing in Southold Town, Suffolk County, New York, in the First Census of the United States, 1790 {853}.

"Sam¹ Howell" was listed as the head of a family consisting of one free white male of 45 years of age and older, one of 10 and under 16, one of under 10, one free white female of 26 and under 45, and two of 10 and under, residing in the Town of Southold, in the Second Census of the United States, 1800 {854}.

Elizabeth (Tuthill) Howell died on 1 Jan 1808 {855}.

Samuel and Elizabeth (Tuthill) Howell were the parents of at least eight children.

+ 216.   i.   ELIZABETH⁵ HOWELL, baptized on 2 Nov 1774 at Mattituck {856}.

217.   ii.   SILAS⁵ HOWELL {857}.

218.   iii.   HANNAH⁵ HOWELL, baptized on 15 Apr 1778 at Mattituck {858}.

219.   iv.   Son⁵ (JOHN HOWELL?), baptized on 2 Feb 1780 at Mattituck {859}. "John Howel", the son of Samuel and Elizabeth, died on 6 Oct 1793, at the age of 14 years and 6 months, and is buried in the Aquebogue Cemetery {860}.

220.   v.   JOSHUA⁵ HOWELL, born on 20 Feb 1780 {861}.

+ 221. vi. SAMUEL⁵ HOWELL, born on 23 Dec 1781 {862}, baptized

---

850. STR, Liber D, 31 left; (III, 60).
851. Id., 32 left; (III, 61).
852. Id., 143 left; (III, 241).
853. HEADS OF FAMILIES.., 1790, NEW YORK, 168.
854. NYG&BR, LVII, 57 (Jan 1926).
855. William F. Howell, Personal communication, from a copy at the SCHS.
856. Craven, op. cit., 282.
857. Alva M. Tuttle, op. cit., 153.
858. Id., 285.
859. Id., 286.
860. Gravestone, Aquebogue Cemetery.
861. William F. Howell, op. cit.
862. Id.

on 4 Jan 1782 at Mattituck {863}.

222. vii.   HARMONY⁵ HOWELL {864}.

223.viii.   USHER⁵ HOWELL {865}.

224. ix.   MILLY⁵ HOWELL {866}.

79. ELIZABETH⁴ HOWELL (Richard³, David², Richard¹), the daughter of Richard³ and Elizabeth (Tuthill) Howell, was born in the vicinity of Mattituck in about 1733.

"Samuel Brown" and "Elizabeth Howel" were married at Mattituck on 7 Dec 1752 {867}. He was born in about 1733.

Samuel Brown was selected to serve as a Fence Viewer for the ensuing year at the Annual Meeting of the Town of Southold on 7 Apr 1761, on 5 Apr 1763, on 3 Apr 1764, and again on 7 Apr 1767 {868}.

Samuel Brown was selected to be a Constable at the Annual Meeting of the Town of Southold held on 5 Apr 1768 {869}.

At the Annual Meeting of the Town of Southold held on 5 Apr 1774, Samuel Brown was elected Collector for the ensuing year, and was "..to give for yᵉ office 5:6:2 Colonel Phineas Faning his Surity" {870}.

Samuel Brown signed the Articles of Association in 1775 as a member of Capt. Hallock's company {871}.

Samuel Brown was listed as the head of a household consisting of one male of 50 years of age and older, one of 16 and under 50, two of under 16, two females of over 16, and one Negro of over 16, residing in Southold Township, Suffolk County, New York, in the Census of 1776 {872}.

Samuel Brown was enumerated as the head of a household of six in the Aquebogue District of Southold, on 22 Aug 1778, by Daniel and Jeremiah Wells {873}.

Samuel Brown, farmer, of the Township of Southold, gave his age as 45 when he signed the Oath of Allegiance and Peaceable Behaviour required by Governor William Tryon in 1778 {874}.

"Elisabeth Brown" received 30s by the will of her father, Richard Howell,

---

863. Craven, op. cit., 288.
864. Alva M. Tuttle, op. cit.
865. Id.
866. Id.
867. Id., 315.
868. STR, Liber D, 129 right, 130 right, 131 left, 131 right; (III, 208-209, 211, 212, 214-215).
869. STR, Liber D, 131 left; (III, 216-217).
870. Id., 134 left; (III, 221-222).
871. Mather, op. cit., 1057.
872. CENSUS OF SUFFOLK COUNTY, 1776, 17.
873. NGSQ, 63, 276 (1975).
874. P.R.O. Colonial Office, Class 5, Vol. 1109, 92.

written on 14 Mch 1783, and proved on 17 Mch 1784 {875}.

"Sam¹ Brown" was listed as the head of a household consisting of one free white male of 16 years of age and upwards, one of under 16, one free white female, and one slave, residing in Southold Town, Suffolk County, New York, in the First Census of the United States, 1790 {876}.

Samuel Brown died on 1 Dec 1792 {877}.

Elizabeth Brown was listed as the head of a family consisting of one free white female of 45 years of age and older, residing in the Town of Riverhead, Suffolk County, New York, in the Second Census of the United States, 1800 {878}.

Samuel and Elizabeth (Howell) Brown were the parents of at least three children.

    i.   JEMIMA BROWN, baptized on 28 Apr 1754 at Mattituck {879}.

    ii.   RICHARD BROWN, baptized on 26 Nov 1758 at Mattituck {880}.

    iii.   DAUGHTER, died on 13 Feb 1777 {881}.

81.EDMUND⁴ HOWELL (Richard³, David², Richard¹), the son of Richard³ and Elizabeth (Tuthill) Howell, was born in about 1739 in the vicinity of Mattituck.

Edmund Howell and Rachel Tuthill were married at Mattituck on 29 Oct 1760 {882}.

Rachel Howell, the wife of Edmund, died on 23 Nov 1774 at the age of 37 {883}.

Edmund Howell and Bethiah Downs were married at Mattituck on 27 Mch 1775 {884}.

Edmund Howell signed the Articles of Association during the summer of 1775 {885}.

Edmund Howell was commissioned as First Lieutenant for the Second Company, Third Regiment of Suffolk County Militia, commanded by Colonel

875. WNYSO, Liber 36, 428-429; (XII, 255-256).
876. HEADS OF FAMILIES.., 1790, NEW YORK, 168.
877. Craven, op. cit., 349
878. NYG&BR, LVII, 56 (Jan 1926).
879. Craven, op. cit., 254.
880. Id., 259.
881. Id., 343.
882. Id., 317; SR, 94; (NYG&BR, XLIX, 162 (Apr 1918)).
883. Id., 324, 339; SR, 46; (NYG&BR, XLVIII, 179 (Apr 1917)).
884. Craven, op. cit., 322.
885. Mather, op. cit., 1057.

Thomas Terry, on 29 Jun 1776 {886}.

Edmund Howell was listed as the head of a family of six residing in Mattituck Parish on 15 Jan 1778 by Lieutenant Isaac Reeve {887}. "Edward Howell" was similarly listed on 25 Aug 1778 {888}.

"Edm^d Howell", farmer, of the Township of Southold, gave his age as 39 when he signed the Oath of Allegiance and Peaceable Behaviour required by Governor William Tryon in 1778 {889}.

Edmund Howell counted votes at the Annual Meeting of the Town of Southold held on 1 Apr 1783 {890}.

By his will of 14 Mch 1783, proved on 17 Mch 1784, Richard Howell left, to his "..eldest son Edmund, the part of my lot I bought of Deacon Colman; Also, all my lands and meadows east of Mapes lane, and south of the Ele branch; Also, my meadow called Muddy Creek meadow; he paying my wife, his mother, five loads of wood yearly at the house where she, my widow, lives." Edmund Howell was also named an executor of this will {891}.

Phebe Howell was listed as the head of a family consisting of one free white male of under 16 years of age, and four free white females, residing in Southold Town, Suffolk County, New York, in the First Census of the United States, 1790 {892}.

The sum of £1 10s was paid "..to Widow Phebe Howel.." by the Town of Riverhead, as recorded on 10 Apr 1793 {893}.

It was recorded, on 1 Apr 1794, that "Jedidiah Aldrich.." was paid "..£1 15s.." for "..house Rent for W^d. Howel.." by the Town of Riverhead {894}.

The Overseers of the Town of Riverhead paid Richard Brown £1 10s "..for Wood for Widow Howell..", and Henry Herrick £2 7s 5d "..for Sundrys for Widow Howell..", as recorded on 30 Mch 1798 {895}.

Phebe Howell was listed as the head of a family consisting of one free white female of 45 years of age and older, and two of 10 and under 16, residing in the Town of Riverhead, Suffolk County, New York, in the Second Census of the United States, 1800 {896}.

Phebe Howell, widow, died on 8 Jly 1804 {897}.

Henry Herrick was paid 13s "..for Wood for Widow Howell..", while Thomas Young was paid 14s for a "Coffin for Widow Howell", and Jason Aldrich was paid 4s for "..diging Grave for Widow Howell.." by the Overseers of the Town

886. Id., op. cit., 993.
887. NGSQ, 63, 281 (1975).
888. Id., 280 (1975).
889. P.R.O. Colonial Office, Class 5, Vol. 1109, 90.
890. STR, Liber D, 139 right; (III, 232).
891. WNYSO, Liber 36, 428-429; (XII, 255-256).
892. HEADS OF FAMILIES.., 1790, NEW YORK, 168.
893. RTR, Liber A, 9; (I, 8).
894. Id., 15; (I, 12).
895. Id., 42; (I, 25-26).
896. NYG&BR, LVII, 56 (Jan 1926).
897. Craven, op. cit., 354.

of Riverhead, as recorded on 29 Mch 1805 {898}.

Edmund and Rachel (Tuthill) Howell were the parents of at least three children.

+ 225. i.   PARNAL[5] HOWELL, baptized at Mattituck on 9 Jan 1765 {899}.

+ 226. ii. ANNA[5] HOWELL, baptized at Mattituck on 17 Dec 1771 {900}.

227. iii.   WILLIAM[5] HOWELL, died 5 Dec 1774, aged 8 months {901}.

"Lieut. Edmund" and Bethiah (Downs) Howell were the parents of at least one child.

+ 228. iv.   MEHITABEL[5] HOWELL, born on 22 Feb 1776 {902}, baptized at Mattituck on 18 Jly 1790 {903}.

"Edmond and Phebe" Howell were the parents of at least four children {904}.

229. v.   DESIRE[5] HOWELL, baptized on 30 May 1790 at Mattituck.

230. vi.   JACOB[5] HOWELL, baptized on 30 May 1790 at Mattituck.

231. vii. KATURAH[5] HOWELL, baptized on 30 May 1790 at Mattituck.

232. viii. CHARITY[5] HOWELL, baptized on 30 May 1790 at Mattituck.

82. JOANNA[4] HOWELL (Richard[3], David[2], Richard[1]), the daughter of Richard[3] and Elizabeth (Tuthill) Howell, was born in the vicinity of Mattituck.

David Terry and Joanna Howell were married at Mattituck on 30 Oct 1760 {905}. He was born in about 1740, probably the son of David and Mehetable (Aldritch) Terry {906}.

David Terry was selected to be one of several "overseers", for the ensuing year, at the Annual Meeting of the Town of Southold, held on 3 Apr 1770 {907}.

"David Terry, Jr." signed the Articles of Association in the summer of

898. RTR, Liber A, 84; (I, 53).
899. Craven, op. cit., 271.
900. Id., 278.
901. Id., 340, 342.
902. Id., 314.
903. Id., 299.
904. Id.
905. Id., 317, SR, 94; (NYG&BR, XLIX, 162 (Apr 1918)).
906. Stuart T. Terry, Terry Manuscript, in the possession of the SCHS, 1993.
907. STR, Liber D, 132 right; (III, 217-218).

1775 as a member of Capt. Josiah Lupton's company {908}.

David Terry was an enlisted man in the Third Regiment of Minute Men, Suffolk County {909}.

"David Terry, Jun'." was listed as the head of a family consisting of one male of 16 and under 50 years of age, two of under 16, one female of above 16, and three of under 16, residing in Southold Township, Suffolk County, New York, in the Census of 1776 {910}.

David Terry, Jr., was listed as the head of a family of seven residing in the Wading River district by Josiah Woodhull on 22 Aug 1778 {911}.

David Terry, Jr., farmer, of the Township of Southold, gave his age as 38 when he signed the Oath of Allegiance and Peaceable Behaviour required by Governor William Tryon in 1778 {912}.

Joanna Terry received 30s by the will of her father, Richard Howell, written on 14 Mch 1783, and proved on 17 Mch 1784 {913}.

A David Terry moved to Cocman's in about 1820. He later moved to Albany, and then to Vermont {914}.

David and Joanna (Howell) Terry were the parents of at least five children {915}.

    i.   JOANNA TERRY, baptized on 11 Jly 1762 at Mattituck {916}.

    ii.   PARSHALL TERRY, born on Long Island, married (1) Zady Goodrich, of Coxsakie, Greene County, New York, eight children, married two other wives, died in the Town of Somerset, Niagara County, New York.

    iii.   GERSHOM TERRY, born on Long Island, married, five children, died in "Clarene", Erie County, New York.

    iv.   DAVID TERRY.

    v.   "PATTY", (MARTHA?), TERRY.

83. MARY[4] HOWELL (Richard[3], David[2], Richard[1]), the daughter of Richard[3] and

---

908. Mather, op. cit., 1056.
909. Id., 997.
910. CENSUS OF SUFFOLK COUNTY, 1776, 23.
911. NGSQ, 63, 283 (1975).
912. P.R.O. Colonial Office, Class 5, Vol. 1109, 86.
913. WNYSO, Liber 36, 428-429; (XII, 255-256).
914. Stuart T. Terry, op. cit.
915. Id.
916. Craven, op. cit., 262.

Elizabeth (Tuthill) Howell, was born in the vicinity of Mattituck in about 1744 {917}.

"amezie Benjeman mary Hall" were married in about Nov 1761 {918}. He was the son of Amaziah and Anna Benjamin, and was born on 16/18 Jan 1741 {919}.

Amaziah Benjamin signed the Articles of Association in Brookhaven Township during the summer of 1775 {920}. On 5 Aug 1776, he was an enlisted man in Capt. Paul Reeve's company of the Third Regiment of Minute Men of Suffolk County, was 35 years of age, 5'3" in stature, and of a dark complexion {921}.

"Amesiah Benjamin" was listed as the head of a family consisting of one male of 16 and under 50 years of age, two of under 16, one female of above 16, and two of under 16, residing in Southold Township, Suffolk County, New York, in the Census of 1776 {922}.

Amaziah Benjamin was enumerated as the head of a family of eight residing in the Aquebogue District of the Town of Southold on 22 Aug 1778 by Daniel and Jeremiah Wells {923}.

Amaziah Benjamin, farmer, of the Township of Southold, gave his age as 40 when he signed the Oath of Allegiance and Peaceable Behaviour required by Governor William Tryon in 1778 {924}.

Mary Benjamin received 30s by the will of her father, Richard Howell, written on 14 Mch 1783, and proved on 17 Mch 1784 {925}.

Amaziah Benjamin was selected to be a Fence Viewer for the ensuing year at the Annual Meeting of the Town of Southold held on 3 Apr 1787 {926}.

"Amiseah Benjamin" was listed as the head of a family consisting of two free white males of 16 years of age and upwards, three of under 16, and two free white females, residing in Southold Town, Suffolk County, New York, in the First Census of the United States, 1790 {927}.

On 1 Apr 1794 "Bethiah Reeve.." was hired out "..to Amaziah Benjamin for...2s 9d per week" under the "Conditions that the Poor of this Town are to be hired out for the Ensuing Year:
The Lowest bidder is to keep them one year and to Wash Lodge Victual and Mend for them During the Said Time and if Compliant Shall be made to the Overseers that any of the poor is abused Such poor May be Removed at the Expence of the Abuser If any Arises by Two bids, the person Shall be Set up again If any person

917. Bicha & Brown, op. cit., 694.
918. Craven, op. cit., 317, SR, 94; (NYG&BR, XLIX, 162 (Apr 1918)).
919. Bicha & Brown, op. cit.
920. Mather, op. cit., 1058.
921. Id., 1009.
922. CENSUS OF SUFFOLK COUNTY, 1776, 24.
923. NGSQ, 63, 276 (1975).
924. P.R.O. Colonial Office, Class 5, Vol. 1109, 91.
925. WNYSO, Liber 36, 428-429; (XII, 255-256).
926. STR, Liber D, 141 right; (III, 238-239).
927. HEADS OF FAMILIES.., 1790, NEW YORK, 168.

chooses to Stay Where They Be the Person or Persons Who bids them of Shall keep them for three Pence in the Week Less" {928}.

On 3 Apr 1795, it was recorded that £9 13s 3d was paid out to Ameziah Benjamin {929}. On 3 Apr 1801, it was similarily recorded that the sum of £5 16s was paid out to Ameziah Benjamin on account of the Overseers of the Poor {930}.

"Ammeriah Benjamin" was listed as the head of a family consisting of one free white male of 45 years of age and older, one free white female of 26 and under 45, and three of under 10, residing in the Town of Riverhead, Suffolk County, New York, in the Second Census of the United States, 1800 {931}.

Ameziah Benjamin was selected to serve as a Fence Viewer for the ensuing year at the Annual Meeting of the Town of Riverhead held on 3 Apr 1804. He was again selected for this position on 1 Apr 1806, and on the first Tuesday of Apr 1811 {932}.

Ear marks for the livestock of Amaziah Benjamin were recorded in "A Coppy, of the Record of Markes on the Ears of Cattle and Sheep River Head, Josep L'hommed" {933}.

Amaziah Benjamin died in 1812 {934}.

Amaziah and Mary (Howell) Benjamin were the parents of at least nine children {935}.

     i.   AMAZIAH BENJAMIN, born on 22 Sep 1764/5, baptized on 6 June 1771 at Mattituck {936}.

    ii.   NELLY P. BENJAMIN, born in 1766.

   iii.   MARY BENJAMIN, baptized on 6 June 1771 at Mattituck {937}.

   iv.   MARTHA BENJAMIN, baptized on 6 June 1771 at Mattituck {938}.

    v.   DAVID BENJAMIN, baptized on 17 Feb 1773 at Mattituck {939}.

---

928. RTR, Liber A, 17; (I, 12-13).
929. Id., 23; (I, 16).
930. Id., 60; (I, 38).
931. NYG&BR, LVI, 330 (Oct 1925).
932. RTR, Liber A, 80, Liber B, 35, 47; (I, 51, 281, 290).
933. Id. (I, 736).
934. Bicha & Brown, op. cit., 694.
935. Id.
936. Craven, op. cit., 278.
937. Id.
938. Id.
939. Craven, op. cit., 279.

vi.   ISAAC BENJAMIN, baptized on 25 May 1774 at Mattituck {940}.

vii.   ISRAEL BENJAMIN, born in about 1777 at Middleroad.

viii.   EZRA BENJAMIN, born in 1781 at Middleroad.

ix.   JEMIMA BENJAMIN.

NOTE: *Three children of Amaziah Benjamin, names not given, were baptized on 22 Oct 1783 at Mattituck {941}.*

84. PHINEAS⁴ HOWELL (Richard³, David², Richard¹), the son of Richard³ and Elizabeth (Tuthill) Howell, was born in the vicinity of Mattituck in about 1746.

"Phinehas Howell" and Mary Brown were married at Mattituck on 2 June 1768 {942}.

Phineas Howell signed the Articles of Association in the Town of Brookhaven during the summer of 1775 {943}.

Phineas Howell was listed as the head of a family consisting of one male of 16 and under 50 years of age, two of under 16, and one female of 16 and above, residing in Southold Township, Suffolk County, New York, in the Census of 1776 {944}.

Phineas Howell, farmer, of the Township of Southold, gave his age as 32 when he signed the Oath of Allegiance and Peaceable Behaviour required by Governor William Tryon in 1778 {945}.

Phineas Howell was enumerated as the head of a family of six persons, residing in Mattituck Parish, on 25 Aug 1778 {946}.

It is said that Phineas Howell removed to Orange County, New York, and "..settled at Brookfield in 1778.." {947} on the Thomas Durland place in the Patent of Wawayanda {948}. It is likely that this actually happened at a later date, since Phineas Howell was paid £11 1s 0d "..for Rebecca Goldsmith.." on 21 Apr 1779 by the Town of Southold. He was also paid £17 1s 6d for her support on 11 Apr 1780 {949}. By 10 Apr 1781, however, James Youngs was paid for her support {950}.

940. Id., 281.
941. Id., 290.
942. Id., 318; SR, 99; (NYG&BR, XLIX, 266 (Jly 1918)).
943. Mather, op. cit., 1058.
944. CENSUS OF SUFFOLK COUNTY, NEW YORK, 1776, 20.
945. P.R.O. Colonial Office, Class 5, Vol. 1109, 86.
946. NGSQ, 63, 280 (1975).
947. Ruttenber and Clark, op. cit., 679.
948. Id., 681.
949. STR, Liber D, 31 right, 31 left; (III, 59, 60).
950. Id., 32 left; (III, 61).

"Phenis Howell" was an enlisted man in the Fourth Regiment of the Orange County militia {951}.

By his will of 14 Mch 1783, proved on 17 Mch 1784, Richard Howell left to his "..second son Phinehas, all the land I bought of Aaron Howell, Samuel Hallock and Peter Hallock; Also, the broad meadow point beach and meadow I bought of the Fannings.." {952}.

"Phineas Howel" was listed as the head of a family consisting of two free white males of 16 years of age and upwards, two of under 16, and three free white females, residing in Minisink Town, Orange County, New York, in the First Census of the United States, 1790 {953}.

On 7 Dec 1793, "..Phinehas Howel of the town of Minisink in the County of Orange and state of New York and Mary his wife.." sold, to Benjamin Smith, "..two certain pieces or parcels of land..the first for a Mill seat..containing forty Eight squair Rods the second for a pond plot..containing one hundred and Eight squair rods of land.." {954}. Benjamin Smith subsequently built a hotel on one of these lots, which were situated in Brookfield, now (1992) Slate Hill, New York. Phineas Howell also sold lands to John Hallock, which the latter gave for the site of the Baptist Church in Brookfield {955}.

On 28 Jan 1796, Phineas and Mary Howell deeded, to their son, Phineas Howell, a plot of land containing about two and one-half acres, in the Town of Minisink {956}. Phineas Howell, Jr., and his wife, Mary, sold this same piece of land to Reuben Cash on 29 Jan 1796 {957}.

The house of Phineas Howell was adjoining to the property of Benjamin Smith in the Town of Minisink in 1798 {958}.

"Phinehas Howell" was listed as the head of a family consisting of one free white male of 45 years of age and older, one of 16 and under 26, one of 10 and under 16, two free white females of 45 and older, and one of 16 and under 26, residing in the Town of Minisink, Orange County, New York, in the Second Census of the United States, 1800 {959}.

On 26 Jan 1807, Phineas Howell deeded to his son, Jason Howell, his farm and homestead, the second of which contained one hundred and twelve acres, excepting "..one acre one quarter & thirty rods of land heretofore conveyed by the said Phineas Howell to his son David Howell, and also about three quarters of Land heretofore conveyed by the said Phineas Howell to Benjamin Smith & now Owned by Joseph Smith.." {960}.

Phineas Howell was listed as the head of a family consisting of one free

951. Roberts, op. cit., 164.
952. WNYSO, Liber 36, 428-429; (XII, 255-256).
953. HEADS OF FAMILIES.., 1790, NEW YORK, 143.
954. Orange County Deeds, Liber F, 347-349.
955. Stickney, HOWELL, #B64.
956. Orange County Deeds, Liber E, 454-455.
957. Id., 437-438.
958. Town of Minisink House Assessment Roll, 1798.
959. NYG&BR, LXIII, 84 (Jan 1932).
960. Orange County Deeds, Liber J, 443-445.

white male of 45 years of age and older, one of 16 and under 26, two of under 10, one free white female of 45 and older, one of 16 and under 26, and one of under 10, residing in the Town of Minisink, Orange County, New York, in the Third Census of the United States, 1810 {961}.

Phineas Howell "..died in 1814, and was buried in the old Baptist graveyard adjoining his farm." {962}.

The legendary Welsh Bible of John Howell, said to have been brought to the New World by him, the reputed father of Richard Howell, is said to have come down in the family of Phineas Howell. The story of this Bible was told by James Peter Howell, in a genealogy he compiled {963}, and repeated in a letter, dated 27 Oct 1884, to James Barnaby Howell, the compiler of a genealogy of another branch of the family, a genealogy of which a copy is on file in the Library of the Daughters of the American Revolution in Washington, D.C. The story relates that Mary (Brown) Howell confided the Bible to her only daughter, Mary Howell, at the time of her death. Mary Howell married, and gave the Bible to her second daughter before she died. This second daughter, in turn, married and, before she died, requested her husband to give the Bible to her younger sister, which he refused to do, twice. After he died, the Bible was said to have been "..spirited away and secreted.." {964}.

Phineas and Mary (Brown) Howell were the parents of at least six children.

+ 233. i. PHINEAS⁵ HOWELL.

+ 234. ii. DAVID⁵ HOWELL, born on 22 Feb 1772 {965}.

  235. iii. MICAH⁵ HOWELL, born on 2 June 1776 {966}, died on 8 June 1776, aged six days {967}.

+ 236. iv. JASON⁵ HOWELL, born on 14 Sep 1777 {968}.

  237. v. MARY⁵ HOWELL.

+ 238. vi. JAMES BROWN⁵ HOWELL, born on 4 Apr 1790 {969}, said to have been the last entry in the legendary Welsh Bible {970}.

---

961. U.S. Census, Minisink, Orange County, NY, 1810, Page 423.

962. Ruttenber & Clark, op. cit., 679.

963. James Peter Howell, op. cit.

964. Letter, James Peter Howell to James Barnaby Howell, cited by Wilbur Franklin Howell, op. cit., iv.

965. Coulter, et. al., op. cit., 61.

966. Craven, op. cit., 314.

967. Id., 339.

968. Stickney, HOWELL, #B95.

969. Family Record of W.B. Howell, courtesy of Boyd C. Anderson, Personal communication, per Ronald Lee Howell, Jr.

970. Letter, James Peter Howell to James Barnaby Howell.

85. KEZIAH[4] HOWELL (Richard[3], David[2], Richard[1]), the daughter of Richard[3] and Elizabeth (Tuthill) Howell, was born in the vicinity of Mattituck.

Ephraim Soper and Keziah Howell were married at Mattituck on 19 May 1768 {971}.

Ephraim Soper signed the Articles of Association in Brookhaven during the summer of 1775 {972}.

"Keziah Sopers" received 30s by the will of her father, Richard Howell, written of 14 Mch 1783, and proved on 17 Mch 1784 {973}.

No listing of the family of Ephraim and Keziah (Howell) Soper has been found or developed.

87. RICHARD[4] HOWELL (Richard[3], David[2], Richard[1]), the son of Richard[3] and Elizabeth (Tuthill) Howell, was born in the vicinity of Mattituck in about 1756.

"Rich[d] Howell", carpenter, of the Township of Southold, gave his age as 22 when he signed the Oath of Allegiance and Peaceable Behaviour required by Governor William Tryon in 1778 {974}.

Richard Howell, Jr., married Rhoda Corwin at Mattituck on 18 Mch 1779 {975}.

"Rody Howell" died on 12 Aug 1784 {976}.

By the will of his father, written on 14 Mch 1783, and proved on 17 Mch 1784, Richard Howell received £30 {977}.

Richard Howell, Jr., married "Mary Orsborn" at Mattituck on 16 Jly 1786 {978}.

Richard Howell was listed as the head of a family consisting of one free white male of 26 and under 45 years of age, two of under 10, one free white female of 26 and under 45, one of 10 and under 16, and one of under 10, residing in the Town of Southold, Suffolk County, New York, in the Second Census of the United States, 1800 {979}.

Richard and Rhoda (Corwin) Howell were the parents of at least one son.

> 239.   i.   JOHN[5] HOWELL, baptized on 3 Aug 1784 at Mattituck {980}.

Richard and Mary (Osborn) Howell were probably the parents of at least one daughter.

---

971. Craven, op. cit., 318, SR, 99; (NYG&BR, XLIX, 266 (Jly 1918)).
972. Mather, op. cit., 1059.
973. WNYSO, Liber 36, 428-429; (XII, 255-256).
974. P.R.O. Colonial Office, Class 5, Vol. 1109, 91.
975. Craven, op. cit., 324.
976. Id., 346.
977. WNYSO, Liber 36, 428-429; (XII, 255-256).
978. Craven, op. cit., 330.
979. NYG&BR, LVII, 57 (Jan 1926).
980. Craven, op. cit., 291.

+ 240. ii.   ELIZABETH^5 HOWELL, born in Jan 1787 {981}.

88. PARSHALL^4 HOWELL (Richard^3, David^2, Richard^1), the son of Richard^3 and
Elizabeth (Tuthill) Howell, was born in the vicinity of Mattituck in about 1760.
    Parshall Howell, cordwainer, gave his age as 18 when he signed the Oath
of Allegiance and Peaceable Behaviour required by Governor William Tryon in
1778 {982}.
    "Pershal Howel" and "Charity Marther" were married at Mattituck on 24
Jan 1782 {983}.
    Richard Howell left, to his "..son, Parshall, the remainder of my lands,
meadows and buildings not yet mentioned..". He was also ordered to pay "..my
wife yearly, 12 bushels of wheat, 10 of corn, 110 pounds of pork, 50 lbs. of beef,
15 lbs. flax, and also keep two cows and six sheep summer and winter, for his
mother; Also, sufficient firewood, with what my son Edmund shall find for her;
Also, a privilege in the orchards and fruits, sufficient for her person. My son
Pearshall to keep my son Abram, as is becoming in a Christian land, during his life.
If he does not provide for Abram, my executors to take sufficient lands willed to
Parshall to support Abram..". Further, he provided for all his "..negroes to be sold,
and sufficient stock to pay my just debts and legacies, and my executors reasonably
for their trouble; the remainder to my son Parshall..", who was made a co-executor
of this will with his brother, Edmund, and his father's "..trusty friend, Daniel
Wells.." {984}.
    Parshall Howell was listed as the head of a family consisting of one free
white male of 16 years of age and upwards, two of under 16, and two free white
females, residing in Southold Town, Suffolk County, New York, in the First
Census of the United States, 1790 {985}.
    Henry Hudson Ju^r. was paid £5 10s "..for Charity Howell.." by the
Overseers of the Poor, Daniel Terry and Richard Hallock, of the Town of
Riverhead, as recorded on 1 Apr 1794 {986}.
    Ezra Halliock was paid £2 9s for "..keeping Charity Howell..", Jedidiah
Corwin was paid £6 17s 9d for "..keeping Charity Howell Child..", "Widow
Elizabeth Brown" was paid £1 6d for "..keeping Charity Howell..", and Jabez
Corwin was paid 11s for "..keeping Charity Howell.." by the Overseers of the
Poor, Town of Riverhead, as recorded on 29 Mch 1805 {987}. Similarly,
David Horton was paid £6 12s 4d "..for keeping Charity Howell..", Joshua Terry
was paid 12s 7d for "..keeping Charity Howell..", and James Terry was paid 12d

981. Jacob E. Mallmann, HISTORICAL PAPERS ON SHELTER ISLAND AND ITS PRESBYTERIAN
CHURCH, 211.
982. P.R.O. Colonial Office, Class 5, Vol. 1109, 82.
983. Craven, op. cit., 327.
984. WNYSO, Liber 36, 428-429; (XII, 255-256).
985. HEADS OF FAMILIES.., 1790, NEW YORK, 168.
986. RTR, Liber A, 15 (I, 12).
987. Id., 83-84; (I, 52-53).

"..for keeping Charity Howell..", as recorded on 28 Mch 1806 {988}. David Horton Ju. was likewise paid £7 7d for "..keeping Charity Howell &c..", as recorded on 3 Apr 1807 {989}, David Horton Ju^r was paid £3 11d 3s "..for articles for & keeping C. Howell..", as recorded on 2 Apr 1808 {990}, and David Horton was paid £7 10s 6d "..for keeping Charity Howell, and sundries.." on 31 Mch 1809. At the same time, John Woodhull was paid £1 6s 8d "..for Articles for Charity Howell.." {991}, and Gershom Edwards was paid £1 "..for articles for Charity Howell.." {992}.

Among the Town poor, Charity Howell was bid off to David Brown on 4 Apr 1809, at 8d per week {993} (NOTE: *Some of the above cited notes may apply to our #233 or #243, Charity Howell*).

Charity Howell was listed as the head of a family consisting of one free white female of 45 years of age and older, and one free white male of 10 and under 16, residing in the Town of Riverhead, Suffolk County, New York, in the Third Census of the United States, 1810 {994}.

Parshall and Charity (Mather) Howell were probably the parents of at least three children.

241. i.   JAMES^5 HOWELL, born on 30 June 1785, died on 21 Feb 1789 at the age of 3 years, 8 months and 22 days, and is buried in the cemetery at the Mattituck Presbyterian Church {995}.

242. ii.   CHARITY^5 HOWELL, born in about 1786, died unmarried on 10 Jan 1849 at the age of 63 {996}.

+ 243. iii. PARSHALL^5 HOWELL, born on 23 Mch 1788 {997}.

90. RICHARD^4 HOWELL (Richard^3, Richard^2, Richard^1), the son of Richard^3 and Patience (Wells) Howell, was born in about 1756, probably in the vicinity of Riverhead.

Richard Howell was listed as the head of a family consisting of one male of 16 and under 50 years of age, one of under 16, one female of 16 and above, and one of under 16, residing in Southold Township, Suffolk County, New York, in the Census of 1776 {998}.

Richard Howell deeded to his "..beloved Brother Merit Howell..certain

988. Id., 87-88; (I, 54-55).
989. Id., 90 (I, 57).
990. Id., 91-92; (I, 58-59).
991. Id., 96; (I, 62).
992. Id.; (I, 63).
993. Id., 97; (I, 63-64).
994. U.S. Census, Riverhead, Suffolk County, NY, 1810, Page 253.
995. Craven, op. cit., 375.
996. RTR; (I, 726).
997. Mr. and Mrs. Larry A. and Kathleen M. (Pollock) McCurdy, Personal communication.
998. CENSUS OF SUFFOLK COUNTY, NEW YORK, 1776, 24.

tracts of land and meadow which were the property of my father Richard Howell late deceased..", including "..one piece called my said Father's Homestead..", by a deed dated 10 Jan 1780 {999}.

Richard Howell was listed as the head of a family of six persons residing in the Aquabogue District of Southold on 22 Aug 1778 by Daniel and Jeremiah Wells, and had been similarly listed, on 16 Jan 1778, by Capt. Jeremiah Wells, and, on 21 Jan 1778, by Ensign John Cleeves Terry {1000}.

"Richd Howell", farmer, of the Township of Southold, gave his age as 32 when he signed the Oath of Allegiance and Peaceable Behaviour required by Governor William Tryon in 1778 {1001}.

"Richd Howell" was listed as the head of a family consisting of two free white males of 16 years of age and upwards, one of under 16, and two free white females, residing in Southold Town, Suffolk County, New York, in the First Census of the United States, 1790 {1002}.

Richard Howell was a witness when letters of administration on the estate of Jeremiah Petty, farmer, of Riverhead, were issued to Hull Osborn, Attorney-at-Law, of Southold, on 1 Sep 1796 {1003}.

"Rich^d. Howel, Sr" was listed as the head of a family consisting of one free white male of 45 years of age and older, one of 16 and under 26, one free white female of 45 and older, and one of 16 and under 26, residing in the Town of Riverhead, Suffolk County, New York, in the Second Census of the United States, 1800 {1004}.

Richard Howell was selected to serve as a Fence Viewer for the ensuing year at the Annual Meeting of the Town of Riverhead on 5 Apr 1803 {1005}.

Richard Howell was listed as the head of a family consisting of one free white male of 45 years of age and older, and one free white female of 45 and older, residing in the Town of Riverhead, Suffolk County, New York, in the Third Census of the United States, 1810 {1006}.

Mary, the wife of Richard Howell, died on 24 Apr 1812, and is buried in Plot 655 in the Riverhead Cemetery, where her tombstone is inscribed, "In memory of Mary wife of Richard Howell who departed this life April 24th 1812 aged 74 years" {1007}.

By his will of 30 Nov 1814, Richard Howell, of Riverhead, left his estate to his sons, Richard and Abner, who were instructed to pay $400 to his daughter, Deborah, the wife of Samuel Jagger. He also named his sons executors of this will,

999. ACKERLY RECORD BOOKS, Book 2, 96-97.
1000. NGSQ, 63, 276, 277 (1975).
1001. P.R.O. Colonial Office, Class 5, Vol. 1109, 82.
1002. HEADS OF FAMILIES.., 1790, NEW YORK, 168.
1003. Suffolk County Letters of Administration, Liber AB, 88; Suffolk County Estates, File #269.
1004. NYG&BR, LVI, 330 (Oct 1925).
1005. RTR, Liber A, 74; (I, 48).
1006. U.S. Census, Riverhead, Suffolk County, NY, 1810, Page 251.
1007. Gravestone, Riverhead Cemetery, from the collection of gravestone inscriptions at the SCHS.

which was proved on 27 May 1823 {1008}.

Richard Howell was listed as a family consisting of one free white male of 45 years of age and older, residing in the Town of Riverhead, Suffolk County, New York, and engaged in agriculture, in the Fourth Census of the United States, 1820 {1009}.

Richard and Mary Howell were the parents of at least three children.

+ 244.   i.   RICHARD[5] HOWELL, born on 2 May 1773.

+ 245.   ii.   DEBORAH[5] HOWELL.

+ 246.   iii. ABNER[5] HOWELL, born on 15 Mch 1781.

92. MERRIT[4] HOWELL (Richard[3], Richard[2], Richard[1]), the son of Richard[3] and Patience (Wells) Howell, was born in about 1750, probably in the vicinity of Riverhead.

"Merret Howel" married "Sarah Leuse" at Mattituck on 25 Nov 1773 {1010}. She was the daughter of Eleazer and Prudence (Youngs) Luce, and was born in about 1755 {1011}.

Merrit Howell, farmer, of the Township of Southold, gave his age as 28 when he signed the Oath of Allegiance and Peaceable Behaviour required by Governor William Tryon in 1778 {1012}.

"Merit Howell" was listed as the head of a family of two residing in the Aquabogue District of Southold on 22 Aug 1778 by Daniel and Jeremiah Wells {1013}.

Merrit Howell was listed as the head of a family consisting of one free white male of 16 years of age and upwards, two of under 16, and three free white females, residing in Southold Town, Suffolk County, New York, in the First Census of the United States, 1790 {1014}.

"Merrit Howel" was selected to become an Overseer of the Highways at the first Annual Meeting of the Town of Riverhead, held on 3 Apr 1792 at the house of John Griffing on Main Street in Riverhead {1015}. He was again selected for this position on 7 Apr 1795, "..his District from the Meeting House to the Rabit Hill..", and on 5 Apr 1796 {1016}.

Merrit Howell was listed as the head of a family consisting of one free white male of 45 years of age and older, one of 16 and under 26, one of 10 and under 16, one free white female of 45 and older, and one of 16 and under 26,

1008. Suffolk County Wills, Liber E, 7-8, Suffolk County Estates, File 1710.
1009. U.S. Census, Riverhead, Suffolk County, NY, 1820, Page 358.
1010. Craven, op. cit., 322.
1011. Charlotte E. Jacques and Alice W. Kappenberg, LUCE ON LONG ISLAND, 8.
1012. P.R.O. Colonial Office, Class 5, Vol. 1109, 85.
1013. NGSQ, 63, 276 (1975).
1014. HEADS OF FAMILIES.., 1790, NEW YORK, 168.
1015. RTR, Liber A, 2; (I, 3).
1016. Id., 28, 30; (I, 17, 20).

residing in the Town of Riverhead, Suffolk County, New York, in the Second Census of the United States, 1800 {1017}.

On 28 Mch 1806, it was recorded that there was paid £10 7s 3d to "Merritt Howell for keeping George Raynor Child" {1018}.

Among "Bills Not Paid April 2ᵈ 1808" was recorded "To Merit Howell, for keeping Hannah Norris, and for sundry artᶜˡˢ..£9 1s 1d" {1019}.

Merrit Howell was listed as the head of a family consisting of one free white male of 45 years of age and older, and one free white female of 45 and older, residing in the Town of Riverhead, Suffolk County, New York, in the Third Census of the United States, 1810 {1020}.

On 29 Mch 1816, it was recorded that "Merit Howell" was paid $25.25 "..in account with the Overseers of the Poor.." {1021}.

In the folk lore of the Town of Riverhead, there is told a story about "..Merit Howell during the dry spell..The exact year of this dry spell has been lost in the mists of antiquity, but it must have been very early in the annals of the town, since Merit Howell was one of Riverhead's first settlers. This was such a dry spell "as never was." Day after day the sun burned a blazing arc across the heavens, and set in the blood-red west. Crops withered and died. Soil turned to a dusty powder. Still there was no rain. One afternoon, defying the blazing heat, Uncle Merit went out into his field and cut his oats, and even as he mopped his brow after his exertions, he espied his neighbor coming toward him across the field.

"Come, Uncle Merit, put away your scythe and go to the house and make yourself tidy, for we go now to the meetin house to pray for rain. 'Tis a grievous dry spell and all the folk of the countryside do agree the time has come to pray for rain. This we must do, and with haste, 'ere our thirsty crops do perish."

So Uncle Merit, leaving his oats in the swath made himself tidy, proceeded to the meeting house, and with all the other folk of the countryside prayed fervently and long that the Lord might send rain to save what remained of the crops. After the last Amen, when they went out again into the summer evening, they saw that the heavens were rent with lightning and thunder muttered out over the Sound. Presently the rains came.

And it rained and rained. It rained as hard as ever the sun had shown, and Uncle Merit's oats, lying in the swath where he had left them, sprouted mightly. For more than a week it rained, and one afternoon Uncle Merit went out into the sodden world to take another look at his oats. As he stood there, watching them sprout still more, under his very eyes, he caught sight of his neighbor making his way across the soggy earth. The two men stood silent for a spell, looking down at Uncle Merit's bedraggled oats.

"Waal, Uncle Merit," remarked his neighbor, "think you, you prayed a leetle too fervent in meetin'...mebbe?"

1017. NYG&BR, LVI, 332 (Oct 1925).
1018. RTR, Liber A, 88; (I, 56).
1019. Id., 96; (I, 62).
1020. U.S. Census, Riverhead, Suffolk County, NY, 1810, Page 252.
1021. RTR, Liber A, 123; (I, 79).

Uncle Merit minced no words..."Take it one time and another," he retorted, "rain does just 'bout as much harm as it does good...take it one time and another!' " {1022}.

By his will of 1 Jan 1818, proved on 6 Oct 1818, Merrit Howell left legacies to his wife, Sarah, and to his daughters, Patience Homan and Sarah Howell, as well as to his grandchildren, Hariot and Uriah Homan, along with lands to his daughters and grandson. The balance of his estate was left to his sons, Merrit and Benjamin {1023}.

Merrit Howell died on 2 Jan 1818, at the age of 67, and is buried in the cemetery at Aquebogue {1024}.

Sarah (Luce) Howell died on 25 Jan 1824, at the age of 69, and is buried beside her husband at Aquebogue {1025}.

Merrit and Sarah (Luce) Howell were the parents of at least four children {1026}.

+ 247. i.   PATIENCE[5] HOWELL, born in about Jly 1777.

+ 248. ii.   SARAH[5] HOWELL, born in about Mar 1781.

+ 249. iii. MERRIT[5] HOWELL, born on 10 Nov 1783.

+ 250. iv.   BENJAMIN[5] HOWELL, born in about 1786.

93. NATHAN[4] HOWELL (Isaac[3], Isaac[2], Richard[1]) may have been the son of Isaac[3] and Mary (Curtice) Howell.

The only mention we have found of Nathan Howell is as a grandson in the will of Isaac Howell, #8 {1027}. It thus seems possible that this was a copyist's error, and that the grandson meant was Nathan Corwin.

95. ISAAC[4] HOWELL (Isaac[3], Isaac[2], Richard[1]), the son of Isaac[3] and Mary (Curtice) Howell, was born in the vicinity of Aquebogue in about 1746. While there are no records extant which identify Isaac[4] Howell as the son of Isaac[3] Howell, his descendants possessed a copy of a certain deed, to Isaac Howell, for a piece of land in the "aquabok Division", dated 10 Mch 1732/3, which, since it came down through Isaac[4] Howell, indicates that he was, indeed, the son of Isaac[3] Howell. Also, family tradition has it that, when his wife wished to name their first son "Abraham", Isaac insisted that he be named "Isaac", since "..his father's name was

1022. Helen Y. Reeve, Riverhead Town - The Record Speaks, 24-25, quoted by Wilbur Franklin Howell, op. cit., 96ff.
1023. Suffolk County Wills, Liber D, 164-165; Suffolk County Estates, File #1433.
1024. Gravestone, Aquebogue Cemetery.
1025. Id.
1026. Jacques & Kappenberg, op. cit., 8, 9.
1027. WNYSO, Liber 21, 465-467; (V, 350-351).

Isaac, and HIS father's name was Isaac also..", and that he had no brother, but had a half-sister named Lois, who married a Schellinger, known by many of the older grandchildren {1028}.

Isaac Howell married Abigail Freeman, who was born in about 1738 {1029}, the daughter of Robert and Mary (Paine) Freeman {1030}.

"Isaak Howell" was a member of the Fourth Regiment of Orange County militia during the Revolutionary War {1031}.

"..about, or after, the close of the Revolutionary War..", Isaac Howell moved "..to the "Green River Country", either in the northwest part of Connecticut or eastern New York. Legal papers still preserved show that he resided in Columbia County, N.Y., in 1793 and made contracts for 2000 acres of land lying in Franklin, Delaware County, N.Y., and in 1795 was a resident there in possession of the tract, in accordance with the contract. Subsequently he subdivided the same between his four sons, and lived with the younger son until his death." {1032}.

Abigail (Freeman) Howell died on 15 Oct 1816, and is buried in a cemetery about two miles south of Franklin, New York {1033}.

Isaac Howell died on 17 Sep 1835, aged 89 years, and is buried beside his wife at Franklin {1034}.

Isaac and Abigail (Freeman) Howell were the parents of eight children {1035}.

+ 251. i.   NANCY[5] HOWELL, born on 20 Nov 1766.

+ 252. ii. ISAAC[5] HOWELL, born on 2 Oct 1768.

+ 253. iii. ABRAHAM[5] HOWELL, born on 5 Jan 1771.

+ 254. iv. POLLY[5] HOWELL.

+ 255. v.   CLARISA[5] HOWELL, born on 8 Jan 1774.

+ 256. vi. SIMEON[5] HOWELL, born on 4 Feb 1776.

+ 257. vii. FANNY[5] HOWELL.

+ 258. viii. JACOB[5] HOWELL, born on 4 Sep 1779.

1028. James Barnaby Howell, op. cit., 3.

1029. Id., 4.

1030. Amanda N. Frink Hawkes, Supplement to James Barnaby Howell's HOWELL GENEALOGY, 18.

1031. Roberts, op. cit., 256.

1032. Hawkes, op. cit, 18.

1033. Id.

1034. Gravestone, Franklin Cemetery, from a photo and rubbing graciously supplied by Nancy (Howell) Ornce.

1035. James Barnaby Howell, op. cit.

96. MICAH[4] HOWELL (Micah[3], Isaac[2], Richard[1]), the son of Micah[3] and Bethia (Reeve) Howell, was born in the vicinity of Mattituck in about 1742.

"Micha Howel & Sarah Row" were married in Mch 1764 {1036}. She was born on 26 Aug 1745.

Sarah Howell was received into communion with the church at Mattituck by the Rev. Nathaniel Barker {1037}.

Micah Howell, Jr., signed the Articles of Association during the summer of 1775 {1038}.

"Micah Howell, Jun'" was listed as the head of a family consisting of one male of 16 and under 50 years of age, one female of 16 and older, and two females of under 16, residing in Southold Township, Suffolk County, New York, in the Census of 1776 {1039}.

Micah Howell, farmer, of the Township of Southold, gave his age as 36 when he signed the Oath of Allegiance and Peaceable Behaviour required by Governor William Tryon in 1778 {1040}.

On 2 Apr 1793, Micah Howell was selected to be a Fence Viewer for the ensuing year, by the Annual Meeting of the Town of Southold {1041}.

Micah Howell, Jr., was listed as the head of a family of four residing in Mattituck Parish on 25 Aug 1778, and had been similarly listed by Lieutenant Isaac Reeve on 15 Jan 1778 {1042}.

By his father's will of 14 Apr 1796, proved on 1 Oct 1799, Micah Howell received real estate and other bequests {1043}.

"Mitchel Howell" was listed as the head of a family consisting of one free white male of 45 years of age and older, one of 16 and under 26, one free white female of 45 and older, and one of 16 and under 26, residing in the Town of Southold, Suffolk County, New York, in the Second Census of the United States, 1800 {1044}.

By his will of 21 Jly 1801, Micah Howell left legacies to his daughters, Bethiah and Christianna, with bequests to his wife, Sarah, who was to have rooms and supplies while she remained his widow, while the bulk of his estate was left to his son, Barnabas. This will, of which Barnabas and Sarah Howell were executors, along with Deacon Jonathan Horton, was proved on 6 Oct 1801 {1045}.

Micah Howell died on 2 Aug 1801 {1046}, and is buried at

1036. SR, 97; (NYG&BR, XLIX, 165 (Apr 1918)).
1037. Craven, op. cit., 114.
1038. Mather, op. cit., 1057.
1039. CENSUS OF SUFFOLK COUNTY, NEW YORK, 1776, 20.
1040. P.R.O. Colonial Office, Class 5, Vol. 1109, 91.
1041. STR, Liber D, 144 right; (III, 244).
1042. NGSQ, 63, 280, 281 (1975).
1043. Suffolk County Wills, Liber B, 77-79; Suffolk County Estates, File #430.
1044. NYG&BR, LVII, 57 (Jan 1926).
1045. Suffolk County Wills, Liber B, 154-155; Suffolk County Estates, File #507.
1046. Craven, op. cit., 353, SR, 66; (NYG&BR, XLVIII, 344 (Oct 1917)).

Mattituck, where his tombstone indicates that he died in his 60th year {1047}.

Sarah (Roe) Howell died on 5 Aug 1819, at the age of 73 years, 11 months, and 10 days, and is buried beside her husband at Mattituck {1048}.

Micah and Sarah (Roe) Howell were the parents of at least four children.

259. i. SARAH[5] HOWELL, born on 15 May 1768, baptized at Mattituck on 18 Sep 1769 {1049}, died on 20 Oct 1789 {1050}, at the age of 21 years, 5 months, and 5 days, and is buried at Mattituck {1051}.

260. ii. BETHIAH[5] HOWELL, baptized at Mattituck on 31 May 1772 {1052}.

+ 261. iii. BARNABAS[5] HOWELL, born in about 1779.

+ 262. iv. CHRISTIANNA[5] HOWELL, born on 23 Jly 1785 {1053}.

97. BETHIA[4] HOWELL (Micah[3], Isaac[2], Richard[1]), the daughter of Micah[3] and Bethia (Reeve) Howell, was born in the vicinity of Mattituck.

Bethia Howell married Jonathan Howell, #43 {1054}.

Bethia (Howell) Howell died on 24 Nov 1786 {1055}.

Jonathan and Bethia (Howell) Howell were the parents of three children, as listed under Jonathan[4] Howell, #43.

98. SILAS[4] HOWELL (Daniel[3], Isaac[2], Richard[1]), the son of Daniel[3] and Sarah (Swesey) Howell, was born in the vicinity of Mattituck on 22 Feb 1750/1 {1056}.

"Silus Howel & Jemime Howel" were married in about Apr 1775 {1057}. Jemima Howell (#61) was the daughter of David[3] and Lydia (Case) Howell, and was born on 10 Jly 1755 {1058}. "Silas and Jemima's home built in 1775 was located on the site of the present (1981) Riverhead Town Hall on

1047. Craven, op. cit., 374.
1048. Id.
1049. Id., 264.
1050. Id., 348.
1051. Id., 374.
1052. Id., 267.
1053. The REGISTER, SCHS, #2, 41 (Fall 1993).
1054. Donnelly, THE REGISTER, SCHS, XVI, 93-96 (Spring 1991).
1055. Craven, op. cit., 347, SR, 57; (NYG&BR, XLVIII, 288 (Jly 1917)).
1056. Book, property of Ruth Ackerly, said to have been written by Dency Youngs (Mrs. Chauncey Howell), cited by Wilbur Franklin Howell, op. cit., 174.
1057. SR, 102; (NYG&BR, XLIX, 269 (Jly 1918)).
1058. Dency Youngs (Mrs. Chauncey Howell) Book.

Howell Avenue." {1059}.

Silas Howell signed the Articles of Association in Brookhaven during the summer of 1775 {1060}. He may also have signed them at the County Hall, Riverhead, Suffolk County, in May 1775 {1061}.

Silas Howell was listed, by Daniel and Jeremiah Wells, as the head of a family of four residing in the Aquabogue district of Southold on 22 Aug 1778, and had been similarly listed by Captain Jeremiah Wells on 16 Jan 1778, and by Ensign John Cleeves Terry on 21 Jan 1778 {1062}.

Silas Howell, carpenter, of the Township of Southold, gave his age as 27 when he signed the Oath of Allegiance and Peaceable Behaviour required by Governor William Tryon in 1778 {1063}.

Silas Howell was listed as the head of household consisting of one free white male of 16 years of age and upwards, two of under 16, five free white females, three other free persons, and two slaves, residing in Southold Town, Suffolk County, New York, in the First Census of the United States, 1790 {1064}.

Letters of administration on the estate of Joseph Howell, yeoman, were issued to his brother, Silas Howell, of Southold, on 23 Nov 1790 {1065}.

"Silas Howell' was selected to servce as one of three "Commissiones of highways" at the Annual Meeting of the Town of Riverhead on 1 Apr 1794 {1066}. He was again selected for this position on 7 Apr 1795, and again on 5 Apr 1796, and on 2 Apr 1799 {1067}.

On 24 Mch 1797, "..a new Road or Publick highway (identified as "River Road").." was "..laid out and established..begining at the Country Road about one Mile to the Westerd of the house of John Griffing Inholder, Thence Running paraller with Peaconneck River, through Land, belonging to..Silas Howells.." by the Commissioners, including Silas Howell {1068}.

On 31 Mch 1797, it was recorded that Silas Howell was paid 10s by the Town of Riverhead {1069}.

On 4 Apr 1797, Silas Howell was selected to serve as one of three Assessors for the ensuing year at the Annual Meeting of the Town of Riverhead {1070}. He was again selected to fill this position on 3 Apr 1798, and on 6 Apr 1802 {1071}.

1059. Wines, op. cit., 48.
1060. Mather, op. cit., 1058.
1061. Id., 1056.
1062. NGSQ, 63, 276, 277 (1975).
1063. P.R.O. Colonial Office, Class 5, Vol. 1109, 82.
1064. HEADS OF FAMILIES.., 1790, NEW YORK, 168.
1065. Suffolk County Letters of Administration, Liber AB, 42; Suffolk County Estates, File #121.
1066. RTR, Liber A, 13; (I, 10).
1067. Id., 26, 32, 50; (I, 17, 20, 31).
1068. Id., 37; (I, 23).
1069. Id., 36; (I, 22).
1070. Id., 36; (I, 23).
1071. Id., 43, 67; (I, 27, 42).

It was recorded, on 30 Mch 1798, that £1 8s was paid to "Silas Howell Assessor for Service &c" {1072}. On 29 Mch 1799, it was similarily recorded that £3 15s was paid to "Silas Howell for Servise" {1073}.

On 8 May 1799, Silas Howell was associated with the laying out of a road later known as Sound Road, Wading River {1074}.

"Silas Howel" was selected to be one of several Fence Viewers at the Annual Meeting of the Town of Riverhead on 5 Apr 1803 {1075}.

"Silus Howell" was listed as the head of a family consisting of one free white male of 45 years of age and older, two of 16 and under 26, two of under 10, two free white females of 45 and older, two of 16 and under 26, one of 10 and under 16, and two of under 10, residing in the Town of Riverhead, Suffolk County, New York, in the Second Census of the United States, 1800 {1076}.

On 29 Mch 1805, it was recorded that there was paid out to "Silas Howell Sundry for Robert Hinkman...£1 17s, and 17s for two pairs of shoes {1077}.

Silas Howell was listed as the head of a family consisting of one free white male of 45 years of age and older, one of 26 and under 45, one of 16 and under 25, one of 10 and under 16, two of under 10, one free white female of 45 and older, three of 16 and under 26, and one of 10 and under 16, residing in the Town of Riverhead, Suffolk County, New York, in the Third Census of the United States, 1810 {1078}.

Jemima (Howell) Howell died on 25 June 1811 in her 57th year {1079}, and is buried in the Aquebogue Cemetery {1080}.

Silas Howell was a witness to the will of Merrit Howell, of Riverhead. This will was written on 1 Jan 1818, and proved on 6 Oct 1818 {1081}.

On 31 Mch 1818, it was recorded that Silas Howell had been paid $3.69 "..in Acc^t. with Overseers of the Poor" {1082}. On 30 Mch 1830, it was similarily recorded that he had been paid 37^1/$_2$¢ {1083}.

Silas Howell was listed as the head of a family consisting of one free white male of 45 years of age and older, two of 18 and under 25, one of 16 and under 18, and one free white female of 25 and under 45, residing in the Town of Riverhead, Suffolk County, New York, in the Fourth Census of the United States, 1820. Of these, three were engaged in agriculture {1084}.

Silas Howell died on 7 Dec 1832, at the age of 81 years, and is buried in

1072. Id., 42; (I, 26).
1073. Id., 48; (I, 30).
1074. Id., 52; (I, 32-33).
1075. Id., 74; (I, 48).
1076. NYG&BR, LVI, 332 (Oct 1925).
1077. RTR, Liber A, 84; (I, 53).
1078. U.S. Census, Riverhead, Suffolk County, NY, 1810, Page 252.
1079. Wilbur Franklin Howell, op. cit., 118.
1080. Gravestone, Aquebogue Cemetery.
1081. Suffolk County Wills, Liber D, 164-165; Suffolk County Estates, File #1433.
1082. RTR, Liber A, 131; (I, 84).
1083. Id., 133[a]; (I, 86).
1084. U.S. Census, Riverhead, Suffolk County, NY, 1820, Page 357.

the Aquebogue Cemetery {1085}.

Silas and Jemima (Howell) Howell were the parents of nine children {1086}.

+ 263. i.   BETHIA⁵ HOWELL, born on 23 Nov 1776.

+ 264. ii.   DANIEL⁵ HOWELL, born on 8 May 1779.

  265. iii.   SARAH⁵ HOWELL, born in Jan 1780.

+ 266. iv.   MEHITABLE⁵ HOWELL, born on 31 Mch 1785.

+ 267. v.   JEMIMA⁵ HOWELL, born on 3 Mch 1788.

+ 268. vi.   SILAS HAMILTON⁵ HOWELL, born on 15 Feb 1790.

  269. vii. POLLY LYDIA⁵ HOWELL, born on 13 Aug 1792.

+ 270. viii. GEORGE⁵ HOWELL, born on 7 Sep 1795.

+ 271. ix.   EARNEST AUGUSTA⁵ HOWELL, born on 22 Jan 1798.

100. JOSEPH⁴ HOWELL (Daniel³, Isaac², Richard¹), the son of Daniel³ and Sarah (Swesey) Howell, was born in the vicinity of Mattituck in about 1757.

Joseph Howell signed the Articles of Association in Brookhaven during the summer of 1775 {1087}.

"Joseph Howel" was a member of Captain Daniel Roe's company, in the Second Regiment of the New York Troops, commanded by Colonel James Clinton, before 1 May 1776 {1088}.

Joseph Howell, farmer, of the Township of Southold, gave his age as 21 when he signed the Oath of Allegiance and Peaceable Behaviour required by Governor William Tryon in 1778 {1089}.

Joseph Howell and Hannah Penny were married at Mattituck on 28 Oct 1779 {1090}. She was the daughter of Nathan and Mary (Paine) Penny, and was dead by 7 Oct 1790, when Joseph Howell was named an heir to the estate of Nathan Penny {1091}.

Joseph Howell and "Sarah Marther" were married at Mattituck on 9 Sep

---

1085. Gravestone, Aquebogue Cemetery.
1086. Wilbur Franklin Howell, op. cit.
1087. Mather, op. cit., 1058.
1088. Id., 1017.
1089. P.R.O. Colonial Office, Class 5, Vol. 1109, 93.
1090. Craven, op. cit., 325.
1091. Wines, op. cit., 31.

1782 {1092}.

Joseph Howell was shot on 12 Nov 1790 {1093}. He is buried at Jamesport, where his gravestone indicates that he died at the age of 43 {1094}.

Letters of administration on the estate of Joseph Howell, yeoman, were issued to his brother, Silas Howell, of Southold, on 23 Nov 1790 {1095}.

Joseph and Hannah (Penny) Howell were probably the parents of at least one son.

272.   i.   JOSEPH⁵ HOWELL.

Joseph and Sarah (Mather) Howell were the parents of at least one son {1096}.

+ 273.   ii.   EBENEZER⁵ HOWELL, born on 29 (sic) Feb 1785.

102. JACOB⁴ HOWELL (Jacob³, Jacob², Richard¹), the son of Jacob³ and Elizabeth (Dimon) Howell, was born in the vicinity of Mattituck.

Jacob Howell was enlisted by Capt. Thomas Terry on 10 Apr 1758 {1097}.

Jacob Howell and Lydia Howell, "Dr to I Hoᴵ", "both of Mattituck", were married at Cutchogue in Aug 1758 {1098}, or on 10 Sep 1758 {1099}.

Jacob Howell, of Roxbury Township, Morris County, New Jersey, was rated at 150 acres, 2 horses, 13 cattle, and 1 pig on the Mch 1779 List of Rateables, and at 1 horse, 12 cattle and 4 pigs on the Feb 1780 List {1100}.

Jacob Howell, of Roxbury Township, Morris County, New Jersey, left, to his wife, Lydia, her right of dower, namely, one-third of his estate, by his will of 19 Mch 1791, proved on 28 June 1794. By this will, he also divided his lands between his sons, Jonathan and Jacob. To his sons, Joshua and Seth, he left £10 each. To each of his daughters, namely, Elizabeth, Sarah, Margaret, Azuba, Lydia, Mary, Dorothy, Patience, Unice, Johannah, and Anna, he left 5s. His sons, Jonathan and Jacob, were named executors of this will {1101}.

Jacob and Lydia (Howell) Howell were the parents of at least fifteen children.

1092. Craven, op. cit. 328.
1093. SR, 60; (NYG&BR, XLVIII, 288 (Jly 1917)).
1094. Gravestone, Jamesport Cemetery, from the SCHS collection of cemetery marking records.
1095. Suffolk County Letters of Administration, Liber AB, 42; Suffolk County Estates, File #121).
1096. Michael A. Howell, Personal communication.
1097. MUSTER ROLLS OF NEW YORK PROVINCIAL TROOPS, 126.
1098. Wayland Jefferson, CUTCHOGUE.., 148.
1099. SR, 93; NYB&GR, XLIX, 161 (Apr 1918).
1100. THE GENEALOGICAL MAGAZINE OF NEW JERSEY (GMNJ), 46, 89 (1971).
1101. New Jersey Wills, Liber 35, 145; (NEW JERSEY ARCHIVES, 37 (Vol. 8, Abstracts of Wills), 187.

+ 274.   i.   JONATHAN[5] HOWELL.

   275. ii.   ELIZABETH[5] HOWELL.

   276. iii.   SARAH[5] HOWELL.

+ 277. iv.   MARGARET[5] HOWELL.

+ 278.   v.   AZUBA[5] HOWELL, born in about 1761.

   279. vi.   LYDIA[5] HOWELL.

   280. vii.   MARY[5] HOWELL.

+ 281. viii. JACOB[5] HOWELL, born in about 1770.

   282. ix.   JOSHUA[5] HOWELL.

   283.   x.   DOROTHY[5] HOWELL.

+ 284. xi.   PATIENCE[5] HOWELL.

+ 285. xii.   EUNICE[5] HOWELL.

   286. xiii. SETH[5] HOWELL.

   287. xiv. JOANNA[5] HOWELL.

+ 288. xv.   ANNA[5] HOWELL.

- END OF FOURTH GENERATION -

- FIFTH GENERATION -

I. Descendants of John[2] Howell.

A. John[3], John[2], Richard[1]

104. JONATHAN[5] HOWELL (John[4]), the son of John[4] Howell, was born on 22 Mch 1758 {1102} at Middle Island.

"Jonat[n] Howell", farmer, of the Township of Brookhaven, gave his age as 19 when he signed the Oath of Allegiance and Peaceable Behaviour required by Governor William Tryon in 1778 {1103}.

Jonathan Howell married Anna Davis, the daughter of David and Anna (Norton) Davis, who was born on 27 Nov 1765 {1104}.

"Jon[n] Howell" was listed as the head of a household consisting of one free white male of 16 years of age and upwards, one free white female, and one other free person, residing in Brookhaven Town, Suffolk County, New York, in the First Census of the United States, 1790 {1105}.

Jonathan Howell was selected to be a Fence Viewer for the ensuing year at the Annual Meeting of the Town of Brookhaven on 3 Apr 1792 {1106}.

"Jonathan Hoel" was listed as possessing real property worth £100, along with personal property worth an additional £100, on the Town of Brookhaven Tax Estimate for 1795 {1107}.

Jonathan Howell was listed as possessing a house and land worth $500, and personal property worth $30, on the Town of Brookhaven Tax Estimate for 1799 {1108}.

"Jonathan Howel" was listed as the head of a family consisting of one free white male of 26 and under 45 years of age, two of under 10, one free white female of 26 and under 45, and one of 10 and under 16, residing in the Town of Brookhaven, Suffolk County, New York, in the Second Census of the United States, 1800 {1109}.

In the Third Census of the United States, 1810, Jonathan Howell was listed as the head of a family consisting of one free white male of 45 years of age and older, two of 10 and under 16, one free white female of 26 and under 45, and two of 16 and under 26, residing in the Town of Brookhaven, Suffolk County, New York {1110}.

1102. Mordecai Homan's New Testament Record.
1103. P.R.O. Colonial Office, Class 5, Vol. 1109, 8.
1104. Bible record, Davis Family Bible, Printed MDCCLXXV, in the possession of Ernest Hawkins, 1942, from a copy in the possession of David A. Overton, 1990.
1105. HEADS OF FAMILIES.., 1790, NEW YORK, 161.
1106. BTR, Liber A, Part III, 238; (A, 103).
1107. Town of Brookhaven Tax Estimate for 1795.
1108. Town of Brookhaven Tax Estimate for 1799.
1109. NYG&BR, LVI, 280 (Jly 1925).
1110. U.S. Census, Brookhaven, Suffolk County, NY, 1810, Page 214.

Jonathan Howell was taxed 27⌐on real property assessed at $215 in 1813 {1111}.

In the Fifth Census of the United States, 1830, Jonathan Howell was listed as the head of a family consisting of one free white male of 70 and under 80 years of age, and one free white female of 60 and under 70, residing in the Town of Brookhaven, Suffolk County, New York {1112}.

Jonathan Howell was listed as the head of a family consisting of one free white male of 80 and under 90 years of age, and one free white female of 70 and under 80, residing in the Town of Brookhaven, Suffolk County, New York, in the Sixth Census of the United States, 1840 {1113}.

Jonathan Howell died on 23 Sep 1840, at the age of 82 years, 6 months and 1 day, and was buried in the Homan Cemetery at South Haven {1114}, and subsequently re-buried in the Brookhaven Village Cemetery {1115}.

Anna (Davis) Howell died on 3 Apr 1843, at the age of 77 years and 5 months {1116}.

Jonathan and Anna (Davis) Howell were the parents of four children {1117}.

+ 289.   i.   NANCY⁶ HOWELL, born in 1792.

290.   ii.   DAVIS⁶ HOWELL, born in 1797.

291.   iii.   NORTON⁶ HOWELL.

292.   iv.   CHARITY⁶ HOWELL.

105. JOHN⁵ HOWELL (John⁴), the son of John⁴ Howell, was born in about November 1762, probably at Middle Island.

John Howell, farmer, of the Township of Brookhaven, gave his age as 15 when he signed the Oath of Allegiance and Peaceable Behaviour required by Governor William Tryon in 1778 {1118}.

John Howell married Martha Benjamin, the daughter of Amaziah and Mary (Howell) Benjamin {1119}. Martha Benjamin was baptized at Mattituck on 6 June 1771 {1120}.

1111. Town of Brookhaven Tax Estimate for 1813, from a copy in the possession of David A. Overton, 1990.
1112. U.S. Census, Brookhaven, Suffolk County, NY, 1830, Page 167.
1113. Id., 1840, Page 273.
1114. Mordecai Homan's New Testament Record.
1115. Harry W. Huson, AMERICAN REVOLUTIONARY WAR PATRIOTS BURIED IN THE TOWN OF BROOKHAVEN.
1116. Mordecai Homan's New Testament Record.
1117. Wilbur Franklin Howell, op. cit., 322.
1118. P.R.O. Colonial Office, Class 5, Vol. 1109, 8.
1119. Bicha & Brown, op. cit., 694.
1120. Craven, op. cit., 278.

"Howell, John, Jun'" was listed as the head of a family consisting of one free white male of 16 years of age and upwards, one of under 16, and one free white female, residing in Brookhaven Town, Suffolk County, New York, in the First Census of the United States, 1790 {1121}.

The real property of John Howell was assessed at £100, while his personal property was assessed at £20, in 1795 {1122}.

John Howell was listed as possessing a house and land worth $430, and personal property worth $50, on the Town of Brookhaven Tax Estimate for 1799 {1123}.

In the Second Census of the United States, 1800, "John Howel" was listed as the head of a family consisting of one free white male of 26 and under 45 years of age, one of 10 and under 16, one of under 10, one free white female of 26 and under 45, and one of under 10, residing in the Town of Brookhaven, Suffolk County, New York {1124}.

John Howell provided bond when letters of administration on the estate of Zophar Garrard, mason, of the Town of Brookhaven, were issued to his son, Gilbert Garrard, on 5 May 1800 {1125}.

John Howell was listed as the head of a family consisting of one free white male of 45 years of age and older, one of 16 and under 26, one of under 10, one free white female of 26 and under 45, one of 10 and under 16 and one of under 10, residing in the Town of Brookhaven, Suffolk County, New York, in the Third Census of the United States, 1810 {1126}.

In the Fourth Census of the United States, 1820, John Howell was listed as the head of a family consisting of one free white male of 45 years of age and older, one of 10 and under 16, and one free white female of 45 and older, residing in the Town of Brookhaven, Suffolk County, New York {1127}.

John Howell provided bond when letters of administration on the estate of Jehiel Brown were issued on 6 Nov 1828 {1128}.

John Howell was listed as the head of a family consisting of one free white male of 60 and under 70 years of age, and one free white female of 60 and under 70, residing in the Town of Brookhaven, Suffolk County, New York, in the Fifth Census of the United States, 1830 {1129}.

Martha (Benjamin) Howell, the wife of John Howell, died on 3 Aug 1836, AE 65, and is buried in the Union Cemetery at Middle Island {1130}.

In the Sixth Census of the United States, 1840, John Howell was listed as the head of a household consisting of one free white male of 70 and under 80 years

1121. HEADS OF FAMILIES.., 1790, NEW YORK, 161.
1122. Town of Brookhaven Tax Estimate for 1795.
1123. Town of Brookhaven Tax Estimate for 1799.
1124. NYG&BR, LVI, 279 (Jly 1925).
1125. Suffolk County Letters of Administration, Liber AB, 146; Suffolk County Estates, File 443-A.
1126. U.S. Census, Brookhaven, Suffolk County, NY, 1810, Page 217.
1127. Id., 1820, Page 341.
1128. Suffolk County Letters of Administration, Liber E, 159; Suffolk County Estates, File #2182.
1129. U.S. Census, 1830, Brookhaven, Suffolk County, NY, Page 159.
1130. Gravestone, Union Cemetery, Middle Island.

of age, and one free white female of 40 and under 50, residing in the Town of Brookhaven, Suffolk County, New York {1131}.

John Howell died on 27 Dec 1842, AE 81, and is buried beside his wife in the Union Cemetery at Middle Island {1132}.

John and Martha (Benjamin) Howell were the parents of five children {1133}.

+ 293.   i.   CHARLES[6] HOWELL, born on 30 Oct 1789.

+ 294.   ii.   JOHN[6] HOWELL, born on 1 Oct 1798.

+ 295.   iii.   AMELIA[6] HOWELL.

   296.   iv.   CHARLOTTE[6] HOWELL(?).

+ 297.   v.   MITCHELL[6] HOWELL, born on 15 Nov 1806.

106. CHARITY[5] HOWELL (John[4]), the daughter of John[4] Howell, was born in the vicinity of Middle Island in about 1764.

Charity Howell married Mordecai Homan {1134}, who was born on 17 Nov 1757, the son of Mordecai and Sarah (Wells (Mills?)) Homan.

"Mordecai Homan 3rd" signed the Articles of Association as a member of the Third Company on 17 May 1775, as did his father and grandfather {1135}.

Mordecai Homan brought back two cannon balls from the Battle of Long Island, which came down to Edgar Homan, along with his musket, knife and New Testament, 1761. The story is told that his wife was peeling potatoes when she saw a young deer eating in the garden. She took up his knife, ran out and killed the deer by cutting its throat {1136}.

Mordecai Homan was probably listed as a member of the family of Mordecai Homan, which consisted of three males of 16 and under 50 years of age, five of under 16, one female of over 16, and two of under 16, residing in Brookhaven Township, Suffolk County, New York, in the Census of 1776 {1137}.

"Mordicah Homan", farmer, of the Town of Brookhaven, gave his age as 20 when he signed the Oath of Allegiance and Peaceable Behaviour required by

1131. Id., 1840, Brookhaven, Suffolk County, NY, Page 282.
1132. Gravestone, Union Cemetery, Middle Island.
1133. Charles Reeve Howell Family Bible, owned by Mrs William Homan, from a copy in the possession of David A. Overton, 1992.
1134. Mordecai Homan's New Testament.
1135. Mather, op. cit., 992.
1136. Edgar Homan, Personal communication, from a copy in the possession of David A. Overton, 1992.
1137. CENSUS OF SUFFOLK COUNTY..1776, 13.

Governor William Tryon in 1778 {1138}.

"Modiccah Homan" was listed as the head of a household consisting of one free white male of 16 years of age and older, one of under 16, four free white females, and one other free person, residing in Brookhaven Town, Suffolk County, New York, in the First Census of the United States, 1790 {1139}.

"Mordeca Homan" was listed as the head of a family consisting of one free white male of 26 and under 45 years of age, one of under 10, one free white female of 26 and under 45, one of 10 and under 16, and four of under 10, residing in the Town of Brookhaven, Suffolk County, New York, in the Second Census of the United States, 1800 {1140}.

Mordecai Homan died at Fire Place on 6 Apr 1829, at the age of 72, and was buried in the burial lot on the family farm. His body was among those taken up and re-buried in the Bellport Cemetery {1141}.

Charity (Howell) Homan died on 21 June 1838, at the age of 74 years, and was buried beside her husband. Her body was among those taken up and re-buried at Bellport {1142}.

Mordecai and Charity (Howell) Homan were the parents of at least three children.

    i.   SILAS HOMAN, born on 8 Aug 1792 {1143}.

    ii.   CHARITY HOMAN, born in about 1795 {1144}.

    iii.   HARRIET HOMAN.

108. ELIZABETH[5] HOWELL (Reeves[4]), the daughter of Reeves[4] and Bathsheba (Clark) Howell, was born at Middle Island on 23 Nov 1763.

Elizabeth, "Betsey", Howell married Nathan Davis {1145}, who was born on 31 Oct 1752, and baptized at Smithtown on 6 Feb 1753, the son of Elnathan and Elizabeth Davis {1146}.

Nathan Davis signed the Articles of Association within the Fourth Company limits in the Town of Brookhaven on 16 May 1775, on 8 Jun 1775, and during the summer of 1775 {1147}.

Nathan Davis, farmer, of the Township of Brookhaven, gave his age as 27 years when he signed the Oath of Allegiance and Peaceable Behaviour required by

1138. P.R.O. Colonial Office, Class 5, Vol. 1109, 10.
1139. HEADS OF FAMILIES.., 1790, NEW YORK, 160.
1140. NYG&BR, LVI, 278 (Jly 1925).
1141. Edgar Homan, op. cit.
1142. Id.
1143. Gravestone, Bellport Cemetery, from Ida A. Maddrah, op. cit.
1144. Mordecai Homan's New Testament Record.
1145. Sarah (Vail) Howell Terry, op. cit.
1146. NYG&BR, XLIV, 282 (Jly 1913).
1147. Mather, op. cit., 1060, 1061, 1058.

Governor William Tryon in 1778 {1148}.

"Nathan Daviss" was listed as the head of a family consisting of one free white male of 16 years of age and upwards, one of under 16, and two free white females, residing in Brookhaven Town, Suffolk County, New York, in the First Census of the United States, 1790 {1149}.

Nathan Davis was listed as the head of a family consisting of one free white male of 45 years of age and older, one of 10 and under 16, two of under 10, one free white female of 45 and older, and one of 10 and under 16, residing in the Town of Brookhaven, Suffolk County, New York, in the Second Census of the United States, 1800 {1150}.

Nathan Davis died on 15 Oct 1843, at the age of 90 years, 11 months, and 15 days, and is buried in the Old Presbyterian Church Cemetery at Manorville, where his gravestone is inscribed "Here he retires to rest | His aged Head | Free from all wars | Slumbers with the dead" {1151}.

Elizabeth, "Betsey", (Howell) Davis died on 3 Oct 1854, at the age of 90 years, 10 months, and 10 days, and is buried beside her husband at Manorville {1152}.

Nathan and Elizabeth (Howell) Davis were the parents of at least four children.

    i.   REEVE DAVIS, born in about 1785.

    ii.   Daughter.

    iii.   Son.

    iv.   Son.

109. ALTHEA[5] HOWELL (Reeves[4]), the daughter of Reeves[5] and Bathsheba (Clark) Howell, was born on 22 Jly 1766 {1153}, in the vicinity of Middle Island.

In 1787, Althea Howell married Daniel Tooker, who was born on 8 Oct 1764, the son of Jonah and Anna (Gerard) Tooker {1154}.

"Dan¹ Tucker" was listed as the head of a family consisting of one free white male of 26 and under 45 years of age, one of 10 and under 16, three of under 10, one free white female of 26 and under 45, and one of under 10, residing in the Town of Brookhaven, Suffolk County, New York, in the Second Census of the

1148. P.R.O Colonial Office, Class 5, Vol. 1109, 15.
1149. HEADS OF FAMILIES.., 1790, NEW YORK, 161.
1150. NYG&BR, LVI, 326 (Oct 1925).
1151. Gravestone, Manorville Cemetery, from Huson, op. cit.
1152. Id.
1153. Tooker Family Bible, from notes of Martha Tooker Overton, in the possession of David A. Overton, 1991.
1154. Id.

United States, 1800 {1155}.

Daniel Tooker, Elder in the Presbyterian Church, died on 15 Jly 1841, at the age of 76 years, 9 months, and 6 days, and is buried in the churchyard cemetery at the Setauket Presbyterian Church {1156}.

Althea (Howell) Tooker, the consort of Elder Daniel Tooker, died on 17 Nov 1845, in the 78th year of her age, and is buried beside her husband at Setauket {1157}.

Daniel and Althea (Howell) Tooker were the parents of nine children {1158}.

    i.   DANIEL TOOKER, born in about 1790.

    ii.   JAMES TOOKER, born on 21 Mch 1793.

    iii.   TIMOTHY BREWSTER TOOKER.

    iv.   HAMILTON TOOKER.

    v.   WILLIAM CLARK TOOKER, born in about 1798.

    vi.   CHARLOTTE G. TOOKER, born on 10 Aug 1800.

    vii.   JONAS TOOKER, born in about 1801.

    viii.   DEBORAH ANN TOOKER.

    ix.   ANGELINE TOOKER.

110. ISAAC REEVES[5] HOWELL (Reeves[4]), the son of Reeves[4] and Bathsheba (Clark) Howell, was born on 19 Feb 1769 {1159}.

Isaac Reeves Howell married Mary, "Polly", Hawkins on 29 Dec 1789 {1160}. She was the daughter of Gershom[5] and Hannah (Brigard (Pritchard?)) Hawkins, and was born on 17 Jly 1771 {1161}.

In the First Census of the United States, 1790, Isaac Howell was listed as the head of a family consisting of one free white male of 16 years of age and upwards, and one free white female, residing in Southold Town, Suffolk County, New York {1162}.

1155. NYG&BR, LVI, 280 (Jly 1925).
1156. Barstow, op. cit., EPITAPHS.
1157. Id.
1158. Tooker Family Bible, op. cit.
1159. Sherwood, op. cit.
1160. Id.
1161. Hawkins, op. cit., 20.
1162. HEADS OF FAMILIES.., 1790, NEW YORK, 168.

Isaac Howell was an executor of the will of his father, Reeves Howell, written on 16 Dec 1797, and proved on 6 Sep 1802. By this will, he was ordered to pay, to his brother, James Howell, "..£60 current money of New York..or give an obligation for the same at the delivery of a deed for his place..". By a codicil to this will, Isaac Reeve Howell was ordered to give to "..William Howell..all the land and timber that shall be between the Granny Road and a certain line to be drawn east and west 10 rods South of S^d Granny Road.." {1163}.

Isaac Howell was assessed as possessing personal property worth $38 on the 1799 Tax Estimate for the Town of Brookhaven {1164}.

On 2 Dec 1799, John Bayles and Daniel Saxton, Commissioners of Highways, Town of Brookhaven, ordered a road to be opened running "..Southerly On the Line Between John Howells an Reve Howells Land until it comes to the Top of the hill North of Isaac Howells House then Takeing the Best of the Ground for a Road East of Isaac Howells House to the Coram Road." {1165}.

Isaac Howell provided bond when letters of administration on the estate of Zophar Garrard, mason, of Brookhaven, were issued to his son, Gilbert Garrard, on 5 May 1800 {1166}.

On 28 June 1800, Isaac Howell was a witness to the will of Gershom Brown, of Brookhaven {1167}.

In the Second Census of the United States, 1800, "Isaac Howel" was listed as the head of a household consisting of one free white male of 26 and under 45 years of age, one free white female of 16 and under 26, two of under 10, and one slave, residing in the Town of Brookhaven, Suffolk County, New York {1168}.

On 6 Apr 1802, Isaac Howell was chosen to serve as an Overseer of Highways, and as a Fence Viewer, for the ensuing year, at the Annual Meeting of the Town of Brookhaven {1169}.

Isaac Howell was an executor of the will of his brother, Daniel Howell, written on 28 Jan 1808, and proved on 23 Feb 1808. His wife, Polly, and his mother, "Bashaby Howell", were witnesses to the signing of this will {1170}.

On 3 Dec 1808, Isaac Howell was a witness to the signing of the will of Caleb M. Hulse, of Brookhaven {1171}.

In the Third Census of the United States, 1810, "Isaac R. Howel" was listed as the head of a household consisting of one free white male of 26 and under 45 years of age, two of under 10, one free white female of 26 and under 45, two of 10 and under 16, two of under 10, and one other free person, residing in the

---

1163. Suffolk County Wills, Liber B, 205-208; Suffolk County Estates, File #554.
1164. Town of Brookhaven Tax Estimate for 1799.
1165. BTR, Book A, Part III, 334; (D, 22-23).
1166. Suffolk County Letters of Administration, Liber AB, 146; Suffolk County Estates, File #443-A.
1167. Suffolk County Wills, Liber B, 158-160.
1168. NYG&BR, LVI, 279 (Jly 1925).
1169. BTR, Book A, Part III, 378; (D, 53-54).
1170. Suffolk County Wills, Liber B, 490-491; Suffolk County Estates, File #795.
1171. Id., Liber C, 61-64.

Town of Brookhaven, Suffolk County, New York {1172}.

Isaac Howell provided bond when letters of administration were issued on the estate of Joshua Davis, mariner, of Brookhaven, on 1 Jan 1812 {1173}.

Isaac Howell was an executor of the will of his brother, William Howell, written on 6 Feb 1812, and proved on 7 May 1812 {1174}.

By his will of 5 Oct 1812, Isaac Howell left, to his wife, Mary Howell, the use of his estate, both real and personal, after his just debts were paid, for the support and upbringing of their children. His real estate was to be divided equally between his three sons, Isaac Reeve Howell, Gershom Hawkins Howell, and William Clark Howell, after the demise or re-marriage of his wife. Each of his daughters, Polly Howell, Alathea Howell, Hannah Howell, and Sally Howell, was to receive one cow, six sheep, and $30 in cash on the day of her marriage, and a residence and support until then. The remainder of his estate was to be divided equally between his three sons. His wife, Mary, was named sole executrix {1175}.

Isaac Reeves Howell died on 27 Oct 1812 {1176}, and is buried in the Union Cemetery at Middle Island, where his gravestone is inscribed "IN Memory of | Mr. ISAAC HOWELL | Who died Oct. 27 1813 | in the 44 year | of his age" {1177}.

Isaac Howell's estate was taxed $2.12 on real property assessed at $1,716 in 1813 {1178}.

When the Commissioners of Common Schools for the Town of Brookhaven met at Coram on 3 Nov 1813 to divide the town into school districts, they decided that District 12 was "..to embrace the Inhabitant of the lower part of Middle Island as far west as Isaac Howells (Deceas^d)..", while District 23 was "..to embrace the Inhabitants of Coram hills as far East as the Widow Howells-" {1179}.

In the Fourth Census of the United States, 1820, Mary Howell was listed as the head of a family consisting of one free white female of 25 and under 45 years of age, two of 10 and under 16, two free white males of 18 and under 25, one of 16 and under 18, and one of under 10, residing in the Town of Brookhaven, Suffolk County, New York {1180}.

On 1 May 1830, Mary Howell, the "Executrix to the Estate of Isaac Howell deceased..", sold, to her son, Gershom Hawkins Howell, a piece of land which was "..a part of lot No. Forety Nine and Containing by Estimation one hundred and Twenty acres.." for $300, by a deed recorded on 8 May 1830 {1181}.

1172. U.S. Census, Brookhaven, Suffolk County, NY, Page 217.
1173. Suffolk County Letters of Administration, Liber C, 190; Suffolk County Estates, File 962.
1174. Suffolk County Wills, Liber C, 233-235; Suffolk County Estates, File #987.
1175. Id., 277-279; Suffolk County Estates, File #1016.
1176. Sherwood, op. cit.
1177. Gravestone, Union Cemetery, Middle Island.
1178. Town of Brookhaven Tax Estimate for 1813.
1179. BTR, Book D, 124-125; (D, 179).
1180. U.S. Census, Brookhaven, Suffolk County, NY, 1820, Page 341.
1181. Suffolk County Deeds, Liber M, 275-276.

Mary (Hawkins) Howell died in Apr 1839 {1182}.

Isaac Reeves and Mary, "Polly", (Hawkins) Howell were the parents of eleven children {1183}.

    298. i.   REEVE[6] HOWELL, born on 1 Sep 1790, died on 30 May 1797.

    299. ii.   ISAAC[6] HOWELL, born on 18 Jly 1792, died on 28 Feb 1797.

    300. iii. SALLY[6] HOWELL, born on 12 Aug 1794, died on 17 Oct 1794.

    301. iv. DANIEL[6] HOWELL, born on 28 Oct 1795, died on 5 Oct 1798.

+ 302. v.   MARY[6] HOWELL, born on 28 Oct 1797.

+ 303. vi.   ALTHEA[6] HOWELL, born on 17 Oct 1799.

+ 304. vii. ISAAC REEVE[6] HOWELL, born on 5 Apr 1802.

+ 305. viii. GERSHOM HAWKINS[6] HAWKINS, born on 28 May 1804.

+ 306. ix.   HANNAH MARIA[6] HOWELL, born on 15 Nov 1806.

+ 307. x.   SARAH ANN[6] HOWELL, born on 18 Dec 1808.

+ 308. xi.   WILLIAM CLARK[6] HOWELL, born on 28 Dec 1811.

111. JAMES[5] HOWELL (Reeves[4]), the son of Reeves[4] and Bathsheba (Clark) Howell, was born in about 1771, probably at Middle Island.

James Howell married Catherine Youngs, the daughter of Daniel and Catherine (Brown) Youngs {1184}, who was born in about 1778, and was baptized at Southold on 5 Jan 1784 {1185}.

James Howell bought land at Middle Island in 1793 when he was about 21. "In 1796, he paid William Tooker £150 for a 'messuage and tract of land' on the north side of the Country Road". It was on this land that he established his home. The land was mortgaged to Daniel Homan for £50 in 1798 {1186}.

James Howell was listed as possessing a house and land worth $150, and personal property worth $12, on the Town of Brookhaven Tax Estimate for 1799 {1187}.

"James Howel" was listed as the head of a family consisting of one free

1182. Sherwood, op. cit.
1183. Id.
1184. Selah Youngs, Jr., YOUNGS FAMILY, 347.
1185. RECORDS OF THE FIRST CHURCH OF SOUTHOLD, 27; NYG&BR, LXV, 54 (Jan 1934).
1186. Grendler, op. cit., Introduction.
1187. Town of Brookhaven Tax Estimate for 1799.

white male of 26 and under 45 years of age, one of under 10, one free white female of 16 and under 26, and two of under 10, residing in the Town of Brookhaven, Suffolk County, New York, in the Second Census of the United States, 1800 {1188}.

On 15 Jan 1802, letters of administration on the estate of Daniel Youngs, cooper, of the Town of Brookhaven, were issued to his son-in-law, James Howell, after his wife, Amy, resigned {1189}.

In the Third Census of the United States, 1810, James Howell was listed as the head of a family consisting of one free white male of 26 and under 45 years of age, one of 10 and under 16, three of under 10, one free white female of 26 and under 45, two of 10 and under 16, and one of under 10, residing in the Town of Brookhaven, Suffolk County, New York {1190}.

On 2 Apr 1811, James Howell was selected to be a Fence Viewer, for the ensuing year, at the Annual Meeting of the Town of Brookhaven, held at the house of Goldsmith Davis, innkeeper {1191}. He was again selected for this office on 7 Apr 1812 {1192}.

James Howell was taxed 32⌐ on real property assessed at $257 in 1813 {1193}.

James Howell was selected to serve as an Overseer of Highways, for the ensuing year, at the Annual Meeting of the Town of Brookhaven on 7 Apr 1818, and again on 3 Apr 1821 {1194}.

Catherine (Youngs) Howell died on 24 Mch 1820, and is buried in the cemetery at the New Village Congregational Church in Centereach, where her gravestone is inscribed, "Caty | wife of James Howell died March 24 1820 | aged 42" {1195}.

In the Fourth Census of the United States, 1820, James Howell was listed as the head of a family consisting of one free white male of 45 years of age and older, two of 18 and under 25, two of 10 and under 16, two of under 10, two free white females of 16 and under 25, one of 10 and under 16, and two of under 10, residing in the Town of Brookhaven, Suffolk County, New York. Three members of the family were engaged in agriculture {1196}.

On 14 Jly 1824, James Howell joined Samuel F. Norton in posting bond when letters of administration were issued on the estate of Israel Ruland, of the Town of Brookhaven {1197}.

On 1 Oct 1825, James Howell married Elizabeth Hurtin, who was born in about Dec 1782, as his second wife. She was a sister of Mrs. Louisa Homan, whose

1188. NYG&BR, LVI, 280 (Jly 1925).
1189. Suffolk County Letters of Administration, Liber C, 34; Suffolk County Estates, File #520.
1190. U.S. Census, Brookhaven, Suffolk County, NY, 1810, Page 221.
1191. BTR, Book D, 78; (D, 144).
1192. Id., 99; (D, 159).
1193. Town of Brookhaven Tax Estimate for 1813.
1194. Id., 155, 175; (D, 208, 228).
1195. NYG&BR, XXI, 75 (Apr 1890).
1196. U.S. Census, Brookhaven, Suffolk County, NY, 1820, Page 340.
1197. Suffolk County Letters of Administration, Liber E, 68; Suffolk County Estates, File #1797.

husband was a minister, and the father of Rebecca and Sarah Homan {1198}.

James Howell was selected to serve as a Fence Viewer, for the ensuing year, at the Annual Meeting of the Town of Brookhaven on 1 Apr 1828, and again on 7 Apr 1829 {1199}.

James Howell was listed as the head of a family consisting of one free white male of 50 and under 60 years of age, two of 10 and under 15, one free white female of 40 and under 50, and two of 15 and under 20, residing in the Town of Brookhaven, Suffolk County, New York, in the Fifth Census of the United States, 1830 {1200}.

In the Sixth Census of the United States, 1840, James Howell was listed as the head of a family consisting of one free white male of 60 and under 70 years of age, one of 20 and under 30, and one free white female of 50 and under 60, residing in the Town of Brookhaven, Suffolk County, New York {1201}.

James Howell died on 23 Sep 1848, and is buried beside his wife in the New Village Congregational Church cemetery at Centereach, where his gravestone is inscribed, "James Howell | died Sept. 23 1848 aged 77 years" {1202}.

On 12 Aug 1870, Elizabeth Howell, 87, was enumerated at New Village in the Town of Brookhaven, Suffolk County, New York, in the Ninth Census of the United States {1203}.

Elizabeth (Hurtin) Howell died on 13 Oct 1875, and is buried beside her husband at Centereach. Her gravestone is inscribed, "Elizabeth | wife of James Howell died Oct 13 1875 | aged 92 years 10 mos." {1204}.

James and Catherine (Youngs) Howell were the parents of eleven children {1205}.

+ 309.   i.   YOUNGS[6] HOWELL, born on 1 Feb 1795.

+ 310.   ii.   NANCY[6] HOWELL, born on 6 Jan 1798.

+ 311.   iii.   CATHERINE[6] HOWELL, born on 21 Feb 1800.

+ 312.   iv.   JAMES[6] HOWELL, born on 9 Jly 1802.

+ 313.   v.   REEVES[6] HOWELL, born on 4 Nov 1804.

+ 314.   vi.   DANIEL BROWN[6] HOWELL, born on 29 Dec 1806.

   315.   vii. ELIZA[6] HOWELL, born in about 1810, died on 1 Feb 1826, and

---

1198. Grendler, op. cit., 3.
1199. BTR, Book D, 234, 238; (D, 290, 296).
1200. U.S. Census, Brookhaven, Suffolk County, NY, 1830, Page 183.
1201. Id., 1840, Page 294.
1202. NYG&BR, XXI, 76 (Apr 1890).
1203. U.S. Census, Brookhaven, Suffolk County, NY, 1870, Dwelling House 1886, Family Number 2035, Page 431.
1204. NYG&BR, XXI, 76 (Apr 1890).
1205. Grendler, op. cit., 3.

is buried in the New Village Congregational Church cemetery at Centereach, where her gravestone is inscribed, "Eliza | daughter of James & Caty Howell | died Feb. 14 1826 AE 16 years." {1206}.

+ 316. viii.   HARRIET ATWOOD[6] HOWELL, born on 5 Jan 1812.

+ 317. ix.   DEBORAH ROE[6] HOWELL, born on 9 Sep 1814.

+ 318. x.   EDMUND WHEELER[6] HOWELL, born on 7 Mch 1817.

+ 319. xi.   RICHARD OAKLEY[6] HOWELL, born on 15 June 1819.

112. DANIEL[5] HOWELL (Reeves[4]), the son of Reeves[4] and Bathsheba (Clark) Howell, was born in about 1773 at Middle Island.

Daniel Howell was enumerated in the household of his father, Reeves Howell, in the Town of Brookhaven, Suffolk County, New York, in the First Census of the United States, 1790 {1207}, and in the Second Census of the United States, 1800 {1208}.

Daniel Howell was a major heir of his father, Reeves Howell, by whose will, written on 16 Dec 1797, and proved on 6 Dec 1802, he inherited his father's homestead, along with the responsibility of keeping a cow for his mother, Bathsheba Howell, providing a home for his unmarried brothers and sisters, and providing his sisters with household furniture at the time of their marriages {1209}.

Daniel Howell married "Patty Stevens" at Westhampton in 1805 {1210}. Martha, "Patty", Stephens {1211}, was the daughter of Edward and Martha (Rogers) Stephens, of Quogue, and was born on 11 May 1779 {1212}.

By his will of 28 Jan 1808, proved on 23 Feb 1808, Daniel Howell left his entire estate to his daughter, Abigail {1213}.

Daniel Howell died on 7 Feb 1808, at the age of 35, and is buried in the Union Cemetery at Middle Island {1214}.

In the Third Census of the United States, 1810, Martha Howell was listed as the head of a family consisting of one free white female of 16 and under 26 years of age, and one of under 10, residing in the Town of Brookhaven, Suffolk County,

1206. NYG&BR, XXI, 75 (Apr 1890).
1207. HEADS OF FAMILIES.., 1790, NEW YORK, 161.
1208. NYG&BR, LVI, 328 (Oct 1925).
1209. Suffolk County Wills, Liber B, 205-208; Suffolk County Estates, File #554.
1210. Westhampton Presbyterian Church records, from a copy in the possession of the SCHS, 1990.
1211. Sherwood, op. cit.
1212. Donnelly, The REGISTER, SCHS, XV, #2, 40-42 (Fall 1989).
1213. Suffolk County Wills, Liber B, 490-491; Suffolk County Estates, File #795.
1214. Gravestone, Union Cemetery, Middle Island.

New York {1215}.

Daniel Howell's Estate was taxed $1.49 on real property assessed at $1,203 in 1813 {1216}.

Martha (Stephens) Howell married Richard Swezey, the son of Christopher and Ann Swezey, as her second husband {1217}.

Edward Stephens, of Quogue, left his daughter, Martha, an annuity by his will of 11 Sep 1832, proved on 18 Feb 1836 {1218}.

Martha (Stephens) Howell Swezey died on 5 Dec 1855, at the age of 76 years, 6 months, and 24 days, and is buried in the Union Cemetery at Middle Island {1219}.

Daniel and Martha (Stephens) Howell were the parents of one daughter.

+ 320.   i.   ABIGAIL[6] HOWELL, born on 2 Feb 1806 {1220}.

Richard and Martha (Stephens) Howell Swezey were the parents of one daughter (Swezey).

            i.   JULIA STEPHENS SWEZEY, born in about 1815 {1221}.

113. DEBORAH[5] HOWELL (Reeves[4]), the daughter of Reeves[4] and Bathsheba (Clark) Howell, was born at Middle Island in about 1777.

Deborah Howell married Ludlow Clark {1222}.

Ludlow Clark was listed as the head of a family consisting of one free white male of 16 and under 26 years of age, one free white female of 16 and under 26, and one of under 10, residing in the Town of Brookhaven, Suffolk County, New York, in the Second Census of the United States, 1800 {1223}.

No other information on the family of Ludlow and Deborah (Howell) Clark has been developed.

114. WILLIAM[5] HOWELL (Reeves[4]), the son of Reeves[4] and Bathsheba (Clark) Howell, was born at Middle Island in about 1785.

William Howell married Phebe Barteau {1224}.

On 1 Apr 1806, William Howell was selected to serve as a Constable for ensuing year by the Annual Meeting of the Town of Brookhaven {1225}. He was again selected for this office, as well as that of an Overseer of Highways, at the

---

1215. U.S. Census, 1810, Brookhaven, Suffolk County, NY, Page 219.
1216. Town of Brookhaven Tax Estimate for 1813.
1217. Richard M. Bayles, SWEZEY HISTORY, THE REGISTER, SCHS, XIV, 72 (Winter 1988).
1218. Suffolk County Wills, Liber G, 190-194.
1219. Gravestone, Union Cemetery, Middle Island.
1220. Id.
1221. Richard M. Bayles, THE REGISTER, SCHS, XIV, 72 (Winter 1988).
1222. Sarah (Vail) Howell Terry, op. cit.
1223. NYG&BR, LVI, 328 (Oct 1925).
1224. Sherwood, op. cit.
1225. BTR, Book D, 11; (D, 102).

Annual Town Meeting on 7 Apr 1807 {1226}.

In the Third Census of the United States, 1810, William Howell was listed as the head of a family consisting of one free white male of 26 and under 45 years of age, one of 10 and under 16, one of under 10, one free white female of 26 and under 45, and one of under 10, residing in the Town of Brookhaven, Suffolk County, New York {1227}.

By his will of 6 Feb 1812, proved on 7 May 1812, William Howell left his estate to his son, William Reeve Howell, and his daughter, Lucinda Howell, with bequests to his wife, Phebe Howell {1228}.

William and Phebe (Barteau) Howell were the parents of at least two children.

+ 321.   i.   WILLIAM REEVE[6] HOWELL, born in about 1807.

+ 322.   ii.   LUCINDA[6] HOWELL, born in about 1808.

116. MARY SARAH[5] HOWELL (Reeve[4]), the daughter of Reeve[4] and Bathsheba (Clark) Howell, was born at Middle Island on 28 Nov 1788.

Mary, "Polly", Howell married Isaac Tooker {1229} on 15 Dec 1815 {1230}.

Isaac and Polly Tooker moved to Orange County, New York, in about 1821 {1231}.

Mary Tooker, the wife of Isaac Tooker, died on 13 Apr 1829, at the age of 40 years, 4 months and 16 days, at Ridgebury, and is buried in the Minisink Methodist Church cemetery at Westtown, New York {1232}.

Isaac Tooker married Lydia Mathers Shay as his second wife. She is buried at Beemerville {1233}.

Isaac Tooker died on 4 May 1861, and is buried beside his first wife at Westtown {1234}.

Isaac and Mary Sarah (Howell) Tooker were the parents of five children {1235}.

     i.   NANCY B. TOOKER, born on 12 Apr 1817 in Suffolk County, married Stephen Tuttle Alward, died at Middletown on 1 Feb

1226. Id., 22; (D, 111).
1227. U.S. Census, Brookhaven, Suffolk County, NY, 1810, Page 217.
1228. Suffolk County Wills, Liber C, 233-235; Suffolk County Estates, File #987.
1229. Sarah (Vail) Howell Terry, op. cit.
1230. Isaac Tooker Family Bible records, from Nellie May Tooker's collection, from C. Evelyn Brown Steuwer's THE TOOKER FAMILY IN AMERICA, 1637-1977, 86, kindly supplied by Stewart M. Aldrich, Historian, Village of Babylon, NY.
1231. Id.
1232. Id., CEMETERIES OF THE TOWN OF MINISINK, 110.
1233. Isaac Tooker Family Bible Records.
1234. Id., CEMETERIES OF THE TOWN OF MINISINK, 110.
1235. Isaac Tooker Family Bible Records.

1894, and is buried at Westtown, in Orange County, New York {1236}.

    ii.   RUTH TOOKER, born on 3 Jly 1820 in Suffolk County, died at birth.

    iii.   DEBORAH TOOKER, born on 3 Jly 1820 in Suffolk County, married Isaac Jefferson.

    iv.   SAMUEL TOOKER, born on 23 Nov 1823 (or 5 Aug 1825) at Ridgebury, married Sarah Snook, who was born on 5 Feb 1837.

    v.   ISAAC TOOKER, born on 23 Jan 1829.

B. Jonathan[3], John[2], Richard[1]

117. JONATHAN[5] HOWELL (Jonathan[4]), the son of Jonathan[4] and Bethiah (Howell) Howell, was born in the vicinity of Mattituck shortly before he was baptized there on 7 Oct 1770 {1237}.

Jonathan Howell was given the bulk of the estate of his father, Jonathan Howell, after bequests to Daniel and Cynthia Howell, by a will written on 25 Aug 1791, and proved on 27 Mch 1793 {1238}.

Jonathan Howell was a witness to the will of William Hallock, of the Town of Riverhead. This will was written on 19 June 1794, and proved on 26 Nov 1794 {1239}.

Jonathan Howell married Elizabeth Hallock, who was born in about 1774, the daughter of Zachariah and Hannah Hallock {1240}. (NOTE: *A record of gravestone inscriptions from the Aquebogue and Jamesport Cemeteries {1241}, in the possession of the Suffolk County Historical Society (1995), and probably the work of Orville B. Ackerly, indicates that Hannah, the wife of Zachariah Hallock, was the daughter of Daniel and Mary Young*).

Jonathan Howell was listed as the head of a household consisting of one free white male of 26 and under 45 years of age, one of 16 and under 26, one of under 10, one free white female of 26 and under 45, two of under 10, and one other free person, residing in the Town of Southold, Suffolk County, New York, in the Second Census of the United States, 1800 {1242}.

1236. Id., CEMETERIES OF THE TOWN OF MINISINK, 101.
1237. Craven, op. cit., 276.
1238. Suffolk County Wills, Liber A, 281-282; Suffolk County Estates, File #203.
1239. Suffolk County Wills, Liber A, 362-365.
1240. Lucius H. Hallock, op. cit., 263.
1241. AQUEBOGUE and JAMESPORT GRAVEYARD RECORDS.
1242. NYG&BR, LVII, 57 (Jan 1926).

John Howell, executor of the will of Jonathan[4] Howell, of the Town of Southold, Suffolk County, New York, received of Jonathan[5] Howell, of the Town of Riverhead, the full sum of £20, current money of said state, the full legacy bequeathed to Cynthia Howell by her father, as shown by a receipt dated 3 Apr 1797, and signed by John Howell {1243} {1244}.

Jonathan Howell was selected to be a Fence Viewer, for the ensuing year, by the Annual Meeting of the Town of Riverhead, held on 3 Apr 1804 {1245}. He was again selected for this office on 2 Apr 1805, and on 1 Apr 1806 {1246}.

Jonathan Howell was a witness to the will of Sylvanus Brown, of the Town of Riverhead, written on 14 Jan 1805, and proved on 26 Mch 1805 {1247}.

"Jon[n] Howel" was listed as the head of a family consisting of one free white male of 45 years of age and older, one of 26 and under 45, one of 10 and under 16, three of under 10, one free white female of 26 and under 45, two(?) of 10 and under 16, and one of under 10, residing in the Town of Riverhead, Suffolk County, New York, in the Third Census of the United States, 1810 {1248}.

Jonathan Howell was listed as the head of a family consisting of one free white male of 45 years of age and older, one of 18 and under 25, one of 16 and under 18, two of 10 and under 16, three of under 10, one free white female of 45 and older, and two of 16 and under 25, residing in the Town of Riverhead, Suffolk County, New York, in the Fourth Census of the United States, 1820. Of these, two were engaged in manufacturing {1249}.

Jonathan Howell "..followed farming all his days." {1250}.

Elizabeth, the wife of Jonathan Howell, died on 3 Dec 1827, in her 54th year, and is buried in the cemetery at the Mattituck Presbyterian Church {1251}.

By his will of 7 Sep 1831, proved on 3 Jan 1832, Jonathan Howell bequeathed $50 to his oldest son, Jonathan Davis Howell. He also bequeathed, to his sons, John, Albert, "Van Renselaer", and Edward Young Howell, $50 each. He bequeathed $10 to his eldest daughter, Betsy, and $20 to his daughter, Bethia. To his daughter, Maria, he bequeathed $50, one-third of the household furniture, and "..a residence in the homestead so long as she remain single..". His younger sons, George and Eli Woodhull Howell, were given his farm and homestead, and the remainder of the estate. Sylvester Howell, of the Town of Southold, was appointed Executor of this will {1252}.

Jonathan Howell died on 16 Sep 1831, and is buried beside his wife at

1243. Receipt, CHAUNCEY PERKINS HOWELL COLLECTION, SCHS.
1244. Wilbur Franklin Howell, op. cit., 413.
1245. RTR, Liber A, 80; (I, 51).
1246. Id., Liber B, 33, 36; (I, 280, 281).
1247. Suffolk County Wills, Liber B, 314-316.
1248. U.S. Census, Riverhead, Suffolk County, NY, 1810, Page 255.
1249. Id., 1820, Page 362.
1250. PORTRAIT AND BIOGRAPHICAL RECORD OF SUFFOLK COUNTY, 183.
1251. Craven, op. cit., 374.
1252. Suffolk County Wills, Liber F, 212-214; Suffolk County Estates, File #2410.

Mattituck, where his gravestone indicates that he died on 16 Sep 1832, at the age of 61 {1253}.

Jonathan and Elizabeth (Hallock) Howell were the parents of ten children.

+ 323.   i.   JONATHAN DAVIS[6] HOWELL, born in about 1797.

+ 324.   ii.   BETSY[6] HOWELL.

+ 325.   iii. JOHN H.[6] HOWELL, born in about 1801.

   326.   iv. BETHIA[6] HOWELL.

   327.   v.   MARIA[6] HOWELL.

+ 328.   vi. ALBERT[6] HOWELL, born in about 1807.

+ 329.   vii. VAN RENSSELAER[6] HOWELL, born on 8 Nov 1808.

+ 330.   viii. EDWARD YOUNG[6] HOWELL, born in about Feb 1811.

+ 331.   ix. GEORGE[6] HOWELL.

+ 332.   x.   ELI WOODHULL[6] HOWELL, born on 16 Mch 1816.

118. DANIEL[5] HOWELL (Jonathan[4]), the son of Jonathan[4] and Bethiah (Howell) Howell, was born in the vicinity of Mattituck shortly before 7 Jly 1782, when he was baptized {1254}.

Daniel Howell married Ester Reeve on 31 Jly 1802 {1255}. She was the daughter of Thomas and Parnel (Hubbard) Reeve, and was baptized on 24 May 1790, with her brothers and sisters {1256}.

On 1 Apr 1817, Daniel Howell was selected to serve as a Fence Viewer for the ensuing year at the Annual Meeting of the Town of Southold {1257}.

Daniel Howell was listed as the head of a family consisting of one free white male of 25 and under 45 years of age, one of 18 and under 25, one of 16 and under 18, one of 10 and under 16, one free white female of 25 and under 45, and one of under 10, residing in the Town of Riverhead, Suffolk County, New York, in the Fourth Census of the United States, 1820 {1258}.

Daniel Howell was listed as the head of a family consisting of one free white male of 40 and under 50 years of age, one free white female of 20 and under

1253. Craven, op. cit., 374.
1254. Id., 288.
1255. Id., 336.
1256. Id., 298.
1257. STR, Liber D, 168 left; (III, 300).
1258. U.S. Census, Riverhead, Suffolk County, NY, 1820, Page 357.

30, and one of 10 and under 15, residing in the Town of Southold, Suffolk County, New York, in the Fifth Census of the United States, 1830 {1259}.

Daniel Howell died on 25 Dec 1849, at the age of 66, and is buried in the cemetery at the Mattituck Presbyterian Church {1260}.

Daniel and Ester (Reeve) Howell were the parents of at least four children.

+ 333. i.   DANIEL[6] HOWELL, baptized at Mattituck on 9 Jly 1809 {1261}.

   334. ii.   CLARISSA[6] HOWELL, baptized at Mattituck on 9 Jly 1809 {1262}.

   335. iii.   HUBBARD[6] HOWELL, baptized at Mattituck on 9 Jly 1809 {1263}.

+ 336. iv.   MARY[6] HOWELL, born on 26 Feb 1822 {1264}.

119. CYNTHIA[5] HOWELL (Jonathan[4]), the daughter of Jonathan[4] and Bethiah (Howell) Howell, was born in about Nov 1786, and was baptized at Mattituck as "Syntha", the daughter of "Jonathan, Jr."on 18 Mch 1787 {1265}.

On 29 Dec 1804, "Syntha Howell" married "Benjamin More" {1266}, who was born on 3 Mch 1780, at Mattituck.

By his will of 2 May 1846, proved on 22 Feb 1858, Benjamin Moore, of the Town of Southold, gave, devised and bequeathed to his "..wife Synthia for and during her natural life or marriage whichever event shall first happen, and no longer, all my real and personal estate whatsoever and wheresoever the same may be..". All his household goods were to be divided among their five daughters, Mehetable, Elizabeth, Helen, Jerusha and Nancy B., after her decease. Each daughter was also left the sum of $50, except for Nancy B., who was left $100. There was also a special restriction on the money left to Mehetable, such that her husband was never to have control of it. The unmarried daughters, Helen and Nancy B., were each to have a home with one of his sons. His real property was to be divided between his sons, Calvin and Grover, after his wife's decease or re-marriage, as was his wearing apparel and "..iron tooth harrow..". The actual distribution of property was modified by a codicil of 26 Feb 1856 {1267}.

Benjamin Moore died on 24 Dec 1857, at the age of 77 years, 9 months,

1259. Id., Southold, Suffolk County, NY, 1830, Page 346.
1260. Craven, op. cit., 375, THE REGISTER, SCHS, XVI, #3, 82 (Winter 1990).
1261. Craven, op. cit., 314.
1262. Id.
1263. Id.
1264. Mallmann, op. cit., 174.
1265. Craven, op. cit., 293.
1266. Id., 336.
1267. Suffolk County Wills, Liber 6, 332-335.

and 21 days, and is buried in the "Old Yard" cemetery at Cutchogue {1268}.

Cynthia, the wife of Benjamin Moore, died on 19 May 1859, at the age of 72 years and 6 months, and is buried beside her husband at Cutchogue {1269}.

Benjamin and Cynthia (Howell) Moore were the parents of at least seven children {1270}.

i.   MEHETABEL MOORE, born on 1 Feb 1806 {1271}, married Platt S. Conklin on 7 Nov 1826 {1272}, died on 29 Dec 1887, and is buried in the cemetery at the Mattituck Presbyterian Church {1273}. He was born on 29 (sic) Feb 1799, the son of Isaac and Elizabeth (Jones) Mulford Conkling {1274}, died on 12 Oct 1885, and is buried beside his wife at Mattituck {1275}.

ii. CALVIN MOORE, born on 4 Mch 1808, married (1) Mary Ann Tuthill on 9 Jan 1832, nine children. She was born on 26 Sep 1808, the daughter of David and Mary (Terry) Tuthill, and died on 11 Oct 1865. He married(2) Hannah (Benjamin) Tuthill, who was born on 28 Aug 1807, the daughter of Isaiah T. and Sarah (Corwin) Benjamin, and was the widow of Isaac T. Tuthill. She died on 5 Oct 1888, while he died on 27 Jan 1886 {1276}, and is buried at Cutchogue in the "New Yard" Cemetery {1277}.

iii. ELIZABETH MOORE, born on 7 May 1811, married Henry Pike, three children {1278}, died on 27 May 1895, and is buried in the cemetery at the Mattituck Presbyterian Church {1279}. Henry Pike was born on 6 Oct 1794, the son of William Henry and Pamela (Osborne) Pike {1280}, died on

---

1268. Gravestone, Cutchogue Old Yard Cemetery, from the collection of gravestone marking records at the SCHS.
1269. Id.
1270. Wilbur Franklin Howell, op. cit., 414.
1271. Craven, op. cit., 363.
1272. RECORDS, FIRST CHURCH OF SOUTHOLD, 49; NYG&BR, 66, 53 (1935).
1273. Craven, op. cit.
1274. A CONKLING GENEALOGY, prepared by Eleazer Mulford Conkling, of Parma, N.Y., from a copy in the Long Island Collection at the East Hampton Library, graciously provided by Dorothy T. King, Librarian.
1275. Craven, op. cit.
1276. Barrington S. Havens, THE REGISTER, SCHS, I, #4, 31 (Mch 1976).
1277. Gravestone, Cutchogue New Yard Cemetery, from the collection of gravestone inscriptions at the SCHS.
1278. Wilbur Franklin Howell, op. cit., 417.
1279. Craven, op. cit., 381.
1280. Wilbur Franklin Howell, op. cit.

25 Sep 1868, and is buried beside his wife at Mattituck

    iv.   GROVER MOORE.

    v.   JERUSHA MOORE, married Benjamin H. Terry.

    vi.   BENJAMIN F. MOORE, born in about 1817, died on 20 May 1840 at the age of 23, and is buried in the "Old Yard" cemetery at Cutchogue {1282}.

    vii.   HELEN MOORE.

    viii.   NANCY B. MOORE.

120. BETHIAH[5] HOWELL (Recompence[4]), the daughter of Recompence[4] and Martha (Horton) Howell, was baptized at Mattituck, on 6 Nov 1774, by the Rev. Joseph Lee {1283}.

    "Bethier Hoel and Wins Osborn" were married on 15 Jly 1802 {1284}.

    Bethiah (Howell) Osborn was the principal heir to her father's estate, with the provision that it pass to her son, Joseph Osborn, after her demise {1285}.

    Wines and Bethiah (Howell) Osborn were the parents of at least one son.

    i.   JOSEPH OSBORN.

121. JEREMIAH[5] HOWELL (Jeremiah[4]), the son of Jeremiah[4] and Elthena (Harris) Howell, was born in about Jly 1775, probably in the Town of Marlborough, Ulster County, New York.

    On 18 Dec 1796, Jeremiah Howell married Catharine Hanyan at St. Andrew's Episcopal Church in Walden, N.Y. {1286}. She was born on 11 Apr 1777, the daughter of David and Elizabeth (Shaw) Hannion {1287}.

    On 1 Sep 1850, Jeremiah Howell, 75, and his wife, Catherine, 73 {1288} were living next door to their son, John, and his wife, Hester

---

1281. Id.

1282. Gravestone, Cutchogue Old Yard Cemetery.

1283. Craven, op. cit., 268.

1284. SR, 110; NYG&BR, XLIX, 277 (Jly 1918).

1285. Suffolk County Wills, Liber C, 512-514; Suffolk County Estates, File #1199.

1286. RECORDS OF CHURCHES IN ULSTER AND ORANGE COUNTY, NEW YORK; 1730-1860, 530, from LDS microfilm #017987.

1287. Mary Ellen Halsey, Personal communication.

1288. U.S. Census, Newburgh, Orange County, NY, 1850, Dwelling House 355, Family Number 382, Page 26.

{1289}, in Newburgh, Orange County, New York, as recorded in Seventh Census of the United States. In 1855, Jeremiah Howell, 80, and his wife, Catherine, both born in Ulster County, were living with their daughter, Catherine, and her husband, Daniel Carver. In 1860, Catherine Howell was living with John McGahey and his wife, Maria. In 1865, she was again living with the Carvers, and reported that she had been the mother of 11 children. In 1870, at age 93, she was living with her daughter, Catherine (Howell) Carver, and her son, Howell Hennion Carver {1290}.

By his will of 4 Sep 1857, probated on 31 Jly 1858, Jeremiah Howell, of the Town of Locke, Cayuga County, New York, gave to his children, Elizabeth Cosman, Isaac Howell, David Howell, James Howell and Catherine Carver, all his railroad company bonds. He left his son, Elliot Howell, two dollars, to be paid two years after his death. He left his grandchildren, David Cummings, Elizabeth Fields, Ann Catherine Cummings, Emily Cummings, Thomas J. Cummings, David Birdsall, James Howell, John Howell, Catherine Hanford, Margaret Rundle and Adelia Howell, one dollar each to be paid one year after his death. To his wife, Catherine Howell, he left the interest on one thousand dollars worth of stock in the Kingston bank, with the bank stock to be divided among his children, Elizabeth Cosman, Isaac Howell, David Howell, James Howell and Catherine Carver, after his wife's death. He left the rest of his estate to these same five children, and named James and David Howell his executors {1291}.

Jeremiah Howell died on 1 Mch 1858, at the age of 82 years and 8 months, and is buried Genoa Village Cemetery {1292}.

Catherine (Hennion) Howell died in 1872, and is buried in the Cedar Hill Cemetery at Millhope {1293}.

Jeremiah and Catherine (Hennion) Howell were the parents of eleven children.

+ 337.   i.   ELIZABETH[6] HOWELL, born in about Oct 1800.

   338. ii.   JEREMIAH[6] HOWELL.

+ 339. iii.   JOHN[6] HOWELL, born in about 1808.

+ 340. iv.   ELLIOTT[6] HOWELL, born in about 1809.

+ 341. v.   DAVID[6] HOWELL, born on 6 Mch 1810.

+ 342. vi.   JAMES[6] HOWELL.

1289. Id., Dwelling House 356, Family Number 383, Page 26.
1290. Mary Ellen Halsey, op. cit.
1291. Cayuga County Wills, Book M, 324-330.
1292. Gravestone, Genoa Village Cemetery, NYG&BR, LIV, 232 (Jly 1923).
1293. Gravestone, Cedar Hill Cemetery, Middlehope, NY, from a photograph graciously supplied by Cheryl Hennion Hahn, 1997.

+ 343. vii.   CATHERINE⁶ HOWELL, born on 14 Oct 1815.

+ 344. viii.   ISAAC⁶ HOWELL, born in about 1822.

+ 345. ix.   ALTHEA⁶ HOWELL, married Mr. Cummings.

+ 346. x.   CHARLOTTE⁶ HOWELL, married Mr. Birdsall.

   347. xi.   Child⁶.

122. JOHN⁵ HOWELL (Jeremiah⁴), the son of Jeremiah⁴ and Elthena (Harris) Howell, was born in about 1780 in the Town of Plattekill.

"Dissatisfied at home, he ran away. Trading his coat for a broad-axe, he learned the ship-carpenter's trade, and hewed his way to success. In 1804, he married Esther Pride, and commenced business at "Crum Elbow", on the west side of the Hudson River, by starting a ship-yard. He built a number of sloops. Then he started a store. Cord-wood was a legal tender at that time, so much so that at one time he had seven thousand cords on hand. Very high prices ruled prior to the close of the war of 1812. Hickory-wood brought twelve dollars per cord. Large quantities of wood were used in the lime-kilns at Hampton and Barnegat. In 1818 he purchased the property and built the house where the family..reside. He retired from active business in 1820. When Robert Fulton came up the Hudson River with his steamboat, the "Clermont", Mr. Howell thought that "all the rocks in 'Crum Elbow' were tumbling in the river". He went out in a small boat, and clambered on board. Fulton was shaving, and roughly demanded his business. He answered, "I have come to see" {1294}.

John Howell located in the Town of Platekill in 1805. His wife, Esther Pride, whose mother was a niece of David Brainard, was born at Haddam, Connecticut, in 1778 {1295}.

John Howell kept his store from 1812 to 1816 {1296}.

On 23 Aug 1850, John Howel, 70, with real property worth $50,000, was enumerated as the head of a family consisting of himself, his wife, Ester, 72, and their daughter, Lydia, 44, residing in the Town of Lloyd, Ulster County, New York, in the Seventh Census of the United States {1297}.

By his will of 3 Oct 1867, probated on 18 Feb 1868, John Howell left most of his farm at Lloyd to his son, John B. Howell, then to his grandsons, Charles Howell and George Howell, children of his daughter, Eliza Longbotham. He left the south part of his house, and the east part of his garden, to his daughters, Lydia Howell and Eliza Longbotham. He also left them his household furniture and

---

1294. Sylvester, op. cit., 136.
1295. Id.
1296. Id.
1297. U.S. Census, Lloyd, Ulster County, NY, 1850, Dwelling House 591, Family Number 618, Page 289.

137

livestock, to be tended by his son, John. The rest of his property was to be equally divided between his three children {1298}.

Hester Howell died on 6 June 1868, AE 90 {1299}.

John and Esther (Pride) Howell were the parents of at least three children {1300}.

+ 347.   i.   LYDIA[6] HOWELL, born on 18 June 1805.

+ 348.   ii.   ELIZA[6] HOWELL, born on 30 Mch 1809.

+ 349.   iii.   JOHN BRAINARD[6] HOWELL, born on 15 Apr 1813.

129. HARMONY[5] HOWELL (John[4]), the daughter of John[4] and Hannah (Kasar) Corwin Howell, was born in the vicinity of Mattituck in about 1795. She was baptized at Mattituck on 29 Apr 1798 {1301}.

Harmony Howell married James Aldridge on 21 Feb 1811 {1302}.

James O. Aldrich died on 18 Feb 1828, in his 39th year, and is buried in the cemetery at the Mattituck Presbyterian Church {1303}.

Harmony (Howell) Aldrich married Bethuel Hallock as her second husband. He was a farmer in West Mattituck, and was born in about 1790. His first wife was Polly Corwin {1304}, the daughter of Rev. Joseph and Mary (Sweezy) Corwin. She died on 30 Jan 1828, at the age of 35, and is buried in the Aquebogue Cemetery {1305}.

Harmony (Howell) Aldrich Hallock died on 26 Mch 1864, at the age of 69, and is buried beside her first husband at Mattituck {1306}.

Bethuel Hallock died on 26 Feb 1866, at the age of 75, and is buried beside his first wife at Aquebogue {1307}.

James O. and Harmony (Howell) Aldrich were the parents of at least five children.

   i.   HENRY ALDRICH {1308}.

   ii.   SOPHRONIA ALDRICH {1309}.

1298. Ulster County Wills, Liber P, 537-539.
1299. Kenneth E. Hasbrouck, DEATH NOTICES | From the Scrapbook of | ELMIRAH FREER | Born 1820, 16, from LDS microfilm #0529190.
1300. Sylvester, op. cit., 136.
1301. Craven, op. cit., 306.
1302. Jefferson, op. cit., 155.
1303. Craven, op. cit., 358.
1304. Lucius H. Hallock, op. cit., 194.
1305. Gravestone, Aquebogue Cemetery.
1306. Craven, op. cit., 358.
1307. Gravestone, Aquebogue Cemetery.
1308. William S. Pelletreau, in Vol. III, A HISTORY OF LONG ISLAND, by Peter Ross, 189.
1309. Id.

iii.   MARIA ALDRICH {1310}.

iv.   POLLY ALDRICH, born on 19 Apr 1815, died on 9 Feb 1820, at the age of 4 years, 9 months, and 21 days, and is buried at Mattituck {1311}.

v.   BETSEY ALDRICH, born on 2 Mch 1817, died on 8 Feb 1820, at the age of 2 years, 11 months, and 6 days, and is buried at Mattituck {1312}.

Bethuel and Harmony (Howell) Aldrich Hallock were the parents of two children {1313}.

vi.   JOHN KASAR HALLOCK, born in 1831, married (1) Mary J. Aldrich, three children, married (2) Joanna Downs, two children {1314}, died on 10 Mch 1875, at the age of 43 {1315}. Mary J. Hallock died in 1862 {1316}.

vii.   BETHUEL EVANDER HALLOCK, born in 1835, married Elizabeth Terry, six children, died in 1861 {1317}.

130. SYLVESTER[5] HOWELL (John[4]), the son of John[4] and Hannah (Kasar) Corwin Howell, was baptized at Mattituck on 1 June 1800 {1318}.

Sylvester Howell was born at the old Howell homestead in Mattituck, and lived there "..throughout his life, his time and energies being devoted to agricultural pursuits." {1319}.

Sylvester Howell married Nancy Young, who was born on 22 Sep 1799, and baptized at Mattituck on 9 Nov 1800, a daughter of Thomas Young {1320}.

Sylvester Howell was listed as the head of a family consisting of one free white male of 20 and under 30 years of age, one of 70 and under 80, one of 10 and under 15, one free white female of 20 and under 30, and one of 70 and under 80, residing in the Town of Southold, Suffolk County, New York, in the Fifth Census

1310. Id.
1311. Craven, op. cit., 358.
1312. Id.
1313. Lucius H. Hallock, op. cit., 194.
1314. Id., 420.
1315. N. Hubbard Cleveland, THE SALMON RECORD SCRAPBOOK, from a copy at the SCHS, 1995.
1316. Lucius H. Hallock, op. cit.
1317. Id., 195.
1318. Craven, op. cit., 307.
1319. Pelletreau, op. cit.
1320. Id.

of the United States, 1830 {1321}.

"In early life Mr. Howell was an old-line Whig in politics and later supported the Republican party." Sylvester and Nancy Howell "..were earnest and consistent members of the Northville church, and were highly respected and esteemed by all who knew them." {1322}.

Sylvester Howell was listed as the head of a family consisting of one free white male of 40 and under 50 years of age, two of under 5, one free white female of 30 and under 40, one of 20 and under 30, and one of 5 and under 10, residing in the Town of Southold, Suffolk County, New York, in the Sixth Census of the United States, 1840 {1323}.

On 31 Jly 1850, Sylvester Howell, 50, farmer, with real property worth $5,000, was enumerated as the head of a family consisting of himself, his wife, Nancy, 49, and their children, Addison, 15, Susan (sic) Young, 13, Sydney, 8, and Chauncey, 4, residing in the Town of Southold, Suffolk County, New York, in the Seventh Census of the United States in 1850 {1324}.

On 3 June 1870, Sylvester Howell, 70, with real estate worth $5,000, and personal property worth $500, was enumerated as the head of a family consisting of himself, his wife, Nancy, 69, and their daughter-in-law, Jemima, 25, residing at Peconic on the Town of Southold, Suffolk County, New York, in the Ninth Census of the United States {1325}.

Sylvester Howell died on 6 Nov 1875, at the age of 76, and is buried in the Laurel Cemetery {1326}.

Nancy (Young) Howell died on 15 Jly 1892, at the age of 92 years, 9 months, and 23 days, and is buried beside her husband in the Laurel Cemetery {1327}.

Sylvester and Nancy (Young) Howell were the parents of six children {1328}.

+ 351.   i.   MARY AUGUSTA[6] HOWELL, born on 27 Mch 1831 {1329}.

  352.   ii.   LEANDER P.[6] HOWELL, born on 18 June 1833, died on 30 Jan 1835, at the age of 1 year, 6 months, and 12 days, and is buried in the family plot in the Laurel Cemetery {1330}.

+ 353.   iii.   ADDISON S.[6] HOWELL, born on 19 Oct 1835.

1321. U.S. Census, Southold, Suffolk County, NY, 1830, Page 346.
1322. Pelletreau, op. cit.
1323. U.S Census, 1840, Southold, Suffolk County, NY, Page 232.
1324. Id., 1850, Dwelling Place 819, Family Number 893, Page 331.
1325. Id., 1870, Dwelling Place 80, Family Number 82, Page 237.
1326. Gravestone, Laurel Cemetery, from the collection of gravestone inscriptions at the SCHS.
1327. Id.
1328. Pelletreau, op. cit.
1329. Gravestone, Laurel Cemetery.
1330. Id.

+ 354. iv.   LEANDER YOUNG[6] HOWELL, born on 10 Dec 1837.

355. v.   SYDNEY C.[6] HOWELL, born on 21 Nov 1841, died on 21 D 1866, at the age of 25 years and 1 month, and is buried in ti family plot at the Laurel Cemetery {1331}.

+ 356. vi.   CHAUNCEY PERKINS[6] HOWELL, born in Oct 1845.

133. JOHN[5] HOWELL (Eli[4]), the son of Eli[4] Howell, was born in about 1792 ii New York State {1332}.

John Howell married Rosabella ---- {1333}.

In the Fourth Census of the United States, 1820, John Howell was listed as the head of a family consisting of one free white male of 26 and under 45 years of age, one of under 10, one free white female of 16 and under 26, and one of under 10, with one person engaging in agriculture, residing in the Town of Mount Pleasant, Wayne County, Pennsylvania {1334}.

John Howell was listed as the head of a family consisting of one free white male of 30 and under 40 years of age, two of 5 and under 10, two of under 5, one free white female of 30 and under 40, and one of 5 and under 10, residing in the Town of Mount Pleasant, Wayne County, Pennsylvania, in the Fifth Census of the United States, 1830 {1335}.

In the Sixth Census of the United States, 1840, John Howell was listed as the head of a family consisting of one free white male of 40 and under 50 years of age, two of 15 and under 20, two of 10 and under 15, one of 5 and under 10, one free white female of 30 and under 40, one of 15 and under 20, one of 10 and under 15, two of 5 and under 10, and two of under 5, residing in the Town of Mount Pleasant, Wayne County, Pennsylvania {1336}.

John Howell, 58, farmer, with real estate worth $1,000, was listed as the head of a family consisting of himself, his wife, Rosabella, 57, and their children, Elizabeth A., 24, Stephen A., 22, John, 20, and Amos, 16, residing in the Town of Mount Pleasant, Wayne County, Pennsylvania, in the Seventh Census of the United States, 1850 {1337}.

Rosabella Howell died on 29 Nov 1852, and is buried at Mount Pleasant {1338}.

John and Rosabella Howell were the parents of six children {1339}.

+ 357. i.   ELISHA[6] HOWELL, born in 1821.

1331. Id.
1332. Scott Sliker, Personal communication.
1333. Id.
1334. U.S. Census, Mount Pleasant, Wayne County, PA, 1820, Page 50.
1335. Id., 1830, Page 208.
1336. Id., 1840, Page 287.
1337. Id., 1850, Dwelling House 210, Family Number 226, Page 27.
1338. Sliker, op. cit.
1339. Id.

358.   ii.   ELIZABETH A.[6] HOWELL, born in about 1826.

359.   iii.   STEPHEN A.[6] HOWELL, born in about 1828.

360.   iv.   JOHN WESLEY[6] HOWELL, born in about 1830.

361.   v.   AMOS[6] HOWELL, born in about 1834.

362.   vi.   Son[6].

134. DAVID[5] HOWELL (Eli[4]), the son of Eli[4] Howell, was born in New York State on 27 Nov 1795 {1340}.

David Howell married Wealthy Campbell, who was born in New York State on 10 Jan 1801 {1341}.

In the Fourth Census of the United States, 1820, David Howell was listed as the head of a family consisting of one free white male of 16 and under 26 years of age, and one free white female of 16 and under 26, with one person engaged in agriculture, residing in the Town of Mount Pleasant, Wayne County, Pennsylvania {1342}.

David Howell was listed as the head of a family consisting of one free white male of 30 and under 40 years of age, three of 5 and under 10, one of under 5, one free white female of 20 and under 30, one of 5 and under 10, and two of under 5, residing in the Town of Mount Pleasant, Wayne County, in the Fifth Census of the United States, 1830 {1343}.

In the Sixth Census of the United States, 1840, David Howell was listed as the head of a family consisting of one free white male of 40 and under 50 years of age, two of 15 and under 20, two of 10 and under 15, one of 5 and under 10, one free white female of 40 and under 50, one of 15 and under 20, one of 10 and under 15, two of 5 and under 10, and two of under 5, residing in the Town of Mount Pleasant, Wayne County, Pennsylvania {1344}.

On 9 Aug 1850, David Howell, 54, farmer, with real estate worth $500, was enumerated as the head of a family consisting of himself, his wife, Wealthy, 49, and their children, Darius, sawyer, 27, Seth, farmer, 23, Thaddeus, farmer, 20, Elizabeth, 20, Rhoda, 18, Albert, farmer, 15, and Ellen, 6, residing in the Town of Mount Pleasant, Wayne County, Pennsylvania, in the Seventh Census of the United States {1345}.

1340. Craig R. Howell, op. cit.
1341. Id.
1342. U.S. Census, Mount Pleasant, Wayne County, Pennsylvania, 1820, Page 51.
1343. Id., 1830, Page 213.
1344. Id., 1840, Page 286.
1345. Id., 1850, Dwelling House 67, Family Number 72, Page 17.

Wealthy Howell died on 8 June 1857, and is buried at Mount Pleasant {1346}.

David Howell married Mary Gates as his second wife. She was born in 1802, and died in 1873 {1347}.

On 27 Jly 1860, David Howell, 65, with real property worth $100, and personal property worth $500, was enumerated as the head of a family consisting of himself, his wife, Mary, 65, and his daughter, Ellen, 17, residing in the Township of Mount Pleasant, Wayne County, Pennsylvania, in the Eighth Census of the United States {1348}.

David Howell died on 17 Feb 1878, and is buried beside his first wife at Mount Pleasant {1349}

David and Wealthy (Campbell) Howell were the parents of twelve children {1350}.

363.   i.   TERESIA LEAVINA[6] HOWELL, born on 8 Feb 1821.

+ 364.   ii.   DARIUS[6] HOWELL, born on 8 Oct 1823.

+ 365.   iii.   THADDEUS C.[6] HOWELL, born on 13 Apr 1824.

366.   iv.   ELI JOHN[6] HOWELL, born on 11 Aug 1825.

+ 367.   v.   SETH[6] HOWELL, born on 7 April 1827.

368.   vi.   ELIZABETH[6] HOWELL, born on 26 Nov 1828, married Calvin Peck, who was born in 1820, in Sep 1851.

369.   vii.   MARY ANN[6] HOWELL, born on 10 Aug 1830, married Hiram Buck in Jly 1852.

370.   x.   RHODA[6] HOWELL, born on 9 May 1832, married Oliver Peck, who was born in 1830, died on 31 Dec 1879.

+ 371. viii.   ALBERT[6] HOWELL, born on 8 Sep 1835.

372.   ix.   JANE A.[6] HOWELL, born on 5 Apr 1837, died on 16 Nov 1844, and is buried at Mount Pleasant.

373.   xi.   ESTHER M.[6] HOWELL, born on 27 Nov 1839, died on 3 Jan 1845, and is buried at Mount Pleasant.

1346. Craig R. Howell, op. cit.
1347. Id.
1348. U.S. Census, Mount Pleasant, Wayne County, PA, 1860, Dwelling House 1818, Page 391.
1349. Craig R. Howell, op. cit.
1350. Id.

374. xii.   ELLEN FLORETTE[6] HOWELL, born on 17 Aug 1844, married
Hiram Buck in Mch 1868.

135.   ELI[5] HOWELL (Eli[4]), the son of Eli[4] Howell, was born in Jly 1814
{1351}.

Eli Howell married Fannie E. McKinney, who was born on 5 Mch 1820
at Providence, Pennsylvania, the daughter of Daniel and Anna (Allen) McKinney
{1352}.

In the Sixth Census of the United States, 1840, Eli Howell was listed as
the head of a family consisting of one free white male of 20 and under 30 years of
age, one of under 5, one free white female of 20 and under 30, and one of under
5, residing in the Town of Manchester, Wayne County, Pennsylvania
{1353}.

On 9 Aug 1850, Eli Howell, laborer, 35, with real estate worth $100, was
listed as the head of a family consisting of himself, his wife, Fanny E., 30, and
their children, Mary A., 12, Daniel A., 9, Harriet A., 7, Wilber E., 4, and Sarah
E., 2, residing in the Town of Mount Pleasant, Wayne County, Pennsylvania, in
the Seventh Census of the United States {1354}.

On 28 June 1860, Eli Howell, farmer, 47, having real estate worth $250,
and personal property worth $140, was listed as the head of a family consisting of
himself, his wife, Fanny, 43, and their children, Amanda, 22, Daniel, 20, Harriet,
17, Wilber, 14, Emory, 6, and M. L., 2, residing in the Town of Lenox,
Susquehanna County, Pennsylvania, in the Eight Census of the United States
{1355}.

Eli Howell, farmer, 56, having real estate worth $1,000, and personal
property worth $450, was listed as the head of a family consisting of himself, his
wife, Fanny E., 50, their son, Emory, 16, and George Long, 45, a laborer, residing
in the Town of Mount Pleasant, Wayne County, Pennsylvania, in the Ninth Census
of the United States, on 18 Jly 1870 {1356}.

On 18 June 1880, Eli Howell, farmer, 65, was enumerated as the head of
a family consisting of himself, his wife, Fannie E., 60, and their grandson, Argus,
12, residing in the Town of Mount Pleasant, Wayne County, Pennsylvania, in
Tenth Census of the United States {1357}.

1351. Sliker, op. cit.
1352. Id.
1353. U.S.Census, Manchester, Wayne County, PA, 1840, Page 282.
1354. Id., Mount Pleasant, Wayne County, PA, 1850, Dwelling House 88, Family Number 95, Page
18.
1355. Id., Lenox, Susquehanna County, PA, 1860, Dwelling House 739, Family Number 740, Page
97.
1356. Id., Mount Pleasant, Wayne County, PA, 1870, Dwelling House 336, Family Number 339, Page
45.
1357. Id., 1880, Dwelling House 251, Family Number 261, Page 28.

Eli Howell died in 1902, and is buried at West Lenox, Pennsylvania {1358}.

Fannie E. Howell died on 21 Jan 1906 at Harford, Pennsylvania, and is buried beside her husband at West Lenox {1359}.

Eli and Fannie E. (McKinney) Howell were the parents of six children {1360}.

375.	i.	MARY AMANDA[6] HOWELL, born in about 1838.
376.	ii.	DANIEL[6] HOWELL, born in about 1840.
+ 377.	iii.	HARRIET ANN[6] HOWELL, born on 6 Apr 1843.
+ 378.	iv.	WILBUR E.[6] HOWELL, born in about 1846.
379.	v.	SARAH[6] HOWELL, born in about 1848.
+ 380.	vi.	EMORY A.[6] HOWELL, born in Aug 1854.

II. Descendants of David [2] Howell.

A. David [3], David [2], Richard [1]

136. DAVID[5] HOWELL (David[4]), the son of David[4] Howell {1361}, was born in 1776 {1362}.

David Howell married Elizabeth Mapes, who was born in 1790, the daughter of Nathan and Mary (Dains) Mapes {1363}.

By his will of 28 Dec 1846, proved on 7 Aug 1848, David Howell left their household furniture, a room of her choice in their house, and a space for a garden, to his beloved wife, Elizabeth. He left a "mountain farm" of about eighty two acres to his son, Abner, excepting a woodland of about five acres, which he left to his son, David V. Howell, to whom he also left his home farm of about sixty acres. He left his daughter, Lois Mariah Howell, a mountain lot of about seven acres, as well as money. His daughter, Frances Jane, was also bequeathed money, as were his four grandchildren, William H. Howell, Charles E. Howell and Phebe Ann Howell, the children of his deceased son, George Howell, and Elizabeth Kohnen, the daughter of Herman Kohnen, when the reached majority. He appointed Abner Howell and George W. Tuthill to be his Executors, and Lois Mariah Howell

---

1358. Sliker, op. cit.
1359. Id.
1360. Id.
1361. George Rogers Howell, op. cit., 322.
1362. THE FAMILY RECORD, op. cit., 146.
1363. Id., 71.

to be his Executrix {1364}.

David Howell died in 1848 {1365}.

On 31 Jly 1850, Elizabeth Howell, 67, with real property worth $4,500, was enumerated as the head of a family consisting of herself and her children, Louisa, 29, Francis J., 21, farmer (sic), and David V., 17, farmer, residing in the Town of Monroe, Orange County, New York, in the Seventh Census of the United States {1366}.

Elizabeth Howell died in 1857 {1367}.

David and Elizabeth (Mapes) Howell were the parents of ten children {1368}.

+ 381.   i.   ABNER[6] HOWELL, born in about 1812.

+ 382.   ii.   GEORGE[6] HOWELL, born in about 1815.

383.   iii.   LOIS MARIAH[6] HOWELL, born in about 1821, never married {1369}.

384.   iv.   SMITH[6] HOWELL, died young.

385.   v.   CHARLES[6] HOWELL, died young.

386.   vi.   ELIZABETH[6] HOWELL, married Herman Kohner, one child, Elizabeth, died before 28 Dec 1846 {1370}.

387.   vii.   JEFFERSON[6] HOWELL, died young.

388. viii.   FRANCES JANE[6] HOWELL, born in about 1829, married Sidney Edson {1371}.

389.   ix.   ALEXANDER[6] HOWELL, died young.

+ 390.   x.   DAVID VAN NESS[6] HOWELL, born in 1833 {1372}.

137. LOIS[5] HOWELL (David[4]), the daughter of David[4] Howell, was born on 17

1364. Orange County Wills, Liber O, 637-644.
1365. THE FAMILY RECORD, 146.
1366. U.S. Census, Monroe, Orange County, NY, 1850, Dwelling House 503, Family Number 503, Page 300.
1367. THE FAMILY RECORD, 146.
1368. Id.
1369. Id.
1370. Id.
1371. Id.
1372. Id.

Apr 1781 {1373}.

On 9 Feb 1798, Lois Howell married William Knap, Jr., who was born on 22 Feb 1776 {1374}.

In his will of 11 Sep 1823, proved on 24 Sep 1823, William Knapp, Jr., of Warwick, mentioned his wife, Lois, his brothers, John and Matthew, his nephews, William, the son of John Knapp, and William, the son of Matthew Knapp, and his niece, Lois Ann Ward {1375}.

William Knap, Jr., died on 17 Sep 1823 {1376}, or 17 Aug 1823, and is buried in the Old School Baptist Cemetery {1377}.

Lois Howell Knapp died on 26 Dec 1856, and is buried beside her husband {1378}.

William, Jr., and Lois (Howell) Knapp apparently had no children.

138. JOANNA[5] HOWELL (David[4]), the daughter of David[4] Howell, was born on 29 Mch 1783 {1379}.

Joanna Howell married (1) Edward Mapes {1380}.

Joanna Howell married (2) Crynes LaRue {1381}.

Crynes and Joanna (Howell) LaRue were the parents of at least one son {1382}.

    i.   WILLIAM H. LARUE, born on 30 Jly 1820, married (1) Eleanor A. Howell (#402), and (2) Jane E. Howell (#407), at least one son, died on 27 Jan 1897.

139. JAMES[5] HOWELL (David[4]), the son of David[4] Howell, was born on 4 Nov 1785 {1383}.

James Howell died on 27 Jan 1815, and is buried in the Howell burial plot in Sugar Loaf village {1384}.

David Howell, of Warwick, mentioned his grand-daughters, the two daughters of James Howell, although he did not name them, in his will of 26 Nov 1816, proved on 31 Mch 1830 {1385}.

1373. Ward Family Bible.
1374. Id.
1375. Orange County Wills, Liber G, 130; Abstracted in EARLY ORANGE COUNTY WILLS, 209.
1376. Ward Family Bible.
1377. Gertrude A. Barber, GRAVEYARD INSCRIPTIONS OF ORANGE COUNTY (GRAVEYARDS), 4, 4.
1378. Id.
1379. Stickney, HOWELL, Last page.
1380. Richard W. Hull, Personal communication.
1381. Stickney, op. cit.
1382. Id.
1383. CEMETERIES OF CHESTER, NEW YORK.., 84.
1384. Id., 84.
1385. Orange County Wills, Liber I, 97.

Deanna Howell, who was born in 1788, died at the age of 22 years, 10 months, and 22 days, and is buried beside James Howell {1386}.

On 4 Feb 1815, letters of administration on the estate of James Howell, of the Town of Monroe, were issued to his widow, Charity, his brother, Josiah, and his friend, John Brooks {1387}.

James Howell was the father of at least two children.

391.   i.   Daughter[6].

392.   ii.   Daughter[6].

140. JOSIAH[5] HOWELL (David[4]), the son of David[4] Howell, was born on 17 Apr 1788 {1388}.

Josiah Howell married Mary Ann Biggar {1389}, who was born on 2 Jly 1788 {1390}, the daughter of John Bigger {1391}.

Josiah Howell was among those to whom letters of administration on the estate of James Howell, late of the Town of Monroe, were issued on 4 Feb 1815 {1392}.

Josiah Howell was an executor of the will of his father, David Howell, written on 26 Nov 1816 and proved on 31 Mch 1830 {1393}.

Josiah Howell was listed as the head of a family consisting of one free white male of 26 and under 45 years of age, one of 10 and under 18, one of under 10, one free white female of 26 and under 45, one of 10 and under 16, and two of under 10, residing in the Town of Goshen, Orange County, New York, in the Fourth Census of the United States, 1820. Of these, one was engaged in agriculture {1394}.

Josiah Howell was a witness to the will of Vincent Wood, written on 4 Sep 1829 and proved on 19 Oct 1830 {1395}.

Josiah Howell was the first postmaster at Sugar Loaf, New York {1396}.

In 1830, Josiah and Mary Ann Howell moved their family to the Town of Chili, in Monroe County, New York, where he became a prosperous farmer {1397}.

1386. CEMETERIES OF CHESTER.., NEW YORK, 84.
1387. Orange County Letters of Administration, Liber D, 239.
1388. Linda S. Flesch, Personal communication.
1389. Id.
1390. Gravestone, North Chili Rural Cemetery, from a listing compiled by Richard T. Halsey, based on an earlier listing made by Mary T. Douglas, graciously supplied by Linda S. Flesch.
1391. Flesch, op. cit.
1392. Orange County Letters of Administration, Liber D, 239.
1393. Orange County Wills, Liber I, 97.
1394. U.S. Census, Goshen, Orange County, 1820, NY, Page 314.
1395. Orange County Wills, Liber I, 146; Abstracted in EARLY ORANGE COUNTY WILLS, 274.
1396. Richard W. Hull, SUGAR LOAF | NEW YORK | 1700-1997 | THE ENDURING VISION, 16.
1397. Flesch, op. cit.

By his will of 20 May 1844, proved on 18 Oct 1847, Josiah Howell left a farm of 327 acres to his son, Edmund W. Howell, whom he also named as his executor. To his son, Charles B. Howell, he left his property of about 220 acres in the Town of Riga. He left his home farm to his son, John Howell. His daughter, Eliza Woods, was to receive the interest on $1500, the principle of which was to go to his grandson, Josiah Howell Woods, after her death. To his daughters, Mary Ann Grunendike and Jane Jameson, he left equal shares of the farm known as the Dibble farm. To his daughter, Amelia Howell, he left securities in the value of $3000 {1398}.

Mary Ann Howell died on 30 Oct 1843, and is buried in the North Chile Rural, or Evergreen, Cemetery in Chili, New York {1399}.

Josiah Howell, of North Chile, Monroe County, New York, formerly of Sugar Loaf, Orange County, died on 27 Aug 1847 {1400} at the age of 59 years, 4 months and 9 days, and is buried beside his wife at Chili {1401}.

Josiah and Mary Ann (Biggar) Howell were the parents of eight children.

+ 393. i.   ELIZA[6] HOWELL, born in about 1811.

  394. ii.   HARRIET[6] HOWELL, born in about 1812, and died in about 1813 {1402}.

+ 395. iii.   MARY ANN[6] HOWELL, born on 27 Jly 1814 {1403}.

+ 396. iv.   EDMUND W.[6] HOWELL, born in 1817.

+ 397. v.   JANE[6] HOWELL, born on 17 Apr 1819 {1404}.

+ 398. vi.   AMELIA[6] HOWELL, born in about 1819 {1405}.

+ 399. vii.   CHARLES B.[6] HOWELL, born in about Nov 1821.

+ 400. viii.   JOHN[6] HOWELL, born in about 1828.

142. JOSEPH B.[5] HOWELL (David[4]), the son of David[4] Howell, was born on 28 May 1794 {1406}.

    Joseph B. Howell married Elizabeth J. Weeden, who was born on 26 May

---

1398. Monroe County Wills, Volume 4, 57-59.
1399. Gravestone, North Chili Rural Cemetery.
1400. GOSHEN INDEPENDENT REPUBLICAN, 10 Sep 1847, cited by Weller, op. cit.
1401. Gravestone, North Chili Rural Cemetery.
1402. Flesch, op. cit.
1403. Id.
1404. Personal Communication, John Jameson.
1405. Flesch, op. cit.
1406. Stickney, HOWELL, #675.

1797 {1407}.

Joseph B. Howell died at Sugar Loaf on 21 Aug 1845 {1408} at the age of 51 years, 2 months, and 23 days, and is buried in the Howell burial plot there {1409}.

Elizabeth J. Howell died on 30 June 1865, at the age of 68 years, 1 month and 4 days, and is buried beside her husband {1410}.

Joseph B. and Elizabeth J. (Weeden) Howell were the parents of nine children {1411}.

401. i.   JAMES H.[6] HOWELL, born on 9 May 1818.

+ 402. ii.   ELEANOR ANN[6] HOWELL, born on 13 Nov 1820.

403. iii. AMZI[6] HOWELL, born on 12 June 1823.

404. iv. THOMAS M.[6] HOWELL, born on 25 Sep 1825.

405. v.   EDWARD[6] HOWELL, born on 15 Nov 1827, died on 20 Dec 1829.

406. vi. DAVID[6] HOWELL, born on 7 Apr 1830, died on 12 Apr 1830.

+ 407. vii. JANE ELIZABETH[6] HOWELL, born on 1 Jly 1831.

408. viii. MARTHA LOUISA[6] HOWELL, born on 14 Jan 1833.

+ 409. ix. JOSEPH BENTON[6] HOWELL, born on 16 Feb 1838.

143. BOADICEA[5] HOWELL (David[4]), the daughter of David[4] Howell, was born on 28 Nov 1796 at Warwick {1412}.

Boadicea Howell married Thomas Ward, who was born in 1788 at Warwick {1413}.

Thomas Ward died on 9 Jan 1854 {1414}.

Boadicea Ward died on 21 Nov 1872 {1415}.

Thomas and Boadicea (Howell) Ward were the parents of eight children {1416}.

1407. Id., #675, Last page.
1408. GOSHEN INDEPENDENT REPUBLICAN, 29 Aug 1845 {750}.
1409. CEMETERIES OF CHESTER, NEW YORK.., 84.
1410. Id.
1411. Stickney, HOWELL, #675.
1412. Ward Family Bible, cited in THE QUARTERLY, OCGS, 6, #3, 17, 18.
1413. Id.
1414. Id.
1415. Id.
1416. Id.

i.   LOIS ANN WARD, born on 20 May 1819, married Philetus W. Demarest on 20 Sep 1838, four children. He was born on 11 Sep 18__.

ii.   WILLIAM HENRY WARD, born on 25 Oct 1820, married Clara Seely on 13 June 1855, five sons, died on 3 Sep 1898. She was born on 13 Mch 1831 and died on 14 Aug 1908.

iii.   MARY JANE WARD, born on 3 Aug 1822, married William B. Welling on 29 Dec 1841, two children. He was born on 12 Jly 1810 and died on 7 Nov 1754, while she died in 1890.

iv.   AMELIA WARD, born on 1 Aug 1825, married Andrew Jackson Jones, no children, died on 24 Dec 1874.

v.   EMILY WARD, born on 1 Aug 1825, married Francis Ellis on 17 (or 19) Dec 1850, four children, died on 22 Sep 1912.

vi.   BROWER COOPER WARD, born at Warwick on 13 Oct 1827, married Gertrude Horton.

vii.   HANNAH WARD, born on 23 May 1833, married William Rysdyk, two children, died 3 Jly 1894.

viii.   FRANCES WARD, born on 20 Jly 1836, died in early teens.

145. MILLICENT[5] HOWELL (John[4]), the daughter of John[4] and Sally (Dougherty) Howell, was born on 10 Jan 1775 {1417}, or 10 Jan 1776 {1418}.

Millicent Howell married Reuben Cash, the son of Daniel and Mary (Tracy) Cash, who was born on 23 Jan 1768 {1419}, or 15 Jan 1769 {1420}, and was a refugee from the Pennamite war in Wyoming, Pennsylvania {1421}. He and his mother escaped the Wyoming massacre of 1778, "..and she led him by the hand through the wilderness to Minisink, he being a small boy at the time." {1422}.

Reuben and Millicent (Howell) Cash "..lived and d. on the farm on the banks of Rutgers Creek..", owned, in 1915, by John Strahan, near Johnsons, New

1417. Stickney, HOWELL, #B83.
1418. Roswell Mead Family Bible, at the Historical Society of Middletown, cited in THE QUARTERLY, OCGS, 11, 28 (Feb 1982).
1419. ANCESTORS OF DR. JAMES CASH COLEMAN.., 12.
1420. Stickney, op. cit.
1421. Id.
1422. Stickney, MINISINK, 170.

York {1423}.

"Meale" was mentioned in the will of her father, John Howell, written on 27 Mch 1789, and proved on 11 Feb 1790 {1424}.

Reuben Cash purchased a gallery pew in the Old School Baptist Church for $30.50 {1425}.

Reuben Cash died on 6 June 1828, at the age of 59 {1426}, and is buried in the Stewartstown Cemetery, south of Ridgebury {1427}.

Millicent (Howell) Cash died on 3 Sep 1838 {1428}, at the age of 63 years, 7 months, and 23 days, and is buried beside her husband in the Stewartstown Cemetery {1429}.

Reuben and Millicent (Howell) Cash were the parents of nine children {1430}.

 i. SALLY CASH, born on 5 Apr 1794, married Samuel Vail, Sr., died on 7 Nov 1845, at the age of 51 years, 7 months, and 2 days, and is buried in the Stewartstown cemetery. Samuel Vail, who was born on 23 Sep 1787, and died on 6 Apr 1855, at the age of 67 years, 6 months, and 13 days, is buried beside his wife {1431}.

 ii. HANNAH CASH, born on 4 Nov 1796, married Roswell Mead, who was born on 15 Jly 1784, the son of Mathew and Phebe (Whelpley) Mead, on 8 Dec 1813 {1432}, or on 5 Dec 1813 {1433}, 6 children {1434}, died on 15 Apr 1868 {1435}.

 iii. FANNY CASH, born on 11 June 1799, married Parmenus Horton, who was born on 13 Dec 1795, the son of Barnabas and Milicent (Howell) Horton, on 16 Nov 1819, 5 children, died on 31 Mch 1838 {1436}.

 iv. MERITT H. CASH, born on 20 Jly 1802, married Hannah Davis on 27 Sep 1841 at the residence of her father, with the Rev. Ralph

---

1423. Id., HOWELL, #B83.
1424. Orange County Wills, Liber A, 82.
1425. OLD SCHOOL BAPTIST CHURCH, SLATE HILL, RECORDS, published in The QUARTERLY, OCGS, 6, #4, 26 (Feb 1977)).
1426. Roswell Mead Family Bible.
1427. Coulter, et al., op. cit., 65.
1428. Roswell Mead Family Bible.
1429. Coulter, et al., op. cit.
1430. Stickney, MINISINK, 170-171, Roswell Mead Family Bible.
1431. Coulter, et al., op. cit.
1432. ANCESTORS OF DR. JAMES CASH COLEMAN.., 10, 12.
1433. Roswell Mead Family Bible.
1434. Ruttenber & Clark, op. cit., 679.
1435. PORTRAIT AND BIOGRAPHICAL RECORD OF ORANGE COUNTY, 1126.
1436. George F. Horton, HORTON GENEALOGY, 118.

Bull presiding {1437}. She was born on 17 Feb 1821, the daughter of Joseph and Elizabeth Davis {1438}, and died on 5 Aug 1847, while he died on 26 Apr 1861 {1439}.

v.   JOHN MORRIS CASH, born on 11 Apr 1805, married Frances Gardner on 23 Jan 1839 {1440}, died on 5 May 1846 {1441}.

vi.   SELAH J. CASH, born on 18 Sep 1807, died on 19 Oct 1833 {1442}.

vii.   JAMES MADISON CASH, born on 1 Jan 1809, died on 29 Jan 1838 {1443}.

viii.   SOLOMON VAN RENSSELAER CASH, born on 20 May 1812, died on 29 May 1836 {1444}.

ix.   PHEBE MILLICENT CASH, born on 4 June 1815, married John Elmer Smith Gardner, died on 26 Aug 1875 {1445}.

146. SARAH[5] HOWELL (John[4]), the daughter of John[4] and Sarah (Dougherty) Howell, was born in about 1779.

"Sally, m. John Roberts, son of the widow Roberts..They lived and d. on the farm now (1914) owned by Ira Roberts a grandson near Johnson, N.Y.." {1446}.

"..Sally wife of John Roberts..died April 26, 1832 in her 54th year..", and is buried in the Stewartstown Cemetery {1447}.

"..John Roberts..died Dec 6, 1859 aged 85 years 5 months.", and is buried beside his wife in the Stewartstown Cemetery {1448}.

John and Sarah, "Sally", (Howell) Roberts were the parents of four

1437. MARRIAGES, WESTTOWN PRESBYTERIAN CHURCH, cited in THE QUARTERLY, OCGS, 16, #1, 5 (May 1986).
1438. Coulter, et al., op. cit.
1439. Roswell Mead Family Bible.
1440. PERSONS MARRIED BY ELDER GABRIEL CONKLIN, from HISTORICAL PAPERS, Warwick Historical Society, No. 2, Part Two, 1933. Reprinted in THE QUARTERLY, OCGS, 7, #4, 30 (Feb 1978), and in WARWICK HISTORICAL PAPERS, Vol. 2, 227.
1441. Roswell Mead Family Bible.
1442. Id.
1443. Id.
1444. Coulter, et al., op. cit.
1445. Id.
1446. Stickney, HOWELL, #B84.
1447. Coulter, et al., op. cit., 65.
1448. Id.

children {1449}.

    i.   ORPHA ROBERTS, born on 6 Feb 1803 {1450}, married John Elisha DuBois, of Westtown, N.Y., the son of Elisha and Elizabeth (Peck) DuBois, on 15 Nov 1827, three children {1451}, died on 13 Oct 1871, at the age of 68 years, 8 months, and 7 days, and is buried beside her husband in the Westtown Presbyterian Church Cemetery {1452}. He was born on 26 Jan 1803 in Warwick, and died on 18 Dec 1888 {1453}.

    ii.   ELIZA ANN ROBERTS, born on 21 Sep 1806, married Joseph Halstead, of Minisink, N.Y., 9 children, died on 22 Jan 1882. He was born on 18 Jan 1803, and died on 23 May 1878 {1454}.

    iii.   JOHN HOWELL ROBERTS, born on 28 June 1813, married Julia Ann Wells on 30 Apr 1836, at least three sons, died on 5 Jan 1889. She was born on 6 May 1820, and died in 1873 {1455}.

    iv.   JEFFREY JEFFERSON ROBERTS, born on 18 Dec 1816, died on 16 Jan 1882 {1456}.

147. JEFFREY[5] HOWELL (John[4]), the son of John[4] and Sarah (Dougherty) Howell, was born on 24 Aug 1780.

    "Jeffre Howell" was a principal heir of his father by his will of 27 Mch 1789, proved on 11 Feb 1790 {1457}.

    "Jeffrey, for his half of his father's lands took the farm now (1914) owned by Frances R. Stickney near Stewarttown. He d. there July 2, 1847, aged 46 years, 10 months and 9 days. Interred in Stewarttown cemetery. He m. Jemima, dau. of Peter Corwin. She d. in Ridgeberry, April 2, 1881. Buried in Stewarttown cemetery. She bequeathed the parsonage to the M.E. church in Ridgeberry. Had seven children all of whom died without children." {1458}.

    "Jeffrey married a daughter of Peter Corwin, Esq., and had seven children;

1449. Stickney, op. cit.
1450. CEMETERIES OF THE TOWN OF MINISINK, 115.
1451. Vivian DuBois Curtis, Personal communication, published in THE QUARTERLY, OCGS, 14, #4, 29 (Feb 1985).
1452. CEMETERIES OF THE TOWN OF MINISINK, 115.
1453. Curtis, op. cit.
1454. Hester Halstead Pier, op. cit.
1455. Ronald Lee Howell, Jr., HOWELL FAMILY ALBUM, 92.
1456. Id.
1457. Orange County Wills, Liber A, 82.
1458. Stickney, HOWELL, #B82.

but by a strange fatality, all died with the consumption before attaining the age of thirty-two years." {1459}.

"Jeffrey Howell died July 2, 1837 aged 46 years. 10 mo. 9 ds", and is buried in the Stewartstown Cemetery south of Ridgebury {1460}.

On 1 Aug 1850, Jemima Howell, 55, with real property worth $1,200, was enumerated as the head of a family consisting of herself and her son, J. Merritt Howell, 18, residing in the Town of Minisink, Orange County, New York, in the Seventh Census of the United States. David Morse, and David Morse, Jr., were residing in the same house {1461}.

Jemima Howell, 65, having real property worth $7000, and personal property worth $2500, was enumerated as the head of a household consisting of herself, her son, John M., 28, postmaster, and George Clawson, 24, teacher, residing in Wawayanda Township in Orange County, New York, in the Eighth Census of the United States, as recorded on 1 Sep 1860 {1462}.

By her will of 23 Mch 1875, proved on 10 June 1881, Jemima Howell left $300 "..for the general improvement of the Howells' Cemetery..in..the town of Waywanda..". She had given a claim of $5000 to her niece, Mary A. Scott, the wife of Rev. A.B. Scott, which she honored. She left most of her real property to the Methodist Episcopal Church in Ridgebury, and her personal property to her sisters, Azubah Carr, Lucetta Hulse, Mary Mullock, and her niece, Arminda Parsons. The remainder of her estate was to be converted into cash, and divided among her sisters, Azubah, the wife of David Carr, Lucetta, the widow of George Hulse, Mary, the wife of Lewis M. Mullock, and her deceased sister, Betsy's, children, i.e., Milton (?) Goble, Elizabeth Goble, Fanny Kelly, the wife of Charles Kelly, and Arminda Parsons, the wife of William Parsons. She reduced the share of her sister, Mary Mullock, and enhanced the share of her sister, Lucetta Hulse, by $200, which she justified by the "..straightened circumstances.." of Lucetta Hulse, and the generous gift of $500 to Mary A. Scott, the daughter of Mary Mullock. Her son-in-law, John M. Talmadge, and her husband's nephew, Erastus Stickney, were named executors of this will {1463}.

By a codicil to this will, dated 26 Apr 1876, Jemima Howell provided that a monument should be provided for her husband, Jeffrey Howell, herself, all their children, namely, Hiram, William, Jeffrey, Jr., Lewis, Sarah Jane, and John M. Howell, and Mary Ann Talmadge. Further, she willed that certain items of her household furniture be given to the Methodist Episcopal parsonage in Ridgebury. She also left $100 each to Francis and Hattie, daughters of Erastus Stickney. Finally, she willed that the rest of her estate be given to the four children of her deceased sister, Betsey Goble, and Lucetta Hulse {1464}. By another codicil,

1459. Id., MINISINK, 170.
1460. Coulter, et. al., op. cit., 66.
1461. U.S.Census, Minisink, Orange County, NY, 1850, Dwelling House 358, Family Number 368, Page 236.
1462. Id., 1860, Dwelling House 2111, Family Number 2370, Page 311.
1463. Orange County Wills, Liber 43, 427ff.
1464. Id., 430-431.

dated 29 Jly 1878, she revoked the provision of this codicil regarding the erection of the monument, since that had been done, and directed that the funds willed for that purpose be divided among her specified heirs {1465}. By yet another codicil, of 18 Oct 1879, she withdrew the appointment of John M. Talmadge as an executor, and replaced him with Franklin B. Ellis {1466}.

"Jemima wife of Jeffrey Howell died April 2, 1881 aged 87 yrs. 22 ds.", and is buried beside her husband in the Stewartstown Cemetery {1467}.

Jeffrey and Jemima (Corwin) Howell were the parents of seven children.

410.   i.   HIRAM[6] HOWELL, born on 15 Sep 1816, died on 24 May 1840, at the age of 23 years, 8 months, and 9 days, and is buried in the Stewartstown Cemetery {1468}.

+ 411.   ii.   MARY ANN[6] HOWELL, born on 5 Aug 1818.

412.   iii.   WILLIAM[6] HOWELL, born on 18 Aug 1820, died on 22 Feb 1843, aged 22 years, 6 months and 4 days, buried in the Stewartstown Cemetery {1469}.

413.   iv.   SARAH JANE[6] HOWELL, born on 10 Aug 1821, died on 14 Mch 1841, aged 19 years, 7 months and 4 days, buried in the Stewartstown Cemetery {1470}.

414.   v.   JEFFREY[6] HOWELL, born on 14 Aug 1822, died on 7 Mch 1847, aged 24 years, 6 months and 21 days, and is buried in the family plot in the Stewartstown Cemetery {1471}.

415.   vi.   LEWIS[6] HOWELL, born on 20 May 1826, died on 22 Mch 1843, aged 16 years, 10 months and 2 days, and is buried in the family plot in the Stewartstown Cemetery {1472}.

416.   vii.   JOHN MERITT[6] HOWELL, born on 10 Oct 1831, died on 19 Sep 1863, aged 31 years, 11 months and 9 days, and is buried in the family plot in the Stewartstown Cemetery {1473}.

148. PHEBE[5] HOWELL (John[4]), the daughter of John[4] and Sarah (Dougherty) Howell, was born in about 1782.

1465. Id., 431-432.
1466. Id., 432-433.
1467. Coulter, et al., op. cit., 66.
1468. Id.
1469. Id.
1470. Id.
1471. Id.
1472. Id.
1473. Id.

"Phebe, m. Eliphalet Stickney, a son of Dr. James and Mary (Belknap) Stickney, of Newburgh, N.Y. They removed to Wayne Co., near Lyons, N.Y., where they lived and d." He was born on 20 Aug 1778 {1474}.

"Eliphalet..married Phebe Howell, who resided near Ridgebury, Orange county, New York. For some time he engaged in teaching school in an academy in Chester, New York, and then removed to Lyons, Wayne county, New York, where he and his wife spent their remaining days." {1475}.

On 30 Nov 1850, "Eliphalet Stigney", farmer, 70, with real property worth $2,800, was listed as the head of a household consisting of himself, his wife, Phebe, 68, their sons, John, 36, and Benjamin, 26, both farmers, John's wife, Elizabeth, 28, and Ellen, 5, and Hannah, 2, the daughters of John and Elizabeth, as well as George Carr, 17, farmer, residing in Lyons Township, Wayne County, New York, in the Seventh Census of the United States {1476}.

Eliphalet Stickney died on 31 Aug 1858, and is buried in the Lyons Rural Cemetery at Lyons, New York {1477}.

Phebe (Howell) Stickney died on 16 June 1861, at the age of 79, and is buried beside her husband at Lyons, New York {1478}.

Eliphalet and Phebe (Howell) Stickney were the parents of six children {1479}.

    i.   ERASTUS STICKNEY, born on 4 May 1810 in the Township of Waywanda, Orange County, NY, married Lucy R. Allen, of Sullivan County, the daughter of Prentice Allen, in 1836, five children, including Charles E. Stickney, was elected to the state legislature in 1856, served from 1846 to 1879 as a Justice of the Peace, died near Stewartstown, N.Y. Lucy R. Stickney died in 1857 {1480}.

    ii.   JOHN STICKNEY, born in about 1814, resided in Arcadia Township, Wayne County, New York, on 26 Jly 1860, at least six children {1481}.

    iii.   JULIA ANN STICKNEY, born 1819, died 1907, married Garret Brink Mapes, who was born in 1817, and died in 1895, both buried in the Stewartstown Cemetery {1482}. They were

1474. Stickney, HOWELL, #B85.
1475. BIOGRAPHICAL AND GENEALOGICAL HISTORY, 743.
1476. U.S.Census, Lyons, Wayne County, NY, 1850, Dwelling House 525, Family Number 535, Page 75.
1477. Gravestone, Lyons Rural Cemetery, courtesy of Deborah Ferrell, assistant to Marjory Allen Perez, Historian, Wayne County, NY (1995).
1478. Id.
1479. PORTRAIT & BIOGRAPHICAL RECORD OF ORANGE COUNTY, 785-786.
1480. BIOGRAPHICAL AND GENEALOGICAL HISTORY, 743.
1481. U.S.Census, Arcadia, Wayne County, NY, 1860, Dwelling House 913, Family Number 988, Page 13.
1482. Coulter, et al., op. cit., 65.

the parents of two children {1483}.

iv.   CHARLES STICKNEY, born in about 1821, married Mary E.
      Barker, of Vienna, N.Y., in 1845 {1484}, at least two
      sons. She died on 3 Aug 1857, at the age of 26, and is buried in
      the Lyons Rural Cemetery {1485}, while he died on 2 Aug
      1881, at the age of 60, and is buried beside his wife at Lyons
      {1486}.

v.   BENJAMIN M. STICKNEY, born in Nov 1825, married Carrie
      Hosford {1487}, at least two daughters, died at Sodus,
      N.Y., on 2 Feb 1890 {1488}, and is buried in the Sodus
      Rural Cemetery {1489}.

vi.   MARY STICKNEY, married a Mr. Cunningham, died in
      Michigan.

149. JOHN[5] HOWELL (John[4]), the son of John[4] and Sarah (Dougherty) Howell,
was born in about 1784.

On 26 Jan 1833, John Howell married Mrs. Ann Knapp, with Elder
Gabriel Conklin, pastor of the Old School Baptist Church from Mch 1832 to Sep
1846, presiding {1490}.

"John Howell, Jr., married the widow of Moses Knapp, and sister of
Alanson Kimball, Esq., but she was accidently drowned, while crossing the outlet
of Binnewater pond, near Pine Ridge, in search of herbs for some medicinal
purpose, June 24, 1834; having been married scarce a year.." {1491}.

"John and his brother, Jeffrey divided their father's lands according to his
will. John took the farm now (1914) owned by the heirs of Erastus Stickney, and
lived and d. there, Feb. 20, 1867. He m. Sally, widow of Moses Knapp, whose
maiden name was Kimball, d. July 24, 1834, one year after marriage, was drowned
in Indigot creek near Johnson, N.Y. while crossing it to gather herbs."
{1492}.

"Mrs. Howell.., we understand, left her home about the middle of the day,
for the purpose of procuring articles for family beer, and it appears, in attempting

1483. THE FAMILY RECORD, 118.
1484. WESTERN ARGUS, 28 May 1845.
1485. Gravestone, Lyons Rural Cemetery.
1486. Id.
1487. Obituary, NEWARK UNION GAZETTE, 17 June 1923.
1488. WAYNE COUNTY ALLIANCE, 5 Feb 1890.
1489. Gravestone, Sodus Rural Cemetery.
1490. PERSONS MARRIED BY ELDER GABRIEL CONKLIN, THE QUARTERLY, OCGS, 7, #4,
29 (Feb 1978), WARWICK HIST. PAPERS, 224.
1491. Stickney, MINISINK, 170.
1492. Stickney, HOWELL, #B81.

to walk, over a large brook, she must have lost her balance and precipitated in the stream below, in which she was found the following evening, drowned, in less than four feet of water." {1493}.

"Anna, wife of John Howell, died May 19, 1834, in the 39th year of her age", and is buried in the Stewartstown Cemetery {1494}.

On 1 Aug 1850, John Howell, 60, farmer, with real estate worth $6,500, was enumerated as the head of a household consisting of himself and his sister, "Hipsiba", 52, residing in the Town of Minisink, Orange County, New York, in the Seventh Census of the United States {1495}.

"John Howell died Feb. 20, 1867 in the 83rd year of his age", and is buried beside his wife in the Stewartstown Cemetery {1496}.

John and Anna (Kimball) Knapp Howell had no children {1497}.

150. BENJAMIN[5] HOWELL (John[4]) was the son of John[4] and Sarah (Dougherty) Howell {1498}.

Benjamin Howell learned the trade of wagon making, as requested by the will of his father, plying the trade at a shop in Ridgebury, New York {1499}.

Benjamin Howell removed to New York.

152. BENJAMIN[5] HOWELL (George[4]), the son of George[4] and Eunice (Horton) Howell, was born on 1 Oct 1776, probably in the Town of Warwick, Orange County, New York {1500}.

Benjamin Howell married Jane Moffat, who was born in about 1780 {1501}.

"Benjamin Howell settled with his family (in Aurora, Illinois) in 1839. He and his wife lived to be more than eighty years of age: both are now deceased. They were the parents of I. M. Howell, Dr. O. D. Howell and William Howell, all at one time citizens of Aurora." {1502}.

On 16 Nov 1850, Benjamin Howell, 74, carpenter, with real estate valued at $500, and his wife, Jane, 70, were residing in Aurora, Illinois, as enumerated in

1493. MINISINK SENTINEL, quoted in the NEWBURGH GAZETTE, 31 May 1834.
1494. Coulter, et al., op. cit., 66.
1495. U.S. Census, Minisink, Orange County, NY, 1850, Dwelling House 391, Family Number 400, Page 238.
1496. Coulter, et al., op. cit., 66.
1497. Stickney, HOWELL, #B81.
1498. Id., #B62.
1499. Id., #B86.
1500. Finch, op. cit., 7.
1501. Id.
1502. COMMEMORATIVE BIOGRAPHICAL AND HISTORICAL RECORD OF KANE COUNTY, ILLINOIS, 940.

the Seventh Census of the United States {1503}.

Benjamin Howell died on 27 Aug 1858, at Aurora, Illinois {1504}. His remains were re-buried in the Spring Lake Cemetery there on 26 Nov 1917 {1505}.

Jane Howell died on 13 Nov 1859, and is re-buried beside her husband in the Spring Lake Cemetery {1506}.

Benjamin and Jane (Moffat) Howell were the parents of at least three children {1507}.

+ 417. i.   WILLIAM M.[6] HOWELL, born in about 1814.

+ 418. ii.   ORRIN DAY[6] HOWELL, born on 18 May 1818.

+ 419. iii. ISAAC M.[6] HOWELL, born in about 1821.

153. LUCINDA[5] HOWELL (George[4]), the daughter of George[4] and Eunice (Horton) Howell, was born on 11 Dec 1778, probably in the Town of Warwick, in Orange County, New York {1508}.

Lucinda Howell married Robert Alexander, of Genoa, Cayuga County, New York, on 9 Apr 1805, as his second wife. He was born on 7 Oct 1766. His first wife was Charlott Norris, who died in 1803 {1509}.

Robert Alexander, Sr., died on 12 Aug 1837, at Alexander's Corners, in the Town of Newfield, Tompkins County, New York {1510}.

Lucinda (Howell) Alexander died on 20 Aug 1859.

Robert and Lucinda (Howell) Alexander were the parents of seven children {1511}.

     i.   GEORGE L. ALEXANDER, born on 9 Oct 1809, married Amelia Van Buskirk, 6 children, died on 26 Oct 1883. Amelia (Van Buskirk) Alexander died on 16 Oct 1889.

    ii.   FANNY ALEXANDER, born in about 1811, married Ransom Hinkley, died on 30 Mch 1836, at the age of 24 years. He died in 1842, aged 35 years.

   iii.   JOHN ALEXANDER, born in about 1813, married Sarah Ann Mead, at least one son, Charles.

1503. U.S.Census, Aurora, Kane County, IL, 1850, Dwelling House 74 (3074?), Family Number 290, Page 208.
1504. Finch, op. cit., 7.
1505. RECORDS FROM EARLY AURORA CEMETERIES.., 77.
1506. Id.
1507. COMM. BIO. & HIST. REC..KANE COUNTY.., 940.
1508. Finch, op. cit., 7.
1509. Id.
1510. Id.
1511. Id.

iv. SALLY ANN ALEXANDER, born in about 1814, married Charles Gillet.

v. CHARLOTTE ALEXANDER, born on 24 Jan 1817, married James Madison Knettles, died 15 Jly 1885, at the age of 68 years, 5 months, and 21 days. He died on 22 May 1884, at the age of 69 years and 9 days.

vi. JEREMIAH ALEXANDER, born on 30 Dec 1818, married Mary Jane McCorn, died on 10 Jan 1866, at the age of 47 years and 11 days. She died on 22 May 1899, at the age of 80 years, 10 months, and 17 days.

vii. ELIZA ANN ALEXANDER, born in about 1822, married David Brooks, died on 12 Sep 1892, and is buried in the Alexander Corners cemetery.

Robert and Charlott (Norris) Alexander were the parents of four children.

(i) RACHEL ALEXANDER, born in about 1796, married Jonah Tooker.

(ii) JOSEPH ALEXANDER, born in about 1799.

(iii) HANNAH ALEXANDER, born in about 1801, married Lewis Townley.

(iv) ROBERT ALEXANDER, JR., born in about 1803, married Christine Snyder.

154. SALLY[5] HOWELL (George[4]), the daughter of George[4] and Eunice (Horton) Howell, was born on 27 Sep 1781, probably in the Town of Warwick, Orange County, New York {1512}.

Sally Howell married Ardon Kingsbury, who was born on 9 Oct 1779, the son of Williard Kingsbury {1513}.

Sally (Howell) Kingsbury died on 25 Dec 1851, and is buried at Elmira, New York {1514}.

Ardon and Sally (Howell) Kingsbury were the parents of at least eight children {1515}.

i. GEORGE KINGSBURY, born in about 1804, married Elizabeth Bancroft, 6 children, died in about 1852. She died in 1881 at the

---

1512. Finch, op. cit., 7.
1513. Id.
1514. Id.
1515. Id.

age of 68 years.

    ii.   PHILO KINGSBURY, born on 31 Jly 1804, died on 11 Apr 1826, at the age of 21 years, 8 months, and 11 days, and is buried at Hector, New York.

    iii.   HORACE KINGSBURY, born in about 1807, married Catherine Coates, at least one child, Sarah.

    iv.   HENRY F. KINGSBURY, born in about 1808.

    v.   LUCINDA KINGSBURY, born on 13 Dec 1812, did not marry, died on 2 Jly 1877.

    vi.   LUCIUS KINGSBURY, born in about 1817.

    vii.   MARY ANN KINGSBURY, born on 10 Jan 1823, died on 9 Mch 1823, at the age of 1 month, and 27 days, and is buried at Hector, New York.

    viii.   OLIVER COMSTOCK KINGSBURY, born on 5 Mch 1827 at Hector, New York, married Mary Ann Chapman, the daughter of Elihu Chapman, 3 children, died on 14 May 1903, at Watkins, New York.

155. MEHITABLE[5] HOWELL (George[4]), the daughter of George[4] and Eunice (Horton) Howell, was born on 24 Aug 1783, probably in the Town of Warwick, Orange County, New York {1516}.

    Mehitable Howell married William Mapes {1517}.

    Mehitable (Howell) Mapes died on 21 Aug 1841 at Hector, New York, and is buried there {1518}.

    William and Mehitable (Howell) Mapes were the parents of at least two children {1519}.

    i.   EUNICE MAPES, born on 14 Mch 1808, died on 23 Feb 1842, at the age of 33 years, 11 months, and 9 days, and is buried beside her mother at Hector.

    ii.   JOHN MAPES, born in about 1835, died in 1841, at the age of 6, and is buried beside his mother at Hector.

1516. Id., 7.
1517. Id.
1518. Id.
1519. Id.

157. ANNA[5] HOWELL (George[4]), the daughter of George[4] and Eunice (Horton) Howell, was born on 21 Sep 1787, probably in the Town of Warwick, Orange County, New York {1520}.

Anna Howell married Lemuel Ferris, ths son of Ahasuerus Ferris, of Genoa, Cayuga County, New York {1521}.

Anna Ferris was living with her son, George, in Genoa, when the Seventh Census of the United States was taken in 1850 {1522}.

In 1851, "aunt Ann ferris on a visit here" at the home of her brother, Jeremiah Howell {1523}.

Lemuel and Anna (Howell) Ferris were the parents of at least one son.

   i.   GEORGE FERRIS, born in about 1822 {1524}.

158. JEMIMA[5] HOWELL (George[4]), the daughter of George[4] and Eunice (Horton) Howell, was born on 6 Apr 1790, probably in the Town of Warwick, Orange County, New York {1525}.

Jemima Howell married David Farlin {1526}.

David Farlin died on 26 Aug 1827 {1527}.

Jemima (Howell) Farlin died on 15 May 1828 {1528}.

David and Jemima (Howell) Farlin were the parents of eight children {1529}.

   i.   HARRIET NEWELL FARLIN, born in about 1812, married Reuben Swift Smith, died before 1839.

   ii.   CHANCY PORTER FARLIN, born on 12 Feb 1814, married Clarinda ---, died before 1884.

   iii.   WILLIAM HOWELL FARLIN, born on 16 Feb 1816, married Mary Melvina Bruster on 6 Feb 1840, 3 children, died on 9 Feb 1895. Mary Melvina, the daughter of Clark and Phebe (Matthews) Bruster, was born on 24 Aug 1820, and died on 11 Mch 1888.

   iv.   SARAH ANN FARLIN, born in about 1818, married Reuben Swift Smith, died in about 1842 {1530}.

1520. Id., 6.
1521. Id., 6, 8.
1522. Id., 8.
1523. Id.
1524. Id.
1525. Id., 8.
1526. Id.
1527. Id.
1528. Id.
1529. Id.
1530. Id., 9.

v.   DAVID VOLNEY FARLIN, born on 12 Feb 1820 in Chautauqua County, New York, married Mary ---, at least 1 child, died on 6 Jly 1875 at Logan (Hector), New York {1531}.

vi.   ELIZA V. FARLIN, born on 15 Feb 1822, died before 1912 {1532}.

vii.   LAURA M. FARLIN, born on 27 Jly 1824, married Mr. Jackson, of Bennetsburg, died in about 1912 {1533}.

viii.   GEORGE LUCIAN FARLIN, born on 7 Oct 1826 {1534}.

160. JEREMIAH[5] HOWELL (George[4]), the son of George[4] and Eunice (Horton) Howell, was born on 4 Dec 1793 {1535}.
   Jeremiah Howell married Asenath Everts in about 1817 {1536}.

"Soon after his marriage Jeremiah Howell bought land in Covert, Seneca County. However there is no record showing he ever lived there. In 1825 he removed from Hector to West Hill, between Elmira & Big Flats in Chemung Co. then in Tioga Co., N.Y.

West Hill is the name locally used for the part nearest to Elmira of a group of hills whose three corners are Elmira to the southeast, Horseheads to the north and Big Flats to the northwest with the Chemung River on the south. In 1852 when the Rhea and Tremble wall map of Chemung County was made, the highest part was designated as Hawes Hill. This at a later time was the site of Harris Hill Glider Field, Harris being the name of an early settler there. West Hill is not as high as Harris Hill and overlooks Elmira rather Big Flats and the Chemung River. In 1822 this area became part of the town of Big Flats when that town was set off from Elmira.

Jeremiah Howell's house on West Hill was probably built about 1825. It was smaller than his father's house in Hector but styled much the same, the larger part having its gable and toward the road and a low story and half wing built at right angles to the larger two story part of the house; an architectural style often used at this time in central N.Y.

The members of Jeremiah's family attended the Presbyterian Church in Elmira.

1531. Id.
1532. Id.
1533. Id.
1534. Id.
1535. Id., 12.
1536. Id.

A record of the texts of sermons heard there and notations of relatives who visited Jeremiah Howell's hospitable home on West Hill are to be found in a diary kept from 1849 through 1854 by Sarah a daughter who later married Artemus Mills of West Hill." {1537}.

On 25 Oct 1850, Jeremiah Howell, 56, farmer, with real property worth $4000, was enumerated as the head of a family consisting of himself, his wife, "Asnatha", 54, and their children, Ann, 28, "Everett", 24, Sarah, 22, Clarissa, 20, Eunice, 17, and Luther, 15, residing in the Town of Big Flats, Chemung County, New York, in the Seventh Census of the United States {1538}.

Jeremiah Howell died on 15 Dec 1851 on West Hill, Elmira, New York, where he was buried, although his stone, and that of his wife, were removed to the Woodlawn Cemetery in Elmira {1539}.

Asenath (Everts) Howell died in 1854 {1540}.

Jeremiah and Asenath (Everts) Howell were the parents of nine children {1541}.

+ 420. i. SIDNEY BURKE[6] HOWELL, born on 7 Dec 1818 in Hector.

421. ii. HANNAH ANN[6] HOWELL, born on 18 Dec 1820, died unmarried on 13 Feb 1885, lived with various relatives after the West Hill house was sold, an exacting woman with a talent for design, was the owner of a Paisley shawl treasured by Jessie Howell Finch {1542}.

+ 422. iii. MARY[6] HOWELL, born on 30 Sep 1823 in Hector.

+ 423. iv. DANIEL EVERTS[6] HOWELL, born on 25 Dec 1825 in Big Flats.

+ 424. v. SARAH[6] HOWELL, born on 30 Oct 1827.

425. vi. CLARISSA AGARD[6] HOWELL, born on 7 Jly 1830, died in Middletown, New York, unmarried, on 24 Nov 1884, attended Miss Thurston's Seminary in Elmira, had a talent for composition and writing {1543}.

+ 426. vii. EUNICE ELIZA[6] HOWELL, born on 12 Dec 1832.

1537. Id.
1538. U.S. Census, Big Flats, Chemung County, NY, 1850, Dwelling House 241 (2201?), Family Number 241 (2213?), Pages 142-143.
1539. Finch, op. cit., 12.
1540. Id.
1541. Id.
1542. Id., 13.
1543. Id.

+ 427. viii.   LUTHER CLARK[6] HOWELL, born on 25 Feb 1835.

  428. ix.   MARTHA BENNETT[6] HOWELL, born on 2 Mch 1837, died on 25 Nov 1846, aged 9 years.

161. HANNAH[5] HOWELL (George[4]), the daughter of George[4] and Eunice (Horton) Howell, was born on 31 Aug 1796 in Delaware County, New York {1544}.

    Hannah Howell married (1) Elijah Webster, and (2) Elihu Chapman as his second wife. He was born on 17 Oct 1796 in Otsego County, N.Y. {1545}.

    Elihu Chapman died on 13 Feb 1866 {1546}.

    Hannah (Howell) Webster Chapman died on 29 Mch 1869, and is buried at Elmira {1547}.

    Elihu and Hannah (Howell) Webster Chapman were the parents of two children {1548}.

      i.   GEORGE CHAPMAN, born in about 1832, married Philinda Rockwell, at least one son, Isaac, died in about 1905.

      ii.   HENRIETTA CHAPMAN, married (1) Abbott Barber, at least one son, Adalaski.

Elihu and Phoebe (?) (Stocum) Chapman were the parents of six children {1549}.

      i.   ORRIN CHAPMAN, born in about 1817, married Mary Chandler Mills, the daughter of Silas and Phoebe Mills, four children, died on 23 Jan 1894 at Big Flats. His wife was born on 20 Aug 1820, and died on 21 Dec 1898.

      ii.   HANNAH CHAPMAN, married Ambrose B. Lockwood, at least four children, died before 1866.

      iii.   PHOEBE CHAPMAN, married S. Palmer Buckbee, two sons.

      iv.   SAMUEL A. CHAPMAN, born 22 Jly 1824, married Mary Howell (#422), the daughter of Jeremiah (#160) Howell.

      v.   SEELEY PERRY CHAPMAN, born on 8 June 1826, married Sarah C. Kingsbury, the daughter of Horace and Catherine Coates Kingsbury, four children, died on 23 Oct 1912. His wife was born

1544. Id., 9.
1545. Id.
1546. Id.
1547. Id.
1548. Id., 10.
1549. Id., 9, 10.

on 5 Nov 1836, and died on 9 Oct 1896.

vi. MARY ANN CHAPMAN, born in about 1829, married Oliver Comstock Kingsbury, at least three children, died in about 1925.

162. GEORGE[5] HOWELL (George[4]), the son of George[4] and Eunice (Horton) Howell, was born on 7 Feb 1802, at about the time his father moved from Delaware County to Cayuga County, before settling at Hector, N.Y. {1550}.

George Howell married Sally Durland, the daughter of Robert Durland. They lived on the Howell homestead at Logan in Hector {1551}.

Sally (Durland) Howell died on 25 Mch 1874, at the age of 78 {1552}.

George Howell died at Logan on 24 Jan 1880 {1553}.

George and Sally (Durland) Howell were the parents of four children {1554}.

+ 429. i. ROBERT D.[6] HOWELL, born in about 1824.

+ 430. ii. EMMA MIRANDA[6] HOWELL, born on 6 Jan 1830.

+ 431. iii. GEORGE OLIVER[6] HOWELL, born on 3 Aug 1834.

+ 432. iv. HARRIET[6] HOWELL, born in about 1840.

164. SAMUEL[5] HOWELL (George[4]), the son of George[4] and Eunice (Horton) Howell, was born on 7 Jly 1810 {1555}.

Samuel Howell married (1) Delilah Brown, who was born in about 1816 in Tompkins County, New York {1556}. He married (2) Urania (Rena) Saxton, who was born in about 1828 in Tompkins County {1557}.

On 2 Sep 1850, Samuel H. Howell, 40, farmer, with real property worth $1200, was enumerated as the head of a family consisting of his wife, Delilah, 34, and their children, Mandana, 16, John B., 14, Eliza Ann, 11, Elizabeth, 6, Emma, 2, and Delilah, 2 months, residing in the Town of Barton, Tioga County, New York, in the Seventh Census of the United States {1558}.

Delilah Howell died on 18 Mch 1861, AE 45, and is buried in the North

1550. Id., 11.
1551. Id.
1552. Id.
1553. Id.
1554. Id.
1555. Id., 7.
1556. New York State Census, Barton, Tioga County, 1855.
1557. Id., 1865.
1558. U.S. Census, Barton, Tioga County, NY, 1850, Dwelling House 465, Family Number 471, Page 31.

Barton Cemetery {1559}.

Samuel Howell died on 1 June 1886, AE 76, and is buried beside his wife in the North Barton Cemetery {1560}.

Samuel H. and Delilah (Brown) Howell were the parents of eight children.

+ 433. i.   MANDANA[6] HOWELL, born on 22 June 1834.

434. ii.   JOHN B.[6] HOWELL, born in about 1836.

435. iii. ELIZA ANN[6] HOWELL, born in about 1839.

436. iv.   ELIZABETH[6] HOWELL, born in about 1844, died on 25 Oct 1862, AE 18, and is buried beside her parents {1561}.

437. v.   EMMA D.[6] HOWELL, born in about 1848.

438. vi.   DELILAH[6] HOWELL, born in about July 1850.

+ 439. vii. CHRISTINA C.[6] HOWELL, born on 18 Jly 1850 {1562}.

440. viii. GEORGE W.[6] HOWELL, born in 1855, died on 23 June 1856, AE 9 months, and is buried in the family plot at the North Barton Cemetery {1563}.

NOTE: *It seems likely that Delilah Howell and Christine Howell were either twins, or the same person. In her obituary {1564}, "Miss Howell", who married Mr. Shipman, was stated to have been the youngest daughter of Samuel Howell. Also, while "Delilah Howell" was listed in the Seventh Census of the United States, 1850, she was not listed in the 1855 Census of New York State, nor in the 1865 Census.*

165. JAMES[5] HOWELL (Benjamin[4]), the son of Benjamin[4] and Sarah (Webster) Howell {1565}, was born on 9 Mch 1785.

In 1813, James Howell was a resident of District No. 4, the Ridgebury District, in the Town of Wawayanda, Orange County, New York {1566}.

James Howell and his wife sold a farm, about one mile south of Ridgebury,

1559. Gravestone, North Barton Cemetery, from a listing in the possession of the Tioga County Historical Society, 1996.
1560. Id.
1561. Gravestone, North Barton Cemetery.
1562. Patricia Shipman, Personal communication.
1563. Gravestone, North Barton Cemetery.
1564. OWEGO GAZETTE, 7 Nov 1912.
1565. Stickney, HOWELL, #B69.
1566. Ruttenber & Clark, op. cit., 682.

New York, to Samuel Bailey, in 1829 {1567}.

James Howell moved with his family to Steuben County, New York {1568}.

On 1 Aug 1850, James Howel, 66, farmer, was enumerated as the head of household consisting of himself, his wife, Ann, 56, His son, Mordeca, 28, farmer, his son's wife, Welthy, 19, and their daughter, Matilda, 1, residing in the Town of Hartsville, Steuben County, New York, in the Seventh Census of the United States {1569}.

James Howell died on 16 Aug 1853, at the age of 68 years, 5 months and 7 days, and is buried in the Hartsville Cemetery {1570}.

Ann Howell died on 27 Oct 1865, and is buried beside her husband {1571}.

James and Ann Howell were the probably the parents of at least one son.

+ 441.   i.   MORDECA[6] HOWELL, born in about 1822.

166. GEORGE W.[5] HOWELL (Benjamin[4]) was the son of Benjamin[4] and Sarah (Webster) Howell, was born in 1786 {1572}.

George W. Howell married Fanny Dunning {1573}, who was born in 1793 {1574}. They lived in Goshen, N.Y. {1575}.

George W. Howell was listed as the head of a family consisting of one free white male of 26 and under 45 years of age, one free white female of 26 and under 45, and three of under 10, residing in the Town of Goshen, Orange County, New York, in the Fourth Census of the United States, 1820 {1576}.

Frances, the wife of George W. Howell, joined the First Presbyterian Church at Goshen, New York, on 4 Aug 1820 {1577}. George W. Howell joined the same church on 4 Nov 1820 {1578}. He was baptized on the following day, 5 Nov 1820 {1579}.

George W. Howell, the Keeper of the Orange County Poorhouse, died on 24 Feb 1845 at the age of 58 {1580}, and is buried in the Slate Hill

---

1567. Stickney, op. cit.
1568. Id.
1569. U.S. Census, Hartsville, Steuben County, NY, 1850, Dwelling House 114, Family Number 117, Page 173.
1570. Gravestone, Hartsville Cemetery, also known as the Comfort-Cline Cemetery, from a collection on LDS microfilm #1479820.
1571. Id.
1572. Barber, GRAVEYARDS, 4, 65.
1573. Finch, op. cit., 4.
1574. Barber, GRAVEYARDS, 4, 65.
1575. Stickney, HOWELL, #B73.
1576. U.S. Census, Goshen, Orange County, NY, 1820, Page 328.
1577. Coleman, op. cit., 62.
1578. Id., 63.
1579. Id., 134.
1580. GOSHEN INDEPENDENT REPUBLICAN, 28 Feb 1845, from Weller, op. cit.

Cemetery {1581}.

Fanny Howell died in 1865, and is buried beside her husband at Slate Hill {1582}.

George W. and Frances (Dunning) Howell were the parents of at least six children.

442. i. FRANCES EVALINA[6] HOWELL, baptized at Goshen on 3 Nov 1821 {1583}.

443. ii. JANE DUNNING[6] HOWELL, baptized at Goshen on 3 Nov 1821 {1584}.

444. iii. JEROMUS[6] HOWELL, baptized at Goshen on 3 Nov 1821 {1585}.

445. iv. SARAH[6] HOWELL, baptized at Goshen on 31 Jly 1824 {1586}.

446. v. ANN MARIA[6] HOWELL, baptized at Goshen on 4 Aug 1827 {1587}.

+ 447. vi. GEORGE[6] HOWELL, baptized at Goshen on 1 Aug 1829 {1588}.

167. BENJAMIN[5] HOWELL (Benjamin[4]) was the son of Benjamin[4] and Sarah (Webster) Howell.

Benjamin Howell moved to New York City {1589}.

168. JOHN[5] HOWELL (Benjamin[4]), the son of Benjamin[4] and Sarah (Webster) Howell, was born in about 1794.

John Howell married Rebecca Ann Clausen, who was born in about 1803. They lived in Goshen, N.Y. {1590}.

John Howell was a land owner at Goshen, "..part of the time with his brother Daniel. As to place of residence, in a deed from Gilbert Jackson and wife, May 5, 1817, conveying lands along the road from the Goshen Court House

1581. Barber, op. cit.
1582. Id.
1583. Coleman, op. cit., 135.
1584. Id.
1585. Id.
1586. Id., 136.
1587. Id., 137.
1588. Id., 138.
1589. Finch, op. cit., 4.
1590. Stickney, HOWELL, #B71.

southerly it is mentioned "by the lands of Major John Howell, dec., near the Episcopal church," " {1591}.

On 25 Nov 1850, "John Howel", 56, shoe merchant, was enumerated as the head of a family consisting of himself, his wife, Rebecca A., 47, and their son, John E., 21, student, residing in the Town of Goshen, Orange County, New York, in the Seventh Census of the United States {1592}.

John Howell, 63, died at Goshen on 8 Jly 1856 {1593}.

John Howell, his wife, Rebecca Ann, and their children, Emily A. and John E. Howell, are all buried in the Slate Hill Cemetery, but no dates are given on their monument {1594}.

John and Rebecca Ann (Clausen) Howell were the parents of at least two children {1595}.

448.   i.   EMILY AUGUSTA[6] HOWELL, born in about 1822, baptized on 6 Aug 1831, died on 31 May 1839 of "Hydrocephalis" at the age of 17 {1596}.

+ 449.   ii.   JOHN E.[6] HOWELL, born in about 1829, baptized on 6 Aug 1831.

169. DANIEL[5] HOWELL (Benjamin[4]) was the son of Benjamin[4] and Sarah (Webster) Howell.

Daniel Howell married Rhoda Ross {1597}.

Daniel Howell "..went to Goshen, N.Y., where the records show him to have been a landowner as late as 1825. In that year he and his wife Rhoda sold to John Howell lands in Belvale {1598}. He then went to New York city." {1599}.

170. CHAUNCEY G.[5] HOWELL (Benjamin[4]) was the son of Benjamin[4] and Sarah (Webster) Howell.

Chauncey Howell moved to Erie County, New York {1600}.

1591. Id.
1592. U.S. Census, Goshen, Orange County, NY, 1850, Dwelling House 411, Family Number 429, Page 182.
1593. GOSHEN INDEPENDENT REPUBLICAN, 11 Jly 1856, from Weller, op. cit.
1594. Barber, GRAVEYARDS, 4, 80.
1595. Coleman, op. cit., 139.
1596. Id., 97.
1597. Finch, op. cit., 4.
1598. Orange County Deeds, Liber Z, 221.
1599. Stickney, HOWELL, #B70.
1600. Id., #B74.

172. HENRY[5] HOWELL (Benjamin[4]) was the son of Benjamin[4] Howell {1601}.

Henry Howell joined the Ridgebury Presbyterian Church on 7 Oct 1820 {1602}.

On 5 May 1841, Henry Howell was a witness, with Isaac Talmadge, to the marriage of Wm. S. Parrot and Miss Doxey {1603}.

Henry D. Howell married Mary Wood in Oct 1841, with Elder Gabriel Conklin officiating {1604}.

In 31 Oct 1846, Henry D. Howell joined the Ridgebury Presbyterian Church {1605}.

Henry Howell went to Illinois {1606}.

173. PRESTON W.[5] HOWELL (Benjamin[4]), the son of Benjamin[4] and Eleanor (Webb) Howell, was born in 1811 {1607}.

On 22 Apr 1839, Preston W. Howell married Jane Dunning {1608}, the daughter of Daniel and Jemima (Hallock) Dunning, of Ridgebury, New York {1609}.

Preston W. Howell joined the church at Ridgebury on 14 Oct 1842 {1610}.

On 15 Nov 1849, "Preston Howell & Lady" were witnesses at the marriage of "Nathaniel Cary of Chemung & Miss Fanny Mills" {1611}.

On 29 Jly 1850, Preston Howell, 39, farmer, with real estate worth $2,000, was enumerated as the head of a family consisting of himself, his wife, Phebe, 35, and their children, Margaret, 9, Sarah, 7, Ann, 4, Fanny, 2, and Allen, 1, residing in the Town of Minisink, Orange County, New York, in the Seventh Census of the United States, 1850 {1612}.

In 1858, P.W. Howell moved to Muscatine County, Iowa, where he became a farmer on Section 21 {1613}.

Preston W. Howell, 48, farmer, having real estate valued at $700, and personal property valued at $100, was listed as the head of a family consisting of

1601. Stickney, HOWELL, #B75.
1602. Coulter, et al., op. cit., 6.
1603. Id., 25.
1604. HISTORICAL PAPERS, WARWICK, NEW YORK, #2, Part 2, reprinted by OCGS as WARWICK HISTORICAL PAPERS, 2, 229.
1605. Coulter, et al., op. cit., 12.
1606. Stickney, op. cit.
1607. THE HISTORY OF MUSCATINE COUNTY, IOWA, 627, cited in THE QUARTERLY, OCGS, 15, #1, 8 (May 1985).
1608. Coulter, et al., op. cit., 24.
1609. Stickney, HOWELL, #B77.
1610. Coulter, et al., op. cit., 12.
1611. Id., 26.
1612. U.S. Census, Minisink, Orange County, NY, 1850, Dwelling House 218, Family Number 220, Page 228.
1613. HISTORY..MUSCATINE COUNTY, IOWA, 627.

his wife, Phebe J., 44, and their daughters, Eleanor A., 17, teacher (of music?), Ann A., 14, and Fanny M., 11, all of whom were born in New York, residing in Bloomington Township, Muscatine County, Iowa, in the Eighth Census of the United States, 1860 {1614}.

Preston W. and Phebe (?) Jane (Dunning) Howell were the parents of eight children.

450. i.   MARGARET[6] HOWELL, born in about 1841.

451. ii.   SARAH EMILY[6] HOWELL, born in about 1843, died at Windsor, N.Y. on 23 Mch 1853, AE 10 {1615}.

452. iii. ELEANOR[6] HOWELL, born in about 1843.

453. iv. MARY[6] HOWELL, born on 20 May 1844, died on 29 Dec 1847, at the age of 3 years, 7 months and 9 days, and is buried in the Ridgebury Cemetery {1616}.

454. v.   ANN A.[6] HOWELL, born in about 1846.

455. vi.   FANNY M.[6] HOWELL, born in about 1848.

456. vii. ELLEN[6] HOWELL, born in about 1849.

457. viii. Child[6], died at 2 months and 20 days, and is buried at Ridgebury {1617}.

176. JOHN[5] HOWELL (Ezra[4]), the son of Ezra[4] and Jane (Chatfield) Howell, was born on 14 Feb 1792 {1618}.

John Howell married Polly Cooley and lived in Blooming Grove, N.Y. {1619}.

177. HUNTTING[5] HOWELL (Ezra[4]), the son of Ezra[4] and Jane (Chatfield) Howell, was born on 6 June 1794 {1620}.

On 9 Aug 1850, "Hunting M. Howel", 55, farmer, with real property worth $5000, was enumerated as the head of a family considering of himself and

1614. U.S. Census, Bloomington, Muscatine County, IA, 1860, Dwelling House 463, Family Number 479, Page 71.
1615. GOSHEN DEMOCRAT, 8 Apr 1853, from Weller, op. cit.
1616. Coulter, et al., op. cit., 39.
1617. Id.
1618. Stickney, HOWELL, #B66.
1619. Id.
1620. Stickney, HOWELL, #B58.

his children, Levi, 20, Juliaett, 17, Cornelia, 12, and Alonzo, 5, residing in the Town of Sterling, Cayuga County, New York, in the Seventh Census of the United States {1621}. His son, Thomas B., 31, farmer, and his wife, Hannah, 23, were residing in the same house {1622}, while his son, Ezra, 27, farmer, was residing with his family in the next house {1623}.

Huntting M. Howell died in about 1876 in Cayuga County, New York {1624}.

Huntting M. Howell was the father of at least six children.

+ 458. i. THOMAS B.[6] HOWELL, born in about 1819.

+ 459. ii. EZRA[6] HOWELL, born in about 1823.

460. iii. LEVI[6] HOWELL, born in about 1830.

461. iv. JULIAETT[6] HOWELL, born in about 1833.

462. v. CORNELIA[6] HOWELL, born in about 1838.

463. vi. ALONZO[6] HOWELL, born in about 1845.

178. HANNAH[5] HOWELL (Ezra[4]), the daughter of Ezra[4] and Jane (Chatfield) Howell, was born on 30 Sep 1796 {1625}.

Hannah Howell married Benjamin Wise {1626}.

180. COE SAYER[5] HOWELL (Ezra[4]), the son of Ezra[4] and Jane (Chatfield) Howell, was born on 24 Mch 1800 {1627}.

On 30 Nov 1838, Coe Sayer Howell married Frances Amelia Stewart, who was born on 9 Aug 1812, the daughter of John and Elizabeth (Bradner) Stewart {1628}.

On 15 Aug 1850, Coe S. Howell, 50, farmer, with real property worth $3,000, was enumerated as the head of a family including himself, his wife, Fannie A., 35, and their children, Anna E., 10, Susan, 7, Emily, 5, Nathan, 3, and Isabell, 1, residing in Town of Blooming Grove, Orange County, New York, in the

---

1621. U.S. Census, Sterling, Cayuga County, NY, 1850, Dwelling House 67, Family Number 68, Page 180.

1622. Id., Family Number 69, Page 180.

1623. Id., Dwelling House 66, Family Number 67, Page 180.

1624. Finch, op. cit., 5.

1625. Stickney, HOWELL, #B58.

1626. Stickney, HOWELL, #B66$^{1}/_{2}$.

1627. Id., #B67$^{1}/_{2}$.

1628. Id.

Seventh Census of the United States, 1850 {1629}.

Coe S. Howell, 60, farmer, was enumerated as the head of a family consisting of himself, his wife, Frances S., 47, and their children, Anna E., 20, Sarah J., 17, Eliza S., 15, Nathan S., 13, and James B. (sic), 11, and residing in Blooming Grove, Orange County, New York, in the Eighth Census of the United States, as recorded on 11 June 1860 {1630}.

Coe S. Howell had a farm of 154 acres in Blooming Grove in 1871 {1631}.

By his will of 22 May 1874, proved on 20 Nov 1890, Coe S. Howell left, to his "..beloved wife Frances A. Howell one equal third part of all.." his personal estate. He left his daughter, Ann Eliza S. Howell, two equal ninth parts of his personal estate. He made a similar bequest to his daughter, Isabella B. Howell. His executors were directed to sell the rest of his personal estate and invest the proceeds for the benefit of Emily S. Stedman, the wife of James Stedman, and her children. He willed that his property in Passaic, New Jersey, be sold, and the proceeds divided between his wife, and his daughters, Ann Eliza S., and Isabella B., in the same proportions as directed for his personal estate. He directed that, if either of these daughters should die before his decease, her share would be divided among her survivors. If she had no survivors, her share would be divided between her sisters and, should any sister be deceased, among that sister's survivors. He left the rest of his estate to his son, Nathan S. Howell, who was named executor of this will, along with his sister, Ann Eliza S. Howell {1632}.

On 21 June 1880, Coe S. Howell, 79, farmer, was enumerated as the head of a household consisting of himself, his wife, Frances, 67, their children, Ann E., 39, and Nathan, 33, their daughter, Emily Steadman, and her children, Belle, 12, James, 10, Harry, 8, and Alice, 2, residing in the Town of Blooming Grove, Orange County, New York, in the Tenth Census of the United States {1633}.

Coe Sayer Howell died on 27 Oct 1890 {1634}, and is buried in the Washingtonville Cemetery {1635}.

By her will of 12 June 1891, proved on 4 Jan 1898, Frances S. Howell divided her property between her son, Nathan S. Howell, and her daughter, Ann Eliza S. Howell, naming them executor and executrix, and explaining that she had not left anything to her other two children, Isabella B. Gardner and Emily S. Stedman, "..for the reason that they.." were "..comfortably provided for in life {1636}.

1629. U.S. Census, Blooming Grove, Orange County, NY, 1850, Dwelling House 24, Family Number 24, Page 320.

1630. Id., 1860, Dwelling House 210, Family Number 216, Page 32.

1631. Orange County Directory, 1871, 121.

1632. Orange County Wills, Liber 54, 215-219.

1633. U.S. Census, Blooming Grove, Orange County, NY, 1880, Enumeration District 1, Family Number 258, Page 33.

1634. Stickney, op. cit.

1635. Gravestone, Washingtonville Cemetery, from the markings copied by Elizabeth Horton and in the possession of the OCGS.

1636. Orange County Wills, Liber 64, 155-158.

Frances A. (Stewart) Howell died on 29 Nov 1897 {1637}, and is buried beside her husband at Washingtonville {1638}.

Coe Sayer and Frances A. (Stewart) Howell were the parents of six children {1639}.

464. i.   ANNA ELIZA⁶ HOWELL, born on 11 Sep 1839 {1640}, died on 12 Sep 1915, and is buried at Washingtonville {1641}.

465. ii.   JOANNA⁶ HOWELL.

466. iii. SARAH JANE⁶ HOWELL, born on 23 Oct 1843, died on 28 Sep 1865 {1642}, and is buried at Washingtonville {1643}.

+ 467. iv. EMILY SAUNDERS⁶ HOWELL, born on 21 Jan 1845 {1644}.

468. v.   NATHAN S.⁶ HOWELL, born on 31 Jan 1847 {1645}, died in 1931, and is buried at Washingtonville {1646}.

+ 469. vi. ISABELLA BORLAND⁶ HOWELL, born on 14 Mch 1849 {1647}.

182. ASA R.⁵ HOWELL (Ezra⁴), the son of Ezra⁴ and Jane (Chatfield) Howell, was born on 8 Mar 1805 {1648}.

Asa R. Howell was licensed as a physician by the Orange County Medical Society in 1826 {1649}.

Asa R. Howell was a physician at Cornwall, New York {1650}, and, later, at Elmira, New York, and St. Louis, Missouri {1651}.

"Dr. A.R. Howell..contracted a fever while acting as a surgeon in the army, near St. Louis I think in '61 or '2, returned to his home in the far west, and

1637. Stickney, op. cit.
1638. Gravestone, Washingtonville Cemetery.
1639. Finch, op. cit., 5.
1640. Ronald L. Stewart, Personal communication.
1641. Gravestone, Washingtonville Cemetery.
1642. Ronald L. Stewart, op. cit.
1643. Gravestone, Washingtonville Cemetery.
1644. Ronald L. Stewart, op. cit.
1645. Id.
1646. Gravestone, Washingtonville Cemetery.
1647. Ronald L. Stewart, op. cit.
1648. Stickney, HOWELL, #B58.
1649. Headley, op. cit., 578.
1650. Stickney, HOWELL, #B66¹/₄.
1651. Finch, op. cit., 5.

died soon after." {1652}.

Asa R. Howell "..died "in the west"; his widow & a dau. Mrs. Blackburn with a dau. Jessie returned to Elmira after his death." {1653}.

Asa R. Howell was the father of at least one child.

470.   i.   Daughter[6].

183. JULIET[5] HOWELL (Ezra[4]), the daughter of Ezra[4] and Jane (Chatfield) Howell, was born on 7 May 1807 {1654}.

Juliet Howell married Harvey Howell {1655}.

186. THOMAS CHATFIELD[5] HOWELL (Ezra[4]), the son of Ezra[4] and Jane (Chatfield) Howell, was born on 18 Jly 1813 {1656}.

On 1 Feb 1843 {1657}, Thomas Chatfield Howell married Mary Bradner Tuthill, who was born on 31 Dec 1818, the daughter of Phineas Tuthill {1658}.

Thomas Howell, 37, farmer, with real estate worth $6,000, was enumerated as the head of a family consisting of himself, his wife, Mary F., 32, and their children, Julie, 6, Frank, 5, and Mary J., 2, and Lucretia Howell, 60, and residing in the Town of Warwick, Orange County, New York, in the Seventh Census of the United States, 1850 {1659}.

Thomas C. Howell had a farm of 130 acres in Blooming Grove in 1871 {1660}

By his will of 30 Mch 1882, proved on 7 May 1891, Thomas C. Howell, of the Town of Blooming Grove, left all his household furniture to his wife, Mary K. Howell, and the remainder of his estate to his son, A. Malcolm Howell, who was also named as executor of this will. By the will, A. Malcolm Howell was directed to pay each of his two brothers, Job T. Howell and Thomas Scott Howell, $200 one year after their father's decease, and $750 to each of his sisters, Mary Jane Howell and Harriet E. Howell, at the same time. He was also to provide his sisters a home until they married {1661}.

Thomas Chatfield Howell died on 20 June 1890 {1662}, and is

1652. Coe S. Howell, Letter of 10 Mch 1867 to Sidney B. Howell, from a copy at the OCGS.
1653. Finch, op. cit.
1654. Stickney, HOWELL, #B58.
1655. Id., #B66³/₄.
1656. Id., #B58.
1657. Tuttle, op. cit., 412.
1658. Stickney, HOWELL, #B68¹/₄.
1659. U.S. Census, Warwick, Orange County, NY, 1850, Dwelling House 23, Family Number 23, Page 53.
1660. Orange County Directory, 1871, 122.
1661. Orange County Wills, Liber 54, 437-440.
1662. Finch, op. cit., 5.

buried in the Washingtonville Cemetery {1663}.

Mary Howell died on 20 Sep 1902 {1664}, and is buried beside her husband {1665}.

Thomas Chatfield and Mary Bradner (Tuthill) Howell may have been the parents of at least seven children {1666}.

471. i. JULIETTE[6] HOWELL, born on 26 Aug 1844, died on 10 Jly 1892, and is buried in the Washingtonville Cemetery {1667}.

472. ii. ASA MALCOLM[6] HOWELL, born on 28 Oct 1845, died in 1929.

473. iii. FRANK[6] HOWELL, born in about 1845.

474. iv. HARRIET E.[6] HOWELL, born on 19 Dec 1851, died unmarried on 12 Apr 1939.

475. v. MARY JANE[6] HOWELL, born on 28 Dec 1847.

+ 476. vi. JOB TUTHILL[6] HOWELL, born on 19 Mch 1853.

477. vii. THOMAS SCOTT[6] HOWELL, born on 24 Oct 1855, died unmarried on 5 Sep 1926.

187. CADWALADER[5] HOWELL (Noble[4]), the son of Noble[4] and Tabitha (Mapes) Howell, was born on 20 Jly 1793 {1668}.

Cadwalader Howell married Catherine Wood {1669}, who was born in about 1791.

On 22 Oct 1850, Cadwalader Howell, 50, farmer, with real property worth $11,850, was enumerated as the head of a household consisting of himself, his wife, Catherine, 45, their sons, Chauncy, 25, and George, 22, artist, and Harriet Collier, 20, and Laura Bostwick, 11, residing in the Town of Ogden, Monroe County, New York, in the Seventh Census of the United States {1670}.

Cadwallader and Catherine Howell moved to Illinois in 1860 {1671}.

Cadwalader Howell, 68, and his wife, Catherine, 69, were enumerated in

1663. Gravestone, Washingtonville Cemetery.
1664, Tuttle, op. cit., 412.
1665. Gravestone, Washingtonville Cemetery.
1666. Tuttle, op. cit., 412.
1667. Gravestone, Washingtonville Cemetery.
1668. Stickney, HOWELL, #B63.
1669. PORTRAIT AND BIOGRAPHICAL RECORD OF HENRY COUNTY, ILLINOIS, 208.
1670. U.S. Census, Ogden, Monroe County, NY, 1850, Dwelling House 156, Family Number 165, Page 92.
1671. PORTRAIT & BIOGRAPHICAL RECORD OF HENRY COUNTY.., 208.

the household of their son, George Howell, 31, farmer, in the Town of Clover, Henry County, Illinois, in the Eighth Census of the United States, 1860 {1672}.

Catherine Howell died in 1869 {1673}, while "Cadwalader Howell, a soldier of the War of 1812, died in Goshen, April 20, 1877, aged 86 years." {1674}.

Cadwalader and Catherine (Wood) Howell were the parents of four children.

+ 478. i. THOMAS JACKSON[6] HOWELL, born on 7 May 1823 {1675}.

+ 479. ii. CHAUNCY[6] HOWELL, born in about 1825.

+ 480. iii. GEORGE[6] HOWELL, born in about 1829, removed to Illinois with the family, was a large man and a railroader, was killed on the railroad {1676}.

+ 481. iv. ELIZABETH[6] HOWELL {1677}, born in about 1833.

188. HANNAH[5] HOWELL (Noble[4]), the daughter of Noble[4] and Tabitha (Mapes) Howell, was born on 2 Jan 1795 {1678}.

Hannah Howell married David McWhorter {1679}.

189. MARY[5] HOWELL (Noble[4]), the daughter of Noble[4] and Tabitha (Mapes) Howell, was born on 10 Feb 1797 {1680}.

Mary Howell married James J. Hallock {1681} in 1818. He was the son of Deacon Jonathan Hallock, and was born in Haverstraw, New York {1682} on 21 Nov 1795.

On 26 Aug 1845, James J. Hallock was issued letters of administration on the estate of Joseph B. Howell (#142), of the Town of Chester {1683}.

1672. U.S. Census, Clover, Henry County, IL, 1860, Dwelling House 2910, Family Number 2795, Page 920.
1673. PORTRAIT & BIOGRAPHICAL RECORD OF HENRY COUNTY.., 208.
1674. Michael A. Leeson, DOCUMENTS AND BIOGRAPHY PERTAINING TO THE SETTLEMENT AND PROGRESS OF STARK COUNTY, ILLINOIS, 553.
1675. PORTRAIT & BIOGRAPHICAL RECORD OF HENRY COUNTY.., 208.
1676. Predmore, op. cit.
1677. Finch, op. cit., 5.
1678. Stickney, HOWELL, #B63.
1679. Finch, op. cit., 5.
1680. Stickney, HOWELL, #B63.
1681. Stickney, HOWELL, #B91.
1682. Lucius H. Hallock, op. cit., 392.
1683. Orange County Letters of Administration, Liber G, 341.

On 7 Oct 1850, James J. Hallock, 53, farmer, was enumerated as the hea of a household consisting of himself and his children, Fanny, 32, William, 2 farmer, Mary, 22, George, 18, farmer, John, 15, farmer, and Caroline, 9, residin in the Town of Chester, Orange County, New York, in the Seventh Census of th United States {1684}.

James J. Hallock died on 7 Apr 1854, at the age of 58 years, 4 months an 17 days, and is buried in the family burying ground on the west side of Sugar Loa Mountain Road {1685}.

Mary (Howell) Hallock died on 25 May 1882, and is buried beside her husband {1686}.

James J. and Mary (Howell) Hallock were the parents of eight children {1687}.

   i.   FANNIE HALLOCK, born in about 1818.

   ii.   ELBERT HALLOCK, born on 6 Sep 1819, married Maria Bartholof in 1845, eight children, died in Jly 1897. She was born on 17 Jly 1825 and died on 8 Mch 1865 {1688}.

   iii. DANIEL HALLOCK.

   iv.   WILLIAM HALLOCK, born in about 1824.

   v.   MARY HALLOCK, born on 6 Sep 1828, died on 10 Aug 1861, at the age of 32 years, 11 months and 4 days, and is buried in the same burying ground as her parents {1689}.

   vi.   JAMES HALLOCK, born in about 1830.

   vii. GEORGE HALLOCK, born in about 1832.

   viii. JOHN HALLOCK, born in about 1835, was a Captain in the U.S. Army, where he was killed.

   ix.   CAROLINE HALLOCK, born in about 1841.

190. ELBERT[5] (or ALBERT) HOWELL (Noble[4]), the son of Noble[4] and Tabitha

---

1684. U.S. Census, Chester, Orange County, NY, 1850, Dwelling House 1637, Family Number 1647, Page 172.
1685. CEMETERIES OF CHESTER, NEW YORK, 86.
1686. Id.
1687. Lucius H. Hallock, op. cit., 392.
1688. Id., 254.
1689. CEMETERIES OF CHESTER, NEW YORK, 86.

(Mapes) Howell, was born on 8 Oct 1798 {1690}.

Elbert Howell married Jemima Smith {1691}.

Elbert and Jemima (Smith) Howell were the parents of six children {1692}.

+ 482.　i.　ELIZABETH[6] HOWELL, born on 23 Aug 1823.

+ 483.　ii.　PHEBE ANN[6] HOWELL, born on 21 Oct 1824.

  484.　iii.　CHARLES[6] HOWELL.

  485.　iv.　BON[6] HOWELL (?).

+ 486.　v.　SARAH J.[6] HOWELL, born on 9 Aug 1829.

+ 487.　vi.　COE[6] HOWELL.

191. FANNY[5] HOWELL (Noble[4]), the daughter of Noble[4] and Tabitha (Mapes) Howell, was born on 6 Dec 1800 {1693}.

On 7 Oct 1850, Fanny Howell, 40, was enumerated as a member of the household of her brother, Peter, in the Town of Chester, Orange County, New York, in the Seventh Census of the United States {1694}.

By her will of 22 Nov 1858, proved on 20 June 1881, Fanny Howell left her estate to her brother, Peter. Her friend, James B. Stevens was named executor of this will {1695}.

Fanny Howell died on 6 Feb 1881, and is buried in the Howell-Hallock burying ground on the west side of Sugar Loaf Mountain Road {1696}.

192. COE[5] HOWELL (Noble[4]), the son of Noble[4] and Tabitha (Mapes) Howell, was born in about 1803.

Coe Howell married Jemima Ann Demarest, who was born in about 1809, the daughter of James and Anna Demarest of Warwick {1697}.

On 1 Oct 1850, Coe Howell, 45, laborer, was enumerated as the head of a family consisting of himself, his wife, Minnie A, 40, and Sarah J., 7, residing in the Town of Chester, Orange County, New York, in the Seventh Census of the

1690. Stickney, HOWELL, #B63.
1691. Id., #B93.
1692. Id.
1693. Id., #B63.
1694. U.S.Census, Chester, Orange County, NY, 1850, Dwelling House 1610, Family Number 1620, Page 170.
1695. Orange County Wills, Liber 43, 442-444.
1696. CEMETERIES OF CHESTER, NEW YORK, 86.
1697. Orange County Deeds, Liber 80, 131-133.

United States, 1850 {1698}.

"Mina Ann", the wife of Coe Howell, died on 28 Dec 1880, at the age of 72 years, and is buried in the family burying ground on the west side of Sugar Loaf Mountain Road {1699}.

By his will of 3 Jan 1881, proved on 3 Apr 1882, Coe Howell left all his estate to his sister, Jane King, and appointed his "..trusty friend James B. Stevens sole executor.." {1700}.

Coe Howell died on 28 Dec 1881, at the age of 79 years, and is buried beside his wife {1701}.

Coe and Mimi (Demarest) Howell did not have any children {1702}.

193. PETER[5] HOWELL (Noble[4]), the son of Noble[4] and Tabitha (Mapes) Howell, was born on 26 Nov 1807 {1703}.

On 7 Oct 1850, Peter Howell, 30, farmer, was enumerated as the head of a household consisting of himself, his mother, "Tabithy", 74, his sisters, Fanny, 40, and Jane, 37, and Joshua Valentine, 10, residing in the Town of Chester, Orange County, New York, in the Seventh Census of the United States {1704}.

Peter Howell was the sole heir of his sister, Fanny, as given in her will of 22 Nov 1858, proved on 20 June 1881 {1705}.

Peter Howell had a farm of 77 acres in Sugar Loaf in 1871 {1706}.

Peter Howell died on 6 Apr 1871, at the age of 63 years and 7 months, and is buried in the family burying ground on the west side of Sugar Loaf Mountain Road {1707}.

194. JANE[5] HOWELL (Noble[4]), the daughter of Noble[4] and Tabitha (Mapes) Howell, was born on 25 Feb 1809 {1708}.

Jane Howell married George King {1709} on 11 Oct 1854 at the First Presbyterian Church in Monroe, New York, before the Rev. D. N. Freeland

1698. U.S. Census, Chester, Orange County, NY, 1850, Dwelling House 1558, Family Number 1568, Page 166.
1699. CEMETERIES OF CHESTER, NEW YORK, 86.
1700. Orange County Wills, Liber 44, 350-353.
1701. CEMETERIES OF CHESTER, NEW YORK, 86.
1702. Finch, op. cit.
1703. Stickney, op. cit.
1704. U.S. Census, Chester, Orange County, NY, Dwelling House 1610, Family Number 1620, Page 170.
1705. Orange County Wills, Liber 43, 442-444.
1706. Orange County Directory, 1871, 122.
1707. CEMETERIES OF CHESTER, NEW YORK, 86.
1708. Stickney, op. cit.
1709. Id., #B90.

{1710}. George King was the son of Joseph and Sarah Ann (Gray) King, of Round Lake, N.Y. {1711}.

George King died on 21 Apr 1870, at the age of 66 years, and is buried in the Monroe cemetery {1712}.

Jane King died on 7 Feb 1895, at the age of 86 years, and is buried beside her husband at Monroe {1713}.

George and Jane (Howell) King were the parents of one daughter {1714}.

    i.   LOUISA KING, married Samuel Holbert.

195. JOHN[5] HOWELL (Noble[4]), the son of Noble[4] and Tabitha (Mapes) Howell was born on 21 Oct 1813 {1715}.

John Howell married Sarah Adams, of Wantage Township, in Sussex County, New Jersey. They removed to Virginia {1716}.

196. LYDIA[5] HOWELL (Noble[4]), the daughter of Noble[4] and Tabitha (Mapes) Howell, was born on 14 Aug 1817 {1717}.

Lydia Howell married Peter Demarest {1718}.

Lydia (Howell) Demarest died on 11 Aug 1875 {1719}.

B. Aaron[3], David[2], Richard[1]

198. AARON[5] HOWELL (Isaiah[4]), the son of Isaiah[4] and Sarah Howell, was born in 1769 {1720}.

Aaron Howell married Sarah Drake {1721}.

Aaron Howell died in 1844 {1722}.

Aaron and Sarah (Drake) Howell were the parents of five children {1723}.

1710. Mrs. C. Arthur Brooks, HISTORY OF THE FIRST PRESBYTERIAN CHURCH, MONROE, NEW YORK, 186.

1711. Predmore, op. cit.

1712. Barber, GRAVEYARDS, 2, 55.

1713. Id.

1714. Predmore, op. cit.

1715. Stickney, HOWELL, #B63.

1716. Id., #B88$^1/_2$.

1717. Id., #B63.

1718. Id., #B87$^1/_2$.

1719. Id.

1720. Marjorie (Mrs. William W.) Sederlund, Personal communication, cited in The QUARTERLY, OCGS, 3, #4, 26 (Feb 1974).

1721. Id.

1722. Id.

1723. Id.

488. i. JESSE[6] HOWELL, married Miss Durland.

489. ii. MARY[6] HOWELL, married Mr. Clark.

490. iii. MARGARET[6] HOWELL, married Mr. Tuthill.

491. iv. AARON[6] HOWELL, married Miss Elsten.

492. v. ELIZABETH[6] HOWELL, married Mr. Baird.

C. Israel[3], David[2], Richard[1]

203. MARY[5] HOWELL (Silas[4]), the daughter of Silas[4] and Mary (Benjamin) Howell, was born on 25 Jly 1775.

On 5 Jan 1798, Mary Howell married David Tuthill {1724}, who was born on 18 June 1764.

David Tuthill died on 30 Oct 1841, at the age of 89 years, 4 months, and 12 days, and is buried at Cutchogue {1725}.

Mary (Howell) Tuthill died on 3 May 1865, at the age of 89 years, 9 months, and 8 days, and is buried beside her husband at Cutchogue {1726}.

David and Mary (Howell) Tuthill were the parents of seven children {1727}.

    i. HULDAH TUTHILL, born on 25 Aug 1800.

    ii. ELMA TUTHILL, born on 28 Oct 1803, married Dr. Joshua Fanning, died on 8 Aug 1870 {1728}.

    iii. JAMES TUTHILL, born on 21 Mch 1805.

    iv. DAVID TUTHILL, born on 26 Aug 1807.

    v. HENRY TUTHILL, died young.

    vi. MARY BENJAMIN TUTHILL, born on 19 Feb 1812, married John T. Luce, 6 children, died on 2 Oct 1898. He was born on 28 Mch 1808, the son of John T. and Rachel (Terry) Luce, and died on 7 Jan 1878 {1729}.

1724. George H. Tuthill, op. cit.
1725. Gravestone, Cutchogue New Yard Cemetery.
1726. Id.
1727. Tuttle, op. cit., 119.
1728. Wilbur Franklin Howell, op. cit., 52.
1729. Mallmann, op. cit., 226.

vii. GEORGE HOWELL TUTHILL, born on 19 Feb 1817, married Jemima Luce, the sister of John T. Luce, in June 1837, 2 children, died on 21 June 1888. She was born on 1 Mch 1820 {1730}.

204. SILAS[5] HOWELL (Silas[4]), the son of Silas[4] and Mary (Benjamin) Howell, was born in about 1766.

Silas Howell married Hannah Woodhull, who was born in about 1776.

Silas Howell was listed as the head of a family consisting of one free white male of 26 and under 45 years of age, one free white female of 26 and under 45, and one of under 10, residing in the Town of Brookhaven, Suffolk County, New York, in the Third Census of the United States, 1810 {1731}.

Silas Howell lived at Setauket, where he died on 15 Apr 1814, at the age of 49, and is buried in the cemetery at the Setauket Presbyterian Church {1732}.

Hannah (Woodhull) Howell married (2) Daniel Jones. She died on 30 Mch 1845, in the 69th year of her age, and is buried beside her first husband at Setauket {1733}.

Silas and Hannah (Woodhull) Howell did not have any children {1734}.

Daniel and Hannah (Woodhull) Howell Jones were the parents of at least one daughter {1735}.

    i.   HARRIET AMANDA JONES.

205. HENRY[5] HOWELL (Silas[4]) was the son of Silas[4] and Mary (Benjamin) Howell {1736}.

Henry Howell was listed as the head of a family consisting of one free white male of 26 and under 45 years of age, one of 16 and under 26, and one free white female of 16 and under 26, residing in the Town of Brookhaven, Suffolk County, New York, in the Third Census of the United States, 1810 {1737}.

Henry Howell was at Oyster Bay, and was drowned {1738}.

Henry Howell was the father of at least one son {1739}.

493.   i.   HENRY[6] HOWELL.

1730. Id.
1731. U.S. Census, Brookhaven, Suffolk County, NY, 1810, Page 224.
1732. Barstow, op. cit., EPITAPHS.
1733. Id.
1734. George H. Tuthill, op. cit.
1735. Barstow, op. cit.
1736. George H. Tuthill, op. cit.
1737. U.S. Census, Brookhaven, Suffolk County, NY, 1810, Page 223.
1738. George H. Tuthill, op. cit.
1739. Id.

206. SARAH[5] HOWELL (Silas[4]) was the daughter of Silas[4] and Mary (Benjamin) Howell {1740}.

On 11 Jly 1787, Sarah, "Sally", Howell married Benjamin Mapes at Wading River. He was born on 27 Jly 1763 {1741}.

Benjamin and Sarah (Howell) Mapes were the parents of seven children {1742}.

    i.   HULDAH MAPES, born in 1788 and died in 1791.

    ii.   BENJAMIN MAPES, born in 1790.

    iii.   SARAH, "SALLY", MAPES, born in 1791.

    iv.   AMY MAPES, born in 1792.

    v.   SILAS HOWELL MAPES, born in 1797, married Hila Ann Wines on 18 Jly 1822, 10 children.

    vi.   LYDIA MAPES, born in 1799.

    vii.   ELMA MAPES, born in 1805.

207. JOSEPH[5] HOWELL (Silas[4]), the son of Silas[4] and Mary (Benjamin) Howell, was born on 19 Dec 1770 {1743}.

On 17 Sep 1797, Joseph Howell married Elizabeth Smith, who was born at Coram {1744}. on 18 Nov 1773, the daughter of John Smith {1745}.

Joseph Howell was listed as the head of a family consisting of one free white male of 26 and under 45 years of age, one free white female of 26 and under 45, and two free white females of under 10, residing in the Town of Riverhead, Suffolk County, New York, in the Second Census of the United States, 1800 {1746}.

Joseph Howell was listed as the head of a household consisting of one free white male of 26 and under 45 years of age, one of under 10, one free white female of 26 and under 45, two of 10 and under 16, two of under 10, and one other free person, residing in the Town of Riverhead, Suffolk County, New York, in the Third Census of the United States, 1810 {1747}.

1740. Id.
1741. THE FAMILY RECORD, 118.
1742. Id.
1743. Wilbur Franklin Howell, op. cit., 8.
1744. Id.
1745. The REGISTER, SCHS, XIII, #2, 46-47 (Fall 1987).
1746. NYG&BR, LVI, 331 (Oct 1925).
1747. U.S. Census, Riverhead, Suffolk County, NY, 1820, Page 358.

Elizabeth (Smith) Howell died on 25 Sep 1819, and is buried in the Baiting Hollow Cemetery {1748}.

Joseph Howell was listed as the head of a family consisting of one free white male of over 45 years of age, one of 10 and under 16, one of under 10, one free white female of 16 and under 25, two of 10 and under 16, and two of under 10, residing in the Town of Riverhead, Suffolk County, New York, in the Fourth Census of the United States, 1820. Of these, one was engaged in agriculture {1749}.

Joseph Howell married Bethia Wines(?), of Manor, as his second wife {1750}.

The will of Joseph Howell, written on 7 Aug 1833, mentions his wife, Bethiah, his daughters, Betsey Blanchard, Abigail Lacy, Sarah Howell and Amelina Howell, and his sons, John Smith Howell and Silon Wines Howell. John Gilmore was named executor of this will. In a codicil to this will, dated 19 Aug 1833, he mentioned his grandsons, Henry and Joseph Birge {1751}.

Joseph Howell died on 5 Sep 1833 at Greenville, Bond County, Illinois {1752}.

Joseph and Elizabeth (Smith) Howell were the parents of nine children {1753}.

494. i. HULDAH[6] HOWELL, born on 16 Aug 1798, died on 26 Aug 1815, at the age of 17 years and 12 days.

+ 495. ii. BETSEY[6] HOWELL, born on 13 Aug 1800.

496. iii. CHARITY[6] HOWELL, born on 17 Oct 1802, not named in her father's will.

497. iv. JOSEPH BENJAMIN[6] HOWELL, born on 14 Dec 1807(?), died on 26 Aug 1826.

+ 498. v. ABIGAIL[6] HOWELL, born on 24 Apr 1810.

+ 499. vi. JOHN SMITH[6] HOWELL, born on 13 Jan 1813.

500. vii. SARAH[6] HOWELL, born on 19 Jly 1815.

501. viii. EVALINA[6] HOWELL, born on 23 Feb 1818.

1748. Gravestone, Baiting Hollow Cemetery.
1749. U.S. Census, Riverhead, Suffolk County, NY, 1820, Page 354.
1750. THE REGISTER, SCHS, XIII, #2, 46-47 (Fall 1987).
1751. Bond County, Illinois, Record Book A-1, 199-205, as reported in the ILLINOIS STATE GENEALOGICAL SOCIETY QUARTERLY, VI, #4, 207 (WINTER 1974).
1752. THE REGISTER, SCHS, XIII, #2, 46-47 (Fall 1987).
1753. Id.

Joseph and Bethia (Wines?) Howell were the parents of at least one child {1754}.

502. ix. SILAS WINES[6] HOWELL.

208. MICAH[5] HOWELL (Silas[4]), the son of Silas[4] and Mary (Benjamin) Howell, was born on 20 Jan 1773 {1755}.

On 11 Oct 1794, Micah Howell married Hannah Lupton, who was born on 29 Dec 1776 {1756}.

Micah Howell removed to Tompkins County in about 1818, and later to Almond, in Allegheny County, New York, as did several of his children {1757}.

Hannah (Lupton) Howell died on 28 May 1841 {1758}.

On 17 Sep 1850, Micah Howell, 77, farmer, was enumerated as a member of the household of his son, Micah, 54, merchant, with real property worth $1000, residing in the Town of Riverhead, Suffolk County, New York {1759}. On 17 Oct 1850, he was enumerated as a member of the household of his daughter, Julia, 42, with real property worth $300, residing in the Town of Almond, Allegheny County, New York, in the Seventh Census of the United States {1760}.

Micah Howell married the widow, Mrs. Cartwright, as his second wife {1761}.

Micah and Hannah (Lupton) Howell were the parents of ten children {1762}.

+ 503. i. MICAH[6] HOWELL, born on 15 Oct 1795.

+ 504. ii. DANIEL[6] HOWELL, born on 28 Oct 1797.

  505. iii. SILAS[6] HOWELL, born on 21 May 1800, died on 7 Oct 1805.

  506. iv. JAMES[6] HOWELL, born on 15 Mch 1803, died on 5 Oct 1805.

+ 507. v. HANNAH[6] HOWELL, born on 11 Feb 1805.

+ 508. vi. JULIA[6] HOWELL, born on 24 Dec 1807.

1754. Id.
1755. Wilbur Franklin Howell, op. cit., 9.
1756. Id.
1757. Id.
1758. Id.
1759. U.S. Census, 1850, Riverhead, Suffolk County, NY, Dwelling House 477, Family Number 523, Page 279.
1760. Id., Almond, Allegheny County, NY, Dwelling House 539, Family Number 604, Page 58.
1761. Wilbur Franklin Howell, op. cit., 9.
1762. Id.

+ 509. vii.   LAURA[6] HOWELL, born on 6 Feb 1810, died on 10 Mch 1854.

+ 510. viii.   GEORGE[6] HOWELL, born on 6 Apr 1812.

+ 511. ix.   LUTHER[6] HOWELL, born on 21 Nov 1813.

  512. x.   ANNA[6] HOWELL, born on 13 Apr 1817, died on 1 Sep 1822.

209. SMITH[5] HOWELL (Silas[4]), the son of Silas[4] and Mary (Benjamin) Howell, was born on 19 Dec 1779 {1763}.
    Smith Howell married Elizabeth Hammond, who was born on 18 Nov 1774 {1764}.
    Smith Howell removed to Pennsylvania {1765}.
    Elizabeth (Hammond) Howell died on 2 Mch 1827 {1766}.
    Smith Howell died on 2 Mch 1854 {1767}.
    Smith and Elizabeth (Hammond) Howell were the parents of seven children {1768}.
+ 513. i.   ELIZA[6] HOWELL.

  514. ii.   HENRY[6] HOWELL, born on 7 June 1803, died on 9 Aug 1805.

+ 515. iii.   SMITH H.[6] HOWELL, born on 22 June 1811.

+ 516. iv.   SYLVESTER[6] HOWELL, born on 22 June 1812.

  517. v.   SYLVANUS[6] HOWELL, born on 23 Dec 1815, died on 21 Aug 1816.

  518. vi.   CHARITY[6] HOWELL.

  519. vii.   ABIGAIL J.[6] HOWELL.

210. BENJAMIN[5] HOWELL (Silas[4]) was the son of Silas[4] and Mary (Benjamin) Howell.
    Benjamin Howell lived and died in New York {1769}.

1763. Id., 48.
1764. Id.
1765. George H. Tuthill, op. cit.
1766. Wilbur Franklin Howell, op. cit.
1767. Id.
1768. Id.
1769. George H. Tuthill, op. cit.

Benjamin Howell had no children {1770}.

211. CHARITY[5] HOWELL (Silas[4]), the daughter of Silas[4] and Mary (Benjamin) Howell, was born on 22 June 1779 {1771}.

On 13 Dec 1804, Charity Howell married Israel Hawkins, who was born on 22 Feb 1776 at Stony Brook, the son of Israel and Phebe (Brush) Hawkins {1772}.

Israel Hawkins died on 11 May 1833, at the age of 57, and is buried in the churchyard cemetery at the Setauket Presbyterian Church {1773}.

On 16 Aug 1850, Charity Hawkins, 70, widow, with real property worth $2000, was enumerated as the head of a household consisting of herself, her daughter, Angeline Petty, 44, widow, with real property worth $200, and Nehemiah A. Petty, 22, residing in the Town of Brookhaven, Suffolk County, New York, in the Seventh Census of the United States {1774}. Henry Wells, 33, carpenter, his wife, Clarissa A., 30, and their children, Amelia, 3, and Edna, 1, were living in the same house {1775}.

Charity (Howell) Hawkins died on 18 Oct 1864, at the age of 85, and is buried beside her husband at Setauket {1776}.

Israel and Charity (Howell) Hawkins were the parents of eight children {1777}.

    i.   Son, died Nov 1805 {1778}.

    ii.   ANGELINA HAWKINS, born 1 Sep 1805, married Beria Petty, who was born on 5 Jly 1805 at Stony Brook, and who became a mariner. One child, who died young. Beria Petty drowned at sea on 5 Jly 1843. Angelina (Hawkins) Petty died on 12 Aug 1869, and is buried at Setauket {1779}.

    iii.   DELIA HAWKINS, born 1 Feb 1808, died 4 Jly 1825, at the age of 17 years, 5 months and 3 days, and is buried at Setauket {1780}.

    iv.   ISRAEL HAWKINS, born on 29 May 1810, married Delia S.

1770. Id.
1771. Wilbur Franklin Howell, op. cit., 53.
1772. Hawkins, op. cit., 34.
1773. Barstow, op. cit, EPITAPHS.
1774. U.S. Census, Brookhaven, Suffolk County, NY, 1850, Dwelling House 536, Family Number 608, Page 181.
1775. Id., Family Number 607, Page 181.
1776. Barstow, op. cit.
1777. Hawkins, op. cit.
1778. Wilbur Franklin Howell, op. cit., 53.
1779. Hawkins, op. cit., 64.
1780. Barstow, op. cit.

Hulse, who was born on 7 Apr 1818, ten children. "They lived in New York City. He died June 13, 1871, and she died May 8, 1883. Both were buried at the Methodist Episcopal Church, Stony Brook." {1781}.

v. SILAS HOWELL HAWKINS, born on 25 Nov 1812, married Hannah M. Smith, was a seaman and lived at St. James. He died on 5 Sep 1856, and is buried at the Episcopal Church, St. James {1782}.

vi. JOHN SHEPERD HAWKINS, born on 13 May 1815, died on 28 Apr 1836, at the age of 20 years, 11 months, and 15 days, and is buried at Setauket {1783}.

vii. EDNA C. HAWKINS, born on 25 Oct 1817, died on 6 Jly 1833, at the age of 15 years, 8 months, and 11 days, and is buried at Setauket {1784}.

viii. CLARISSA HAWKINS, born on 9 Jly 1820, married Henry Wells on 22 Jan 1845. He was a carpenter, and was born on 22 Jan 1817. Three children. "He died March 29, 1888. She died April 25, 1898. Both are buried at the Presbyterian Church at Setauket." {1785}.

212. AZUBA⁵ HOWELL (Silas⁴) was the daughter of Silas⁴ and Mary (Benjamin) Howell {1786}.

   Azuba Howell married Abner⁵ Howell, #246, as his first wife {1787}, and died shortly thereafter.

213. ESTHER⁵ HOWELL (Israel⁴), the daughter of Israel⁴ and Tabitha (Hulse) Howell, was born on 10 Oct 1770 {1788}, and baptized on 6 Mch 1771 at Mattituck {1789}.

   On 27 Dec 1792, Esther Howell married Nathaniel Homan at Mattituck {1790}.

1781. Hawkins, 64, 65.
1782. Id., 65.
1783. Barstow, op. cit.
1784. Id.
1785. Hawkins, op. cit.
1786. George H. Tuthill, op. cit.
1787. Id.
1788. Ida A. Maddrah, op. cit.
1789. Craven, op. cit., 277.
1790. Id., 333.

Esther (Howell) Homan married (2) Nathan R. Barteau, who owned a fine farm {1791}.

Esther (Howell) Homan Barteau married (3) a Mr. Mills, who had a farm at Middle Island {1792}.

Esther (Howell) Homan Barteau Mills married (4) Rev. Jonathan Robinson, who was born on 4 Jly 1774, a cousin of her brother David's wife {1793}.

Mrs. Jonathan Robinson attended the funeral of her nephew, David Porter Howell, on 23 Oct 1834 {1794}.

Rev. Jonathan Robinson died on 16 Jan 1848, at the age of 93 years, 6 months and 12 days, and is buried beside his first wife, Hannah, in the Riverhead Cemetery {1795}.

Nathaniel and Esther (Howell) Homan were the parents of six children {1796}.

i.   TABATHA HOMAN, lived with her uncle, David Howell after her father died, married William Riley Sprague.

ii. EUNICE HOMAN, married Benjamin Sprague.

iii. AMY HOMAN, married Mr. Henessee.

iv. LYDIA HOMAN, never married, lived with her mother and Nathan R. Barteau.

v.   HANNAH HOMAN, born on 5 Oct 1805, married John Murphy on 28 June 1823 at the Grace Episcopal Church in Flushing, New York, three children, died on 6 June 1888 (NOTE: *Hannah (Homan) Murphy was the grandmother of Ida A. Maddrah*).

vi. ESTHER HOMAN, at age 15, went to live at the home of her uncle, David Howell's, where she lived for one year, never married.

214. DAVID[5] HOWELL (Israel[4]), the son of Israel[4] and Tabitha (Hulse) Howell, was baptized at Mattituck on 24 Nov 1773 {1797}.

David Howell married Joanna Wells, who was born on 25 Jan 1779, the

---

1791. Ida A. Maddrah, op. cit.
1792. Id.
1793. Id.
1794. Id.
1795. Id.
1796. Id.
1797. Craven, op. cit., 281.

daughter of Obadiah and Joanna (Downs) Wells {1798}.

"David Howell was no doubt born on the Newton farm but when it was sold, the Howells removed to Deep Hole, a mile south of the main road, and built and continued there. Their farm was still a part of the first lot; was in fact the s. end reserved, and within the original e. and w: lines..Mr. Howell - he married Joanna Wells, daughter of Obadiah..and they reared their family of eight daughters and one son" {1799}.

David Howell was listed as the head of a family consisting of one free white male of 26 and under 45 years of age, one of 18 and under 25, one of 16 and under 18, one of under 10, one free white female of 26 and under 45, one of 10 and under 16, and 4 of under 10, residing in the Town of Riverhead, Suffolk County, New York, in the Third Census of the United States, 1810 {1800}.

David Howell was listed as the head of a family consisting of one free white male of 45 years of age and older, one of 18 and under 25, one of 16 and under 18, one of under 10, one free white female of 45 and older, one of 25 and under 45, two of 10 and under 16, and three of under 10, residing in the Town of Riverhead, Suffolk County, New York, in the Fourth Census of the United States, 1820. Of these, 2 were engaged in agriculture {1801}.

In "A CENSUS OF BAITING HOLLOW PARISH BY FAMILIES - January 1, 1825", David Howell was listed as the head of a family of 3 males and 9 females {1802}.

David Howell was listed as the head of a family consisting of one free white male of 50 and under 60 years of age, one of 20 and under 30, one of 15 and under 20, one free white female of 50 and under 60, one of 40 and under 50, one of 20 and under 30, two of 15 and under 20, one of 10 and under 15, and two of 5 and under 10, residing in the Town of Riverhead, Suffolk County, New York, in the Fifth Census of the United States, 1830 {1803}.

David Howell was listed as the head of a family consisting of one free white male of 60 and under 70 years of age, one of 10 and under 15, one free white female of 60 and under 70, one of 50 and under 60, and two of 15 and under 20, residing in the Town of Riverhead, Suffolk County, New York, in the Sixth Census of the United States, 1840 {1804}.

On 15 Sep 1850, the household of David Howell, 76, farmer, having property worth $4,000, was listed as including Johannah, 70, and Nancy, 71, along with Wm. H. Moon, 14, and George Edwards, 9, and being in the Town of Riverhead, Suffolk County, New York, in the Seventh Census of the United States {1805}.

1798. Wilbur Franklin Howell, op. cit., 62.
1799. Young, op. cit., VII, #4, 98 (March 1982).
1800. U.S. Census, Riverhead, Suffolk County, NY, 1810, Page 252.
1801. Id., 1820, Page 365.
1802. THE REGISTER, SCHS, VII, #4, 89 (March 1982).
1803. U.S. Census, Riverhead, Suffolk County, NY, 1830, Page 241.
1804. Id., 1840, Page 241.
1805. Id., 1850, Dwelling House 452, Family Number 494, Page 278.

David Howell died on 8 Sep 1852 {1806}.

Joanna (Wells) Howell died on 31 Oct 1860 {1807}.

David and Joanna (Wells) Howell were the parents of twelve children {1808}.

+ 520. i.   HANNAH[6] HOWELL, born on 19 Nov 1798.

    521. ii.   ABIGAIL[6] HOWELL, born on 28 Nov 1800.

+ 522. iii.   ISRAEL[6] HOWELL, born on 9 Mch 1803.

+ 523. iv.   LOUISE[6] HOWELL, born on 9 Mch 1805.

    524. v.   EMELINE[6] HOWELL, born on 12 Mch 1808.

+ 525. vi.   TABITHA[6] HOWELL, born on 19 May 1810.

    526. vii.   ESTHER[6] HOWELL, born on 4 June 1812.

    527. viii.   DAVID PORTER[6] HOWELL, born on 30 Dec 1815, died on 22 Oct 1834, in his 20th year, and is buried in the Baiting Hollow Cemetery {1809}.

    528. ix.   SYLVESTER[6] HOWELL, born on 20 Jly 1817, died on 17 Mch 1818, and is buried beside his brother, David P., in the Baiting Hollow Cemetery {1810}.

+ 529. x.   PHYLINDA B.[6] HOWELL, born on 12 Aug 1819.

    530. xi.   HULDAH[6] HOWELL, born on 9 Dec 1821.

    531. xii.   MARY O.[6] HOWELL, born on 25 Mch 1825, died on 20 Jan 1851.

215. HANNAH[5] HOWELL (Israel[4]), the daughter of Israel[4] and Tabitha (Hulse) Howell, was born on 25 Jan 1779 {1811}, and baptized at Mattituck on 28 Jly 1780 {1812}.

1806. Wilbur Franklin Howell, op. cit., 62.
1807. Id.
1808. Faris, op. cit., 259-260.
1809. Gravestone, Baiting Hollow Cemetery.
1810. Id.
1811. Ida A. Maddrah, op. cit.
1812. Craven, op. cit., 286.

Hannah Howell was called Nancy {1813}. As such, she was reported as dwelling in the house of her brother, David, in the Seventh Census of the United States, 1850 {1814}.

By her will of 7 Mch 1840, proved on 18 Mch 1851, Nancy Howell, of the Town of Riverhead, left $100 to her sister, Esther Robinson, and $100 to her niece, Hannah Phillips. All her landed property was left to her nephew, Israel Howell, after he had paid all her bills. He was also named a co-executor, with Abel Corwin {1815}.

Hannah, "Nancy", Howell died on 20 Jan 1851 {1816}.

216. ELIZABETH[5] HOWELL (Samuel[4]), the daughter of Samuel[4] and Elizabeth (Tuthill) Howell, was baptized at Mattituck on 2 Nov 1774 {1817}.

On 30 May 1793, Elizabeth Howell married Sylvanus Brown, who was born on 7 Apr 1774, the son of Sylvanus and Hannah (Rackett) Brown, as his second wife. His first wife was Elizabeth Terry, the daughter of John and Temperance Terry {1818}, who was baptized at Mattituck on 9 Nov 1766 {1819}, and who died on 25 Jly 1792, at the age of 26 {1820}.

Sylvanus Brown died on 16 May 1802 {1821}.

Elizabeth (Howell) Brown died on 10 Aug 1854, and is buried at Mattituck {1822}.

Sylvanus and Elizabeth (Terry) Brown were the parents of five children {1823}.

    i.   HANNAH BROWN, baptized at Mattituck on 14 May 1786 {1824}.

    ii.   TEMPERANCE CONKLIN BROWN, baptized at Mattituck on 5 Oct 1788 {1825}.

    iii.   ELIZABETH BROWN, baptized at Mattituck on 17 Jly 1792 {1826}.

1813. Ida A. Maddrah, op. cit.
1814. U.S. Census, Riverhead, Suffolk County, NY, 1850, Dwelling House 452, Family Number 494, Page 278.
1815. Suffolk County Wills, Liber 5, 190-191; Suffolk County Estates, File #4072.
1816. Ida A. Maddrah, op. cit.
1817. Craven, op. cit., 282.
1818. Wilbur Franklin Howell, op. cit., 68ff.
1819. Craven, op. cit., 272.
1820. Wilbur Franklin Howell, op. cit., 68ff.
1821. Id.
1822. Craven, op. cit., 360.
1823. Wilbur Franklin Howell, op. cit.
1824. Craven, op. cit., 292.
1825. Id., 295.
1826. Id., 302.

iv.   ESTHER BROWN, baptized at Mattituck on 17 Jly 1792 {1827}.

v.   SAMUEL BROWN.

Sylvanus and Elizabeth (Howell) Brown were the parents of five children.

vi.   SYLVANUS BROWN, baptized at Mattituck on 14 June 1795 {1828}.

vii.   IRA BROWN, baptized at Mattituck on 4 Oct 1801 {1829}.

viii.   PERMERIA BROWN, baptized at Mattituck on 4 Oct 1801 {1830}.

ix.   HULDEY BROWN, baptized at Mattituck on 4 Oct 1801 {1831}.

x.   DANIEL BROWN, baptized at Mattituck on 4 Oct 1801 {1832}.

221. SAMUEL⁵ HOWELL (Samuel⁴), the son of Samuel⁴ and Elizabeth (Tuthill) Howell, was born on 23 Dec 1781 {1833}, and was baptized at Mattituck on 4 Jan 1782 {1834}.

Samuel Howell married Charity Davis in 1812. She was the daughter of Phineas and Sybel Davis, and was born on 1 Jan 1793 at Yaphank {1835}.

Samuel Howell was listed as the head of a family consisting of one free white male of 26 and under 45 years of age, one of under 10, one free white female of 26 and under 45, and two of under 10, residing in the Town of Smithtown, Suffolk County, New York, in the Fourth Census of the United States, 1820 {1836}.

In the Sixth Census of the United States, 1840, Samuel Howell was listed as the head of a family consisting of one free white male of 50 and under 60 years of age, one of 15 and under 20, one free white female of 30 and under 40, and one

1827. Id.
1828. Id., 305.
1829. Id., 308.
1830. Id.
1831. Id.
1832. Id.
1833. William F. Howell, op. cit.
1834. Craven, op. cit., 288.
1835. Ruth Isabelle (Davis) Ferris, PHINEAS DAVIS OF LONG ISLAND AND HIS DESCENDANTS, in the possession of the SCHS, 1997.
1836. U.S. Census, Smithtown, Suffolk County, NY, 1830, Page 317.

of 10 and under 15, residing in the Town of Smithtown, Suffolk County, New York {1837}.

On 26 Aug 1850, Samuel Howell, carpenter, 60, was listed as the head of a family consisting of himself and his wife, Charity, 50, residing in the Town of Smithtown, Suffolk County, New York, in the Seventh Census of the United States {1838}.

Samuel Howell died in 1861 {1839}.

Charity Howell died on 2 Aug 1871 {1840}.

Samuel and Charity (Davis) Howell were the parents of six children {1841}.

+ 532.   i.   ELIZABETH[6] HOWELL, born on 4 June 1813.

+ 533.   ii.   JOHN DAVIS[6] HOWELL, born on 18 Sep 1815.

+ 534.   iii. MARIA AMELIA[6] HOWELL, born on 30 Jan 1817.

+ 535.   iv.   HIRAM BENJAMIN[6] HOWELL, born on 21 May 1820.

+ 536.   v.   HARRIET MALVINA[6] HOWELL, born on 2 June 1822.

+ 537.   vi.   HARVEY WARREN[6] HOWELL, born on 8 Feb 1826.

D. Richard[3], David[2], Richard[1]

225. PARNAL[5] HOWELL (Edmund[4]), the daughter of Edmund[4] and Rachel (Tuthill) Howell, was born in about 1762, and was baptized at Mattituck on 9 Jan 1765 {1842}.

On 24 June 1779, Parnell Howell married James Reeve at Mattituck {1843}. He was the son of Thomas and Keziah Reeve {1844}, and was born in about Sep 1751.

James Reeve signed the Articles of Association {1845}.

James Reeve, 24, of a dark complexion and 5' 6" tall, was an Ensign in Capt. Paul Reeve's Company of Suffolk County Minute Men on 5 Aug 1776 {1846}.

1837. Id., 1840, Page 249.
1838. Id., 1850, Dwelling House 67, Family Number 75, Page 127.
1839. William F. Howell, op. cit.
1840. Ferris, op. cit.
1841. Id.
1842. Craven, op cit., 271.
1843. Id., 325.
1844. Id., 384.
1845. Mather, op. cit., 1057.
1846. Id., 1009.

James Reeve IV, farmer, of the Town of Southold, gave his age as 27 when he signed the Oath of Allegiance and Peaceable Behaviour required by Governor William Tryon in 1778 {1847}.

In the First Census of the United States, 1790, James Reeves was listed as the head of a family consisting of one free white male of 16 years of age and over, two of under 16, and three free white females, residing in Southold Town, Suffolk County, New York {1848}.

James Reeve was listed as the head of a household consisting of one free white male of 45 years of age and over, two of 16 and under 26, one of under 10, one free white female of 26 and under 45, one of 16 and under 26, two of 10 and under 16, and two of under 10, residing in the Town of Southold, Suffolk County, New York, in the Second Census of the United States, 1800 {1849}.

By his will of 29 Jly 1807, proved on 7 Oct 1807, James Reeve left most of his homestead to his son, Jesse, with bequests to his wife, "Pernal". His home was reserved for the use of his eight children, and the rest of his property was to be divided equally between them {1850}.

James Reeve died on 13 Aug 1807, in his 56th year {1851}, and is buried in the cemetery at the Mattituck Presbyterian Church {1852}.

Parnel (Howell) Reeve died on 4 Nov 1828, at the age of 66, and is buried beside her husband at Mattituck {1853}.

James and Parnell (Howell) Reeve were the parents of eight children {1854}.

    i.   LAVINIA REEVE, born in about 1779, married Joshua Corwin at Mattituck on 5 Mch 1803 {1855}, died on 26 Dec 1809.

    ii.   JESSE REEVE, born in about 1781, married (1) Betsey, who died 26 Dec 1822 in her 36th year, married (2) Polly Aldrich, who died 29 Dec 1875, age 74. He died on 25 Jly 1845 in his 64th year. All three are buried at Mattituck {1856}.

    iii.   JAMES REEVE.

    iv.   PARNEL REEVE.

1847. P.R.O. Colonial Office, Class 5, Vol. 1109, 88.
1848. HEADS OF FAMILIES.., 1790, NEW YORK, 169.
1849. NYG&BR, LVII, 56 (Jan 1926).
1850. Suffolk County Wills, Liber B, 462-464.
1851. Craven, op. cit., 355.
1852. Id.
1853. Id.
1854. Baker, op. cit., 397-398.
1855. Craven, op. cit., 336.
1856. Id., 384.

v. KEZIAH REEVE, baptized at Mattituck on 20 June 1790

vi. EDMUND REEVE, born on 20 Nov 1792, baptized at Mattituck on 24 Mch 1793 {1858}, married Jerusha Hammond, who died on 10 Dec 1867 and is buried in the cemetery at the Mattituck Presbyterian Church. He died on 15 Oct 1852, at the age of 59 years, 10 months and 25 days, and is buried beside his wife at Mattituck {1859}.

vii. HANNAH REEVE, baptized at Mattituck on 1 Nov 1807 {1860}.

viii. ANNA REEVE, baptized at Mattituck on 1 Nov 1808 {1861}.

228. MEHITABEL[5] HOWELL (Edmund[4]), the daughter of Edmund[4] and Bethiah (Downs) Howell, was born in the vicinity of Mattituck on 22 Feb 1776 {1862}, and baptized there on 18 Jly 1790 {1863}.

"Mahitable" Howell and Henry Corwin, Jr., were married at Mattituck on 8 Feb 1797 {1864}. He was the son of Henry and Bethiah (Reeve) Corwin, and was born on 21 Oct 1774.

"Hen[y] Corwin" was listed as the head of a family consisting of one free white male of 26 and under 45 years of age, two of under 10, and one free white female of 26 and under 45, residing in the Town of Southold, Suffolk County, New York, in the Second Census of the United States, 1800 {1865}.

Henry Corwin died on 27 Jun 1847, at the age of 72 years, 8 months, and 6 days, and is buried in the Aquebogue Cemetery {1866}.

Mehitabel (Howell) Corwin died on 18 Aug 1850, at the age of 75 years, 6 months, and 5 days, and is buried beside her husband at Aquebogue {1867}.

Henry and Mehitabel (Howell) Corwin were the parents of at least two children.

i. OLIVER CORWIN, born on 25 June 1800.

1857. Craven, op. cit., 299.
1858. Id., 303.
1859. Id., 384.
1860. Id., 311.
1861. Id.
1862. Id., 314.
1863. Id., 299.
1864. Id., 334.
1865. NYG&BR, LVII, 56 (Jan 1926).
1866. Gravestone, Aquebogue Cemetery.
1867. Id.

ii.   HALSEY CORWIN, born in about Nov 1806.

233. PHINEAS⁵ HOWELL (Phineas⁴) was the son of Phineas⁴ and Mary (Brown) Howell.
     Phineas Howell married Mary Dowd {1868}.
     "Phinehas Howell" was listed as the head of a family consisting of one free white male of over 45 years of age, one of 16 and under 26, two of under 10, and one free white female of under 10, residing in the Town of Minisink, Orange County, New York, in the Third Census of the United States, 1810 {1869}.
     Phineas and Mary (Dowd) Howell were the parents of at least three children {1870}.
     538. i.   WILLIAM D.⁶ HOWELL.

     539. ii.   MARY⁶ HOWELL.

     540. iii. RICHARD D.⁶ HOWELL.

234. DAVID⁵ HOWELL (Phineas⁴), the son of Phineas⁴ and Mary (Brown) Howell, was born on 22 Feb 1772 {1871}.
     David Howell died on 12 Jan 1798, at the age of 26 years {1872}, and is buried in a private cemetery on a hill behind the farmhouse occupied by Jonathan Decker in 1914 on the Ridgebury-Slate Hill Road {1873}.

236. JASON⁵ HOWELL (Phineas⁴), the son of Phineas⁴ and Mary (Brown) Howell, was born on 14 Sep 1777 {1874}.
     Jason Howell married (1) Mary Hulp (?) {1875}, and (2) Lydia Allison, who was born in about 1790, the daughter of James Allison {1876}.
     By a deed recorded in 1807 {1877}, Jason Howell received the farm of his father, "..now owned by the estate of T. T. Durland in 1914.." {1878}.
     In the Third Census of the United States, 1810, Jason Howell was listed

---

1868. Mary E. Wheelock, HOWELL GENEALOGY, 7, from a copy in the possession of the State Historical Society of Wisconsin, 1992.
1869. U.S. Census, Minisink, Orange County, NY, 1810, Page 423.
1870. Wheelock, op. cit., 7.
1871. Coulter, et al., 61.
1872. Id.
1873. Stickney, HOWELL, #B105.
1874. Id., #B95.
1875. Wheelock, op. cit., 7.
1876. Stickney, HOWELL, #B103.
1877. Orange County Deeds, Liber J, 443-445.
1878. Stickney, op. cit.

as the head of a family consisting of one free white male of 26 and under 45 years of age, three of under 10, two free white females of under 10, residing in the Town of Minisink, Orange County, New York {1879}.

Jason Howell was listed as the head of a family consisting of one free white male of 26 and under 45 years of age, one of 10 and under 16, four of under 10, and one free white female of 26 and under 45, residing in the Town of Minisink, Orange County, New York, in the Fourth Census of the United States, 1820 {1880}.

By a deed of 22 Jan 1820, recorded on 28 Feb 1822, Jason Howell gave his children, Rosette, David, Livinia and Martha Howell, title to a "..certain piece of land, lying in the..Town of Minisink.." {1881}.

Upon the death of James Allison, "..an action was brought to secure a division of of his real estate and Peter Holbert, David Moore and Duncan Hulse, commissioners appointed by the court, set apart to her fourteen acres in one tract and seven in another. In 1831 Jason and his wife Lydia deeded the said tracts to John Holbert who at that time owned the farm now (1914) B. S. Ellsworth's." {1882}.

Jason Howell died on 8 Jan 1844, at the age of 66 years, 3 months and 24 days, and is buried in the family burial ground near the Old School Baptist Church 3n Slate Hill, New York {1883}.

On 30 Jly 1850, Lydia Howell, 41, was enumerated as the head of a family consisting of herself, and her son, Daniel, 38, tailor, residing in the Town of Minisink, Orange County, New York, in the Seventh Census of the United States {1884}.

"Next on the right (past an old house on the left as you entered the east side of the village of Brookfield, now (1918) Slate Hill, near the bridge, and formerly occupied by William Carter, Abram Spears, and a family by the name of VanZelle, and past the home of Vincent Casterlin) was the home of the Jason Howell family, consisting of Aunt Lydia, as she was familiarly called, and three sons, Daniel, Gabriel, and Walter. The first two were tailors by trade, who continued in business in the village up to the 60's" {1885}.

On 6 Sep 1860, Lydia Howell, 71, was enumerated as the head of a family consisting of herself and her son, Gabriel, 45, taylor, residing in the Town of Wawayanda, Orange County, New York, in the Eighth Census of the United States {1886}.

1879. U.S. Census, Minisink, Orange County, NY, 1810, Page 423.
1880. Id., 1820, Page 245.
1881. Orange County Deeds, Liber V, 400-401.
1882. Stickney, op. cit., #B103.
1883. Id.
1884. U.S. Census, Minisink, Orange County, NY, 1850, Dwelling House 292, Family Number 295, Page 232.
1885. Jacob Oakley Austin, WANTAGE RECORDER, 1918, from a copy in the possession of the Orange County Genealogical Society, published in THE QUARTERLY, OCGS, 6, #4, 28 (Feb 1977)).
1886. U.S. Census, Wawayanda, Orange County, NY, 1860, Dwelling House 2273, Family Number 2539, Page 335.

Lydia (Allison) Howell died on 22 Mch 1865, in the 76th year of her age, and is buried beside her husband at Slate Hill {1887}.

Jason and Mary (Hulp?) Howell were the parents of four children {1888}.

541. i.   ROSETTA[6] HOWELL.

542. ii. DAVID[6] HOWELL, born in about 1805, never married, died on 16 Mch 1836, at the age of 31 years, and is buried in the family plot at the O. S. Baptist Church in Slate Hill, New York {1889}.

543. iii. LAVINIA[6] HOWELL.

544. iv. MARTHA, "PATTY",[6] HOWELL.

Jason and Lydia (Allison) Howell were the parents of five children.

545. vi. MELTON B.[6] HOWELL, born in about 1810, never married, died on 15 Mch 1827 in the 18th year of his age, and is buried in the family plot at the O. S. Baptist Church {1890}.

546. vii. DANIEL T.[6] HOWELL, born in about 1812, never married, died on 8 Jly 1860, in the 49th year of his age, and is buried in the family plot at the O. S. Baptist Church {1891}.

547. ix. SARAH M.[6] HOWELL, born in about Jan 1815, died on 18 Mch 1824, at the age of 9 years and 2 months, and is buried in the family plot at Slate Hill {1892}.

548.viii. GABRIEL A.[6] HOWELL, born on 17 Apr 1816, never married, was a dealer in dry goods, groceries and general merchandise at Denton in New Hampton in 1871 {1893}, went to Binghamton, New York where he worked as a tailor, bought the family burial plot from T. T. Durland, erected a neat monument there, died on 16 Feb 1883, and is buried in the family plot {1894}.

+ 549. v.   WALTER S.[6] HOWELL, born in about 1819.

1887. Stickney, op. cit.
1888. Wheelock, op. cit., 7.
1889. Stickney, HOWELL, #B111.
1890. Id., #B112.
1891. Id., #B114.
1892. Id., #B113.
1893. Orange County Directory, 1871, 121.
1894. Id., #B115.

238. JAMES BROWN[5] HOWELL (Phineas[4]), the son of Phineas[4] and Mary (Brown) Howell, was born on 4 Apr 1790 {1895}, and his is said to have been the last name entered in the Welsh Bible of John Howell {1896}.

On 4 June 1807, James Brown Howell married Sarah Stage, who was born on 25 Dec 1789 in New York State {1897}, or Mary Stager {1898}.

James Brown Howell died on 25 Oct 1831 in Niagara County, New York {1899}.

Sarah Howell died on 4 Jul 1861 at Pittsford, Hillsdale County, Michigan, and is buried in an unmarked grave near Osseo, Michigan {1900}.

James Brown and Sarah (Stage) Howell were the parents of eleven children {1901}.

+ 550. i.   MICHAEL B.[6] HOWELL, born on 4 May 1808.

+ 551. ii.   OLSER D.[6] HOWELL, born on 5 Feb 1810.

+ 552. iii. JAMES PETER[6] HOWELL, born on 21 Jan 1812.

+ 553. iv.   SALLY J.[6] HOWELL, born on 30 Jan 1814.

+ 554. v.   WILLIAM L.[6] HOWELL, born on 29 Apr 1816.

  555. vi.   DAVID[6] HOWELL, born on 20 Jly 1818.

  556. vii. MARY A.[6] HOWELL, born on 27 June 1820.

+ 557. viii. WALTER B.[6] HOWELL, born on 25 Dec 1822.

+ 558. ix.   JULIA[6] HOWELL, born on 5 May 1825.

  559. x.   HARRIET[6] HOWELL, born on 23 Jan 1828, and died on 30 Jan 1828.

  560. xi.   GILBERT[6] HOWELL, born on 7 Sep 1829, and died on the same day.

240. ELIZABETH[5] HOWELL (Richard[4]), the daughter of Richard[4] and Mary

---

1895. Family Record of W.B. Howell.
1896. James Peter Howell, op. cit., 7.
1897. Gwendolyn J. Howell, op. cit.
1898. James Peter Howell, op. cit., 7.
1899. James W. Howell, Personal communication.
1900. Id.
1901. Family Record of W.B. Howell.

(Osborn) Howell, was born in Jan 1787 {1902}.

Elizabeth Howell married Richard Brown, who was born in Feb 1786, the son of Richard and Deziah (Hudson) Brown {1903}.

Elizabeth Brown died on 8 Aug 1853 {1904}.

Richard Brown died on 17 Apr 1855 {1905}.

Richard and Elizabeth (Howell) Brown were the parents of five children {1906}.

    i.   OLIVER BROWN, born on 10 May 1813, died on 21 Jan 1889.

    ii.   AMANDA BROWN, married (1) William Dicks on 8 Nov 1840, two children, both died young, married (2) James Crouter.

    iii.   CHARLES BROWN, born in May 1819, died on 25 Feb 1835.

    iv.   DANIEL BROWN, born in Feb 1822, died on 12 Sep 1840.

    v.   ELIZABETH BROWN, born in Oct 1828, died on 9 Dec 1835.

243. PARSHALL[5] HOWELL (Parshall[4]), who was probably the son of Parshall[4] and Charity (Mather) Howell, was born on 23 Mch 1788 {1907}.

On 2 Sep 1810, Parshall Howell married Elizabeth Horton, who was born on 29 May 1795, the daughter of William Horton {1908}. At that time, he was residing near Johnson, New York, in the Town of Minisink {1909}, in School District Number 2 {1910}.

On 13 June 1813, letters of administration on the estate of William Horton, of Minisink, were issued to his son-in-law, Parshall Howell, and his friend, William Lain {1911}.

Parshall Howell removed his family to Hainesville, in Sandyston Township, Sussex County, New Jersey, where they were living on 11 May 1824, when he and his wife, Elizabeth, sold property near Westtown, New York, to David Lain {1912}. In Hainesville, he built a dwelling and a store, and was a merchant there for many years, being succeeded by John Everitt and then by John

1902. Mallmann, op. cit., 211.
1903. Id.
1904. Id.
1905. Id.
1906. Id.
1907. McCurdy, op. cit.
1908. Id.
1909. Stickney, HOWELL, #B102.
1910. McCurdy, op. cit.
1911. Orange County Letters of Administration, Liber D, 156, cited in THE QUARTERLY, O.C.G.S., 13, #4, 28 (Feb 1984).
1912. Orange County Deeds, Liber Y, 33.

Westbrook {1913}.

On 10 June 1836, Parshall Howell bought 320 acres in Section 21 (East half) of White Oak Township, Ingham County, Michigan, property which he later sold to Julius Stevens, whose descendants, in 1983, still owned the property, which was listed as a Michigan Centennial Farm {1914}.

During the month of September, 1838, Parshall Howell and his family settled on a farm in Dexter Township, Washtenaw County, Michigan {1915}.

Parshall Howell owned a store and lot in the Village of East Unadilla, Livingston County, Michigan, which property he bequeathed to his son, Charles, by his will of 22 May 1844 {1916}.

Parshall Howell bequeathed his lands in Ingham County, or the proceeds of the sale of them, to his daughters, "Hetty" and Louisa. His farm in Dexter Township was to be divided between his sons, Chauncy, Benjamin and Nelson Howell, and his daughter, "Mandy" Howell, after the demise or remarriage of his wife, Elizabeth {1917}.

Parshall Howell died on 30 Aug 1849, and was buried in a private cemetery on his farm. His body was taken up from there when the farm was sold, and removed to the Hamlin Township Cemetery, Eaton Rapids, Michigan {1918}.

On 3 Oct 1850, Elizabeth Howell, 56, having real property valued at $3500, was enumerated as the head of a family consisting of herself, her children, Nelson, 19 (sic), Louisa, 23, Chauncy, 19, Amanda, 15, all of whom were born in New Jersey, and Benjamin, 12, who was born in Michigan. The family was residing in Dexter Township, Washington County, Michigan {1919}.

Elizabeth (Horton) Howell died on 12 May 1863, and is buried beside her husband at Eaton Rapids {1920}.

Parshall and Elizabeth (Horton) Howell were the parents of thirteen children {1921}.

+ 561.   i.   JOHN[6] HOWELL, born on 1 Dec 1811.

+ 562.   ii. WILLIAM HORTON[6] HOWELL, born on 10 Sep 1813.

+ 563.   iii. MARIAH[6] HOWELL, born on 28 Feb 1815.

+ 564.   iv. ELIZA ANN[6] HOWELL, born on 19 Jan 1817.

1913. McCurdy, op. cit.
1914. Id.
1915. Id.
1916. Id.
1917. Id.
1918. Id.
1919. U.S. Census, Dexter Township, Washtenaw County, MI, 1850, Dwelling House 97, Family Number 97, Page 517R.
1920. Id.
1921. Id.

565. v. CHARLES[6] HOWELL, born on 16 Apr 1820.

+ 566. vi. GEORGE[6] HOWELL, born on 25 Feb 1822.

+ 567. vii. CHARLES[6] HOWELL, born on 8 Jan 1824.

+ 568. viii. MEHITABLE[6] HOWELL, born on 20 Sep 1825.

+ 569. ix. LOUISA[6] HOWELL, born on 31 Oct 1827.

+ 570. x. CHAUNCY[6] HOWELL, born on 3 Aug 1831.

+ 571. xi. NELSON[6] HOWELL, born on 19 Jly 1833.

572. xii. AMANDA[6] HOWELL, born on 15 Mch 1835, died on 2 Dec 1853, and is buried beside her parents at Eaton Rapids.

573.xiii. BENJAMIN[6] HOWELL, born on 5 Oct 1838, died on 23 May 1854, and is buried beside his parents at Eaton Rapids.

III. Descendants of Richard[2] Howell.

A. Richard[3], Richard[2], Richard[1]

244. RICHARD[5] HOWELL (Richard[4]), the son of Richard[4] and Mary Howell, was born on 2 May 1773, probably at Riverhead.

Richard Howell, Jr. married Charity Youngs at Mattituck on 14 June 1795 {1922}. She was the daughter of Christopher and Anna (Wells) Youngs {1923}, and was born on 11 Apr 1766.

Charity Howell was mentioned in the will of her father, Christopher Youngs, of Riverhead, written on 25 Jly 1799, and proved on 11 June 1800 {1924}.

On 1 Apr 1800, Richard Howell, Jr., was selected as one of several Overseers of High Ways for the ensuing year at the Annual Meeting of the Town of Riverhead. On 7 Apr 1829, he was similarly selected for the 6th School District and, on 6 Apr 1830, for District Number 7, for which he was again selected on 5 Apr 1831. He was again selected for this position on the first Tuesday of Apr 1811, and, for District Number 2, on 4 Apr 1826 {1925}.

Richard Howell, Jr., was selected to be one of several Fence Viewers for the ensuing year at the Annual Meeting of the Town of Riverhead held on 4 Apr

1922. Craven, op. cit., 334.
1923. Wines, op. cit., 38.
1924. Suffolk County Wills, Liber B, 91-93.
1925. RTR, Liber B, 47, 85, 91, 95, 97; (I, 290, 319, 323, 326, 328).

1809 at the Court House. He was again selected for this position on 3 Apr 1810, on the first Tuesday of Apr 1812, on 6 Apr 1813, and on 5 Apr 1814 {1926}.

"Richd Howell, Jur" was listed as the head of a family consisting of one free white male of 26 and under 45 years of age, and one free white female of 26 and under 45, residing in the Town of Riverhead, Suffolk County, New York, in the Second Census of the United States, 1800 {1927}.

In the Third Census of the United States, 1810, Richard Howell was listed as the head of a family consisting of one free white male of 26 and under 45 years of age, and one free white female of 26 and under 45, residing in the Town of Riverhead, Suffolk County, New York {1928}.

Richard Howell was listed as the head of a household consisting of one free white male of 45 years of age and older, one of 10 and under 16, and one free white female of 45 and older, residing in the Town of Riverhead, Suffolk County, New York, in the Fourth Census of the United States, 1820. One of these was engaged in agriculture {1929}.

In the Fifth Census of the United States, 1830, Richard Howell was listed as the head of a household consisting of one free white male of 50 and under 60 years of age, one of 15 and under 20, and one free white female of 60 and under 70, residing in the Town of Riverhead, Suffolk County, New York {1930}.

By his will of 27 Nov 1834, proved on 15 Aug 1840, Richard Howell left his estate to his wife, Charity, for her widowhood. Part of it was then to go to Daniel Howell Reeves, "..if he stay and care for testator and wife while living..". If not, then the same part was to go to Richard Howell's brother, Abner Howell, and his sister, Deborah Jagger. He also left land to his nephews, Josiah Howell, and to David Wells Howell. Further, he left legacies to Anna Hutchinson, Keziah Davis, Charity Wells, Polly Mosier, Hannah Overton, and Emma Smith. The balance of the estate was then left to his brother and his sister. Daniel Howell Reeves and Sidney L. Griffin were named as executors of this will {1931}.

Richard Howell died on 9 June 1840, at the age of 67 years, 1 month, and 7 days, and is buried in the Aquebogue Cemetery {1932}.

Charity (Youngs) Howell died on 7 June 1845, at the age of 79, years, 1 month, and 27 days, and is buried beside her husband in the Aquebogue Cemetery {1933}.

Richard and Charity (Youngs) Howell had no children.

1926. Id., 44, 45, 49, 53, 55; (I, 287, 288, 291, 296, 298).
1927. NYG&BR, LVI, 330 (Oct 1925).
1928. U.S. Census, Riverhead, Suffolk County, NY, 1810, Page 251.
1929. Id., 1820, Page 358.
1930. U.S. Census, Riverhead, Suffolk County, NY, 1830, Page 238.
1931. Suffolk County Wills, Liber H, 278-282; Suffolk County Estates, File #3113.
1932. Gravestone, Aquebogue Cemetery.
1933. Id.

245. DEBORAH⁵ HOWELL (Richard⁴), the daughter of Richard⁴ and Mary Howell, was probably born in the vicinity of Riverhead before 1776.

Deborah Howell married Samuel Jagger. He was the son of James and Jane Jagger, and was born in about 1775 {1934}.

Samuel Jagger died on 10 Mch 1845 {1935}.

Samuel and Deborah (Howell) Jagger were the parents of at least six children {1936}.

    i.   JANE JAGGER, married Sylvanus White {1937}.

    ii.   PHEBE JAGGER, born in about 1804, married Jeremiah Squires {1938} on 11 Dec 1824, four children, died on 9 Apr 1872 in her 68th year, and is buried in the Southampton Cemetery {1939}.

    iii.   MARY JAGGER, born on 12 Oct 1808, married Capt. Austin Herrick {1940}.

    iv.   MARIA JAGGER, married ----- Terry.

    v.   DEBORAH JAGGER.

    vi.   SAMUEL HAMPTON JAGGER, born in about 1816, married Elizabeth Fithian, who was born in about 1822, the daughter of Jonathan {1941} and Abbie (Sayre) Fithian {1942}, two children, was the minister at Marlborough, N.Y., for several years until his health prevented his continuing, when he retired to Newburgh {1943}.

246. ABNER⁵ HOWELL (Richard⁴), the son of Richard⁴ and Mary Howell, was born on 15 Mch 1781, in the vicinity of Riverhead.

Abner Howell married Azuba Howell (#212), the daughter of Silas⁴ and Mary (Benjamin) Howell, as his first wife {1944}.

Abner Howell was selected to serve as one of several Overseers of high

1934. George Rogers Howell, op. cit., 328.
1935. Id.
1936. Id.
1937. Id., 405.
1938. Id., 388.
1939. Richard A. Squires, Personal communication.
1940. George Rogers Howell, op. cit., 295.
1941. Id., 328-329.
1942. Rattray, op. cit., 332.
1943. George Rogers Howell, op. cit., 328-329.
1944. George H. Tuthill, op. cit.

ways at the Annual Meeting of the Town of Riverhead held on 3 Apr 1804 {1945}.

On 29 Mch 1805, it was recorded that the Overseers of the Poor received £46 16s from "..Abner Howell Collector" {1946}. On 28 Mch 1806, the Overseers received of "Abner Howell Collector in full of the Rate Book for the year 1804..£13 5s" {1947}. At the same time, it was recorded that he received £1 12s 10d "..for Collecting 178 doll" {1948}. He was recorded as having been paid 50¢ on 31 Mch 1825. On 26 Mch 1827, he was recorded as having been paid 25¢, and $3.25 on 31 Mch 1828, 25¢ on 30 Mch 1830, 25¢ on 29 Mch 1831, $5.04 in 1836, $5.00 in 1837, $17.74 on 29 Mch 1838, $3.00 in 1839, $3.00 and $86.29 in 1840 {1949}. He shared $2.00 with Zachariah Hallock in 1841 {1950}.

On 28 Sep 1805, Abner Howell was a witness to the will of Lewis Stanbrough, of Riverhead, which was proved on 28 Dec 1808 {1951}.

Abner Howell married his cousin, Sarah, "Sally", Howell, (#248), as his second wife {1952}. She was the daughter of Merrit and Sarah (Luce) Howell, and was born in about Mch 1781.

Abner Howell was listed as the head of a family consisting of one free white male of 26 and under 45 years of age, one of under 10, one free white female of 26 and under 45, and one of under 10, residing in the Town of Riverhead, Suffolk County, New York, in the Third Census of the United States, 1810 {1953}.

At the 24th Annual Town Meeting at the Court House 1815, Abner Howell was selected to serve as a Fence Viewer for the ensuing year {1954}. He was again selected to serve in this office at the 25th Annual Meeting of the Electors of the Town of Riverhead on 2 Apr 1816, as well as on 1 Apr 1817, on 7 Apr 1818, on 6 Apr 1819, on 4 Apr 1820, on 3 Apr 1821, on 2 Apr 1822, on 1 Apr 1823, on 6 Apr 1824, on 5 Apr 1825, on 4 Apr 1826, on 3 Apr 1827, on 1 Apr 1828 {1955}.

Sarah Howell received lands, and other legacies, by the will of her father, Merrit Howell, of Riverhead, written on 1 Jan 1818, and proved on 6 Oct 1818 {1956}.

1945. RTR, Liber A, 80; (I, 51).
1946. Id., 83; (I, 52).
1947. Id., 87; (I, 55).
1948. Id., 88; (I, 56).
1949. Id., 139[a], 140[a], 143, 145, 149, 151, 161, 164, 166, 167, 169, 170; (I, 93, 94, 97, 98, 102, 104, 112, 114, 116, 116, 118, 119).
1950. Id., 172; (I, 120).
1951. Suffolk County Wills, Liber B, 542-543.
1952. SUFFOLK GAZETTE, 17 Mch 1806; NYG&BR, 24, 87 (Jan 1893).
1953. U.S. Census, Riverhead, Suffolk County, NY, 1810, Page 251.
1954. RTR, Liber B, 59; (I, 299).
1955. Id., 63, 65, 67, 69, 71, 73, 75, 77, 80, 83, 85, 87, 89; (I, 301, 303, 305, 306, 308, 310, 311, 313, 314, 317, 319, 321, 322).
1956. Suffolk County Wills, Liber D, 164-165; Suffolk County Estates, File #1433.

Abner Howell was listed as the head of a family consisting of one free white male of 26 and under 45 years of age, one of under 10, one free white female of 26 and under 45, one of 10 and under 16, and one of under 10, residing in the Town of Riverhead, Suffolk County, New York, in the Fourth Census of the United States, 1820. One member of the family was engaged in agriculture {1957}.

On 8 May 1822, Abner Howell was a witness to a deed by which Benjamin Homan and Benjamin Howell sold, to Merrit Howell, a tract of cedar swamp of about 10 acres. This tract was bounded, on the north, by 10 acres "..that was given to the said Benjamin Homan and Abner Howell by Will from Merrit Howell deceased.." {1958}.

By the will of his father, Richard Howell, of Riverhead, written on 30 Nov 1814, and proved on 27 May 1823, Abner Howell divided the estate with his brother, Richard Howell, paying his share of $400 to their sister, Deborah Jagger {1959}.

On 2 Mch 1824, Abner Howell witnessed an agreement by which Benjamin Homan granted, to Jasper Vail, a cartway across his land to a certain piece of meadow which he, Benjamin Homan, had sold to Jasper Vail {1960}.

Abner Howell was listed as the head of a family consisting of one free white male of 40 and under 50 years of age, one free white female of 40 and under 50, one of 15 and under 20, and one of 10 and under 15, residing in the Town of Riverhead, Suffolk County, New York, in the Fifth Census of the United States, 1830 {1961}.

On 6 Apr 1835, Abner Howell was selected to serve as one of three Commissioners of Highways at the Annual Meeting of the Town of Riverhead {1962}. He was again selected to serve in this position on 5 Apr 1836, on 4 Apr 1837, on 3 Apr 1838, and on 2 Apr 1839 {1963}.

Abner Howell was a Commissioner of Highways on 12 Jan 1837, when a highway was laid out from Riverhead to the Middle Road, which ultimately became the southern end of Roanoke Avenue {1964}. He was also a Commissioner on 9 Nov 1837 when a highway was laid out from the Post Road to James Port, later to become Washington Avenue or West Jamesport Lane {1965}.

On 3 Apr 1838, Abner Howell was selected to serve as the Overseer of Highways for District Number 7 for the ensuing year by the Annual Meeting of the Town of Riverhead {1966}.

In the Sixth Census of the United States, 1840, Abner Howell was listed as the head of a household consisting of one free white male of 40 and under 50

1957. U.S. Census, Riverhead, Suffolk County, NY, 1820, Page 358.
1958. ACKERLY RECORD BOOKS, Book 2, 105.
1959. Suffolk County Wills, Liber E, 7-8; Suffolk County Estates, File #1710.
1960. ACKERLY RECORD BOOKS, Book 2, 107-108.
1961. U.S. Census, Riverhead, Suffolk County, NY, 1830, Page 238.
1962. RTR, Liber B, 107; (I, 335).
1963. Id., 109, 113, 115, 118; (I, 336, 339, 341, 343).
1964. Id., 112; (I, 338).
1965. Id., 100, (I, 329-330).
1966. Id., 115; (I, 340).

years of age, two of 20 and under 30, one free white female of 50 and under 60, one of 20 and under 30, and one of under 5, residing in the Town of Riverhead, Suffolk County, New York {1967}.

As of 5 Apr 1842, Abner Howell was paid $4.99 as "..Int^t. on his Note due from Com^n. H. W. (Commissioners of Highways)" {1968}. At this time, there was also paid $71.29 "To Bal Due on Abner Howells Note" {1969}.

As of 28 Mch 1843, $50.00 was "Paid Abnor Howell on Note", as well as $128.81 "To Bal du Zacoriah Hallock & Abner Howell on Notes 1842 Ma[r]ch 29" {1970}.

By his will of 9 Aug 1843, Abner Howell left, to his wife, "Salley", "..part of my farm..as long as she remains my widow..". His son, Josiah, was to receive the eastern part of his farm, while his son, David W., was to receive the western part. He also left legacies to his grandsons, "Lusha Erl Mosly" and "Thomas Nelson Mosly", as well as $100 each to his grand-daughters, Christiana Howell and "Azuba Mosly". His sons, Josiah and David W., were named as executors of this will, which was proved on 18 Mch 1851 {1971}.

At the Annual Town Meeting at the Court House in Riverhead on 2 Apr 1850, it was "Voted That the Town Confer the honour on Mr Abnor Howell of his calling the Highway Runing from the village of Riverhead to Middle Road by the name Abnor Street by his request he putting guide boards at his own expence" {1972}.

On 17 Sep 1850, Abner Howell, 60, farmer, and his wife, Sarah, 60, were living in the same dwelling house as their son, Josiah, 38, and his wife, Amanda, 34, and their children, Christiana, 12, Mary M., 8, Sarah A., 6, and Henrietta, 2, when the Seventh Census of the United States was taken {1973}.

Abner Howell died on 28 Jan 1851, at the age of 69 years, 10 months, and 13 days, and is buried in the Aquebogue Cemetery {1974}.

Sarah (Howell) Howell died on 5 Jan 1862, at the age of 80 years and 10 months, and is buried beside her husband in the Aquebogue Cemetery {1975}.

Abner and Sarah (Howell) Howell were the parents of at least four children.

+ 574. i. MARY W.[6] HOWELL, born in about Nov 1807.

+ 575. ii. JOSIAH[6] HOWELL, born on 14 Jan 1810.

1967. U.S. Census, Riverhead, Suffolk County, NY, 1840, Page 239.
1968. RTR, Liber B, 174; (I, 123).
1969. Id.; (I, 124).
1970. Id., 175; (I, 125).
1971. Suffolk County Wills, Liber 5, 191-193; Suffolk County Estates, File #4073.
1972. RTR, Liber B, 141; (I, 360).
1973. U.S. Census, Riverhead, Suffolk County, NY, 1850, Dwelling House 465, Family Number 509, Page 279.
1974. Gravestone, Aquebogue Cemetery.
1975. Id.

576. iii.   NELSON A.[6] HOWELL, born on 27 Jan 1814 {1976}, died on 8 Sep 1824, in his 11th year, and is buried in the Riverhead Cemetery {1977}.

+ 577. iv.   DAVID WELLS[6] HOWELL, born on 30 Jan 1821 {1978}.

247. PATIENCE[5] HOWELL (Merrit[4]), the daughter of Merrit[4] and Sarah (Luce) Howell, was born in about July 1777 in the vicinity of Riverhead.

Patience Howell married Benjamin Homan, who was born in about 1777.

On 8 May 1822, Benjamin Homan, with Benjamin Howell, sold, to Merrit Howell, a tract of cedar swamp of about 10 acres, bounded, on the north, by 10 acres "..that was given to the said Benjamin Homan and Abner Howell by Will from Merrit Howell deceased.." {1979}.

Benjamin Homan died on 6 May 1831, at the age of 55, and is buried in the Aquebogue Cemetery {1980}.

On 5 Sep 1850, Patience Homan, 73, with real property worth $2500, was enumerated as the head of a family consisting of herself, and her daughter, Sarah, 45, residing in the Town of Riverhead, Suffolk County, New York, in the Seventh Census of the United States {1981}.

Patience (Howell) Homan died on 7 Apr 1854, at the age of 76 years and 9 months, and is buried beside her husband at Aquebogue {1982}.

Benjamin and Patience (Howell) Homan were the parents of six children.

i.   URIAH HOMAN, born on 24 Nov 1798, died on 30 Dec 1872, and is buried the family plot at Riverhead {1983}.

ii.   HARRIET HOMAN, born in about 1800, married Daniel Terry Wells, died on 13 Sep 1877, at the age of 77, and is buried in the Aquebogue Cemetery {1984}.

iii.   SARAH HOMAN, born in about 1805, died on 17 Sep 1873, and is buried at Aquebogue {1985}.

iv.   MALINDA HOMAN.

1976. Mrs. Robert E. (Lois Ann Shaffer) Pawson, Personal communication.
1977. Gravestone, Riverhead Cemetery.
1978. Pawson, op. cit.
1979. ACKERLY RECORD BOOKS, Book 2, 105.
1980. Gravestone, Aquebogue Cemetery.
1981. U.S. Census, Riverhead, Suffolk County, NY, Dwelling House 145, Family Number 165, Page 258.
1982. Gravestone, Aquebogue Cemetery.
1983. Gravestone, Riverhead Cemetery.
1984. Gravestone, Aquebogue Cemetery.
1985. Id.

v. HULDAH HOMAN.

vi. BENJAMIN MILLS HOMAN.

248. SARAH[5] HOWELL (Merrit[4]), the daughter of Merrit[4] and Sarah (Luce) Howell, was born in the vicinity of Riverhead in about Mch 1781.

Sarah, "Sally", Howell married her cousin, Abner Howell (#246), the son of Richard[4] and Mary Howell {1986}, as his second wife.

Sarah (Howell) Howell died on 5 Jan 1862, at the age of 80 years and 10 months, and is buried beside her husband in the Aquebogue Cemetery {1987}.

Abner and Sarah (Howell) Howell were the parents of at least four children, as listed under #246, Abner[5] Howell.

249. MERRITT[5] HOWELL (Merritt[4]), the son of Merritt[4] and Sarah (Luce) Howell, was born on 10 Nov 1783 {1988}.

Merritt Howell married Eleanor Luce, who was born on 25 Nov 1786, the daughter of Capt. Abraham and Jemima (Tuthill) Luce {1989}.

On 3 Apr 1807, it was recorded that £8 18s 5d was paid to "Merritt Howell Ju for keeping George Raynor Child" {1990}.

"Merrit Howell, Jr." was listed as the head of a family consisting of one free white male of 16 and under 26 years of age, one free white female of 16 and under 26, and three of under 10, residing in the Town of Riverhead, Suffolk County, New York, in the Third Census of the United States, 1810 {1991}.

As "Poor bid off at Vendue", Martha Lupton was bid off to "Merit Howell Ju[r]." at 5s 6d per week on 3 Apr 1810 {1992}. On 6 Apr 1813, Deborah Moore was bid off to Merrit Howell Ju[r]. at 10s per week {1993}. On 4 Apr 1815, Peter Wells was bid off to "Merit Howell Jr." for 2s 8d per week {1994}.

In the Fourth Census of the United States, 1820, "Merret Howell" was listed as the head of a family consisting of one free white male of 45 years of age and over, one of 16 and under 26, one of under 10, one free white female of 26 and under 45, one of 16 and under 26, two of 10 and under 16, and three of under 10, residing in the Town of Riverhead, Suffolk County, New York. Of these, one was

---

1986. SUFFOLK GAZETTE, 17 Mch 1806; NYG&BR, XXIV, 87 (Apr 1893).
1987. Gravestone, Aquebogue Cemetery.
1988. Jacques and Kappenberg, op. cit., 13, Mallmann, op. cit., 214.
1989. Id.
1990. RTR, Liber A, 90; (I, 57).
1991. U.S. Census, Riverhead, Suffolk County, NY, 1810, Page 252.
1992. RTR, Liber A, 101; (I, 68).
1993. Id., 113; (I, 75).
1994. Id., 121; (I, 79).

engaged in agriculture {1995}.

On 30 Mch 1826, it was recorded that Merit Howell was paid $15.00 in account with the Overseers of the Poor {1996}.

Charity Howell was hired out to Merit Howell for 29¢ on 4 Apr 1826 {1997} and, on 5 Apr 1831, Sally Lupton was hired out to Merritt Howell for 75¢ {1998}.

"Merit Howell" was listed as the head of a family consisting of one free white male of 70 and under 80 years of age, one of 40 and under 50, one of 15 and under 20, one of 10 and under 15, one free white female of 40 and under 50, one of 15 and under 20, two of 10 and under 15, and two of under 5, residing in the Town of Riverhead, Suffolk County, New York, in the Fifth Census of the United States, 1830 {1999}.

In the Sixth Census of the United States, 1840, "Merrett Howell" was listed as the head of a family consisting of one free white male of 50 and under 60 years of age, one of 20 and under 30, one of 15 and under 20, one free white female of 50 and under 60, one of 20 and under 30, one of 15 and under 20, and one of 10 and under 15, residing in the Town of Riverhead, Suffolk County, New York {2000}.

It was recorded that Merit Howell was paid $10.00 on behalf of the Commissioners of Highways in 1840 {2001}.

On 5 Sep 1850, Merritt Howell, 66, was listed as the head of a household consisting of himself, his wife, Eleanor, 63, Elbert H. Howell (sic), 6, and Pricilla White, 12, residing in the Town of Riverhead, Suffolk County, New York, in the Seventh Census of the United States {2002}.

In his will of 7 Feb 1853, proved on 29 Dec 1857, Merritt Howell mentioned his daughters, Sally Edwards, Jemima Howell, Betsey Smith, Fanny B. Terry, Harriet N. Hallock, and Frances M. Hallock, as well as his son, Hampton F. Howell, and his grandsons, Henry H. Howell, Merritt H. Smith, Theodore B. Terry, Elbert H., James H., and Chancy A. Edwards. In a codicil to this will, dated 11 Nov 1857, he mentioned his grand-daughter, Sarepta E. Edwards {2003}.

By her will of 25 Oct 1854, proved on 3 Mch 1856, Eleanor Howell left land in Riverhead to her daughters, Jemima, the wife of David Howell, Fanny B., the wife of Partial (sic) Terry, of Ohio, Betsey, the wife of Rockwell Smith, Sarah, the wife of David Horton, Harriet, the wife of Herman Hallock, and Frances M., the wife of Sylvester Hallock {2004}.

1995, U.S. Census, Riverhead, Suffolk County, NY, 1820, Page 357.

1996. RTR, Liber A, 141; (I, 95).

1997. Id., Liber B, 85; (I, 319).

1998. Id., 97; (I, 328).

1999. U.S. Census, Riverhead, Suffolk County, NY, 1830, Page 236.

2000. Id., 1840, Page 236.

2001. RTR, Liber A, 170; (I, 119).

2002. U.S. Census, Riverhead, Suffolk County, NY, 1850, Dwelling House 188, Family Number 208, Page 261.

2003. Suffolk County Wills, Liber 6, 309-320; Suffolk County Estates, File #4860.

2004. Id., 16-18; Suffolk County Estates, File #4614.

Eleanor (Luce) Howell died on 31 Oct 1854, and is buried in the Riverhead Cemetery {2005}.

Merrit Howell died on 4 Dec 1857, and is buried beside his wife at Riverhead {2006}.

Merrit and Eleanor (Luce) Howell were the parents of eleven children {2007}.

578. i. BUEL[6] HOWELL, born on 8 June 1804, died on 1 Dec 1806, and is buried in the Aquebogue Cemetery {2008}.

+ 579. ii. JEMIMA[6] HOWELL, born on 26 Jly 1806.

580. iii. ELEANOR[6] HOWELL, born on 21 Aug 1808, died on 19 Jan 1823, and is buried at Aquebogue {2009}.

+ 581. iv. FANNY[6] HOWELL, born on 4 Oct 1810.

+ 582. v. HAMPTON F.[6] HOWELL, born on 10 Sep 1812.

+ 583. vi. BETSEY[6] HOWELL, born on 1 May 1814.

+ 584. vii. SALLY[6] HOWELL, born on 26 Sep 1816.

+ 585. viii. HARRIET[6] HOWELL, born on 28 May 1819.

586. ix. MERRITT B.[6] HOWELL, born on 21 Apr 1824, died on 31 Dec 1825, and is buried at Aquebogue {2010}.

+ 587. x. FRANCES M.[6] HOWELL, born on 25 Feb 1826.

588. xi. ELEANOR LUETA[6] HOWELL, born on 19 Aug 1829, died on 29 Dec 1830, and is buried at Riverhead {2011}.

250. BENJAMIN[5] HOWELL (Merrit[4]), the son of Merrit[4] and Sarah (Luce) Howell, was born in about 1786 in the vicinity of Riverhead.

Benjamin Howell married Huldah Hallock on 10 Dec 1807 at Riverhead before the Rev. Daniel Youngs {2012}. She was the daughter of Daniel and

2005. Gravestone, Riverhead Cemetery; Jacques & Kappenberg, op. cit., 13.
2006. Id.
2007. Jacques & Kappenberg, op. cit., 13; Mallmann, op. cit., 214.
2008. Gravestone, Aquebogue Cemetery.
2009. Id.
2010. Id.
2011. Gravestone, Riverhead Cemetery.
2012. SUFFOLK GAZETTE, 28 Dec 1807; NYG&BR, 24, 161 (1893).

Mary (Wells) Hallock, and was born on 18 Apr 1788 {2013}.

On 8 Feb 1808, Benjamin Howell was a witness to a deed by which Benjamin Horton and Stephen Griffing sold a "..lot of land..lying about one hundred rods easterly from the Court House.." to Merrit Howell {2014}.

Benjamin Howell was listed as the head of a family consisting of one free white male of 16 and under 26 years of age, one of under 10, and one free white female of 16 and under 26, residing in the Town of Riverhead, Suffolk County, New York, in the Third Census of the United States, 1810 {2015}.

With his brother, Merrit Howell, Jr., Benjamin Howell was an executor of the will of his father, Merrit Howell, written on 1 Jan 1818, and proved on 6 Oct 1818, by which he and his brother divided their father's estate, after bequests to their mother, sisters, and a niece and nephew {2016}.

Benjamin Howell was a witness to a deed by which Abraham Luce, John P. Luce and David Hulse sold, to Merrit Howell, a lot of about 25 acres, at Halsey's Manor, in the Town of Brookhaven, on 12 Nov 1819 {2017}.

Benjamin Howell was listed as the head of a family consisting of one free white male of 26 and under 45 years of age, one of 10 and under 16, one free white female of 25 and under 45, one of 16 and under 26, and two of under 10, residing in the Town of Riverhead, Suffolk County, New York, in the Fourth Census of the United States, 1820. One member of the family was engaged in manufacturing {2018}.

Benjamin Howell sold, to his brother, Merrit Howell, a certain piece of land, of about 35 acres, in the Town of Riverhead, bounded "Northerly by the Cliff, Easterly by the land of Richard Howell, Southerly by the North Road, and Westerly by the land of Manly Wells." {2019}, as well as another piece of land, containing about 7 acres, "..at a place called broad meadows..in the town of Southampton..", and yet another piece, of about 8 acres of land, "..at a place called Muddy Creek..", in 1822 {2020}.

With his brother-in-law, Benjamin Homan, and their wives, Patience Homan and Huldah Howell, Benjamin Howell sold a lot of about 10 acres, from his father's estate, to his brother, Merrit Howell, on 20 May 1822 {2021}.

Benjamin Howell was listed as the head of a family consisting of one free white male of 40 and under 50 years of age, one of 20 and under 30, one free white female of 40 and under 50, one of 15 and under 20, and one of 10 and under 15, residing in the Town of Riverhead, Suffolk County, New York, in the Fifth Census of the United States, 1830 {2022}.

2013. Lucius H. Hallock, op. cit., 369.
2014. ACKERLY RECORD BOOKS, Book 2, 99.
2015. U.S. Census, Riverhead, Suffolk County, NY, 1810, Page 252.
2016. Suffolk County Wills, Liber D, 164-165; Suffolk County Estates, File #1433.
2017. ACKERLY RECORD BOOKS, Book 2, 103.
2018. U.S. Census, Riverhead, Suffolk County, NY, 1820, Page 358.
2019. ACKERLY RECORD BOOKS, Book 2, 103-104.
2020. Id., 106-107.
2021. ACKERLY RECORD BOOKS, Book 2, 105.
2022. U.S. Census, Riverhead, Suffolk County, NY, 1830, Page 238.

On 5 Apr 1836, Benjamin Howell was selected to serve as the Overseer of Highways for District Number 7 by the Annual Meeting of the Town of Riverhead {2023}.

In the Sixth Census of the United States, 1840, Benjamin Howell was listed as the head of a family consisting of one free white male of 50 and under 60 years of age, one of 30 and under 40, one free white female of 50 and under 60, one of 30 and under 40, and one of 20 and under 30, residing in the Town of Riverhead, Suffolk County, New York {2024}.

On 17 Sep 1850, Benjamin Howell, 60, farmer, and his wife, Huldah, 60, were living in the same dwelling house, in the Town of Riverhead, Suffolk County, New York, as their son, Alfred L., 40, and his wife, Anna, 36, in the Seventh Census of the United States {2025}.

Huldah (Hallock) Howell died on 6 Oct 1856, at the age of 69 years and 6 months, and is buried in the Aquebogue Cemetery {2026}.

Benjamin Howell died on 23 Dec 1866, at the age of 80, and is buried beside his wife in the Aquebogue Cemetery {2027}.

Benjamin and Huldah (Hallock) Howell were the parents of at least three children.

+ 589.   i.   ALFRED L.[6] HOWELL, born in about 1810.

  590.   ii.   HULDAH MARIA[6] HOWELL, born in about 1815, died on 7 May 1871, in the 57th year of her life, and is buried in the Aquebogue Cemetery {2028}.

+ 591. iii.   JULIETTE[6] HOWELL, born in about 1816 {2029}.

IV. Descendants of Isaac [2] Howell.

A. Isaac [3], Isaac [2], Richard [1]

251. NANCY[5] HOWELL (Isaac[4]), the daughter of Isaac[4] and Abigail (Freeman) Howell was born on 20 Nov 1766 {2030}.

Nancy Howell married Elijah St. John, who was born on 12 Nov 1766, at Sharon, Connecticut {2031}.

2023. RTR, Liber B, 110; (I, 337).
2024. U.S. Census, Riverhead, Suffolk County, NY, 1840, Page 245.
2025. Id., 1850, Dwelling House 461, Family Number 504, Page 278.
2026. Gravestone, Aquebogue Cemetery.
2027. Id.
2028. Id.
2029. Lucius H. Hallock, op. cit., 369.
2030. James Barnaby Howell, op. cit., 4.
2031. Id.

Nancy (Howell) St. John died on 3 June 1853 {2032}.

Elijah and Nancy (Howell) St. John were the parents of eight children {2033}.

    i.   PHILO ST. JOHN, born on 30 Jly 1790.

    ii.   MYRON ST. JOHN, born on 12 June 1792.

    iii.   CLARISSA ST. JOHN, born on 18 Sep 1795.

    iv.   NANCY ST. JOHN, born on 11 Jly 1797.

    v.   PAMELIA ST. JOHN, born on 5 Dec 1799.

    vi.   FANNY ST. JOHN, born on 21 Jly 1802.

    vii. ABIGAIL ST. JOHN, born on 17 Jly 1804.

    viii. E. HOWELL ST. JOHN, born on 22 Dec 1806.

252. ISAAC[5] HOWELL (Isaac[4]), the son of Isaac[4] and Abigail (Freeman) Howell, was born on 2 Oct 1768 {2034}.

On 8 Sep 1793, Isaac Howell married, at Sharon, Connecticut, Bathsheba Holland, who was born on 12 Oct 1777 {2035}.

Isaac Howell died on 7 Jan 1840 {2036}, and is buried in the cemetery at Franklin, New York {2037}.

Isaac and Bathsheba (Holland) Howell were the parents of twelve children {2038}.

592.   i.   SOPHIA[6] HOWELL, born on 16 June 1795, died on 3 Jly 1795.

+ 593. ii.   SAMUEL[6] HOWELL, born on 30 Apr 1797.

+ 594. iii. ABIGAIL[6] HOWELL, born on 19 Mch 1799.

595.   iv. EDWIN[6] HOWELL, born on 30 Jan 1801, died on 15 Apr 1809.

+ 596. v.   CYNTHIA[6] HOWELL, born on 21 Apr 1803.

2032. Id.
2033. Id., 4, 5.
2034. Id., 4.
2035. Id., 5.
2036. Id., 4.
2037. Nancy Allen (Howell) Ornce, Personal communication.
2038. James Barnaby Howell, op. cit., 5.

+ 597. vi.   ISAAC[6] HOWELL, born on 20 Feb 1805.

598. vii.   ALTHEA[6] HOWELL, born on 8 May 1807, died on 22 Oct 1809.

+ 599. viii.   EDWIN[6] HOWELL, born on 20 Aug 1809.

+ 600. ix.   ALTHEA[6] HOWELL, born on 8 Mch 1812.

+ 601. x.   JULIA[6] HOWELL, born on 15 Mch 1814.

602. xi.   HARRIET[6] HOWELL, born on 25 Dec 1816, died on 1 Jan 1835.

+ 603. xii.   MARIA[6] HOWELL, born on 19 Jan 1820.

253. ABRAHAM[5] HOWELL (Isaac[4]), the son of Isaac[4] and Abigail (Freeman) Howell, was born on 5 Jan 1771 {2039}.

In August 1796, Abraham Howell married Polly Little, who was born on 20 Mch 1780 {2040}.

Polly (Little) Howell died on 21 Aug 1810 {2041}.

On 1 Aug 1811, Abraham Howell married (2) Sarah Fisk, who was born on 3 Mch 1795 {2042}.

On 18 Sep 1850, "Abram Howell, 79" and his wife, Sally, 65, were enumerated in the household of their son, Sanuel H. Howell, in the Seventh Census of the United States {2043}.

Abraham Howell died on 8 Jan 1860 at Delavan, New York, and is buried there {2044}.

Sally Howell died in 1863, and is buried beside her husband at Delevan {2045}.

Abraham and Polly (Little) Howell were the parents of six children {2046}.

+ 604. i.   ALFRED MILTON[6] HOWELL, born on 28 Nov 1799.

+ 605. ii.   HENRY[6] HOWELL, born on 5 Feb 1802.

+ 606. iii.   NOAH BUCKLEY[6] HOWELL, born on 22 Oct 1803.

2039. Id., 4.
2040. Id., 5.
2041. Ornce, op. cit.
2042. James Barnaby Howell, op. cit., 5.
2043. U.S. Census, Yorkshire, Cattaraugus County, NY, 1850, Dwelling House 1308, Family Number 1379, Page 465.
2044. Ornce, op. cit.
2045. Gertrude A. Barber, CATTARAUGUS COUNTY, N.Y., CEMETERIES.
2046. James Barnaby Howell, op. cit., 5.

+ 607. iv.   NANCY[6] HOWELL, born on 25 Jan 1806.

+ 608. v.   RALPH[6] HOWELL, born on 8 Feb 1808.

+ 609. vi.   ABRAHAM P.[6] HOWELL, born on 19 Feb 1810.

Abraham and Sally (Fisk) Howell were the parents of seven children {2047}.
+ 610. vii.   FRANCES[6] HOWELL, born on 9 Feb 1813.

+ 611. viii.   BETSEY[6] HOWELL, born on 13 Mch 1814.

+ 612. ix.   POLLY[6] HOWELL, born on 29 Jly 1816 {2048}.

+ 613. x.   SAMUEL HAWKINS[6] HOWELL, born on 25 Apr 1818 {2049}.

+ 614. xi.   URIAH F.[6] HOWELL, born on 25 Jan 1820 {2050}.

  615. xii.   EUSEBIA[6] HOWELL.

+ 616. xiii.   SARAH ANN[6] HOWELL.

254. POLLY[5] HOWELL (Isaac[4]) was the daughter of Isaac[4] and Abigail (Freeman) Howell {2051}.
        Polly Howell mrried Mr. Barnaby {2052}.
        Polly (Howell) Barnaby was the mother of five children {2053}.
        i.   JAMES BARNABY, married Susan Elliott, no children.

        ii.   SABRINA BARNABY, born on 17 Apr 1797, married Sylvanus Halsey on 8 Nov 1821 {2054}, four children, died on 14 Feb 1853.

        iii.   AMBROSE BARNABY.

        iv.   MARY BARNABY.

2047. Id., 6.
2048. Ornce, op. cit.
2049. Id.
2050. Id.
2051. James Barnaby Howell, op. cit., 6.
2052. Id.
2053. Id.
2054. Id., 13.

v. HOWELL BARNABY.

255. CLARISA[5] HOWELL (Isaac[4]), the daughter of Isaac[4] and Abigail (Freeman) Howell, was born on 8 Jan 1774 {2055}.

On 7 Sep 1795 {2056}, Clarisa Howell married Col. Silas Fitch at New Canaan, Connecticut {2057}. He was born on 28 Jan 1773 {2058}.

Silas Fitch died on 15 Feb 1857 {2059}, at Fabius, New York {2060}.

Clarisa (Howell) Fitch died on 4 Aug 1862 {2061}, at Fabius {2062}.

Silas and Clarisa (Howell) Fitch were the parents of ten children {2063}.

i.   SALLY FITCH, born on 4 Jly 1797, married Abel Bostwick, who was born on 7 Mch 1798, at Franklin, New York, five children {2064}, died in 1869.

ii. CLARISA FITCH, born on 26 Jly 1799, married Sidney Hastings, six children {2065}, died in 1869.

iii. ALMIRON FITCH, born on 8 Aug 1801, married Caroline Case on 11 June 1826 at Franklin, New York, two children {2066}, died on 9 Jan 1877.

iv. SAPHRONIA FITCH, born on 29 Oct 1803, married Horace Mann on 22 Feb 1825 at Franklin, New York, four children {2067}, died on 25 Feb 1891.

v.   EMELINE FITCH, born on 25 Mch 1806, married Ephraim Clough at Fabius, New York, six children {2068}, died on 21 Mch 1894.

2055. Id., 5.
2056. Id. 6.
2057. Hawkes, op. cit., 19.
2058. James Barnaby Howell, op. cit., 6.
2059. Id.
2060. Hawkes, op. cit., 19.
2061. Id.
2062. Id., 18.
2063. James Barnaby Howell, op. cit., 6.
2064. Id., 14.
2065. Id., 13, 14.
2066. Id., 14.
2067. Id.
2068. Id.

vi.   ESTHER FITCH, born on 13 Feb 1809, married Charles Fox, three children {2069}, died on 22 Sep 1860.

vii.   SILAS FITCH, born on 26 Feb 1811, died on 7 Feb 1812.

viii.   SILAS FITCH, born on 15 Mch 1813, married Mary A. White on 30 Mch 1842, seven children {2070}, died on 26 Oct 1885 {2071}.

ix.   NANCY FITCH, born on 9 June 1815, married (1) Charles R. Torrey on 24 Sep 1848 {2072}, one child, married (2) John Moses in May 1854, one child {2073}, died on 5 Aug 1887.

x.   JULIA ANN FITCH, born on 18 May 1819, married George O'Blemeis, no children {2074}, died on 7 Dec 1893.

256. SIMEON[5] HOWELL (Isaac[4]), the son of Isaac[4] and Abigail (Freeman) Howell, was born on 4 Feb 1776 {2075}.

In 1800, at Franklin, New York, Simeon Howell married Rhoda McCall, who was born in about 1781 {2076}.

Rhoda (McCall) Howell died on 22 May 1820 {2077}.

Simeon Howell married (2) Mrs. Mary Mulford at New Hartford in 1820. She was born on 18 Jan 1786 {2078}.

Simeon Howell died on 21 Nov 1856 {2079}.

Mary (----) Mulford Howell died on 6 May 1867 {2080}.

Simeon and Rhoda (McCall) Howell were the parents of eight children {2081}.

617.   i.   ESTHER[6] HOWELL, born on 28 Nov 1801, died on 22 Nov 1852.

+ 618.   ii.   EMILY[6] HOWELL, born on 2 Apr 1803.

2069. Id.
2070. Id.
2071. Id., 6.
2072. Id., 14.
2073. Id., 15.
2074. Id.
2075. Id., 4.
2076. Id., 6.
2077. Id.
2078. Id., 7.
2079. Id., 4.
2080. Id., 7.
2081. Id., 6.

+ 619. iii.   POLLY[6] HOWELL, born on 11 Nov 1804.

+ 620. iv.   DANIEL[6] HOWELL, born on 26 Oct 1807.

+ 621. v.   SUSAN[6] HOWELL, born on 30 Nov 1809.

+ 622. vi.   CLARISA[6] HOWELL, born on 5 Apr 1814.

623. vii.   FANNY[6] HOWELL, born on 3 Apr 1816.

+ 624. viii.   JANE[6] HOWELL, born on 1 Jan 1818.

Simeon and Mary (----) Mulford Howell were the parents of four children {2082}.

+ 625. ix.   SARAH[6] HOWELL, born on 27 Nov 1821.

626. x.   CAROLINE[6] HOWELL, born on 15 Jan 1823.

627. xi.   FRANCES[6] HOWELL, born on 18 Feb 1825.

+ 628. xii.   ELIZABETH[6] HOWELL, born on 17 Aug 1828.

257. FANNY[5] HOWELL (Isaac[4]) was the daughter of Isaac[4] and Abigail (Freeman) Howell {2083}.

Fanny Howell married Mr. Pierce {2084}.

Fanny (Howell) Pierce was the mother of at least one child {2085}.

i.   FANNY PIERCE, married Mr. Parmely, two children {2086}.

258. JACOB[5] HOWELL (Isaac[4]), the son of Isaac[4] and Abigail (Freeman) Howell, was born on 4 Sep 1779 {2087}.

On 27 Dec 1804, at Franklin, New York, Jacob Howell married Betsey McCall, who was born on 7 Nov 1785 {2088}.

Jacob Howell died on 16 June 1838 {2089}.

Betsey Howell died on 23 June 1869 {2090}.

2082. Id., 7.
2083. Id., 4.
2084. Id., 7.
2085. Id.
2086. Id., 16.
2087. Id., 4.
2088. Id., 7.
2089. Id., 4.
2090. Id., 7.

Jacob and Betsey (McCall) Howell were the parents of eleven children {2091}.

+ 629. i.   PAMELIA[6] HOWELL, born on 21 Dec 1805.

   630. ii.   SIMEON F.[6] HOWELL, born on 17 Nov 1807.

+ 631. iii. ANNA E.[6] HOWELL, born on 23 Dec 1809.

   632. iv. ELIHU McCALL[6] HOWELL, born on 8 Nov 1811.

+ 633. v.   JAMES BARNABY[6] HOWELL, born on 4 Dec 1813.

+ 634. vi. ALVAH LORENZO[6] HOWELL, born on 22 Sep 1815.

+ 635. vii. MARIANNE[6] HOWELL, born on 12 Jly 1817.

+ 636. viii. ELIZABETH C.[6] HOWELL, born on 22 June 1819.

+ 637. ix. JACOB W.[6] HOWELL, born on 3 Sep 1821.

+ 638. x.   BETSEY U.[6] HOWELL, born on 1 Apr 1824.

+ 639. xi. HENRY[6] HOWELL, born on 9 Feb 1829.

B. Micah[3], Isaac[2], Richard[1]

261. BARNABAS[5] HOWELL (Micah[4]), the son of Micah[4] and Sarah (Roe) Howell, was born in about 1779.

Barnabas Howell was the principal heir, as well as an executor, of the will of his father, written on 21 Jly 1801, and proved on 6 Oct 1801 {2092}.

On 2 Dec 1801, "Barnibus Howell (married) "Mehittible Wines" {2093}.

In the Third Census of the United States, 1810, Barnabus Howell was listed as the head of a family consisting of one free white male of 26 and under 45 years of age, four of under 10, and one free white female of 26 and under 45, residing in the Town of Southold, Suffolk County, New York {2094}.

Barnabus Howell was listed as the head of a family consisting of one free white male of 26 and under 45 years of age, two of 10 and under 16, two of under 10, one free white female of 26 and under 45, and two of under 10, residing in the

---

2091. Id.
2092. Suffolk County Wills, Liber B, 154-155; Suffolk County Estates, File #507.
2093. SR, 110; NYG&BR, XLIX, 277 (Jly 1918).
2094. U.S. Census, Southold, Suffolk County, NY, 1810, Page 257.

Town of Southold, Suffolk County, New York, in the Fourth Census of the United States, 1820 {2095}.

By his will of 15 Jly 1822, proved on 1 Oct 1822, Barnabas Howell left certain property to his wife, Hetty, with furniture, in lieu of dower, said property to pass to his son, Hampton, at her death or remarriage, with the balance to be sold for her benefit {2096}.

Barnabas Howell died on 4 Sep 1822, at the age of 43, and is buried in the cemetery at the Mattituck Presbyterian Church {2097}.

"Mahet¹ Howell" was listed as the head of a family consisting of one free white female of 40 and under 50 years of age, and one of 15 and under 20, residing in the Town of Southold, Suffolk County, New York, in the Fifth Census of the United States, 1830 {2098}.

On 10 Jly 1850, Mehitabel Howell, 70, with real property worth $200, was listed as the head of a family consisting of herself in the Seventh Census of the United States. She was residing in the Town of Southold, Suffolk County, New York {2099}.

Mehetable Howell died on 24 Sep 1858, in her 80th year, and is buried beside her husband at Mattituck {2100}.

Barnabas and Mehetable (Wines) Howell were the parents of at least three children.

640. i.   CLARISSA⁶ HOWELL, born on 23 Sep 1816, died on 4 Mch 1817, and is buried beside her parents at Mattituck {2101}.

641. ii. HAMPTON⁶ HOWELL.

642. iii. BARNABUS W.⁶ HOWELL.

262. CHRISTIANNA⁵ HOWELL (Micah⁴), the daughter of Micah⁴ and Sarah (Roe) Howell, was born on 23 Jly 1785 {2102}.

"Mr. Zachariah Hallock, Jun., married Miss Christiana Howell, the daughter of Mr. Micah Howell, deceased.." in about 1810 {2103}. He was born on 12 May 1776 {2104}, the son of Zachariah and Hannah (Youngs) Hallock. Christianna Howell was his second wife, his first having been Mary Aldrich {2105}, who was born on 29 Jly 1783 {2106}. She died on

2095. Id., 1820, Page 257.
2096. Suffolk County Wills, Liber D, 374-375; Suffolk County Estates, File #1654.
2097. Craven, op. cit., 374.
2098. U.S. Census, Southold, Suffolk County, NY, 1830, Page 346.
2099. Id., NY, 1850, Dwelling House 43, Family Number 46, Page 283.
2100. Craven, op. cit.
2101. Id.
2102. THE REGISTER, SCHS, XIX, #2, 41 (Fall 1993).
2103. SUFFOLK GAZETTE, 17 Mch 1810.
2104. THE REGISTER, SCHS, XIX, #2, 41 (Fall 1993).
2105. Lucius H. Hallock, op. cit., 641.

7 Nov 1809, in the 26th year of her age, and is buried in the cemetery at Aquebogue {2107}.

Zachariah Hallock was a farmer who lived at Northville, New York {2108}.

Zachariah Hallock died on 4 Nov 1854, at the age of 78, and is buried beside his wives at Aquebogue {2109}.

Christianna (Howell) Hallock died on 6 May 1860, at the age of 75, and is buried beside her husband at Aquebogue {2110}.

Zachariah and Mary (Aldrich) Hallock were the parents of four children {2111}. Zachariah and Christianna (Howell) Hallock did not have any children.

    i.   HANNAH HALLOCK, born on 22 Jly 1802, married Rogers Aldrich, of Jamesport, on 23 Jan 1833, 6 children, died on 12 Oct 1849. Her husband was born on 8 May 1806, and died on 16 Oct 1889 {2112}.

    ii.   HERMAN HALLOCK, born on 24 June 1804 {2113}, married Arminda Young in 1828, 6 children, died in 1881 {2114}.

    iii.   MARY OWEN HALLOCK, born on 12 Oct 1806 {2115}, died on 7 Jan 1823, at the age of 17, and is buried in the cemetery at Aquebogue {2116}.

    iv.   ZACHARIAH HALLOCK, born on 15 Mch 1809, married Arletta Young in 1833, died in 1864. His wife was born on 11 Feb 1816, and died in 1883 {2117}.

C. Daniel [3], Isaac [2], Richard [1]

263. BETHIA[5] HOWELL (Silas[4]), the daughter of Silas[4] and Jemima[4] (Howell)

2106. THE REGISTER, SCHS, XIX, #2, 41 (Fall 1993).
2107. Gravestone, Aquebogue Cemetery.
2108. Lucius H. Hallock, op. cit.
2109. Gravestone, Aquebogue Cemetery.
2110. Id.
2111. Lucius H. Hallock, op. cit.
2112. Id., 333.
2113. THE REGISTER, SCHS, XIX, #2, 41 (Fall 1993).
2114. Lucius H. Hallock, op. cit., 361.
2115. THE REGISTER, SCHS XIX, #2, 41 (fALL 1993).
2116. Gravestone, Aquebogue Cemetery.
2117. Lucius H. Hallock, op. cit.

Howell, was born on 23 Nov 1776 {2118}.

On 20 June 1796, Bethia Howell married Joshua Livingston Wells, who was born on 13 June 1776, the son of Paul and Anna Wells {2119}.

Joshua L. Wells was a farmer at Aquebogue, a repairer and painter of carriages, who made his own varnish, and who made ploughs, carts, stage coaches and riding chairs {2120}.

On 4 Sep 1850, Joshua L. Wells, 73, farmer, and his wife, Bethia, 73, were enumerated as a family residing in the Town of Riverhead, Suffolk County, New York, in the Seventh Census of the United States {2121}.

Joshua L. Wells died on 13 June 1855, at the age of 78 years and 9 months, and is buried in the Aquebogue Cemetery {2122}.

Bethia (Howell) Wells died on 13 Jan 1863, at the age of 86 years, 1 month and 20 days, and is buried beside her husband at Aquebogue {2123}.

Joshua Livingston and Bethia (Howell) Wells were the parents of at least one child {2124}.

    i.   EURYSTHEUS HOWELL WELLS, born in about 1797, married Mary E. Corwin, who was born in about 1800, the daughter of Capt. Jedidiah and Mary (Luce) Corwin, died on 9 Apr 1880, at the age of 83, and is buried in the Aquebogue Cemetery, while she died on 25 Apr 1880, at the age of 80, and is buried beside her husband at Aquebogue {2125}.

264. DANIEL⁵ HOWELL (Silas⁴), the son of Silas⁴ and Jemima⁴ (Howell) Howell, was born on 8 May 1778 {2126}.

In 1806, Daniel Howell married Mary Young, who was born on 4 Aug 1788, the daughter of Rev. Daniel and Mary (Halsey) Young {2127}.

Mary (Youngs) Howell died on 10 Jan 1807, at the age of 19, and is buried in the Aquebogue Cemetery {2128}.

Daniel Howell married (2) Phebe Young, who was born on 25 Dec 1789, the sister of his first wife {2129}.

2118. Wilbur Franklin Howell, op. cit., 119.

2119. Id.

2120. Id.

2121. U.S. Census, Riverhead, Suffolk County, NY, 1850, Dwelling House 103, Family Number 119, Page.

2122. Gravestone, Aquebogue Cemetery.

2123. Id.

2124. Wilbur Franklin Howell, op. cit.

2125. Gravestone, Aquebogue Cemetery.

2126. Charles Ransom Howell Family Bible, in the possession of the Nassau County Museum, from a copy at the New York Genealogical & Biographical Society, a copy of which was kindly provided to me by Henry Hoff via Harry Macy.

2127. Id.

2128. Gravestone, Aquebogue Cemetery.

2129. Charles Ransom Howell Family Bible.

Daniel Howell "..served as a soldier in the War of 1812.." {2130}.

A payment of $2.00 to Daniel Howell in account with the Overseers of the Poor of the Town of Riverhead was recorded on 31 Mch 1825 {2131}.

In the Fifth Census of the United States, 1830, Daniel Howell was listed as the head of a family consisting of one free white male of 40 and under 50 years of age, one of 20 and under 30, one of 10 and under 15, one free white female of 40 and under 50, and one of 15 and under 20, residing in the Town of Riverhead, Suffolk County, New York {2132}.

On 2 Apr 1833, Daniel Howell was chosen to serve as the Overseer of Highways for the ensuing year, for Road District Number 10 of the Town of Riverhead {2133}. He was again chosen for this position on 1 Apr 1834, on 2 Apr 1844, on 7 Apr 1846, and on 6 Apr 1847 {2134}.

Daniel Howell was listed as the head of a family consisting of one free white male of 60 and under 70 years of age, one of 15 and under 20, one free white female of 40 and under 50, and one of 20 and under 30, residing in the Town of Riverhead, Suffolk County, New York, in the Sixth Census of the United States, 1840 {2135}.

Phebe (Youngs) Howell died on 18 Feb 1849, at the age of 59 years, 1 month, and 24 days, and is buried at Aquebogue {2136}.

On 5 Sep 1850, Daniel Howell, 71, was enumerated with the household of his son, Charles R., in the Town of Riverhead, Suffolk County, New York in the Seventh Census of the United States {2137}.

Daniel Howell died on 27 Apr 1854 at the age of 75, and is buried beside his wives at Aquebogue {2138}.

Daniel and Mary (Youngs) Howell were the parents of one son {2139}.

+ 643.   i.   CHARLES RANSOM[6] HOWELL, born on 1 Jan 1807.

Daniel and Phebe (Youngs) Howell were the parents of one daughter {2140}.

644.   ii.   POLLY MARIA[6] HOWELL, born on 5 May 1815, died on 24 Oct 1843, at the age of 28 years, 5 months, and 19 days, and is buried at Aquebogue {2141}.

2130. PORTRAIT & BIOGRAPHICAL RECORD OF SUFFOLK COUNTY, 489.
2131. RTR, Liber A, 139a (I, 92); 140a (I, 93).
2132. U.S. Census, Riverhead, Suffolk County, NY, 1830, Page 236.
2133. RTR, Liber B, 103; (I, 332).
2134. Id., 105, 127, 132, 134; (I, 333, 350, 353, 355).
2135. U.S. Census, Riverhead, Suffolk County, NY, 1840, Page 236.
2136. Gravestone, Aquebogue Cemetery.
2137. U.S. Census, Riverhead, Suffolk County, NY, 1850, Dwelling House 150, Family Number 170, Page 258.
2138. Gravestone, Aquebogue Cemetery.
2139. Wilbur Franklin Howell, op. cit., 129.
2140. Id.
2141. Gravestone, Aquebogue Cemetery.

266. MEHITABLE⁵ HOWELL (Silas⁴), the daughter of Silas⁴ and Jemima⁴ (Howell) Howell, was born on 31 Mch 1785 {2142}.

Mehitable Howell married Bartlett Griffing, the son of John and Anna Griffing {2143}.

Deacon Bartlett Griffing died on 25 Jly 1855, at the age of 82 years, and is buried in the Aquebogue Cemetery {2144}.

Mehitable (Howell) Griffing died on 23 Jly 1867, and is buried beside her husband at Aquebogue {2145}.

Deacon Bartlett and Mehitable (Howell) Griffing were the parents of one daughter {2146}.

    i.   JEMIMA⁶ GRIFFING.

267. JEMIMA⁵ HOWELL (Silas⁴), the daughter of Silas⁴ and Jemima⁴ (Howell) Howell, was born on 3 Mch 1788 {2147}.

Jemima Howell married James Moore, who was born on 2 Sep 1786, the son of James and Cathy Moore {2148}.

On 2 Sep 1850, James Moore, 63, farmer, with real property worth $1000, was enumerated as the head of a family consisting of himself, his wife, Jemima, 62, and their son, Silas, 38, seaman, residing in the Town of Riverhead, Suffolk County, New York, in the Seventh Census of the United States {2149}.

Jemima (Howell) Moore died on 14 Apr 1857, at the age of 59 years, 1 month, and 14 days, and is buried in the Aquebogue Cemetery {2150}.

James Moore died on 7 May 1862, at the age of 75 years, and is buried beside his wife at Aquebogue {2151}.

James and Jemima (Howell) Moore were the parents of three children {2152}.

    i.   SILAS MOORE, born in about 1812.

    ii.   HARRIET MOORE.

    iii.   Child.

2142. Id., 138.
2143. Wilbur Franklin Howell, op. cit., 138.
2144. Gravestone, Aquebogue Cemetery.
2145. Id.
2146. Wilbur Franklin Howell, op. cit.
2147. Id., 118.
2148. Id., 143.
2149. U.S. Census, Riverhead, Suffolk County, NY, 1850, Dwelling House 4, Family Number 5, Page 250.
2150. Gravestone, Aquebogue Cemetery.
2151. Id.
2152. Wilbur Franklin Howell, op. cit., 129.

268. SILAS HAMILTON[5] HOWELL (Silas[4]), the son of Silas[4] and Jemima[4] (Howell) Howell, was born on 15 Feb 1790 {2153}.

Silas Hamilton Howell married Mary, "Polly", Griffing {2154}. She was the daughter of Nathaniel and Mary (Albertson) Griffing {2155}, and was given a legacy by his will of 22 Mch 1822, probated on 18 June 1823 {2156}.

Silas Howell, Jr. was listed as the head of a family consisting of one free white male of 26 and under 45 years of age, one of under 10, one free white female of 26 and under 45, and one of under 10, residing in the Town of Riverhead, Suffolk County, New York, in the Fourth Census of the United States, 1820 {2157}.

On 31 Mch 1825, it was recorded that Silas H. Howell was paid $2.25 in account with the Overseers of the Poor (1050). He was similarily paid $2.25 in 1829 {2158}.

On 4 Apr 1826, Silas H. Howell was selected to serve as one of several Fence Viewers at the Annual Meeting of the Town of Riverhead {2159}. He was similarily selected on 3 Apr 1827, and on 1 Apr 1828 {2160}.

Silas H. Howell was selected to serve as one of four Assessors at the Annual Meeting of the Town of Riverhead held in the County Hall on 4 Apr 1826 {2161}.

On 6 Apr 1830, Silas H. Howell was selected to serve as one of three Commissioners of Highways for the ensuing year at the Annual Meeting of the Town of Riverhead {2162}. He was again selected for this position on 5 Apr 1831, on 3 Apr 1832, on 5 Apr 1841, on 5 Apr 1842, on 4 Apr 1843, on 2 Apr 1844, on 1 Apr 1845, on 7 Apr 1846, on 6 Apr 1847. He was the sole Commissioner of Highways after 1846 {2163}.

In the Fifth Census of the United States, 1830, S. H. Howell was listed as the head of a family consisting of one free white male of 40 and under 50 years of age, one of 10 and under 15, one of 5 and under 10, one of under 5, one free white female of 40 to 50, one of 15 and under 20, one of 10 and under 15, and one of 5 and under 10, residing in the Town of Riverhead, Suffolk County, New York {2164}.

In 1831, Silas H. Howell was paid $4.00 as a Commissioner of Highways.

2153. Id., 144.
2154. Id.
2155. Clara J. Stone, GENEALOGY OF THE DESCENDANTS OF JASPER GRIFFING, 21.
2156. Suffolk County Wills, Liber E, 13-14.
2157. U.S. Census, Riverhead, Suffolk County, NY, 1820, Page 357.
2158. RTR, Liber A, 147*; (I, 100).
2159. RTR, Liber B, 85; (I, 319).
2160. Id., 87, 89; (I, 321, 322).
2161. Id., Liber B, 86; (I, 320).
2162. Id., 96; (I, 327).
2163. Id., 98, 102, 122, 124, 126, 128, 130, 132, 134; (I, 329, 331, 346, 347, 349, 350, 352, 354, 355). ·
2164. U.S. Census, Riverhead, Suffolk County, NY, 1830, Page 236.

He was similarily paid $2.76 in 1832, and $7.00 in 1833 {2165}.

Silas H. Howell was selected to serve as the Overseer of Highways for Road District Number 4 by the Annual Meeting of the Town of Riverhead held at the Court House on 2 Apr 1833 {2166}.

Silas H. Howell was listed as the head of a family consisting of one free white male of 50 and under 60 years of age, one of 20 and under 30, one of 15 and under 20, one free white female of 50 and under 60, one of 20 and under 30, one of 15 and under 20, and one of 5 and under 10, residing in the Town of Riverhead, Suffolk County, New York, in the Sixth Census of the United States, 1840 {2167}.

In 1842, Silas H. Howell was paid $3.00 in account with the Supervisor, Town of Riverhead. A similar payment of $5.00 was recorded on 28 Mch 1843, one of $4.00 on 26 Mch 1844, one of $5.00 on 25 Mch 1845, one of $5.00 on 30 Mch 1846, and another of $5.00 on 28 Mch 1848 {2168}.

On 5 Sep 1850, Silas H. Howell, 60, farmer, with real property worth $3,500, was listed as the head of a family consisting of himself, his wife, Mary, 61, and their children, George, 21, and Emily, 18, residing in the Town of Riverhead, Suffolk County, New York, in the Seventh Census of the United States {2169}.

Mary (Griffing) Howell died on 25 Dec 1851, at the age of 63 years and 3 days, and is buried in the Aquebogue Cemetery {2170}.

Silas Hamilton Howell died on 21 Jan 1852, at the age of 61 years, 11 months, and 6 days, and is buried beside his wife at Aquebogue {2171}.

Silas Hamilton and Mary (Griffing) Howell were the parents of six children {2172}.

645.   i.   MARY ALBERTSON[6] HOWELL, born on 31 Jly 1817, died on 10 June 1845, at the age of 27 years, 10 months, and 10 days, and is buried at Aquebogue {2173}.

+ 646.   ii.   DANIEL GRIFFING[6] HOWELL, born on 21 Oct 1819.

+ 647.   iii.   CHARITY J.[6] HOWELL, born on 13 Dec 1821.

648.   iv.   SILAS HAMILTON[6] HOWELL, born in about 1824, was an unmarried teacher when he died on 10 May 1848 {2174}

2165. RTR, Liber A, 151, 153, 155; (I, 104, 106, 108).
2166. Id., Liber B, 103; (I, 332).
2167. U.S. Census, Riverhead, Suffolk County, NY, 1840, Page 236.
2168. RTR, Liber A, 174, 176, 179, 186, 191, 195; (I, 123, 126, 129, 136, 140, 144).
2169. U.S. Census, Riverhead, Suffolk County, NY, 1850, Dwelling House 146, Family Number 166, Page 258.
2170. Gravestone, Aquebogue Cemetery.
2171. Id.
2172. Wilbur Franklin Howell, op. cit.
2173. Gravestone, Aquebogue Cemetery.
2174. RTR, (I, 725).

in the 24th year of his age, and is buried at Aquebogue {2175}.

+ 649. v. GEORGE N.[6] HOWELL, born on 23 Mch 1829.

+ 650. vi. EMILY S.[6] HOWELL, born in about 1832.

270. GEORGE[5] HOWELL (Silas[4]), the son of Silas[4] and Jemima (Howell) Howell, was born on 7 Sep 1796 {2176}.

On 28 Dec 1820, George Howell married Polly B. Wells, who was born on 10 Jly 1797 {2177}.

On 5 Apr 1842, George Howell was selected to be the Overseer of Roads for Road District No. 4 of the Town of Riverhead for the ensuing year. He was again selected for this position on 4 Apr 1843, on 2 Apr 1844, on 1 Apr 1845, on 7 Apr 1846, on 6 Apr 1847, on 4 Apr 1848, on 3 Apr 1849, on 2 Apr 1850, on 1 Apr 1851, on 6 Apr 1852, on 5 Apr 1853, and on 4 Apr 1854 {2178}.

Polly B. Howell lost her eyesight about Christmas in 1848 {2179}.

On 5 Sep 1850, George Howell, 54, farmer, with real property worth $6,000, was enumerated as the head of a family consisting of himself, his wife, Polly B., 53, and their sons, Wm. S., 20, teacher, and Joshua M., 18, residing in the Town of Riverhead, Suffolk County, New York, in the Seventh Census of the United States {2180}.

George Howell was shot by Augustus Terry, who was apparently an escaped maniac, on 12 Oct 1859, but was not seriously hurt {2181}.

On 17 Feb 1864, David F. Vail, George Howell and J. Henry Perkins were appointed as a committee to act with the Supervisor and Town Clerk to procure the men and money to meet the town quota under the call of President Lincoln for a draft of 500,000 men {2182}.

On 5 Apr 1864, 3 votes were cast for George Howell to be Town Clerk, and 182 votes for him to be Justice of the Peace. Nathan Corwin was elected to both offices {2183}.

George Howell died on 13 Nov 1871, at the age of 76 years, 2 months,

2175. Gravestone, Aquebogue Cemetery.
2176. NYG&BR, 81, 142 (1950), Wilbur Franklin Howell, op. cit., 174.
2177. Id., 144 (1950); Wilbur Fanklin Howell, op. cit.
2178. RTR, Liber B, 124, 126, 128, 130, 132, 134, 138, 140, 142, 144, 148, 154, 166; (I, 347, 348, 350, 351, 353, 355, 357, 359, 360, 362, 364, 369, 376).
2179. Edna J. Raynor, Notes, in the file of Wilbur Franklin Howell, in the possession of the SCHS, 1992.
2180. U.S. Census, Riverhead, Suffolk County, NY, 1850, Dwelling House 147, Family Number 167, Page 258.
2181. Edna J. Raynor, op. cit.
2182. RTR, Liber B, 272, Liber C, 9; (I, 444, 554).
2183. Id., Liber B, 277; (I, 446).

and 6 days, was buried in the Aquebogue Cemetery {2184}, but is now buried at Riverhead {2185}.

Polly B. Howell died on 7 Mch 1872, at the age of 74 years and 8 months, was buried at Aquebogue {2186}, but is now buried beside her husband at Riverhead {2187}.

George and Polly B. (Wells) Howell were the parents of nine children {2188}.

651. i.   EDNA JANE[6] HOWELL, born on 30 Sep 1821, died on 22 Mch 1841, was buried in the Aquebogue Cemetery {2189}, but was re-buried at Riverhead {2190}.

\+ 652. ii.   JOHN FRANKLIN[6] HOWELL, born on 11 Mch 1824.

\+ 653. iii. JOSEPH CHAUNCEY[6] HOWELL, born on 14 Jan 1827.

\+ 654. iv. WILLIAM SIDNEY[6] HOWELL, born on 16 Jan 1830.

\+ 655. v.   JOSHUA M.[6] HOWELL, born on 24 Oct 1832.

656. vi.   GEORGE WASHINGTON[6] HOWELL, born on 24 Oct 1832, died on 14 Nov 1832, at the age of 2 months and 4 days, was buried in the Aquebogue Cemetery {2191}, but was re-buried at Riverhead {2192}.

657. vii. LYDIA MARIE[6] HOWELL, born on 20 Dec 1834, died on 28 Aug 1835, was buried at Aquebogue {2193}, but was re-buried at Riverhead {2194}.

\+ 658. viii. ROSELINE V.[6] HOWELL, born on 9 Mch 1838.

\+ 659. ix. EDNA JANE[6] HOWELL, born on 14 Sep 1841.

271. EARNEST AUGUSTA[5] HOWELL (Silas[4]), the daughter of Silas[4] and Jemima[4]

2184. Gravestone, Aquebogue Cemetery.
2185. Id., Riverhead Cemetery.
2186. Gravestone, Aquebogue Cemetery.
2187. Id., Riverhead Cemetery.
2188. NYG&BR, LXXXI, 142, 144 (Apr 1950); Wilbur Franklin Howell, op. cit., 174.
2189. Gravestone, Aquebogue Cemetery.
2190. Id., Riverhead Cemetery.
2191. Gravestone, Aquebogue Cemetery.
2192. Id., Riverhead Cemetery.
2193. Gravestone, Aquebogue Cemetery.
2194. Id., Riverhead Cemetery.

(Howell) Howell, was born on 22 Jan 1798 {2195}.

On 2 Nov 1816, Earnest Augusta Howell married James Wells, Jr., who was born on 3 Dec 1795 {2196}, the son of James and Lydia (Terry) Wells.

On 5 Sep 1850, Jas. Wells, 54, farmer, with real property worth $5000, was enumerated as the head of a household consisting of himself, his wife, Earnest A., 51, their children, Lydia J., 18, and George S., 8, and Andrew McDonald, 22, laborer, residing in the Town of Riverhead, Suffolk County, New York, in the Seventh Census of the United States {2197}.

Earnest Augusta (Howell) Wells died on 17 Aug 1876, at the age of 78 years, 6 months, and 26 days, and is buried in the Aquebogue Cemetery {2198}.

James Wells died on 26 Apr 1877, at the age of 81 years, 4 months, and 23 days, and is buried beside his wife at Aquebogue {2199}.

James and Earnest Augusta (Howell) Wells were the parents of six children {2200}.

> i.   JOSHUA LIVINGSTON WELLS, born on 30 Oct 1817, married Frances Puah Terry, died on 15 Mch 1882.
>
> ii. JANE FRANCES WELLS, born on 3 Feb 1820, married Alden Wells, died on 6 Jly 1842.
>
> iii. JAMES MADISON WELLS, born on 10 Jan 1822, died on 10 Oct 1828.
>
> iv. Infant, born on 29 Jly 1824, died on 5 Aug 1824.
>
> v.   LYDIA JEMIMA WELLS, born on 24 Sep 1832, married Joshua B. Griffin, died on 24 June 1888.
>
> vi. GEORGE L. WELLS, born on 12 Sep 1842, married Mary Teresa Young.

273. EBENEZER[5] HOWELL (Joseph[4]), the son of Joseph[4] and Sarah (Mather) Howell, was born on 29 Feb(sic) 1785 {2201}.

On 6 Dec 1812, Ebenezer Howell married Sarah Holmes, who was born on 7 Jan 1791 {2202}.

2195. Wilbur Franklin Howell, op. cit., 186.

2196. Id.

2197. U.S. Census, Riverhead, Suffolk County, NY, 1850, Dwelling House 151, Family Number 171, Page 258.

2198. Gravestone, Aquebogue Cemetery.

2199. Id.

2200. Wilbur Franklin Howell, op. cit., 186.

2201. Ebenezer Howell Family Bible, in the possession of Michael A. Howell, 1995.

2202. Id.

Sarah Howell died on 25 Feb 1824 {2203}.

On 8 May 1827, Ebenezer Howell married Elizabeth Johnston, who was born on 1 Apr 1795, the daughter of Samuel and Elizabeth (Miller) Johnston {2204}.

Ebenezer Howell was a carpenter, and he maintained a home in Rockland County and later in Brooklyn {2205}.

Ebenezer and Sarah (Holmes) Howell were the parents of five children {2206}.

+ 660. i.   JOSEPH MARTHERS[6] HOWELL, born on 16 Feb 1814 at Newburgh.

+ 661. ii.   JOHN H.[6] HOWELL, born on 20 Apr 1816.

+ 662. iii. SARAH JANE[6] HOWELL, born on 9 Jan 1819.

+ 663. iv. FRANCES[6] HOWELL, born on 7 Dec 1820.

  664. v.   ANN ELIZA[6] HOWELL, born on 14 Jly 1823.

Ebenezer and Elizabeth (Johnston) Howell were the parents of five children {2207}.

+ 665. vi. MARY[6] HOWELL, born on 2 Mch 1828.

+ 666. vii. CHARLES[6] HOWELL, born on 30 Jan 1830.

  667.viii. EBENEZER[6] HOWELL, JR., born on 1 Mch 1831 (sic), died on 6 Jly 1833, at the age of 1 year, 4 months, and 6 days.

+ 668. ix. ANNA[6] HOWELL, born on 11 Apr 1834.

  669. x.   JULIETTE[6] HOWELL, born on 17 Jly 1836, died on 15 Sep 1840, at the age of 4 years and 1 month.

V. Descendants of Jacob[2] Howell.

A. Jacob[3], Jacob[2], Richard[1].

274. JONATHAN[5] HOWELL (Jacob[4]) was the son of Jacob[4] and Lydia (Howell)

2203. Id.
2204. Id.
2205. Michael A. Howell, op. cit.
2206. Ebenezer Howell Family Bible.
2207. Id.

Howell.

By his will of 5 Sep 1812, proved on 22 Oct 1812, Jonathan Howell, of Chester Township, Morris County, New Jersey, left, to his brother, Joshua, $100, to his nephew, Jonathan, son of his brother, Joshua, $200, to his sister, Margaret Mulford, $20, to his sister, Eunis Swezey, $20, to his sisters, Azuba Hopkins, Patience Dolley, and Anney Howell, $5 each, to his nephew, Jonathan Howell Swezey, $50, and, to his brother, Jacob, $2.50. He also left $10 to the First Congregational Church in Chester for a bell, and provided that any residue should be divided between his brother, Joshua, and his sisters {2208}.

277. MARGARET⁵ HOWELL (Jacob⁴) was the daughter of Jacob⁴ and Lydia (Howell) Howell.

Margaret Howell was referred to as "Market Mulford" in the will of her brother, Jonathan Howell, of Chester Township, Morris County, New Jersey, written on 5 Sep 1812, and proved on 22 Oct 1812, by which she inherited $20 {2209}.

278. AZUBA⁵ HOWELL (Jacob⁴), the daughter of Jacob⁴ and Lydia (Howell) Howell, was born on 1 Aug 1761 {2210}.

Azuba Howell married John Hopkins, who was born in 1755 {2211},the son of William and Sarah (Langstaff) Hopkins {2212}.

Azuba Hopkins was bequeathed $5 by the will of her brother, Jonathan Howell, of Chester Township, Morris County, New Jersey, written on 5 Sep 1812, and proved on 22 Oct 1812 {2213}.

John Hopkins died on 15 Mch 1833, and is buried in a small cemetery north of East Palmyra {2214}.

Azuba Hopkins died on 1 Apr 1845, at the age of 83 years, 8 months and 18 days, and is buried beside her husband {2215}.

John and Azuba (Howell) Hopkins were the parents of eight children {2216}.

    i.   JOHN HOPKINS.

    ii.   JONAH HOPKINS, born in 1782.

    iii.   SARAH HOPKINS, born in 1784, married Timothy van Winkle.

2208. NEW JERSEY ARCHIVES, (Vol. 12, Abstracts of Wills), 192-193.
2209. Id.
2210. Ruth E. Parker, Personal communication.
2211. Irene M. Hopkins, Personal communication.
2212. David Faris, op. cit., 153.
2213. NEW JERSEY ARCHIVES, op. cit.
2214. Wayne County, N.Y., Cemeteries, from L.D.S. microfilm 0813654.
2215. Id.
2216. Hopkins, op. cit.

iv.   BENJAMIN HOPKINS.

v.   TRUMAN HOPKINS.

vi.   ELIZABETH S. HOPKINS.

vii.   MARIETTA HOPKINS, married Robert Patrick.

viii.   HANNAH HOPKINS, married Mr. Esterly.

281. JACOB[5] HOWELL (Jacob[4]) was the son of Jacob[4] and Lydia (Howell) Howell, and was born on 15 June 1770 {2217}.

Jacob Howell married Hannah Moore(s), who was born on 27 Aug 1778 {2218}.

Jacob Howell was bequeathed $2.50 by the will of his brother, Jonathan Howell, of Chester Township, Morris County, New Jersey, written on 5 Sep 1812, and proved on 22 Oct 1812 {2219}.

Jacob Howell died on 19 May 1845, at the age of 75 years, and is buried in the East Palmyra Cemetery {2220}.

Hannah (Moore) Howell died 27 June 1864, at the age of 85 years, and is buried beside her husband at East Palmyra {2221}. Most of her children are mentioned in her will of 26 Jan 1864, proved on 12 Sep 1864 {2222}.

Jacob and Hannah (Moore) Howell were the parents of fourteen children {2223}.

+ 670.   i.   AZUBA[6] HOWELL, born on 14 Nov 1799.

+ 671.   ii.   WILLIAM[6] HOWELL, born on 25 Dec 1800.

  672.   iii.   ISAIAH[6] HOWELL, born on 20 Jly 1802.

+ 673.   iv.   PHOEBE G.[6] HOWELL, born on 19 Jly 1803.

  674.   v.   RACHEL[6] HOWELL, born on 4 Sep 1804.

+ 675.   vi.   MARGARET[6] HOWELL, born on 24 Sep 1806.

2217. Alice Howell, Personal communication.
2218. Id.
2219. NEW JERSEY ARCHIVES, op. cit.
2220. East Palmyra Cemetery records, p. 3$^{1}/_{2}$, from Wayne County Cemetery Records, L.D.S. microfilm 0813654.
2221. Id.
2222. Wayne County (NY) Wills, Liber K, Page 264-266.
2223. Wayne County (NY) Surrogate Records, File #0608; Parker, op. cit.

+ 676. vii.   JACOB⁶ HOWELL, born on 3 Apr 1810.

+ 677. viii. ABIGAIL⁶ HOWELL, born on 20 May 1811.

+ 678. ix.   ISAAC⁶ HOWELL, born on 11 Nov 1812.

  679. x.   HYLEASA⁶ HOWELL, born on 23 Oct 1814, died in Aug 1816,
              and is buried in the East Palmyra Cemetery {2224}.

+ 680. xi.   JOHN L.⁶ HOWELL, born on 11 Feb 1816.

+ 681. xii.   SAMUEL⁶ HOWELL, born on 3 Sep 1817.

+ 682. xiii. MARTIN⁶ HOWELL.

  683. xiv.   MARION⁶ HOWELL.

  684. xv.   HANNAH⁶ HOWELL, born on 3 Sep 1822.

282. JOSHUA⁵ HOWELL (Jacob⁴) was the son of Jacob⁴ and Lydia (Howell) Howell.
    Joshua Howell was bequeathed $100 by the will of his brother, Jonathan Howell, of Chester Township, Morris County, New Jersey, written on 5 Sep 1812, and proved on 22 Oct 1812 {2225}.
    Joshua Howell was the father of at least one son.

+ 685. i.   JONATHAN⁶ HOWELL.

284. PATIENCE⁵ HOWELL (Jacob⁴) was the daughter of Jacob⁴ and Lydia (Howell) Howell.
    Patience Dolley was bequeathed $5 by the will of her brother, Jonathan Howell, of Chester Township, Morris County, New Jersey, written on 5 Sep 1812, and proved on 22 Oct 1812 {2226}.

285. EUNICE⁵ HOWELL (Jacob⁴) was the daughter of Jacob⁴ and Lydia (Howell) Howell.
    Eunice Swezey was bequeathed $20 by the will of her brother, Jonathan Howell, of Chester Township, Morris County, New Jersey, written on 5 Sep 1812,

---

2224. East Palmyra Cemetery records.
2225. NEW JERSEY ARCHIVES, op. cit.
2226. Id.

and proved on 22 Oct 1812 {2227}.

Eunice (Howell) Swezey was the mother of at least one son.

    i.   JONATHAN HOWELL SWEZEY.

291. ANNA[5] HOWELL (Jacob[4]) was the daughter of Jacob[4] and Lydia (Howell) Howell.

"Anney Howel" was bequeathed $5 by the will of her brother, Jonathan Howell, of Chester Township, Morris County, New Jersey, written on 5 Sep 1812, and proved on 22 Oct 1812 {2228}.

- END OF FIFTH GENERATION -

2227. Id.
2228. Id.

- SIXTH GENERATION -

I. Descendants of John[2] Howell -

A. John[3], John[2], Richard[1]

1. Jonathan[5], John[4]

289. NANCY[6] HOWELL (Jonathan[5], John[4]), the daughter of Jonathan[5] and Anna (Davis) Howell, was born at Middle Island in about June 1792.

Nancy Howell married Isaac Hulse as his second wife {2227}. He was born on 21 June 1796.

On 3 Aug 1850, Isaac Hulse, 54, farmer, was enumerated as the head of a household consisting of himself, his wife, Nancy, 58, his daughters, Harriet, 19, and Emily, 17, and Chas. Brown, 19, laborer, residing in the Town of Brookhaven, Suffolk County, New York, in the Seventh Census of the United States {2228}.

Nancy (Howell) Hulse died on 28 Jan 1862, at the age of 69 years and 7 months, and is buried beside her husband at Middle Island {2229}.

Isaac Hulse died on 17 Aug 1870, at the age of 74 years, 1 month, and 27 days, and is buried in the Union Cemetery at Middle Island {2230}.

2. John[5], John[4]

293. CHARLES[6] HOWELL (John[5], John[4]), the son of John[5] and Martha (Benjamin) Howell, was born on 3 Oct 1789 {2231}.

On 31 Dec 1816, Charles Howell married Deborah Reeve, who was born on 4 Oct 1793 {2232}, the daughter of Isaac and Anna (Howell) Reeve {2233}.

Charles Howell was listed as the head of a family consisting of one free white male of 26 and under 45, one free white female of 26 and under 45, and one of under 10, residing in the Town of Brookhaven, Suffolk County, New York, in the Fourth Census of the United States, 1820 {2234}.

2227. Wilbur Franklin Howell, op. cit., 322.
2228. U.S. Census, Brookhaven, Suffolk County, NY, 1850, Dwelling House 336, Family Number 372, Page 210.
2229. Id.
2230. Gravestone, Union Cemetery, Middle Island.
2231. Charles Reeve Howell Family Bible.
2232. Id.
2233. Wilbur Franklin Howell, op. cit., 259.
2234. U.S. Census, Brookhaven, Suffolk County, NY, 1820, Page 341.

In the Fifth Census of the United States, 1830, Charles Howell was listed as the head of a household consisting of one free white male of 40 and under 50 years of age, two of five and under 10, one of under 5, and one free white female of 20 and under 30, residing in the Town of Brookhaven, Suffolk County, New York {2235}.

Charles Howell was listed as the head of a family consisting of one free white male of 50 and under 60 years of age, two of 15 and under 20, one of 10 and under 15, one of 5 and under 10, one free white female of 40 and under 50, one of 20 and under 30, and one of 15 and under 20, residing in the Town of Brookhaven, Suffolk County, New York, in the Sixth Census of the United States, 1840 {2236}.

Charles Howell died on 13 Dec 1849, at the age of 60 years, 1 month, and 14 days, and is buried in the Union Cemetery at Middle Island {2237}.

On 23 Aug 1850, Deborah Howell, 57, with real property worth $1,000, was listed as the head of a family consisting of herself, and her children, Charles R., 22, farmer, Edmund H., 18, farmer, and Charlotte, 27, residing in the Town of Brookhaven, Suffolk County, New York, in the Seventh Census of the United States, 1850 {2238}.

"at a Meeting of the Board of Trustees of the Town of Brookhaven on tuesday the 2d day of March 1852.." it was "-decided that Mrs. Deborah Howell have 50 cts per week for keeping her son Davis Howell from last meeting to Town Meeting-" {2239}.

Deborah (Reeve) Howell died on 5 Sep 1881, at the age of 87 years and 11 months, and is buried in the Yaphank Cemetery {2240}.

Charles and Deborah (Reeve) Howell were the parents of seven children {2241}.

+ 686. i.   DEBORAH ANN[7] HOWELL, born on 15 Feb 1818.

+ 687. ii.   FRANKLYN[7] HOWELL, born on 6 Nov 1820.

+ 688. iii. CHARLOTTE[7] HOWELL, born on 21 Dec 1823.

  689. iv.   DAVIS[7] HOWELL, born on 25 May 1825, died on 27 Sep 1877, at the age of 52 years, 4 months, and 2 days, and is buried in the Yaphank Cemetery. He was a deaf mute.

  690. v.   CHARLES REEVE[7] HOWELL, born on 1 Aug 1829, member,

---

2235. Id., 1830, Page 185.
2236. Id., 1840, Page 283.
2237. Gravestone, Union Cemetery, Middle Island.
2238. U.S. Census, Brookhaven, Suffolk County, NY, 1850, Dwelling House 664, Family Number 754, Page 238.
2239. BTR, Book D, 416 (D, 472).
2240. Gravestone, Yaphank Cemetery, from the William F. Howell collection of cemetery markings.
2241. Charles Reeve Howell Family Bible.

Company C, 2nd U.S. Cavalry, died on 17 Oct 1864 at Andersonville.

+ 691. vi.   EDMUND[7] HOWELL, born on 5 Apr 1832.

692. vii.   MARY[7] HOWELL, born on 3 June 1836, died on 5 Jly 1836.

294. JOHN[6] HOWELL (John[5], John[4]), the son of John[5] and Martha (Benjamin) Howell, was born on 1 Oct 1791 at Middle Island {2242}.

On 4 Jan 1814, John Howell married Elizabeth, "Betsey", Wells, who was born on 30 Aug 1791, the daughter of Rev. Manley and Mary (Benjamin) Wells {2243}.

In 1828, John Howell "..thinking it would be best for him as,, his family was Large to movve to moriches a village on the south side of Long Island in Brookhaven town where he Bought part of a griss,, mill and tended it him self with his sons to-help him for 9 or 10 years;; when he traided his part of the Mill for a small farm joining the said mill, and Bilt a haus thereon in 1835." He was living there on 1 Jan 1852 {2244}.

John Howell was listed as the head of a family consisting of one free white male of 30 and under 40 years of age, one of 10 and under 15, one of under 5, one free white female of 30 and under 40, and three of 5 and under 10, residing in the Town of Brookhaven, Suffolk County, New York, in the Fifth Census of the United States, 1830 {2245}.

In the Sixth Census of the United States, 1840, John Howell was listed as the head of a family consisting of one free white male of 40 and under 50 years of age, one of 15 and under 20, two of 10 and under 15, two of 5 and under 10, one of under 5, one free white female of 40 and under 50, one of 5 and under 10, and one of under 5, residing in the Town of Brookhaven, Suffolk County, New York {2246}.

On 7 Aug 1850, John Howell, 59, farmer, with real property worth $500, was listed as the head of a family consisting of himself, his wife, Betsey, 55, and their children, Betsey, 19, Hannah, 12, Mitchell, 17, Charles, 14, and Hampton Y., 22, pedler, residing in the Town of Brookhaven, Suffolk County, New York, in the Seventh Census of the United States {2247}.

Elizabeth, "Betsey", (Wells) Howell died on 7 June 1862, at the age of 65 years, 9 months, and 8 days, and is buried in the Mount Pleasant Cemetery at

---

2242. Wilbur Franklin Howell, op. cit., 263.
2243. Id.
2244. John Howell, Personal communication, included in Wilbur Franklin Howell, op. cit., 287ff.
2245. U.S. Census, Brookhaven, Suffolk County, NY, 1830, Page 159.
2246. Id., 1840, Page 278.
2247. Id., 1850, Dwelling House 82, Family Number 93, Page 193.

Center Moriches {2248}.

John Howell died on 4 Jly 1867, at the age of 75 years, 9 months, and 3 days, and is buried beside his wife at Center Moriches {2249}.

John and Elizabeth (Wells) Howell were the parents of nine children {2250}.

+ 693. i. WILLIAM BENJAMIN[7] HOWELL, born on 3 Nov 1816.

+ 694. ii. ELIZABETH[7] HOWELL, born on 1 Sep 1818.

+ 695. iii. JOHN FRANKLIN[7] HOWELL, born on 2 Apr 1822.

+ 696. iv. NATHANIEL WELLS[7] HOWELL, born on 19 Mch 1824.

+ 697. v. HAMPTON YOUNGS[7] HOWELL, born on 17 Aug 1826.

+ 698. vi. ELECTA AMELIA[7] HOWELL, born on 17 June 1830.

+ 699. vii. J. MITCHELL[7] HOWELL, born on 24 Dec 1833.

+ 700. viii. CHARLES MANLEY[7] HOWELL, born on 20 Nov 1835.

+ 701. ix. HANNAH MARIA[7] HOWELL, born on 26 Nov 1838.

295. AMELIA[6] HOWELL (John[5], John[4]), the daughter of John[5] and Martha (Benjamin) Howell, was probably born at Middle Island in about 1800.

Amelia Howell married William Jarvis Sweezey {2251}, who was born in about 1798.

On 12 Aug 1850, W[m] J. Swezey, 52, laborer, was enumerated as the head of a family consisting of himself, his wife, Amelia, 50, and their children, Stephen, 28, seaman, with real property worth $700, Warren, 26, W[m] E., 18, and Moses, 16, residing in the Town of Brookhaven, Suffolk County, New York, in the Seventh Census of the United States {2252}.

William Jarvis and Amelia (Howell) Sweezey were the parents of seven children {2253}.

i. STEPHEN JARVIS SWEEZEY, born in about 1822.

2248. Gravestone, Mount Pleasant Cemetery, Center Moriches, from the collection of Osborn Shaw, in the office of David A. Overton, Historian, Town of Brookhaven.
2249. Id.
2250. Wilbur Franklin Howell, op. cit.
2251. Id., 319.
2252. U.S. Census, Brookhaven, Suffolk County, NY, 1850, Dwelling House 253, Family Number 279, Page 204.
2253. Wilbur Franklin Howell, op. cit.

ii. JOHN WARREN SWEEZEY, born on 20 May 1824 at Middle Island, married Phebe Hawkins in 1851, who was born on 29 Sep 1815 at Islip, the daughter of Selah and Rachel (Rose) Hawkins, three children. He died on 8 Feb 1887 at Brooklyn, where she died on 29 May 1903. Both are buried in the Woodlawn Cemetery at Bellport {2254}.

iii. WILLIAM EGBERT SWEEZEY, born in about 1832, married Hannah Elizabeth Hulse, who was born on 26 Feb 1834, the daughter of Amos and Hannah (Hawkins) Hulse {2255}.

iv. ELIZABETH ELMORE SWEEZEY.

v. ANNIE AUGUSTA SWEEZEY.

vi. ELECTA JANE SWEEZEY.

vii. MOSES SWEEZEY, born on 15 Apr 1834, married Jane E. Hawkins on 23 Jan 1858 at Brookhaven, three children. She was born on 20 Sep 1839 at Fireplace, the daughter of Samuel Conklin and Jerusha Ann (Rogers) Hawkins. He died on 3 Apr 1865, on the battlefield at Sweert's Creek, VA, and she married (2) Franklin A. Smith, who died on 21 June 1921, on 9 Mch 1871. She died on 8 Feb 1924 at East Hampton, and is buried at Brookhaven {2256}.

297. MITCHELL[6] HOWELL (John[5], John[4]), the son of John[5] and Martha (Benjamin) Howell, was born on 15 Nov 1806 {2257}.
 Mitchell Howell married Martha Allen {2258}.
 Mitchell Howell died on 26 Feb 1877, at the age of 70 years, 3 months, and 11 days {2259}.

3. Isaac Reeve[5], Reeves[4]

302. MARY[6] HOWELL (Isaac Reeve[5], Reeves[4]), the daughter of Isaac Reeve[5] and

2254. Hawkins, op. cit., 93.
2255. Id.
2256. Id., 154-155.
2257. Charles Reeve Howell Family Bible.
2258. Wilbur Franklin Howell, op. cit., 256.
2259. Charles Reeve Howell Family Bible.

Mary (Hawkins) Howell, was born on 28 Oct 1797 {2260} in the vicinity of Middle Island.

On 12 Apr 1812, Mary Howell married Overton Dayton {2261}, who was born in about 1790, the son of Henry and Susan (Overton) Dayton {2262}.

Overton Dayton was listed as the head of a family consisting of one free white male of 26 and under 45 years of age, two of under 10, one free white female of 16 and under 26, one of 10 and under 16, and two of under 10, residing in the Town of Brookhaven, Suffolk County, New York, in the Fourth Census of the United States, 1820. Of these, one was engaged in agriculture {2263}.

In the Fifth Census of the United States, 1830, Overton Dayton was listed as the head of a family consisting of one free white male of 40 and under 50 years of age, one of 10 and under 15, one of under 5, one free white female of 30 and under 40, one of 15 and under 20, one of 10 and under 15, two of 5 and under 10, and two of under 5, residing in the City of Brooklyn, Kings County, New York {2264}.

On 20 Aug 1850, Overton Dayton, laborer, 60, was listed as the head of a family consisting of himself, his wife, Mary, 52, and their daughter, Phebe, 12, residing in the dwelling house of Nelson Monsell, 42, seaman, in Town of Brookhaven, Suffolk County, New York, in the Seventh Census of the United States, 1850 {2265}.

Overton and Mary (Howell) Dayton were the parents of ten children {2266}.

    i.   MARY DAYTON, married Mr. Terrel.

    ii.   JASON DAYTON.

    iii.   HENRIETTA DAYTON, married Mr. Roper.

    iv.   NANCY DAYTON, married Mr. Prasser.

    v.   CATHRYN DAYTON, married Mr. James.

    vi.   SARAH DAYTON, married (1) Mr. Griffin, and (2) Mr. Corwin.

    x.   VIOLETTA DAYTON, married Mr. Quinn.

2260. Sherwood, op. cit.
2261. Id.
2262. Jacobus, Donald Lines, and Dayton, Arthur Bliss, THE EARLY DAYTONS AND DESCENDANTS OF HENRY, JR., 35.
2263. U.S. Census, Brookhaven, Suffolk County, NY, 1820, Page 346.
2264. Id., Brooklyn, Kings County, NY, 1830, Page 284.
2265. Id., Brookhaven, Suffolk County, NY, 1850, Dwelling House 555, Family Number 626, Page 226.
2266. Sherwood, op. cit.

vii.   RUTH DAYTON, married Mr. McCanth.

viii.   PHEBE DAYTON, born in about 1838, died young.

ix.   HARRIET DAYTON.

303. ALTHEA[6] HOWELL (Isaac Reeve[5], Reeves[4]), the daughter of Isaac Reeve[5] and Mary (Hawkins) Howell, was born on 17 Oct 1799 {2267}, probably at Middle Island.

On 11 Jan 1817, Althea Howell married Thomas Jarvis {2268}.

Althea (Howell) Jarvis married John (William?) Gladwich as her second husband {2269}.

John Gladwish was listed as the head of a family consisting of one free white male of 30 and under 40 years of age, one of 15 and under 20, one of under 5, one free white female of 30 and under 40, one of 15 and under 20, and one of 5 and under 10, residing in the Third Ward in the City of Brooklyn, in the Sixth Census of the United States, 1840 {2270}.

On 4 Sep 1850, John Gladwish, 55, shoemaker, Althea Gladwish, 51, and George Gladwish, 10, were listed with the household of Frederick H. Smith in the Town of Smithtown, Suffolk County, New York, in the Seventh Census of the United States {2271}.

Thomas and Althea (Howell) Jarvis were the parents of two children {2272}.

i.   HANNAH ANN JARVIS.

ii.   THOMAS JARVIS.

John and Althea (Howell) Jarvis Gladwish were the parents of three children {2273}.

i (iii).   ALTHEA GLADWISH, born in about 1833, married Jonas Nichols, who was born in about 1832, resided in the house of James Nichols, on 1 June 1850 {2274}.

ii (iv).   EDWARD GLADWISH, married Susan French.

iii (v).   GEORGE GLADWISH, born in about 1840.

2267. Id.
2268. Id.
2269. Id.
2270. U.S. Census, 3rd Ward, Brooklyn, Kings County, NY, 1840, Page 462.
2271. Id., Smithtown, Suffolk County, NY, 1850, Dwelling House 125, Family Number 189, Page 133.
2272. Sherwood, op. cit.
2273. Id.
2274. U.S. Census, Smithtown, Sufolk County, NY, 1850, Dwelling House 54, Family Number 60, Page 125.

304. ISAAC REEVE[6] HOWELL (Isaac Reeve[5], Reeves[4]), the son of Isaac Reeve[5] and Mary (Hawkins) Howell, was born on 5 Apr 1802 {2275} at Middle Island.

On 2 Dec 1824, Isaac Reeve Howell married Hannah Raynor, who was born on 10 Aug 1801 at Saint George's Manor, the daughter of Joseph and Phebe (Robinson) Raynor {2276}.

Isaac Howell was listed as the head of a family consisting of one free white male of 20 and under 30 years of age, three of 5 and under, and one free white female of 20 and under 30, residing in the Town of Brookhaven, Suffolk County, New York, in the Fifth Census of the United States, 1830 {2277}.

Isaac R. Howell was listed as the head of a family consisting of one free white male of 30 and under 40 years of age, two of 10 and under 15, one of 5 and under 10, one of under 5, one free white female of 30 and under 40, one of 5 and under 10, and one of under 5, residing in the Town of Southold, Suffolk County, New York, in the Sixth Census of the United States, 1840 {2278}.

On 31 Jly 1850, Isaac R. Howell, 47, farmer, of the Town of Southold, Suffolk County, New York, having property worth $1,500, was enumerated as the head of a family including Hannah, 47, his wife, and their children, Isaac R., 24, farmer, with property worth $500, Cyrus F., 17, farmer, Mary, 15, Sereno, 12, Miriam, 11, Frances, 8, and Hannah S., 5, in the Seventh Census of the United States {2279}.

Isaac R. Howell was, at one time, an Elder of the Mattituck Presbyterian Church {2280}.

Hannah (Raynor) Howell died on 21 Aug 1852 at Mattituck, and is buried in the cemetery at the Mattituck Presbyterian Church {2281}.

Isaac Reeve Howell married (2) Margaret Robinson as his second wife, and (3) Jane Davis as his third wife {2282}.

Isaac Reeve Howell died at Mattituck on 28 May 1863, and is buried there beside his first wife {2283}.

Isaac Reeve and Hannah (Raynor) Howell were the parents of fifteen children {2284}.

+ 702. i. ISAAC REEVE[7] HOWELL, born on 10 Sep 1825.

2275. Sherwood, op. cit.
2276. Id.
2277. U.S. Census, Brookhaven, Suffolk County, NY, 1830, Page 185.
2278. Id., Southold, Suffolk County, NY, 1840, Page 207.
2279. Id., 1850, Dwelling Place 859, Family Number 936, Page 334.
2280. Craven, op. cit., 185.
2281. Id., 375.
2282. Sherwood, op. cit.
2283. Craven, op. cit.
2284. Sherwood, op. cit.

+ 703. ii.   JOSEPH RAYNOR[7] HOWELL, born on 25 Oct 1826 {2285}.

704. iii.   Daughter[7], died young.

705. iv.   GERSHOM HAWKINS[7] HOWELL, died young.

706. v.   WILLIAM WALLACE[7] HOWELL, died young.

707. vi.   AUSTIN ROE[7] HOWELL, died young.

708. vii.   HANNAH[7] HOWELL, died young.

709. viii.   PHEBE[7] HOWELL, twin of Hannah, died young.

+ 710. ix.   CYRUS FANCHER[7] HOWELL, born on 3 Jan 1833.

711. x.   EDWIN[7] HOWELL, died young.

+ 712. xi.   MARY ANN[7] HOWELL, born in about 1835.

+ 713. xii.   SERENO BERNELL[7] HOWELL, born in about 1838.

+ 714. xiii.   MIRIAM AUGUSTA[7] HOWELL, born in about 1839.

+ 715. xiv.   FRANCES AMANDA[7] HOWELL, born on 3 May 1841.

+ 716. xv.   HANNAH SMITH[7] HOWELL, born on 31 Jan 1845.

305. GERSHOM HAWKINS[6] HOWELL (Isaac Reeves[5], Reeves[4]), the son of Isaac Reeves[5] and Mary (Hawkins) Howell, was born on 28 May 1804 {2286} at Middle Island.

On 18 Nov 1824, Gershom Hawkins Howell married Lydia Conklin (378), the daughter of Lewis and Lydia (Tuthill) Conklin, who was born on 8 Oct 1800 {2287}.

On 1 May 1830, Gershom H. Howell purchased, for $300, a piece of land which was "..a part of lot No. Forty Nine Containing by Estimation one hundred and Twenty acres.." from his mother, Mary Howell, the "Executrix to the Estate

2285. Franklin Bowditch Dexter, BIOGRAPHICAL NOTICES OF GRADUATES OF YALE COLLEGE.., 396, M.N. Whitmore, STATISTICS OF THE CLASS OF 1854, OF YALE COLLEGE, 20.
2286. Sherwood, op. cit.
2287. Mallmann, op. cit., 301.

of Isaac Howell deceased..", by a deed recorded on 8 May 1830 {2288}.

Gershom Howell was listed as the head of a family consisting of one free white male of 20 and under 30 years of age, two of 15 and under 20, one of under 5, and one free white female of 20 and under 30, residing in the Town of Brookhaven, Suffolk County, New York, in the Fifth Census of the United States, 1830 {2289}.

Gershom Hawkins Howell moved, with his family, to Mattituck, probably by 1839. It is likely that they lived in "The old house..that belonged to Ebenezer Webb in 1762 and to John Horton in 1788, belonged to Richard Howell in 1816, and to Gershom Howell in 1839.." {2290}. "North of the lake, between it and the highway, dwelt..Gershom Howell, carpenter, father of Joel C. Howell,..in the old house with its back to the road, now (1906) occupied by Edward Worthington, which is often called the Elymas Reeve house..In 1849 Gershom Howell sold to Parthenia Reeve, daughter of Elymas, and after that Elymas moved to the house that commonly bears his name." {2291}.

Gershom H. Howell was listed as the head of a family consisting of one free white male of 30 and under 40 years of age, one of 5 and under 10, two free white females of 30 and under 40, and two of under 5, residing in the Town of Southold, Suffolk County, New York, in the Sixth Census of the United States, 1840 {2292}.

On 1 Aug 1850, the family of Gershom H. Howell, 45, carpenter, of the Town of Southold, Suffolk County, New York, was listed as consisting of himself, his wife, Lydia, 50, and their children, Joel, 18, laborer, Sarah, 15, Lucy, 11, and Alfred, 8, in the Seventh Census of the United States {2293}.

Gershom H. Howell was a witness to the will of his brother, William C. Howell, written on 10 Sep 1856, and proved on 7 Oct 1856 {2294}.

Gershom Hawkins Howell was, undoubtedly, the "Uncle Gershom" who shared his recollections of the early history of this family with Grace Lillian (Hammond) Sherwood {2295}.

On 8 June 1870, Gershom Howell, 66, carpenter, with real property worth $200, was enumerated as the head of a family consisting of himself, his wife, Lydia, 69, and their daughter, Sarah, 34, and their grand-daughter, Nellie, 14, residing at Mattituck in the Town of Southold, Suffolk County, New York, in the Ninth Census of the United States {2296}.

Lydia (Conklin) Howell died on 16 Dec 1880 {2297} at Mattituck,

---

2288. Suffolk County Deeds, Liber M, 275-276.

2289. U.S. Census, Brookhaven, Suffolk County, NY, 1830, Page 185.

2290. Craven, op. cit., 204-205.

2291. Id., 203.

2292. U.S. Census, Southold, Suffolk County, NY, 1840, Page 208.

2293. Id., 1850, Family Number 937, Dwelling House 860, Page 334.

2294. Suffolk County Wills, Liber 10, 121; Suffolk County Estates, File #4713.

2295. Sherwood, op. cit.

2296. U.S. Census, Southold, Suffolk County, NY, 1870, Dwelling House 143, Family Number 146, Page 241.

2297. Mallmann, op. cit., 301.

and is buried in the churchyard cemetery there {2298}.

Gershom Hawkins Howell died on 26 Jan 1889 {2299}, and is buried beside his wife at Mattituck {2300}.

Gershom Hawkins and Lydia (Conklin)·Howell were the parents of seven children {2301}.

717. i.   WILLIAM L.[7] HOWELL, born on 27 Feb 1825, died on 26 Mch 1825.

718. ii.   LYDIA C.[7] HOWELL, born on 16 May 1826, died on 3 June 1826.

719. iii. WILLIAM L.[7] HOWELL, born on 15 Apr 1829, died on 15 May 1829.

+ 720. iv. JOEL CONKLIN[7] HOWELL, born on 12 Jly 1832.

721. v.   SARAH[7] HOWELL, born on 18 Jly 1835, died on 26 Aug 1901, buried at Mattituck {2302}. The story is told of Sarah that, having been jilted in love, she declared that she would go to bed, and never get up again, and she did just that, living at one time in the home of her brother, Joel, and being waited on by everyone. This intrigued her grand-nephew, Edward F. Howell, so much that he decided he would try to see if she would put her feet on the floor. Therefore, on one July 4th, while serving her dinner, he surreptitiously placed a firecracker with a long fuse under her bed. When he came back to take away her dishes, he lit the fuse and left. Soon, there was a loud "Bang!", and Sarah was on her feet, yelling and screaming. Edward was reprimanded by his grandfather, Joel, for having done this, but Sarah did not change her ways, and remained in bed for the rest of her life {2303}.

722. vi. LUCY ANN[7] HOWELL, born on 16 Dec 1837.

+ 723. vii. ALFRED B.[7] HOWELL, born on 10 Apr 1842.

306. HANNAH MARIA[6] HOWELL (Isaac Reeve[5], Reeves[4]), the daughter of Isaac

---

2298. Craven, op. cit., 375.
2299. Edna Howell Yeager, Personal communication.
2300. Craven, op. cit., 375.
2301. Mallmann, op. cit., 301, 302.
2302. Craven, op. cit., 375.
2303. Yeager, op. cit.

Reeve[5] and Mary (Hawkins) Howell, was born on 15 Nov 1806 {2304}, at Middle Island.

On 15 May 1826, "Hannah M. Howel" married John Swezey at Middle Island {2305}. He was the son of James and Ṣarah (Tuthill) Swezey, and was born in 1802 {2306}.

"John Sweezey" was listed as the head of a family consisting of one free white male of 20 and under 30 years of age, one of 10 and under 15, one of under 5, one free white female of 20 and under 30, one of under 5, and one of 50 and under 60, residing in the Town of Brookhaven, Suffolk County, New York, in the Fifth Census of the United States, 1830 {2307}.

In the Sixth Census of the United States, 1840, "John Swezey" was listed as the head of a family consisting of one free white male of 30 and under 40 years of age, one of 10 and under 15, two of 5 and under 10, two of under 5, one free white female of 30 and under 40, and one of 5 and under 10, residing in the Town of Brookhaven, Suffolk County, New York {2308}.

John Swezey died in 1843 {2309}.

On 17 Jly 1850, Hannah Swezey, 44, widow, with real property worth $1,500, was listed as the head of a family including herself and her children, William C., 17, Mary A., 15, Daniel H., 13, and Gershom H., 9, all "In school", residing in the Town of Brookhaven, Suffolk County, New York, in the Seventh Census of the United States, 1850 {2310}. Her son, James, 23, was listed with the household of Lewis Hulse {2311}, while her son, Isaac R., 11, also in school, was listed with the household of Daniel and Nancy (Howell) Terry {2312}.

Hannah (Howell) Swezey married John C. Bond as her second husband {2313}.

"Hannah Bond, 60" was listed as a member of the household of James Swezey, 33, farmer, in the Town of Brookhaven, Suffolk County, New York, in the Eighth Census of the United States, 1860 {2314}.

In Jly 1870, Hannah (Howell) Swezey Bond married Daniel Terry as her third husband. He was the man in whose household her son, Isaac R., was residing in 1850, and from whom Isaac R. had complained of receiving many beatings (1238). On 10 Aug 1870, Daniel Terry, farmer, 70, with real property worth

2304. Sherwood, op. cit.
2305. THE AMERICAN GENEALOGIST (TAG), XIX, 111 (1943).
2306. C. Eugene Swezey, Personal communication.
2307. U.S. Census, Brookhaven, Suffolk County, NY, 1830, Page 186.
2308. Id., Brookhaven, Suffolk County, NY, 1840, Page 284.
2309. C. Eugene Swezey, op. cit.
2310. U.S. Census, Brookhaven, Suffolk County, NY, 1850, Dwelling House 35, Family Number 38, Page 148.
2311. Id., Dwelling House 327, Family Number 367, Page 167.
2312. Id., Dwelling House 643, Family Number 731, Page 232.
2313. Sherwood, op. cit.
2314. U.S. Census, Brookhaven, Suffolk County, NY, 1860, Dwelling House 1395, Family Number 862, Page 862.

$3,000, and personal property worth $500, was enumerated as the head of family consisting of himself, his wife, Hannah, 63, Franklin Terry, 10, and William Swezey, 4, residing in Holtsville in the Town of Brookhaven, Suffolk County, New York, in the Ninth Census of the United States {2315}.

John and Hannah (Howell) Swezey were the parents of six children {2316}.

    i.   JAMES SWEZEY, born in 1827.

    ii.   WILLIAM CLARK SWEZEY, born in 1833, married Maria Hallock, died at sea.

    iii.   MARY A. SWEZEY, born in 1835, married C. Wesley Ruland.

    iv.   DANIEL HOWELL SWEZEY, born in 1837, died at sea.

    v.   ISAAC REEVES SWEZEY, born in 1839, married Adelaide Kent.

    vi.   GERSHOM HAWKINS SWEZEY, born on 6 May 1841, married Harriet S. Kent.

307. SARAH ANN[6] HOWELL (Isaac Reeves[5], Reeves[4]), the daughter of Isaac Reeves[5] and Mary (Hawkins) Howell, was born on 18 Dec 1808 {2317} at Middle Island.

Sarah Ann Howell married (1) William Booth, however, this proved to be an invalid marriage, as she discovered when she found a letter from his wife in England in a coat of his which she was mending. She then went to live with her sister, where her first son, George Lafayette Booth, was born {2318}.

On 29 Jly 1842, Sarah Ann (Howell) Booth married (2) Brewster Pedrick as his second wife. He was the son of Josiah and Sarah Elizabeth (Ruland) Pedrick, and was born on 18 Apr 1802 in the Town of Huntington.

Brewster Pedrick was a farmer for most of his life, although "..at one time he was engaged in the mercantile business at Smithtown Landing." {2319}. His first wife was Sarah M. Darling.

Brewster Pedrick first appeared in the Census of the United States in 1830, when he was listed as the head of a family consisting of one free white male of 20 and under 30 years of age, three of under 5, and one free white female of 20 and under 30, residing in the Town of Huntington, Suffolk County, New York {2320}.

2315. Id., 1870, Dwelling House 1777, Family Number 1926, Page 425.
2316. John Swezey Family Bible, in the possession of Mrs. Hazel Monsell, 1970, information generously provided by C. Eugene Swezey.
2317. Sherwood, op. cit.
2318. Bessie A. Rowland, Personal communication.
2319. PORTRAIT AND BIOGRAPHICAL RECORD OF SUFFOLK COUNTY, 956.
2320. U.S. Census, Huntington, Suffolk County, 1830, NY, Page 331.

In the Sixth Census of the United States, 1840, Brewster Pedrick was listed as the head of a family consisting of one free white male of 30 and under 40 years of age, one of 15 and under 20, one of 10 and under 15, one of under 5, one free white female of 30 and under 40, two of 5 and under 10, and one of under 5, residing in the Town of Islip, Suffolk County, New York {2321}.

On 28 Aug 1850, Brewster Pedrick, 48, farmer, was listed as the head of a family including himself, his wife, Sarah, 41, his children, Josiah, 13, and Phebe, 10, his wife's son, George L., 11, and their children, Isaac B., 5, Allethia, 4, and Ellen J., 1, residing in the Town of Smithtown, Suffolk County, New York, in the Seventh Census of the United States {2322}.

On 7 June 1860, Brewster Pedrick, 58, farmer, was listed as the head of a family consisting of himself, his wife, Sarah, 51, her son, George L. Booth, 20, amd their children, Isaac M., 15, Althea, 13, and Ellen F. Pedrick, 11, residing in the Town of Smithtown, Suffolk County, New York, in the Eighth Census of the United States {2323}.

On 2 June 1870, Brewster Pedrick, 68, farmer, with real property worth $5000, and personal property worth $500, was enumerated as the head of a household consisting of himself, his wife, Sarah, 61, their daughter, Ella F., 21, and Phebe Nichols, 7, residing in the Town of Smithtown, Suffolk County, New York, in the Ninth Census of the United States {2324}.

Brewster Pedrick died on 27 Aug 1883, at the age of 81 years and 4 months {2325}, and is buried in the cemetery at the Hauppauge United Methodist Church {2326}.

Sarah Ann (Howell) Booth Pedrick died at Hauppauge on 8 Feb 1895, at about 4:00 P.M., with "Senility" being given as the cause of her death {2327}. She is buried beside her husband at Hauppauge {2328}.

Brewster and Sarah Ann (Howell) Booth Pedrick were the parents of three children {2329}.

    i.   ISAAC BREWSTER PEDRICK, born on 20 Sep 1844, married Eugenia W. Bunce on 18 May 1868 at Commack, three children, died on 17 Nov 1911, and is buried in the Huntington Rural Cemetery.

    ii.   JESSIE ALTHEA PEDRICK, born on 2 Sep 1846 at Bayport, married Thomas Barton Cornell on 5 Nov 1865 at Commack, six children, died on 6 Jan 1921 at South Apalachin, New York, and

2321. Id., Smithtown, Suffolk County, NY, 1840, Page 203.
2322. Id., 1850, Dwelling House 113, Family Number 125, Page 130.
2323. Id., 1860, Dwelling House 138, Family Number 146, Page 183.
2324. Id., 1870, Dwelling House 34, Family Number 35, Page 125.
2325. #60, Register of Deaths, Town of Smithtown.
2326. Gravestone, Hauppauge United Methodist Church Cemetery.
2327. #831, Register of Deaths, Town of Smithtown.
2328. Gravestone, Hauppauge United Methodist Church Cemetery.
2329. Cornell Family Bible, in the possession of Charles Rowland, 1997.

is buried at Hauppauge {2330}. NOTE: *Jessie Althea Pedrick was the great-grandmother of the compiler, Thomas H. Donnelly.*

    iii.   ELLEN FRANCES PEDRICK, born on 6 May 1849, married Benjamin F. Prince on 27 Nov 1873, three children.

William and Sarah Ann (Howell) Booth were the parents of one son.

    i.   GEORGE LAFAYETTE BOOTH, born on 16 Aug 1839 at Brooklyn, enlisted in Company H, 127th Regiment, New York Volunteer Infantry on 21 Aug 1862, mustered out on 8 Jly 1865 {2331}, married (1) Catherine Griffith on 20 Dec 1865 {2332}, four children. She died on 16 Oct 1878, and is buried in the cemetery at the Hauppauge United Methodist Church {2333}. On 16 Jan 1882 {2334}, he married (2) Celia (Blydenburg) Hawkins {2335}. He died on 17 Feb 1919 at Smithtown Branch {2336}, and is buried beside his first wife, and his daughter, Edith, at Hauppauge {2337}.

Brewster and Sarah M. (Darling) Pedrick were the parents of eight children {2338}.

    i.   GARRET PEDRICK, born on 14 Mch 1825, married Elsey F. Howell in Mch 1849, and died in 1889.

    ii.   LEANDER PEDRICK, born on 26 Aug 1827, died on 12 Apr 1828.

    iii.   EMMET PEDRICK, born on 31 Oct 1829, married (1) Mary Ann Taylor in 1847, married (2) Reumah A. ---, married (3) Matilda J. --- , died on 26 June 1901, and is buried in the cemetery at the Hauppauge United Methodist Church {2339}.

    iv.   MARY CELIA PEDRICK, born on 2 Apr 1832, married James Nicoll, died on 12 Aug 1912, and is buried at Hauppauge (1255).

2330. Gravestone, Hauppauge United Methodist Church Cemetery.
2331. U.S. Pension File 873419.
2332. Bessie A. Rowland, op. cit.
2333. Gravestone, Hauppauge United Methodist Church Cemetery.
2334. Cornell Family Bible.
2335. Hawkins, op. cit., 68.
2336. Newspaper clipping, 21 Feb 1919, from Orville B. Ackerley's Obituary Book III, p. 139, in the LONG ISLAND COLLECTION at the East Hampton Library.
2337. Gravestone, Hauppauge United Methodist Church Cemetery.
2338. Rowland, op. cit.
2339. Gravestone, Hauppauge United Methodist Church Cemetery.

v.   SARAH ELIZABETH PEDRICK, born on 11 June 1834, married George Gilson on 25 Dec 1851, died in about 1907.

vi.   WILLIAM HENRY PEDRICK, born on 5 Apr 1836, died on 20 Jly 1837.

vii. JOSIAH PEDRICK, born on 5 Oct 1837, married Maria Brush on 25 Apr 1862, died on 7 Apr 1919.

viii. PHEBE PEDRICK, born on 11 Feb 1840, married Merwins Thompson in June 1863, died on 11 Jly 1863.

308. WILLIAM CLARK[6] HOWELL (Isaac Reeves[5], Reeves[4]), the son of Isaac Reeves[5] and Mary (Hawkins) Howell, was born on 28 Dec 1811 {2340} at Middle Island.

In 1833 {2341}, William Clark Howell married Violetta Youngs {2342}, who was born on 13 Oct 1812.

William C. Howell was listed as the head of a family consisting of one free white male of 20 and under 30 years of age, one of 5 and under 10, two of under 5, one free white female of 30 and under 40, and one of 20 and under 30, residing in the Town of Brookhaven, Suffolk County, New York, in the Sixth Census of the United States, 1840 {2343}.

"Wm. C. Howell", 37, house carpenter, was listed as the head of a family consisting of himself, his wife, "Fidelia, 35", and their children, Wm. Platt, 16, James, 13, Sarah, 7, and Elisha, 4, residing in the 11th Ward, New York City, in the Seventh Census of the United States, 1850 {2344}.

Violetta A. Howell died on 31 Dec 1850, at the age of 38 years, 2 months, and 18 days, and is buried in the churchyard cemetery at the Hauppauge United Methodist Church {2345}.

William C. Howell, of the Town of Brookhaven, left, to his wife, Rebecca, the use of his house and lot, as long as she remained his wife, by his will of 10 Sep 1856, as proved on 7 Oct 1856. His sons, Alfred Youngs Howell and Daniel Howell, and his daughter, Sarah Philletta, were to have the above house and lot when Rebecca was no longer his wife {2346}.

William Clark and Violetta A. (Youngs) Howell were the parents of five children {2347}.

2340. Sherwood, op. cit.
2341. John Swezey Family Bible.
2342. Sherwood, op. cit.
2343. U.S. Census, Brookhaven, Suffolk County, NY, 1840, Page 286.
2344. Id., 11th Ward, New York, New York County, NY, 1850, Dwelling House 399, Family Number 1714, Page 226.
2345. Gravestone, Hauppauge United Methodist Church Cemetery.
2346. Suffolk County Wills, Liber 6, 121; Suffolk County Estates, File #4713.
2347. Sherwood, op. cit.

724. i.   WILLAM PLATT[7] HOWELL, born in about 1834.

725. ii.   JAMES[7] HOWELL, born in about 1837.

726. iii. ALFRED YOUNGS[7] HOWELL, born in about 1839, died on 2 Apr 1864 as a member of Company D, 2nd Minnesota Infantry, and is buried in the family plot at Hauppauge {2348}.

727. iv. SARAH VIOLETTA[7] HOWELL, born on 3 Mch 1843, died on 8 June 1913, and is buried in the cemetery at the Hauppauge United Methodist Church {2349}.

+ 728. v.   DANIEL ELIAS[7] HOWELL, born on 13 Oct 1846 {2350}.

4. James[5], Reeves[4]

309. YOUNGS[6] HOWELL (James[5]), the son of James[5] and Catherine (Youngs) Howell, was born on 1 Feb 1795 {2351}.

The marriage of Youngs Howell to Mary Homan, who was born on 30 Sep 1797, the daughter of Joseph and Temperance (Corey) Homan, was reported as having taken place at Patchogue {2352}.

"Yongs Howell" pledged $3.00 toward the building of the First Congregational Church of New Village on 7 Feb 1818 {2353}.

Youngs Howell was listed as the head of a family consisting of one free white male of 30 and under 40 years of age, one of 5 and under 10, one of under five, one free white female of 30 and under 40, one of 10 and under 15, and one of under 5, residing in the Town of Brookhaven, Suffolk County, New York, in the Fifth Census of the United States, 1830 {2354}.

In the Sixth Census of the United States, 1840, Youngs Howell was listed as the head of a family consisting of one free white male of 40 and under 50 years of age, one of 30 and under 40, three of 5 and under 10, two of under 5, one free white female of 40 and under 50, one of 10 and under 15, and two of 5 and under 10, residing in the Town of Brookhaven, Suffolk County, New York {2355}.

On 15 Aug 1850, the family of Youngs Howell, 55, laborer, was listed as

2348. Gravestone, Hauppauge United Methodist Church Cemetery.
2349. Id.
2350. Frederick Kinsman Smith, THE FAMILY OF RICHARD SMITH.., 427.
2351. Grendler, op. cit., 3.
2352. SUFFOLK COUNTY RECORDER, 16 Nov 1816.
2353. David A. Overton, The REGISTER, SCHS, Volume XV, 67 (Winter 1989).
2354. U.S. Census, Brookhaven, Suffolk County, NY, 1830, Page 183.
2355. Id., 1840, Page 302.

including Mary, 52, and James B., 13, in the Seventh Census of the United States {2356}. His son, Jesse S., 11, was listed in the household of Joseph Tooker, 35 {2357}.

Mary (Homan) Howell died on 30 Mch 1862, and is buried in the cemetery at the Setauket Presbyterian Church {2358}.

Youngs Howell died on 23 Mch 1876, at the age of 81 years, 1 month and 23 days, and is buried beside his wife at Setauket {2359}.

Youngs and Mary (Homan) Howell were the parents of eleven children {2360}.

+ 729.   i.   JOSEPH N.[7] HOWELL, born on 4 Oct 1817.

730.   ii.   MARY ANN[7] HOWELL, born on 28 Apr 1819, died on 26 Oct 1821, and is buried in the New Village Congregational Church Cemetery at Centereach {2361}.

731.   iii.   ALDEN[7] HOWELL, born on 6 Mch 1821, died on 28 Oct 1821, and is buried at Centereach {2362}.

+ 732.   iv.   TEMPERANCE[7] HOWELL, born on 24 May 1823.

733.   v.   DANIEL YOUNGS[7] HOWELL, born on 1 Aug 1825.

+ 734.   vi.   ANN ELIZA[7] HOWELL, born on 19 Feb 1828.

735.   vii.   SARAH L.[7] HOWELL, born on 21 June 1830, died on 14 Aug 1831, and is buried at Centereach {2363}.

736. viii.   ELIHU PLATT[7] HOWELL, born on 16 June 1832.

737.   ix.   HANNAH[7] HOWELL, born on 10 May 1835, died on 12 Feb 1848, and is buried at Centereach {2364}.

+ 738.   x.   JAMES BENJAMIN[7] HOWELL, born on 11 May 1837.

+ 739.   xi.   JESSE S.[7] HOWELL, born on 21 Dec 1839.

2356. Id., 1850, Dwelling Place 497, Family Number 562, Page 178.
2357. Id., Dwelling Place 497, Family Number 563, Page 180.
2358. Barstow, op. cit.
2359. Id.
2360. Youngs Howell Family Bible, in the possession of Charles Henry Howell, 1961.
2361. NYG&BR, XXI, 75 (Apr 1890).
2362. Id.
2363. Id.
2364. Id.

310. NANCY[6] HOWELL (James[5]), the daughter of James[5] and Catherine (Youngs) Howell, was born on 6 Jan 1798 {2365}.

In 1822, at the Middle Island church, Nancy Howell married Daniel Terry, who was born on 13 Oct 1800 {2366}.

On 22 Aug 1850, Daniel Terry, 49, farmer, with real property worth $2,500, was enumerated as the head of a family including himself, his wife, Nancy, 52, and their children, Sydney, 25, farmer, Brewster, 19, farmer, and Charlotte, 17, and her cousin, Isaac R. Sweezy, 11, residing in the Town of Brookhaven, Suffolk County, New York, in the Seventh Census of the United States, 1850 {2367}.

Nancy (Howell) Terry died on 4 Mch 1869 {2368}.

Daniel Terry married Hannah Maria (Howell) Swezey Bond (#306) as his second wife {2369} in Jly 1870 {2370}.

On 10 Aug 1870, Daniel Terry, 70, farmer, with real property worth $3000, and personal property worth $500, was enumerated as the head of a household consisting of himself, his wife, Hannah, 63, his grandson, Franklin, 10, and William Swezey, 4, residing in the Town of Brookhaven, Suffolk County, New York, in the Ninth Census of the United States {2371}.

Daniel Terry died in Jly 1876, and is buried at Holtville, near the Long Island Railroad {2372}.

Daniel and Nancy (Howell) Terry were the parents of seven children {2373}.

    i.   MARY TERRY.

    ii.   ELIZA TERRY.

    iii.   SYDNEY TERRY, born in about 1825.

    iv.   BREWSTER TERRY, born in about 1831, died on 13 Sep 1862, and is buried in the cemetery at the New Village Congregational Church at Centereach, where his gravestone is inscribed "Brewster Terry | died Sept. 13 1862 in his 31st year" {2374}.

    v.   CHARLOTTE TERRY, born on 13 May 1833, married Azariah

---

2365. Grendler, op. cit., 6.
2366. Id.
2367. U.S. Census, Brookhaven, Suffolk County, NY, 1850, Dwelling House 643, Family Number 731, Page 232.
2368. Grendler, op. cit., 6.
2369. Swezey, op. cit.
2370. John Swezey Family Bible.
2371. U.S. Census, Brookhaven, Suffolk County, NY, 1870, Dwelling House 1777, Family Number 1926, Page 425.
2372. Grendler, op. cit.
2373. Id.
2374. NYG&BR, XXI, 76 (Apr 1890).

Franklin Hawkins, the son of Samuel Alwood and Eliza (Hammond) Hawkins, two children, died on 12 May 1868 {2375}.

vi. MARGRETTE TERRY, born in about Apr 1836, died on 17 June 1839 and is buried at Centereach, where her epitaph reads "Margrette | daughter of Daniel & Nancy Terry | died, June 17, 1839, aged 3 years 2 mos" {2376}.

vii. ALBERT M. TERRY, born on 6 Oct 1838, died on 25 June 1839, and is buried at Centereach, where his gravestone is inscribed "Albert M. | son of Daniel & Nancy Terry | died June 25 1839 aged 8 mos 19 days" {2377}.

311. CATHERINE[6] HOWELL (James[5]), the daughter of James[5] and Catherine (Youngs) Howell, was born on 21 Feb 1800 {2378}.

On 21 Dec 1820, Catherine Howell married Scudder Terry, who was born on 2 Mch 1798, the son of Daniel and Lydia (Homan) Terry {2379}.

On 22 Aug 1850, Scudder Terry, 52, farmer, with real property worth $2000, was enumerated as the head of a household consisting of himself, his wife, Cath., 50, their children, Emeline, 16, Maria, 13, and Sarah, 10, and Chas. Logan, 12, residing in the Town of Brookhaven, Suffolk County, New York, in the Seventh Census of the United States {2380}.

Catherine (Howell) Terry died on 3 Mch 1898 {2381}.

Scudder Terry died on 10 Apr 1866 {2382}.

Scudder and Catherine (Howell) Terry were the parents of eight children {2383}.

i. AUSTIN ROE TERRY, born on 3 Dec 1821, died on 21 Apr 1822.

ii. SCUDDER HOMAN TERRY, born on 23 Apr 1823.

iii. ELIZA CATHERINE TERRY, born on 31 Apr (Jly?) 1826, married Azariah Hawkins Smith as his second wife in 1843, two children, died on 22 Jly 1912, and is buried in the cemetery at the

2375. Hawkins, op. cit., 110.
2376. NYG&BR, XXI, 76 (Apr 1890).
2377. Id.
2378. Grendler, op. cit., 7.
2379. Id.
2380. U.S. Census, Brookhaven, Suffolk County, 1850, Dwelling House 633, Family Number 720, Page 231.
2381. Grendler, op. cit.
2382. Id.
2383. Id.

New Village Congregational Church in Centereach. Azariah Hawkins Smith was born on 1 Mch 1815, the son of Lemuel and Mary (Alwood) Smith, married (1) Catherine Hawkins, who was born on 26 Apr 1816, the daughter of Benjamin and Deliverance (Tuthill) Hawkins, one child, died on 9 Jun 1847 {2384}.

iv.   RUTH ROE TERRY, born on 8 Apr 1829.

v.   HARRIET EMELINE TERRY, born on 25 Aug 1833.

vi.   MARIA JANE TERRY, born on 7 Sep 1836.

vii.   LYDIA TERRY, born on 2 Dec 1838, died on 28 June 1839.

viii.   SARAH REBECCA TERRY, born on 6 May 1840.

312. JAMES[6] HOWELL (James[5], Reeves[4]), the son of James[5] and Catherine (Youngs) Howell, was born on 9 Jly 1802 {2385}, probably at New Village.

James Howell married Louisa Terrell {2386}, who was born on 3 Jly 1803 {2387}. He "..was prominently identified with farming pursuits throughout life, and proved himself worthy of the high esteem which was accorded him as one of the old residents of the community. He was a man whose pleasant, genial nature made him friends, and in the relations of life he bore himself as a kind husband and father and a true friend, as well as an honest man of business." {2388}.

In the Sixth Census of the United States, 1840, "James Howell, Jr." was listed as the head of family consisting of one free white male of 30 and under 40 years of age, one of 15 and under 20, one of 5 and under 10, one of under 5, one free white female of 30 and under 40, two of 15 and under 20, three of 10 and under 15, and one of 5 and under 10, residing in the Town of Brookhaven, Suffolk County, New York {2389}.

James Howell died on 30 June 1853, and is buried in the cemetery at the New Village Congregational Church in Centereach, where his gravestone is inscribed "James Howell | died June 30 1853 aged 50 years | 11 months & 21 days" {2390}.

Louisa Howell died on 5 Jly 1887, and is buried beside her husband at

2384. Hawkins, op. cit., 44; Smith, op. cit., 397.
2385. Grendler, op. cit., 21.
2386. Id.
2387. Gravestone, New Village Cemetery, Centereach, from the William F. Howell collection of cemetery markings.
2388. PORTRAIT & BIOGRAPHICAL RECORD OF SUFFOLK COUNTY, 293.
2389. U.S. Census, 1840, Brookhaven, Suffolk County, NY, Page 296.
2390. NYG&BR, 21, 74 (1890).

Centereach {2391}.

James and Louisa (Terrell) Howell were the parents of at least seven children {2392}.

+ 740.   i.   CATHERINE[7] HOWELL, born on 16 Mch 1824.

+ 741.   ii.   JAMES ADDISON[7] HOWELL, born in about 1826.

  742.   iii.   SIDNEY SMITH[7] HOWELL.

+ 743.   iv.   WILLIAM SANDFORD[7] HOWELL, born on 1 Jan 1834.

+ 744.   v.   WALTER CARLE[7] HOWELL, born in about 1839.

+ 745.   vi.   SUSAN[7] HOWELL, born in about 1841.

  746.   vii.   ISAAC CONKLIN[7] HOWELL.

313. REEVES[6] HOWELL (James[5], Reeves[4]), the son of James[5] and Catherine (Youngs) Howell, was born on 4 Nov 1804 {2393}, probably at New Village.

On 30 Nov 1826, Reeves Howell married Phebe Gates {2394}, who was born on 8 Nov 1807 {2395}.

Reeve Howell was listed as the head of a family consisting of one free white male of 20 and under 30 years of age, one of under 5, and one free white female of 20 and under 30, residing in the Town of Brookhaven, Suffolk County, New York, in the Fifth Census of the United States, 1830 {2396}.

In the Sixth Census of the United States, 1840, Reeves Howell was listed as the head of a family consisting of one free white male of 30 and under 40 years of age, one of 15 and under 20, one of 10 and under 15, one of 5 and under 10, one of under 5, one free white female of 30 and under 40, one of 10 and under 15, and one of under 10, residing in the Town of Brookhaven, Suffolk County, New York {2397}.

On 21 Aug 1850, Reeves Howell, 41, farmer, with real property worth $1,500, was enumerated as the head of a family including himself, his wife, Phebe, 43, and their children, Shepard R., 23, ship carpenter, William S., 20, seaman, Phebe A., 13, and Theodore B., 11, residing in the Town of Brookhaven, Suffolk

2391. Gravestone, New Village Cemetery, Centereach.
2392. Grendler, op. cit., 21.
2393. Grendler, op. cit., 24.
2394. RECORD OF MARRIAGES PERFORMED BY REV. ZACHARIAH GREENE, 20.
2395. Grendler, op. cit.
2396. U.S. Census, Brookhaven, Suffolk County, NY, 1830, Page 183.
2397. Id., 1840, Page 295.

County, New York, in the Seventh Census of the United States, 1850 {2398}.

On 12 Aug 1870, Reeve Howell, 66, farmer, with real property worth $3000, and personal property worth $300, was enumerated at New Village in the Town of Brookhaven, Suffolk County, New York in the Ninth Census of the United States {2399}.

Phebe Howell died on 1 May 1878, and is buried in the cemetery at the New Village Congregational Church in Centereach {2400}.

Reeves Howell died on 20 Apr 1893, and is buried beside his wife at Centereach {2401}.

Reeves and Phebe (Gates) Howell were the parents of at least five children {2402}.

747.   i.   SHEPARD REEVES[7] HOWELL, born on 25 Aug 1827, died on 3 Jly 1854, and is buried at Centereach, where his tombstone is inscribed "Shepherd Reeves Howell | died July 8, 1854 AE 26 years 10 months | 13 days" {2403}.

748.   ii.   WILLIAM S.[7] HOWELL, born in about 1830.

749.   iii.   JONAH[7] HOWELL, born 18 Apr 1836, died on 25 Nov 1836, and is buried at Centereach, where his epitaph reads "Josiah | Son of Reeves & Phebe Howell | died Nov. 25 1836 aged 7 mos 7 days" {2404}.

+ 750.   iv.   PHEBE ANN[7] HOWELL, born in about 1837.

751.   v.   THEODORE B.[7] HOWELL, born in about 1839.

314. DANIEL BROWN[6] HOWELL (James[5], Reeves[4]), the son of James[5] and Catherine (Youngs) Howell, was born on 29 Dec 1806 at New Village {2405}.

On Sep 17, 1829, Daniel Brown Howell married Caroline Hawkins {2406}. She was the daughter of James and Mary (Bayles) Hawkins, and was born at Setauket on 11 Nov 1803 {2407}.

"Brown Howell" was listed as the head of a family consisting of one free

2398. Id., 1850, Dwelling House 589, Family Number 666, Page 228.
2399. Id., 1870, Dwelling House 1878, Family Number 2027, Page 431.
2400. Gravestone, New Village Cemetery, Centereach.
2401. Id.
2402. Grendler, op. cit.
2403. NYG&BR, XXI, 75 (Apr 1890).
2404. Id.
2405. Grendler, op. cit., 25.
2406. RECORD OF MARRIAGES PERFORMED BY REV. ZACHARIAH GREENE, 21.
2407. Hawkins, op. cit., 94.

white male of 20 and under 30 years, one of under 5, and one free white female of 20 and under 30, residing in the Town of Brookhaven, Suffolk County, New York, in the Fifth Census of the United States, 1830 {2408}.

In the Sixth Census of the United States,. 1840, "Brown Howell" was listed as the head of a family consisting of one free white male of 20 and under 30 years of age, one of 10 and under 15, two of five and under 10, one free white female of 30 and under 40, and one of under 5, residing in the Town of Brookhaven, Suffolk County, New York {2409}.

On 21 Aug 1850, Daniel B. Howell, 43, farmer, with real property worth $1,000, was enumerated as the head of a family including himself, his wife, Caroline, 47, and their children, Celah, 20, seaman, Daniel B., 15, seaman, Mary M., 13, and Frances, 7, residing in the Town of Brookhaven, Suffolk County, New York, in the Seventh Census of the United States, 1850 {2410}.

Daniel Brown Howell died on 14 Apr 1852, and is buried in the cemetery at the New Village Congregational Church, where his epitaph reads "D. Brown Howell | died April 14, 1852 aged 45 years | 3 mos. 15 days" {2411}.

Caroline Howell died on 4 Nov 1876, and is buried beside her husband at Centereach, where her gravestone is inscribed "Caroline | wife of Daniel Brown Howell | born Nov. 11, 1803 died Nov 4, 1876 {2412}.

Daniel Brown and Caroline (Hawkins) Howell were the parents of five children {2413}.

+ 752. i. SELAH[7] HOWELL, born in about 1830.

753. ii. CHARLES[7] HOWELL, born in about June 1832, died on 3 Oct 1840, and is buried at Centereach, where his tombstone is inscribed "Charles | son of D.B. & Caroline Howell - died Oct. 3, 1840 AE 8 years 4 mos" {2414}.

+ 754. iii. DANIEL B.[7] HOWELL, born in about 1835.

+ 755. iv. MARY MELISSA[7] HOWELL, born on 22 Jan 1838.

756. v. FRANCES EMILY[7] HOWELL, born on 4 Mch 1843, died on 8 June 1857, and is buried at Centereach, where her epitaph reads "Frances E. | daughter of D.B. & Caroline Howell | died June 8, 1857 AE 14 years 3 mos. 4 days" {2415}.

2408. U.S Census, Brookhaven, Suffolk County, NY, 1830, Page 183.
2409. Id., 1840, Page 296.
2410. Id., 1850, Dwelling House 630, Family Number 717, Page 231.
2411. NYG&BER, XXI, 75 (Apr 1890).
2412. Id.
2413. Grendler, op. cit.
2414. NYG&BR, XXI, 75 (Apr 1890).
2415. Id.

316. HARRIET ATWOOD[6] HOWELL (James[5], Reeves[4]), the daughter of James[5] and Catherine (Youngs) Howell, was born on 5 Jan 1812 at New Village {2416}.

On 23 Nov 1831, Harriet Atwood Howell married David Brewster Bayles {2417}, who was born at the old Bayles homestead in South Setauket on 10 Jan 1808 {2418}.

"David Brewster Bayles was one of the pioneer ship builders of Long Island. He built the largest sailing vessel at that time, the "Adorna" which was the largest ship ever built on Long Island. He was an Elder in the Setauket Presbyterian Church for nearly 50 years and at the time of his death the session of the church adopted resolutions appraising his faithfulness in the service of God and the Church" {2419}.

David Brewster Bayles died on 12 Dec 1892 {2420}, and is buried in the cemetery at the Setauket Presbyterian Church {2421}.

Harriet Bayles died on 31 Jan 1912 {2422}, and is buried beside her husband at Setauket {2423}.

David Brewster and Harriet Atwood (Howell) Bayles were the parents of two children {2424}.

     i.   DANIEL HOMAN BAYLES, born in about 1832, married (1) Sarah Matilda Woodhull, born on 29 Feb 1836, died on 16 June 1858, and is buried at Setauket {2425}, no children, married (2) Esther MacGregor, who died on 15 Feb 1916, aged 75, three children. Daniel Homan Bayles died on 14 Sep 1910, and is buried in the Woodlawn Cemetery in Newburgh, New York.

    ii.   ENCY LORETTA BAYLES, born on 1 Oct 1836, married Capt. Charles S. Jones, who was born on 23 Mch 1831, died at Havana, Cuba, on 19 Dec 1859, and is buried at Setauket, three children. Ency Loretta Jones died on 10 Jan 1910, and is buried beside her husband at Setauket {2426}.

317. DEBORAH ROE[6] HOWELL (James[5], Reeves[4]), the daughter of James[5] and

2416. Grendler, op. cit., 30.
2417. RECORD OF MARRIAGES PERFORMED BY REV. ZACHARIAH GREENE, 22.
2418. Grendler, op. cit.
2419. Id.
2420. Id.
2421. Barstow, op. cit, EPITAPHS.
2422. Grendler, op. cit.
2423. Barstow, op. cit.
2424. Grendler, op. cit.
2425. Barstow, op. cit.
2426. Id.

Catherine (Youngs) Howell, was born on 9 Sep 1814 at New Village {2427}.

On 1 Sep 1832, Deborah Roe Howell married Joel L'Hommedieu, who was born on 2 Sep 1808 {2428}.

On 16 Aug 1850, Joel L'Hommedieu, 39, shoemaker, was enumerated as the head of a household including himself, his wife, Deborah, 36, and their children, Bathsheba, 16, Edmund H., 14, Susan C., 12, James A., 10, Martha A., 8, John W., 6, and Richard W., 2, residing in the Town of Brookhaven, Suffolk County, New York, in the Seventh Census of the United States, 1850 {2429}.

Deborah Roe L'Hommedieu died on 19 June 1850 {2430}.

Joel L'Hommedieu died on 28 Apr 1872, and is buried in the cemetery at the Methodist Church in Setauket {2431}.

Joel and Deborah Roe (Howell) L'Hommedieu were the parents of fourteen children {2432}.

    i.   BATHSHEBA CLARK L'HOMMEDIEU, born on 31 Dec 1833, married George Washington Terrell, who was born on 19 Jan 1832, the son of Richard Clinton and Harriet (Hawkins) Terrell, on 13 Feb 1852, two children, died on 12 Nov 1904, while he died on 4 Oct 1908 {2433}.

    ii.   EDMUND HENRY L'HOMMEDIEU, born on 18 Nov 1835, married Josephine Vernon, four children, died on 21 Jly 1862.

    iii.   SUSAN CATHERINE L'HOMMEDIEU, born on 20 Aug 1837, married William Henry Terrell, who was born on 24 Nov 1836, the brother of George Washington Terrell, on 16 Dec 1857, three children, died on 7 Mch 1914, while he died on 17 Aug 1892 {2434}.

    iv.   JAMES ADELBERT L'HOMMEDIEU, born on 15 Jan 1840, married Lavinia Thomas in Jan 1865, one child, died on 11 Sep 1901.

    v.   MARTHA ANN L'HOMMEDIEU, born on 27 Jan 1842, married John James Van Brunt on 24 Apr 1859, four children, died on 16 Apr 1884.

2427. Grendler, op. cit., 34.
2428. Id.
2429. U.S. Census, Brookhaven, Suffolk County, NY, 1850, Dwelling House 512, Family Number 579, Page 179.
2430. Grendler, op. cit., 34.
2431. Id.
2432. Id.
2433. Hawkins, op. cit., 94.
2434. Id.

vi.   JOHN WELLS L'HOMMEDIEU, born on 23 Oct 1843, married Messelina Esther Rowland on 10 Jan 1865, two children, died in 1939.

vii.   MARY ELIZA L'HOMMEDIEU, born in 1846, died in 1848.

viii.   RICHARD WALLACE L'HOMMEDIEU, born on 12 Mch 1848, married Sarah E. Reeves, three children, lost at sea on 7 Sep 1874.

ix.   JOEL WELLINGTON L'HOMMEDIEU, born on 3 Aug 1850, married (1) Elvira H. Bunce, three children, married (2) Celia L'Hommedieu, disappeared.

x.   HARRIET L'HOMMEDIEU, born in 1852, died young.

xi.   CHARLES L'HOMMEDIEU, died young.

xii.   DANIEL ROE L'HOMMEDIEU, born on 30 Aug 1856, married Thirza J. Blydenburgh on 15 Oct 1877, three children, died on 6 Dec 1944.

xiii.   IDA LORETTA L'HOMMEDIEU, born in 1858, died young.

xiv.   DEBORAH L'HOMMEDIEU, born in 1860, died young.

318. EDMUND WHEELER[6] HOWELL (James[5], Reeves[4]), the son of James[5] and Catherine (Youngs) Howell, was born at New Village, now (1993) Centereach, on 7 Mch 1817 {2435}.

On 5 Oct 1835, Edmund Wheeler Howell married Sarah Vail, who was born at Riverhead on 29 June 1818, the daughter of John and Elizabeth (Edwards) Vail. Her father owned a small sailing vessel and earned his livelihood transporting people and goods to New York and elsewhere on Long Island Sound. Sarah made many trips with him {2436}, since her mother died on 28 Feb 1824, and he did not remarry until 1826 {2437}.

Edmund Howell was a shoemaker and worked at that trade all his life {2438}.

Edmund Howell was listed as the head of a family consisting of one free

---

2435. Grendler, op. cit., 3.
2436. Anonymous biographical sketch, SARAH (VAIL) HOWELL TERRY, from the records of the Utah Howell family, a copy of which was generously provided by C. Merrill Howell, of Cedar City, Utah.
2437. THE REGISTER, SCHS, XIII, #4, 104-105 (Spring 1988).
2438. SARAH (VAIL) HOWELL TERRY Biography.

white male of 20 and under 30 years of age, one of 5 and under 10, one free white female of 20 and under 30, and one of under 5, residing in the Town of Riverhead, Suffolk County, New York, in the Sixth Census of the United States, 1840 {2439}.

Edmund Howell became a convert to the Church of Jesus Christ of Latter-day Saints in about 1841. His wife, Sarah, became a convert in 1842. At that time, she had been suffering for about a month from a neuralgia in her head. When she was going to be baptized, the Elder told her to cast the bandages from her head. She did so, and traveled seven and one half miles in a bad wind and was baptized in ocean water in Long Island Sound, by Elder Bisbee. From that very hour, the neuralgia left her and never bothered her for the rest of her life {2440}.

During the latter part of 1844, Edmund and Sarah Howell moved, with their children, Willis, Harriet and George, to New York, where Mary was born. While living there, they attempted to accumulate the means to move west. To aid in doing so, Edmund Howell went into partnership with another shoemaker who, after a short time, sold all the assets of the partnership, and disappeared with the earnings. It took the family some time to recover from this disaster {2441}.

In 1846, after burying their son, George, the family moved to Saint Louis, where Emily Ann was born and died {2442}.

In 1848, the family left Saint Louis and moved to Honey Creek, Pottawatomie County, Iowa, where Sarah Elizabeth was born and died {2443}.

On 13 June 1851, Edmund W. Howell, of Honey Creek, Iowa, sent a letter to his brother, Richard O. Howell, saying "Tell Ben Smith he must hurry and sell his place so as to come on in time to go next spring with me for I would like his company very much and I should expect to see some dried blackberries and whortleberries and some Long Island dried apples from them old orchards where you and me used to play so much. You know where Ring and Kitty used to be harnessed sometimes before our little waggon and our stick horses. I thinks of them old times very often and would like to be there again. As for the comforts of this life I would as soon live on Long Island for this world's happiness as any part of the world I have been in. We had to work pretty hard but it was healthy and we felt more like it there than we do here. If we could have this good land there and them salt water fish and oysters and clams and such like things it would be most too good. I don't know but I should "apostatise" and go back there" {2444}.

On 23 Mch 1853, Edmund W. Howell, of Honey Creek, Iowa, sold his property on Long Island to his brother, Richard Oakley Howell {2445}.

Before they joined a company under William Miller, and later under Capt.

2439. U.S. Census, Riverhead, Suffolk County, NY, 1840, Page 234.
2440. SARAH (VAIL) HOWELL TERRY Biography.
2441. Id.
2442. Id.
2443. Id.
2444. LONG ISLAND FORUM, Nov. 1946.
2445. Grendler, op. cit., $42^1/_2$.

Wood, Edmund Howell earned a yoke of oxen and a yoke of cows, a wagon, and provisions with which to continue their journey across the plains. In May of 1852, they left Council Bluffs for Utah. When they reached the Platte River, the company suffered an outbreak of cholera, and both Edmund Howell and his daughter, Harriet, were victims. In spite of these hardships, the company continued on its way across the plains and arrived in the Salt Lake Valley in the Fall of 1852 {2446}.

Edmund Wheeler Howell died on 10 Jly 1852 {2447}.

On 27 Jan 1853, Sarah (Vail) Howell married Otis Lysander Terry as his plural wife. They lived at Cottonwood for 2-3 years, until a plague of crickets came, when they moved into Ogden for one year. They returned to Cottonwood, where Edmund L., Fanny M., Charles and Celestia Terry were born. At that time, the Johnston army invaded Utah, and Willis became a member of a company formed to defend the people {2448}.

The family moved to Fairview, Utah, on 28 Dec 1860, where Sarah (Vail) Howell Terry spent a quiet, unassuming life. She was Treasurer of the Relief Society from the time of its organization in 1868 until 1893 {2449}.

Sarah (Vail) Howell Terry died at Fairview on 14 Jly 1917, and is buried there {2450}.

Edmund Wheeler and Sarah (Vail) Howell were the parents of seven children {2451}.

+ 757. i.   ELIAS WILLIS[7] HOWELL, born on 29 Apr 1837 at Riverhead.

758. ii.   HARRIET MARIE[7] HOWELL, born on 8 June 1839 at Riverhead, died on 18 Jly 1852 on the Platte River.

759. iii. GEORGE EDWARD[7] HOWELL, born on 28 Mch 1842 at Riverhead, died on 3 Jly 1845 at New York.

+ 760. iv. MARY LOVINA[7] HOWELL, born on 27 Nov 1844 at New York.

761. v.   EMILY ANNA[7] HOWELL, born on 1 May 1847 at Saint Louis, died on 8 Feb 1848 at Saint Louis.

762. vi. SARAH ELIZABETH[7] HOWELL, born on 4 Mch 1849 at Honey Creek, Iowa, died on 10 Aug 1850 at Honey Creek.

+ 763. vii. OPHELIA ANN[7] HOWELL, born on 16 Jan 1852 at Honey Creek.

2446. SARAH (VAIL) HOWELL TERRY Biography.
2447. Grendler, op. cit.
2448. SARAH (VAIL) HOWELL TERRY Biography.
2449. Id.
2450. Edmund Wheeler Howell Family Records.
2451. THE REGISTER, SCHS, XIV, #3, 79-80 (Winter 1988).

Otis Lysander and Sarah (Vail) Howell Terry were the parents of four children {2452}.

    i.   EDMUND L. TERRY, born on 20 Apr 1854 at Cottonwood, Utah.

    ii.   FANNY M. TERRY, born on 10 May 1856 at Cottonwood.

    iii.   CHARLES A. TERRY, born on 3 May 1858 at Cottonwood.

    iv.   CELESTIA M. TERRY, born on 28 Dec 1860 at Cottonwood.

319. RICHARD OAKLEY[6] HOWELL (James[5], Reeves[4]), the son of James[5] and Catherine (Youngs) Howell, was born on 15 June 1819 at Mooney Pond, Farmingville {2453}.

Richard Oakley Howell began his education in 1825 in the first district schoolhouse in New Village, a schoolhouse which had been built in 1813 {2454}.

Richard Oakley Howell received his license to teach in the common schools of the Town of Brookhaven in 1839. He taught school at New Village, later Lake Grove, now Centereach, and at Farmingville and at Commack {2455}.

On 18 June 1840, Richard Oakley Howell married Rebecca Tuttle Homan, who was born in about 1818 at Middle Island. She was also a teacher, and had taught school at Wading River {2456}.

In 1840, Richard Howell wrote his wife, Rebecca, in the following stately manner, "Most esteemed and ever dear wife, I now spend a few leisure minutes in writing to you my dearest earthly friend.." {2457}.

On 19 Jly 1850, the family of Richard O. Howell, 30, farmer, of the Town of Brookhaven, Suffolk County, New York, having property worth $1,500, was listed as including his wife, Rebecca, 31, James O., 5, and Elbert, 9 months, in the Seventh Census of the United States, 1850 {2458}.

The house and farm of Richard Oakley Howell were located to the west of the farm of his father. He mended boots and shoes for his neighbors in a tiny shop in one corner of his barn {2459}.

Richard Oakley Howell was a member of the New Village Congregational Church, and Deacon, for 40 years. He also served as Sunday School Superintendent, and was a chorister. With his wife, he withdrew from the church

---

2452. Id.
2453. Grendler, op. cit., 43.
2454. Id., Introduction.
2455. Id., 43.
2456. Id.
2457. Id.
2458. U.S. Census, Brookhaven, Suffolk County, NY, 1850, Family Number 89, Dwelling House 82, Page 151.
2459. Grendler, op. cit., Introduction.

because of some disaffection. He and his wife then joined the Selden Presbyterian Church, where he served as a lay preacher and as Superintendent of Sunday School for ten years. Fire destroyed the church building and the congregation disbanded {2460}.

Richard O. and Rebecca T. Howell were listed as members of the First Congregational Church of New Village on 1 May 1858. They were erased from the church rolls by their request on 6 May 1882 {2461}.

On 12 Aug 1870, Richard O. Howell, 57, farmer, with real property worth $4000, and personal property worth $1000, was enumerated at New Village in the Town of Brookhaven, Suffolk County, New York, as the head of a family consisting of himself, his wife, Rebecca T., 52, and their son, William C., 17, in the Ninth Census of the United States {2462}.

Richard Oakley Howell was remembered as "Grandfather sitting in a high-backed rush-bottomed chair tilted against the wall, his legs curled around the rungs, reading his Bible of a Sunday morning before church and singing hymns. He was always singing. Grandma used to say his singing drove trouble away.." by Caroline Howell Grendler {2463}.

Rebecca Tuttle Howell died in 1898, and is buried in the New Village Cemetery at Centereach {2464}.

Richard Oakley Howell died on 27 Nov 1899 {2465}, and is buried beside his wife at Centereach {2466}.

Richard Oakley and Rebecca Tuttle (Homan) Howell were the parents of three children {2467}.
+ 764.   i.   JAMES OLIVER[7] HOWELL, born on 26 Sep 1844.

+ 765.   ii.   ELBERT RICHARD[7] HOWELL, born on 13 Aug 1849.

+ 766.   iii.   WILLIAM EDMUND CORWIN[7] HOWELL, born on 23 Jan 1853.

5. Daniel [5], Reeves [4]

320. ABIGAIL[6] HOWELL (Daniel[5], Reeves[4]), the daughter of Daniel[5] and Martha (Stephens) Howell, was born on 2 Feb 1806 {2468} at Quogue {2469}.

2460. Id., 43.
2461. David A. Overton, The REGISTER, SCHS, XV, #3, 72 (Winter 1989).
2462. U.S. Census, Brookhaven, Suffolk County, NY, 1870, Dwelling House 1885, Family Number 2034, Page 431.
2463. Grendler, op. cit., Introduction.
2464. Gravestone, New Village Church Cemetery, Centereach.
2465. Grendler, op. cit., 43.
2466. Gravestone, New Village Church Cemetery, Centereach.
2467. Grendler, op. cit., 43.
2468. Gravestone, Union Cemetery, Middle Island.

Abigail Howell inherited the entire estate of her father, Daniel Howell, by his will of 28 Jan 1808, proved on 23 Feb 1808 {2470}.

In 1822, Abigail Howell married John Buckingham, who was born in 1798, the son of Jonas and Deborah (Homan) Buckingham. He became a skilled mechanic who built flour and saw mills {2471}.

John Buckingham was elected a Constable at the Annual Meeting of the Town of Brookhaven on 2 Apr 1822, on 1 Apr 1823, and again on 5 Apr 1825 {2472}.

In the Fifth Census of the United States, 1830, John Buckingham was enumerated as the head of a household consisting of one free white male of 20 and under 30 years of age, two of under 5, one free white female of 50 and under 60, and one of 20 and under 30, and located in the Town of Brookhaven, Suffolk County, New York {2473}.

John Buckingham died in 1852, at the age of 54, and is buried in the Union Cemetery at Middle Island {2474}.

In the Fall of 1857, Abigail Buckingham, and her son, Daniel Howell Buckingham, leased the old homestead, which she had inherited from her father, to William C. Bartlett, a famous lawyer from New York City, who purchased it in 1861 {2475}.

Abigail Buckingham is said to have married Aaron Ketcham {2476}.

Abigail (Howell) Buckingham Ketcham (?) married Jacob Meserole, who was born in about 1797.

On 6 Aug 1870, Jacob Meserole, 73, shoemaker, with real property worth $1000, was enumerated as the head of a family consisting of himself and his wife, Abigail, 63, residing in Port Jefferson, in the Town of Brookhaven, Suffolk County, New York, in the Ninth Census of the United States {2477}.

Abigail (Howell) Buckingham Ketcham (?) Meserole died on 31 Aug 1897 at Port Jefferson {2478}, and is buried beside her first husband at Middle Island {2479}.

John and Abigail (Howell) Buckingham were the parents of eight children {2480}.

    i.   MARGARET BUCKINGHAM, born on 22 Oct 1822, died in

2469. #3140, Register of Deaths, Town of Brookhaven, from a copy graciously provided by Lillian Paul, Registrar.

2470. Suffolk County Wills, Liber B, 490-491; Suffolk County Estates, File #795.

2471. Frederick W. Chapman, THE BUCKINGHAM FAMILY.., 31.

2472. BTR, Book D, 183, 193, 210; (D, 238, 250, 267).

2473. U.S. Census, Brookhaven, Suffolk County, NY, 1830, Page 186.

2474. Gravestone, Union Cemetery, Middle Island.

2475. Daniel H. Buckingham, AUTOBIOGRAPHY, 1.

2476. Wilbur Franklin Howell, op. cit., 363.

2477. U.S. Census, Brookhaven, Suffolk County, NY, 1870, Dwelling House 1680, Family Number 1811, Page 418.

2478. #3140, Register of Deaths, Town of Brookhaven.

2479. Gravestone, Union Cemetery, Middle Island.

2480. Chapman, op. cit.

infancy.

ii.   DANIEL HOWELL BUCKINGHAM, born on 27 Dec 1823, married (1) Hannah M. Gerard on 8 Jan 1850, one child. Hannah (Gerard) Buckingham died on 27 Feb 1851 {2481}, at the age of 22, and is buried in the Union Cemetery at Middle Island {2482}. He married (2) Sarah M. Gerard on 29 Jan 1853 {2483}, nine children, died in 1913 at the age of 86, and is buried near his wives at Middle Island {2484}. Sarah M. Buckingham died in 1874, at the age of 39, and is buried in the family plot at Middle Island {2485}.

iii.   JOHN BUELL BUCKINGHAM, born on 27 Nov 1827, married Mary L. Merchant, four children, resided at Providence, Rhode Island {2486}.

iv.   JONAS EDWARD BUCKINGHAM, born on 29 Jan 1831, married Julia M. Davis, on 30 May 1855, three children {2487}.

v.   CHARRY AMANDA BUCKINGHAM, born on 20 Sep 1833, married David Davis on 25 Apr 1854, three children {2488}.

vi.   MARY ELLEN BUCKINGHAM, born on 10 Oct 1836.

vii.   GEORGE ALLEN BUCKINGHAM, born on 7 Jly 1839, married Sarah Jane Titus on 16 Jly 1863, one child {2489}.

viii.   CHARLES EUGENE BUCKINGHAM, born on 15 Aug 1850, died on 10 Dec 1854, and is buried in the family plot in the Union Cemetery at Middle Island {2490}.

2481. Id., 38.
2482. Gravestone, Union Cemetery, Middle Island.
2483. Chapman, op. cit., 38.
2484. Gravestone, Union Cemetery, Middle Island.
2485. Id.
2486. Chapman, op. cit, 39.
2487. Id.
2488. Id.
2489. Id.
2490. Gravestone, Union Cemetery, Middle Island.

6. William⁵, Reeves⁴

321. WILLIAM REEVE⁶ HOWELL (William⁵, Reeves⁴), the son of William⁵ and Phebe (Barteau) Howell was born in about 1806.

William R. Howell died on 22 June 1831, at the age of 25 years, and is buried in the Union Cemetery at Middle Island {2491}.

322. LUCINDA⁶ HOWELL (William⁵, Reeves⁴), the daughter of William⁵ and Phebe (Barteau) Howell, was born in about 1807.

Lucinda Howell married "John Ruland" {2492}.

In the Fifth Census of the United States, 1830, John Rowland was enumerated as the head of a family consisting of two free white males of 20 and under 30 years of age, one of 5 and under 10, and one free white female, residing in the Town of Brookhaven, Suffolk County, New York {2493}.

Lucinda Rowland, the wife of John E. Rowland, died on 19 Dec 1831, at the age of 24, and is buried in the Union Cemetery at Middle Island {2494}.

B. Jonathan³, John², Richard¹.

1. Jonathan⁵, Jonathan⁴.

323. JONATHAN DAVIS⁶ HOWELL (Jonathan⁵, Jonathan⁴), the son of Jonathan⁵ and Elizabeth (Hallock) Howell, "..was born in Suffolk County in 1797, and in early life was the owner of a sloop that plied between Long Island and the city of New York, it being used principally in the transportation of wood, a business in which he was extensively interested, and up to the time of his death, in 1869, he was engaged in the coal and wood trade in that city." {2495}.

Jonathan Davis Howell married Louise Howell (#523), who was born on 8 Mch 1805, the daughter of David (#214) and Joanna (Wells) Howell.

By his father's will of 7 Sep 1831, proved on 3 Jan 1832, Jonathan Davis Howell, the eldest son, inherited $50 {2496}.

On 26 Jly 1850, Jonathan D. Howell, 54, wood merchant, having real property valued at $3000, was enumerated as the head of a household consisting of himself, his wife, Louisa, 45, their children, Charles, 21, boat builder, Davis, 17, boat builder, Porter, 15, clerk, George, 9, Theodore, 7, and Hampton, 3, and

2491. Id.
2492. Sherwood, op. cit.
2493. U.S. Census, Brookhaven, Suffolk County, NY, 1830, Page 164.
2494. Gravestone, Union Cemetery, Middle Island.
2495. PORTRAIT AND BIOGRAPHICAL RECORD OF SUFFOLK COUNTY, 182.
2496. Suffolk County Wills, Liber F, 212-214; Suffolk County Estates, File #2410.

Margaret Lenan, 20, and Esberitta Willis, 22, boat builder, residing in the Thirteenth Ward, in New York City, in the Seventh Census of the United States {2497}.

In 1852-1853, "Jonath. D. Howell" was dealer in lumber at 78 Rutgers Street in New York City, with a residence at 9 Mangin Street {2498}.

Jonathan Davis and Louise (Howell) Howell were the parents of at least seven sons {2499}.

+ 767.   i.   THADDEUS P.[7] HOWELL, born in about 1827.

+ 768.   ii.   CHARLES E.[7] HOWELL, born in about 1829.

+ 769.   iii. JONATHAN D.[7] HOWELL, born on about 1833.

+ 770.   iv. DAVID PORTER[7] HOWELL, born in about 1835.

+ 771.   v.   BENJAMIN F.[7] HOWELL, born on 5 Sep 1838.

+ 772.   vi. GEORGE[7] HOWELL, born in about 1841.

  773. vii. THEODORE[7] HOWELL, born in about 1843.

  774.viii. HAMPTON[7] HOWELL, born in about 1847.

324. BETSEY[6] HOWELL (Jonathan[5], Jonathan[4]) was the daughter of Jonathan[5] and Elizabeth (Hallock) Howell.

Betsey Howell married Eleazer Luce, who was born in about 1783, the son of Rev. Eleazer, Jr., and Mehetable (Downs) Luce. He became a minister, and they removed to Allegheny County {2500}.

We have no information on the family of Eleazer and Betsey (Howell) Luce.

325. JOHN H.[6] HOWELL (Jonathan[5], Jonathan[4]), the son of Jonathan[5] and Elizabeth (Hallock) Howell, was born in about 1801.

John H. Howell married Millicent Benjamin, who was born in 1799, the daughter of Amaziah and Achsa (Sweezy) Benjamin {2501}.

"For years..", John H. Howell "..was one of the well-to-do agriculturists

2497. U.S. Census, 13th Ward, New York, NY, 1850, Dwelling House 54, Family Number 184, Page 139.

2498. THE NEW YORK DIRECTORY, for 1853-1854, Charles R. Rode, 161 Broadway, late Doggett & Rode, 319.

2499. PORTRAIT & BIOGRAPHICAL RECORD OF SUFFOLK COUNTY, 183.

2500. Jaques & Kappenberg, op.cit., 9.

2501. Bicha & Brown, op. cit., 722.

of this section, and later successfully in fishing. Although in his day the implements used in farming were rude and unhandy, the soil was rich and the crops yielded rich return. When well along in years he was enabled to retire from labor and sit down to enjoy the fruits of his early years. He was especially interested in church work, and was an active member of the Presbyterian Church." {2502}.

In the Sixth Census of the United States, 1840, John H. Howell was enumerated as the head of a family consisting of one free white male of 30 and under 40 years of age, three of 5 and under 10, and one free white female of 30 and under 40, residing in the Town of Brookhaven, Suffolk County, New York {2503}.

On 7 Aug 1850, John H. Howell, 48, farmer, was enumerated as the head of a family consisting of himself, his wife, Milicent, 48, and their children, Egbert, 19, Hiram, 17, George, 14, and Achsa M., 8, residing in the Town of Brookhaven, Suffolk County, New York,in the Seventh Census of the United States, 1850 {2504}.

On 25 Jly 1870, John H. Howell, 68, farmer, with real property worth $300, and personal property worth $800, was enumerated as the head of a family consisting of himself and his wife, "Melissa", 69, residing at East Moriches in the Town of Brookhaven, Suffolk County, New York, in the Ninth Census of the United States {2505}.

John H. Howell died on 26 Aug 1884, at the age of 86 years and 6 months, and is buried in the Mount Pleasant Cemetery at Central Moriches {2506}.

Millicent Howell died on 31 Jan 1885, at the age of 86 years, and is buried beside her husband at Central Moriches {2507}.

John H. and Millicent (Benjamin) Howell were the parents of at least four children {2508}.

+ 775. i. JOHN EGBERT[7] HOWELL, born in about 1830.

+ 776. ii. HIRAM F.[7] HOWELL, born on 3 Sep 1832.

+ 777. iii. GEORGE[7] HOWELL, born in about 1836.

+ 778. iv. ACHSA[7] HOWELL, born in about 1842.

328. ALBERT[6] HOWELL (Jonathan[5], Jonathan[4]), the son of Jonathan[5] and

2502. PORTRAIT AND BIOGRAPHICAL RECORD OF SUFFOLK COUNTY, 672.
2503. U.S. Census, Brookhaven, Suffolk County, NY, 1840, Page 279.
2504. Id., 1850, Dwelling House 73, Family Number 83, Page 193.
2505. Id., 1870, Dwelling House 1203, Family Number 1288, Page 388.
2506. Gravestone, Mount Pleasant Cemetery, Center Moriches, the markings having been graciously provided by Theodore M. Sanford, III.
2507. Id.
2508. Wilbur Franklin Howell, op. cit., 214.

Elizabeth (Hallock) Howell, was born in about 1807.

In the Sixth Census of the United States, 1840, Albert Howell was listed as the head of a family consisting of one free white male of 30 and under 40 years of age, one of 5 and under 10, one free white female of 30 and under 40, and one of 5 and under 10, residing in the Town of Southold, Suffolk County, New York {2509}.

On 12 Jly 1850, Albert Howell, 43, farmer, having real property worth $1,500, was enumerated as the head of a family including himself, his wife, Hannah, 45, and their children, John, 17, laborer, and Betsey, 15, residing in the Town of Southold, Suffolk County, New York, in the Seventh Census of the United States, 1850 {2510}.

Hannah Howell, 54, of Cutchogue, died on 6 Jly 1861 {2511}.

Albert Howell married Mary A. Rowland at Cutchogue on 11 Nov 1862 {2512}.

Albert Howell and Mary E. Luther, both of Greenport, were married on 7 Jly 1870 {2513}.

On 28 Jly 1870, Albert Howell, 65, farmer, with real property worth $3000, and personal property worth $500, was enumerated as the head of a family consisting of himself, his wife, Mary, and his son, John, 30, farmer, with real property worth $700, residing at Cutchogue in the Town of Southold, Suffolk County, New York in the Ninth Census of the United States {2514}.

By his will of 25 Feb 1878, proved on 5 June 1893, Albert Howell left the residue of his estate to his son John A. Howell, whom he designated as sole executor, after his just debts, funeral and burial expenses and legacies to his daughter, Betsey Jane Tuthill, and his grandchildren, Joshua, John, and Martha Tuthill, and Hannah H. Terry, were paid. He designated Alonzo O. Tuthill as guardian of his children {2515}.

Albert and Hannah (Aldrich) Howell were the parents of at least two children.

+ 779. i. JOHN A.[7] HOWELL, born on 26 Mch 1833 {2516}.

+ 780. ii. BETSEY JANE[7] HOWELL, born in about 1835.

329. VAN RENSSELAER[6] HOWELL (Jonathan[5], Jonathan[4]), the son of Jonathan[5] and Elizabeth (Hallock) Howell, was born on 8 Nov 1808.

2509. U.S. Census, Southold, Suffolk County, NY, 1840, Page 231.

2510. Id., 1850, Dwelling House 125, Family Number 130, Page 288.

2511. N. Hubbard Cleveland, op. cit.

2512. SAG HARBOR CORRECTOR, 22 Nov 1862.

2513. Cleveland, op. cit.

2514. U.S. Census, Southold, Suffolk County, NY, 1870, Dwelling House 957, Family Number 1035, Page 291.

2515. Suffolk County Wills, Liber 28, 152-156; Suffolk County Estates, File #12456.

2516. Gravestone, Cutchogue New Yard Cemetery.

Van Rensselaer Howell married Mary Ann Terry, who was born on 18 Dec 1810, the daughter of Isaac Terry, at Riverhead before Rev. Luce {2517}.

In the Sixth Census of the United States, 1840, "Renssalear Howell" was listed as the head of a family consisting of one free white male of 30 and under 40 years of age, one of 10 and under 15, and two of under 5, and one free white female of 20 and under 30, residing in the Town of Southold, Suffolk County, New York {2518}.

On 11 Jly 1850, Van Rensselaer Howell, 42, farmer, having real property worth $2,500, was enumerated as the head of a household including himself, his wife, Mary A., 39, and their children, Isaac T., 12, Gilbert V., 10, Maria J., 7, and the laborer, James Henderson, 21, residing in the Town of Southold, Suffolk County, New York, in the Seventh Census of the United States, 1850 {2519}.

On 20 June 1870, "Rensellaer" Howell, 62, farmer, with real property worth $6000, and personal property worth $500, was enumerated as the head of a household consisting of himself and his wife, Mary, 59, and their domestic servant, Ruth Raynor, 14, residing at Peconic in the Town of Southold, Suffolk County, New York, in the Ninth Census of the United States {2520}.

By his will of 25 Jan 1889, proved on 22 Oct 1894, Van Rensselaer Howell left his farm at Moriches, and other property, to his son, Isaac T. Howell, his homestead farm, and other property, to his daughter, Maria J. Billard, and property and cash to his son, Gilbert V. Howell, whom he named as a co-executor of this will, with his son-in-law, Barnabas F. Billard {2521}.

Van Rensselaer Howell died on 25 Sep 1894, and is buried in the Cutchogue New Yard cemetery {2522}.

Mary Ann (Terry) Howell died on 31 Dec 1895, and is buried beside her husband at Cutchogue {2523}.

Van Rensselaer and Mary Ann (Terry) Howell were the parents of seven children.

+ 781.   i.   ISAAC T.[7] HOWELL, born in about 1838.

+ 782.   ii.   GILBERT VAN RENSSELAER[7] HOWELL, born on 23 Sep 1839.

+ 783.   iii.   MARIA J.[7] HOWELL, born on 2 Jan 1843.

    784.   iv.   ELIZABETH[7] HOWELL.

2517. THE REPUBLICAN WATCHMAN, Sag Harbor, 12 Feb 1831.
2518. U.S. Census, Southold, Suffolk County, NY, 1840, Page 212.
2519. Id., 1850, Dwelling House 85, Family Number 88, Page 285.
2520. Id., 1870, Dwelling House 396, Family Number 413, Page 256.
2521. Suffolk County Wills, Liber 30, 101ff; Suffolk County Estates, File #12921.
2522. Gravestone, Cutchogue New Yard Cemetery.
2523. Id.

+ 785. v. GEORGE H.⁷ HOWELL.

786. vi. JOHN⁷ HOWELL.

787. vii. MARY E.⁷ HOWELL.

330. EDWARD YOUNG⁶ HOWELL (Jonathan⁵, Jonathan⁴), the son of Jonathan⁵ and Elizabeth (Hallock) Howell, was born in about Feb 1811.

Edward Y. Howell married Sarah, who was born on 13 Feb 1812.

Sarah Howell died on 23 May 1863, at the age of 51 years, 3 months and 10 days, and is buried in the Cutchogue "Old Yard" Cemetery {2524}.

On 20 June 1870, "Youngs" Howell, 57, farmer, with real property worth $2000, was enumerated as the head of a household consisting of himself, his wife, Jemima, 45, his daughter, Emma, 26, seamstress, and their domestic servant, Libbie Miller, 20, residing at Peconic in the Town of Southold, Suffolk County, New York, in the Ninth Census of the United States {2525}.

Edward Y. Howell died on 31 Aug 1892, at the age of 81 years and 6 months, and is buried beside his wife at Cutchogue {2526}.

Edward Young and Sarah Howell may have been the parents of at least one daughter.

+ 788. i. EMMA⁷ HOWELL, born in about 1844.

331. GEORGE⁶ HOWELL (Jonathan⁵, Jonathan⁴), the son of Jonathan⁵ and Elizabeth (Hallock) Howell, was born on 1 Nov 1809.

On 4 Dec 1833, George Howell, of Mattituck, married Harriet Penny, of Southold {2527}.

In the Sixth Census of the United States, 1840, George Howell was listed as the head of a household consisting of one free white male of 30 and under 40 years of age, one free white female of 30 and under 40, and one of under 5, residing in the Town of Southold, Suffolk County, New York {2528}.

On 10 Jly 1850, George Howell, 41, farmer, with real property worth $1,000, was enumerated as the head of a family including himself, his wife, Harriet, 42, and their daughter, Frances E., 14, residing in the Town of Southold, Suffolk County, New York, in the Seventh Census of the United States {2529}.

On 16 June 1870, George Howell, 60, farmer, with real property worth

2524. Gravestone, Cutchogue Old Yard Cemetery.
2525. U.S. Census, Southold, Suffolk County, NY, 1870, Dwelling House 385, Family Number 403, Page 256.
2526. Gravestone, Cutchogue Old Yard Cemetery.
2527. Cleveland, op. cit.
2528. U.S. Census, Southold, Suffolk County, NY, 1840, Page 210.
2529. Id., 1850, Dwelling House 30, Family Number 33, Page 282.

$2000, and personal property worth $300, was enumerated as the head of a family consisting of himself and his wife, Harriet, 62, residing in Cutchogue in the Town of Southold, Suffolk County, New York, in the Ninth Census of the United States {2530}.

George Howell, 65, of Cutchogue, died on 26 Nov 1874 {2531}.

George and Harriet (Penny) Howell were the parents of at least one daughter.

789.   i.   FRANCES E.[7] HOWELL, born in about 1836.

332. ELI WOODHULL[6] HOWELL (Jonathan[5], Jonathan[4]), the son of Jonathan[5] and Elizabeth (Hallock) Howell, was born on 16 Mch 1816.

On 11 Dec 1845, Eli Woodhull Howell married Julia Ann Tuthill, who was born on 31 Mch 1824, the daughter of Elisha and Susanna (Wells) Tuthill {2532}.

On 9 Jly 1850, E. Woodhull Howell, 30, seaman, and his wife, Julia Ann, 24, were enumerated as a family residing in the Town of Southold, Suffolk County, New York, in the Seventh Census of the United States {2533}.

Eli W. Howell was a farmer residing at Southold in 1868-9 {2534}.

On 9 Jly 1870, Eli Howell, 53, farmer, with real property worth $2500, and personal property worth $500, was enumerated as the head of a household consisting of himself, his wife, Julia, 45, their daughter, Annie, 8, and Daniel Wells, 17, a farm laborer, residing at Southold in the Town of Southold, Suffolk County, New York {2535}.

By his will of 24 June 1875, proved on 8 Dec 1891, Eli W. Howell left the use of his estate to his wife, Julia A. Howell, except for $1,000, which he left to their daughter, Annie W. Howell, who was to receive the rest of the estate after the decease of her mother, who was named executor of the estate {2536}.

Eli W. Howell died on 5 Nov 1891, and is buried in the Willow Hill Cemetery {2537}.

Julia A. (Tuthill) Howell died on 21 Sep 1898, and is buried beside her husband at Willow Hill {2538}.

Eli Woodhull and Julia Ann (Tuthill) Howell were the parents of at least three children.

2530. Id., 1870, Dwelling House 313, Family Number 333, Page 252.

2531. Cleveland, op. cit.

2532. Tuttle, op. cit., 151, 351.

2533. U.S. Census, Southold, Suffolk County, NY, 1850, Dwelling House 9, Family Number 11, Page 281.

2534. D. Curtin, CURTIN'S DIRECTORY OF SUFFOLK COUNTY, from THE REGISTER, SCHS, XIX, #3, 82 (Winter 1993).

2535. U.S. Census, Southold, Suffolk County, NY, 1870, Dwelling House 573, Family Number 599, Page 266.

2536. Suffolk County Wills, Liber 26, 183ff; Suffolk County Estates, File Number #11955.

2537. Gravestone, Willow Hill Cemetery, from the collection of cemetery markings at the SCHS.

2538. Id.

790. i. SUSAN E.[7] HOWELL, born on 4 Apr 1850, died on 17 Apr 1850, at he age of 13 days, and is buried at Willow Hill {2539}.

791. ii. SON[7], died as an infant on 28 Feb 1854 {2540}.

+ 792. iii. ANNIE WOODHULL[7] HOWELL, born on 17 Mch 1862 {2541}.

2. Daniel [5], Jonathan [4]

333. DANIEL[6] HOWELL (Daniel[5], Jonathan[4]), the son of Daniel[5] and Esther (Reeve) Howell, was baptized at Mattituck on 9 Jly 1809, along with his sister, Clarissa, and his brother, Hubbard {2542}.

336. MARY[6] HOWELL (Daniel[5], Jonathan[4]), the daughter of Daniel and Esther (Reeve) Howell, was born on 26 Feb 1822 {2543}.

On 9 Oct 1847, Mary Howell married Charles W. Overton, who was born on 7 June 1824, the son of Charles T. and Rachel (Moore) Overton {2544}.

Charles W. and Mary (Howell) Overton were the parents of two children {2545}.

  i. ALBRO HOWELL OVERTON, born on 29 Oct 1848, died on 29 Jly 1849.

  ii. CHARLES HANFORD OVERTON, born on 6 Feb 1855, married Cora Ackerson, four children, died on 9 Dec 1885.

3. Jeremiah [5], Jeremiah [4]

337. ELIZABETH[6] HOWELL (Jeremiah[5], Jeremiah[4]), the daughter of Jeremiah[5] and Catherine (Hennion) Howell, was born in about Oct 1800.

Elizabeth Howell married John D. Cosman {2546}.

2539. Id.
2540. Id.
2541. Wilbur Franklin Howell, op. cit., 420.
2542. Craven, op. cit., 314.
2543. Mallmann, op. cit., 174.
2544. Id.
2545. Id.
2546. Gravestone, Genoa Village Cemetery, NYG&BR, LIV, 229 (Jly 1923).

Elizabeth (Howell) Cosman died on 1 Jly 1859, at the age of 58 years and 9 months, and is buried in the Genoa Village Cemetery {2547}.

339. JOHN[6] HOWELL (Jeremiah[5], Jeremiah[4]), the son of Jeremiah[5] and Catherine (Hennion) Howell, was born in about 1808, although his gravestone seems to indicate 8 Jly 1804 {2548}.

On 1 Sep 1850, John Howell, 42, mechanic, with real property worth $3,400, was enumerated as the head of a family including himself, his wife, Hester, 43, and their children, Catherine, 16, Margaret, 14, and Adelia, 9, residing in Newburgh, Orange County, New York, in the Seventh Census of the United States {2549}.

John Howell died on 2 Nov 1855, and is buried in the Cedar Hill Cemetery at Millhope, New York {2550}.

By her will of 20 Jly 1877, proved on 18 Nov 1880, Hester Ann Howell, left a legacy of $200 to her grandson, Fred Rundell, a bequest which she eliminated by a codicil dated 15 Apr 1878. The remainder of her estate was to be divided into four equal parts, one quarter going to her son, James Howell, another to her son, John, yet another to her daughter, Catherine B. Handford, and the fourth quarter being divided between Arminta and Mary T. Bloomer, children of her deceased daughter, Delia Bloomer. By the codicil noted, Arminta was also to have her gold watch. She appointed her sons, James and John, to be executors of this will {2551}.

Hester Ann Howell died on 13 Oct 1880, and is buried beside her husband at Middlehope {2552}.

John and Hester Howell were the parents of five children.

+ 793.   i.   JAMES[7] HOWELL, born in 1826 {2553}.

+ 794.   ii.   JOHN[7] HOWELL, born in 1831 {2554}.

+ 795.   iii.   CATHERINE[7] HOWELL, born in 1833 {2555}.

+ 796.   iv.   MARGARETTA C.[7] HOWELL, born in 1835 {2556}.

2547. Id.
2548. Gravestone, Cedar Hill Cemetery, Middlehope, NY.
2549. U.S. Census, Newburgh, Orange County, NY, 1850, Dwelling House 356, Family Number 383, Page 26.
2550. Gravestone, Cedar Hill Cemetery, Millhope, NY.
2551. Orange County Wills, Liber 43, 157-161.
2552. Gravestone, Cedar Hill Cemetery, Middlehope, NY.
2553. Id.
2554. Id.
2555. Id.
2556. Id.

+ 797.   v.   ADELIA[7] HOWELL, born on 21 Sep 1840 {2557}.

340. ELLIOTT[6] HOWELL (Jeremiah[5], Jeremiah[4]), the son of Jeremiah[5] and Catherine (Hennion) Howell, was born in about 1809.

On 15 Mch 1832, Mr. Elliot Howell, of Marlborough, Ulster County, married Miss Nancy Bloomer, of Newburgh {2558}.

Nancy Howell, the wife of Elliott Howell, died on 2 Jly 1836, at the age of 31 years, 7 months and 16 days, and is buried in the Balmville cemetery {2559}.

Jane Howell, the wife of Elliott, died on 27 Feb 1839, at the age of 29 years and 7 days, and is buried in the Balmville cemetery {2560}.

Elliott Howell married (3) Edith Lent, who was born on 2 Sep 1810, the daughter of Jacob and Martha Lent {2561}.

On 1 June 1839, Jeremiah Howell, of the Town of Locke, in Cayuga County, New York, sold, to Elliott Howell, of the Town of Marlborough, in Ulster County, New York, for $3,000, two lots of land in Marlborough, one of 72 acres and twenty pershes, and the other of 10 acres {2562}.

On 29 Jly 1850, Elliott Howell, 41, farmer, with real property worth $3000, was enumerated as the head of a household consisting of himself, his wife, Edith, 39, his children, Catherine, 16, and Henry, 14, and John Spafford, 16, residing in the Town of Locke, Cayuga County, New York, in the Seventh Census of the United States {2563}.

By his father's will of 4 Sep 1857, proved on 31 Jly 1858, Elliott Howell was bequeathed the sum of one dollar to be paid to him within a year of his father's death {2564}. With his brothers, Isaac and James, he was also a beneficiary of his brother, David, share and share alike {2565}.

Edith Howell died on 8 Feb 1886, at the age of 75 years, 5 months and 6 days, and is buried in the Fleming Hill Cemetery in the Town of Fleming, Cayuga County, New York {2566}.

Elliott Howell died on 29 Sep 1890, at the age of 81, and is buried beside his third wife {2567}.

2557. Dorothy G. Tuttle, Personal communication, from LDS microfilm #1553485.
2558. NEWBURGH GAZETTE, 17 Mch 1832.
2559. INSCRIPTIONS IN THE BALMVILLE BURYING GROUND, Publication #9, Historical Society of Newburgh Bay & the Highlands, from RECORDS FROM NEWBURGH, NEW WINDSOR, AND OTHER NEARBY TOWNS, OCGS, 90.
2560. Id.
2561. Added notes, Fleming Hill Cemetery, from L.D.S. Microfilm #1435221.
2562. Ulster County Deeds, Liber 53, 17-18.
2563. U.S. Census, Locke, Cayuga County, NY, 1850, Dwelling House 249, Family Number 254, Page 103.
2564. Cayuga County Wills, Book M, 324-330.
2565. Id., Book W, 525-531.
2566. Gravestone, Fleming Hill Cemetery, from L.D.S. Microfilm #1435221.
2567. Id.

Elliott and Nancy (Bloomer) Howell were the parents of at least two children.

+ 798.　i.　CATHERINE[7] HOWELL, born in about June 1833.

799.　ii.　HENRY W.[7] HOWELL, born in about 1836, died on 7 Mch 1851, at the age of 16, and is buried beside his father in the Fleming Hill Cemetery {2568}.

341. DAVID[6] HOWELL (Jeremiah[5], Jeremiah[4]), the son of Jeremiah[5] and Catherine (Hennion) Howell, was born on 6 Mch 1810.

On 17 Jly 1850, David Howell, 37, farmer, with real estate worth $6000, was enumerated as the head of a household consisting of himself, Seth Roberts, 67, laborer, and Eliza Taylor, 21, residing in the Town of Locke, Cayuga County, New York, in the Seventh Census of the United States {2569}.

David Howell was a major heir of his father, dividing most of the estate with his brothers, Isaac and James, and his sisters, Elizabeth Cosman and Catherine Carver {2570}.

By his will of 1 Jan 1874, proved on 4 May 1874, David Howell left his property to be divided share and share alike between his brothers, Isaac, James and Elliott Howell {2571}.

David Howell died on 12 Jan 1874, at the age of 63 years, 10 months, and 6 days, and is buried in the Genoa Village Cemetery {2572}.

It appears that David Howell never married.

342. JAMES[6] HOWELL (Jeremiah[5], Jeremiah[4]), the son of Jeremiah[5] and Catherine (Hennion) Howell, was born in 1813.

Lucy B. Howell, who was born in 1823, died in 1867, and is buried in the Genoa village cemetery {2573}.

James Howell died on 8 Oct 1884 {2574}.

James and Lucy B. Howell were the parents of at least two children {2575}.

800.　i.　EVA[7] HOWELL, married Mr. Niblo.

801.　ii.　JESSIE[7] HOWELL, born in about 1870.

2568. Id.
2569. U.S. Census, 1850, Locke, Cayuga County, NY, Dwelling House 36, Family Number 37, Page 90.
2570. Cayuga County Wills, Book M, 324-330.
2571. Id., Book W, 525-531.
2572. Gravestone, Genoa Village Cemetery, NYG&BR, LVI, 232 (Jly 1923).
2573. Id., from L.D.S. Microfilm #1435221.
2574. Petition, Jessie Howell to Surrogate's Court, Cayuga County, from L.D.S. Microfilm #869876.
2575. Id.

343. CATHERINE⁶ HOWELL (Jeremiah⁵, Jeremiah⁴), the daughter of Jeremiah⁵ and Catherine (Hennion) Howell, was born on 14 Oct 1815 {2576}.

Catherine Howell married Daniel Carver, who was born in Claverack, Columbia County, New York, on 10 Feb 1810, the son of John Carver {2577}.

"Before farming at Newburgh, Daniel Carver kept a store in town, and also in Allegheny County. He was the grandson of a Hessian soldier." {2578}.

Daniel Carver kept a store at Carver's Corners, then in Cuba, but in Genessee County in 1895. In 1842 or 1843, he moved to Newburgh, where he ran a general store on Water Street. He bought a farm near Newburgh and moved there in 1853. In politics, he was a Republican and, in religion, belonged to the Methodist Episcopal church {2579}.

On 1 Nov 1850, Daniel Carver, 40, merchant, with real property worth $1000, was enumerated as the head of a household consisting of himself, his wife, Catherine, 36, their son, Daniel S., 2, and Isaac V. Ostrander, 16, clerk, residing in the Town of Newburgh, Orange County, New York, in the Seventh Census of the United States {2580}.

Daniel Carver died on 17 Jan 1867, and is buried in the Cedar Hill cemetery at Middlehope {2581}.

Catherine Carver died in 1899, and is buried beside her husband in the Cedar Hill Cemetery {2582}.

Daniel and Catherine (Howell) Carver were the parents of four children {2583}.

    i.   SARAH E. CARVER, born on 29 Oct 1838, died on 15 May 1839, aged 6 months and 17 days, and is buried in the Cedar Hill Cemetery {2584}.

    ii.   DANIEL S. CARVER, born on 30 May 1848, died on 24 Feb 1869, aged 20 years, 8 months, and 25 days, and is buried at Middlehope {2585}.

    iii.   CATHERINE F. CARVER, born on 29 Aug 1850, married Samuel J. Wait.

    iv.   HOWELL HENNION CARVER, born on 11 Oct 1856, married

---

2576. Mary Ellen Halsey, op. cit.
2577. PORTRAIT AND BIOGRAPHICAL RECORD OF ORANGE COUNTY, NEW YORK, 215.
2578. Halsey, op. cit.
2579. PORTRAIT & BIOGRAPHICAL RECORD OF ORANGE COUNTY, 215.
2580. U.S. Census, Newburgh, Orange County, NY, 1850, Dwelling House 1621, Family Number 1612, Page 107.
2581. Gravestone, Cedar Hill Cemetery, Middlehope, NY.
2582. Id.
2583. PORTRAIT & BIOGRAPHICAL RECORD OF ORANGE COUNTY, 215.
2584. Gravestone, Cedar Hill Cemetery, Middlehope, NY.
2585. Id.

Gertrude Deyo Bloomer, of Balmsville {2586}, on 5 Mch 1874, three children. She died in 10 Sep 1909, while he died in 1936. Both are buried at Middlehope {2587}.

344. ISAAC[6] HOWELL (Jeremiah[5], Jeremiah[4]), the son of Jeremiah[5] and Catherine (Hennion) Howell, was born in about 1822.

On 22 Jly 1850, Isaac Howell, 28, farmer, with real estate worth $2500, was enumerated as the head of a family consisting of himself, his wife, Jane, 22, and their daughter, Elizabeth, $^{10}/_{12}$, residing in the town of Scipio, Cayuga County, New York, in the Seventh Census of the United States {2588}.

Isaac Howell was a major heir to the estate of his father {2589}. He also divided the estate of his brother, David, with his other brothers, James and Elliott, and was the executor of the will {2590}.

Isaac Howell died on 1 Feb 1895 {2591}, and is buried in the Lakeview Cemetery {2592}.

Joanna (Beardsley) Howell died in 1895, and is buried beside her husband in the Lakeview Cemetery {2593}.

Isaac and Jane Howell were the parents of at least four children {2594}.

+ 802.   i.   ELIZABETH[7] HOWELL, born in Sep 1849.

+ 803.   ii.   FRANK[7] HOWELL, born in 1851.

+ 804.   iii.   JEROME[7] HOWELL, born in 1853.

   805.   iv.   LLOYD[7] HOWELL.

345. ALTHEA[6] HOWELL (Jeremiah[5], Jeremiah[4]) was the daughter of Jeremiah[5] and Catherine (Hennion) Howell.

Althea Howell married Mr. Cummings.

Mr. and Althea (Howell) Cummings were the parents of five children {2595}.

2586. Mary Ellen Halsey, op. cit.
2587. Gravestones, Cedar Hill Cemetery, Middlehope, NY.
2588. U.S. Census, Scipio, Cayuga County, NY, 1850, Dwelling House 169, Family Number 176, Page 179.
2589. Cayuga County Wills, Book M, 324-330.
2590. Id., Book W, 525-531.
2591. Petition, Frank Howell to Surrogate's Court, Cayuga County, Box 384, from L.D.S. Microfilm #875073.
2592. Gravestone, Lakeview Cemetery, from L.D.S. Microfilm #1435221.
2593. Id.
2594. Petition, Frank Howell.
2595. Cayuga County Wills, Book M, 324-330.

     i.   DAVID CUMMINGS.

    ii.   ELIZABETH CUMMINGS, married Mr. Fields?

   iii.   ANN CATHERINE CUMMINGS.

   iv.   EMILY CUMMINGS.

    v.   THOMAS J. CUMMINGS.

346. CHARLOTTE[6] HOWELL (Jeremiah[5], Jeremiah[4]), was the daughter of Jeremiah[5] and Catherine (Hennion) Howell.
    Charlotte Howell married Mr. Birdsall.
    Mr. and Charlotte (Howell) Birdsall were the parents of at least one son {2596}.
     i.   DAVID BIRDSALL.

4. John[5], Jeremiah[4]

348. LYDIA[6] HOWELL (John[5], Jeremiah[4]), the daughter of John[5] and Esther (Pride) Howell, was born on 18 June 1805 {2597}.
    On 23 Aug 1850, Lydia Howell, 44, was enumerated as a member of her father's household in the Town of Lloyd, Ulster County, New York, in the Seventh Census of the United States {2598}.
    By her will of 20 Aug 1877, proved on 16 Apr 1894, Lydia Howell left her copy of Appleton's American Cyclopedia to Henry N. Brush and her household furniture, watch, jewelry, wearing apparel, articles of adornment and other books to her sister, Eliza H. Longbotham. She divided the rest of her estate into two equal shares, one of which was to go to her sister, while the other, less the amounts she had advanced to her brother, John B. Howell, and costs of discharging of discharging a $2000 mortgage on the farm he had inherited from their father, was to provide income to her brother during his lifetime, and was then to be divided among his children in equal shares. She named Henry N. Brush and George H. Howell executors of this will {2599}.
    Lydia Howell never married {2600}. She died at the age of 80 on

---

2596. Id.
2597. Sylvester, op. cit., II, 136.
2598. U.S. Census, Lloyd, Ulster County, NY, 1850, Dwelling House 591, Family Number 618, Page 289.
2599. Ulster County Wills, Liber 2, 601-606.
2600. Sylvester, op. cit.

a Friday morning in 1894 {2601}.

349. ELIZA[6] HOWELL (John[5], Jeremiah[4]), the daughter of John[5] and Esther (Pride) Howell, was born on 30 Mch 1809 {2602}.

On 4 Mch 1829, Eliza Howell married James H. Longbottom, who was a manufacturer of woolens in Marlborough {2603}.

James H. Longbottom died in 1858 {2604}.

James H. and Eliza (Howell) Longbottom were the parents of four children {2605}.

    i.   JOHN BRAINARD LONGBOTTOM, baptized by Phineas Rice {2606}, changed name to John Brainard Howard, entered the army as a private, rose to the rank of colonel, married Christiana Howard, four children, died in 1876.

    ii.   ESTHER LONGBOTTOM, married Henry N. Brush, no children. She was a witness to the will of Lydia Howell (#348) when she was living at 201 Amity Street in Brooklyn, New York. On 16 Apr 1894, she was at Nassau, on New Providence in the Bahamas. Her signature was attested to by the other witness, Mary E. Brush {2607}.

+ 806. iii.   GEORGE LONGBOTTOM, changed name to GEORGE[7] HOWELL, married, three children, moved to Nebraska.

+ 807. iv.   CHARLES LONGBOTTOM, changed name to CHARLES[7] HOWELL, married, three children, moved to Iowa.

350. JOHN BRAINARD[6] HOWELL (John[5], Jeremiah[4]), the son of John[5] and Esther (Pride) Howell, was born on 15 Apr 1813 {2608}.

On 16 Sep 1835, John Brainard Howell married Phebe J. Watkins, the daughter of Eliada and Chlorine Watkins {2609}, who was born in about 1816.

2601. Kenneth E. Hasbrouck, DEATH NOTICES | From the Scrapbook of | ELMIRAH FREER, p. 39.

2602. Sylvester, op. cit.

2603. Id., 125.

2604. Id., 136.

2605. Id.

2606. NEWBURGH, N.Y., CIRCUIT OF THE METHODIST EPISCOPAL CHURCH, Historical Papers, #8, Historical Society of Newburgh Bay and the Highlands, THE QUARTERLY, OCGS, 18, #2, 14 (Aug 1988).

2607. Ulster County Wills, Liber 2, 604-605.

2608. Sylvester, op. cit., II, 136.

2609. Id.

John B. Howell, of New Paltz, was baptized in the Newburgh Circuit of the Methodist Episcopal Church in 1832 by Rev. Hiram Wing {2610}.

On 23 Aug 1850, John B. Howel, 39, farmer, was enumerated as the head of a household consisting of himself, his wife, Phebe, 34, and their children, Watkins, 12, Hester, 10, Brainard, 8, and Linsey, 5, residing in the Town of Lloyd, Ulster County, New York, in the Seventh Census of the United States {2611}.

John B. Howell served as an Assemblyman in the winter of 1854 {2612}.

On 10 May 1875, John B. Howell was a Trustee of the Methodist Episcopal Church of Highland {2613}.

John B. Howell served as a Justice of the Peace for many years, and was the Supervisor, Town of Lloyd, in 1875 {2614}.

John Brainard and Phebe J. (Watkins) Howell were the parents of four children {2615}.

808.   i.   WATKINS[7] HOWELL, born in Mch 1838, died in Jan 1851.

+ 809. ii.   HESTER[7] HOWELL, born in Oct 1839.

+ 810. iii. BRAINARD[7] HOWELL, born in June 1842.

811.   iv.   LINSEY[7] HOWELL, born in Sep 1844, died on 24 Aug 1865, from a disease contracted in the army.

5. Sylvester[5], John[4]

351. MARY AUGUSTA[6] HOWELL (Sylvester[5], John[4]), the daughter of Sylvester[5] and Nancy (Young) Howell, was born on 27 Mch 1831.

Mary Augusta Howell married Rev. Charles S. Brown {2616}, who was born on 7 Feb 1825.

Rev. Charles S. Brown died on 14 Nov 1880, and is buried in the Laurel Cemetery {2617}.

Mary A. (Howell) Brown died on 10 Jan 1890, and is buried beside her

2610. NEWBURGH, N.Y., CIRCUIT OF THE METHODIST EPISCOPAL CHURCH, .., THE QUARTERLY, OCGS, 18, #3, 23 (Nov 1988).
2611. U.S. Census, Lloyd, Ulster County, NY, 1850, Dwelling House 590, Family Number 617, Page 289.
2612. Sylvester, op. cit., Part I, 101, Part II, 136.
2613. Id., Part II, 129.
2614. Id., 136.
2615. Id.
2616. Pelletreau, op. cit., 189; LONG ISLAND STAR, 3 Apr 1850, reported in THE REGISTER, SCHS, XVI, #3, 86 (Winter 1990).
2617. Gravestone, Laurel Cemetery.

husband in the Laurel Cemetery {2618}.

Rev. Charles S. and Mary A. (Howell) Brown were the parents of six children {2619}.

- i. FANNIE SEWARD BROWN, born on 30 Oct 1851, married William S. Dalzell, of Cold Spring {2620}, three children {2621}, died on 5 Apr 1888, and is buried in the Laurel Cemetery.

- ii. MARY ALICE BROWN, born on 4 Jan 1854, died on 25 Jan 1906.

- iii. NANCY ELOISE BROWN, born on 31 Dec 1856, married Frank P. Dalzell, of Cold Spring {2622}, died on 5 Mch 1936.

- iv. CHARLES HOWELL BROWN, born on 24 Sep 1859, drowned on 27 June 1874, at the age of 14 years, 9 months, and 3 days, and is buried in the Laurel Cemetery.

- v. CARRIE BROWN, born on 1 Nov 1863, died on 23 Feb 1867, and is buried in the Laurel Cemetery.

- vi. HELEN M. BROWN, born on 8 Feb 1869, died on 4 Oct 1934 {2623}.

353. ADDISON S.[6] HOWELL (Sylvester[5], John[4]), the son of Sylvester[5] and Nancy (Young) Howell, was born on 15 Oct 1835.

Addison Howell married Jemima Jennings {2624}, who was born in Jan 1837 {2625}.

Addison Howell died on 13 Feb 1866, and is buried in the Laurel Cemetery {2626}.

Jemima Howell died on 10 Nov 1894, and is buried beside her husband in the Laurel Cemetery {2627}.

Addison and Jemima (Jennings) Howell had no children {2628}.

2618. Id.
2619. Pelletreau, op. cit.; Gravestones, Laurel Cemetery.
2620. Pelletreau, op. cit.
2621. Bessie L. Hallock, op. cit.
2622. Id.
2623. Id.
2624. Id.
2625. Id.
2626. Gravestone, Laurel Cemetery.
2627. Id.
2628. Bessie L. Hallock, op. cit.

354. LEANDER YOUNG[6] HOWELL (Sylvester[5], John[4]), the son of Sylvester[5] and Nancy (Young) Howell, was born on 10 Dec 1837.

Leander Young Howell married Emily Elnore Corwin {2629}, on 30 Jan 1859 {2630}.

Leander Y. Howell died on 25 Feb 1866, at the age of 28 years, 2 months, and 15 days, and is buried in the Laurel Cemetery {2631}.

Leander Young and Emily Elnore (Corwin) Howell were the parents of one child {2632}.

   812.   i.   LUCY CORWIN[7] HOWELL, born on 1 Jly 1863 at West Mattituck, graduated from the Bridgehampton Academy and was later a teacher there, never married, "..was one of the most competent and popular members of the faculty of the Riverhead High School.." {2633}, died on 11 Apr 1945 {2634}.

356. CHAUNCEY PERKINS[6] HOWELL (Sylvester[5], John[4]), the son of Sylvester[5] and Nancy (Young) Howell, was born on 5 Oct 1845 {2635}.

"On the home farm Chauncey P. Howell was reared to agricultural pursuits and early became familiar familiar with all the duties of farm life. His literary education was obtained in the Franklinville and Northville Academies, and he also took a course at the Eastman Business College in Poughkeepsie, New York. On his return home he resumed farming, and later succeeded to the old homestead, which he is now successfully operating." {2636}.

On 24 Nov 1868, Chauncey P. Howell married Marietta Young, of Aquebogue (1329), the daughter of Joshua and Sophronia (Benjamin) Young, who was born on 27 June 1846 {2637}.

On 3 June 1870, Chauncy Howell, 25, farmer, with personal property worth $200, was enumerated as the head of a household consisting of himself and his wife, Marietta, 22, as well as James Allen, 11, and Theodore Corwin, 25, farm laborer, residing at Peconic in the Town of Southold, Suffolk County, New York, in the same house as his father's family, in the Ninth Census of the United States {2638}.

Chauncey P. Howell was Superintendent of the Sunday School at the Sound

2629. Pelletreau, op. cit.
2630. Bessie L. Hallock, op. cit.
2631. Gravestone, Laurel Cemetery.
2632. Pelletreau, op. cit.
2633. SUFFOLK COUNTY REVIEW, 11 (?) Apr 1945.
2634. Suffolk County Estates, #194 P 1945.
2635. Mallmann, op. cit., 236.
2636. Pelletreau, op. cit.
2637. Mallmann, op. cit.
2638. U.S. Census, Southold, Suffolk County, NY, 1870, Dwelling House 80, Family Number 83, Page 237.

Avenue church for 13 years {2639}.

"The family.." of Chauncey P. and Marietta Howell held "..membership in the Northville church, of which Mr. Howell.." was "..a deacon, and they.." were "..people of prominence in the community...In his political affiliations Mr. Howell.." was "..a Republican, and.." took "..an active interest in public affairs." {2640}.

Marietta Howell died on 17 June 1903, at the age of 56 years, 11 months, and 20 days, and is buried in the Sound Avenue Cemetery {2641}.

Chauncey Perkins Howell died on 24 Sep 1920, at the age of 74 years, 11 months, and 19 days, and is buried beside his wife in the Sound Avenue Cemetery {2642}.

Chauncey Perkins and Marietta (Youngs) Howell were the parents of four children {2643}.

813.   i.   ADDIE E.[7] HOWELL, born on 19 Nov 1870, died on 20 Aug 1873, at the age of 2 years and 9 months, and is buried in the Sound Avenue Cemetery {2644}.

814.   ii.   ALICE JEANNETTE[7] HOWELL, born on 12 Aug 1872, died on 15 Aug 1873, at the age of 1 year, 1 month, and 3 days, and is buried in the Sound Avenue Cemetery {2645}.

+ 815.   iii.   MARY AUGUSTA[7] HOWELL, born on 6 Jan 1875.

+ 816.   iv.   ELIZABETH[7] HOWELL, born on 22 Sep 1881.

6. John [5], Eli [4]

357. ELISHA[6] HOWELL (John[5], Eli[4]), the son of John[5] and Rosabella Howell, was born in about 1821 {2646}.

Elisha K. Howell married Rosetta Keen, the daughter of Capt. Mathias and Anna (Reeves) Keen {2647}.

Elisha K. Howell served "..nine months in the Union army during the Civil war as a member of company D, 179th Pennsylvania Volunteer Infantry. When his term of enlistment had expired he was honorably discharged at Harrisburg,

2639. Wilbur Franklin Howell, op. cit. 405.
2640. Pelletreau, op. cit., 189, 190.
2641. Wilbur Franklin Howell, op. cit.
2642. Id.
2643. Mallmann, op. cit.
2644. Wilbur Franklin Howell, op. cit.
2645. Id.
2646. Sliker, op. cit.
2647. COMMEMORATIVE BIOGRAPHICAL RECORD OF NORTHEASTERN PENNSYLVANIA, 975.

Pennsylvania" {2648}.

Elisha Howell, 29, farmer, was enumerated as the head of a family consisting of himself, his wife, Rosetta, 33, and their children, Charles H., 7, Helen A., 4, and Thomas, 1, residing in the Town of Mount Pleasant, Wayne County, Pennsylvania, in the Seventh Census of the United States, 1850 {2649}.

Elisha K. Howell died on 22 Aug 1888 {2650}.

Letters of administration on the estate of Elisha K. Howell were issued to George W. Kent on 31 Jly 1889, with Rosetta R. Howell, and Thomas N. Howell, acting as sureties {2651}.

Elisha K. and Rosetta R. (Keen) Howell were the parents of five children {2652}.

+ 817. i. CHARLES H.[7] HOWELL, born on 2 Apr 1842.

+ 818. ii. HELEN A.[7] HOWELL, born in about 1846.

819. iii. THOMAS N.[7] HOWELL, born in about 1849.

+ 820. iv. MARY[7] HOWELL.

+ 821. v. ROSA[7] HOWELL.

7. David [5], Eli [4]

364. DARIUS[6] HOWELL (David[5], Eli[4]), the son of David[5] and Wealthy (Campbell) Howell, was born on 8 Oct 1823 {2653}.

On 27 Jly 1860, "Davis Howell", 40, lumber merchant, with real property worth $1000, and personal property worth $600, was enumerated as the head of a household consisting of himself, his brother, "Thadius Howell", 35, farmer, his brother's wife, Lucinda, 35, and their children, Ella, 4, and Rachel, 2, residing in the Town of Mount Pleasant, Wayne County, Pennsylvania, in the Eighth Census of the United States {2654}.

Darius Howell died on 9 Sep 1879. Letters of administration on his estate were issued to Albert Howell on 25 Sep 1879, with Thadeus C. Howell, and Seth Howell, acting as sureties {2655}.

2648. Id.
2649. U.S. Census, Mount Pleasant, Wayne County, PA, 1850, Dwelling House 211, Family Number 227, Page 27.
2650. Wayne County (PA) Wills, Book 5, 100.
2651. Id.
2652. COMM. BIO. RECORD..NORTHEASTERN PENNSYLVANIA, 975.
2653. Craig R. Howell, op. cit.
2654. U.S. Census, Mount Pleasant, Wayne County, PA, 1860, Dwelling House 1810, Page 390.
2655. Wayne County (PA) Wills, Book 3, 418.

365. THADEUS C.[6] HOWELL (David[5], Eli[4]), the son of David[5] and Wealthy (Campbell) Howell, was born on 13 Apr 1824 {2656}.

On 21 Sep 1854, Thaddeus C. Howell married Lucinda N. Bigelow {2657}.

On 27 Jly 1860, "Thadius Howell", 35, his wife, Lucinda, 35, and their children, Ella, 4, and Rachel, 2, were residing at the home of his brother, "Davis Howell", in Mount Pleasant, Wayne County, Pennsylvania, when the Eighth Census of the United States was taken {2658}.

By his will of 25 Apr 1880, proved on 2 June 1880, Thadeus C. Howell left all his property to his "..beloved wife Lucinda N.", whom he also named as his Executrix {2659}.

Thadeus C. Howell died on 1 May 1880 {2660}.

Thadeus C. and Lucinda N. Howell were the parents of at least two children.

822. i. ELLA[7] HOWELL, born in about 1856.

823. ii. RACHEL[7] HOWELL, born in about 1858.

367. SETH[6] HOWELL (David[5], Eli[4]), the son of David[5] and Wealthy (Campbell) Howell, was born on 7 April 1827 in Mount Pleasant Township, Wayne County, Pennsylvania {2661}.

On 16 Feb 1852, Seth Howell married Mary Buck {2662}, of Nicholson, Wyoming County, Pennsylvania, the daughter of John and Mary Buck {2663}, and was born in Aug 1833 {2664}. They resided in the town of Mount Pleasant for a year, then moved to Starucca, where he was employed in the tannery of Osborn & Strong for a year {2665}.

"In 1854..", the family "..removed to Dane county, Wis., and after following farming there for three years..went to Richland county.." There, they purchased a tract of timberland which he cleared and converted into a good farm. He continued its cultivation until Jly 1862, when he enlisted in Company B, 20th Wisconsin Volunteer Infantry. "The regiment was assigned to the Western Army on the Missouri river, where he did duty as a train guard during the battle of Pea Ridge. His health giving way before his three years had expired, he was ordered to the hospital, where he remained until honorably discharged at the close of the war,

2656. Craig R. Howell, op. cit.
2657. Id.
2658. U.S. Census, Mount Pleasant, Wayne County, PA, 1860, Dwelling House 1810, Page 390.
2659. Wayne County (PA) Wills, Book 3, 453-454.
2660. Id.
2661. Craig R. Howell, op. cit.
2662. Id.
2663. COMM. BIO. REC..NORTHEASTERN PENNSYLVANIA, 1458.
2664. U.S. Census, Scott, Wayne County, PA, 1900, Enumeration District 128, Sheet 6, Dwelling House 118, Family Number 122.
2665. COMM. BIO. RECORD..NORTHEASTERN PENNSYLVANIA, 1458.

July 5, 1865." {2666}.

"During his absence Mrs. Howell..removed to Towersville, Crawford Co(unty), Wis(consin), for the purpose of providing her children with better educational privileges..On his return from the army..", Seth Howell sold his farm in Richland County, and purchased another near Towersville. "He never recovered his health, and during the five years he made that place his home he was unable to perform any manual labor. Selling out in the spring of 1871, he and his family moved to DeKalb county, Mo., in a wagon drawn by two yoke of oxen, camping out at night by the wayside, and making the journey in four weeks. For two years he engaged in farming in that county and for the same length was similarly employed in Davis county, Mo. On account of his own and his wife's health, he disposed of his property there, and returned to Lenoxville, Susquehanna Co., Penn., where he engaged in agricultural pursuits for one year. The following two years were spent at Nicholson, Wyoming Co., Penn.,and in March, 1879, he came to Scott township, Wayne county, where he purchased 100 acres of woodland, and with the aid of his two sons cleared and converted it into a fine farm. Upon this place he spent his remaining days.." {2667}.

Seth Howell was a Democrat in politics. While in the west, "..he held several local offices, and in Scott township served as treasurer." {2668}.

Seth Howell "..and his estimable wife were faithful members of the Methodist Episcopal Church while in the West. After coming to Scott township they joined the Evangelical Church" {2669}.

By his will of 16 June 1893, proved on 16 Aug 1893, Seth Howell left all his property to his wife, Mary, whom he appointed Executrix {2670}.

Seth Howell died on 19 Jly 1893 {2671}.

On 9 June 1900, Mary Howell, 66, farmer, was enumerated as the head of a household consisting of herself, her daughter, Clara, 47, her son, Adelbert, 43, farm laborer, his wife, Iola, 27, their daughter, Liza, 6, and Clara's children, Mary B., 16, and Frank Curtis, 13, residing in Scott Township, Wayne County, Pennsylvania, in the Twelfth Census of the United States {2672}.

Seth and Mary (Buck) Howell were the parents of three children {2673}.

+ 824. i.   CLARA A.[7] HOWELL, born in Nov 1852.

+ 825. ii.   ADELBERT C.[7] HOWELL, born on 29 Dec 1856.

+ 826. iii. OLIVER P.[7] HOWELL, born on 24 Oct 1858.

2666. Id.
2667. Id.
2668. Id.
2669. Id.
2670. Wayne County (PA) Wills, Book 5, 520-521.
2671. Id.
2672. U.S. Census, op. cit.
2673. COMM. BIO. RECORD..NORTHEASTERN PENNSYLVANIA, 1458-1459.

370. ALBERT C.[6] HOWELL (David[5], Eli[4]), the son of David[5] and Wealthy (Campbell) Howell, was born on 8 Sep 1834 {2674}.

On 3 Jly 1859, Albert C. Howell married Delila(h) Rutledge, who was born on 24 May 1832, the daughter of Alexander and Mary Ann (LaTourette) Rutledge {2675}.

On 11 Jly 1860, Albert Howell, 24, farmer, with real property worth $900, and personal property worth $400, was enumerated as the head of a family consisting of himself, his wife, Delilah, 21, and their son, Vasti, $^4/_{12}$, residing in the Town of Mount Pleasant, Wayne County, Pennsylvania, in the Eighth Census of the United States {2676}.

Letters of administration on the estate of Darius Howell were issued to Albert Howell on 25 Sep 1879 {2677}.

Delilah Howell died on 15 Feb 1892, and is buried at Galilee, Wayne County, Pennsylvania {2678}.

Albert and Delilah (Rutledge) Howell were the parents of seven children {2679}.

827.   i.   VASHTI[7] HOWELL, born on 20 Apr 1860.

828.   ii.   RHODA E.[7] HOWELL, born on 5 Sep 1862, married J.A. Lent.

829.   iii.   ORLANDA J.[7] HOWELL, born on 5 May 1866, married Nora Baker.

830.   iv.   MARY F.[7] HOWELL, born on 20 May 1868, married Jefferson Baldwin.

831.   v.   REBECCA[7] HOWELL, married Stephen Mitchell.

832.   vi.   LILLIE[7] HOWELL, born in about 1876, married John Codgen.

+ 833.   vii.   PERRY C., "RENO",[7] HOWELL, born on 9 Dec 1878.

8. Eli [5], Eli [4].

377. HARRIET ANN[6] HOWELL (Eli[5], Eli[4]), the daughter of Eli[5] and Fannie (McKinney) Howell, was born on 6 Apr 1843 {2680}.

2674. Craig R. Howell, op. cit.
2675. Id.
2676. U.S. Census, Mount Pleasant, Wayne County, PA, 1860, Dwelling House 2400, Page 216.
2677. Wayne County Wills, Book 3, 418.
2678. Craig R. Howell, op. cit.
2679. Id.
2680. Sliker, op. cit.

Harriet Ann Howell married Moses Webb Cox, Jr., as his second wife. His first wife was her sister, Mary Amanda Howell (#375). He was born on 27 Oct 1828 at Greenfield, Pennsylvania, the son of Moses Webb and Phebe (Cobb) Cox {2681}.

Moses Webb Cox, Jr., died on 7 Feb 1917 at Dunmore, Pennsylvania, and is buried at Clifford, Pennsylvania {2682}.

Harriet Ann Cox died on 19 Apr 1919 at Dunmore, and is buried beside her husband {2683}.

Moses Webb and Harriet Ann (Howell) Cox were the parents of five children {2684}.

    i.   HATTIE JANE COX, born on 26 Feb 1865, died on 17 Nov 1868.

    ii.   SARAH H. COX, born on 28 Jly 1866.

    iii.   ELLA ELIZABETH COX, born on 24 Jly 1868, died on 3 Nov 1937.

    iv.   MYRTIE MARIA COX, born on 23 Aug 1873 at Kingsley, Pennsylvania, married John Casper Dommermuth on 25 May 1892 at Avoca, Pennsylvania, five children, died on 17 Feb 1951 at Binghamton, New York, and is buried at Clifford, Pennsylvania. He was born on 20 Apr 1863 at Aldenville, Pennsylvania, died on 26 Dec 1937 at Binghamton, and is buried beside his wife at Clifford. NOTE: *Myrtie Maria (Cox) Dommermuth was the great-great-grandmother of (Richard) Scott Sliker.*

    v.   HATTIE M. COX, born on 23 Apr 1876, died in 1955.

378. WILBUR E.[6] HOWELL (Eli[5], Eli[4]), the son of Eli[5] and Fannie (McKinney) Howell, was born in about 1846 {2685}.

On 7 June 1867, Wilbur E. Howell married Mary Gaylord at Waymart, Pennsylvania. She was born in about 1848 {2686}.

On 18 Jly 1870, "Nilbur Howell", 24, laborer, was enumerated as the head of a family consisting of himself, his wife, Mary, 22, and their children, Argus, 2, and Milo, $^{10}/_{12}$, residing in the Town of Mount Pleasant, Wayne County,

---

2681. Id.
2682. Id.
2683. Id.
2684. Id.
2685. Sliker, op. cit.
2686. Id.

Pennsylvania, in the Eighth Census of the United States {2687}.

On 1 June 1880, Wilber Howell, 36, lumberman, was enumerated as the head of a family consisting of himself, his wife, Mary, 32, and their children, Argus, 12, Milo, 10, and Willie, 7, residing in the Town of Clifford, Susquehanna County, Pennsylvania, in the Tenth Census of the United States {2688}.

Wilbur E. and Mary (Gaylord) Howell were the parents of three children {2689}.

+ 834.   i.   ARGUS[7] HOWELL, born in Jan 1868.

   835.   ii.   MILO[7] HOWELL, born in Aug 1869.

   836.   iii.   WILLIE[7] HOWELL, born in about 1873.

380. EMORY A.[6] HOWELL (Eli[5], Eli[4]), the son of Eli[5] and Fannie (McKinney) Howell, was born in Aug 1854 {2690}.

On 8 June 1880, Emery Howell, 25, laborer, was enumerated as the head of a family consisting of himself, his wife, Marian, 20, and their children, Lewis, 2, and Arba, 1, residing in the Town of Mount Pleasant, Wayne County, Pennsylvania, in the Tenth Census of the United States {2691}.

On 6 June 1900, Emery A. Howell, 45, lumberman, was enumerated as the head of a household consisting of himself, his wife, Marion D., 33, their children, Lewis A., 22, teamster, Arba E., 20, teamster, Alta M., 12, and Guy W., 10, and their boarders, Alton W. Swingle, 48, engineer, Joseph R. Burdick, 23, teamster, Fred Widman, 32, sawyer, Williams Michles, 26, engineer, Frank Baker, 24, teamster, Frank Hinkley, 28, lumberman, Charles Bryce, 23, saw mill hand, and Nicholas C. Crandall, 28, lumberman, residing in the Town of Clifford, Susquehanna County, Pennsylvania, in the Twelfth Census of the United States {2692}.

Emery A. and Marion D. Howell were the parents of seven children {2693}.

   837.   i.   LEWIS A.[7] HOWELL, born in Feb 1878.

   838.   ii.   ARBA E.[7] HOWELL, born in May 1879.

   839.   iii.   ALTA M.[7] HOWELL, born in Jan 1888.

2687. U.S. Census, Mount Pleasant, Wayne County, PA, 1870, Dwelling House 334, Family Number 337, Page 45.

2688. Id., Clifford, Susquehanna County, PA, 1880, Dwelling House 285, Family Number 297, Page 27.

2689. Sliker, op. cit.

2690. Sliker, op. cit.

2691. U.S. Census, Mount Pleasant, Wayne County, Pennsylvania, 1880, Dwelling House 99, Family Number 104, Page 12.

2692. Id., 1900, Enumeration District 80, Sheet 4, Line 19.

2693. Sliker, op. cit.

840. iv.   GUY W.[7] HOWELL, born in Nov 1889.

841. v.   Child[7].

842. vi.   Child[7].

843. vii.   Child[7].

II. Descendants of David[2] Howell -

A. David[3], David[2], Richard[1]

1. David[5], David[4]

381. ABNER[6] HOWELL (David[5], David[4]),the son of David[5] {2694} and Elizabeth (Mapes) Howell {2695}, was born in about 1812.

Letters of administration on the estate of George Howell, of Goshen, were issued to his father-in-law, Joshua D. Mapes, and his brother, Abner Howell, both of Monroe, on 14 Oct 1845 {2696}.

On 24 Jly 1850, Abner Howell, 38, farmer, with real estate worth $1500, was enumerated as the head of a household consisting of himself, Harrison (?) Howell, 11, who was probably his nephew, and Mary Woodruff, 18, residing in Monroe Township, Orange County, New York, in the Seventh Census of the United States {2697}.

Abner Howell married Mary Jewell {2698}.

On 27 Jly 1860, Abner Howell, 45, farmer, with real property worth $2400, and personal property worth $700, was enumerated as the head of a family consisting of himself, his wife, Mary, 30, their children, Mary T., 2, and Ella T., $9/_{12}$, residing in Monroe Township, Orange County, in the Eighth Census of the United States {2699}.

Letters of administration on the estate of Abner Howell, late of Monroe, were issued to his brother, David V. Howell, on 30 Oct 1866 {2700}.

Abner and Mary (Jewell) Howell were the parents of at least two children.

844. i.   MARY T.[7] HOWELL, born in about 1858.

2694. George Rogers Howell, op. cit., 322.
2695. THE FAMILY RECORD, 146.
2696. Orange County Letters of Administration, Liber G, 347.
2697. U.S. Census, Monroe, Orange County, NY, 1850, Dwelling House 170, Family Number 170, Page 278.
2698. THE FAMILY RECORD, 146.
2699. U.S. Census, Monroe, Orange County, NY, 1860, Dwelling House 1202, Family Number 1249, Page 357.
2700. Orange County Letters of Administration, Liber L, 92.

845. ii. ELLA T.[7] HOWELL, born in about Oct 1859.

382. GEORGE[6] HOWELL (David[5], David[4]),the son of David[5] {2701} and Elizabeth (Mapes) Howell {2702}, was born in about 1815.

George Howell married Julia Ann Mapes, the daughter of Joshua and Phebe (Beach) Mapes {2703}.

George Howell, aged about 30, died on 8 Oct 1845 {2704}.

Julia Ann Howell, the wife of George Howell, died at Monroe in Oct 1845 {2705}.

Letters of administration on the estate of George Howell were issued to Joshua D. Mapes, his father-in-law, and Abner Howell, his brother, on 14 Oct 1845 {2706}.

In 1845, letters of guardianship of the estates of Harrison, Phebe Ann, and Charles Howell were issued to Joshua Mapes, their grandfather {2707}.

On 31 Jly 1850, Charles Howel, 8, and Phoebe Howel, 6, were enumerated as members of the household of Julius Mapes, 68, farmer, residing in the Town of Monroe, Orange County, New York, in the Seventh Census of the United States {2708}, while Harrison, 11, had been enumerated in the household of his uncle, Abner Howell (#384) {2709}.

George and Julia Ann (Mapes) Howell were the parents of three children {2710}.

846. i. WILLIAM H. HARRISON[7] HOWELL, born in about 1839.

847. ii. CHARLES EZRA[7] HOWELL, born in about 1842.

+ 848. iii. PHOEBE ANN[7] HOWELL, born in about 1844.

390. DAVID VAN NESS[6] HOWELL (David[5], David[4]), the son of David[5] and Elizabeth (Mapes) Howell, was born in 1834 {2711}.

In 1861, D. Vanness Howell pledged $10.00 to the organ fund at the First Presbyterian Church, Monroe, New York {2712}.

2701. George Rogers Howell, op. cit.
2702. THE FAMILY RECORD, 146.
2703. PORTRAIT & BIOGRAPHICAL RECORD OF ORANGE COUNTY, 799.
2704. GOSHEN INDEPENDENT REPUBLICAN, 17 Oct 1845, cited by Weller, op. cit.
2705. Id.
2706. Orange County Letters of Administration, Liber G, 347.
2707. Orange County Letters of Guardianship, Liber D, 301, 302, 303.
2708. U.S. Census, Monroe, Orange County, NY, 1850, Dwelling House 501, Family Number 510 (sic), Page 300.
2709. Id.,
2710. PORTRAIT & BIOGRAPHICAL RECORD OF ORANGE COUNTY, 799.
2711. THE FAMILY REGISTER, 146.
2712. Mrs. C. Arthur Brooks, op. cit., 131.

David V. Howell was issued letters of administration on the estate of his brother, Abner, on 30 Oct 1866 {2713}.

David V. Howell, 26, was enumerated as a member of the household of his brother, Abner Howell (#381) on 27 Jly 1860 {2714}.

In 1871, David V. Howell, 26, was a farmer with 57 acres at Monroe {2715}.

2. Josiah [5], David [4]

393. ELIZA[6] HOWELL (Josiah[5], David[4]) was the daughter of Josiah[5] and Mary Ann (Biggar) Howell, was born in about 1811 {2716}.

On 5 Oct 1831, Eliza Howell was married to David M.E. Wood, a merchant from Sugar Loaf in Orange County, N.Y., before the Rev. Mr. Penney at Rochester, N.Y. {2717}.

By her father's will of 20 May 1844, proved on 18 Oct 1847, Eliza Woods was to receive the interest on $1500, the principal of which was to go to her son, Josiah Howell Woods, on her death {2718}.

David M.E. and Eliza (Howell) Woods were the parents of at least one child.

    i.   JOSIAH HOWELL WOODS.

395. MARY ANN[6] HOWELL (Josiah[5], David[4]), the daughter of Josiah[5] and Mary Ann (Biggar) Howell, was born on 27 Jly 1814 at Sugar Loaf in Orange County, New York {2719}.

On 5 June 1839, Mary Ann Howell married Reuben Alesworth Grunendike {2720}. He was the son of John and Elizabeth (Anderson) Grunendike, and was born on 25 Apr 1818 in the Town of Chili, Monroe County, New York. Prior to their marriage, he had attended the Genessee Wesleyan Seminary at Lima. He was especially fond of study and religious argument {2721}.

Mary Ann Grunendike was bequeathed an equal share of the farm, known as the Dibble farm, with her sister, Jane Jameson, by the will of her father, written

2713. Orange County Letters of Administration, Liber G, 347.
2714. U.S. Census, Monroe, Orange County, NY, 1860, Dwelling House 1202, Family Number 1249, Page 357.
2715. ORANGE COUNTY DIRECTORY, 1871, 121.
2716. Flesch, op. cit.
2717. ORANGE COUNTY PATRIOT, 29 Oct 1831, from MARRIAGES & DEATHS IN THE..PATRIOT, copied by Gertrude Barber.
2718. Monroe County Wills, Volume 4, 57-59.
2719. Flesch, op. cit.
2720..Id.
2721. Mrs. Mary E. Haworth, op. cit.

on 20 May 1844, and proved on 18 Oct 1847 {2722}.

After a few years of marriage, Reuben and Mary Ann Grunendike sold their lands in the Town of Chili. With his brother-in-law, Charles Howell, he established a large flour mill near LeRoy, New York, where they made Genessee Valley Flour. Unfortunately, they lost the mill in the financial crisis of 1856-7, so the family returned to Chili, where they joined in a lawsuit against her brother, Edmund, to recover her full inheritance from her father's estate. After this succeeded, they moved to Chicago in Mch 1861. After losing a substantial part of their property, they moved to Salem, IL, in Aug 1861, where they lived with his cousins, Samuel Grunendike and John Brokaw {2723}.

Reuben A. Grunendike enlisted in Company A, 49th Illinois Volunteer Regiment, and took part in the battles at Fort Henry and Fort Donaldson, and was wounded in the side during the Battle of Shiloh. He spent several months in hospitals at Cincinnati, Jefferson Barracks, Saint Louis and Rock Island, but was discharged only one month before his three year term of enlistment expired. In the Spring of 1866, they family moved to Litchfield, IL, where they took in boarders. He ultimately obtained a contract for carrying the mail, and a pension {2724}.

Mary Ann Grunendike died on 9 Aug 1881 at Litchfield, IL {2725}, and is buried there {2726}.

After the death of his wife, Reuben A. Grunendike moved to Kansas, where he lived with his oldest daughter, Eliza E. Reynolds, and took a claim for 160 acres of land. His health failed him, however, and, in 1890, he went to live at the home of his youngest son, Frank Parks Grunendike, in Decatur, IL. He died there on 9 Sep 1891. He is buried beside his wife in Litchfield {2727}.

Reuben Alesworth and Mary Ann (Howell) Grunendike were the parents of six children {2728}.

    i.   ELIZA E. GRUNENDIKE, born on 10 Feb 1841 at Chili, married (1) Erskine Wood, two children, married (2) John Marion Reynolds, three children, died in 1915. NOTE: *Eliza E. (Grunendike) Wood Reynolds was the great-grandmother of Linda S. (Kalb) Flesch.*

    ii.   MARY ELORIA GRUNENDIKE, born on 2 Aug 1845 at Chili, married George D. Haworth, died in 1927.

    iii.   JOHN HOWELL GRUNENDIKE, born on 27 Feb 1851 at LeRoy, died in the same year.

2722. Monroe County Wills, op. cit.
2723. Haworth, op. cit.
2724. Id.
2725. Flesch, op. cit.
2726. Haworth, op. cit.
2727. Id.
2728. Haworth, op. cit., Flesch, op. cit.

iv. FRED ALESWORTH GRUNENDIKE, born on 3 Sep 1853 at LeRoy, died in 1909.

v. EDWARD HOWELL GRUNENDIKE, born on 17 Mch 1856 at LeRoy, married Mary Booth, óne child, died in 1934.

vi. FRANK PARKS GRUNENDIKE, born on 24 Oct 1859 at Chili, married Fredericka Eilers, four children, died in 1941.

396. EDMUND W.[6] HOWELL (Josiah[5], David[4]), the son of Josiah[5] and Mary Ann (Biggar) Howell, was born in 1816 {2729}.

Edmund W. Howell married Jane Orcutt, who was born in 1817 {2730}.

Josiah Howell left his farm of 327 acres in North Chili to his son, Edmund W. Howell, by his will of 20 May 1844, proved on 18 Oct 1847. Edmund W. Howell was named executor of this will {2731}.

Edmund Howell was sued by some of his siblings for failure to distribute the full extent of his father's bequeathed personal property {2732}.

On 18 Oct 1850, Edmond Howell, 33, farmer, with real property worth $20,000, was enumerated as the head of a household consisting of himself, his wife, Jane G., 32, their children, James A., 4, and Helyn H.(?), 2, and five farm laborers, residing in the Town of Chili, Monroe County, New York, in the Seventh Census of the United States {2733}.

Edmund W. Howell died in 1890, and is buried in the North Chili Rural Cemetery, also known as Evergreen Cemetery {2734}.

Jane O. Howell died in 1904, and is buried beside her husband {2735}.

Edmund W. and Jane G. Howell were the parents of at least two children.

+ 849. i. JAMES A.[7] HOWELL, born in about 1846.

850. ii. SELWYN H.[7] HOWELL, born in about 1848.

397. JANE[6] HOWELL (Josiah[5], David[4]), the daughter of Josiah[5] and Mary Ann (Biggar) Howell, was born on 17 Oct 1819 {2736}.

On 3 May 1843, Jane Howell married Isaac Hemingway Jameson, who was

2729. Gravestone, North Chili Rural Cemetery.
2730. Id.
2731. Monroe County Wills, op. cit.
2732. Haworth, op. cit.
2733. U.S. Census, Chili, Monroe County, N.Y., 1850, Dwelling House 237, Family Number 237, Page 297.
2734. Gravestone, North Chili Rural Cemetery.
2735; Id.
2736. John Jameson, Personal communication.

born on 12 Oct 1818 {2737}.

By his will of 20 May 1844, proved on 18 Oct 1847, Josiah Howell left his daughter, Jane Jameson, an equal share in the farm, known as the Dibble farm, with her sister, Mary Ann Grunendike {2738}.

Isaac Hemingway Jameson died on 14 May 1869 at Jacksonville, Florida {2739}.

Jane Jameson died on 16 May 1896 at Chicago, Illinois {2740}.

Isaac Hemingway and Jane (Howell) Jameson were the parents of six children {2741}.

    i.   FRANCIS MARION JAMESON, born on 6 May 1844 at Churchville, New York, married Ione Everett Warren on 5 Sep 1867, two children, died on 10 Mch 1899 at Batavia, New York, and is buried in the Elmwood Cemetery there. She was born on 6 Mch 1845 at Batavia, and died there on 1 Feb 1916.

    ii.   CHARLES DEWITT JAMESON, born on 30 Aug 1847, died on 30 Dec 1868 at Jacksonville, Florida, and is buried at Churchville.

    iii.   AMANDA ELIZABETH JAMESON, born on 21 Jly 1849 at Churchville, married Charles M. Ellis on 29 Sep 1869, one child, died in about 1910. He was born in Maine in about 1841, and died in 1933.

    iv.   ALBERT LITTLE JAMESON, born on 23 Nov 1852 at Churchville, married Helen M. Barber on 16 Oct 1878, died on 14 Feb 1938 at Rochester, New York. She was born on 5 Jly 1857 at Rochester, and died in about 1906.

    v.   GEORGE HOWELL JAMESON, born on 23 May 1856 at Churchville, married Jennie E. Rice on 6 Nov 1876, two children, died before 1920. She was born on 26 Apr 1854 at Rochester, and died there on 15 Mch 1923.

    vi.   MARION LOUISE JAMESON, born on 29 Jan 1860 at Hamilton, Ontario, married Louis C. Heusner on 5 Jan 1881, five children, died after 1910. He was born on 15 Apr 1854 at Rochester, and died after 1910.

398. AMELIA[6] HOWELL (Josiah[5], David[4]), the daughter of Josiah[5] and Mary Ann

2737. Id.
2738. Monroe County Wills, op. cit.
2739. Jameson, op. cit.
2740. Id.
2741. Id.

(Biggar) Howell, was born in about 1819 {2742}.

Amelia Howell married Eber Orcutt {2743}.

399. CHARLES B.[6] HOWELL (Josiah[5], David[4]), the son of Josiah[5] and Mary Ann (Biggar) Howell, was born in about Nov 1821.

Charles B. Howell married Emily Wood {2744}.

Charles B. Howell was a partner in the Howell and Grunendike flour mill near LeRoy with Reuben A. Grunendike {2745}.

Charles B. Howell died on 5 Aug 1860, at the age of 38 years and 9 months, and is buried in the North Chili Rural Cemetery {2746}.

Charles B. and Emily (Wood) Howell were the parents of at least one son, who died at about age 2, and is buried in the North Chili Rural Cemetery {2747}.

400. JOHN[6] HOWELL (Josiah[5], David[4]), the son of Josiah[5] and Mary Ann (Biggar) Howell, was born in about 1828.

John Howell inherited his father's home farm by his will of 20 May 1844, proved on 18 Oct 1847 {2748}.

John Howell married Frances Walker {2749}.

On 24 Oct 1850, John Howell, 22, farmer, with real property worth $9600, was enumerated as the head of a family consisting of himself, his wife, Frances C., 21, Martha Jameson, 12, and two farm laborers, Charles Clark, 23, and Isaac Kimble, 24, residing in the Town of Chili, Monroe County, N.Y., in the Seventh Census of the United States {2750}.

3. Joseph B. [5], David [4]

402. ELEANOR ANN[6] HOWELL (Joseph B.[5], David[4]), the daughter of Joseph B.[5] and Elizabeth J. (Weeden) Howell, was born on 13 Nov 1820 {2751}.

Eleanor Ann Howell married William H. LaRue, who was born on 30 Jly 1820, the son of Crynes and Joanna (Howell)(#138) LaRue.

2742. Flesch, op. cit.
2743. Id.
2744. Flesch. op. cit.
2745. Haworth, op. cit.
2746. Gravestone, North Chili Rural Cemetery
2747. Id.
2748. Monroe County Wills, op. cit.
2749. Flesch, op. cit.
2750. U.S. Census, 1850, Chili, Monroe County, N.Y., Dwelling House 310, Family Number 310, Page 302.
2751. Stickney, HOWELL, #668.

On 2 Aug 1848, William H. Laroe was appointed the guardian of the estates of Joseph B., Jane Elizabeth and Martha L. Howell, minor children of Joseph B. Howell (#142), deceased {2752}.

Eleanor Ann LaRue died on 21 Jan 1854 {2753}, and is probably the E.A.L. buried in the Howell burial plot in Sugar Loaf village {2754}.

407. JANE ELIZABETH[6] HOWELL (Joseph B.[5], David[4]), the daughter of Joseph B.[5] and Elizabeth J. (Weeden) Howell was born on 1 Jly 1831 {2755}.

Jane Elizabeth Howell married William H. LaRue as his second wife {2756}.

Jane Elizabeth LaRue died on 18 May 1893 {2757}.

William H. LaRue died on 27 Jan 1896 {2758}.

William H. and Jane E. (Howell) LaRue were the parents of at least one child.

    i.   FRED BENTON LARUE, born on 3 Feb 1859, married Mary E. Knapp on 14 Jan 1880, one son, died on 27 Dec 1887 {2759}.

409. JOSEPH BENTON[6] HOWELL (Joseph B.[5], David[4]), the son of Joseph B.[5] and Elizabeth Jane (Weeden) Howell, was born on 16 Feb 1838 {2760}.

Joseph Benton Howell died on 2 Sep 1859 {2761}.

4. Jeffrey [5], John [4].

411. MARY ANN[6] HOWELL (Jeffrey[5], John[4]), the daughter of Jeffrey[5] and Jemima (Corwin) Howell, was born on 5 Aug 1818.

Mary Ann Howell and John M. Talmadge, both of Minisink, were married before Elder Gabriel Conklin on 12 Oct 1839 {2762}. He was born on 1 Mch 1816, the son of Isaac and Mary (Hurd) Talmadge {2763}.

2752. Orange County Letters of Guardianship, Liber E, 168-170.
2753. Stickney, op. cit.
2754. CEMETERIES OF CHESTER, NEW YORK.., 84.
2755. Stickney, HOWELL, #673.
2756. Stickney, HOWELL, Last page.
2757. Id., #673.
2758. Id., Last page.
2759. Id.
2760. Id., #675.
2761. Id.
2762. "Persons Married by Elder Gabriel Conklin", from HISTORICAL PAPERS, WARWICK, N.Y., No. 2, Part Two, 1933, reprinted in WARWICK HISTORICAL PAPERS, OCGS, 1998, 218.
2763. PORTRAIT AND BIOGRAPHICAL RECORD OF ORANGE COUNTY, NEW YORK, 682.

Mary Ann Talmadge died on 10 Jan 1841, at the age of 22 years, 5 months, and 5 days, and is buried in the Stewartstown Cemetery {2764}.

John M. Talmadge married (2) Lydia A. Tuttle. She died in Feb 1882 {2765}.

John M. and Mary Ann (Howell) Talmadge did not have any children.

5. Benjamin[5], George[4].

417. WILLIAM M.[6] HOWELL (Benjamin[5], George[4]), the son of Benjamin[5] and Jane (Moffat) Howell, was born in about 1814.

William Howell, of Hector, N.Y., married Esther St. John on 21 Apr 1839 at New Canaan, Connecticut {2766}.

On 15 Nov 1850, William M. Howell, 36, farmer, with real property worth $1100, was enumerated as the head of a family including himself, his wife, Ester, 33, and their children, Samuel M., 12, and Wales Mead, 11, both born in New York State, residing in Aurora, Illinois, in the Seventh Census of the United States {2767}.

W. M. Howell, who with Hiram Scrafford, were the grain dealers, Howell & Scrafford, at Allen's warehouse, was residing at 7 South Root Street in Aurora in 1868 {2768}.

William M. and Esther (St. John) Howell were the parents of at least two children.

   851.   i.   SAMUEL M.[7] HOWELL, born in about 1838.

   852.   ii.   WALES MEAD[7] HOWELL, born in about 1839.

418. ORRIN DAY[6] HOWELL (Benjamin[5], George[4]), the son of Benjamin[5] and Jane (Moffat) Howell, was born on 18 May 1818 in Tompkins County, New York {2769}.

Orrin Day Howell "..acquired his literary education in the common schools and remained at home until eighteen years of age, when, with a cousin, he drove from Elmira, New York, across the country to Aurora, Illinois..In that city.." he "..engaged in school-teaching and in boyish mood he delivered there the first temperance lecture ever given in the town. Returning to New York the following

---

2764. Coulter, et al., op. cit., 66.

2765. PORTRAIT & BIOGRAPHICAL RECORD OF ORANGE COUNTY.., 682.

2766. Finch, op. cit., 7.

2767. U.S. Census, Aurora, Kane County, IL, 1850, Dwelling House 272, Family Number 288, Page 208.

2768. FIRST ANNUAL GAZETEER AND DIRECTORY OF THE CITY OF AURORA, 91.

2769. BIOGRAPHICAL DICTIONARY AND PORTRAIT GALLERY OF THE REPRESENTATIVE MEN OF THE UNITED STATES, ILLINOIS VOLUME, 349.

summer he entered the Albany Medical College, where he was graduated in the class of 1838. He began practice in West Dryden, New York, where he remained for a year, after which he went to Saugerties..where he lived for a year and a half." {2770}.

On 27 Oct 1839, while still at West Dryden, O. D. Howell married Cornelia More, of Moresville, New York. They removed to that place after they left Saugerties. In 1854, he returned to Aurora, where he soon became the foremost physician {2771}.

On 30 Sep 1850, Orrin D. Howell, 31, physician, with real property worth $800, was enumerated as the head of a family consisting of himself, his wife, Cornelia, 30, and their children, Mary Ann, 10, Anna, 7, and Moie (?), 5, residing in the Town of Roxbury, Delaware County, New York, in the Seventh Census of the United States {2772}.

On 16 June 1860, Dr. O.D. Howell, 42, physician, was enumerated as the head of a household consisting of himself, his wife, Cornelia, 42, and their children, Marion, 19, Annie, 17, Edward, 8, and Frank, 2, and their servant, Kate Ward, 18, residing in the Town of Aurora, Kane County, Illinois, in the Eighth Census of the United States {2773}.

O. D. Howell was one of the corporators of the Aurora Gas, Light & Coke Company, which was chartered by the Legislature, on 20 Feb 1861, to manufacture and sell gas, tar and coke, exclusively, for twenty years {2774}.

"Among the public positions which he held were those of surgeon of the Chicago, Burlington & Quincy Railroad Company, and the United States examining surgeon for pensions..He served in the army as surgeon during the Rebellion" {2775}.

In 1867, Dr. Francis B. Blackman began his study of medicine in the office of Dr. O. D. Howell {2776}.

In 1868, Dr. O. D. Howell had his office at 24 Main Street, and his home at 74 Main Street, in Aurora {2777}. In 1884, his office was at the same location, while his residence was on the southeast corner of Root and Main Streets {2778}.

"In addition to his practice Dr. Howell became interested in financial matters..He was a stockholder in the private banking house of Bishop & Coulter, and when it was merged into the Union National Bank he was made vice-president. The bank has since liquidated. He also became one of the founders of the Aurora

---

2770. Id.
2771. Id.
2772. U.S. Census, Roxbury, Delaware County, NY, 1850, Dwelling House 1486, Family Number 1488, Page 406.
2773. Id., Aurora, Kane County, IL, 1860, Dwelling House 902, Family Number 773, Page 343.
2774. COMMEMORATIVE BIOGRAPHICAL AND HISTORICAL RECORD OF KANE COUNTY, ILLINOIS, 946.
2775. Id., 887-888.
2776. Id., 702.
2777. FIRST ANNUAL GAZETEER & DIRECTORY OF THE CITY OF AURORA, 91.
2778. HOLLAND'S AURORA CITY DIRECTORY FOR THE YEARS 1880-84, 163.

National Bank and was its first president, serving thus until his life's labors were ended." {2779}.

Dr. O. D. Howell died of pneumonia on 19 Apr 1887 at Aurora {2780}, and is buried in the family plot at the Spring Lake Cemetery in Aurora {2781}.

Cornelia M. Howell died on 21 Jan 1895, at the age of 76 years and 8 months, and is buried beside her husband {2782}.

Dr. O. D. and Cornelia (More) Howell were the parents of at least four children.

+ 853. i.   MARION[7] HOWELL {2783}, born in about 1841.

+ 854. ii.   ANNIE[7] HOWELL {2784}, born on 22 Dec 1842.

+ 855. iii. EDWIN BEN[7] HOWELL, born on 17 Sep 1852 at Moresville, New York {2785}.

   856. iv. FRANK[7] HOWELL, born in about June 1858, died on 4 Dec 1860 of malignant scarlitina {2786}, was re-buried in the Spring Lake Cemetery at Aurora, Illinois, on 17 Jly 1888 {2787}.

419. ISAAC M.[6] HOWELL (Benjamin[5], George[4]), the son of Benjamin[5] and Jane (Moffat) Howell, was born in New York in about 1821.

On 2 Apr 1850, I. M. Howell was selected to be a commissioner of highways for the Township of Aurora for the ensuing year {2788}.

On 15 Nov 1850, I. M. Howell, 29, was enumerated as the head of a family including himself, his wife, Cornelia, 29, and their children, William, 5, Lydia, 3, and Spooner, 1, residing in Aurora Township, Kane County, Illinois, in the Seventh Census of the United States {2789}.

In 1868, I. M. Howell, of Howell & Shoemaker, was a lumber dealer in Aurora, residing at 78 Third Avenue {2790}. In 1880, he was a dealer in lumber, lath and shingles, having been established since 1861, at 8 Fox Street. He

2779. BIO. DICTIONARY AND PORTRAIT GALLERY ..REPRESENTATIVE MEN.., 349.
2780. Id., 350.
2781. SPRING LAKE CEMETERY, AURORA, ILLINOIS, Section II, Surname Index H-P, 46.
2782. Id., 45.
2783. BIO. DICTIONARY AND PORTRAIT GALLERY ..REPRESENTATIVE MEN.., 350.
2784. Id.
2785. Id., 349.
2786. Aurora Cemetery Book, 5-6, from a copy at the Aurora Public Library.
2787. Id., 48-49.
2788. COMMEMORATIVE BIOGRAPHICAL AND HISTORICAL RECORD OF KANE COUNTY, ILLINOIS, 931.
2789. U.S. Census, Aurora, Kane County, IL, 1850, Dwelling House 289, Family Number 3073, Page 208.
2790. FIRST ANNUAL GAZETEER & DIRECTORY OF THE CITY OF AURORA, 91.

also served as a township school trustee {2791}.

"On the southeast corner of Fox and Water streets stood a one-story office building occupied by I.M. Howell, who had a lumber yard there. The lumber piles extended on Fox street nearly to Broadway" {2792}.

I.M. Howell died on 8 Nov 1881, and is buried in the family plot at the Spring Lake Cemetery {2793}.

Mrs. I.M. Howell died on 10 Jly 1891, at the age of 68 years, 8 months, and 4 days, and is buried beside her husband {2794}.

Isaac M. and Cornelia Howell were the parents of at least three children.

857.   i.   WILLIAM[7] HOWELL, born in about 1845.

858.   ii.   LYDIA[7] HOWELL, born in about 1847.

859.   iii.   SPOONER[7] HOWELL, born in about 1849.

6. Jeremiah[5], George[4]

420. SYDNEY BURKE[6] HOWELL (Jeremiah[5], George[4]), the son of Jeremiah[5] and Asenath (Edwards) Howell, was born on 7 Dec 1818 at Hector, New York {2795}.

Sidney B. Howell married Isabel Swartwood at Starkey, N.Y., in 1855 {2796}.

For many years, Sidney B. Howell had a retail furniture business in Painted Post, New York {2797}.

Sydney Burke and Isabel (Swartwood) Howell were the parents of two children {2798}.

860.   i.   HENRY PARTRIDGE[7] HOWELL, born on 12 Apr 1856, never married, died on 19 Feb 1899 at Manistique, MI.

861.   ii.   JENNIE KIRK[7] HOWELL, born on 22 Aug 1863, never married, died on 14 Aug 1953 at Elmira.

422. MARY[6] HOWELL (Jeremiah[5], George[4]), the daughter of Jeremiah[5] and

---

2791. HOLLAND'S AURORA CITY DIRECTORY FOR THE YEARS 1880-84, 163.
2792. Charles Pierce Burton, THEN & NOW, AURORA BEACON NEWS, 28 Mch 1944.
2793. SPRING LAKE CEMETERY, AURORA.., Surname Index H-P, 45.
2794. Id., 46.
2795. Finch, op. cit., 12.
2796. Id., 13.
2797. Id.
2798. Id.

Asenath (Edwards) Howell, was born on 30 Sep 1823 {2799} at Hector {2800}.

Mary Howell married Samuel A. Chapman, who was born on 22 June 1824, the son of Elihu Chapman and his first wife, who was a Stocum (Kingsbury Genealogy says "Susan", son Samuel's Death Certificate says "Phoebe", while son Seeley's says "Mary") {2801}.

Samuel A. and Mary Chapman resided on West Hill, Elmira, New York {2802}.

Mary Chapman died in 1896 {2803}.

Samuel A. Chapman died on 17 Dec 1906 {2804}.

Samuel A. and Mary (Howell) Chapman were the parents of four children {2805}.

    i.   JUDSON CHAPMAN, born in 1853, died in 1854.

    ii.   EDWARD CHAPMAN, born in 1856, died in 1866.

    iii.   ANNA BELLE CHAPMAN, born on 23 Jan 1862, married (1) Charles A. Fox, one child, married (2) Josiah Gregory, died 14 Mch 1926.

    iv.   ALICE CHAPMAN, born on 2 Sep 1865, married William R. Van Horn as his second wife, three children born at Elmira, died on 17 Jly 1927.

423. DANIEL EVERTS[6] HOWELL (Jeremiah[5], George[4]), the son of Jeremiah[5] and Asenath (Edwards) Howell, was born on 24 Dec 1825 at West Hill in Big Flats, New York {2806}.

On 20 Mch 1860, Daniel E. Howell married Fatima Minier {2807}.

At six feet, D. Everts Howell was the tallest of the sons of Jeremiah Howell. He was a farmer, then a cattle buyer, and then a fruit grower, his house being on West Hill Street on a triangle of land bounded by the road to West Hill and the present Hart Street in Elmira. He became a charter member of the Lake Street Presbyterian Church when it was formed from the First Presbyterian Church of Elmira due to dissension in the Civil War {2808}.

Fatima Howell, and her daughter-in-law, Marion, were charter members

2799. Id., 12.
2800. Id., 13.
2801. Id., 9.
2802. Id.
2803. Id.
2804. Id.
2805. Id.
2806. Id., 14.
2807. Id.
2808. Id.

of the Walnut Street Literary Club, later called Sorosis {2809}.

Everts Howell died on his farm on 15 Feb 1907 {2810}.

Fatima Howell died on 30 Nov 1910 {2811}.

Daniel Everts and Fatima (Minier) Howell were the parents of three sons {2812}.

+ 862.   i.   FRED MINIER[7] HOWELL, born on 25 Nov 1860.

+ 863.   ii.   SIDNEY LLEWELLYN[7] HOWELL, born on 6 Mch 1866.

+ 864.   iii.   CHESTER EVERTS[7] HOWELL, born on 12 Aug 1867.

424. SARAH[6] HOWELL (Jeremiah[5], George[4]), the daughter of Jeremiah[5] and Asenath (Edwards) Howell, was born on 30 Oct 1827 {2813}.

From 1849 through 1854, Sarah Howell kept a diary in which she recorded the texts of sermons heard at the Presbyterian Church in Elmira, and visits of relatives to the family home {2814}.

On 16 Oct 1855, Sarah Howell married Artemus Mills, of West Hill. He was born on 28 Aug 1825, the son of Silas and Phoebe (Chandler) Mills {2815}.

Sarah Mills died on 15 Aug 1882 {2816}.

Artemus Mills died on 9 Jan 1889 {2817}.

Artemus and Sarah (Howell) Mills were the parents of two children {2818}.

    i.   FRANK HOWELL MILLS, born on 30 Oct 1856, married Hattie B. Everts on 24 Dec 1888, three children, died on 11 Mch 1926. She was born on 5 Dec 1872.

    ii.   HOLLIS MILLS, born in 1860, died in 1877.

426. EUNICE ELIZA[6] HOWELL (Jeremiah[5], George[4]), the son of Jeremiah[5] and Asenath (Edwards) Howell, was born on 12 Dec 1832 {2819}.

Eunice Eliza Howell married Abbott Barber as his second wife. His first

---

2809. Id.
2810. Id.
2811. Id.
2812. Id.
2813. Id., 12.
2814. Id.
2815. Id., 13.
2816. Id., 12.
2817. Id., 13.
2818. Id.
2819. Id.

wife was her cousin, Henrietta Chapman {2820}.

On 17 Aug 1850, Abbott Barber, 20, mason, was enumerated with the household of Edward Payne, 30, mason, residing in Elmira in Chemung County, New York, in the Seventh Census of the United States. He was born in New Jersey in about 1830 {2821}.

Abbott Barber married four times {2822}.

Eunice Eliza Barber died on 28 Oct 1889 {2823}.

Abbott and Henrietta (Chapman) Barber were the parents of one son {2824}.

    i.   ADALASKI BARBER.

Abbott and Eunice Eliza (Howell) Barber had no children {2825}.

427. LUTHER CLARK[6] HOWELL (Jeremiah[5], George[4]), the son of Jeremiah[5] and Asenath (Edwards) Howell, was born on 25 Feb 1835 {2826}.

Luther Clark Howell joined the 2nd Massachusetts Regiment, formed at Amherst College at the beginning of the Civil War. "His letters written to the family during the War are in the keeping of the Hitchcock Memorial Room at Amherst with the agreement that they are available for use to any of our family." {2827}.

"With the letters are a number of small photographs of his friends of the war period. Luther was first a Lieut. and then a Captain in this Mass. Regt. Before attending Amherst, he had studied at Alfred, NY. Luther survived the War but died of a fever at Haynesville, Alabama 14 Oct. 1866. His betrothed was Miss Clark who later kept a private school for girls at Plainfield, N.J. where Luther's niece Jennie Howell and her adopted sister Isabel Arnold were teachers" {2828}.

7. George[5], George[4]

429. ROBERT D.[6] HOWELL (George[5], George[4]), the son of George[5] and Sally (Durland) Howell, was born in 1824 at Hector {2829}.

Robert D. Howell married Elizabeth Hager, who was born in 1835, the

2820. Id.
2821. U.S. Census, Elmira, Chemung County, New York, 1850, Dwelling House 827, Family Number 900, Page 254.
2822. Finch, op. cit.
2823. Id.
2824. Finch, op. cit., 10.
2825. Id., 13.
2826. Id., 12.
2827. Id., 13.
2828. Id., 14.
2829. Id., 11.

daughter of Henry and Liza Hager of Reynoldsville {2830}.

Robert D. Howell died in 1901, while Elizabeth Howell died in 1912 {2831}.

Robert D. and Elizabeth (Hager) Howell were the parents of seven children {2832}.

+ 865.   i.   HELEN E.[7] HOWELL, born in 1856.

+ 866.   ii.   HENRY C.[7] HOWELL, born on 6 Jly 1858.

+ 867.   iii.   IDA B.[7] HOWELL, born on 20 Sep 1861.

+ 868.   iv.   LUCY[7] HOWELL, born in 1866.

+ 869.   v.   OAKLEY DURLAND[7] HOWELL, born in about 1869.

+ 870.   vi.   SARAH[7] HOWELL, born in 1872.

+ 871. vii.   GEORGE O.[7] HOWELL.

430. EMMA MIRANDA[6] HOWELL (George[5], George[4]), the daughter of George[5] and Sally (Durland) Howell, was born on 30 Jan 1830 {2833}.

Emma Miranda Howell married Professor A. C. Huff, who was born in 1832 {2834}.

Emma Miranda Huff died on 29 Aug 1904 {2835}.

Professor A. C. Huff died in 1910 {2836}.

Professor A. C. and Emma Miranda (Howell) Huff were the parents of at least four children {2837}.

     i.   ADA HUFF, died young.

    ii.   EDA HUFF, died young.

   iii.   MINNIE J. HUFF, died young.

   iv.   CARRIE HUFF, died young.

2830. Id.
2831. Id.
2832. Id.
2833. Id.
2834. Id.
2835. Id.
2836. Id.
2837. Id.

431. GEORGE OLIVER[6] HOWELL (George[5], George[4]), the son of George[5] and Sally (Durland) Howell, was born on 3 Aug 1834 {2838}.

George Oliver Howell married Lucy Rowland, who was born on 30 Apr 1835 {2839}.

George Oliver Howell died on 2 Apr 1872 {2840}.

George Oliver and Lucy (Rowland) Howell were the parents of five children {2841}.

+ 872.   i.   FRANK E.[7] HOWELL, born on 16 May 1856.

   873.   ii.   CARRIE A.[7] HOWELL, born on 24 Sep 1857, died on 19 Nov 1866.

+ 874. iii.   FRED S.[7] HOWELL, born on 15 May 1865.

+ 875. iv.   CORA M.[7] HOWELL, born on 6 Nov 1867.

+ 876. v.   GEORGIA OLIVER[7] HOWELL, born on 4 Nov 1872.

432. HARRIET[6] HOWELL (George[5], George[4]), the daughter of George[5] and Sally (Durland) Howell, was born in about 1840 {2842}.

Harriet Howell married Harry Ely 2nd {2843}.

Harry and Harriet (Howell) Ely were the parents of five children {2844}.

     i.   GEORGE ELY.

     ii.   EDWARD ELY.

    iii.   FRANK ELY.

    iv.   RICHARD ELY, married Mabel Matthews.

     v.   CLARENCE ELY.

2838. Id.
2839. Id.
2840. Id.
2841. Id., 11, 12.
2842. Id., 12.
2843. Id.
2844. Id.

8. Samuel[5], George[4]

433. MANDANA[6] HOWELL (Samuel[5], George[4]), the daughter of Samuel H. and Delilah (Brown) Howell, was born on 22 June 1834.

Mandana Howell married Nathaniel Brister {2845}.

Mandana (Howell) Brister died on 2 Jly 1856, at the age of 21 years, 8 months, and 10 days {2846}.

439. CHRISTINE C.[6] HOWELL (Samuel[5], George[4]), the daughter of Samuel[5] and Delilah (Brown) Howell, was born on 18 Jly 1850 {2847}.

Christine C. Howell married Harvey D. Shipman, who was born on 21 Aug 1847, the son of Shalor Shipman {2848}.

Miss Howell, the youngest daughter of Samuel Howell, who married Mr. Shipman, died in about Sep 1912 {2849}.

Christine (Howell) Shipman died on 3 Oct 1912 {2850}.

Harvey D. and Christine C. (Howell) Shipman were the parents of three sons {2851}.

    i.   WALTER SHIPMAN, born on 27 Aug 1872, married Grace Dickerson on 21 Sep 1892, one child, died on 27 Jan 1928. She was born on 22 Feb 1883, the daughter of Orson and Elizabeth (Coleman) Dickerson, and died on 23 Jan 1903.

    ii.   MYRON SHIPMAN, born on 11 May 1877, married Jennie Maltby, who was born on 7 June 1871 and died on 11 Jan 1921, one child died young.

    iii.   RALPH SHIPMAN, born on 11 Oct 1882, married Estella Gibson, who died on 12 May 1916, one child, who moved to Los Angeles with his father after his mother's death.

NOTE: *When the household of Samuel H. Howell was enumerated on 2 Sep 1850, "Delilah Howell", 2 months of age, was listed as a member. She was not listed in either the 1855 or the 1865 Census of New York State. Since Christine would have been approximately two months old at that time, and she was not listed in the Seventh Census of the United States, 1850, it would seem that her name had not been chosen when that census was taken, and Delilah, her mother's name, was*

2845. Notes, Tioga County Historical Society, 1996.
2846. Id.
2847. Shipman, op. cit.
2848. Id.
2849. OWEGO GAZETTE, 7 Nov 1912.
2850. Shipman, op. cit.
2851. Id.

tentatively listed.

9. James⁵, Benjamin⁴.

441. MORDECA⁶ HOWELL (James⁵, Benjamin⁴), the son of James⁵ and Ann Howell, was born in about 1822.

On 1 Aug 1850, Mordeca Howell, 28, farmer, with his wife, Welthy, 19, and their daughter, Matilda, 1, was listed as a member of his father's family residing in the Town of Hartsville, Steuben County, New York, in the Seventh Census of the United States {2852}.

Mordeca and Welthy Howell were the parents of at least one child.

877.   i.   MATILDA⁷ HOWELL, born in about 1849.

10. George W. ⁵, Benjamin⁴.

447. GEORGE⁶ HOWELL (George W.⁵, Benjamin⁴), the son of George W.⁵ (473) and Frances (Dunning) Howell, was born on 5 May 1829 {2853}, and baptized on 1 Aug 1829 at Goshen {2854}.

Dr. George Howell married Sarah L. Skidmore, who was born on 9 May 1835, the daughter of Luther and Esther Ann (Whipple) Skidmore {2855}.

In 1868-9, George Howell was a dentist in Riverhead {2856}.

On 10 June 1870, George Howell, 41, dentist, was enumerated as the head of a family consisting of himself, his wife, Sarah L., 35, their children, Levi L., 13, and Ann W., 10, both of whom attended school, and a domestic servant, Julia E. Hulse, 21, residing in Riverhead in Suffolk County, New York, in the Ninth Census of the United States {2857}. They were living in the same house as the family of Luther Skidmore, 62, blind maker, Sarah's father {2858}.

On 4 Apr 1871, Dr. George Howell received 218 votes as a candidate for the office of Inspector of Elections in District Number 2 of the Town of Riverhead, but was not elected {2859}.

2852. U.S. Census, Hartsville, Steuben County, NY, 1850, Dwelling House 114, Family Number 117, Page 173.

2853. Gravestone, Riverhead Cemetery.

2854. Coleman, op. cit., 138.

2855. Warren Skidmore, THOMAS SKIDMORE (SCUDAMORE), 1605-1684.., 156.

2856. D. Curtin, CURTIN'S DIRECTORY OF LONG ISLAND, from THE REGISTER, SCHS, XI, #3, 75 (Winter 1985).

2857. U.S. Census, Riverhead, Suffolk County, NY, 1870, Dwelling House 122, Family Number 134, Page 69.

2858. Id., Family Number 133, Page 69.

2859. RTR, Liber B, 328; (I, 480).

Hon. Dr. George Howell was a member of the New York State Legislature {2860}.

Dr. George Howell died on 28 Jly 1879, and is buried in Plot 240 at the Riverhead Cemetery {2861}.

Sarah L. (Skidmore) Howell died on 17 Jly 1881, and is buried beside her husband at Riverhead {2862}.

Dr. George and Sarah L. (Skidmore) Howell were the parents of two children.

+ 878. i.   LEVI L.[7] HOWELL, born on 3 Apr 1856.

  879. ii. ANNA W.[7] HOWELL, born on 19 Nov 1860, died on 5 Feb 1932, and is buried in the family plot at Riverhead {2863}.

11. John [5], Benjamin [4].

449. JOHN E.[6] HOWELL (John[5], Benjamin[4]), the son of John[5] and Rebecca Ann (Clausen) Howell, was born in about 1829.

John E. Howell was baptized on 6 Aug 1831 {2864}.

On 25 Nov 1850, John E. Howell, 21, student, was enumerated with his father's family in the Seventh Census of the United States {2865}.

John E. Howell, 42, lawyer, having real property worth $15,000, and personal property worth $25,000, was enumerated as the head of a household consisting of himself, his mother, Rebecca, 67, Margaret Murrow, 35, domestic servant who was born in Ireland, and Lewis Miller, 22, a black coachman who was born in Virginia, on 20 June 1870. They were residing in the Town of Goshen in Orange County, New York {2866}.

In 1871, John E. Howell, attorney and counsellor at law, had an office on Main Street opposite the Orange Hotel in Goshen, and a residence there on South street near Church. A John E. Howell also had a farm of 200 acres near Goshen {2867}.

"John E. Howell lived the largest part of his life in Goshen, N.Y.. where he was at one time a celebrated financier and had millions of dollars on mortages in surrounding farm lands. He was ruined by the great decline in prices of real estate following the civil war, and retired to Branchville, N.J., where he lived alone a d. March 2, 1900, unmarried. He wrote and published some volumes of very

---

2860. Skidmore, op. cit.
2861. Gravestone, Riverhead Cemetery.
2862. Id.
2863. Id.
2864. Coleman, op. cit., 139.
2865. U.S. Census, Goshen, Orange County, NY, 1850, Dwelling House 411, Family Number 429, Page 209.
2866. Id., 1870, Dwelling House 198, Family Number 228, Page 473.
2867. Orange County Directory, 1871, 121.

good poetry {2868}.

12. Huntting[5], Ezra [4].

458. THOMAS B.[6] HOWELL (Huntting[5], Ezra[4]), the son of Huntting[5] Howell, was born in about 1819.

On 9 Aug 1850, Thomas B. Howell, 31, farmer, was enumerated as the head of a family consisting of himself, and his wife, Hannah, 23, residing in the Town of Sterling, Cayuga County, New York, in the Seventh Census of the United States {2869}.

459. EZRA[6] HOWELL (Huntting[5], Ezra[4]), the son of Huntting[5] Howell, was born in about 1823.

On 9 Aug 1850, Ezra Howell, 27, farmer, with real property worth $1500, was enumerated as the head of a household consisting of himself, his wife, Julia, 29, their son, Marquis, 2, and Samuel Wright, 18, farmer, residing in the Town of Sterling, Cayuga County, New York, in the Seventh Census of the United States {2870}.

Ezra and Julia Howell were the parents of at least one child.
    880.   i.   MARQUIS[7] HOWELL, born in about 1848.

13. Coe Sayer [5], Ezra [4]

467. EMILY SAUNDERS[6] HOWELL (Coe Sayer[5], Ezra[4]), the daughter of Coe Sayer[5] and Frances A. (Stewart) Howell, was born on 21 Jan 1845 {2871}.

Emily Howell married James Steadman {2872}.

On 21 June 1880, Emily Steadman, 35, with her children, Belle, 12, James, 10, Harry, 8, and Alice, 2, was enumerated in the household of her parents in the town of Blooming Grove, Orange County, New York, in the Tenth Census of the United States {2873}.

James and Emily (Howell) Steadman were the parents of at least four children.

2868. Stickney, HOWELL, #B98.
2869. U.S. Census, Sterling, Cayuga County, NY, 1850, Dwelling House 67, Family Number 68, Page 180.
2870. Id., Dwelling House 66, Family Number 67, Page 180.
2871. Stewart, op. cit.
2872. Orange County Wills, Liber 54, 215-219.
2873. U.S. Census, Blooming Grove, Orange County, NY, 1880, Enumeration District 1, Family Number 258, Page 33.

i. BELLE STEADMAN, born in about 1868.

ii. JAMES STEADMAN, born in about 1870.

iii. HARRY STEADMAN, born in about 1872.

iv. ALICE STEADMAN, born in about 1878.

469. ISABELLA BORLAND[7], "BELLE", HOWELL (Coe Sayer[5], Ezra[4]), the daughter of Coe Sayer[5] and Frances A. (Stewart) Howell {2874}, was born on 14 Mch 1849 {2875}.

On 19 Nov 1879, Belle Howell married Merit H. C. Gardner, who was born on 17 Sep 1848 {2876}, the son of John E. Smith and Phebe Millicent (Cash) Gardner. They lived on the place formerly owned by Reuben Cash. He was a Republican, and the family worshiped at the Presbyterian church {2877}.

Merit H. C. and Belle (Howell) Gardner were the parents of two children {2878}.

i. COE SMITH GARDNER, born on 20 Aug 1880.

ii. IRA NATHAN GARDNER, born on 20 Dec 1883, at Johnsons, New York, educated at Stewarttown and Westtown, then in the public schools at Middletown, graduated in 1903, graduated from New York Law School in 1906 {2879}.

14. Thomas Chatfield[5], Ezra[4]

476. JOB TUTHILL[6] HOWELL (Thomas Chatfield[5], Ezra[4]), the son of Thomas Chatfield[5] and Mary Bradner (Tuthill) Howell, was born on 19 Mch 1853 {2880}.

On 8 Sep 1880, Job T. Howell married Elizabeth, "Libbie", Crane McGarrah before the Rev. D.N. Freeland at the Monroe Presbyterian Church {2881}.

Mrs. Job T. Howell was baptized by the Rev. T.B. Thomas on 17 Sep

2874. Stickney, HOWELL, #B66$^1/_2$.
2875. Stewart, op. cit.
2876. Stickney, HOWELL, #B67$^1/_2$.
2877. PORTRAIT AND BIOGRAPHICAL RECORD OF ORANGE COUNTY, NEW YORK, 810-813.
2878. Id.
2879. Headley, op. cit., 844.
2880. Tuttle, op. cit., 412.
2881. Mrs. C. Arthur Brooks, HISTORY OF THE FIRST PRESBYTERIAN CHURCH, MONROE, NEW YORK, 191.

1892 {2882}. She became a member of the church by her profession of faith on 17 Sep 1897 {2883}. She was President of the Ladies Aid Society in 1919 {2884}.

15. Cadwallader[5], Noble [4]

478. THOMAS JACKSON[6] HOWELL (Cadwallader[5], Noble[4]), the son of Cadwallader[5] and Catherine (Wood) Howell, was born in Orange County, New York, on 7 May 1823 {2885}.

On 4 Nov 1850, Thomas Howell, 27, farmer, was enumerated in the household of Thomas Jackson, in the town of Blooming Grove, Orange County, New York, in the Seventh Census of the United States {2886}.

On 22 Nov 1855, Thomas J. Howell married Matilda Cornelia Post, who was born in Orange County on 30 Jly 1828 {2887}, the daughter of Gen. P. S. and Mary D. (Coe) Post {2888}.

"Mr. Howell..made his home with an uncle from the time he was 18 months old until the year 1856, receiving a common-school education. At the age of 30 years he left his uncle for one year, and engaged in the creamery business in Morristown, N. J. He then resided with his uncle again for two years, from whom he received for his services his farm and personal effects. He came to Illinois in 1856, settling in Woodhull, and building the first house in the place. He purchased the half of section 7, in company with his brother, George Howell. He also bought 40 acres in the northern part of the same section, a quarter of section 29, in 1859; also 110 acres since then, and a quarter of section 24, 80 acres on section 12, and 80 acres acres on section 32. In 1880 he became a member of of the Farmers' Bank firm..As a farmer and as a dealer in fine horses and high-grade stock, Mr. Howell has been eminently successful..He is a Republican;..the first Republican surveyor of the township of Clover. For the past 19 years he has been a Trustee of the Presbyterian Church, to which body his wife and daughter also belong." {2889}.

On 10 Aug 1860, T.J. Howell, 36, farmer, was enumerated as the head of a household consisting of himself, his wife, Matilda, 31, their daughter, Carry, 4, and William Doyle, 15, farm laborer, residing in the Town of Clover, Henry

2882. Id., 111, 119.
2883. Id., 212, 236.
2884. Id., 170.
2885. PORTRAIT & BIOGRAPHICAL RECORD OF HENRY COUNTY, ILLINOIS, 208.
2886. U.S. Census, Blooming Grove, Orange County, NY, 1850, Dwelling House 822, Family Number 822, Page 55.
2887. THE HISTORY OF HENRY COUNTY, ILLINOIS; ITS TAX-PAYERS AND VOTERS, 329.
2888. PORTRAIT & BIOGRAPHICAL RECORD OF HENRY COUNTY.., 208.
2889. Id.

County, Illinois, in the Eighth Census of the United States {2890}.

The Howell family resided on Section 29, Clover Township, in Henry County, Illinois {2891}.

By his will of 11 Sep 1893, proved on 23 Oct 1893, Thomas J. Howell left his property to his "..beloved wife..". He included a bequest of $2000 to his grandson, Howell N. Brownlee, to be paid him on reaching 22 years of age. He also left $800 for the erection of a family monument. He named his wife Executrix, and his friend, W. C. Stickney, Executor, of this will {2892}.

By her will of 23 Apr 1898, proved on 3 Nov 1904, Matilda C. Howell left all her property to her daughter, Carrie P. Brownlee, whom she also named as Executrix {2893}.

Thomas Jackson and Matilda C. (Post) Howell were the parents of two children {2894}.

+ 881.   i.   CARRIE P.[7] HOWELL, born in about 1856.

  882.   ii.   SCHUYLER P.[7] HOWELL, born in about 1861, died in 1878 at the age of 17 years, at Rock Island.

479. CHAUNCY[6] HOWELL (Cadwalader[5], Noble[4]), the son of Cadwalader[5] and Catherine (Wood) Howell, was born in about 1825 in New York State.

On 12 Sep 1860, Chancy Howell, 34, farmer, with real estate worth $2600, and personal property worth $900, was enumerated as the head of a family consisting of himself, his wife, Edlia, 33, and their children, Samuel, 9, and DeWitt, 5, all of whom were born in New York state, in the Eighth Census of the United States. They were residing in the Town of Oxford, Henry County, Illinois {2895}.

Chauncy and Edlia Howell were the parents of at least two children.

  883.   i.   SAMUEL[7] HOWELL, born in about 1841.

  884.   ii.   DEWITT[7] HOWELL, born in about 1845.

480. GEORGE[6] HOWELL (Cadwalader[6], Noble[5]), the son of Cadwalader[5] and Catherine (Wood) Howell, was born in about 1828.

On 14 Aug 1860, George Howell, 31, farmer, was enumerated as the head

2890. U.S. Census, Clover, Henry County, IL, 1860, Dwelling House 2799, Family Number 2685, Page 903.
2891. Id.
2892. Henry County (IL) Wills, Book E, 271-272.
2893. Id., Book J, 24-25.
2894. PORTRAIT & BIO. ALBUM..HENRY COUNTY.., 209.
2895. U.S. Census, Oxford, Henry County, IL, 1860, Dwelling House 3929, Family Number 3843, Page 1064.

of a family consisting of himself and his parents, Cadawalader, 68, and Catherine, 69, residing in the Town of Clover, Henry County, Illinois, in the Eighth Census of the United States {2896}.

George Howell was a large man who became a railroader and was killed on the railroad {2897}.

481. ELIZABETH[6] HOWELL (Cadwalader[5], Noble[4]), the daughter of Cadwalader[5] and Catherine (Wood) Howell, was born in about 1833.

On 4 Nov 1850, Elizabeth Howell, 17, was enumerated in the household of Thomas Jackson, in the town of Blooming Grove, Orange County, New York, in the Seventh Census of the United States {2898}.

16. Elbert[5], Noble[4]

482. ELIZABETH[6] HOWELL (Elbert[5], Noble[4]), the daughter of Elbert[5] and Jemima (Smith) Howell, was born on 23 Aug 1823 {2899}.

Elizabeth Howell married John Demerest {2900}.

483. PHEBE ANN[6] HOWELL (Elbert[5], Noble[4]), the daughter of Elbert[5] and Jemima (Smith) Howell, was born on 21 Oct 1824 {2901}.

Phebe Ann Howell married John Bates {2902}.

Phebe Ann Bates died on 16 Apr 1900 {2903}.

John and Phebe Ann (Howell) Bates were the parents of six children {2904}.

    i.   EMILY BATES, married Jesse Holbert.

    ii.   ADELINE BATES, did not marry.

    iii.   JULIA BATES, married Will Balduron.

    iv.   GEORGE BATES.

2896. U.S. Census, Clover, Henry County, IL, 1860, Dwelling House 2910, Family Number 2795, Page 920.
2897. Predmore, op. cit.
2898. U.S. Census, Blooming Grove, Orange County, NY, 1850, Dwelling House 822, Family Number 822, Page 55.
2899. Stickney, HOWELL, #B116.
2900. Predmore, op. cit.
2901. Stickney, HOWELL, #B117.
2902. Predmore, op. cit.
2903. Id.
2904. Id.

v.   FRANCES AUGUSTA BATES.

vi.   CHARLES WILLIAM BATES.

486. SARAH J.[6] HOWELL (Elbert[5], Noble[4]), the daughter of Elbert[5] and Jemima (Smith) Howell, was born on 9 Aug 1829 {2905}.
   Sarah J. Howell married Gibson Kent {2906}.

487. COE[6] HOWELL (Elbert[5], Noble[4]) was the son of Elbert[5] and Jemima (Smith) Howell {2907}.
   Coe Howell married Nettie Langdon {2908}.

B. Israel[3], David[2], Richard[1].

1. Joseph[5], Silas[4].

495. BETSEY[6] HOWELL (Joseph[5], Silas[4]), the daughter of Joseph[5] and Elizabeth (Smith) Howell, was born 13 Aug 1800 {2909}.
   Betsey Howell married Seth Blanchard {2910}.
   Betsey Blanchard died on 18 Oct 1846 {2911}.

498. ABIGAIL[6] HOWELL (Joseph[5], Silas[4]), the daughter of Joseph[5] and Elizabeth (Smith) Howell, was born on 24 Apr 1810 {2912}.
   On 11 Oct 1827, at Greenville, IL, Abigail Howell married Dr. Alexander Robert Thompson Lacey, who was born on 1 Feb 1804 in Sullivan County, N.Y., the son of Daniel and Esther (Taylor) Lacey {2913}.
   Abigail Lacey died on 9 Nov 1832 at Lancaster, WI {2914}.
   Dr. Alexander Lacey died on 5 Sep 1853 at Oregon City, OR {2915}.
   Dr. Alexander Robert Thompson and Abigail (Howell) Lacey were the

2905. Stickney, HOWELL, #B120.
2906. Predmore, op. cit.
2907. Stickney, HOWELL, #B121.
2908. Predmore, op. cit.
2909. THE REGISTER, SCHS, XIII, #2, 46-47 (Fall 1987).
2910. Wilbur Franklin Howell, op. cit., 8.
2911. Id.
2912. THE REGISTER, SCHS, XIII, op. cit.
2913. Id.
2914. Id.
2915. Id.

parents of at least one child {2916}.

      i.   SARAH CORNELIA LACEY, married Peter Holt Hatch.

499. JOHN SMITH⁶ HOWELL (Joseph⁵, Silas⁴), the son of Joseph⁵ and Elizab
(Smith) Howell, was born on 13 Jan 1813 {2917}.

      On 7 Nov 1838, John S. Howell married Hannah Goldsmith, who w
born at Mattituck on 2 Sep 1819, the daughter of Benjamin, Jr., and Elizabe
(Terry) Goldsmith {2918}.

      On 10 Jly 1850, John S. Howell, 37, farmer, with real property won
$3,300, was enumerated as the head of a family consisting of himself, his wife
Anna, 30, their son, H.G., 10, and Margaret, 20, residing in the Town o
Southold, Suffolk County, New York, in the Seventh Census of the United States
1850 {2919}.

      On 20 June 1870, John Howell, 56, farmer, with real property worth
$6000, and personal property worth $3000, was enumerated as the head of a family
consisting of himself and his wife, Hannah, 50, residing at Peconic in the Town of
Southold, Suffolk County, New York, in the Ninth Census of the United States
{2920}.

      John S. Howell died on 27 Sep 1891, at the age of 78 years, and is buried
in the Willow Hill Cemetery {2921}.

      Hannah P. Howell died on 11 Feb 1902, at the age of 83 {2922},
and is buried beside her husband in the Willow Hill Cemetery {2923}.

      John Smith and Hannah P. (Goldsmith) Howell were the parents of at least
one son {2924}.

   885.   i.   HENRY G.⁷ HOWELL, born in about 1840.

2. Micah⁵, Silas⁴

503. MICAH⁶ HOWELL (Micah⁵, Silas⁴), the son of Micah⁵ and Hannah (Lupton)
Howell, was born on 15 Oct 1795 {2925}.

      On 2 Dec 1815, Micah Howell married Anna Youngs, who was born on

---

2916. Id.
2917. Id.
2918. Id.
2919. U.S. Census, Southold, Suffolk County, NY, 1850, Dwelling House 69, Family Number 73, Page
284.
2920. Id., 1870, Dwelling House 375, Family Number 394, Page 255.
2921. Gravestone, Willow Hill Cemetery.
2922. THE REGISTER, SCHS, XIII, op. cit.
2923. Gravestone, Willow Hill Cemetery.
2924. Id.
2925. Wilbur Franklin Howell, op. cit., 10.

29 Oct 1797, the daughter of Jeremiah and Mehitable (Wells) Youngs {2926}.

Micah Howell was listed as the head of a family consisting of one free white male of 16 and under 26 years of age, one free white female of 16 and under 26, and one of under 10, residing in then Town of Riverhead, Suffolk County, New York, in the Fourth Census of the United States, 1820. One of these was employed in agriculture {2927}.

In the 1 Jan 1825 Census of Baiting Hollow, Micah Howell was listed as the head of a family consisting of one male and two females {2928}.

"Micah Howell was a g(reat) grandson of the Israel Howell that lived on the Newton farm. He came to B(aiting) H(ollow) and after a short time, opened a general country store. Was postmaster for many years, the second one in the place, Benj. F. Young being the first. His commission was signed by Amos Kimball, P.M. General. The first year's profits according to papers left (I think, speaking from memory, in 1838) was very nearly $5. But Mr. Howell was a popular man; he gossiped no gossip, and kept friends and customers. Before he came to Baiting Hollow proper, he lived in the Country Road section, a little ways west of the Forge, but he came to North Road before 1825" {2929}. Micah Howell "..lived on the corner and kept a store in what had been Silas' house, which he had moved along side of one he had built." {2930}.

In the Fifth Census of the United States, 1830, Micah Howell was listed as the head of a family consisting of one free white male of 30 and under 40 years of age, one of 15 and under 20, and one free white female of 20 and under 30, residing in the Town of Riverhead, Suffolk County, New York {2931}.

Micah Howell was listed as the head of a family consisting of one free white male of 40 and under 50 years of age, residing in the Town of Riverhead, Suffolk County, New York, in the Sixth Census of the United States, 1840 {2932}.

On 17 Sep 1850, Micah Howell, 54, merchant, with real property worth $10,500, was enumerated as the head of a family consisting of himself, his wife, Anna, 52, their daughter, Lucetta P., 19, and his father, Micah, 77, residing in the Town of Riverhead, Suffolk County, New York, in the Seventh Census of the United States {2933}.

Anna Howell died on 31 Mch 1853, at the age of 55 years, and is buried in the Baiting Hollow Cemetery {2934}.

Micah Howell died on 30 Nov 1865, at the age of 70 years, 1 month, and

2926. Id.
2927. U.S. Census, Riverhead, Suffolk County, NY, 1820, Page 354.
2928. THE REGISTER, SCHS, VII, #4, 89 (March 1982).
2929. James Franklin Young, op. cit., VII, #4, 96 (Mch 1982).
2930. Id., VIII, #1, 9 (June 1982).
2931. U.S. Census, Riverhead, Suffolk County, NY, 1830, 241.
2932. Id., 1840, Page 246.
2933. Id., 1850, Dwelling House 477, Family Number 523, Page 279.
2934. Gravestone, Baiting Hollow Cemetery.

15 days, and is buried beside his wife in the Baiting Hollow Cemetery {2935}.

Micah and Anna (Youngs) Howell were the parents of four children {2936}.

+ 886. i. SAREPTA[7] HOWELL, born on 12 Sep 1816.

887. ii. HANNAH M.[7] HOWELL, born on 24 Sep 1821, died on 22 Dec 1825, at the age of 4 years and 3 months {2937}.

+ 888. iii. POLLY MARIA[7] HOWELL, born on 20 Apr 1827.

+ 889. iv. LUCETTA PRISCILLA[7] HOWELL, born on 10 Aug 1831.

504. DANIEL[6] HOWELL (Micah[5], Silas[4]), the son of Micah[5] and Hannah (Lupton) Howell, was born on 28 Oct 1797 {2938}.

On 16 Sep 1823, Daniel Howell married Jemima Howell (#579), who was born on 26 Jly 1806, the daughter of Merritt (#249) and Eleanor (Luce) Howell {2939}.

In the 1 Jan 1825 Census of Baiting Hollow, Daniel Howell was listed as the head of a family consisting of two males and two females {2940}.

Daniel Howell was listed as the head of a family consisting of one free white male of 30 and under 40 years of age, one of 10 and under 15, one of under 5, one free white female of 20 and under 30, one of 5 and under 10, and one of under 5, residing in the Town of Riverhead, Suffolk County, New York, in the Fifth Census of the United States, 1830 {2941}.

Daniel Howell was the brother of Micah Howell, "..and lived next farm west. He had a much larger farm. His wife, Jemima (daughter Merritt Howell) distantly related, but they lived long and reared their family. H.H. Howell of Aquebogue, their only son, for many terms a successful teacher. Would it sound queer to you? He was (is) not a college man; others had undoubtedly taken larger shares of books, but I say, in all candor, my best teacher." {2942}.

In the Sixth Census of the United States, 1840, Daniel Howell, Jr. was listed as the head of a family consisting of one free white male of 40 and under 50 years of age, one of 10 and under 15, one free white female of 30 and under 40, one of 15 and under 20, one of 10 and under 15, and one of 5 and under 10, residing in the Town of Riverhead, Suffolk County, New York {2943}.

2935. Id.
2936. Wilbur Franklin Howell, op. cit., 10.
2937. Gravestone, Baiting Hollow Cemetery.
2938. Wilbur Franklin Howell, op. cit., 9.
2939. Mallmann, op. cit., 226.
2940. THE REGISTER, SCHS, VII, #4, 89 (March 1982).
2941. U.S. Census, Riverhead, Suffolk County, NY, 1830, Page 241.
2942. James Franklin Young, op. cit., VII, #4, 96 (March 1982).
2943. U.S. Census, Riverhead, Suffolk County, NY, 1840, Page 246.

On 21 Sep 1850, Daniel Howell, 52, farmer, with real property worth $3,500, was enumerated as the head of a family consisting of himself, his wife, Jemima L., 43, and their children, Electa H., 16, Marinda Ann, 9, and Harrison H., 20, residing in the Town of Riverhead, Suffolk County, New York, in the Seventh Census of the United States {2944}.

Jemima L. Howell died on 22 Oct 1857, at the age of 51 years, 2 months, and 26 days, and is buried in the Baiting Hollow Cemetery {2945}.

Daniel Howell died on 17 Mch 1871, at the age of 73 years, 4 months, and 19 days, and is buried in the Baiting Hollow Cemetery {2946}.

Daniel and Jemima L. (Howell) Howell were the parents of five children {2947}.

+ 890. i. ELEANOR[7] HOWELL, born on 15 May 1825.

+ 891. ii. HANNAH ROSETTA[7] HOWELL, born on 28 Sep 1828.

+ 892. iii. HENRY HARRISON[7] HOWELL, born on 31 Mch 1830.

+ 893. iv. ELECTA H.[7] HOWELL, born on 7 Mch 1834.

+ 894. v. MARINDA ANN[7] HOWELL, born on 21 Feb 1841.

507. HANNAH[6] HOWELL (Micah[5], Silas[4]), the daughter of Micah[5] and Hannah (Lupton) Howell, was born on 11 Feb 1805 {2948}.

Hannah Howell married the Rev. Thomas Storms Anderson on 16 Jly 1829 {2949}.

Rev. Thomas S. Anderson died at Almond on 15 Sep 1841 {2950}.

On 17 Oct 1850, Hannah Anderson, 45, was enumerated as the head of a family consisting of herself and her son, LaRoy S. Anderson, 9, residing in the Town of Almond in Allegheny County, New York, in the Seventh Census of the United States. They were residing in the same house as her father and her sister, Julia {2951}.

Hannah Anderson died on 27 Mch 1897 {2952}.

Rev. Thomas S. and Hannah (Howell) Anderson were the parents of at

2944. Id, 1850, Dwelling House 481, Family Number 527, Page 280.
2945. Gravestone, Baiting Hollow Cemetery.
2946. Id.
2947. Mallmann, op. cit., 226.
2948. Laura Ann (Stearns) Benjamin, personal communication, to Julia (Howell) Benjamin, to Bessie Hallock, who supplied it to the Riverhead Town Historian's office. Generously provided by Justine Warner Wells.
2949. Id.
2950. Id.
2951. U.S. Census, Almond, Allegheny County, NY, 1850, Dwelling House 539, Family Number 605, Page 58.
2952. Laura Ann (Stearns) Benjamin, op. cit.

least one son.

     i.   LAROY S. ANDERSON, born in about 1841.

508. JULIA[6] HOWELL (Micah[5], Silas[4]), the daughter of Micah[5] and Hannah (Lupton) Howell, was born on 24 Dec 1807 {2953}.

    On 17 Oct 1850, Julia Howell, 42, with real property worth $300, was enumerated as the head of a family consisting of herself and her father, Micah, 77, farmer, residing in the Town of Almond, Allegheny County, New York, in the Seventh Census of the United States. Her sister, Hannah Anderson, with her son, LaRoy Anderson, was residing in the same house {2954}.

    On 24 Aug 1851, Julia Howell, "..of Allegany County N. York", married Nathan Benjamin {2955}.

    Julia Benjamin died on 2 Apr 1877 {2956}.

    Nathan Benjamin died on 15 June 1885, at the age of 70 years and 2 months, and is buried in the Baiting Hollow Cemetery {2957}.

    Nathan and Julia (Howell) Benjamin were the parents of at least one son {2958}.

    i. DAVID BENJAMIN.

509. LAURA[6] HOWELL (Micah[5], Silas[4]), the daughter of Micah[5] and Hannah (Lupton) Howell, was born on 6 Feb 1810 {2959}.

    On 11 Apr 1833, Laura Howell married Calvin Stearns, who was born on 31 Dec 1809 {2960}.

    On 18 Nov 1850, Calvin Stearns, 40, farmer, with real property worth $5000, was enumerated as the head of a family consisting of himself, his wife, Laura, 40, and their children, Israel, 14, Laura A., 13, Mary L., 11, Calvin L., 9, Susan E., 7, all of whom had attended school, and Eliza J., 5, George W., 4, Frances M., 2, and Charles B., $^6/_{12}$, residing on the Town of Almond, Allegheny County, New York, in the Seventh Census of the United States {2961}.

    Laura Stearns died on 10 Mch 1854, at the age of 44 {2962}.

2953. Wilbur Franklin Howell, op. cit., 9.

2954. U.S. Census, Almond, Allegheny County, NY, 1850, Dwelling House 539, Family Number 604, Page 58.

2955. Christopher Young's Marriage Record, 5, printed by the SCHS, 1975.

2956. Wilbur Franklin Howell, op. cit.

2957. Bicha and Brown, op. cit., 783.

2958. Wilbur Franklin Howell, op. cit., 32ff.

2959. Id., 9.

2960. Id.

2961. U.S. Census, Almond, Allegheny County, NY, 1850, Dwelling House 778, Family Number 862, Page 74.

2962. Wilbur Franklin Howell, op. cit.

Calvin Stearns died on 8 May 1862, while serving under General Grant {2963}.

Calvin and Laura (Howell) Stearns were the parents of ten children {2964}.

    i.   ISRAEL HOWELL STEARNS, born in about 1836.

    ii.   LAURA ANNA STEARNS was born on 12 May 1837 at Almond, N.Y., married John B.W. Benjamin, the son of Nathan Benjamin on 14 Mch 1855 {2965}, seven children, died on 30 Jly 1921, at the age of 84 years, 2 months, and 18 days, and is buried in the Baiting Hollow Cemetery {2966}.

    iii.   MARY LOUISE STEARNS, born in about 1839.

    iv.   CALVIN LEANDER STEARNS, born in about 1841.

    v.   SUSAN ELVIRA STEARNS, born in about 1843.

    vi.   ELIZA JANE STEARNS, born in about 1845.

    vii.   GEORGE WASHINGTON STEARNS, born in about 1846.

    viii.   FRANCES MARIA STEARNS, born in about 1848.

    ix.   CHARLES BENJAMIN STEARNS, born in about May 1850.

    x.   SARAH HANNAH STEARNS.

510. GEORGE[6] HOWELL (Micah[5], Silas[4]), the son of Micah[5] and Hannah (Lupton) Howell, was born on 6 Apr 1812 {2967}.

George Howell married Elizabeth Wygant {2968}.

On 15 Oct 1850, George Howell, 37, innkeeper, with real property worth $1400, was enumerated as the head of a household consisting of himself, his wife, Eliza, 33, and eight boarders, in the Town of Almond, Allegheny County, New York, in the Seventh Census of the United States {2969}.

George Howell died on 3 Jan 1892, at the age of 80 years {2970}.

2963. Id.
2964. Id., 40.
2965. Bicha and Brown, op. cit., 783.
2966. Id., 854.
2967. Wilbur Franklin Howell, op. cit.
2968. Id.
2969. U.S. Census, Almond, Allegheny County, NY, 1850, Dwelling House 558, Family Number 630, Page 59.
2970. Wilbur Franklin Howell, op. cit.

511. LUTHER[6] HOWELL (Micah[5], Silas[4]), the son of Micah[5] and Hannah (Lupton) Howell, was born on 21 Nov 1813 {2971}.
Luther Howell married Sarah Newcomb {2972}.
Luther Howell died on 6 Sep 1863 {2973}.

3. Smith[5], Silas[4]

513. ELIZA[6] HOWELL (Smith[5], Silas[4]) was the daughter of Smith[5] and Elizabeth (Hammond) Howell {2974}.
Eliza Howell married Clark Terry {2975}.

515. SMITH H.[6] HOWELL (Smith[5], Silas[4]), the son of Smith[5] and Elizabeth (Hammond) Howell, was born on 22 June 1811 {2976}.
Smith H. Howell died on 7 Mch 1839 {2977}.
Smith H. Howell was the father of at least two sons {2978}.
  895.   i.   ADDISON M.[7] HOWELL, born on 7 Mch 1834.

  896.   ii.   WARREN S.[7] HOWELL, born on 28 Sep 1836.

516. SYLVESTER[6] HOWELL (Smith[5], Silas[4]), the son of Smith[5] and Elizabeth (Hammond) Howell, was born on 22 June 1812 {2979}.
Sylvester H. Howell died on 8 Feb 1861 {2980}.
Sylvester H. Howell was the father of at least two children {2981}.
  897.   i.   SYLVESTER W.[7] HOWELL, born in 1843.

  898.   ii.   SARAH A.[7] HOWELL, born on 12 Dec 1851.

4. David[5], Israel[4]

520. HANNAH[6] HOWELL (David[5], Israel[4]), the daughter of David[5] and Joanna

---

2971. Id.
2972. Id.
2973. Id.
2974. Id., 48.
2975. Id.
2976. Id.
2977. Id., 49.
2978. Id.
2979. Id., 48.
2980. Id., 50.
2981. Id.

(Wells) Howell, was born on 19 Nov 1798 {2982}.

Hannah Howell married Samuel Harrison {2983}.

522. ISRAEL[6] HOWELL (David[5], Israel[4]), the son of David[5] and Joanna (Wells) Howell, was born on 9 Mch 1803 {2984}.

Israel Howell married Arletta Corwin {2985}, who was born in about 1805.

In the Sixth Census of the United States, 1840, Israel Howell was listed as the head of a family consisting of one free white male of 30 and under 40 years of age, one of 20 and under 30, one of 5 and under 10, one free white female of 30 and under 40, residing in the Town of Riverhead, Suffolk County, New York {2986}.

On 12 Sep 1850, Israel Howell, 47, with real property worth $25,000, was enumerated as the head of a household including himself, his wife, Arletta, 45, and John Brown, 11, residing in the Town of Riverhead, Suffolk County, New York, in the Seventh Census of the United States, 1850 {2987}.

Israel Howell was the principal heir of his aunt, Nancy Howell (#215), and an executor of her will, written on 7 Mch 1840, and proved on 18 Mch 1851 {2988}.

Arletta Howell, the aunt of Joseph William Corwin, died at Northville on 2 Nov 1870, at the age of 75 years and 9 months {2989}, or on 5 Nov 1870, in the 65th year of her age, and is buried in Plot 237 in the Riverhead Cemetery {2990}.

Israel Howell died on 1 Mch 1878, in the 76th year of his age, and is buried beside his wife at Riverhead {2991}.

Israel and Arletta (Corwin) Howell did not have any children.

523. LOUISE[6] HOWELL (David[5], Israel[4]), the daughter of David[5] and Joanna (Wells) Howell, was born on 8 Mch 1805 {2992}.

Louise Howell married Jonathan Davis Howell (#323), who was born in 1797, the son of Jonathan (#117) and Elizabeth (Hallock) Howell {2993}.

Jonathan Davis and Louise (Howell) Howell were the parents of at least

2982. David Faris, op. cit., 259.
2983. Id.
2984. Id.
2985. Wilbur Franklin Howell, op. cit., 62.
2986. U.S. Census, Riverhead, Suffolk County, NY, 1840, Page 246.
2987. Id., 1850, Dwelling House 354, Family Number, Page 272.
2988. Suffolk County Wills, Liber 5, 190-191; Suffolk County Estates, File #4072.
2989. HEMPSTEAD INQUIRER, 18 Nov 1870.
2990. Gravestone, Riverhead Cemetery.
2991. Id.
2992. Faris, op. cit., 260.
2993. PORTRAIT & BIOGRAPHICAL RECORD OF SUFFOLK COUNTY.., 182-183.

seven sons, as listed under #323, Jonathan Davis Howell.

525. TABITHA⁶ HOWELL (David⁵, Israel⁴), the daughter of David⁵ and Joanna (Wells) Howell, was born on 19 May 1810 {2994}.

Tabitha Howell married George Edwards {2995}, who was born in 1808, the son of Daniel {2996} and Sarah (Sherman) Edwards {2997}.

George E. Edwards, aged 42 years, of Sag Harbor, died in about Apr 1850 {2998}.

On 13 Aug 1850, Tabitha Edwards, 40, was enumerated as the head of a family consisting of herself and her children, Mary E., 17, Abel S., 12, George E., 9, Sarah J., 7, and Charles A., ¹¹/₁₂, residing in the Town of Southampton, Suffolk County, New York, in the Seventh Census of the United States {2999}.

George E. and Tabitha (Howell) Edwards were the parents of eight children {3000}.

      i.   MARY EMILY EDWARDS, born on 28 May 1833, married John Strong on 22 Oct 1756, at least four children, died on 5 May 1896. John Strong was born on 14 Feb 1827, the son of Sylvanus {3001} and Mary (Howell) Strong {3002}, and died on 5 Sep 1895 {3003}.

     ii.   ABEL SMITH EDWARDS, born in 1838, married Sarah A. Jagger, twelve children {3004}.

   iii.   CHARLES EDWARDS.

    iv.   GEORGE EDWARDS, born in 1841, died in 1863.

     v.   SARAH J. EDWARDS, born in about 1843, married Henry Lewis Osborn on 8 Apr 1863 {3005}, three children. Henry L. Osborn was born on 13 May 1834 {3006}.

2994. Faris, op. cit.
2995. Id.
2996. Rattray, op. cit., 315.
2997. Id., 314.
2998. Id., 315.
2999. U.S. Census, Southampton, Suffolk County, NY, 1850, Dwelling House 887, Family Number 968, Page 396.
3000. Rattray, op. cit.
3001. Id., 569.
3002. Id., 568.
3003. Id., 569.
3004. Id., 316.
3005. EHTR, V, 544.
3006. Rattray, op. cit., 505.

vi. THEODORE EDWARDS.

vii. DANIEL EDWARDS.

viii. CHARLES A. EDWARDS, born on 3 Sep 1849 {3007}.

529. PHYLINDA B.[6] HOWELL (David[5], Israel[4]), the daughter of David[5] and Joanna (Wells) Howell, was born on 12 Aug 1819 {3008}.
Phylinda B. Howell married Ebenezer Payne {3009}.
On 24 Aug 1850, Ebenezer Payne, 43, farmer, was enumerated as the head of a family consisting of himself, his wife, Philinda, 31, and their daughter, Sarah, 12, residing in the Town of Southampton, Suffolk County, New York, in the Seventh Census of the United States {3010}.
On 12 Jly 1870, Ebenezer Payne, 62, farmer, with real property worth $1500, and personal property worth $850, was enumerated as the head of a family consisting of himself, his wife, Philander, 50, and their son, Gilbert, 17, residing in the Town of Southampton, Suffolk County, New York, in the Ninth Census of the United States {3011}.
Ebenezer and Phylinda B. (Howell) Payne were the parents of at least two children.

i. SARAH PAYNE, born in about 1838.

ii. GILBERT PAYNE, born in about 1853.

5. Samuel[5], Samuel[4]

532. ELIZABETH[6] HOWELL (Samuel[5], Samuel[4]), the daughter of Samuel[5] and Charity (Davis) Howell, was born on 4 June 1813 {3012}.
Elizabeth Howell married William Senier {3013}, or Raynor {3014}.
William and Elizabeth (Howell) Raynor(?) were the parents of four children {3015}.

i. WILLIAM E. RAYNOR, died on 18 Nov 1861.

3007. Southampton Births, from THE REGISTER, SCHS, XXI, 27 (Summer 1995).
3008. Faris, op. cit.
3009. Id.
3010. U.S. Census, Southampton, Suffolk County, NY, 1850, Dwelling House 1149, Family Number 1247, Page 413.
3011. Id., 1870, Dwelling House 810, Family Number 839, Page 199.
3012. Ruth Isabelle (Davis) Ferris, op. cit.
3013. Id.
3014. Janice Linda (Howell) Derr, Personal communication.
3015. Ferris, op. cit.

ii.   SAMUEL R. RAYNOR, died on 17 Nov 1868.

iii.   JAMES J. RAYNOR, died on 29 Dec 1872.

iv.   MARTHA H. RAYNOR, born on 7 Jly 1845.

533. JOHN DAVIS[6] HOWELL (Samuel[5], Samuel[4]), the son of Samuel[5] and Charity (Davis) Howell, was born on 18 Sep 1815 {3016}.

     John Davis Howell married Caroline, who was born in about 1835, and who was pregnant when he left for California during the Gold Rush {3017}.

     John Davis Howell sailed to California on a ship carrying lumber from Long Island, abandoned the ship to join the Gold Rush, and died in San Francisco on 20 Mch 1850 {3018}.

     Caroline Howell married (2) James Jewell {3019}.

     On 3 June 1880, James H. Jewell, 49, farmer, was enumerated as the head of a family consisting of himself, his wife, Carrie E., 48, and their children, George E, 19, sailor, Henry, 17, farm laborer, Sarah L., 14, Carrie E., 12, Josephine, 9, and Lillie, 7, residing in the Town of Smithtown, Suffolk County, New York, in the Tenth Census of the United States {3020}.

     John Davis and Caroline Howell were the parents of one son {3021}.

+ 899.   i.   WILLIAM SHEPARD[7] HOWELL, born in 1850.

James and Caroline Howell Jewell were the parents of six children.

         i.   GEORGE E. JEWELL, born in about 1861.

         ii.   HENRY JEWELL, born in about 1863.

         iii.   SARAH L. JEWELL, born in about 1866.

         iv.   CAROLINE JEWELL, born in about 1868, married Samuel Gould, inherited the St. James Hotel in 1905 {3022}.

         v.   JOSEPHINE JEWELL, born in about 1871.

         vi.   LILLIE JEWELL, born in about 1873.

3016. Id.
3017. Derr, op. cit.
3018. Id.
3019. Id.
3020. U.S. Census, Smithtown, Suffolk County, N.Y., 1880, Dwelling House 27, Family Number 31, Enumeration District 326, Page 4.
3021. Derr, op. cit.
3022. Id.

534. MARIA AMELIA[6] HOWELL (Samuel[5], Samuel[4]), the daughter of Samuel[5] and Charity (Davis) Howell, was born on 30 Jan 1817 {3023}.

Maria Amelia Howell married (1) John Sterling {3024}.

On 1 Jan 1854 {3025}, or on 10 Jan 1854, in New York before Rev. King, Maria Amelia (Howell) Sterling married (2) Charles W. Train, who was born on 20 Feb 1812 {3026}.

Maria Amelia (Howell) Sterling Train died on 24 (or 30) Oct 1892 {3027}.

John and Maria Amelia (Howell) Sterling were the parents of six children {3028}.

   i.   GEORGE STERLING.

   ii.   WILL (WILHAM {3029}) STERLING.

   iii. JOHN STERLING.

   iv. KATE STERLING.

   v.   JANE A. STERLING.

   vi. CHARITY MALVINA STERLING, married (1) John O'Neil, six children (one adopted), married (2) James Beckwith, died on 12 Feb 1931, and is buried in the Newton Cemetery.

Charles W. and Maria Amelia (Howell) Sterling Train were the parents of three children {3030}.

   i.   ADELAIDE TRAIN, born in 1855, married Horace Fordhan.

   ii.   HENRY WELD TRAIN, born on 12 Jly 1857 at Lakeland, married Hattie Howell on 23 Apr 1884 at Patchogue, two children. Hattie Howell was born on 28 Aug 1861, and died on 5 Jly 1950.

   iii. JOSEPHINE AMELIA TRAIN, born on 26 Sep 1860, married John Dickerson of Islip, five children, died in 1908.

535. HIRAM BENJAMIN[6] HOWELL (Samuel[5], Samuel[4]), the son of Samuel[5] and

---

3023. Ferris, op. cit.
3024. Id.
3025. Derr, op. cit.
3026. Ferris, op. cit.
3027. Derr, op. cit.
3028. Ferris, op. cit.
3029. Derr, op. cit.
3030. Ferris, op. cit.

Charity (Davis) Howell, was born on 21 May 1820 {3031}.

Hiram Benjamin Howell married Sarah Jewell {3032}, who was born in 1827 {3033}.

Hiram Benjamin Howell was a Justice of the Peace in 1863-1869, and in 1872-1885 {3034}.

On 12 Jly 1870, Hiram Howel, 50, house carpenter, with real property worth $2000, and personal property worth $200, was enumerated as the head of a family consisting of himself, his wife, Sarah, 40, and their daughter, Emma, 16, who was attending school, residing in the Town of Smithtown, Suffolk County, New York, in the Ninth Census of the United States {3035}.

On 3 June 1880, Hiram Howell, 57, carpenter, was enumerated as the head of a household consisting of himself, his wife, Sarah, 53, James Wason, 38, a boarder who was an artist and portrait painter, and Nellie Crowell, 9, residing in the Town of Smithtown, Suffolk County, New York, in the Tenth Census of the United States {3036}.

Hiram Benjamin and Sarah (Jewell) Howell were the parents of at least three children {3037}.

900.   i.   THOMAS NICOLL[7] HOWELL, born in 1842.

901.   ii.   EMMA[7] HOWELL, born in about 1854.

902.   iii. SARAH L.[7] HOWELL

536. HARRIET MALVINA[6] HOWELL (Samuel[5], Samuel[4]), the daughter of Samuel[5] and Charity (Davis) Howell, was born on 2 June 1822 {3038}.

Harriet Malvina Howell married William Henry Lowden, who was born on 17 Nov 1814 {3039}.

William Henry Lowden died on 28 Feb 1865 {3040}.

William Henry and Harriet Malvina (Howell) Lowden were the parents of six children {3041}.

    i.   ELIZABETH CLOCK LOWDEN, born on 7 Jan 1843.

    ii.   AMELIA FRANCES LOWDEN, born on 16 Dec 1845, died on

3031. Id.
3032. Id.
3033. Derr, op. cit.
3034. Id.
3035. U.S. Census, Smithtown, Suffolk County, NY, 1870, Dwelling House 333, Family Number 329, Page 142.
3036. Id., 1880, Dwelling House 28, Family Number 32, Enumeration District 326, Page 5.
3037. Derr, op. cit.
3038. Id.
3039. Ferris, op. cit.
3040. Id.
3041. Id.

23 Aug 1846.

iii.   AMOS HENRY LOWDEN, born on 15 Feb 1848, married Emma Cordelia Williams of New Village on 25 May 1870.

iv.   HIRAM ALBERT LOWDEN, born on 25 Nov 1851, married Ella Smith at Islip on 22 Oct 1873.

v.   GEORGE WILLIAM LOWDEN, born on 29 Dec 1854, married Anna Leona Burwill at Tarrytown on 29 Dec 1882, died in 1931.

vi.   FRED T. LOWDEN, born on 12 Jly 1857, married Annie Eugenia Hudson at Brooklyn on 24 Dec 1884.

537. HARVEY WARREN[6] HOWELL (Samuel[5], Samuel[4]), the son of Samuel[5] and Charity (Davis) Howell, was born on 8 Feb 1826 {3042}.

On 15 Nov 1847, Harry W. Howell, 20, married (1) Nancy Newton, 17 {3043}, the daughter of Sylvester Newton {3044}.

On 21 Aug 1850, it was recorded {3045} that Harvey W. Howell, 24, farmer, and his wife, Nancy, were living in the same house as his mother-in-law, Martha A. Newton, 37, in the Town of Brookhaven, in Suffolk County, NY, when the Seventh Census of the United States was taken {3046}.

Nancy Howell died on 24 Aug 1850, and is buried in the Phineas Davis plot at the Newton Cemetery.

Harvey Warren Howell married (2) Mary Gould {3047}, who was born in about 1827.

On 14 June 1870, Harvey Howell, 44, farmer, with real property worth $5000, and personal property worth $1000, was enumerated as the head of a household consisting of himself, his wife, Mary, 43, their son, Warren, 1, Kate McCarthy, 20, domestic servant, and Albert Hammond, 23, farmer laborer, residing at Cutchogue in the Town of Southold, Suffolk County, New York, in the Ninth Census of the United States {3048}.

Harvey Warren and Mary (Gould) Howell were the parents of two children {3049}.

+ 903.   i.   LOTTIE[7] HOWELL.

3042. Id.
3043. BROOKHAVEN MARRIAGES, from THE REGISTER, SCHS, XVIII, #2, 43 (Fall 1992).
3044. Ferris, op. cit.
3045. U.S. Census, Brookhaven, Suffolk County, NY, 1850, Dwelling House 609, Family Number 642, Page 230.
3046. Id., Family Number 641, Page 230.
3047. Ferris, op. cit.
3048. U.S. Census, Southold, Suffolk County, NY, 1870, Dwelling House 216, Family Number 228, Page 246.
3049. Ferris, op. cit.

904.   ii.   WARREN[7] HOWELL, born in about 1869.

6. Jason[5], Phineas[4]

549. WALTER S.[6] HOWELL (Jason[5], Phineas[4]), the son of Jason [5] and Lydia (Allison) Howell, was born in about 1819.

Walter Howell married Arminda (?) Tompkins. They lived on a farm south of Slate Hill. Later, they moved to Binghamton {3050}.

On 30 Jly 1850, Walter S. Howell, 31, farmer, was enumerated as the head of a family consisting of himself, his wife, Arminda, 24, and his brother, Gabriel, 34, tailor, residing in the Town of Minisink, Orange County, New York, in the Seventh Census of the United States {3051}.

In 1871, Walter S. Howell was a dealer in dry goods, groceries and general merchandise at Pine Island {3052}.

Walter Howell was the father of three children {3053}.

905.   i.   SON.

906.   ii.   DAUGHTER.

907.   iii.   DAUGHTER.

7. James Brown[5], Phineas[4]

550. MICHAEL B.[6] HOWELL (James Brown[5], Phineas[4]), the son of James Brown[5] and Sarah (Stage) Howell, was born on 4 May 1808 {3054}.

When quite young, Michael B. Howell worked for seven years on the Erie Canal {3055}.

Michael B. Howell married Lydia Coomer {3056}.

Michael B. Howell came to Michigan in August 1837. Although not an ordained minister, he preached for several years, promulgating the faith of the Baptist Church {3057}.

On 22 Aug 1850, Michael B. Howell, 42, farmer, with real estate worth

---

3050. Stickney, HOWELL, #B110.
3051. U.S. Census, Minisink, Orange County, NY, 1850, Dwelling House 293, Family Number 296, Page 232.
3052. Orange County Directory, 1871, 122.
3053. Stickney, op. cit.
3054. Family Record of W.B. Howell.
3055. PORTRAIT & BIOGRAPHICAL ALBUM OF BARRY & EATON COUNTIES, MICHIGAN, 763.
3056. Id.
3057. Id.

$700, was enumerated as the head of a family consisting of himself, his wife, Lydia, 38, and their children, William, 18, farmer, John, 14, Caroline, 12, Chauncy, 9, Emeline, 6, Eveline, 6, Charles, 4, Emily, 2, and Oliver, 1 month, and residing in Jefferson Township, Hillsdale County, Michigan, in the Seventh Census of the United States. Of the children, William and John were born in New York, while the others were born in Michigan {3058}.

Lydia Howell died on 18 Jly 1869 {3059}.

Michael B. Howell died on 23 Jan 1878 {3060}.

Michael B. and Lydia (Coomer) Howell were the parents of at least ten children {3061}.

+ 908. i. WILLIAM C.[7] HOWELL, born on 20 Jan 1833 {3062}.

  909. ii. JOHN[7] HOWELL, born in about 1834.

  910. iii. CAROLINE[7] HOWELL, born in about 1838.

+ 911. iv. CHAUNCY[7] HOWELL, born in about 1840.

+ 912. v. EMELINE[7] HOWELL, born in about 1844, twin to Eveline.

  913. vi. EVELINE[7] HOWELL, born in about 1844, twin to Emeline.

  914. vii. CHARLES C.[7] HOWELL, born in about 1846.

  915. viii. EMILY[7] HOWELL, born in about 1848.

  916. ix. OLIVER[7] HOWELL, born in about Jly 1850.

  917. x. CLINTON[7] HOWELL, born in about 1855.

551. OLSER D.[6] HOWELL (James Brown[5], Phineas[4]), the son of James Brown[5] and Sarah (Stage) Howell, was born on 5 Feb 1810 {3063}.

    Olser D. Howell married Hannah Savins {3064}, who was born in New York State in 1820 {3065}.

    On 3 Sep 1850, Olser D. Howell, 41, farmer, with real estate worth $800, was enumerated as the head of a family residing in Portland Township, Ionia

3058. U.S. Census, 1850, Jefferson, Hillsdale County, MI, Dwelling House 114, Family Number 117, Page 380.
3059. PORTRAIT & BIOGRAPHICAL ALBUM..BERRY & EATON COUNTIES.., 763.
3060. Id.
3061. James W. Howell, op. cit.
3062. PORTRAIT & BIOGRAPHICAL ALBUM..BARRY & EATON COUNTIES.., 763.
3063. Ronald Lee Howell, Jr., op. cit., 139.
3064. IONIA COUNTY RECORD OF DEATH, #5739.
3065. Ronald Lee Howell, Jr., op. cit., 139.

County, Michigan, and consisting of himself, his wife, Hannah, 30, and their children, James, 11, Erastus, 8, Henry, 6, Henryetta, 6, Hiram, 4, Mary, 2, and William, 1, as well as Nelson P. Gabins, 22, in the Seventh Census of the United States {3066}.

Olser D. Howell was a farmer residing in Portland Township, Ionia County, Michigan in 1872 {3067}.

Olser D. and Hannah (Savins) Howell were the parents of eleven children {3068}.

918.   i.   JAMES R.[7] HOWELL, born in about 1839.

+ 919.   ii.   ERASTUS M.[7] HOWELL, born in about 1842.

920.   iii.   HENRIETTA M.[7] HOWELL, born in about 1845, twin to Henry.

921.   iv.   HENRY O.[7] HOWELL, born in about 1845, twin to Henrietta.

922.   v.   HIRAM C.[7] HOWELL, born in about 1847.

923.   vi.   MARY E.[7] HOWELL, born in about 1848.

924.   vii.   WILLIAM W.[7] HOWELL, born in about 1849.

925.   viii. LUCINDA M.[7] HOWELL, born in about 1850.

926.   ix.   ANDREW J.[7] HOWELL, born in about 1852.

+ 927.   x.   WALTER W.[7] HOWELL, born on 4 Apr 1854.

928.   xi.   HANNAH J.[7] HOWELL, born in about 1856.

552. JAMES PETER[6] HOWELL (James Brown[5], Phineas[4]), the son of James Brown[5] and Sarah (Stage) Howell, was born on 21 Jan 1812 {3069}.

On 9 Nov 1836, at Pittsford, Michigan, James Peter Howell married Emily Perrin, who was born on 8 Jly 1814 at Woodstock, Connecticut, the daughter of John and Bethesda (Skinner) Perrin {3070}.

On 13 Aug 1850, James P. Howell, 38, farmer, with real estate worth $800, was enumerated as the head of a family residing in Pittsford Township, Hillsdale County, Michigan, and consisting of himself, his wife, Emily, 36, and

---

3066. U.S. Census, Portland, Ionia County, MI, 1850, Dwelling House 240, Family Number 240, Page 140R.
3067. 1872 IONIA COUNTY DIRECTORY.
3068. James W. Howell, op. cit.
3069. Gwendolyn J. (Mrs. Arthur H.) Howell, op. cit.
3070. Id.

their children, Mary, 9, Walter, 7, Armilla, 5, Elvira, 3, and Alma, 1, all of whom were born in Michigan, as well as Cynthia J. Smith, 15, Timothy D. Perrin, 26, sawyer, and John Perrin, Jr., 8 months, in the Seventh Census of the United States {3071}.

Emily Howell died on 6 Aug 1891 {3072}, and is buried in the Greenwood Cemetery in Hillsdale County, Michigan {3073}.

James Peter Howell died on 5 Jly 1899 in Wayne Township, Cass County, Michigan {3074}, and is buried near his wife in the Greenwood Cemetery {3075}.

James Peter and Emily (Perrin) Howell were the parents of nine children {3076}.

929. i.   MARY[7] HOWELL, born on 13 Jan 1839, died on 29 Jan 1839.

930. ii.   MARY[7] HOWELL, born on 15 Dec 1840, died on 20 Sep 1859, and is buried near her parents in the Greenwood Cemetery {3077}.

931. iii. WALTER[7] HOWELL, born on 30 Aug 1842.

+ 932. iv. ARMILLA[7] HOWELL, born on 26 June 1845.

933. v.   ELVIRA[7] HOWELL, born on 23 Mch 1847, died on 3 Aug 1851, and is buried near her parents in the Greenwood Cemetery {3078}.

934. vi.   ALMA[7] HOWELL, born on 10 Jan 1849.

935. vii. EMILY[7] HOWELL, born on 21 Mch 1851.

936. viii. JULIA[7] HOWELL, born on 3 May 1853.

+ 937. ix. JAMES CLAIR[7] HOWELL, born on 13 Feb 1855.

938. x.   JANE[7] HOWELL, born on 5 Jly 1857.

553. SALLY J.[6] HOWELL (James Brown[5], Phineas[4]), the daughter of James

3071. U.S. Census, Pittsford, Hillsdale County, MI, 1850, Dwelling House 150, Family Number 150, Page 366.
3072. Ronald Lee Howell, Jr., op. cit., 124.
3073. HILLSDALE COUNTY, MICHIGAN, BURIALS, 304.
3074. Gwendolyn J. Howell, op. cit.
3075. HILLSDALE COUNTY, MICHIGAN, BURIALS, 304.
3076. James W. Howell, op. cit.
3077. HILLSDALE COUNTY, MICHIGAN, BURIALS, 304.
3078. Id.

Brown[5] and Sally (Stage) Howell, was born on 30 Jan 1814 {3079}.

      Sally J. Howell married Mr. Leonard {3080}.

      Sally J. Leonard died on 23 Apr 1889 {3081}.

554. WILLIAM L.[6] HOWELL (James Brown[5], Phineas[4]), the son of James Brown[5] and Sarah (Stage) Howell, was born on 29 Apr 1816 {3082}.

      In about 1836, William L. Howell married Belinda S. Taft, who was born in about 1816 {3083}.

      On 15 Nov 1850, William L. Howell, 34, shoemaker, was enumerated as the head of a family consisting of himself, his wife, Belinda S., 34, and their children, Mary E., 13, Michael S., 11, James C., 9, Wesley, 6, and DeWitt, 1, and residing in Adams Township, Hillsdale County, Michigan, in the Seventh Census of the United States {3084}.

      Belinda S. Howell died on 30 June 1868 in North Shade Township, Gratiot County, Michigan {3085}.

      In 1869, William L. Howell married (2) Hannah Coit, who was born in 1825 {3086}.

      William L. Howell died on 12 Jan 1893 in North Shade Township {3087}.

      Hannah Howell died in 1898 {3088}.

      William L. and Belinda S. (Taft) Howell were the parents of eight children {3089}.

+ 939. i.   MARY E.[7] HOWELL, born on 1 Aug 1837.

+ 940. ii.   MICHAEL S.[7] HOWELL, born on 11 Aug 1839.

+ 941. iii. JAMES C.[7] HOWELL, born on 7 June 1841.

+ 942. iv. WESLEY[7] HOWELL, born in 1844.

+ 943. v.   DEWITT[7] HOWELL, born in 1849.

+ 944. vi. WILLIAM H.[7] HOWELL, born in 1852.

3079. Family Record of W.B. Howell.
3080. Id.
3081. Id.
3082. Ronald Lee Howell, Jr., op. cit., 146.
3083. Id., 129.
3084. U.S. Census, Adams, Hillsdale County, MI, 1850, Dwelling House 84, Family Number 86, Page 463.
3085. Ronald Lee Howell, Jr., op. cit., 129.
3086. Id.
3087. Id.
3088. Id.
3089. Id.

+ 945. vii.   CORDELIA[7] HOWELL, born in 1854.

+ 946. viii.   EMILY[7] HOWELL, born in 1856.

557. WALTER B.[6] HOWELL (James Brown[5], Phineas[4]), the son of James Brown[5] and Sarah (Stage) Howell, was born on 25 Dec 1822 in Ontario County, New York {3090}.

On 7 Aug 1845, at Jefferson, Michigan, Walter B. Howell married Elvira Johnson, who was born on 5 Sep 1822 in Allegheny County, New York {3091}.

On 21 Aug 1850, Walter D. Howell, 27, farmer, with real estate worth $400, was enumerated as the head of a family residing in Jefferson Township, Hillsdale County, Michigan, and consisting of himself, his wife, Alvira, 27, and their daughter, Eunice A., 2, in the Seventh Census of the United States {3092}.

Walter B. Howell died on 28 Aug 1885 in North Star, Michigan {3093}.

Elvira Howell died on 20 Mch 1891 {3094}.

Walter B. and Elvira (Johnson) Howell were the parents of at least one child {3095}.

+ 947. i.   ELVIRA AMANDA[7] HOWELL, born 8 Jly 1852.

Walter B. and Elvira (Johnson) were the adoptive parents of one child {3096}.

  948. ii.   EUNICE ANN BASSETT HOWELL, born on 6 Aug 1848, died on 5 Jly 1880.

558. JULIA[6] HOWELL (James Brown[5], Phineas[4]), the daughter of James Brown[5] and Sally (Stage) Howell, was born on 5 May 1825 at Phelps, New York {3097}.

On 17 Aug 1842, Julia Howell married George W. Duryee at Florida, Michigan. He was born on 22 Jan 1820 at Seneca Falls, New York, the son of William and Sarah (Groot) Duryee, and died on 3 May 1865 at General Hospital No. 1, in Nashville, Tennessee {3098}.

3090. James W. Howell, op. cit.
3091. Id.
3092. U.S. Census, Jefferson, Hillsdale County, MI, 1850, Dwelling House 86, Family Number 89, Page 378.
3093. James W. Howell, op. cit.
3094. Id.
3095. Id.
3096. Id.
3097. Family Record of W.B. Howell.
3098. Tad David Campbell, Personal communication, via Ronald Lee Howell, Jr.

Julia Duryee died on 7 Mch 1899 and is buried in the East Hill Cemetery in Jefferson Township, Hillsdale County, Michigan {3099}.

George W. and Julia (Howell) Duryee were the parents of children {3100}.

i. JAMES H. DURYEE, born on 30 Apr 1843 in Michigan and died on 10 Jly 1910 at Los Angeles.

ii. SARAH AMELIA DURYEE, born on 12 Sep 1845, married (1) Charles Carpenter on 7 Feb 1864, two children, both given up for adoption after her husband died on 26 Sep 1868, married (2) James Jacob Stubblefield in June 1910 at Los Amgeles, no children, died on 29 Jly 1933. Charles Carpenter was born in about 1832, while James Jacob Stubblefield was born in about 1844, and died in 1924. (NOTE. *Sarah Amelia Duryee was the great-great-great grandmother of Tad David Campbell*).

iii. BYRON WILLIAM DURYEE, born on 6 Mch 1848, married Francis Anna Taylor on 26 Feb 1870 at Osseo, Michigan, seven children, died on 11 Feb 1886 at Ridgeville, Indiana.

iv. SUSAN M. DURYEE, born on 21 Sep 1850, married Robert Henry Brenenstul on 30 June 1867 at Osseo, two children, died on 29 Aug 1908 at Cleveland, Ohio.

v. GEORGE H. DURYEE, born on 17 Mch 1855 at Osseo, married Dora D. Huff on 11 Oct 1874, three children, died on 16 Oct 1915 at Hillsdale, Michigan. Dora D. Huff was born in 1849, and died in 1922.

vi. ADONIRAM JUSTIN DURYEE, born on 9 Sep 1857 at Osseo, married (1) Caroline Thobold on 24 Sep 1877 at Plainwell, Michigan, four children, married (2) Sarah Potter on 22 Sep 1888 at Rome City, Indiana.

8. Parshall⁵, Parshall⁴

561. JOHN⁶ HOWELL (Parshall⁵, Parshall⁴), the son of Parshall⁵ and Elizabeth (Horton) Howell, was born on 1 Dec 1811, in the Town of Minisink, Orange County, New York {3101}.

On 8 Feb 1833, John Howell married Mariett Decker, who was born on

---

3099. Id.
3100. Id.
3101. Larry A. & Kathleen M. McCurdy, op. cit.

9 Nov 1814 {3102}.

"In 1838, John and his father with their families moved to Michigan where John is listed as one of the original settlers of Ingham County. He purchased 80 acres in Stockbridge Township from Hiram & Elizabeth Macy (East $^{1}/_{2}$ of the North $^{1}/_{4}$ of 12 T 1 N R 2 E). He also owned 40 acres across the road from this property in Livingston County" {3103}.

On 30 Jly 1850, John Howell, 38, farmer, with real estate worth $1000, was enumerated as the head of a family residing in Stockbridge Township, Ingham County, Michigan, and consisting of himself, his wife, Marietta, 36, and their children, Abigail E., 16, Parson (sic), 14, Emily J., 12, William H., 9, Athaline, 7, James E., 4, and Sarah M., 1, in the Seventh Census of the United States. Of the children, the first three were born in New Jersey, and the others in Michigan {3104}.

Mariett (Decker) Howell died on 19 Sep 1888, and is buried in the Plainfield Cemetery in Livingston County, Michigan {3105}.

John Howell died on 13 Mch 1896, and is buried beside his wife in the Plainfield Cemetery {3106}.

John and Mariett (Decker) Howell were the parents of nine children {3107}.

949.   i.   ABIGAIL ELIZABETH[7] HOWELL, born on 18 Dec 1833.

+ 950.   ii.   PARSHALL[7] HOWELL, Jr., born on 24 Jan 1836.

951.   iii.   EMELE JANE[7] HOWELL, born on 9 June 1836.

952.   iv.   WILLIAM HORTEN[7] HOWELL, born on 7 June 1841.

953.   v.   ATHALINE[7] HOWELL, born on 14 Aug 1843, died on 20 Feb 1889, and is buried in the Plainfield Cemetery.

954.   vi.   JAMES ELWOOD[7] HOWELL, born on 10 Apr 1846, died on 30 May 1874, and is buried in the Plainfield Cemetery.

955.   vii.   SARAH MARIAH[7] HOWELL, born on 16 Dec 1848, died on 15 Aug 1940, and is buried in the Plainfield Cemetery.

956. viii.   ZELLA ETT[7] HOWELL, born on 24 June 1851.

3102. Id.
3103. Id.
3104. U.S. Census, Stockbridge, Ingham County, MI, 1850, Dwelling House 211, Family Number 211, Page 28.
3105. McCurdy, op. cit.
3106. Id.
3107. Id.

957.   ix.   ISAAC WESTBROOK[7] HOWELL, born on 24 Sep 1853, died on
12 May 1890, and is buried in the Plainfield Cemetery.

562. WILLIAM HORTON[6] HOWELL (Parshall[5], Parshall[4]), the son of Parshall[5]
and Elizabeth (Horton) Howell, was born on 10 Sep 1813 {3108}.

On 18 June 1844, William Horton Howell married Jane Sophia Hackett,
who was born in about 1826 {3109}.

William H. Howell was an executor of his father's will of 22 May 1844
{3110}.

563. MARIAH[6] HOWELL (Parshall[5], Parshall[4]), the son of Parshall[5] and Elizabeth
(Horton) Howell, was born on 28 Feb 1815 {3111}.

Mariah Howell married David K. Wood, who was born in about 1815
{3112}.

564. ELIZA ANN[6] HOWELL (Parshall[5], Parshall[4]), the daughter of Parshall[5] and
Elizabeth (Horton) Howell, was born on 19 Jan 1817 {3113}.

On 3 Aug 1835, in Orange County, New York, Elizabeth Ann Howell
married James Reeves, who was born on 24 Sep 1812, the son of Howell and
Elizabeth (Wood) Reeves {3114}.

James Reeves died on 9 Jan 1875, at the age of 62, and is buried in the
North Stockbridge Cemetery in Stockbridge Township, Ingham County, Michigan
{3115}.

Elizabeth Ann Reeves died on 16 Dec 1890, and is buried beside her
husband {3116}.

James and Elizabeth Ann (Howell) Reeves were the parents of twelve
children {3117}.

         i.   HOWELL REEVES, born on 20 Jly 1836, married Emily Topping
              on 1 Jan 1859, two children, died on 24 Jan 1919. Emily Topping
              was born on 24 Oct 1837.

        ii.   MARY REEVES, born on 11 Feb 1838, married James B. Soules
              at Chardstock, Dorsetshire, England, on 23 May 1861, three

3108. Id.
3109. Id.
3110. Id.
3111. Id.
3112. Id.
3113. Id.
3114. Id.
3115. Id.
3116. Id.
3117. Id.

children, died on 28 Oct 1874, while he died on 29 Nov 1906.

iii. CAROLINE REEVES, born on 20 Jly 1840, married William H. Ives on 20 June 1858 in Stockbridge Township, Michigan, at least one child, died on 16 Sep 1899 at age 59, while he died in Mch 1906.

iv. CHARLES REEVES, born on 16 Apr 1843, died on 25 Aug 1845 at age 2.

v. MEHITABLE, "HETTIE", REEVES, born on 21 Dec 1844, married Frank Smead on 29 Mch 1866, at least one child.

vi. ALICE REEVES, born on 22 Mch 1847, married Frank G. Baker on 12 Dec 1865, two children, died on 2 May 1922. Frank G. Baker was born on 12 Dec 1844, and died on 30 Oct 1924.

vii. HORTON REEVES, born on 31 May 1849, married Helen B. Gaylord on 31 Oct 1877, at least one child.

viii. ORTANCE REEVES, born on 18 Apr 1851, married Robert Henry Mitteer, three children, died 11 Mch 1938.

ix. CLARA REEVES, born on 10 June 1853, married Hiram Mort on 27 Oct 1880 at Stockbridge, four children. Hiram Mort died on 20 Sep 1923.

x. DAYTON E. REEVES, born on 2 Sep 1856, married Flora Westfall on 19 Apr 1883 at Stockbridge, three children, died on 19 Jly 1894.

xi. ADA ANN REEVES, born on 11 Jly 1859, died on 24 Jan 1863.

xii. OVA REEVES, born on 25 Apr 1862, married Nicholas Conklin on 11 Feb 1890 at Stockbridge, at least one child, died on 6 Aug 1906.

566. GEORGE W.[6] HOWELL (Parshall[5], Parshall[4]), the son of Parshall[5] and Elizabeth (Horton) Howell, was born on 26 Feb 1822 {3118}.

On 13 May 1843, at Unadilla, Michigan, George Howell married Hellen Belle Coleman, who was born on 25 Dec 1825, the daughter of David and Bethiah

---

3118. Gregory A. Inman, Personal communication.

(Howell) Coleman {3119}.

George Howell was an executor of his father's will of 22 May 1844 {3120}.

On 1 Oct 1850, George Howell, 29, farmer, with real property worth $2000, was enumerated as the head of a family consisting of himself, his wife, Helen, 24, and their children, Mary, 7, Susan M., 5, Helen A., 3, and Catharine F., $^2/_{12}$, residing in Dexter Township, Washtenaw County, Michigan, in the Seventh Census of the United States {3121}.

Hellen B. Howell died on 5 Aug 1895 at Greenville, Montcalm County, Michigan, at 69 years of age {3122}.

George Howell died on 21 Jan 1899, at the age of 76 years {3123}.

George and Hellen (Coleman) Howell were the parents of nine children {3124}.

+ 958. i.   MARY ELIZABETH[7] HOWELL, born on 18 Mch 1844.

959. ii.   SUSAN MARIA[7] HOWELL, born on 19 Jan 1846, died on 20 Mch 1865 in Ionia County, Michigan.

+ 960. iii.   HELLEN AMANDA[7] HOWELL, born on 2 Nov 1848.

+ 961. iv.   CATHERINE JANE, "JANNIE"[7], HOWELL, born on 23 Aug 1850.

+ 962. v.   IDA MARIAN[7] HOWELL, born on 5 Dec 1853.

+ 963. vi.   GEORGE DAVID[7] HOWELL, born on 29 May 1855.

+ 964. vii. WILLIAM BENNIE[7], HOWELL, born on 23 Mch 1858.

965. viii. MEHITABLE COLEMAN, "BELLE"[7], HOWELL, born on 17 Aug 1862, and died on 14 Jly 1908.

966. ix.   MYRTLE LENA[7] HOWELL, born on 17 Dec 1866, died on 22 Aug 1874.

+ 967. x.   FREDERICK JAMES, "FREDDIE"[7], HOWELL, born on 25 June 1869.

3119. Id.
3120. McCurdy, op. cit.
3121. U.S. Census, Dexter, Washtenaw County, MI, 1850, Dwelling House 3, Family Number 3, Page 511.
3122. Inman, op. cit.
3123. Id.
3124. Id.

567. CHARLES[6] HOWELL (Parshall[5], Parshall[4]), the son of Parshall[5] and Elizabeth (Horton) Howell, was born on 8 Jan 1824 {3125}.

By his father's will of 22 May 1844, Charles Howell inherited "..the equal undivided half of my store and lot in the village of East Unadilla in the County of Livingston in the state aforesaid (Michigan) - known as the "John Drake" property.." {3126}.

On 3 Oct 1850, Charles Howell, 27, merchant, was listed as the head of a family consisting of himself and his wife, Fanny M., 25, residing in Dexter Township, Washtenaw County, Michigan, in the Seventh Census of the United States {3127}.

568. MEHITABLE[6] HOWELL (Parshall[5], Parshall[4]), the daughter of Parshall[5] and Elizabeth (Horton) Howell, was born on 20 Sep 1825 {3128}.

On 15 Mch 1847, Mehitable, "Hetty", Howell married John Dunning, who was born in New York state in about 1812 {3129}.

By her father's will of 22 May 1844, "Hetty Howell" was to inherit, with her sister, Louisa, a "..tract of land situated in the county of Ingham in aforesaid being the East half of the section number twenty-one in Township No. Two East..provided that the said premises shall be sold by me during my life time then the proceeds of such sale is to belong and be given.." to the two sisters {3130}.

Mehitable Dunning died on 12 Aug 1866, and is buried in the Unadilla Cemetery in Unadilla Township, Livingston County, Michigan {3131}.

John and Mehitable (Howell) Dunning were the parents of at least one child {3132}.

    i.   FLORA A. DUNNING, born in about 1849.

569. LOUISA[6] HOWELL (Parshall[5], Parshall[4]), the daughter of Parshall[5] and Elizabeth (Horton) Howell, was born on 31 Oct 1827 {3133}.

By her father's will of 22 May 1844, Louisa was to inherit, with her sister, Hetty, a "..tract of land situated in the county of Ingham in aforesaid being the East half of the section number twenty-one in Township No. Two East. To have and to hold the same together with all profit and income thereof to them..provided that the said premises shall be sold by me during my life time then the proceeds of such sale

3125. McCurdy, op. cit.
3126. Id.
3127. U.S. Census, Dexter, Washtenaw County, MI, 1850, Dwelling House 96, Family Number 96, Page 517R.
3128. McCurdy, op. cit.
3129. Id.
3130. Id.
3131. Id.
3132. Id.
3133. Id.

is to belong and be given to them the said Hetty and Louisa." {3134}.

In about 1853, Luiza Howell married Owen Chapman, who was born in about 1828 {3135}.

Owen and Luiza (Howell) Chapman were the parents of three children {3136}.

    i.   AMANADA CHAPMAN, born in about 1854.

    ii.   FRANK CHAPMAN, born in about 1856.

    iii.   FREDRICK CHAPMAN, born in about 1859.

570. CHAUNCY[6] HOWELL (Parshall[5], Parshall[4]), the son of Parshall[5] and Elizabeth (Horton) Howell, was born on 3 Aug 1831 {3137}.

With his siblings, Benjamin, Nelson and Mandy, Chauncy Howell was to inherit the "..remainder of all my said farm in the Township of Dexter..after the decease or marriage of my said wife..provided that if my said wife should die or marry before the youngest of the said children shall arrive at the age of twenty one years. Then the said property shall be and remain in the hands of my executors..for the support of them the said Chauncy, Benjamin, Nelson and Manda. Until the youngest of them shall arrive at the years of his majority then, to be equally divided..between the said four children so many of them as shall then be living." {3138}.

In about 1863, Chauncy Howell married (1) Mary Ann ---- , who was born in New York state in about 1838. She died before 1880 at age 41, after which he married (2) Lelia ---- , who was born in about 1837 {3139}.

Chauncy and Mary Ann Howell were the parents of three children {3140}.

968.   i.   JAMES[7] HOWELL, born in about 1866.

969.   ii.   SAMUEL B.[7] HOWELL, born on 30 Sep 1867 at Dexter, Michigan, died on 3 Oct 1867.

970.   iii.   FRANCIS AMANDA[7] HOWELL, born on 15 Oct 1868.

571. NELSON[6] HOWELL (Parshall[5], Parshall[4]), the son of Parshall[5] and Elizabeth

---

3134. Id.
3135. Id.
3136. Id.
3137. Id.
3138. Id.
3139. Id.
3140. Id.

(Horton) Howell, was born on 19 Jly 1833 {3141}.

With his siblings, Chauncy, Amanda, and Benjamin, Nelson Howell was to share in the residue of his father's estate, as stated under Chauncy Howell (#570) {3142}.

In about 1862, Nelson Howell married Elvira Clark, who was born in about 1835 in New York State {3143}.

Nelson Howell died on 12 Jan 1912, and is buried in the Hamlin Township Cemetery at Eaton Rapids, Eaton County, Michigan {3144}.

Nelson and Elvira (Clark) Howell were the parents of five children {3145}.

971.   i.   FLORA[7] HOWELL, born in about 1863.

972.   ii.   ORA ANNIE[7] HOWELL, born on 23 May 1867.

973. iii.   MEHITABLE C., "BELL"[7], HOWELL, born on 20 Dec 1870.

974.   iv.   ELMIRA[7] HOWELL, born on 24 Mch 1873.

975.   v.   MARY[7] HOWELL, born in Nov 1876, died in Sep 1877.

III. Descendants of Richard[2] Howell -

A. Richard[3], Richard[2], Richard[1].

1. Abner[5], Richard[4]

574. MARY W.[6] HOWELL (Abner[5], Richard[4]), the daughter of Abner[5] and Sarah (Howell) Howell, was born in about Nov 1807.

Mary W. Howell married Nathan K. Moseley.

Mary W. Moseley died on 3 Sep 1842, at the age of 35 years and 10 months, and is buried in the Aquebogue Cemetery {3146}.

Nathan K. and Mary W. (Howell) Moseley were the parents of at least three children {3147}.

     i.   AZUBA ANN MOSELEY, born on 18 Nov 1830. On 13 Mch 1847 {3148}, at Aquebogue, she married Daniel Benjamin,

---

3141. Id.
3142. Id.
3143. Id.
3144. Id.
3145. Id.
3146. Gravestone, Aquebogue Cemetery.
3147. Wilbur Franklin Howell, op. cit., 93.
3148. RTR (Printed records, 729).

who was born on 25 May 1822, the son of Daniel and Rebecca (Young) Benjamin, nine children, died 31 Jan 1904, at the age of 73 years, 2 months, and 13 days, at Middleroad. He died on 4 May 1900, and is buried in the Baiting Hollow Cemetery {3149}.

ii.   LUCIUS K. MOSELEY, married Sarah Ann Benjamin, who was born on 9 Oct 1835, the daughter of Daniel and Rebecca (Young) Benjamin {3150}.

iii.   THOMAS NELSON MOSELEY, born on 25 Mch 1839, married Maron Edwards on 15 Nov 1862, four children, died on 25 Nov 1873 {3151}, at the age of 34 years and 8 months, and is buried in the Riverhead Cemetery {3152}. She was born on 23 Feb 1845, the daughter of Spafford and Mary Sophia (Raynor) Edwards. On 18 Mch 1902, she married (2) Henry W. Brown, who died on 6 Jly 1913, while she died on 25 Jly 1921, and is buried beside her first husband at Riverhead {3153}.

575. JOSIAH[6] HOWELL (Abner[5], Richard[4]), the son of Abner[5] and Sarah (Howell) Howell, was born on 14 Jan 1810.

Josiah Howell married Amanda Wells at Riverhead {3154}.

On 17 Sep 1850, Josiah Howell, 38, farmer, with real property worth $1,500, was listed as the head of a family including himself, his wife, Amanda, 34, and their children, Christiana, 12, Mary M., 8, Sarah A., 6, and Henrietta, 2, residing in the Town of Riverhead, Suffolk County, New York, in the same house as his parents, in the Seventh Census of the United States, 1850 {3155}.

On 23 Jly 1870, Josiah Howell, 60, farmer, with real property worth $4000, and personal property worth $800, was enumerated as the head of a family consisting of himself, Sarah M., 55, and his children, Henrietta, 22, and Henry J., 18, residing in the Town of Riverhead, Suffolk County, New York, in the Ninth Census of the United States {3156}.

Josiah Howell died on 14 Oct 1872, and is buried in the Riverhead Cemetery {3157}.

3149. Bicha and Brown, op. cit., 855.
3150. Id., 785.
3151. Mary E. Moseley, Personal communication, in the possession of the Suffolk County Historical Society, 1993.
3152. Gravestone, Riverhead Cemetery.
3153. Moseley, op. cit.
3154. LONG ISLAND FARMER.., 11 Nov 1835.
3155. U.S. Census, Riverhead, Suffolk County, NY, 1850, Dwelling House 465, Family Number, Page 279.
3156. Id., 1870, Dwelling House 585, Family Number 636, Page 103.
3157. Gravestone, Riverhead Cemetery.

Amanda A. Howell died on 7 Nov 1885, and is buried beside her husband at Riverhead {3158}.

Josiah and Amanda A. (Wells) Howell were the parents of five children {3159}.

+ 976.   i.   CHRISTIANA[7] HOWELL, born on 7 Nov 1837 {3160}.

+ 977.   ii.   MARY MEHETABLE[7] HOWELL, born on 3 Oct 1841 {3161}.

   978.   iii.   SARAH AMANDA[7] HOWELL, born in about Aug 1844, died on 7 Nov 1867, at the age of 23 years and 3 months, was buried in the Aquebogue Cemetery {3162}, and is re-buried in the family plot at the Riverhead Cemetery {3163}.

+ 979.   iv.   HENRIETTA[7] HOWELL, born in about 1848.

+ 980.   v.   HENRY JOSIAH[7] HOWELL, born in 1851.

577. DAVID WELLS[6] HOWELL (Abner[5], Richard[4]), the son of Abner[5] and Sarah (Howell) Howell, was born on 30 Jan 1821.

On 31 Dec 1840, David Wells Howell married Joanna Warner {3164}, who was born on 21 Jan 1823, the daughter of Daniel and Jemima (Benjamin) Warner {3165}.

On 17 Sep 1850, David W. Howell, 29, farmer, with real property worth $600, was listed as the head of a family including himself, and his wife, Joanna, 26, residing in the Town of Riverhead, Suffolk County, New York, in the Seventh Census of the United States {3166}.

Joanna Howell died on 26 Sep 1861, at the age of 38 years, 8 months, and 5 days, and is buried in the Aquebogue Cemetery {3167}.

On 29 Mch 1862, David Wells Howell married (2) Sarah Robinson {3168}.

On 25 Jly 1870, David W. Howell, 48, farmer, with real property worth $1,500, and personal property worth $400, was enumerated as the head of a family

3158. Id.
3159. Wilbur Franklin Howell, op. cit., 94.
3160. Tuttle, op. cit., 347.
3161. Id., 149.
3162. Gravestone, Aquebogue Cemetery.
3163. Gravestone, Riverhead Cemetery.
3164. Wells, op. cit., 25
3165. Id.
3166. U.S. Census, Riverhead, Suffolk County, NY, 1850, Dwelling House 464, Family Number 508, Page 279.
3167. Gravestone, Aquebogue Cemetery.
3168. Mrs. Robert E. Pawson, op. cit., 18.

consisting of himself, his wife, Sarah A., 27, and their children, Herbert W., 7, and Richard S., 4, residing in East Moriches in the Town of Brookhaven, Suffolk County, New York, in the Ninth Census of the United States, 1870 {3169}.

David Wells and Sarah A. (Robinson) Howell were the parents of five children {3170}.

+ 981.   i.   HERBERT W.[7] HOWELL, born on 7 Jan 1863.

982.   ii.   RICHARD S.[7] HOWELL, born on 7 Dec 1865.

983.   iii.   MARY ELIOT[7] HOWELL, born on 2 Dec 1867.

984.   iv.   JOHN ABNER[7] HOWELL, born on 29 Mch 1868, died on 3 Jly 1869.

985.   v.   JUSTIN[7] HOWELL, disappeared in his mother's boat.

2. Merritt[5], Merritt[4]

579. JEMIMA[6] HOWELL (Merritt[5], Merritt[4]), the daughter of Merritt[5] and Eleanor (Luce) Howell, was born on 26 Jly 1806 {3171}.

On 16 Sep 1823, Jemima Howell married Daniel Howell (#504), who was born on 23 Oct 1797, the son of Micah (#208) and Hannah (Lupton) Howell {3172}.

Jemima Howell died on 22 Oct 1857 {3173}, at the age of 51 years, 2 months, and 26 days, and is buried in the cemetery at Baiting Hollow {3174}.

Daniel Howell died on 17 Mch 1871, at the age of 73 years, 4 months and 19 days, and is buried beside his wife at Baiting Hollow {3175}.

Daniel and Jemima (Howell) Howell were the parents of five children, as given under #504, Daniel Howell.

581. FANNY B.[6] HOWELL (Merritt[5], Merritt[4]), the daughter of Merritt[5] and Eleanor (Luce) Howell, was born on 4 Oct 1810 {3176}.

3169. U.S. Census, Brookhaven, Suffolk County, NY, 1870, Dwelling House 1232, Family Number 1317, Page 389.
3170. Pawson, op. cit.
3171. Mallmann, op. cit., 226.
3172. Mallmann, op. cit., 226, Wilbur Franklin Howell, 9.
3173. Mallmann, op. cit.
3174. Gravestone, Baiting Hollow Cemetery.
3175. Id.
3176. Mallmann, op. cit., 214.

Fanny B. Howell married Rev. Parshall Terry {3177}.

On 13 June 1860, Parshall Terry, 53, Congregationalist minister, was enumerated as the head of a family consisting of himself, his wife, Fanny B., 49, and their children, Theodore B., 17, and Josephine, 10, residing in Thompson Township, Geauga County, Ohio, in the Eighth Census of the United States {3178}.

Rev. Parshall and Fanny B. (Howell) Terry were the parents of at least two children.

    i.   THEODORE B. TERRY, born in about 1843.

    ii.   JOSEPHINE TERRY, born in about 1850.

582. HAMPTON F.[6] HOWELL (Merritt[5], Merritt[4]), the son of Merritt[5] and Eleanor (Luce) Howell, was born on 10 Sep 1812 {3179}.

Hampton F. Howell married Maria Raynor {3180}, who was born on 23 Mch 1822 {3181}.

At a Special Town Meeting held at the Court House in Riverhead on 27 Aug 1862, Hampton F. Howell voted in favor of paying a $125 bounty to volunteers for the service of the United States {3182}.

On 25 June 1870, Hampton Howell, 57, retired farmer, with real property worth $3000, and personal property worth $6000, was enumerated as the head of a household consisting of himself, his wife, Maria, 47, Philetus Foster, 46, seaman, his wife, Sarah, 37, and their daughter, Dina, 4, residing in the Town of Riverhead, Suffolk County, New York, in the Ninth Census of the United States {3183}.

Hampton F. Howell died on 17 Jly 1885, and is buried in the Plot 1 at the Riverhead Cemetery {3184}.

Maria Howell died on 1 Feb 1888, and is buried beside her husband at Riverhead {3185}.

Hampton F. and Maria (Raynor) Howell did not have any children {3186}.

3177. Id.
3178. U.S. Census, Thompson, Geauga County, Ohio, 1860, Dwelling House 388, Family Number 362, Page 630.
3179. Mallmann, op. cit., 214.
3180. Id.
3181. Gravestone, Riverhead Cemetery.
3182. RTR, Liber B, 254-256, Liber C, 2-3; (I, 433-434, 550-551).
3183. U.S. Census, Riverhead, Suffolk County, NY, 1850, Dwelling House 215, Family Number 237, Page 76.
3184. Gravestone, Riverhead Cemetery.
3185. Id.
3186. Mallmann, op. cit., 214.

583. BETSEY[6] HOWELL (Merritt[5], Merritt[4]), the daughter of Merritt[5] and Eleanor (Luce) Howell, was born on 1 May 1814 {3187}.

Betsey Howell married J. Rock Smith, who was born on 9 Apr 1809, the son of John and Sarah (Corwin) Smith {3188}.

On 12 Sep 1850, John R. Smith, 41, farmer, with real property worth $1500, was enumerated as the head of a family consisting of himself, his wife, Betsey, 36, and their children, Sarah, 17, Merritt, 14, Amelia A., 11, John H., 8, Floyd E., 2, and Gertrude I., 2, and a servant, Adelia, 19, residing in the Town of Riverhead, Suffolk County, New York, in the Seventh Census of the United States {3189}.

On 16 Jly 1870, John R. Smith, 61, farmer, with real estate worth $3,000, and personal property worth $500, was enumerated as the head of a family consisting of himself, his wife, Betsey, 56, and their son, Floyd, 25, residing in the Town of Riverhead, Suffolk County, New York, in the Ninth Census of the United States {3190}.

J. Rock Smith died on 19 Apr 1881 {3191}.

J. Rock and Betsey (Howell) Smith were the parents of six children {3192}.

    i.   SARAH C. SMITH, born in 1833, married James Fordham, six children.

    ii.   MERRITT H. SMITH, born in 1835, married Ellen Robbins, one daughter, Jennie R., who married Hermon H. Wells.

    iii.   AMELIA A. SMITH, born in 1838, married Albert Norton, four children.

    iv.   JOHN H. SMITH, born in 1840, died in 1864.

    v.   FLOYD E. SMITH, born in 1842, married Emily Jason on 26 Sep 1896.

    vi.   GERTRUDE I. SMITH, married Ardin Wicks, three children.

584. SALLY[6] HOWELL (Merritt[5], Merritt[4]), the daughter of Meritt[5] and Eleanor (Luce) Howell, was born on 26 Sep 1816 {3193}.

3187. Id., 227.
3188. Id.
3189. U.S. Census, Riverhead, Suffolk County, NY, 1850, Dwelling House 353, Family Number 388, Page 272.
3190. Id., 1870, Dwelling House 493, Family Number 536, Page 96.
3191. Mallmann, op. cit.
3192. Id.
3193. Id., 214.

Sally Howell married (1) Sells Hallock Edwards, and (2) David Horton {3194}.

Sells Hallock Edwards, 36, farmer, of Baiting Hollow, died on 5 May 1848 {3195}.

On 16 Jly 1870, David Horton, 53, farmer, with real estate worth $1500, and personal property worth $360, was enumerated as the head of a family consisting of himself, his wife, Sarah, 53, and a daughter, Rosa J., 14, residing in the Town of Riverhead, Suffolk County, New York, in the Ninth Census of the United States {3196}.

Hallock and Sally (Howell) Edwards were the parents of four children {3197}, one of whom was born on 2 Oct 1847 {3198}.

    i.   ELBERT H. EDWARDS, born in about 1844.

    ii.   JAMES H. EDWARDS.

    iii.   CHANCY AEZEL EDWARDS, born on 2 Oct 1847, married [Mary] Agnes Warner on 14 Dec 1870, four children, died on 6 Oct 1898 of complications from tuberculosis. Agnes Warner was born on 18 Dec 1851, and died on 15 Jan 1922 at Brooklyn. She and her husband are buried in the Cedar Hill Cemetery at Port Jefferson {3199}.

    iv.   SAREPTA EDWARDS.

David Horton was the father of at least one daughter.

    i.   ROSA J. HORTON, born in about 1856.

585. HARRIET B.[6] HOWELL (Merritt[5], Merritt[4]), the daughter of Merritt[5] and Eleanor (Luce) Howell, was born on 28 May 1819 {3200}.

On the morning of 20 Oct 1841, Harriet B. Howell was married to Herman Hallock, of Rocky Point, by the Rev. Charles C. Knowles {3201}.

On 23 Jly 1850, Herman Hallock, 38, farmer, with real property worth $6000, was enumerated as the head of a household consisting of himself, his wife, Harriet H., 31, their daughter, Roselean, 2, and a servant, David Jack, 12, residing in the Town of Brookhaven, Suffolk County, New York, in the Seventh

3194. Id.
3195. Riverhead Deaths, RTR; (I, 725); See also THE REGISTER, SCHS, XX, #3, 72 (Winter 1994).
3196. U.S. Census, Riverhead, Suffolk County, NY, 1870, Dwelling House 498, Family Number 541, Page 96.
3197. Suffolk County Wills, Liber 6, 309-320; Suffolk County Estates, File #4860.
3198. Riverhead Births, RTR, (I, 717); See also, THE REGISTER, SCHS, XX, #1, 20 (Summer 1994).
3199. Wells, op. cit., 77.
3200. Mallmann, op. cit., 214.
3201. REPUBLICAN WATCHMAN, 30 Oct 1841.

Census of the United States {3202}.

Herman and Harriet (Howell) Hallock were the parents of at least one child.

    i.   ROSALINE HALLOCK, born on 4 Oct 1847 {3203}.

587. FRANCES M.[6] HOWELL (Merritt[5], Merritt[4]), the daughter of Merritt[5] and Eleanor (Luce) Howell, was born on 25 Feb 1826 {3204}.

On 13 Nov 1844, Frances M. Howell married Sylvester Hallock, who was born on 27 Feb 1816, the son of Samuel B. and Betsey Hallock, of Rocky Point {3205}.

On 4 Jly 1870, Sylvester Hallock, 52, farmer, with real property worth $15,000, and personal property worth $2000, was enumerated as the head of a family consisting of himself, his wife, Mary F., 41, and their children, Josephine, 17, Meritt S., 12, and Samuel H., 12, residing at Wading River in the Town of Riverhead, Suffolk County, New York, in the Ninth Census of the United States {3206}.

Sylvester and Frances M. (Howell) Hallock were the parents of four children {3207}.

    i.   ANNA ADELIA HALLOCK, born on 5 Nov 1846, married Samuel Hulse, who was born on 13 Dec 1846 (sic) and died on 9 Apr 1907, one child, died on 8 Dec 1922 {3208}.

    ii.   JOSEPHINE HALLOCK, born on 17 Feb 1853 at Rocky Point, married Charles Edward Woodhull, the son of Rev. John Woodhull, on 28 Jly 1891, one child, died on 19 Nov 1915 {3209}.

    iii.   SAMUEL HEATHCOTE HALLOCK, born on 20 Jan 1858.

    iv.   MERRITT SYLVESTER HALLOCK, born on 20 Jan 1858, married Annie A. Hallock, the daughter of Daniel Wells and Fannie J. (Wells) Hallock {3210}, on 19 Nov 1879, two

3202. U.S. Census, Brookhaven, Suffolk County, NY, 1850, Dwelling House 123, Family Number 130, Page 153.
3203. BROOKHAVEN BIRTHS, from THE REGISTER, SCHS, XVII, 14 (Summer 1991-Spring 1992).
3204. Mallmann, op. cit., 214.
3205. Lucius H. Hallock, op. cit., 598.
3206. U.S. Census, Riverhead, Suffolk County, NY, 1870, Dwelling House 685, Family Number 542, Page 342.
3207. Lucius H. Hallock, op. cit., 598.
3208. Id., 174.
3209. Id., 436.
3210. Id., 613.

children. She was born on 19 Nov 1860, and died on 5 Dec 1926 {3211}.

3. Benjamin⁵, Merritt⁴

589. ALFRED L.⁶ HOWELL (Benjamin⁵, Merritt⁴), the son of Benjamin⁵ and Huldah (Hallock) Howell, was born in about 1810.

On 20 Dec 1836, Alfred Howell, of Riverhead, was married to Ann W. Young, the youngest daughter of Luther and Abigail (Wells) Young {3212}, by her brother, Rev. Christopher Young, at his residence at Wading River {3213}.

On 17 Sep 1850, Alfred L. Howell, 40, farmer, with real property worth $1000, was enumerated as the head of a family consisting of himself and his wife, Anna, 36, residing in the same house in Riverhead as his parents {3214}.

On 23 Jly 1870, Alfred Howell, 60, retired farmer, with real property worth $1200, and personal property worth $200, was enumerated as the head of a family consisting of himself and his wife, Anna, 60, residing in the Town of Riverhead, Suffolk County, New York, in the Ninth Census of the United States {3215}. Samuel Gordon, 30, farm laborer, his wife, Susan, 25, and their daughter, Jane, 4, were living in the same house {3216}.

Ann W. Howell died on 3 Nov 1895, and is buried at Aquebogue {3217}.

591. JULIETTE⁶ HOWELL (Benjamin⁵, Merritt⁴), the daughter of Benjamin⁵ and Huldah (Hallock) Howell, was born in about 1816.

On 8 Nov 1835, Juliette Howell married Moses Benjamin, who was born on 6 Feb 1812, the son of David and Deziah (Terry) Benjamin {3218}.

On 17 Sep 1850, Moses Benjamin, 38, farmer, having real property worth $1500, was enumerated as the head of a family consisting of himself, his wife, Julietta, 34, and their children, Horace, 13, Phebe J., 11, Alonzo, 8, Angeline, 5, all of whom had attended school, and David, 1, residing in the Town of Riverhead,

---

3211. Id., 501.
3212. Gravestone, Aquebogue Cemetery.
3213. Christopher Young's Marriage Record, 12.
3214. U.S. Census, Riverhead, Suffolk County, NY, 1850, Dwelling House 461, Family Number 505, Page 278.
3215. Id., 1870, Dwelling House 594, Family Number 643, Page 103.
3216. Id., Family Number 644, Page 103.
3217. Gravestone, Aquebogue Cemetery.
3218. Bicha and Brown, op. cit., 779.

Suffolk County, New York, in the Seventh Census of the United States {3219}.

Juliette Benjamin died on 7 Nov 1885, at the age of 69 years, 8 months, and 22 days, and is buried in the Aquebogue Cemetery {3220}.

Deacon Moses Benjamin died on 13 Mch 1898, at the age of 86 years, 1 month, and 7 days, and is buried beside his wife at Aquebogue {3221}.

Moses and Juliette (Howell) Benjamin were the parents of eight children {3222}.

i.   JOSEPH HOWELL BENJAMIN.

ii. HORACE H. BENJAMIN, born on 13 Sep 1837, married (1) Sarah Richards, six children. She was born on 9 Apr 1838, and died on 13 Apr 1891. He married (2) Frances ---- , who was born in 1851 and died on 22 Dec 1937. He died on 27 Jan 1914, and is buried beside his first wife in the Riverhead Cemetery {3223}.

iii. PHEBE JANE BENJAMIN, born on 24 May 1840, married Charles W. Hallock on 24 Dec 1859, seven children, died in 1925, and is buried at Riverhead. He was born in 1838 and died in 1922.

iv. ALONZO HALLOCK BENJAMIN, born on 15 Jly 1842, married Esther Jemima Jennings on 18 Dec 1859, two children, died on 15 Aug 1916. His wife, whose name is recorded as Sarah Melvina Benjamin, was born in 1848 and died on 16 Mch 1920 {3224}.

v.   ANGELINE, "LENA", AUGUSTA BENJAMIN, born on 4 Mch 1845, married John Corwin Young in 1870, two children, died in 1880.

vi. DAVID H. BENJAMIN, born 8 June 1849, married Emma C. White on 11 May 1872, died on 20 May 1895.

vii. MARY ESTELLE BENJAMIN, born on 23 Aug 1853, married John D. Briggs, two children.

3219. U.S. Census, Riverhead, Suffolk County, NY, 1850, Dwelling House 468, Family Number 513, Page 279.
3220. Bicha and Brown, op. cit.
3221. Id.
3222. Id.
3223. Id., 852.
3224. Id., 852, 853.

viii. FANNIE BENJAMIN, married Mr. Terry, five children.

IV. Descendants of Isaac [2] Howell.

A. Isaac [3], Isaac [2], Richard [1].

1. Isaac [5], Isaac [4]

593. SAMUEL[6] HOWELL (Isaac[5], Isaac[4]), the son of Isaac[5] and Bathsheba (Holland) Howell, was born on 30 Apr 1797 {3225}, at Franklin, New York {3226}.

On 1 Oct 1823, Samuel Howell married Elizabeth, "Betsey", Delia Olmsted at East Meredith, New York {3227}. She was born on 7 Dec 1801, the daughter of Lewis and Sarah (Bennett) Olmstead {3228}.

Samuel Howell died on 9 Dec 1874 at Windsor, New York {3229}, and is buried in the Spring Forest Cemetery at Binghamton, New York {3230}.

Elizabeth Delia Howell died on 14 Feb 1898, and is buried beside her husband {3231}.

Samuel and Delia (Olmsted) Howell were the parents of seven children {3232}.

+ 986. i. AMANDA[7] HOWELL, born on 23 Aug 1824.

+ 987. ii. GEORGE[7] HOWELL, born on 30 Oct 1825.

+ 988. iii. DELIA[7] HOWELL, born on 9 May 1829.

+ 989. iv. EMMA[7] HOWELL, born on 7 Dec 1830.

+ 990. v. HOLLAND S.[7] HOWELL, born on 11 Sep 1832.

+ 991. vi. ISAAC N.[7] HOWELL, born on 11 Feb 1834.

+ 992. vii. MARY[7] HOWELL, born on 11 May 1838.

3225. James Barnaby Howell, op. cit., 5.
3226. Hawkes, op. cit., 19.
3227. James Barnaby Howell, op. cit., 9.
3228. Hawkes, op. cit.
3229. James Barnaby Howell, op. cit., 4.
3230. Hawkes, op. cit.
3231. Id.
3232. James Barnaby Howell, op. cit., 9.

594. ABIGAIL⁶ HOWELL (Isaac⁵, Isaac⁴), the daughter of Isaac⁵ and Bathsheba (Holland) Howell, was born on 19 Mch 1799 {3233}.

On 13 Jan 1819, Abigail Howell married Allis Brown at Franklin, New York, who was born on 19 Mch 1797 {3234}.

Abigail Brown died on 2 Sep 1885 {3235}.

Allis and Abigail (Howell) Brown were the parents of eleven children {3236}.

    i.   IVORY HOLLAND BROWN, born on 7 Mch 1820.

    ii.   MARTHA BROWN, born on 30 Nov 1821.

    iii.   HENRY A. BROWN, born on 18 Feb 1823, died on 5 Oct 1857.

    iv.   JONAS H. BROWN, born on 11 Feb 1825, died on 5 Apr 1825.

    v.   MARY BROWN, born on 27 Aug 1826, died on 3 May 1849.

    vi.   JONAS H. BROWN, born on 27 June 1828, died on 28 June 1858.

    vii.   AMELIA A. BROWN, born on 15 Nov 1830.

    viii.   ISAAC H. BROWN, born on 29 June 1833, died on 16 Aug 1839.

    ix.   ALLIS EUGENE BROWN, born on 2 Nov 1835, died on 29 Mch 1862.

    x.   FREDERICK WM. BROWN, born on 10 Sep 1838.

    xi.   ISAAC H. BROWN, born on 9 Apr 1840, died on 11 Sep 1850.

596. CYNTHIA⁶ HOWELL (Isaac⁵, Isaac⁴), the daughter of Isaac⁵ and Bathsheba (Holland) Howell, was born on 21 Apr 1803 {3237}.

Cynthia Howell married Dewey Case {3238}.

Cynthia Case died in 1856 {3239}.

3233. Id., 5.
3234. Id., 9.
3235. Id., 5.
3236. Id., 9.
3237. Id., 5.
3238. Id., 9.
3239. Id., 5.

Dewey and Cynthia (Howell) Case were the parents of two children {3240}.

    i.   ADALINE CASE, born in 1824.

    ii.   CHESTER CASE, born in 1826.

597. ISAAC[6] HOWELL (Isaac[5], Isaac[4]), the son of Isaac[5] and Bathsheba (Holland) Howell, was born on 20 Feb 1805 {3241}.

    Isaac Howell married Deborah Ketchum {3242}.

    Isaac Howell died in 1884 {3243}, at Grand Island, California {3244}.

    Isaac and Deborah (Ketchum) Howell were the parents of three children {3245}.

993.   i.   EDWIN[7] HOWELL.

994.   ii.   MYRON[7] HOWELL.

995.   iii.   DAUGHTER[7].

599. EDWIN[6] HOWELL (Isaac[5], Isaac[4]), the son of Isaac[5] and Bathsheba (Holland) Howell, was born on 20 Aug 1809 {3246}.

    On 11 Jan 1838, Edwin Howell married Maria Rockwell at New Lisbon, New York. She was born on 18 Feb 1817 {3247}.

    Maria Howell died on 1 Jan 1879 {3248}.

    Edwin Howell died on 22 Feb 1891 {3249}, at East 82nd Street, New York, N.Y. {3250}.

    Edwin and Maria (Rockwell) Howell were the parents of four children {3251}.

996.   i.   HARRIET E.[7] HOWELL, born on 12 Nov 1838, died on 12 Oct 1850.

997.   ii.   ELLEN L.[7] HOWELL, born on 19 Oct 1840, died on 20 Jan

---

3240. Id., 10.
3241. Id., 5.
3242. Id., 10.
3243. Id., 5.
3244. Hawkes, op. cit., 18.
3245. James Barnaby Howell, op. cit., 10.
3246. Id., 5.
3247. Id., 10.
3248. Id.
3249. Id., 5.
3250. Hawkes, op. cit., 18.
3251. James Barnaby Howell, op. cit., 10.

1841.

998. iii. HELOTUS R.[7] HOWELL, born on 10 Aug 1843, died on 30 Aug 1863.

999. iv. ADA L.[7] HOWELL, born on 2 Jly 1850.

600. ALTHEA[6] HOWELL (Isaac[5], Isaac[4]), the daughter of Isaac[5] and Bathsheba (Holland) Howell, was born on 8 Mch 1812 {3252}.

On 30 Nov 1840, Althea Howell married Wm. H. Johnson, who was born on 19 Apr 1806 {3253}.

Wm. H. Johnson died on 19 May 1889 {3254}.

Althea Johnson died on 30 Aug 1898 {3255}.

Wm. H. and Althea (Howell) Johnson were the parents of two children {3256}.

   i.   NELLIE E. JOHNSON, born on 10 Nov 1844, died in 1900.

   ii. CLARENCE JOHNSON, born on 25 Dec 1850, died on 10 Feb 1856.

601. JULIA[6] HOWELL (Isaac[5], Isaac[4]), the daughter of Isaac[5] and Bathsheba (Holland) Howell, was born on 15 Mch 1814 {3257}.

Julia Howell married Hewit Fitch {3258}.

On 14 Oct 1850, Hewit Fitch, 45, clergyman, was enumerated as the head of a household consisting of himself, his wife, Julia, 24 (sic), their children, Fayette, 16, Henry, 14, Harriet, 13, Edgar, 9, Isaac, 6, and Linus, 1, and Mary Ann Harrington, 16, residing in the Town of New Lisbon, Otsego County, New York, in the Seventh Census of the United States {3259}.

Julia Fitch died on 9 Mch 1885 {3260}.

Hewit and Julia (Howell) Fitch were the parents of at least seven children {3261}.

   i.   FAYETTE FINCH, born in about 1834.

3252. Id., 5.
3253. Id., 10.
3254. Id.
3255. Id., 5.
3256. Id., 10.
3257. Id., 5.
3258. Id., 10.
3259. U.S. Census, New Lisbon, Otsego County, NY, 1850, Dwelling House 1473, Family Number 1599, Page 299.
3260. James Barnaby Howell, op. cit., 5.
3261. Id., 10.

ii.   HENRY FITCH, born in about 1836.

iii.   HARRIET FITCH, born in about 1837.

iv.   DAVID FITCH.

v.   EDGAR FITCH, born in about 1841.

vi.   ISAAC FITCH, born in about 1843.

vii.   LINUS FITCH, born in about 1849.

603. MARIA E.^{6} HOWELL (Isaac^5, Isaac^4), the daughter of Isaac^5 and Bathsheba (Holland) Howell, was born on 19 Jan 1820 {3262}.

Maria E. Howell married E. Orlando Wheelock {3263}, who was born on 8 Oct 1817, the son of Luther and Nancy (St. John) Wheelock {3264}.

E. Orlando Wheelock died on 21 Apr 1891 {3265}.

Maria Wheelock died on 10 Feb 1903 {3266}.

E. Orlando and Maria E. (Howell) Wheelock were the parents of seven children {3267}.

i.   EDWIN WHEELOCK, born on 20 Dec 1842, died on 22 Apr 1845.

ii.   JULIA M. WHEELOCK, born on 29 Nov 1844.

iii.   HARRIET E. WHEELOCK, born on 16 Aug 1849, died on 22 Mch 1901.

iv.   EUGENE O. WHEELOCK, born on 18 Sep 1851, died on 22 June 1921.

v.   CARRIE A. WHEELOCK, born on 2 Aug 1856, died on 19 May 1858.

vi.   HENRY H. WHEELOCK, born on 26 Dec 1858.

vii.   CLARENCE WHEELOCK, born on 26 Dec 1858, died on 5 Jan

3262. Id., 5.
3263. Id., 10.
3264. Id., 8.
3265. Id.
3266. Id., 5.
3267. Id., 10.

1859.

2. Abraham⁵, Isaac⁴

604. ALFRED MILTON⁶ HOWELL (Abraham⁵, Isaac⁴), the son of Abraham⁵ and
Polly (Little) Howell, was born on 28 Nov 1799 {3268}.

On 11 Mch 1830, Alfred Milton Howell married Patience Bowen, who was
born on 31 Mch 1804 {3269}.

On 13 Sep 1850, Alfred Howell, 49, farmer, having real property valued
at $1400, was enumerated as the head of a family consisting of himself, his wife,
Patience, 46, and their children, James B., 19, Maria L., 18, Harriet M., 15,
Alfred M., 12, Helen L., 8, and Nathaniel M., 5, residing in the Town of
Yorkshire, Cattaraugus County, New York, in the Seventh Census of the United
States {3270}.

Alfred M. Howell died on 25 Dec 1861, and is buried in the McKinstry
Cemetery at Delevan, New York {3271}.

Patience Howell died on 12 Jan 187? {3272}.

Alfred Milton and Patience (Bowen) Howell were the parents of nine
children {3273}.

  1000. i. JAMES BOWEN⁷ HOWELL, born on 2 Mch 1831, died of
         tuberculosis at the age of 23, and is buried in the Yorkshire
         Cemetery.

  1001. ii. MARIA LOVITIA⁷ HOWELL, born on 24 Apr 1832, married
         Arnold Bowen, died on 12 Feb 1920, while he died in Sep 1908.

  1002. iii. HANNAH LOUISA⁷ HOWELL, born on 27 Oct 1833, died on
         21 Feb 1837.

  1003. iv. HARRIET MARINDA⁷ HOWELL, born on 15 Sep 1835, died on
         1 Aug 1857.

  1004. v. MARYETTE⁷ HOWELL, born on 15 June 1837, died on 25 June
         1837.

+ 1005. vi. ALFRED MILTON⁷ HOWELL, born on 15 Sep 1838.

3268. Id., 5.
3269. Ornce, op. cit.
3270. U.S Census, Yorkshire, Cattaraugus County, NY, 1850, Dwelling House 1184, Family Number
1194, Page 456.
3271. Ornce, op. cit.
3272. Id.
3273. Duane A. Howell, per Gordon Adams.

1006. vii.   ALBERT FRANKLIN[7] HOWELL, born on 27 June 1840, served the Civil War as a First Lieutenant, died on 14 Sep 1888, and is buried in the Yorkshire Cemetery.

1007. viii. HELEN LOUISA[7] HOWELL, born on 18 Aug 1842, married Lot Holland, eight children, died on 26 Jly 1935.

+ 1008. ix. NATHANIEL MILFORD[7] HOWELL, born on 24 Oct 1844.

605. HENRY[6] HOWELL (Abraham[5], Isaac[4]), the son of Abraham[5] and Polly (Little) Howell, was born on 5 Feb 1802 {3274} at Franklin, New York {3275}.

On 24 Feb 1833, Henry Howell married Delia Wheat {3276}.

A Henry Howell, 48, farmer, and Fayette Howell, 8, were enumerated with the family of Clark Nichols in the Seventh Census of the United States on 30 Aug 1850 {3277}.

In Mch 1852, Henry Howell married (2) Sylvia Johnson {3278}, who was born on 23 Nov 1822 {3279}.

Henry Howell died on 29 Nov 1886, and is buried in the Maple Grove Cemetery at Delevan {3280}.

Sylvia Howell died on 21 Apr 1894 {3281}.

Henry Howell was the father of six children {3282}.

1009. i.   ANGELINE[7] HOWELL, born in about 1839.

1010. ii.   HERSEBA[7] HOWELL.

1011. iii. ABRAHAM[7] HOWELL.

1012. iv.   CAREY J.[7] HOWELL.

1013. v.   PAMELIA[7] HOWELL.

1014. vi.   MARTHA[7] HOWELL.

3274. Id., 5.
3275. Ornce, op. cit.
3276. Id.
3277. U.S. Census, Sardinia, Erie County, NY, 1850, Dwelling House 1559, Family Number 1601, Page 105.
3278. Ornce, op. cit.
3279. Gravestone, Delevan Village Cemetery.
3280. Ornce, op. cit., Gertrude A. Barber, CATTARAUGUS COUNTY, N.Y., CEMETERIES.
3281. Barber, CATTARAUGUS COUNTY, N.Y., CEMETERIES.
3282. James Barnaby Howell, op. cit., 11.

606. NOAH BUCKLEY[6] HOWELL (Abraham[5], Isaac[4]), the son of Abraham[5] and Polly (Little) Howell, was born on 22 Oct 1803 {3283}.

Noah Buckley Howell married Sarah Johnson {3284}.

Buckley and Sarah (Johnson) Howell were the parents of two children {3285}.

    1015   i.   AMBROSIA[7] HOWELL.

    1016. ii.   MARY[7] HOWELL.

607. NANCY[6] HOWELL (Abraham[5], Isaac[4]), the daughter of Abraham[5] and Polly (Little) Howell, was born on 25 Jan 1806 {3286}.

Nancy Howell married Clark Nichols at Franklin. He was born in Rhode Island on 15 Jan 1797 {3287}.

On 30 Aug 1850, Clark Nichols, 53, farmer, with real property valued at $5500, was enumerated as the head of a family consisting of himself, his wife, Nancy, 44, and their children, Henry, 21, farmer, Caroline, 17, Elmira, 15, George, 12, Olive, 11, Elbert, 8, and Alice, 3, residing in the Town of Sardinia, Erie County, New York. Also living in the dwelling house were her brother, Henry Howell, 48, and Fayette Howell, 8 {3288}.

Nancy Nichols died on 23 Apr 1879 {3289}.

Clark and Nancy (Howell) Nichols were the parents of eight children {3290}.

      i.   LUTHER NICHOLS, born on 21 Apr 1827.

     ii.   HENRY NICHOLS, born on 26 Dec 1828.

    iii.   CAROLINE NICHOLS, born on 17 Nov 1833.

    iv.   ELMINA NICHOLS, born on 5 Jly 1835.

     v.   GEORGE NICHOLS, born in about 1838.

    vi.   OLIVE NICHOLS, born on 6 Feb 1840.

   vii. ELBERT NICHOLS, born in about 1842.

3283. Id., 5.
3284. Ornce, op. cit.
3285. James Barnaby Howell, op. cit., 11.
3286. Id., 5.
3287. Id., 11.
3288. U.S. Census, Sardinia, Erie County, NY, 1850, Dwelling House 1559, Family Number 1601, Page 105.
3289. James Barnaby Howell, op. cit., 5.
3290. Id., 11.

viii.   ALICE NICHOLS, born on 31 Jan 1847.

608. RALPH[6] HOWELL (Abraham[5], Isaac[4]), the son of Abraham[5] and Polly (Little) Howell, was born on 8 Feb 1808 {3291}.

Ralph Howell married Clarisa Kingsley at Dunkirk {3292}.

On 30 Aug 1850, Ralph L. Howell, 42, forwarding merchant, was enumerated as the head of a household consisting of himself, his wife, Clarisa, 36, their daughters, Mary E., 14, and Eliza, 11, and Jacob Kingsley, 75, Diathey Kingsley, 66, and Helen McGonquer, 16, residing in the Town of Pomfret, Chatauqua County, New York, in the Seventh Census of the United States {3293}.

Ralph L. Howell died on 25 Oct 1880, and is buried at Lockport, New York {3294}.

Ralph and Clarisa (Kingsley) Howell were the parents of two children {3295}.

1017. i.   MARY[7] HOWELL, born on 6 Aug 1836.

1018. ii.   ELOISE[7] HOWELL, born on 15 Sep 1839.

609. ABRAHAM PAYNE[6] HOWELL (Abraham[5], Isaac[4]), the son of Abraham[5] and Polly (Little) Howell, was born on 19 Feb 1810 {3296}.

Abraham Payne Howell died on 7 Jan 1853 {3297}.

Abraham Payne Howell was the father of two children {3298}.

1019. i.   CAREY J.[7] HOWELL.

1020. ii.   SARAH[7] HOWELL.

610. FRANCES[6] HOWELL (Abraham[5], Isaac[4]), the daughter of Abraham[5] and Sally (Fisk) Howell, was born on 9 Feb 1813 {3299}.

On 24 Apr 1846 {3300}, Frances Howell married George W. Horton {3301}.

3291. Id., 5.
3292. Id., 11.
3293. U.S. Census, Pomfret, Chatauqua County, NY, 1850, Dwelling House 121, Family Number 122, Page 194.
3294. James Barnaby Howell, op. cit., 5.
3295. Id., 11.
3296. Id., 5.
3297. Id.
3298. Id., 5, 12.
3299. Id., 5.
3300. Ornce, op. cit.
3301. James Barnaby Howell, op. cit., 12.

Frances Horton died after 1886, and is buried at Newfane, New York {3302}.

George W. and Frances (Howell) Horton were the parents of three children {3303}.

    i.   FRANKLIN HORTON.

    ii.   SARAH HORTON.

    iii.   CHARLES HORTON.

611. BETSEY[6] HOWELL (Abraham[5], Isaac[4]), the daughter of Abraham[5] and Sally (Fisk) Howell, was born on 13 Mch 1814 {3304}.

On 6 Nov 1831, Betsey Howell married Ira Wheeler, who was born on 26 Sep 1806 {3305}.

Ira Wheeler died in 1843 {3306}.

In June 1847, Betsey (Howell) Wheeler married Wm. R. Forsaith {3307}.

Betsey (Howell) Wheeler Forsaith died on 18 Jly 1879 {3308}.

Ira and Betsey (Howell) Wheeler were the parents of four children {3309}.

    i.   MELISA WHEELER, born on 18 Nov 1832, died in Mch 1879.

    ii.   LOUISA WHEELER, born in Apr 1834.

    iii.   ANNETTE WHEELER, born on 11 Jly 1838, died in 1866.

    iv.   MILTON WHEELER, born on 29 Jan 1840, died on 1 Jan 1924.

Wm. R. and Betsey (Howell) Wheeler Forsaith were the parents of six children {3310}.

    v.   WARREN FORSAITH, born on 18 Mch 1849.

    vi.   CLINTON FORSAITH, born on 10 Oct 1850.

    vii.   FRANK FORSAITH, born on 17 Oct 1852, died in 1900.

3302. Id., 5.
3303. Id., 12.
3304. Id., 5.
3305. Id., 12.
3306. Id.
3307. Id.
3308. Id., 5.
3309. Id.
3310. Id.

viii.   EUGENE FORSAITH, born on 7 Mch 1855.

ix.   MARY FORSAITH, born on 25 Dec 1857.

x.   WILLIE FORSAITH, born on 31 Oct 1859.

612. POLLY[6] HOWELL (Abraham[5], Isaac[4]), the daughter of Abraham[5] and Sally (Fisk) Howell {3311}, was born on 29 Jly 1816 at Franklin, New York {3312}.

On 1 June 1842, Polly Howell married Alonzo Cook {3313}.

On 18 Sep 1850, Alonzo H. Cook, 34, farmer, having real property valued at $1400, was enumerated as the head of a household consisting of himself, his wife, Polly, 33, their children, Philitas, 7, Sally, 2, and Melissa, 1, and her niece, Angeline Howell, 11, residing in the Town of Yorkshire, Cattaraugus County, New York, in the Seventh Census of the United States {3314}.

Polly Cook died on 20 Sep 1895, and is buried in the Maple Grove Cemetery at Delevan, New York {3315}.

Alonzo and Polly (Howell) Cook were the parents of six children {3316}.

i.   PHILETUS COOK, born on 26 Mch 1842.

ii.   MARIA COOK, born on 10 Sep 1845.

iii.   AURELIA COOK, born on 28 May 1847.

iv.   BELA H. COOK, born on 12 Feb 1849.

v.   MARY COOK, born on 31 Aug 1855.

vi.   SARAH COOK, born on 31 Aug 1855.

613. SAMUEL HAWKINS[6] HOWELL (Abraham[5], Isaac[4]), the son of Abraham[5] and Sally (Fisk) Howell {3317}, was born on 25 Apr 1818 {3318}.

In 1845, Samuel Hawkins Howell married (1) Harriet Chapen, who was

3311. Id., 6.
3312. Ornce, op. cit.
3313. Id.
3314. U.S. Census, Yorkshire, Cattaraugus County, NY, 1850, Dwelling House 1306, Family Number 1317, Page 465.
3315. Ornce, op. cit.
3316. James Barnaby Howell, op. cit., 12.
3317. Id., 6.
3318. Ornce, op. cit.

born on 9 May 1825 {3319}.

On 18 Sep 1850, Samuel H. Howell, 32, farmer, with real property worth $1,300, was enumerated as the head of a family consisting of himself, his wife, Harriet, 25, their daughter, Ercilia, 4, and his parents, Abram, 79, and Sally, 65, residing in the Town of Yorkshire, Cattaraugus County, New York, in the Seventh Census of the United States {3320}.

Harriet Howell died on 23 Aug 1853, at the age of 28 years, 3 months, and 14 days, and is buried in the Delevan Village Cemetery {3321}, now the Maple Grove Cemetery {3322}.

On 6 June 1856, Samuel Hawkins Howell married Eveline Meech, who was born at Arcade, New York, on 13 Jan 1815, the daughter of Silas and Lydia (Parker) Meech {3323}.

Eveline Howell died on 6 Dec 1893 at Delevan, New York {3324}, and is buried in the Delevan Village Cemetery {3325}.

Samuel Hawkins Howell died on 16 Apr 1906, and is buried in the Maple Grove Cemetery at Delevan {3326}.

Samuel Hawkins and Harriet (Chapen) Howell were the parents of one son {3327}.

1021. i. JOSEPH[7] HOWELL, born on 21 Dec 1848.

Samuel Hawkins and Eveline (Meech) Howell were the parents of three children {3328}.

1022. ii. HARRIET ELLEN[7] HOWELL, born on 26 Dec 1856 at Delevan, died on 5 Jan 1942, and is buried in the Maple Grove Cemetery.

1023. iii. MARY AMNA[7] HOWELL, born on 14 Jan 1859 at Delevan, died on 6 Feb 1919, and is buried in the Maple Grove Cemetery {3329}.

+ 1024. iv. RALPH MILLARD[7] HOWELL, born on 8 Dec 1860.

614. URIAH FLYNT[6] HOWELL (Abraham[5], Isaac[4]), the son of Abraham[5] and

3319. Id.
3320. U.S. Census, Yorkshire, Cattaraugus County, NY, 1850, Dwelling House 1308, Family Number 1379, Page 465.
3321. Barber, CATTARAUGUS COUNTY, N.Y., CEMETERIES.
3322. Ornce, op. cit.
3323. Id.
3324. Id.
3325. Barber, op. cit.
3326. Ornce, op. cit.
3327. Id.
3328. Id.
3329. Barber, op. cit.

Sally (Fisk) Howell {3330}, was born on 25 Jan 1820 at Delevan, New York {3331}.

Uriah Flynt Howell married Nancy Smith. They apparently resided in Indiana for a time around 1854, returned to New York by 1858, then returned to Indiana by 1865, and ultimately settled in Michigan by 1870 {3332}.

On 18 Sep 1850, a Uriah Howell, 27, wagon maker, was enumerated with the household of William Cady, 26, grocer, residing in the Town of Orrion, Oakland County, Michigan, in the Seventh Census of the United States {3333}.

On 16 Dec 1861, Uriah Flynt Howell enlisted in Company K, 105th New York Infantry {3334}.

Uriah Flynt Howell, who was a member of the I.O.O.F., died on 5 Apr 1874, possibly in Michigan, but is buried in the Maple Grove Cemetery at Delevan {3335}.

Uriah F. Howell was the father of seven children {3336}.

+ 1025. i. SARAH[7] HOWELL, born in about 1853.

  1026. ii. JOSEPH[7] HOWELL.

  1027. iii. BYRON[7] HOWELL, born on 26 Apr 1855 in Indiana, never married, died on 23 June 1927 at Georgetown, Michigan.

+ 1028. iv. WALTER[7] HOWELL, born on 22 May 1858.

+ 1029. v. GEORGE[7] HOWELL, born in 1865.

  1030. vi. ALLIS[7] HOWELL, born on 19 Mch 1870 at Chickaming, Berrien County, Michigan, and died there on 22 Apr 1870.

+ 1031. vii. EVA LINA[7] HOWELL, born on 1 Aug 1871.

616. SARAH ANN[6] HOWELL (Abraham[5], Isaac[4]), the daughter of Abraham[5] and Sally (Fisk) Howell {3337}, was born on 8 Jly 1827 at Delevan, New York {3338}.

On 23 Apr 1848, Sarah Ann Howell married George W. White in

3330. James Barnaby Howell, op. cit., 6.
3331. Ornce, op. cit.
3332. Gordon Adams, Personal communication.
3333. U.S. Census, Orrion, Oakland County, MI, 1850, Dwelling House 1792, Family Number 1828, Page 137.
3334. Gordon Adams, op. cit.
3335. Ornce, op. cit., Barber, op. cit.
3336. James Barnaby Howell, op. cit., 12, 13, Adams, op. cit.
3337. James Barnaby Howell, op. cit., 6.
3338. Ornce, op. cit.

Cattaraugus County {3339}.

Sarah Ann White is buried at Omro, Wisconsin {3340}.

George W. and Sarah Ann (Howell) White were the parents of four children {3341}.

    i.   GORDICE WHITE, born on 3 Nov 1851.

    ii.   FORDICE WHITE, born on 3 Nov 1851.

    iii.   CLARA WHITE, born on 4 Nov 1853.

    iv.   ZULA WHITE, born on 23 Mch 1865.

3. Simeon [5], Isaac [4]

618. EMILY[6] HOWELL (Simeon[5], Isaac[4]), the daughter of Simeon[5] and Rhoda (McCall) Howell, was born on 2 Apr 1803 {3342}.

On 28 Sep 1823, Emily Howell married Nathan Edgerton {3343}.

Emily Edgerton died in Jly 1850 {3344}.

Nathan and Emily (Howell) Edgerton were the parents of two children {3345}.

    i.   EDWARD EDGERTON, born on 26 Apr 1829, died in Nov 1900.

    ii.   MARIA EDGERTON, born on 24 Dec 1839, died on 5 Feb 1920.

619. POLLY[6] HOWELL (Simeon[5], Isaac[4]), the daughter of Simeon[5] and Rhoda (McCall) Howell, was born on 11 Nov 1804 {3346}.

On 7 Sep 1823, Polly Howell married Hiram McCall {3347}.

On 2 Aug 1850, Hiram McCall, 50, farmer, having real property valued at $4500, was enumerated as the head of a family consisting of himself, His wife, Polly, 47, and their children, Samuel, 20, farmer, having real property valued at $1500, Mary J., 18, and Helen E., 13, residing in the Town of Lisle, Broome

---

3339. James Barnaby Howell, op. cit., 13.
3340. Ornce, op. cit.
3341. James Barnaby Howell, op. cit.
3342. Id., 6.
3343. Id., 15.
3344. Id., 6.
3345. Id., 15.
3346. Id., 6.
3347. Id., 15.

County, New York, in the Seventh Census of the United States {3348}.

Polly McCall died on 14 June 1888 {3349}.

Hiram and Polly (Howell) McCall were the parents of four children {3350}.

    i.   SIMEON McCALL, born on 28 June 1824, died in 1882.

    ii.   SAMUEL McCALL, born on 28 Jan 1830, died on 20 May 1862.

    iii.   MARY JANE McCALL, born on 20 Nov 1832.

    iv.   HELEN E. McCALL, born on 3 Apr 1837.

620. DANIEL[6] HOWELL (Simeon[5], Isaac[4]), the son of Simeon[5] and Rhoda (McCall) Howell, was born on 26 Oct 1807 {3351}.

On 21 Sep 1828, Daniel Howell married Elizabeth Jones {3352}.

Daniel Howell died on 2 Dec 1890 {3353}.

Daniel and Elizabeth (Jones) Howell had no children {3354}.

621. SUSAN[6] HOWELL (Simeon[5], Isaac[4]), the daughter of Simeon[5] and Rhoda (McCall) Howell, was born on 30 Nov 1809 {3355}.

In 1842, Susan Howell married Alexander McDowell {3356}.

On 7 Aug 1850, Alexander McDowell, 31, lawyer, having real property worth $700, and his wife, Susan, 35, were enumerated as a family residing in the Town of Lisle, Broome County, New York, in the Seventh Census of the United States {3357}.

Susan McDowell died in Dec 1882 {3358}.

Alexander and Susan (Howell) McDowell had no children {3359}.

622. CLARISA[6] HOWELL (Simeon[5], Isaac[4]), the daughter of Simeon[5] and Rhoda

3348. U.S. Census, Lisle, Broome County, NY, 1850, Dwelling House 677, Family Number 706, Page 276.
3349. James Barnaby Howell, op. cit, 6.
3350. Id., 15.
3351. Id., 6.
3352. Id., 15.
3353. Id., 6.
3354. Id., 15.
3355. Id., 6.
3356. Id., 15.
3357. U.S. Census, Lisle, Broome County, NY, 1850, Dwelling House 852, Family Number 883, Page 285.
3358. James Barnaby Howell, op. cit., 6.
3359. Id., 15.

(McCall) Howell, was born on 5 Apr 1814 {3360}.

On 3 Nov 1839, Clarisa Howell married Fosket M. Putney {3361}.

Clarisa Putney died on 12 Mch 1855 {3362}.

Fosket M. Putney died in 1887 {3363}.

Fosket M. and Clarisa (Howell) Putney were the parents of one son {3364}.

    i.   FRANK HOWELL PUTNEY.

624. JANE[6] HOWELL (Simeon[5], Isaac[4]), the daughter of Simeon[5] and Rhoda (McCall) Howell, was born on 1 Jan 1818 {3365}.

On 27 Oct 1837, Jane Howell married Henry Lockwood {3366}.

Henry and Jane (Howell) Lockwood were the parents of three children {3367}.

    i.   BYRON LOCKWOOD.

    ii.   HENRY LOCKWOOD.

    iii.   MORTIMER LOCKWOOD.

625. SARAH[6] HOWELL (Simeon[5], Isaac[4]), the daughter of Simeon[5] and Mary (----) Mulford Howell, was born on 27 Nov 1821 {3368}.

On 12 Sep 1843, Sarah Howell married John Townsend {3369}.

Col. John Townsend died on 15 Dec 1905 {3370}.

Col. John and Sarah (Howell) Townsend were the parents of three children {3371}.

    i.   CHARLES W. TOWNSEND, born on 17 Aug 1844.

    ii.   WILLIAM TOWNSEND, born on 22 Aug 1848.

    iii.   JOHN HENRY TOWNSEND, born on 3 Jan 1853.

3360. Id., 6.
3361. Id., 15.
3362. Id., 6.
3363. Id., 15.
3364. Id.
3365. Id., 6.
3366. Id., 15.
3367. Id.
3368. Id., 7.
3369. Id., 15.
3370. Id., 15.
3371. Id., 16.

628. ELIZABETH[6] HOWELL (Simeon[5], Isaac[4]), the daughter of Simeon[5] and Mary (----) Mulford Howell, was born on 17 Aug 1828 {3372}.

In Sep 1851, Elizabeth Howell married Martin Nevius Kline {3373}.

Martin Nevius and Elizabeth (Howell) Kline were the parents of two children {3374}.

     i.   MARY KLINE, born in Jly 1853.

     ii.   NELLIE KLINE, born in Jan 1861.

4. Jacob[5], Isaac[4]

629. PAMELIA[6] HOWELL (Jacob[5], Isaac[4]), the daughter of Jacob[5] and Betsey (McCall) Howell, was born on 21 Dec 1805 {3375}.

On 27 Aug 1827, Pamelia Howell married John Thompson {3376}.

Pamelia Thompson died on 13 Feb 1882 in Iowa {3377}.

John and Pamelia (Howell) Thompson were the parents of one son {3378}.

     i.   CLARK THOMPSON, born in 1828, died on 2 Dec 1882.

631. ANN ELIZA[6] HOWELL (Jacob[5], Isaac[4]), the daughter of Jacob[5] and Betsey (McCall) Howell, was born on 23 Dec 1809 {3379}.

On 5 Dec 1845, Ann Elizabeth Howell married Wm. H. Main {3380}.

Ann Eliza Main died on 17 Apr 1880 at Bloomington, Illinois {3381}.

Wm. H. Main died in June 1884 {3382}.

Wm. H. and Ann Eliza (Howell) Main had no children {3383}.

633. JAMES BARNABY[6] HOWELL (Jacob[5], Isaac[4]), the son of Jacob[5] and Betsey

3372. Id., 7.
3373. Id., 16.
3374. Id.
3375. Id., 7.
3376. Id., 16.
3377. Id., 7.
3378. Id., 16.
3379. Id., 7.
3380. Id., 16.
3381. Id., 7.
3382. Id., 16.
3383. Id.

(McCall) Howell, was born on 4 Dec 1813 {3384}.

"James B. Howell settled in Rockford (IL) November 8, 1843. His business was that of a wool-carder and cloth-dresser. When the first dam was completed, Mr. Howell operated a carding and fulling machine on the south side of State street. He erected a building in 1846, and began business in 1848, and continued there until the dam went out in 1851. He then removed his machinery to New Milford. He returned to Rockford; and some years later he formed a partnership with his brother-in-law, M. H. Regan, in the lumber business." {3385}.

On 1 May 1851, James Barnaby Howell married Louisa Dewey {3386}, the sister of M. H. Regan's first wife {3387}.

Louisa Howell died on 4 Jly 1856 {3388}.

"After Huntington & Barnes book store was destroyed by fire, Mr. Howell engaged in the book trade. His stand was the east store in Metropolitan Hall block, which for many years was occupied by B. R. Waldo, in the same line of trade. L. A. Trowbridge began business as a clerk in this store in 1861." {3389}.

In 1900, Mr. Howell was treasurer of the township school fund, a post he had held since 1888, succeeding his daughter, Ella. He was a constituent member of the State Street Baptist church {3390}.

On 1 June 1900, J.B. Howell, 86, was enumerated as the head of a family consisting of himself {3391}.

James Barnaby Howell died on 26 Mch 1901 at Rockford, Illinois {3392}.

James Barnaby and Louisa (Dewey) Howell were the parents of one daughter {3393}.

+ 1032. i.   ELLA ELIZABETH[7] HOWELL, born on 6 Mch 1852.

634. ALVAH LORENZO[6] HOWELL (Jacob[5], Isaac[4]), the son of Jacob[5] and Betsey (McCall) Howell, was born on 22 Sep 1815 {3394}.

On 13 Mch 1848, A. Lorenzo Howell married Phebe Case {3395}.

On 30 Jly 1850, A.L. Howell, 34, carpenter, with real property worth $2000, was enumerated as the head of a household consisting of himself, his wife,

3384. Id., 7.
3385. Charles Church, HISTORY OF ROCKFORD AND WINNEBAGO COUNTY, ILLINOIS, 273.
3386. James Barnaby Howell, op. cit., 16.
3387. Church, op. cit.
3388. James Barnaby Howell, op. cit., 16.
3389. Church, op. cit., 273, 274.
3390. Id., 274.
3391. U.S. Census, Rockford, Winnebago County, IL, 1900, Dwelling House 2, Family Number 3, Enumeration District 131, Sheet Number 1.
3392. James Barnaby Howell, op. cit., 7.
3393. Id., 16.
3394. Id., 7.
3395. Id., 16.

Phebe, 25, and Maria Howell, 25, all of whom were born in New York State, but were residing in Beloit, Rock County, Wisconsin, in the Seventh Census of the United States {3396}.

Alvah Lorenzo Howell died on 30 Apr 1851 at Beloit, Wisconsin {3397}.

Phebe Howell died in Dec 1881 {3398}.

A. Lorenzo and Phebe (Case) Howell did not have any children {3399}.

635. MARIANNE[6] HOWELL (Jacob[5], Isaac[4]), the daughter of Jacob[5] and Betsey (McCall) Howell, was born on 12 Jly 1817 {3400}.

On 1 June 1900, Marianne Howell, 83, was enumerated as a boarder with the family of her niece, Mrs. Ellis W. (Ella H.) Pyle {3401}.

636. ELIZABETH C.[6] HOWELL (Jacob[5], Isaac[4]), the daughter of Jacob[5] and Betsey (McCall) Howell, was born on 22 June 1819 {3402}.

On 6 Jan 1840, Elizabeth Howell married Homer Bostwick {3403}.

Homer Bostwick died on 8 Dec 1892 {3404}.

Elizabeth Bostwick died on 18 Jan 1899 at Batavia, New York {3405}.

Homer and Elizabeth C. (Howell) Bostwick were the parents of two children {3406}.

    i.   JULIA E. BOSTWICK, born on 20 Jly 1844, died on 13 Aug 1925.

    ii.   JAMES G. BOSTWICK, born on 16 Feb 1849, died on 22 Jan 1922.

637. JACOB WARREN[6] HOWELL (Jacob[5], Isaac[4]), the son of Jacob[5] and Betsey

---

3396. U.S. Census, Beloit, Rock County, WI, 1850, Dwelling House 301, Family Number 319, Page 395.
3397. James Barnaby Howell, op. cit., 7.
3398. Id., 16.
3399. Id.
3400. Id., 7.
3401. U.S. Census, Rockford, Winnebago County, IL, 1900, Dwelling House 2, Family Number 4, Enumeration District 131, Sheet Number 1.
3402. James Barnaby Howell, op. cit., 7.
3403. Id., 16.
3404. Id.
3405. Id., 7.
3406. Id., 16.

(McCall) Howell, was born on 3 Sep 1821 {3407}.

In May 1849, J. Warren Howell married Paulina Rockwell, who was born in 1829 {3408}.

Paulina Howell died on 15 Aug 1854 {3409}.

On 3 Oct 1855, J. Warren Howell married Mary C. Richardson, who was born in Jan 1836 {3410}.

Jacob W. Howell died on 21 May 1898, at "Santa Cruz & B. Newcastle, Cal." {3411}.

Mary C. Howell died on 22 Sep 1906 {3412}.

Jacob Warren and Paulina (Rockwell) Howell were the parents of two children {3413}.

1033. i.   JAMES R.[7] HOWELL, born on 24 Mch 1851, died on 6 June 1884.

1034. ii.   ALICE P.[7] HOWELL, born on 28 Aug 1853.

Jacob Warren and Mary C. (Richardson) Howell were the parents of four children {3414}.

1035. iii.   FRANK[7] HOWELL, born on 28 May 1858.

1036. iv.   MINNIE[7] HOWELL, born on 24 Mch 1860.

1037. v.   HARRY[7] HOWELL, born on 14 Feb 1869.

1038. vi.   GERTRUDE[7] HOWELL, born on 16 Nov 1874.

638. BETSEY URANIA[6] HOWELL (Jacob[5], Isaac[4]), the daughter of Jacob[5] and Betsey (McCall) Howell, was born on 1 Apr 1824 {3415}.

On 12 Dec 1850, Urania Howell married Alson L. Ames, who was born on 28 Mch 1818 {3416}.

Betsey U. Ames died on 11 Feb 1875 in Edgar County, Illinois {3417}.

Alson L. Ames died on 9 Mch 1900 {3418}.

3407. Id., 7.
3408. Id., 16.
3409. Id.
3410. Id., 17.
3411. Id., 7.
3412. Id., 17.
3413. Id.
3414. Id.
3415. Id., 7.
3416. Id., 17.
3417. Id., 7.
3418. Id., 17.

Alson L. and Betsey U. (Howell) Ames were the parents of four children {3419}.

    i.   EDGAR L. AMES, born on 7 Sep 1851, died on 31 Mch 1925.

    ii.   URA H. AMES, born on 13 Aug 1857.

    iii.   IDA L. AMES, born on 26 Nov 1862.

    iv.   HELEN E. AMES, born on 24 Mch 1866, died on 16 Jly 1895.

639. HENRY[6] HOWELL (Jacob[5], Isaac[4]), the son of Jacob[5] and Betsey (McCall) Howell, was born on 9 Feb 1829 {3420}.

On 14 Nov 1865, Henry Howell married Mary E. Strather, who was born on 5 Aug 1843 {3421}.

Henry Howell died on 22 May 1899 at Rock Rapids, Iowa {3422}.

Henry and Mary E. (Strather) Howell were the parents of three children {3423}.

1039. i.   FANNIE BELL[7] HOWELL, born on 10 Mch 1868, died on 3 Sep 1875.

1040. ii.   GRACE MARIA[7] HOWELL, born on 21 Sep 1872.

1041. iii.   HOMER THERON[7] HOWELL, born on 10 Oct 1879, died in 1917.

B. Daniel[3], Isaac[2], Richard[1]

1. Daniel[5], Silas[4]

643. CHARLES RANSOM[6] HOWELL (Daniel[5], Silas[4]), the son of Daniel[5] and Mary (Youngs) Howell, was born on 1 Jan 1807 {3424}.

On 9 Dec 1829, Charles Ransom Howell married Elizabeth, "Betsy", Corwin, who was born on 16 Sep 1810, the daughter of Jabez Corwin {3425}.

Charles R. Howell was listed as the head of a family consisting of one free

---

3419. Id.
3420. Id., 7.
3421. Id., 17.
3422. Id., 7.
3423. Id., 17.
3424. Charles Ransom Howell Family Bible.
3425. Edwin Tanjore Corwin, THE CORWIN GENEALOGY, 57.

white male of 30 and under 40 years of age, one of 5 and under 10, one free white female of 20 and under 30, and one of under 5, residing in the Town of Riverhead, Suffolk County, New York, in the Sixth Census of the United States, 1840 {3426}.

In the Seventh Census of the United States, 1850, Charles R. Howell, 43, was listed as the head of a family consisting of himself, his wife, Betsy, 40, their children, Charles H., 18, Mary, 12, Sarah, 10, and Daniel H., 2, and his father, Daniel, 71 {3427}.

On 29 Mch 1859, it was recorded that Charles R. Howell was paid $5.00 owed to him by the Town of Riverhead {3428}.

Charles R. Howell voted "Yea" on a resolution to grant a bounty of $125 to volunteers for the service of the United States on 27 Aug 1862 {3429}.

It was recorded that Charles R. Howell purchased a $100 bond to help raise funds to cover war-related expenses of the Town of Riverhead {3430}.

Charles R. Howell, yeoman, was on the 1860 Jurors List for the Town of Riverhead {3431}.

On 20 June 1870, Ransom Howell, 63, farmer, having real property worth $5000, and personal property worth $600, was enumerated as the head of a family consisting of himself, his wife, Betsey, 60, and their children, Mary E., 32, and Daniel H., 22, seaman, residing in the village and Town of Riverhead, Suffolk County, New York, in the Ninth Census of the United States {3432}.

Charles R. Howell died on 25 Jly 1870, at the age of 63 years, 6 months, and 24 days, and is buried in Plot 206 in the Riverhead Cemetery {3433}.

Betsy, the wife of Charles R. Howell, died on 1 Aug 1877, at the age of 66 years, 10 months, and 15 days, and is buried beside her husband at Riverhead {3434}.

Charles Ransom and Elizabeth (Corwin) Howell were the parents of five children {3435}.

1042. i. DANIEL HALSEY[7] HOWELL, born on 16 Jan 1831, died on 29 Jan 1838, at the age of 7 years and 13 days, and is buried in the Aquebogue Cemetery {3436}.

+ 1043. ii. CHARLES HENRY[7] HOWELL, born on 18 Jly 1832.

3426. U.S. Census, Riverhead, Suffolk County, NY, 1840, Page 236.
3427. Id., 1850, Dwelling House 150, Family Number 170, Page 258.
3428. RTR, Liber A, 266; (I, 188).
3429. Id., Liber B, 256, Liber C, 3; (I, 434, 551).
3430. Id., 25; (I, 564).
3431. Id., (I, 710).
3432. U.S. Census, Riverhead, Suffolk County, NY, 1870, Dwelling House 187, Family Number 208, Page 74.
3433. Gravestone, Riverhead Cemetery.
3434. Id.
3435. Charles Ransom Howell Family Bible.
3436. Gravestone, Aquebogue Cemetery.

1044. iii.   MARY ELIZABETH[7] HOWELL, born on 29 May 1838, never married, died on 28 Mch 1915, and is buried in the Riverhead Cemetery {3437}.

+ 1045. iv.   SARAH BETHIAH[7] HOWELL, born on 21 Sep 1840.

+ 1046. v.   DANIEL HALSEY[7] HOWELL, born on 9 Mch 1848.

2. Silas Hamilton[5], Silas[4]

646. DANIEL GRIFFING[6] HOWELL (Silas Hamilton[5], Silas[4]), the son of Silas Hamilton[5] and Mary (Griffing) Howell, was born on 21 Oct 1819 {3438}.

Daniel G. Howell married Jemima Amanda Benjamin at the Moriches Presbyterian Church. She was born on 8 Apr 1826, the daughter of Usher and Jemima (Reeves) Benjamin {3439}.

Daniel G. Howell "..was a farmer by occupation and followed that calling for the most part. In 1842 he was made a lieutenant in the State militia, and the following year was promoted to the rank of captain. For many years he was a member of the Methodist Church" {3440}.

On 23 Mch 1848, Daniel G. Howell was a witness to an agreement by the owners of the Mill Dam at the Village of Upper Mills to grant the use of the Mill Dam as a public way {3441}.

On 4 Apr 1848, Daniel G. Howell was chosen to be the Commissioner of Highways for the Town of Riverhead {3442}. He was again selected for this office on 3 Apr 1849, on 1 Apr 1851, on 6 Apr 1852, and on 5 Apr 1853 {3443}. He was nominated to serve in this capacity on 4 Apr 1854, and on 3 Apr 1855 {3444}, but was not chosen.

Daniel G. Howell, yeoman, was listed on the 1848 Jurors List for the Town of Riverhead {3445}. He was also listed on the 1851 List, the 1854 List, the 1857 List, the 1860 List, and the 1863 List {3446}.

It was recorded on 27 Mch 1849 that a bill of $5.00 was paid to Daniel G. Howell, another of $4.00 on 26 Mch 1850, yet another of $5.00 on 25 Mch 1851, and still another of $5.00 on 28 Mch 1854 {3447}.

3437. Gravestone, Riverhead Cemetery.
3438. Wilbur Franklin Howell, op. cit., 146.
3439. Bicha and Brown, op. cit., 775.
3440. PORTRAIT & BIOGRAPHICAL RECORD OF SUFFOLK COUNTY.., 548.
3441. RTR, Liber B, 136; (I, 356).
3442. Id., 140; (I, 358).
3443. Id., 140, 145, 150a, 157; (I, 359, 363, 365, 371).
3444. Id., 170, 181; (I, 379, 385).
3445. Id., (I, 698).
3446. Id., (I, 700, 704, 707, 710, 713).
3447. Id., Liber A, 199, 202, 207, 226; (I, 147, 149, 153, 166).

On 5 Sep 1850, Daniel G. Howell, 30, farmer, with real property worth $800, was listed as the head of a family consisting of himself, his wife, Jemima, 25, and their son, Charles H., 2 months, residing in the Town of Riverhead, Suffolk County, New York, in the Seventh Census of the United States {3448}.

As Commissioner of Highways, Daniel G. Howell declared the North Road to be a public highway on 10 Sep 1852 {3449}, laid out a public highway commencing "..on the Middle Road at a certain Road known as Nathan Benjamins Road and running a Northwest course until it strikes the highway running from the Northroad to the Upper Mills.." by 1 Nov 1852 {3450}, laid out "..the road running from the Middle Road to the Highway that runs from the North Road to the Upper Mills.." {3451}, and declared that "Road district No 4 shall extend to the Middle Road and district No 7 shall extend half mile north of the Middle Road.." on 21 Mch 1853 {3452}. In response to the "..application..of twelve reputable freemen.." of the Town of Riverhead, he "..laid out a public highways three rods in width..opposite the centre of the North end of the Suffolk Road on the Middle Road and running North thirty five (35) degrees west to the Northeast part of a Pond and then running north twenty three (23) degrees west untill it strikes the North Road opposite the centre of a Road leading to the Sound near the house of James W. Youngs.." by 4 Mch 1853 {3453}. Likewise, he laid out a "..highway to commence on the public road leading from the Cannungum Mills to the Country Road and to run Westerly by the Land of the Long Island Rail Road Company on the South side of Said Land and parallel with it to the turn offtract known as Hulses turn off the running the course of Said turnoff untill it strikes the RiverRoad.." by 1 Nov 1853 {3454}.

It was recorded that Daniel G. Howell purchased bonds 233 and 234, worth $150, and bearing date 1 Jly 1864 {3455}.

Daniel G. Howell received 243 votes as a candidate for Inspector of Elections in Election District No 2 of the Town of Riverhead on 7 Apr 1868, as did Orlando O. Wells {3456}.

On 25 June 1870, Daniel Howell, 50, having real property worth $3000, and personal property worth $1000, was enumerated as the head of a family consisting of himself, his wife, Jemima, and their sons, Charles H., 19, fisherman, Francis G., 14, and Usher B., 9, who had attended school, residing in the village and Town of Riverhead, Suffolk County, New York, in the Ninth Census of the

---

3448. U.S. Census, Riverhead, Suffolk County, N.Y., 1850, Dwelling House 144, Family Number 164, Page 258.
3449. RTR, Liber B, 151; (I, 367).
3450. Id., 152; (I, 368).
3451. Id., 164; (I, 375).
3452. Id., 152; (I, 368).
3453. Id., 158-159; (I, 371-372).
3454. Id., 163; (I, 374).
3455. Id., 250; (I, 675).
3456. Id., 305; (I, 465).

United States {3457}.

On 26 Mch 1871, it was recorded that Daniel G. Howell was paid $1.50 in account of the Commissioners of Highways ot the Town of Riverhead {3458}.

Jemima A. Howell died on 15 Dec 1884, and is buried in Plot 321 in the Riverhead Cemetery {3459}.

Daniel G. Howell died on 16 Mch 1895, and is buried beside his wife at Riverhead {3460}.

Daniel Griffing and Jemima Amanda (Benjamin) Howell were the parents of four children {3461}.

+ 1047. i.   CHARLES HAMILTON[7] HOWELL, born on 9 Apr 1850 {3462}.

   1048. ii.   HENRY G.[7] HOWELL, born on 28 Jan 1853, died on 16 Aug 1853, and is buried beside his parents in the Riverhead Cemetery {3463}.

+ 1049. iii.   FRANCIS GRIFFING[7] HOWELL, born on 20 Jan 1855.

+ 1050. iv.   USHER B.[7] HOWELL, born on 17 Dec 1858.

647. CHARITY J.[6] HOWELL (Silas Hamilton[5], Silas[4]), the daughter of Silas Hamilton[5] and Mary (Griffing) Howell, was born on 13 Dec 1821 {3464}.

Charity J. Howell married Noah Wilson Youngs of Northville in April 1842. He was born on 25 Aug 1819, the son of Noah and Keziah (Reeve) Youngs. "He was a corporal of the Militia Company, a Democrat in politics, and resided on the farm, which was his father's" {3465}.

Charity J. Youngs died on 18 Mch 1845 at the age of 23 years, 3 months, and 5 days, and is buried in the Aquebogue Cemetery {3466}.

On 28 Nov 1846 {3467}, Noah Wilson Youngs married Dency Jane Luce, who was born on 14 Feb 1828, the daughter of Hallock and Sarah (Fanning) Luce {3468}.

3457. U.S. Census, Riverhead, Suffolk County, NY, 1870, Dwelling House 235, Family Number 258, Page 77.
3458. Id., Liber C, 84; (I, 607).
3459. Gravestone, Riverhead Cemetery.
3460. Id.
3461. Wilbur Franklin Howell, op. cit., 146.
3462. PORTRAIT & BIOGRAPHICAL RECORD OF SUFFOLK COUNTY.., 548.
3463. Gravestone, Riverhead Cemetery.
3464. Wilbur Franklin Howell, op. cit., 144.
3465. Selah Youngs, Jr., op. cit., 233.
3466. Gravestone, Aquebogue Cemetery.
3467. Selah Youngs, Jr., op. cit.
3468. Jacques and Kappenberg, op. cit., 16.

Noah Wilson Youngs died on 29 Jan 1887, and is buried in the Northville Cemetery {3469}.

Dency Jane (Luce) Youngs died on 1 Sep 1893, and is buried beside her husband at Northville {3470}.

Noah Wilson and Charity J. (Howell) Youngs had no children, but he and Dency Jane (Luce) Youngs were the parents of six children {3471}.

     i.   HENRY WILSON YOUNGS, born on 17 Dec 1847, married Anna Ayers.

    ii.   DRUSILLA YOUNGS, born on 7 Jly 1849, died on 3 Nov 1927, unmarried.

   iii. EDNA A. YOUNGS, born on 1 Apr 1851, married George C. Hallock on 1 Dec 1869, four children, died in 1925 {3472}.

   iv. LEANDER EDSON YOUNGS, born on 24 Nov 1854, married Georgianna M. Hallock, two children, died on 18 Nov 1919 {3473}.

    v.   DANIEL R. YOUNGS, born on 16 Mch 1868, married Mary E. F. Costello on 28 June 1905.

   vi. SARAH KEZIAH YOUNGS, born on 20 Aug 1871, married Herman Halsey Hallock on 16 Oct 1898, four children {3474}.

649. GEORGE N.[6] HOWELL (Silas Hamilton[5], Silas[4]), the son of Silas Hamilton[5] and Mary (Griffing) Howell, was born on 23 Mch 1829 {3475}.

George N. Howell married Mary E. Reeve {3476}, who was born in 1831 {3477}.

George N. Howell ran a hardware store on Main Street in Riverhead, and lived on Main Street near the railroad {3478}.

On 9 June 1870, Geo. N. Howell, 40, retired merchant, with real property

---

3469. Id., 16.
3470. Id.
3471. Id., 16, 17.
3472. Lucius H. Hallock, op. cit., 316.
3473. Id., 328.
3474. Id., 362.
3475. Wilbur Franklin Howell, op. cit., 153.
3476. Id.
3477. Gravestone, Riverhead Cemetery.
3478. CURTIN'S DIRECTORY OF LONG ISLAND, THE REGISTER, SCHS, XI, #3, 75 (Winter 1985).

worth $12000, and personal property worth $200, was enumerated as the head of a family consisting of himself, his wife, Mary E., 37, and their children, Ida, 8, and Hattie, 6, residing in the Town of Riverhead, Suffolk County, New York, in the Ninth Census of the United States {3479}.

George N. Howell died on 5 Feb 1891 {3480}, and is buried in Plot 432 in the Riverhead Cemetery {3481}.

Mary E. (Reeve) Howell died on 30 Nov 1919 {3482}, and is buried beside her husband at Riverhead {3483}.

George N. and Mary E. (Reeve) Howell were the parents of four children {3484}.

1051. i.   IDA E.[7] HOWELL, born on 23 Mch 1858, did not marry, died on 9 Nov 1946 {3485}, and is buried beside her parents at Riverhead {3486}.

1052. ii.   HATTIE[7] HOWELL, born on 9 Nov 1862, married David Nelson Gay, no children, died on 14 May 1888, and is buried in Plot 205 in the Riverhead Cemetery {3487}. He was born on 22 Feb 1855, died on 26 Nov 1926, and is buried beside his wife at Riverhead {3488}.

1053. iii.   EMILY[7] HOWELL, married, two children.

1054. iv.   HOWARD S.[7] HOWELL, born in 1873, married Lillian Woodhull, no children.

650. EMILY S.[6] HOWELL (Silas Hamilton[5], Silas[4]), the daughter of Silas Hamilton[5] and Mary (Griffing) Howell, was born in about May 1832.

Emily S. Howell married George Orry Reeve, the son of Orry and Otsey Reeve {3489}.

Emily S. Reeve died on 24 Jan 1870, at the age of 37 years and 8 months, and is buried in the Aquebogue Cemetery {3490}.

On 7 Jly 1870, George O. Reeve, 41, farmer, having real property valued

---

3479. U.S. Census, Riverhead, Suffolk County, NY, 1870, Dwelling House 93, Family Number 102, Page 67.
3480. Wilbur Franklin Howell, op. cit., 153.
3481. Gravestone, Riverhead Cemetery.
3482. Suffolk County Estates, File #23842.
3483. Gravestone, Riverhead Cemetery.
3484. Wilbur Franklin Howell, op. cit.
3485. Suffolk County Estates, File #651 P 1946.
3486. Gravestone, Riverhead Cemetery.
3487. Id.
3488. Id.
3489. Baker, op. cit., 432.
3490. Gravestone, Aquebogue Cemetery.

at $7000, and personal property valued at $900, was enumerated as the head of a household consisting of himself, his mother, Otsey Reeve, 60, his children, Mary A., 13, and George, Jr., 2, as well as Thomas Brown, 18, farm laborer, and Mary Smith, 17, domestic servant, residing in the Town of Riverhead, Suffolk County, New York, in the Ninth Census of the United States {3491}.

George Orry and Emily S. (Howell) Reeve were the parents of six children {3492}.

<ul>
<li>i.   CARRIE REEVE, born on 2 Jly 1858, died on 17 Jan 1860, at the age of 1 year, 6 months, and 15 days, and is buried in the Aquebogue Cemetery {3493}.</li>
</ul>

<ul>
<li>ii.   MARY ADELE REEVE, born in about Nov 1860, died on 23 Mch 1864, at the age of 3 years and 5 months, and is buried in the Aquebogue Cemetery {3494}.</li>
</ul>

<ul>
<li>iii.   EDDIE REEVE, born in about Apr 1861 (?), died on 29 Apr 1862, at the age of 1 year, and is buried in the Aquebogue Cemetery {3495}.</li>
</ul>

<ul>
<li>iv.   DAUGHTER, died on 16 Mch 1863, and is buried in the Aquebogue Cemetery {3496}.</li>
</ul>

<ul>
<li>v.   GEORGE REEVE, born in about 1868.</li>
</ul>

<ul>
<li>vi.   CHAUNCEY T. REEVE.</li>
</ul>

3. George[5], Silas[4]

652. JOHN FRANKLIN[6] HOWELL (George[5], Silas[4]), the son of George[5] and Polly B. (Wells) Howell, was born on 11 Mch 1824 {3497}.

On 11 Jan 1844, John F. Howell married Lucretia Jane Jennings, who was born in about Apr 1822, the daughter of Nicholas and Lucretia (Terry) Jennings {3498}.

On 5 Sep 1850, John F. Howell, 26, farmer, was enumerated as the head of a family consisting of himself, his wife, Lucretia J., 26, and their children,

---

3491. U.S. Census, Riverhead, Suffolk County, NY, 1870, Dwelling House 365, Family Number 402, Page 86.
3492. Wilbur Franklin Howell, op. cit., 154.
3493. Gravestone, Aquebogue Cemetery.
3494. Id.
3495. Id.
3496. Id.
3497. Wilbur Franklin Howell, op. cit., 175.
3498. Id.

Lydia M., 6, and John, 4, residing in the Town of Riverhead, Suffolk County, New York, in the Seventh Census of the United States {3499}.

On 20 June 1870, John F. Howell, 46, farmer, was enumerated as the head of a family consisting of himself, his wife, Jane, 46, and their children, Lydia Wood, 25, and Willie, 14, residing in the Town of Riverhead, Suffolk County, New York, in the Ninth Census of the United States {3500}.

Lucretia Jane Howell died on 10 Feb 1887 {3501}, and is buried in the Aquebogue Cemetery {3502}.

John Franklin Howell died on 9 Mch 1910, and is buried beside his wife in the Aquebogue Cemetery {3503}.

John Franklin and Lucretia Jane (Jennings) Howell were the parents of four children {3504}.

+ 1055. i. LYDIA MARIA[7] HOWELL, born on 19 Nov 1844.

   1056. ii. JOHN LEROY[7] HOWELL, born on 8 Sep 1846, said to have died of typhus in London, England, on 16 June 1867, at the age of 20 years, 8 months, and 7 days, and to have had his body returned by his brother-in-law, Dr. Webster C. Wood, and buried in the Aquebogue Cemetery {3505}.

   1057. iii. FRANK WILLARD[7] HOWELL, born on 13 Nov 1852, died on 20 Jan 1857, at the age of 4 years, 2 months, and 7 days, and is buried in the Aquebogue Cemetery {3506}.

+ 1058. iv. WILLIAM HENRY[7] HOWELL, born on 15 Apr 1856.

653. JOSEPH CHAUNCEY[6] HOWELL (George[5], Silas[4]), the son of George[5] and Polly B. (Wells) Howell, was born on 14 Jan 1827 {3507}.

On 16 Nov 1848, Joseph C. Howell married Dency Maria Youngs, who was born on 24 Nov 1829, the daughter of Aseph and Parnell (Corwin) Youngs {3508}.

On 5 Sep 1850, Joseph C. Howell, 23, farmer, was enumerated as the head of a family consisting of himself, his wife, Dency, 20, and their son, George W., 6 months, residing in the Town of Riverhead, Suffolk County, New York, in the

3499. U.S. Census, Riverhead, Suffolk County, NY, 1850, Dwelling House 148, Family Number 168, Page 258.
3500. Id., 1870, Dwelling House 212, Family Number 234, Page 75.
3501. Id.
3502. Gravestone, Aquebogue Cemetery.
3503. Wilbur Franklin Howell, op. cit.
3504. Id.
3505. Gravestone, Aquebogue Cemetery.
3506. Id.
3507. Wilbur Franklin Howell, op. cit., 180.
3508. Selah Youngs, Jr., op. cit., 170.

Seventh Census of the United States {3509}.

On 25 June 1870, Jo⁵. C. Howell, 43, farm laborer, having personal property worth $500, was enumerated as the head of a family consisting of himself, his wife, Dency M., 39, and their children, George W., 17, who was a clerk in a store, and Ellen A., 15, residing in the village and Town of Riverhead, Suffolk County, New York, in the Ninth Census of the United States {3510}.

J. Chauncey Howell was killed by a Long Island Railroad train on 21 Nov 1896 {3511}, and is buried in Plot 85 in the Riverhead Cemetery {3512}.

Dency M. Howell died on 10 June 1897, and is buried beside her husband at Riverhead {3513}.

Joseph Chauncey and Dency Maria (Youngs) Howell were the parents of four children {3514}.

 1059. i. GEORGE WILBUR[7] HOWELL, born on 27 Nov 1849, died on 21 Feb 1852, at the age of 2 years, 2 months, and 24 days, and was buried in the Aquebogue Cemetery {3515}, was later removed by Edna Jane Raynor, and is now buried in Plot 85 in the Riverhead Cemetery {3516}.

 1060. ii. DANIEL MONROE[7] HOWELL, born on 23 Sep 1851, died on 26 Nov 1851, at the age of 2 months, and 3 days, and was likewise first buried in the Aquebogue Cemetery {3517}, but is now buried in Plot 85 in the Riverhead Cemetery {3518}.

+ 1061. iii. GEORGE WILBUR[7] HOWELL, born on 26 Dec 1852.

+ 1062. iv. ELLEN ADELAIDE[7] HOWELL, born on 29 Dec 1854.

654. WILLIAM SIDNEY[6] HOWELL (George[5], Silas[4]), the son of George[5] and Polly B. (Wells) Howell, was born on 16 Jan 1830 {3519}.

3509. U.S. Census, Riverhead, Suffolk County, New York, 1850, Dwelling House 149, Family NUmber 169, Page 158.
3510. U.S. Census, Riverhead, Suffolk County, NY, 1870, Dwelling House 186, Family Number 207, Page 74.
3511. Wilbur Franklin Howell, op. cit.
3512. Gravestone, Riverhead Cemetery.
3513. Id.
3514. NYG&BR, LXXXI, 143 (Apr 1950).
3515. Gravestone, Aquebogue Cemetery.
3516. Gravestone, Riverhead Cemetery.
3517. Gravestone, Aquebogue Cemetery.
3518. Gravestone, Riverhead Cemetery.
3519. NYG&BR, LXXXI, 142 (Apr 1950).

On 8 Aug 1855, William S. Howell married Louisa King {3520}, who was born in about 1825.

Wm. S. Howell, M.D., died in New York on 6 Jan 1874, and is buried in Plot 158 in the Riverhead Cemetery {3521}.

Louisa Howell died on 20 May 1894, AE 70 years, and is buried beside her husband at Riverhead {3522}.

655. JOSHUA M.[6] HOWELL (George[5], Silas[4]), the son of George[5] and Polly B. (Wells) Howell, was born on 24 Oct 1832 {3523}.

On 1 Jan 1857, Joshua M. Howell married Selina Downs {3524}, who was born on 14 Nov 1835 {3525}.

Joshua M. Howell died on 19 Nov 1865, was buried in the Aquebogue Cemetery {3526}, and is now buried in Plot 171 in the Riverhead Cemetery {3527}.

Selina Downs Howell died on 19 Jan 1910, and is buried beside her husband at Riverhead {3528}.

Joshua M. and Selina (Downs) Howell were the parents of one child.

+ 1063.   i.   JOHN D.[7] HOWELL, born on 20 Feb 1858.

658. ROSALINE V.[6] HOWELL (George[5], Silas[4]), the daughter of George[5] and Polly B. (Wells) Howell, was born on 9 Mch 1838 {3529}.

On 19 Nov 1859, Rosaline V. Howell married Eugene Hallock, who was born on 16 Sep 1838, the son of Joseph Edwin and Amanda (Tuthill) Hallock {3530}.

Eugene Hallock died on 3 June 1904, and is buried in the Sound Avenue Cemetery {3531}.

Rosaline V. Hallock died on 27 Sep 1910, and is buried beside her husband {3532}.

Eugene and Rosaline V. (Howell) Hallock were the parents of four children {3533}.

3520. Id., 144 (Apr 1950).
3521. Gravestone, Riverhead Cemetery.
3522. Id.
3523. NYG&BR, LXXXI, 142 (Apr 1950).
3524. Id., 144 (Apr 1950).
3525. Gravestone, Riverhead Cemetery.
3526. Gravestone, Aquebogue Cemetery.
3527. Gravestone, Riverhead Cemetery.
3528. Gravestone, Riverhead Cemetery.
3529. NYG&BR, LXXXI, 142 (Apr 1950).
3530. Wilbur Franklin Howell, op. cit., 185.
3531. Id.
3532. Id.
3533. Id.

i.   KITTIE KETURAH HALLOCK, born on 26 Jly 1863, never married, died on 1 Apr 1943.

ii.   JOSEPH EDWIN HALLOCK, born on 27 Jan 1868, married Helen Evers, died on 30 May 1949.

iii.   FREDERICK W. HALLOCK, born on 3 Mch 1872, married Mrs. Helen Dayton Culver, died on 16 May 1912.

iv.   ARCHIBALD HALLOCK, born on 11 Dec 1874, died on 11 Mch 1875.

659. EDNA JANE[6] HOWELL (George[5], Silas[4]), the daughter of George[5] and Polly B. (Wells) Howell, was born on 14 Sep 1841 {3534}.

On 28 Dec 1867, Edna J. Howell married Edgar Raynor {3535}, who was born on 20 Aug 1830, the son of Joseph Raynor {3536}.

On 20 June 1870, Edgar Raynor, 39, photographer, with personal property worth $500, and Edna Raynor, 29, were enumerated as members of the household of her father, George Howell, in the Town of Riverhead, Suffolk County, New York, in the Ninth Census of the United States {3537}.

Edgar Raynor died on 5 Mch 1900, and is buried in Plot 70 in the Riverhead Cemetery {3538}.

Edna Jane Raynor died on 23 Mch 1913, and is buried beside her husband at Riverhead {3539}.

Edgar and Edna Jane (Howell) Raynor had no children {3540}.

4. Ebenezer[5], Joseph[4]

660. JOSEPH MARTHERS[6] HOWELL (Ebenezer[5], Joseph[4]), the son of Ebenezer[5] and Sarah (Holmes) Howell, was born at Newburgh, New York, on 16 Feb 1814 {3541}.

Joseph M. Howell came to New Orleans in Nov 1833 {3542}.

On 15 Jly 1841 at New Orleans, Joseph Marthers Howell married Marie

3534. NYG&BR, LXXXI, 142 (Apr 1950).
3535. Id., 144 (Apr 1950).
3536. Wilbur Franklin Howell, op. cit., 174ff.
3537. U.S. Census, Riverhead, Suffolk County, NY, 1870, Dwelling House 185, Family Number 206, Page 74.
3538. Gravestone, Riverhead Cemetery.
3539. Id.
3540. Wilbur Franklin Howell, op. cit., 174.
3541. Michael A. Howell, Personal communication.
3542. Id.

Rose Pacaud, who was born on 28 Sep 1823, the daughter of Jacques Alexis and Marie Josepha (Maestre) Pacaud {3543}.

On 5 Oct 1843, Joseph M. Howell completed the purchase of Vault #28 in the new Cypress Grove Firemen's Cemetery, where the majority of his family were later to be buried {3544}.

Joseph M. Howell, who was "5 feet, 4 inches high, of fair complexion, blue eyes, light hair, and by occupation a builder", enlisted for service in the Mexican-American War on 7 May 1846. He served as First Lieutenant in Company B, commanded by Capt. Thomas Glenn, in the First, or "Washington", Regiment, commanded by Col. J. B. Walton. He was discharged on 4 Aug 1846, when the Louisiana Volunteers were disbanded {3545}.

Joseph M. Howell was a builder in New Orleans and, on 27 Apr 1848, a contract for the brickwork on the New Orleans Custom House was signed with the firm of Mitchell, Howell and Coats. The partner, John Mitchell, had participated in the building of the United States Mint at New Orleans in 1835. Moses H. Coats transferred his interest in this contract to Joseph M. Howell on 20 Feb 1849 for $1500 {3546}. Coats was relatively close to Joseph M. Howell, having married Azelie Irene Pacaud, the sister of Mrs. Howell {3547}.

Joseph and Marie Howell lived at 78 Gasquet Street in New Orleans until 7 Aug 1857, when they moved to Corpus Christi, where he was a co-partner, with Capt. Samuel W. Fullerton, in a ranching venture. Joseph M. Howell was taken prisoner, on or about 17 Mch 1864, possibly because he had served on a county committee which had recommended secession, by Union troops who landed at the mouth of the Oso. The Howell family returned to New Orleans on 24 June 1864, and lived there, at 92 Pleasant Street, until Joseph's death {3548}.

After the Civil War, Joseph M. Howell was required to come before the Supervisor of Registration to take an Oath of Allegiance so that he might be allowed to vote as a citizen of the United States {3549}.

Joseph Marthers Howell died on 2 Mch 1876 at New Orleans, where he had spent much of his life as a builder {3550}.

On 16 Nov 1887, Marie Rose Howell, who lived at 434½ Anunciation Street, filed for a pension as a widow of a Mexican-American War veteran, a claim which was handled by Washington attorney, A.M. Kenaday {3551}.

Marie Rose Howell died at New Orleans, where her residence was listed as at 414 Constance Street, on 8 Nov 1889 {3552}.

Joseph Marthers and Marie Rose (Pacaud) Howell were the parents of

---

3543. Id.
3544. Id.
3545. Id.
3546. Samuel Wilson, Jr., A HISTORY OF THE U.S. CUSTOMHOUSE IN NEW ORLEANS, 24.
3547. Michael A. Howell, op. cit.
3548. Id.
3549. Id.
3550. Id.
3551. Id.
3552. Id.

twelve children {3553}.

1064. i.   SARAH JANE[7] HOWELL, born on 8 May 1842, never married, died on 9 Sep 1872, was interred in Vault #28 at Cypress Grove, and moved to the Metairie Cemetery in 1953.

+ 1065. ii.   AZELIE FRANCES[7] HOWELL, born on 31 Jan 1844.

+ 1066. iii.   MARY ROSALINE[7] HOWELL, born in June 1847.

+ 1067. iv.   JOSEPH[7] HOWELL, born in 1848.

+ 1068. v.   FERDINAND COATES[7] HOWELL, born on 9 Dec 1852.

1069. vi.   CARMELETE W.[7] HOWELL, born on 31 Jan 1854, died on 10 June 1854, was interred at Cypress Grove and later moved to the Metairie Cemetery.

+ 1070. vii.   PAMELIA IRENE[7] HOWELL, born on 4 Apr 1854.

+ 1071. viii.   PHILOMENE PATTERSON[7] HOWELL, born in about Jan 1858.

+ 1072. ix.   GEORGIA MYER[7] HOWELL, born on 12 Aug 1860.

+ 1073. x.   SUSIE WATERS[7] HOWELL, born in Mch 1863.

+ 1074. xi.   CARRIE LEE[7] HOWELL, born in about 1866.

1075. xii.   RACHEL ADELINE[7] HOWELL, born in Oct 1868, died on 18 Feb 1869, was interred at Cypress Grove and later moved to the Metairie Cemetery.

661. JOHN H.[6] HOWELL (Ebenezer[5], Joseph[4]), the son of Ebenezer[5] and Sarah (Holmes) Howell, was born on 20 Apr 1816 {3554}.

John H. Howell moved to Binghamton, where he was a resident on his farm for six years before he died on 27 Jly 1889 {3555}.

John H. Howell probably never married {3556}.

662. SARAH JANE[6] HOWELL (Ebenezer[5], Joseph[4]), the daughter of Ebenezer[5] and

---

3553. Id.
3554. Ebenezer Howell Family Bible.
3555. Michael A. Howell, op. cit.
3556. Id.

Sarah (Holmes) Howell, was born on 9 Jan 1819 {3557}.

Sarah Jane Howell married Henry Lozier {3558}.

Henry Lozier died on 10 Oct 1892, at the age of 84 years, and is buried in the Rossville New Cemetery {3559}.

Sarah Jane, the wife of Henry Lozier, died on 8 Feb 1906, and is buried beside her husband at Rossville {3560}.

Henry and Sarah Jane (Howell) Lozier had no children {3561}.

663. FRANCES[6] HOWELL (Ebenezer[5], Joseph[4]), the daughter of Ebenezer[5] and Sarah (Holmes) Howell, was born on 7 Dec 1820, probably in Newburgh, New York {3562}.

On 25 Aug 1847, Frances Howell married John Milton Haight, who was born in about 1812, before the Rev. Zephaniah N. Lewis, minister of the Methodist Episcopal Church {3563}.

"John A. Hait, 36, jeweller" was enumerated as the head of a household consisting of himself, his wife, Frances, 40, Ann Howell, 16, Frances Wilburn, 18, Charles Cashman, 50, furniture, Mary Cashman, 41, and Samuel Dougherty, 20, residing in Newburgh, Orange County, New York, in the Seventh Census of the United States, 1850 {3564}.

John M. Haight died on 15 Mch 1852 {3565}.

On 15 Sep 1862, Frances (Howell) Haight married Mr. William A. Lane, a widower of Haverstraw in Rockland County, New York {3566}, who was born on 15 Sep 1816 at Yorktown, New York. She was said to be "..an estimable lady, a devoted member of the Methodist Episcopal Church, and a woman who stood high in the estimation of everyone." {3567}.

"In early life Mr. Lane was not interested in religious matters, but his second wife, who was an active church worker, was influential in arousing his interest, and he connected himself with the Methodist Episcopal Church, of which he was a member for twenty-five years before his death." {3568}.

Frances (Howell) Haight Lane died on 4 Apr 1878 {3569}, and is

3557. Ebenezer Howell Family Bible.
3558. Michael A. Howell, op. cit.
3559. ROSSVILLE CEMETERY RECORDS, from a copy at the OCGS, published in RECORDS FROM NEWBURGH.., 2, 206, OCGS, 1997.
3560. Id.
3561. U.S. Census, Newburgh, Orange County, NY, 1900, Enumeration District 46, Sheet Number 12, Line 12.
3562. Michael A. Howell, op. cit.
3563. THE NEWBURGH TELEGRAPH, 26 Aug 1847.
3564. U.S. Census, Newburgh, Orange County, N.Y., 1850, Dwelling House 1400, Family Number 1581, Page 105.
3565. George and Virginia Gardner, THE WHIG PRESS DEATH NOTICES, 1851-1865.
3566. Michael A. Howell, op. cit.
3567. ROCKLAND & ORANGE COUNTY BIOGRAPHIES & PORTRAITS OF CITIZENS, 316.
3568. Id., 315.
3569. Id., 316.

buried in the Mount Repose Cemetery in Haverstraw, next to other members of the Lane family {3570}.

William A. Lane died on 3 Dec 1889 {3571}.

665. MARY[6] HOWELL (Ebenezer[5], Joseph[4]), the daughter of Ebenezer[5] and Elizabeth (Johnson) Howell, was born on 2 Mch 1828, probably at Newburgh, New York {3572}.

On 26 Nov 1856, Mary Howell married Peter Havens Clark, who was born on 24 Sep 1823, and christened on 6 Nov 1823 at Clarkstown, New York, the son of Moses D. and Nancy (Brower) Clark, as his second wife. His first wife was Maria van Houten, whom he married at the Kakiat Brick Church on 18 Sep 1845 {3573}.

Peter Havens Clark died on 10 Jly 1884 {3574}.

Mary Clark died on 29 June 1919 {3575}.

Peter Havens and Maria (Van Houten) Clark were the parents of one son {3576}.

    i.   ALFRED VAN HOUTEN CLARK, born on 1 Nov 1847, married Anna Eichoff on 18 Apr 1881, died on 20 Feb 1928, while she died on 29 Dec 1947.

Peter Havens and Mary (Howell) Clark were the parents of three children {3577}.

    ii.   ADA GUSTINA CLARK, born on 27 Dec 1861, married Walter S. Seaman, died on 4 Nov 1918, while he died on 18 Sep 1932.

    iii.   WILBUR CLARENCE CLARK, born on 1 Oct 1864.

    iv.   LILLIE FLORENCE CLARK, born on 1 Oct 1864, died on 20 Aug 1950.

666. CHARLES[6] HOWELL (Ebenezer[5], Joseph[4]), the son of Ebenezer[5] and Elizabeth (Johnston) Howell, was born on 30 Jan 1830, probably at Newburgh, New York {3578}.

Charles Howell married Maria W. Philips, who was born in Jly 1831, the

---

3570. Michael A. Howell, op. cit.
3571. ROCKLAND & ORANGE COUNTY BIOGRAPHIES & PORTRAITS OF CITIZENS, 315.
3572. Michael A. Howell, op. cit.
3573. Id.
3574. Id.
3575. Id.
3576. Id.
3577. Id.
3578. Id.

daughter of John D. and Harriet Philips {3579}.

Charles Howell became a dancing teacher and, as such, went by the name of "Charles H. Rivers". He may have been a dancer on stage, and used this as his stage name {3580}. He established a dancing school at Gothic Hall, on Washington Street, in Brooklyn. Later, in about 1851, he established the Rivers' Academy of Dancing, located at Court and State Streets in Nyack, New York, where he continued until about 1901, after which he taught privately and in various schools. For forty years, he had an annual exhibition in the Academy of Music. He taught many professional dancers their methods, and invented many styles of dancing for them. He was also the founder of the American Society for Professional Dancers {3581}.

After he gave up public teaching, Charles Howell devoted much of his time to his farm at New City, New York {3582}.

Maria W. Howell died on 5 Sep 1901 at Leonia, New Jersey {3583}.

Charles Howell died on 30 Jan 1911 at the home of his daughter, Maria Howell Downing, in Rutherford, New Jersey {3584}, and is buried under the name, Charles H. Rivers, in the Oak Hill Cemetery at Nyack, New York {3585}.

Charles and Maria W. (Philips) Howell were the parents of eight children {3586}.

+ 1076. i.   CHARLES E.[7] HOWELL, born on 21 Jan 1859.

+ 1077. ii.   HENRY F.[7] HOWELL, born in 1860 in Brooklyn.

+ 1078. iii.   WILLIAM P.[7] HOWELL, born in 1862 in Brooklyn.

+ 1079. iv.   MARIA ANTOINETTE[7] HOWELL, born in Jly 1864 in Brooklyn.

   1080. v.   IRENE W.[7] HOWELL, born in 1867 in Brooklyn.

+ 1081. vi.   EUGENE M.[7] HOWELL, born in 1869 in Brooklyn.

+ 1082. vii.   FRANK L.[7] HOWELL, born in 1872 in Brooklyn.

   1083.viii.   FREDERICK C.[7] HOWELL, born in 1874 in Brooklyn.

3579. Id.
3580. Id.
3581. NYACK JOURNAL, 1 Feb 1911.
3582. Id.
3583. Michael A. Howell, op. cit.
3584. NYACK JOURNAL, 1 Feb 1911.
3585. Michael A. Howell, op. cit.
3586. Id.

668. ANNA[6] HOWELL (Ebenezer[5], Joseph[4]), the daughter of Ebenezer[5] and Elizabeth (Johnston) Howell, was born on 11 Apr 1834, probably at Newburgh, New York {3587}.

Ann Howell, 16, was enumerated in the household of "John A. Hait" in Newburgh, Orange County, New York, the Seventh Census of the United States, 1850 {3588}.

Anna Howell married John Jenkins, who was born in Lancaster, England on 11 Feb 1833, the son of John and Hannah (Roddis) Jenkins {3589}.

John Jenkins served with the 14th Regiment in the Civil War, and was wounded at the Battle of the Wilderness {3590}.

Ann Jenkins, of 134 Stone Avenue, Brooklyn, New York, died on 2 Jly 1901 of stomach cancer, and is buried in the Evergreen Cemetery in Brooklyn {3591}.

John Jenkins died of nephritis on 2 Jly 1904 at the Willis Sanitarium in Brooklyn, where he had been residing at 1453 Pacific Street, and is buried beside his wife in the Evergreen Cemetery {3592}.

John and Anna (Howell) Jenkins were the parents of four children {3593}.

    i.   JOHN W. JENKINS, born in Oct 1869, married in 1892, died on 10 Oct 1952, and is buried in the Evergreen Cemetery. His wife, Ada, was born in Oct 1874, died in May 1951, and is buried near him.

    ii.   WILLIAM M. JENKINS, born in Jly 1870, married in 1895, three children. His wife, Agnes, was born on 1 Jan 1878, died on 4 Oct 1948, and is buried in the Holy Rood Catholic Cemetery in Westbury, Connecticut. He died in Dec 1954, and is buried near her.

    iii.   ALBERT H. JENKINS, born on 14 Sep 1873, never married, died on 1 Nov 1936, and is buried in the Evergreen Cemetery.

    iv.   THOMAS JENKINS, born in Sep 1874, and died on 8 Jly 1942. His wife, Clara A., was born in Sep 1873.

3587. Id.
3588. U.S. Census, Newburgh, Orange County, NY, 1850, Dwelling House 1604, Family Number 1581, Page 105.
3589. Michael A. Howell, op. cit.
3590. Id.
3591. Id.
3592. Id.
3593. Id.

V. Descendants of Jacob² Howell -

A. Jacob³, Jacob², Richard¹ -

1. Jacob⁵, Jacob⁴

670. AZUBA⁶ HOWELL (Jacob⁵, Jacob⁴), the daughter of Jacob⁵ and Hannah (Moore) Howell, was born on 14 Nov 1799 {3594}.

> Azuba Howell married Jesse T(h)roop {3595}.
> Azuba Throop died on 6 Sep 1875 {3596}.
> Jesse and Azuba (Howell) Throop were the parents of four children {3597}.

> > i. JENNIE THROOP.

> > ii. SUSAN THROOP, married Mr. Walton.

> > iii. DELIA THROOP, married Mr. Jordan.

> > iv. LEWIS THROOP.

671. WILLIAM⁶ HOWELL (Jacob⁵, Jacob⁴), the son of Jacob⁵ and Hannah (Moore) Howell, was born on 25 Dec 1800 {3598}.

> William Howell was a schoolmate of Joseph Smith, the founder of the Church of Jesus Christ of Latter Day Saints. Also, he worked on the construction of the Erie Canal {3599}.

> William Howell married Cynthia Sherman. They lived in Oramel, Allegany County, New York {3600}.

> On 10 Oct 1850, William Howell, 50, farmer, who was born in New Jersey, was enumerated as the head of a family consisting of himself, his wife, Cynthia, 44, and their children, Israel, 13, Wᵐ A., 5, and Aurilla, 3, residing in the Town of Marion, Wayne County, New York, in the Seventh Census of the United States {3601}.

> William and Cynthia (Sherman) Howell were the parents of five children {3602}.

3594. Alice Howell, Personal communication.
3595. Id.
3596. Id.
3597. Id.
3598. Id.
3599. Id.
3600. Id.
3601. U.S. Census, Marion, Wayne County, NY, 1850, Dwelling House 1645, Family Number 1730, Page 234.
3602. Alice Howell, op. cit.

+   1084. i. GIDEON⁷ HOWELL, born on 9 Sep 1824.

   1085. ii. NORMAN⁷ HOWELL.

+   1086. iii. ISRAEL⁷ HOWELL, born on 17 Feb 1838.

   1087. iv. WILLIAM⁷ HOWELL, born in about 1845.

   1088. v. MARY⁷ HOWELL.

673. PHOEBE⁶ HOWELL (Jacob⁵, Jacob⁴), the daughter of Jacob⁵ and Hannah (Moore) Howell, was born on 19 Jly 1803 {3603}.
      Phoebe G. Howell married Howell Reeves. They lived in Marion, Wayne County, New York {3604}.
      Howell and Phoebe G. (Howell) Reeves were the parents of four children {3605}.
         i. STEPHEN REEVES.

        ii. HARLAN REEVES.

       iii. FANNY REEVES, married Mr. Rice.

        iv. CHARLES REEVES.

675. MARGARET⁶ HOWELL (Jacob⁵, Jacob⁴), the daughter of Jacob⁵ and Hannah (Moore) Howell, was born on 24 Sep 1806 {3606}.
      On 30 Dec 1830, Margaret Howell married her cousin, John Moore(s) {3607}.
      John Moore died on 11 Mch 1854, at the age of 51, and is buried in the East Palmyra Cemetery {3608}.
      Margaret Moore died on 14 Dec 1873, at the age of 67, and is buried beside her husband at East Palmyra {3609}.
      John and Margaret (Howell) Moore were the parents of eight children {3610}.
         i.   HARRIET MOORE, born on 12 Nov 1832, married Mr. Loomis.

3603. Id.
3604. Ruth E. Parker, Personal communication.
3605. Alice Howell, op. cit.
3606. Id.
3607. Id.
3608. Gravestone, East Palmyra Cemetery, from Wayne County, N.Y., cemeteries, LDS Microfilm #0813654.
3609. Id.
3610. Alice Howell, op. cit.

ii. LOUISA CERLISTA MOORE, born on 16 Nov 1834, died on 9 Jly 1836.

iii. ISAAC MOORE, born on 10 Sep 1836, five children, died on 2 Nov 1907 at Walworth, New York, interred at Port Gibson.

iv. MALINDA MOORE, born on 13 Sep 1837, married Josiah Hamilink, eight children, died on 15 Dec 1880.

v. EMILY ADELINE MOORE, born on 21 May 1839, married John Wellemeyer, three children, died on 27 Apr 1912.

vi. ROBERT FRANKLIN MOORE, born on 3 May 1842, died on 14 Sep 1844.

vii. ALICE LA VELLE MOORE, born on 11 Nov 1845, married Lindley Bratt, two children, died on 25 Apr 1889.

viii. MARTHA MOORE, born on 27 June 1847, married Stephen Snyder, one child, died on 13 May 1874, in her 36th year, and is buried in Lot 103 in the East Palmyra Cemetery {3611}.

ix. MARY ELIZABETH MOORE, born on 17 Dec 1849, died on 9 Oct 1854.

676. JACOB[6] HOWELL (Jacob[5], Jacob[4]), the son of Jacob[5] and Hannah (Moore) Howell, was born on 3 Apr 1810 {3612}.

Jacob Howell married Emily Fosket in 1828. They lived in Pontiac, Michigan {3613}.

On 28 Aug 1850, Jacob Howell, 47, farmer, was enumerated as the head of a family consisting of himself, his wife, Emily, and their children, Myron, 17, Almira, 15, Charles, 10, George, 8, Allen, 6, Amanda, 3, and Evelina, 1, residing in Pontiac Township, Oakland County, Michigan, in the Seventh Census of the United States {3614}.

Jacob Howell died on 28 Aug 1873 {3615}.

Jacob and Emily (Fosket) Howell were the parents of nine children {3616}.

3611. Gravestone, East Palmyra Cemetery.
3612. Alice Howell, op. cit.
3613. Ruth E. Parker, op. cit.
3614. U.S. Census, Pontiac, Oakland County, Michigan, 1850, Dwelling House 1357, Family Number 1382, Page 105.
3615. Parker, op. cit.
3616. Id.

1089. i. HARRIET[7] HOWELL, born on 15 Jly 1829, died on 5 Sep 1830, at the age of 1 year, 1 month and 21 days, and is buried in a small cemetery north of East Palmyra {3617}.

1090. ii. ORSON[7] HOWELL, born on 25 Mch 1831, died on 28 Aug 1837, at the age of 6 years, 5 months and 3 days, and is buried near his sister {3618}.

1091. iii. MYRON[7] HOWELL, born in about 1833.

1092. iv. ALMIRA[7] HOWELL, born in about 1835.

1093. v. CHARLES[7] HOWELL, born in about 1840.

1094. vi. GEORGE[7] HOWELL, born in about 1842.

1095. vii. ALLEN[7] HOWELL, born in about 1844.

1096.viii. AMANDA[7] HOWELL, born in about 1847.

1097. ix. EVELINA[7] HOWELL, born in about 1849.

677. ABIGAIL[6] HOWELL (Jacob[5], Jacob[4]), the daughter of Jacob[5] and Hannah (Moore) Howell, was born on 20 May 1811 {3619}.

On 4 Feb 1829, Abigail Howell married John W. Van Winkle. They lived in Sodus, New York {3620}.

Abigail Van Winkle died on 22 Oct 1894 {3621}.

John W. and Abigail (Howell) Van Winkle were the parents of two children {3622}.

    i. HANNAH VAN WINKLE, married Mr. Steger.

    ii. JOHN VAN WINKLE.

678. ISAAC[6] HOWELL (Jacob[5], Jacob[4]), the son of Jacob[5] and Hannah (Moore) Howell, was born on 11 Nov 1812 {3623}.

3617. From Wayne County Cemeteries, L.D.S. microfilm 0813654.
3618. Id.
3619. Alice Howell, op. cit.
3620. Parker, op. cit.
3621. Id.
3622. Alice Howell, op. cit.
3623. Id.

Isaac Howell fought in the Civil War. He was living in Palmyra in 1864 {3624}.

Isaac Howell was the father of three children {3625}.

1098. i.   PETER CHRYSLER[7] HOWELL.

1099. ii.   APHELIA[7] HOWELL, married Mr. Butts, two children.

1100. iii.   KATHERINE[7] HOWELL, married Mr. Patrick, one child.

680. JOHN L.[6] HOWELL (Jacob[5], Jacob[4]), the son of Jacob[5] and Hannah (Moore) Howell, was born on 11 Feb 1816 {3626}.

John L. Howell was living in Vermontville, Eaton County, Michigan in 1864 {3627}.

681. SAMUEL[6] HOWELL (Jacob[5], Jacob[4]), the son of Jacob[5] and Hannah (Moore) Howell, was born on 3 Sep 1817 {3628}.

On 16 Sep 1846, Samuel Howell married Nancy Scullen {3629}, who was born on 31 Jan 1825.

On 28 June 1860, Samuel Howell, 42, farmer, with real estate worth $500, was enumerated as the head of a family consisting of himself, his wife, Nancy, 35, and their children, Augusta, 12, Cornelia, 10, Cyrus L., 8, Lucy H., 6, Riley B., 2, and Fanny, 1, residing in the Town of Williamson, Wayne County, New York, in the Eighth Census of the United States {3630}.

Samuel Howell was living in Williamson, Wayne County, New York, in 1864 {3631}.

Nancy W. Howell died on 21 Dec 1890, at the age of 65 years, 10 months and 21 days, and is buried in the East Williamson Cemetery {3632}.

"Mr. Howell..spent nearly his entire life of ninety-two years in Wayne County. For many years, his home was at East Williamson, but for the past few years he had resided in Sodus, the last three years having been passed with his daughter, Mrs. Cornelia Daily, at Alton. Mr. Howell was unusually active for a man of his years..Mr. Howell possessed an excellent disposition. He was always

3624. Parker, op. cit.
3625. Alice Howell, op. cit.
3626. Id.
3627. Parker, op. cit.
3628. Alice Howell, op. cit.
3629. Diane Howell Friis, Personal communication.
3630. U.S. Census, Williamson, Wayne County, N.Y., 1860, Dwelling House 360, Family Number 378, Page 44.
3631. Parker, op. cit.
3632. Gravestone, East Williamson Cemetery, from a listing in the possession of the Historian, Wayne County, 1995.

cheerful and optimistic.." {3633}.

Samuel Howell died on 14 Oct 1909, at the home of his grand-daughter, Mrs. John Cole, in Sodus, New York {3634}, at the age of 92 years, 1 month, and 19 days, and is buried beside his wife at East Williamson {3635}.

Samuel and Nancy W. (Scullens) Howell were the parents of eight children {3636}.

1101. i. AUGUSTA[7] HOWELL, born in about 1848, married Mr. Myers.

1102. ii. CORNELIA[7] HOWELL, born in about 1850, married Mr. Dailey.

1103. iii. CYRUS LYMAN[7] HOWELL, born in about 1852.

1104. iv. LUCIA H.[7] HOWELL, born in about 1854, married Nelson Briggs.

1105. v. RILEY B.[7] HOWELL, born in about 1858.

+ 1106. vi. FANNY J.[7] HOWELL, born on 9 Apr 1859.

+ 1107. vii. SYLVESTER[7] HOWELL, born on 15 Aug 1861.

1108. viii. FREDERIC[7] HOWELL, born in about 1868.

682. MARTIN[6] HOWELL (Jacob[5], Jacob[4]) was the son of Jacob[5] and Hannah (Moore) Howell {3637}.

Martin Howell was living in Elizabeth, New Jersey, in 1864 {3638}.

- END OF SIXTH GENERATION -

3633. Obituary, Samuel Howell, SODUS RECORD, 22 Oct 1909.
3634. Id.
3635. Gravestone, East Williamson Cemetery.
3636. Friis, op. cit.
3637. Parker, op. cit.
3638. Id.

I. Descendants of John² Howell -

A. John⁴, John³, John², Richard¹

1. Charles⁶, John⁵

686. DEBORAH ANN⁷ HOWELL (Charles⁶), the daughter of Charles⁶ and Deborah (Reeve) Howell, was born on 15 Feb 1818 {3639}.

Deborah Ann Howell married John Hammond {3640} on 24 Dec 1844. He was born on 25 Nov 1814 at Yaphank, the son of Daniel and Ruth (Mills) Hammond. He learned the trade of shoe-making with his father, but followed the sea as a young man, making voyages to the South Seas, New Zealand, and the South Pacific, as a member of the crew of the vessels, THAMES, of Sag Harbor, and HONQUA, of New Bedford, and others. He was a skillful navigator in the merchant service from 1843 to 1848. He became a conductor on the Long Island Railroad in 1848, and served as such until 1851, when he returned to shoe-making, which he followed until his death {3641}.

On 29 Jly 1870, John Hammond, 55, shoemaker, having real property worth $500, was enumerated as the head of a family consisting of himself, his wife, Deborah, 51, and their children, Edward R., 20, and Ruth, 16, residing at Yaphank in the Town of Brookhaven, Suffolk County, New York, in the Ninth Census of the United States {3642}.

John Hammond died on 16 Aug 1895 at Yaphank {3643}.

John and Deborah Ann (Howell) Hammond were the parents of four children {3644}.

     i.   GEORGE E. HAMMOND, born on 18 Nov 1845.

     ii.   EDMUND HAMMOND, born on 28 Jly 1849.

     iii.   RUTH F. HAMMOND, born on 19 Feb 1854.

     iv.   CHARLES FOREST HAMMOND, born on 28 Feb 1864, died on 3 Mch 1864.

3639. Charles Reeve Howell Family Bible.

3640. Id.

3641. Frederick S. Hammond, HISTORY AND GENEALOGIES OF THE HAMMOND FAMILIES IN AMERICA, 2, 408, 409.

3642. U.S. Census, Brookhaven, Suffolk County, NY, 1870, Dwelling House 1396, Family Number 1493, Page 398.

3643. Hammond, op. cit., 409.

3644. Id.

687. FRANKLYN[7] HOWELL (Charles[6]), the son of Charles[6] and Deborah (Reeve) Howell, was born on 6 Nov 1820 {3645}.

Franklin Howell, 27, and Hannah Davis, 14, were married on 5 Feb 1848 {3646}.

Franklyn Howell was a deaf mute who lived in Port Jefferson {3647}.

On 23 Aug 1850, Franklin Howell, shoemaker, 31, with real property worth $200, was enumerated as the head of a family consisting of himself, and Hannah, 16, residing in the Town of Brookhaven, Suffolk County, New York, in the Seventh Census of the United States {3648}.

On 15 Aug 1870, Franklin Howell, shoemaker, 50, was enumerated as the head of a household, in Selden in the Town of Brookhaven, Suffolk County, New York, consisting of himself, his wife, Hannah A., 36, and their children, Emma E., 19, George G., 16, Walton F., 15, Lydia, 13, William L., 11, and Clara B., 6, in the Ninth Census of the United States {3649}.

Franklin Howell died in 1888, and is buried in the Cedar Hill Cemetery at Port Jefferson {3650}.

Hannah Howell died in 1899, and is buried beside her husband at Port Jefferson {3651}.

Franklin and Hannah (Davis) Howell were the parents of at least six children.

1109. i.   EMMA E.[8] HOWELL, born in about 1851.

1110. ii. GEORGE G.[8] HOWELL, born in about 1854.

1111. iii. WALTON F.[8] HOWELL, born in about 1855.

1112. iv. LYDIA[8] HOWELL, born in about 1857.

1113. v.   WILLIAM L.[8] HOWELL, born in about 1859.

1114. vi. CLARA B.[8] HOWELL, born in about 1864.

688. CHARLOTTE[7] HOWELL (Charles[6]), the daughter of Charles[6] and Deborah (Reeve) Howell, was born on 21 Dec 1823 {3652}.

3645. Charles Reeve Howell Family Bible.
3646. BROOKHAVEN MARRIAGES, from THE REGISTER, SCHS, XVIII, #2, 44 (Fall 1992).
3647. Charles Reeve Howell Family Bible.
3648. U.S. Census, Brookhaven, Suffolk County, NY, 1850, Dwelling House 683, Family Number 775, Page 234.
3649. Id., 1870, Dwelling House 1898, Family Number 2146, Page 432.
3650. Gravestone, Cedar Hill Cemetery, Port Jefferson, from the William F. Howell collection of cemetery markings (579).
3651. Id.
3652. Charles Reeve Howell Family Bible.

On 23 Aug 1850, Charlotte Howell, 27, was enumerated as a member of her mother's family in the Seventh Census of the United States, 1850 {3653}.

Charlotte Howell married Franklyn H. Ward at Yaphank {3654}.

Charlotte Ward became a deaf mute {3655}.

Franklyn and Charlotte (Howell) Ward were the parents of at least one son.

    i.   CHARLES W. WARD.

691. EDMUND[7] HOWELL (Charles[6]), the son of Charles[6] and Deborah (Reeve) Howell, was born on 5 Apr 1832 {3656}.

On 23 Aug 1850, Edmund H. Howell, 18, was enumerated as a member of his mother's family in the Seventh Census of the United States, 1850 {3657}.

Edmund Howell married Charlotte Petty {3658}. She was born on 14 Feb 1841, the daughter of Mitchell and Angeline (Mills) Petty {3659}.

Edmund Howell "..followed the sea in coastwise trade until he was thirty years of age. He then was for several years active in the city of Newark, New Jersey, in the house moving business, and in the latter part of his life returned to the old house at Yaphank, and also built a considerable number of houses in that vicinity..", where he was still living there at the age of ninety-two {3660}.

Charlotte A. Howell died on 29 Oct 1918, at the age of 77 years, 7 months, and 15 days, and is buried in the Yaphank Cemetery {3661}.

Edmund Howell died on 18 Apr 1928 {3662}.

Edmund and Charlotte A. (Petty) Howell were the parents of six children {3663}.

1115. i.   ELMER WINFIELD[8] HOWELL, born on 28 Sep 1861, married Lizzie Brown, the daughter of George S. Brown, in 1887, two children, was in the construction business in Babylon, died 11 Oct 1954.

1116. ii.   CHARLOTTE[8] HOWELL, born on 16 Sep 1863, married

---

3653. U.S. Census, Brookhaven, Suffolk County, NY, 1850, Dwelling House 664, Family Number 754, Page 238.

3654. LONG ISLAND STAR, 9 Sep 1857, from THE REGISTER, SCHS, XIX, #2, 44 (Fall 1993).

3655. Charles Reeve Howell Family Bible.

3656. Id.

3657. U.S. Census, op. cit.

3658. Henry Isham Hazelton, THE BOROUGHS OF BROOKLYN AND QUEENS COUNTIES OF NASSAU AND SUFFOLK LONG ISLAND, NEW YORK, 1609-1924, V, 284.

3659. Wilbur Franklin Howell, op. cit., 260.

3660. Hazelton, op. cit.

3661. Wilbur Franklin Howell, op. cit., 260.

3662. Suffolk County Estates, File #30284.

3663. Hazelton, op. cit.

Fernando Willis Edwards on 28 Feb 1883 {3664}.

1117. iii.   CECILLA M.[8] HOWELL, born on 25 Dec 1867.

1118. iv.   ARCHIE R.[8] HOWELL, born on 10 Feb 1871.

1119. v.   FRED S.[8] HOWELL, born on 6 Jly 1874.

1120. vi.   EDMUND F.[8] HOWELL, born on 7 Jan 1877.

2. John [6], John [5]

693. WILLIAM BENJAMIN[7] HOWELL (John[6]), the son of John[6] and Elizabeth (Wells) Howell, was born on 3 Nov 1816 {3665}.
    William Benjamin Howell married Hannah Peck {3666}, who was born on 2 Mch 1815 {3667}.
    William B. Howell was listed as the head of a family consisting of one free white male of 20 and under 30 years of age, one of under 5, and one free white female of 20 and under 30, residing in the Town of Brookhaven, Suffolk County, New York, 1840 {3668}.
    On 7 Aug 1850, William B. Howell, 34, seaman, was enumerated as the head of a family consisting of himself, his wife, Hannah M., 35, and their children, Benj. F., 11, George W., 6, Thadias P., 4, and Emma, 2, residing in the Town of Brookhaven, Suffolk County, New York, in the Seventh Census of the United States {3669}.
    On 22 Jly 1870, William B. Howell, 53, farmer, with real property worth $3,000, and personal property worth $800, was enumerated as the head of a family consisting of himself, his wife, Hannah M., 55, and their children, George W., 27, seaman, Thadeus P., 24, farm laborer, Judson P., 17, and Jesse L., 10, residing in Center Moriches in the Town of Brookhaven, Suffolk County, New York, in the Ninth Census of the United States {3670}.
    Hannah M. Howell died on 19 Jan 1880, and is buried in the Mount Pleasant Cemetery at Center Moriches {3671}.
    William B. Howell died on 17 May 1883, and is buried beside his wife at Center Moriches {3672}.

3664. Gertrude A. Barber, MARRIAGES OF SUFFOLK COUNTY, N.Y.
3665. Wilbur Franklin Howell, op. cit., 265.
3666. Id.
3667. Gravestone, Mount Pleasant Cemetery, Center Moriches.
3668. U.S. Census, Brookhaven, Suffolk County, NY, 1840, Page 279.
3669. Id., 1850, Dwelling House 76, Family Number 86, Page 193.
3670. Id., 1870, Dwelling House 1131, Family Number 1212, Page 384.
3671. Gravestone, Mount Pleasant Cemetery, Center Moriches.
3672. Id., from the William F. Howell collection of cemetery markings.

William Benjamin and Hannah (Peck) Howell were the parents of six children {3673}.

1121. i. BENJAMIN FRANKLIN[8] HOWELL, born in about 1839.

1122. ii. GEORGE WASHINGTON[8] HOWELL, born on 30 Nov 1843, married Ida Trencher, died on 2 Oct 1881, at the age of 38, and is buried in the Mount Pleasant Cemetery in Center Moriches {3674}.

1123. iii. THADDEUS PECK[8] HOWELL, born on 14 Feb 1848, never married.

1124. iv. EMMA G.[8] HOWELL, married Morton Jones.

1125. v. JUDSON P.[8] HOWELL, born on 15 Sep 1853, married, died on 22 Mch 1932 {3675}, and is buried at Center Moriches.

1126. vi. JESSE L.[8] HOWELL, born in 1860, died on 27 Feb 1943 {3676}, and is buried in the Mount Pleasant Cemetery at Center Moriches {3677}.

694. ELIZABETH[7] HOWELL (John[6]), the daughter of John[6] and Elizabeth (Wells) Howell, was born on 1 Sep 1818 {3678}.

Elizabeth Howell married William M. Bishop. They were residing in Sauk Center, Stearns County, Minnesota, in 1883 {3679}.

William M. and Elizabeth (Howell) Bishop were the parents of two children {3680}.

i. SARAH JANE BISHOP, born on 9 Aug 1838, married Hugh Smith.

ii. GEORGE MITCHELL BISHOP.

695. JOHN FRANKLIN[7] HOWELL (John[6]), the son of John[6] and Elizabeth (Wells) Howell, was born on 7 Apr 1822 {3681}.

On 20 Nov 1849, John Franklin Howell married Mary A. Halsey, who was

3673. Wilbur Franklin Howell, op. cit., 265.
3674. Gravestone, Mount Pleasant Cemetery, Center Moriches.
3675. Suffolk County Estates, File #107 A 1932.
3676. Id., File #132 A 1943.
3677. Gravestone, Mount Pleasant Cemetery, Center Moriches.
3678. Wilbur Franklin Howell, op. cit., 257, 263.
3679. Id., 278.
3680. Id., 257.
3681. Id., 276.

born on 4 Apr 1829, the daughter of Hiram and Melissa (Tuttle) Halsey {3682}.

On 7 Aug 1850, Franklin Howell, 28, boat builder, with real property worth $800, was enumerated as the head of a family consisting of himself and his wife, Mary A., 21, residing in the Town of Brookhaven, Suffolk County, New York, in the Seventh Census of the United States {3683}.

On 25 Jly 1870, John F. Howell, 48, marketman, with real property worth $2,000, and personal property worth $3,000, was enumerated as the head of a family consisting of himself, and his wife, Mary, 42, residing in East Moriches in the Town of Brookhaven, Suffolk County, New York, in the Ninth Census of the United States {3684}. William Waley, 20, and Ella Waley, 19, were dwelling in the same house {3685}.

John Franklin and Mary A. (Halsey) Howell were the parents of two children {3686}.

1127.   i.   MARY ELEANOR[8] HOWELL, born on 24 Oct 1850, married William A. Whaley, who was born on 19 Aug 1850, the son of George and Margaret Whaley, on 6 Sep 1869, three children. William A. Whaley died on 15 Feb 1935, while Mary Eleanor, "Ella", died on 27 Jan 1943. Both are buried at Center Moriches {3687}.

1128.   ii.   FRANCES JANE[8] HOWELL, born on 30 Jan 1855, died on 12 Feb 1855, and is buried near her parents in the Mount Pleasant Cemetery in Center Moriches {3688}.

696. NATHANIEL WELLS[7] HOWELL (John[6]), the son of John[5] and Elizabeth (Wells) Howell, was born on 19 Mch 1824 {3689}.

Nathaniel Wells Howell married Hulda Albertson {3690}.

On 8 Aug 1850, Nathaniel Howell, 27, fisherman, with real property worth $500, was enumerated as the head of a family consisting of himself and his wife, Huldah, 20, residing in the Town of Brookhaven, Suffolk County, New York, in the Seventh Census of the United States, 1850 {3691}.

On 2 June 1870, N.W. Howell, 46, farmer, with real property worth

---

3682. Id.
3683. U.S. Census, Brookhaven, Suffolk County, NY, 1850, Dwelling House 77, Family Number 87, Page 193.
3684. Id., 1870, Dwelling House 1201, Family Number 1285, Page 388.
3685. Id., Family Number 1286, Page 388.
3686. Wilbur Franklin Howell, op. cit., 276.
3687. Id., 277 (?).
3688. Gravestone, Mount Pleasant Cemetery, Center Moriches.
3689. Wilbur Franklin Howell, op. cit., 257, 263.
3690. Id.
3691. U.S. Census, Brookhaven, Suffolk County, NY, 1850, Dwelling House 125, Family Number 139, Page 196.

$3000, and personal property worth $1000, was enumerated as the head of a family consisting of himself, his wife, Huldah, 44, and their daughter, Carrie M., 7, residing in Amagansett in the Town of East Hampton, Suffolk County, New York, in the Ninth Census of the United States {3692}. Hervey King, 37, farm laborer, with property worth $200, was residing in the same dwelling, as were his wife, Adelia, 27, and their children, Alice, 9, and Everett, 4 {3693}.

Hulda M. Howell died in 1888 {3694}.

Nathaniel W. Howell married Anne Edwards as his second wife {3695}.

Nathaniel Wells Howell died on 10 Feb 1907 {3696}.

Nathaniel Wells and Huldah (Albertson) Howell were the parents of at least two children {3697}.

1129. i.   EDGAR F.[8] HOWELL, born on 17 Nov 1846 at Eastport, married Lucy Lent in 1865, four children, was a merchant and became Postmaster {3698}.

1130. ii.   CARRIE M.[8] HOWELL, born on 7 Sep 1866.

Nathaniel Wells and Anne (Edwards) Howell were the parents of one son.

1131. iii. NATHANIEL ROBINSON[8] HOWELL, born on 15 June 1888, married Elizabeth Valentine Conway, the daughter of Thomas and Katherine (Hutton) Valentine, on 1 Jly 1922. She was born on 29 Jly 1887, and died on 10 Nov 1962 {3699}, and is buried in the Woodlawn Cemetery at Bellport {3700}. He was the Historian of the Town of Islip {3701}. He died on 29 Dec 1956 {3702}.

697. HAMPTON YOUNGS[7] HOWELL (John[6]), the son of John[6] and Elizabeth (Wells) Howell, was born on 17 Aug 1826 {3703}.

Hampton Youngs Howell "..folowed the water for a Living, ketching eels

3692. Id., East Hampton, Suffolk County, NY, 1870, Dwelling House 27, Family Number 33, Page 444.
3693. Id., Family Number 32, Page 444.
3694. PORTRAIT & BIOGRAPHICAL RECORD OF SUFFOLK COUNTY, 609.
3695. Wilbur Franklin Howell, op. cit., 263.
3696. Id.
3697. Id., 281.
3698. PORTRAIT & BIOGRAPHICAL RECORD OF SUFFOLK COUNTY, 609.
3699. Suffolk County Estates, File #1252 P 1962.
3700. Gravestone, Woodlawn Cemetery, Bellport, from the William F. Howell collection of cemetery markings.
3701. Wilbur Franklin Howell, op. cit.
3702. Suffolk County Estates, File #53 P 1957.
3703. Wilbur Franklin Howell, op. cit., 257, 263.

and fish untill the age of 20 years.." {3704}.

"In the year 1846. July 20. I was taken ill so that I could not do much work untill January 1847. and then I went to tend store for John Cornell in -- Warter vill with N. W. Howell in pardenship where I staid untill April 1848. at that time Mr. Cornell discontinued keeping store and I went to take charge of a store in Speonk town of South Hampton owned by H. H. Rogers where I staid and tended store untill Feb. 8, 1849. when I left Mr. Rogers, and went to my Brothers, for the perpus of a going to chool where I staid 2 or 3 weeks as the chool house was old and the wether cold I cought a violent cold and had to leave the chool and find my way home where I staid untill April when I went to New Park and Bought a Lot of Books and thought I would travil around and see the country,, But I soon found that this would not do for me so I stop this traid in June 1849, and cummensed cutting flags, and gathern master work seed,, untill September and then I cummensed Pediling drugs, from the store of John W. Smith, Hempstead, L. Island with a horse an wagon their the Island to all the stores and Doctors whole sail and reatail, and got orders for soap and candles at 5 percent commision and continued this until Oct. 1850 to March 1851 when I was taken with the Measles whitch I thought would end my life, But..I am yet alive and unto the Lord I owe my Life and strength." {3705}.

On 7 Aug 1850, Hampton Y. Howell, 22, pedler, was enumerated with the household of his father, John Howell, in the Seventh Census of the United States, 1850 {3706}.

Hampton Y. Howell married Elizabeth Wakeman {3707}. (NOTE: *Hampton Howell married Mrs. Elizabeth Webber* {3708}).

Hampton Howell died on 8 Jly 1863, and is buried in the Mount Pleasant Cemetery in Center Moriches {3709}.

Hampton Youngs and Elizabeth (Wakeman) Webber Howell were the parents of four children {3710}.

1132.   i.   WALLACE HAMPTON[8] HOWELL, born on 26 Jly 1853, married Eugenie Munier, who was born on 19 Jly 1857, the daughter of Charles and Mary (Rolland) Munier, three children.

1133.   ii.   CHARLES W.[8] HOWELL, born in 1855.

1134.   iii.   HENRY W.[8] HOWELL, born in 1858, died in 1859, and is buried

3704. Hampton Youngs Howell, Personal communication, given by Wilbur Franklin Howell, op. cit., 287.
3705. Id.
3706. U.S. Census, Brookhaven, Suffolk County, NY, 1850, Dwelling House 82, Family Number 93, Page 193.
3707. Wilbur Franklin Howell, op. cit., 287.
3708. LONG ISLAND STAR, 9 Feb 1853, from THE REGISTER, SCHS, XVIII, #1, 24 (Summer 1992).
3709. Gravestone, Mount Pleasant Cemetery, Center Moriches.
3710. Wilbur Franklin Howell, op. cit.

in the Mount Pleasant Cemetery at Center Moriches {3711}.

1135. iv.   CORA BELL[8] HOWELL.

698. ELECTA AMELIA[7] HOWELL (John[6]), the daughter of John[6] and Elizabeth (Wells) Howell, was born on 17 June 1830 {3712}.
 Electa Amelia Howell married Lewis Terry {3713}.
 On 23 Jly 1870, Lewis Terry, 41, farmer, having real property valued at $2000, and personal property valued at $500, was enumerated as the head of a family consisting of himself, his wife, Electa, 40, and their children, Millard, 14, Cornelia, 12, Adelia, 10, and Herbert, 8, residing in the Town of Brookhaven, Suffolk County, New York, in the Ninth Census of the United States {3714}.
 Electa Amelia Terry died in 1919 {3715}.
 Lewis and Electa Amelia (Howell) Terry were the parents of at least four children.

   i.   MILLARD TERRY, born in about 1856.

   ii.   CORNELIA TERRY, born in about 1858.

   iii.   ADELIA TERRY, born in about 1860.

   iv.   HERBERT TERRY, born in about 1862.

699. J. MITCHELL[7] HOWELL (John[6]), the son of John[6] and Elizabeth (Wells) Howell, was born on 24 Dec 1833 {3716}.
 On 7 Aug 1850, Mitchell Howell, 17, was enumerated as a member of his father's family in the Seventh Census of the United States, 1850 {3717}.
 Mitchell Howell married Mary E. Mott, who was born on 17 June 1839, the daughter of Ezra and Melinda (Smith) Mott {3718}.
 J. Mitchell and Mary E. (Mott) Howell were the parents of seven children {3719}.

1136. i.   STELLA[8] HOWELL.

3711. Gravestone, Mount Pleasant Cemetery, Center Moriches.
3712. Wilbur Franklin Howell, op. cit., 263.
3713. Id.
3714. U.S. Census, Brookhaven, Suffolk County, NY, 1870, Dwelling House 1165, Family Number 1247, Page 385.
3715. Wilbur Franklin Howell, op. cit.
3716. Id., 257, 263.
3717. U.S. Census, Brookhaven, Suffolk County, NY, 1850, Dwelling House 82, Family Number 93, Page 193.
3718. Wilbur Franklin Howell, op. cit., 295.
3719. Id.

1137. ii.   BURTON[8] HOWELL.

1138. iii. AUGUSTUS[8] HOWELL.

1139. iv.   EDWARD S.[8] HOWELL.

1140. v.   JOHN[8] HOWELL.

1141. vi.   FRANK[8] HOWELL.

1142. vii. CHARLES[8] HOWELL.

700. CHARLES MANLEY[7] HOWELL (John[6]), the son of John[6] and Elizabeth (Wells) Howell, was born on 20 Nov 1835 {3720}.

On 7 Aug 1850, Charles Howell, 14, was enumerated as a member of his father's family in the Seventh Census of the United States {3721}.

Charles Manley Howell married Mary J. Havens {3722}, who was born on 28 June 1833, the daughter of Daniel Tuthill and Betsey (Raynor) Havens {3723}.

On 4 Aug 1870, Charles Howell, 35, ship carpenter, with real property worth $800, and personal property worth $100, was enumerated as the head of a family consisting of himself, his wife, Mary, 36, and their children, William, 12, Winnie, 10, Gussie, 7, Charles, 6, Ada, 4, and Frank, 1, residing at East Marion in the Town of Southold, Suffolk County, New York, in the Ninth Census of the United States {3724}.

Charles M. Howell and his sons were oystermen living on Main Street in Dividing Creek, New Jersey, in 1900 {3725}.

Charles M. Howell was drowned, with his son, Leolin, his daughter, Winnie E., her husband, Albert B. Lamb, and their adopted son, John Scullinger, on 5 Jly 1902 when their gasoline engine-powered skiff was swamped in rough seas at Jones Inlet off Hempstead, Long Island, New York {3726}.

Charles Manley and Mary J. (Havens) Howell were the parents of seven children {3727}.

3720. Id., 263.
3721. U.S. Census, Brookhaven, Suffolk County, NY, Dwelling House 82, Family Number 93, Page 193.
3722. Wilbur Franklin Howell, op. cit.
3723. Mallmann, op. cit., 167.
3724. U.S. Census, Southold, Suffolk County, NY, 1870, Dwelling House 1166, Family Number 1268, Page 303.
3725. Id., Cumberland County, NJ, 1900, Dwelling House 58.
3726. RIVERHEAD RECORD, 5 Jly 1902, PATCHOGUE ADVANCE, 18 Jly 1902, BRIDGETON (NJ) PIONEER, 17 Jly 1902, Margaret Louise Mints, THE GREAT WILDERNESS, copies of all graciously provided by Joy Titmus.
3727. Joy Titmus, Personal communication, via Ronald Lee Howell, Jr.

1143. i. WILLIAM[8] HOWELL, born in 1858.

1144. ii. WINNIE E.[8] HOWELL, born in Sep 1861, married her cousin, Albert B. Lamb, who was born in Jan 1855, the son of Elisha Rodman and Matilda R. (Havens) Lamb, one adopted son. All were drowned on 5 Jly 1902.

1145. iii. GUSSIE[8] HOWELL, born in 1863.

1146. iv. CHARLES H.[8] HOWELL, born in Dec 1864, married Lillie E. --- , at least two children.

1147. v. ADA[8] HOWELL, born in about 1866.

1148. vi. FRANK[8] HOWELL, born in about 1869.

1149. vii. LEOLIN[8] HOWELL, born in Aug 1879.

701. HANNAH MARIA[7] HOWELL (John[6]), the daughter of John[6] and Elizabeth (Wells) Howell, was born on 26 Nov 1838 {3728}.

Hannah Howell, 12, was enumerated in her father's family on 7 Aug 1850 in the Seventh Census of the United States {3729}.

Hannah Maria Howell married Joshua Penny {3730}.

Hannah Maria Penny died on 4 June 1896 {3731}.

B. Reeves[4], John[3], John[2], Richard[1]

1. Isaac Reeve[6], Isaac Reeve[5]

702. ISAAC REEVE[7] HOWELL (Isaac Reeve[6]), the son of Isaac Reeve[6] and Hannah (Raynor) Howell, was born on 10 Sep 1825 {3732}, at Middle Island.

On 31 Jly 1850, Isaac R. Howell, 24, farmer, with real property valued at $500, was enumerated with the family of his father in the Seventh Census of the

---

3728. Wilbur Franklin Howell, op. cit., 263.
3729. U.S. Census, Brookhaven, Suffolk County, NY, 1850, Dwelling House 82, Family Number 93, Page 193.
3730. Wilbur Franklin Howell, op. cit.
3731. Id.
3732. Craven, op. cit., 375.

United States {3733}.

Isaac Reeve Howell married Abigail Ann Cox, who was born on 4 Feb 1831, the daughter of Samuel and Bethiah (Reeve) Cox {3734}.

Isaac Reeve Howell was a Trustee of the Mattituck Society at the time of its organization on 21 Mch 1854 {3735}.

"In 1856 one acre for a new site for the Mattituck schoolhouse was purchased of Barnabas Wines for $275.00. This lot was next east of the old site. The building was erected the next year, the plans being made by Isaac R. Howell, Jr., and the contract for building being awarded to B. T. Corwin for $591.00." {3736}.

Isaac R. Howell, Jr., became a bayman and built a house near the shore. On 2 Apr 1868, as he was crossing Peconic Bay to Red Cedar Point to get shellfish, his boat capsized, and he was drowned before the eyes of his wife, Abbie Ann {3737}. He is buried in the cemetery at the Mattituck Presbyterian Church {3738}.

By his will of 24 Oct 1859, Isaac R. Howell, Jr., bequeathed to his "..wife Abbie Ann the use of all my property both real and personal estate during her natural life, so long as she remains my widow and in case of her marriage I give and bequeath to my said wife the sum of Five Hundred Dollars in lieu of her dower in my real estate." He left this property to his children, George Herbert Howell and Mary Emma Howell, with two-thirds to go to George Herbert and one-third to go to Mary Emma. His wife, Abbie Ann, and his friend, J. Frank Horton, were named executors of this will {3739}.

On 2 June 1870, Abby Howell, 39, with real property worth $5000, and personal property worth $1500, was enumerated as the head of a family consisting of herself and her children, George, 15, farmer, Mary, 11 (sic), and Sarah, 8, all of whom attended school, residing in Mattituck in the Town of Southold, Suffolk County, New York, in the Ninth Census of the United States {3740}.

On 6 Feb 1874, Thomas Reeve married Mrs. Abbie A. Howell {3741}.

Abigail Ann (Cox) Howell Reeve died on 29 Dec 1913 {3742}.

Isaac Reeve and Abigail Ann (Cox) Howell were the parents of three children {3743}.

3733. U.S. Census, Southold, Suffolk County, NY, 1850, Dwelling House 859, Family Number 936, Page 334.
3734. Wilbur Franklin Howell, op. cit., 367.
3735. Craven, op. cit., 176-177.
3736. Id., 200.
3737. Edna Howell Yeager, Personal communication.
3738. Craven, op. cit.
3739. Suffolk County Wills, Liber 10, 27-28; Suffolk County Estates, File #6458.
3740. U.S. Census, Southold, Suffolk County, NY, 1870, Dwelling House 27, Family Number 29, Page 234.
3741. Gertrude A. Barber, MARRIAGES OF SUFFOLK COUNTY.
3742. Wilbur Franklin Howell, op. cit.
3743. Id.

1150. i. MARY EMMA[8] HOWELL, born on 11 Nov 1852.

1151. ii. GEORGE HERBERT[8] HOWELL, born on 14 Apr 1855, married Mary E. Brown on 21 Feb 1878 {3744}, three children, died on 14 Apr 1955. Mary E. Howell died on 1 June 1935, and is buried at Middletown, NY {3745}.

1152. iii. SARAH ELIZABETH[8] HOWELL, born on 26 Aug 1862, married H. Halsey Reeve {3746}, who was born on 5 May 1859, the son of Thomas E. and Caroline (Hallock) Reeve. With his father, he established an extensive greenhouse in Mattituck {3747}.

703. JOSEPH RAYNOR[7] HOWELL (Isaac Reeve[6]), the son of Isaac Reeve[6] and Hannah (Raynor) Howell, was born at Middle Island on 25 Oct 1826. He entered Yale College as a sophomore in 1851, and graduated in the Class of 1854 {3748}.

Soon after his graduation, Joseph Raynor Howell commenced teaching at Franklinville, Long Island, New York {3749}. He became Principal of the Franklinville Academy {3750}, and continued teaching there until a few days before his death {3751}.

On 16 Oct 1854, Joseph Raynor Howell married Harmony Etta Squires, who was born on 6 Oct 1831 {3752}, the daughter of Seth and Harmony (Wines) Squires {3753}.

"While watching at the bedside of a dying brother, he contracted the typhus fever and died of that disease on the 13th of Sept., 1855" {3754}.

Joseph Raynor Howell died in Squiretown {3755}, and is buried in the cemetery at Good Ground {3756}.

Harmony Etta (Squires) Howell married (2) William H. Clark, of Center Moriches {3757}, on 28 Sep 1875. On 31 Dec 1894, she married (3) Benjamin Alvah Horton as his second wife {3758}.

3744. N. Hubbard Cleveland, op. cit.
3745. Wilbur Franklin Howell, op. cit., 368.
3746. Owen J. Cook, Personal communication.
3747. Lucius H. Hallock, op. cit., 203.
3748. M.N. Whitmore, op. cit.
3749. Id.
3750. Franklin Bowditch Dexter, op. cit.
3751. Whitmore, op. cit.
3752. David M. Squires, Personal communication.
3753. Tiger Gardiner, Personal communication.
3754. Whitmore, op. cit.
3755. Dexter, op. cit.
3756. Squires, op. cit.
3757. Dexter, op. cit.
3758. Squires, op. cit.

Joseph Raynor and Harmony Etta (Squires) Howell did not have any children.

710. CYRUS FANCHER[7] HOWELL (Isaac Reeve[6]), the son of Isaac Reeve[6] and Hannah (Raynor) Howell, was born on 3 Jan 1833 at Middle Island.

On 31 Jly 1850, Cyrus F. Howell, 17, farmer, was enumerated with the family of his father in the Seventh Census of the United States {3759}.

Cyrus Fancher Howell married Caroline Halsey {3760}.

Cyrus Fancher Howell died on 10 Sep 1855 at Mattituck, at the age of 22 years, 8 months, and 7 days, and is buried in the cemetery at the Mattituck Presbyterian Church {3761}. He was, most likely, the brother at whose bedside Joseph Raynor Howell (#703) became infected with typhus.

Caroline M. Howell, age 28, died at Southold in 1857 {3762}.

712. MARY ANN[7] HOWELL (Isaac Reeve[6]), the daughter of Isaac Reeve[6] and Hannah (Raynor) Howell, was born at Middle Island in about 1835.

On 31 Jly 1850, Mary Howell, 15, was residing in the home of her father, as reported in the Seventh Census of the United States {3763}.

Mary Ann Howell married Henry N. Chapman, who was born in 1823 {3764}.

On 2 June 1870, Henry Chapman, 47, farmer, with real property worth $1000, was enumerated as the head of a household consisting of himself, his wife, Mary, 35, George Howell, 18, farm laborer, and Edward Howell, 5, residing at Mattituck in the Town of Southold, Suffolk County, New York, in the Ninth Census of the United States {3765}.

Henry N. Chapman died in 1899 {3766}.

Mary Ann Chapman died in 1912 {3767}.

Henry N. and Mary Ann (Howell) Chapman were the parents of one adopted son {3768}.

    i.   EDWARD OLIN CHAPMAN, married Frances Octavia Hammond

3759. U.S. Census, Southold, Suffolk County, NY, 1850, Dwelling House 859, Family Number 936, Page 334.
3760. Sherwood, op. cit.
3761. Craven, op. cit., 375.
3762. LONG ISLAND STAR, 30 Sep 1857, from THE REGISTER, SCHS, XIX, #2, 45 (Fall 1993).
3763. U.S. Census, Southold, Suffolk County, NY, 1850, Dwelling House 859, Family Number 936, Page 334.
3764. Wilbur Franklin Howell, op. cit., 380.
3765. U.S. Census, Southold, Suffolk County, NY, 1870, Dwelling House 25, Family Number 27, Page 234.
3766. Wilbur Franklin Howell, op. cit., 380.
3767. Id.
3768. Id.

as his second wife on 7 Jan 1897 {3769}.

713. SERENO BERNELL[7] HOWELL (Isaac Reeve[6]), the son of Isaac Reeve[6] and Hannah (Raynor) Howell, was born in about 1838.

On 31 Jly 1850, Sereno Howell, 12, was residing in the home of his father, as recorded in the Seventh Census of the United States {3770}.

"Sareno Howell" married Miss Elizabeth Kent at Mattituck {3771}. She was born in England in about 1840.

On 2 June 1870, Sereno Howell, 32, farmer, with real property worth $1500, and personal property worth $200, was enumerated as the head of a family consisting of himself, his wife, Elizabeth, 30, and their children, Laura, 10, Sereno, 8, Florence, 6, Frederick, 3, and Anna, 5 months, residing at Mattituck in the Town of Southold, Suffolk County, New York {3772}.

Sereno Bernell and Elizabeth (Kent) Howell were the parents of five children.

   1153. i.   LAURA[8] HOWELL, born in about 1860.

   1154. ii.   SERENO[8] HOWELL, born in about 1862.

   1155. iii.   FLORENCE[8] HOWELL, born in about 1864.

   1156. iv.   FREDERICK[8] HOWELL, born in about 1867.

   1157. v.   ANNA[8] HOWELL, born in Jan 1870.

714. MIRIAM AUGUSTA[7] HOWELL (Isaac Reeve[6]), the daughter of Isaac Reeves[6] and Hannah (Raynor) Howell, was born in about 1839.

Miriam Howell, 11, was enumerated in the household of her father in the Seventh Census of the United States, as recorded on 31 Jly 1850 {3773}.

Miriam Augusta Howell married Asa Clinton York, of Mattituck {3774}.

Asa Clinton York was a witness to the will of Isaac R. Howell, Jr., written on 24 Oct 1859 {3775}.

On 4 June 1870, Clinton York, 36, carpenter, with real property worth $900, was enumerated as the head of a family consisting of himself, his wife,

3769. Hammond, op. cit., 674.
3770. U.S. Census, Southold, Suffolk County, NY, 1850, Dwelling House 859, Family Number 936, Page 334.
3771. LONG ISLAND STAR, 20 Jly 1859.
3772. U.S. Census, Southold, Suffolk County, NY, 1870, Dwelling House 30, Family Number 32, Page 234.
3773. Id., 1850, Dwelling House 859, Family Number 936, Page 334.
3774. Sherwood, op. cit.
3775. Suffolk County Wills, Liber 10, 27-28.

Miriam, 30, and their children, Charles, 14, Frank, 13, Minnie, 7, and Henry, $^8/_{12}$, residing at Mattituck in the Town of Southold, Suffolk County, New York, in the Ninth Census of the United States {3776}.

Asa Clinton and Miriam Augusta (Howell) York were the parents of at least eight children.

    i.   CHARLES YORK, born in about 1856.

    ii.   FRANK YORK, born in about 1857.

    iii.   BENJAMIN F. YORK, born on 14 Nov 1858, died on 11 Mch 1859, at the age of 4 months and 25 days, and is buried in the cemetery at the Mattituck Presbyterian Church {3777}.

    iv.   MARY EMILY YORK, born on 25 Sep 1859, died on 23 May 1869, at the age of 9 years, 8 months, and 28 days, and is buried beside her siblings at Mattituck {3778}.

    v.   I. HOWELL YORK, born on 23 Apr 1861, died on 29 May 1869, at the age of 8 years, 1 month, and 6 days, and is buried beside his siblings at Mattituck {3779}.

    vi.   MINNIE YORK, born in about 1863.

    vii.   LUCY H. YORK, born on 30 Nov 1864, died on 7 Sep 1868, at the age of 3 years, 9 months, and 7 days, and is buried beside her siblings at Mattituck {3780}.

    viii. HENRY YORK, born in Oct 1869.

715. FRANCES AMANDA[7] HOWELL (Isaac Reeve[6]), the daughter of Isaac Reeve[6] and Hannah (Raynor) Howell, was born on 3 May 1841 {3781}.

Frances Howell, 8, was enumerated with the family of her father in the Seventh Census of the United States, as recorded on 31 Jly 1850 {3782}.

On 22 Nov 1859, Frances Amanda, "Fannie", Howell married Samuel Mowbray Hammond, who was born at New Village, now (1994) Centereach, on 10

3776. U.S. Census, Southold, Suffolk County, NY, 1870, Dwelling House 91, Family Number 94, Page 238.

3777. Craven, op. cit., 396.

3778. Id.

3779. Id., 395.

3780. Craven, op. cit., 396.

3781. Sherwood, op. cit.

3782. U.S. Census, Southold, Suffolk County, NY, 1850, Dwelling House 859, Family Number 936, Page 334.

Mch 1833, the son of Rev. Mowbray S. and Laura (Hallock) Hammond {3783}.

Samuel Mowbray Hammond went to sea at the age of sixteen, but returned home after a few months. "He went South soon after his return, and spent three years, mainly in Virginia and South Carolina, where he was engaged in taking daguerrotypes and teaching. During this period in the South, he experienced religion, and upon his return home in 1853 he began to tell his experience and exhort. His eloquent words resulted in a revival of religion, and he saw clearly that his true field of labor was in the ministry. To secure means for his education, he again returned to Virginia and taught school." {3784}.

"In 1855 he received a license to exhort, and in 1856 a local preacher's license from the York, Va., circuit. When he had earned enough money to continue his education he returned North and entered Fort Plain (N. Y.) Seminary, where he remained a year, when he entered the Biblical Institute at Concord, N. H., where he graduated in 1859. After his graduation he was supply preacher at Freeport, Long Island, some months, and then he joined the New York Eastern Conference at its session in 1860. He then preached at Freeport and Bethel, L. I., the remainder of the year, at Southold, L. I., 1861-62; Riverhead, L. I., 1863-64; Nostrand Avenue, Brooklyn, N. Y., 1865-67; New Canaan, Conn., 1868-70; Hamden, Conn., 1871; Freeport, L. I., 1872-1874; Port Chester, N. Y., 1875-77; New Rochelle, N. Y., 1878-80; East Pearl Street, New Haven, Conn., 1885-87; New Britain, Conn., 1844; Ansonia, Conn., 1885-87, and Torrington, Conn., 1888, until his death." {3785}.

"He was an eloquent preacher, a fluent and convincing writer, and a man whose everyday life and example added greatly to the weight of his words. He truly believed and practiced what he preached; a kind, loving husband and father, a true friend and adviser, a fearless, noble example of American manhood; his good deeds live after him." {3786}.

Samuel Mowbray Hammond died on 2 Jan 1892 at Torrington, Connecticut {3787}.

Fanny Howell Hammond was cited by Wilbur Franklin Howell {3788}.

Samuel Mowbray and Frances Amanda, "Fannie", (Howell) Hammond were the parents of fourteen children {3789}.

    i.   FRANCES OCTAVIA HAMMOND, born on 5 Aug 1860, married Edward Olin Chapman, the adopted son of Henry and Mary Ann (Howell) (#714) Chapman, on 7 Jan 1887, as his

---

3783. Sherwood, op. cit.
3784. Hammond, op. cit., 546.
3785. Id., 546-547.
3786. Id., 547.
3787. Id., 546.
3788. Wilbur Franklin Howell, op. cit., vi.
3789. Hammond, op. cit., 548.

second wife {3790}.

ii. GRACE MOWBRAY HAMMOND, born on 22 Mch 1862, died on 19 Apr 1862, at the age of 18 days, and is buried in the cemetery at the New Village Congregational Church in Centereach {3791}.

iii. MARION LINCOLN HAMMOND, born on 27 Apr 1865.

iv. FREDERIC H. L. HAMMOND, born on 13 Oct 1866.

v. HALLIE HAMMOND, born on 12 Dec 1868, died on 20 Jan 1870.

vi. SAMUEL M. HAMMOND, born on 24 Oct 1870.

vii. GRACE LILLIAN HAMMOND, born on 1 Jly 1872 at Freeport, New York, graduated from the New Britain State Normal School in 1894, was a teacher at Stamford, Connecticut, until Dec 1900, married Herbert F. Sherwood, of Stamford, who was a journalist on the staff of the *New York Herald Tribune*, on 6 Mch 1901, resided at East Orange, New Jersey {3792}.

viii. EDITH CARY HAMMOND, born on 14 Mch 1874 at Freeport, graduated from the New Britain State Normal School in 1894, was a teacher at Stamford.

ix. ELEANOR SUMMERFIELD HAMMOND, born on 28 Dec 1875 at Port Chester, New York, resided with her mother at New Haven.

x. ETHEL WILLIS HAMMOND, born on 27 June 1877 at Port Chester, was a stenographer employed at Bridgeport, Connecticut.

xi. JOSEPH HOWELL HAMMOND, born on 17 Dec 1878, died on 22 Dec 1878.

xii. CYRUS FANCHER HAMMOND, born on 17 Dec 1878, died on 29 Dec 1878.

xiii. BLANCHE GARFIELD HAMMOND, born on 8 Apr 1880 at New Rochelle, New York, graduated from the New Haven Normal

3790. Id., 674.
3791. NYG&BR, 21, 78 (Apr 1890).
3792. Hammond, op. cit., 676.

School in 1900, was a teacher in Branford, Connecticut.

xiv.   CHARLES GLOVER HAMMOND, born on 11 Mch 1887 at Ansonia.

716. HANNAH SMITH[7] HOWELL (Isaac Reeve[6]), the daughter of Isaac Reeve[6] and Hannah (Raynor) Howell, was born on 30 Jun 1845.

On 31 Jly 1850, Hannah S. Howell, 5, was enumerated with the family of her father in the Seventh Census of the United States {3793}.

On 2 Mch 1865, Hannah Howell married Orlando Smith, who was born at Smithtown on 8 Jly 1835, the son of Howard Smith {3794}.

On 2 June 1870, Orlando Smith, 35, fisherman, was enumerated as the head of a family consisting of himself, his wife, Hannah, 24, and their child, Henrietta, $^3/_{12}$, and Melinda Smith, 70, residing at Mattituck in the Town of Southold, Suffolk County, New York, in the Ninth Census of the United States {3795}. Living in the same house was Mehetable Conklin, 55, with real property worth $1200 {3796}.

Hannah Smith died at Southold on 21 Dec 1899, at the age of 53 years, 6 months, and 21 days {3797}.

Orlando Smith died at Southold on 15 Dec 1902, at the age of 67 years, 5 months, and 7 days {3798}.

Orlando and Hannah (Howell) Smith were the parents of three children {3799}.

i.   HENRIETTA SMITH, born in Mch 1870, married Mr. Fickeissen, died in 1906.

ii.   SERENO H. SMITH, married Amarette Hallock in Feb 1912. She was born in 1878 {3800}, the daughter of Charles W. and Phebe Jane (Benjamin) Hallock {3801}.

iii.   ARTHUR SMITH.

3793. U.S. Census, Southold, Suffolk County, NY, 1850, Dwelling House 859, Family Number 936, Page 334.
3794. Wilbur Franklin Howell, op. cit., 370.
3795. U.S. Census, Southold, Suffolk County, NY, 1870, Dwelling House 22, Family Number 23, Page 234.
3796. Id., Family Number 24, Page 234.
3797. Wilbur Franklin Howell, op. cit.
3798. Id.
3799. Id.
3800. Lucius H. Hallock, op. cit., 163.
3801. Id., 216.

2. Gershom Hawkins[6], Isaac Reeve[5]

720. JOEL CONKLIN[7] HOWELL (Gershom Hawkins[6]), the son of Gershom Hawkins[6] and Lydia (Conklin) Howell, was born on 12 Jly 1832 {3802}.

On 1 Aug 1850, Joel Howell, 18, laborer, was enumerated in the household of his father in the Seventh Census of the United States {3803}.

On 24 Sep 1854, Joel Conklin Howell married Phebe Huldah Carter, who was born on 21 Sep 1834, the daughter of Silas and Selina (Raynor) Carter {3804}.

On 2 June 1870, Joel Howell, 37, book agent, with real property worth $700, was enumerated as the head of a family consisting of himself, his wife, Phebe, 35, and their children, Nellie, 14, Thomas, 12, Silas, 10, Lillie, 9, Earnest, 3, and Carrie, 1, residing in Mattituck in the Town of Southold, Suffolk County, New York, in the Ninth Census of the United States {3805}.

Joel Conklin Howell died on 21 Sep 1919 {3806}, and is buried in the cemetery at the Mattituck Presbyterian Church {3807}.

Phebe Huldah Howell died on 11 Jly 1921 at Mattituck {3808}, and is buried beside her husband at Mattituck {3809}.

Joel Conklin and Phebe H. (Carter) Howell were the parents of seven children {3810}.

1158. i. RINELCHE, "NELLIE", HALLOCK[8] HOWELL, born on 3 Jan 1856, was counted twice in the 1870 Census {3811}, married Willard Fletcher Hallock on 8 Nov 1876, four children. He was born in Jly 1855, the son of Joel Hallock, and died on 12 Nov 1897. She later married (2) William Corbin Arnold {3812}.

1159. ii. THOMAS HENRY[8] HOWELL, born on 10 Dec 1857, married Grace Amanda Tripp, who was born on 21 Sep 1863, the daughter of Gideon and Betsey (Brewster) Tripp, on 21 Dec 1882, two children. He was a Captain in the New England Steamship

---

3802. Mallmann, op. cit., 302-303.
3803. U.S. Census, Southold, Suffolk County, NY, 1850, Dwelling House 860, Family Number 937, Page 334.
3804. Mallmann, op. cit., 303.
3805. U.S. Census, Southold, Suffolk County, NY, 1870, Dwelling House 28, Family Number 30, Page 234.
3806. Suffolk County Estates, File #23866.
3807. Gravestone, Mattituck Presbyterian Church Cemetery, from the cemetery markings collected by William F. Howell (579).
3808. Edna Howell Yeager, Personal communication.
3809. Gravestone, Mattituck Presbyterian Church Cemetery.
3810. Mallmann, op. cit.
3811. U.S. Census, Southold, Suffolk County, NY, 1870, Dwelling House 28, Family Number 30, Page 234, Id., Dwelling House 143, Family Number 146, Page 241.
3812. Mallmann, op. cit., 304, Wilbur Franklin Howell, op. cit., 384.

Company, and lived in New London, Connecticut, where he died on 19 Mch 1922 {3813}.

1160. iii.   SILAS HAWKINS[8] HOWELL, born on 13 Jly 1859, married Lizzie C. Dunham, who was born on 1 Oct 1861, the daughter of William H. and Caroline (Griffin) Dunham, on 1 Sep 1886, two children {3814}.

1161. iv.   LYDIA C.[8] HOWELL, born on 15 Apr 1861, married F. Porter Howell (#1229) on 17 Mch 1880 , five children {3815}, died on 5 Feb 1927 {3816}. He was born on 17 Jly 1859, the son of Hiram (#776) and Belinda (Raynor) Howell, died on 9 Sep 1936 {3817}, and is buried in the Riverhead Cemetery {3818}. NOTE: *F. Porter and Lydia C. Howell were the grandparents of Edna Howell Yeager* {3819}.

1162. v.   JOEL ERNEST[8] HOWELL, born on 17 Jly 1866, married Sydney R. Burgess, who was born on 22 Feb 1868, the daughter of Robert and Sarah (Donnelley) Burgess, three children, died on 12 Aug 1946 {3820}.

1163. vi.   CAROLINE AMANDA[8] HOWELL, born on 14 Aug 1868, married Arthur Horace Tuthill, who was born on 28 May 1858, the son of Daniel and Caroline (Wells) Tuthill, on 8 Sep 1886, four children, died on 14 Jan 1950, while he died on 19 Dec 1899 {3821}.

1164. vii.   ALFRED V. B.[8] HOWELL, born on 13 Feb 1871, married (1) Bertha Vail on 10 Nov 1898, one child, married (2) Agnes or Allison Eberhardt, of Scranton, died in Mch 1953 {3822}.

723. ALFRED B.[7] HOWELL (Gershom Hawkins[6]), the son of Gershom Hawkins[6] and Lydia (Conklin) Howell, was born on 10 Apr 1842 {3823}.

    Alfred Howell, 8, was enumerated with his father's family in the Seventh

3813. Mallmann, op. cit., 304, Wilbur Franklin Howell, op. cit., 391.
3814. Mallmann, op. cit., 304, Wilbur Franklin Howell, op. cit., 393.
3815. Mallmann, op. cit., 304.
3816. Yeager, op. cit.
3817. Suffolk County Estates, File #407 P 1936.
3818. Gravestone, Riverhead Cemetery.
3819. Yeager, op. cit.
3820. Mallmann, op. cit., 304, Wilbur Franklin Howell, op. cit., 396.
3821. Mallmann, op. cit., 304, Alva M. Tuttle, op. cit., 46.
3822. Wilbur Franklin Howell, op. cit., 401.
3823. Mallmann, op. cit., 302.

Census of the United States {3824}.

On 1 Jan 1875, Alfred B. Howell married Cassie Wiggins, of Greenport {3825}.

Alfred B. Howell died on 9 June 1932 {3826}.

3. William Clark [6], Isaac Reeves [5]

728. DANIEL ELIAS[7] HOWELL (William Clark[7], Isaac Reeves[6], Reeves[5]), the son of William Clark[6] and Violetta A. (Youngs) Howell, was born on 13 Oct 1846 {3827}.

On 6 Jly 1878, Daniel Elias Howell married Augusta May Tubbs, who was born on 23 Jan 1863, the daughter of John Henry and Anna Amelia (Smith) Hubbs {3828}.

Daniel Elias Howell died on 17 Oct 1917 {3829}.

Augusta May Howell died in 1937 {3830}.

Daniel Elias and Augusta May (Tubbs) Howell were the parents of two children {3831}.

    1165. i.   LILLIAN MAY[8] HOWELL, born on 2 Sep 1879, married Oscar Wahlberg, who was born in 1881, on 20 Mch 1918, no children, died in 1937.

    1166. ii.   ANNA JEANETTE[8] HOWELL, born on 17 May 1889, married Arthur E. Smith, the son of George Smith, on 4 Nov 1908.

4. Youngs [6], James [5]

729. JOSEPH N.[7] HOWELL (Youngs[6], James[5], Reeves[4]), the son of Youngs[6] and Mary (Homan) Howell, was born on 5 Aug 1817 {3832}.

On 16 Mch 1850, "..at Hempstead, by the Rev. N. W. Thomas, Mr. Joseph Howell of Brookhaven.." was married "..to Miss Sarah Emily Arthur, of Smithtown." {3833}. She was born on 14 Aug 1815 {3834}.

3824. U.S. Census, Southold, Suffolk County, NY, 1850, Dwelling House 860, Family Number 937, Page 334.
3825. Cleveland, op. cit., Gertrude A. Barber, MARRIAGES OF SUFFOLK COUNTY, N.Y.
3826. Suffolk County Estates, File #313 D 1932.
3827. Frederic Kinsman Smith, THE FAMILY OF RICHARD SMITH.., 427.
3828. Id.
3829. Id.
3830. Id.
3831. Id.
3832. Grendler, op. cit., 3.
3833. LONG ISLAND FARMER, 26 Mch 1850.

On 12 Jly 1870, Joseph Howel, 51, farmer, with real property worth $3000, and personal property worth $300, was enumerated as the head of a household consisting of himself, his wife, Emily, 53, their son, Arthur, 19, and Henrietta Burns, 14, residing in the Town of Smithtown, Suffolk County, New York, in the Ninth Census of the United States {3835}.

Joseph N. Howell died on 5 Apr 1892 {3836}, and is buried in the cemetery at the Smithtown Presbyterian Church {3837}.

Sarah Howell died on 10 Jan 1901 {3838}, and is buried beside her husband at Smithtown {3839}.

Joseph N. and Sarah Emily (Arthur) Howell were the parents of one child {3840}.

1167. i. ARTHUR V.[8] HOWELL, born on 20 Jan 1850, married Bertha J. Tyler, who was born in 1852, the daughter of William Tyler, on 26 Nov 1873 {3841}, two children, died on 2 Nov 1876 at Warrens, WI, and is buried in the family plot at Smithtown. Bertha J. Howell died on 10 Jly 1925, and is buried beside her husband at Smithtown {3842}.

732. TEMPERANCE[7] HOWELL (Youngs[6]), the daughter of Youngs[6] and Mary (Homan) Howell, was born on 23 May 1823 {3843}.

Temperance Howell married Joseph Tooker {3844}.

On 15 Aug 1850, Joseph Tooker, 35, having real property valued at $2000, was enumerated as the head of a family consisting of himself, his wife, Temperance, 28, their son, Charles H., 9, and her brother, Jesse S. Howell, 11, residing in the Town of Brookhaven, Suffolk County, New York, in the Seventh Census of the United States {3845}.

Joseph and Temperance (Howell) Tooker were the parents of at least one son.

i. CHARLES H. TOOKER, born in about 1841.

3834. Grendler, op. cit., 4.

3835. U.S. Census, Smithtown, Suffolk County, NY, Dwelling House 419, Family Number 413, Page 147.

3836. Grendler, op. cit.

3837. Gravestone, Smithtown Presbyterian Church Cemetery, from the collection of cemetery markings of William F. Howell.

3838. Grendler, op. cit.

3839. Gravestone, Smithtown Presbyterian Church Cemetery.

3840. Grendler, op. cit.

3841. SAG HARBOR EXPRESS, 27 Nov 1873.

3842. Gravestone, Smithtown Presbyterian Church Cemetery.

3843. Grendler, op. cit., 3.

3844. Id.

3845. U.S. Census, Brookhaven, Suffolk County, NY, 1850, Dwelling House 525, Family Number 594, Page 180.

734. ANN ELIZABETH[7] HOWELL (Youngs[6]), the daughter of Youngs[6] and Mary (Homan) Howell, was born on 19 Feb 1828 {3846}.

Ann Elizabeth Howell married Mr. Matthews {3847}.

738. JAMES BENJAMIN[7] HOWELL (Youngs[6], James[5], Reeves[4]), the son of Youngs[6] and Mary (Homan) Howell, was born on 11 May 1837 {3848}.

On 15 Aug 1850, James B. Howell, 13, was enumerated with the family of his father in the Seventh Census of the United States {3849}.

On 28 Aug 1858, James Benjamin Howell was baptized into the Caroline Church of Setauket {3850}.

739. JESSE S.[7] HOWELL (Youngs[6]), the son of Youngs[6] and Mary (Homan) Howell, was born on 21 Dec 1839 {3851}.

Jesse S. Howell was residing in the household of his sister, Temperance Tooker on 15 Aug 1850, as recorded in the Seventh Census of the United States {3852}.

On 14 May 1863, Jesse Howell married Mary F. Jayne {3853}.

"Jesse S. Howell was a Captain owned a vessel jointly with Captains Al and Shephard Hulse which plied between New York and South America." {3854}.

Jesse S. Howell died on 21 Jly 1878, and is buried in the Cedar Hill Cemetery at Port Jefferson {3855}.

Jesse S. and Mary Frances (Jayne) Howell were the parents of five children {3856}.

1168.　i.　CHARLES HENRY[8] HOWELL, born on 5 Dec 1865, married Jenny Brewster, who was born in 1875, the daughter of Frederick and Mary (Rowland) Brewster, two children, died in 1962, and is buried in the cemetery at the Setauket Presbyterian Church, while she died in 1967, and is buried beside her husband at Setauket {3857}.

3846. Grendler, op. cit.
3847. Id.
3848. Id., 4.
3849. U.S. Census, Brookhaven, Suffolk County, NY, 1850, Dwelling House 497, Family Number 562, Page 178.
3850. THE REGISTER, SCHS, XIII, #2, 59 (Fall 1987).
3851. Grendler, op. cit.
3852. U.S. Census, Brookhaven, Suffolk County, NY, 1850, Dwelling House 497, Family Number 563, Page 178.
3853. REPUBLICAN WATCHMAN, 17 June 1863.
3854. Grendler, op. cit.
3855. Gravestone, Cedar Hill Cemetery, Port Jefferson.
3856. Grendler, op. cit.
3857. Barstow, op. cit., EPITAPHS.

1169. ii.   MINOR S.[8] HOWELL, born on 16 Apr 1872, died on 22 Aug 1872, and is buried in the Cedar Hill Cemetery at Port Jefferson {3858}.

1170. iii.   JOHN DICKERSON[8] HOWELL, born in 1874, died on 27 Apr 1947 {3859}, and is buried in the Cedar Hill Cemetery at Port Jefferson {3860}.

1171. iv.   JESSE H.[8] HOWELL, born in 1878, married Gertrude Rowley.

1172. v.   SYLVESTER[8] HOWELL.

5. James [6], James [5]

740. CATHERINE[7] HOWELL (James[6]), the daughter of James[6] and Louisa (Terrell) Howell, was born on 16 Mch 1824 {3861}.

On 29 Jly 1848, Catherine Howell married Micah Wells {3862}, who was born on 30 Mch 1822, the son of Thomas Wells {3863}.

On 20 Jly 1870, Michael E. Wells, 48, farmer, with real property worth $1500, and personal property worth $200, was enumerated as the head of a family consisting of himself, his wife, Catherine, 46, and their son, Henry T., 16, mariner, residing at Sag Harbor in the Town of Southampton, Suffolk County, New York, in the Ninth Census of the United States {3864}.

Catherine Wells died on 5 Dec 1871 {3865}.

Micah E. Wells married (2) Chary Robinson {3866}.

Micah Edmund and Catherine (Howell) Wells were the parents of three children {3867}.

i.   WILLIAM S. WELLS, born on 11 Aug 1851, died on 2 Mch 1859.

ii.   HENRY T. WELLS, born on 11 May 1854, married Annie E. Mott, of New London, Connecticut, on 13 Jan 1876.

3858. Gravestone, Cedar Hill Cemetery, Port Jefferson.
3859. Suffolk County Estates, File #202 A 1947.
3860. Gravestone, Cedar Hill Cemetery, Port Jefferson.
3861. Grendler, op. cit., 24.
3862. BROOKHAVEN MARRIAGES, from THE REGISTER, SCHS, XVIII, #2, 46 (Fall 1992).
3863. Grendler, op. cit.
3864. U.S. Census, Southampton, Suffolk County, NY, 1870, Dwelling House 963, Family Number 982, Page 207.
3865. Grendler, op. cit.
3866. Id.
3867. Id.

iii.   SARAH WELLS, born on 15 Jan 1859, died on 15 May 1859.

741. JAMES ADDISON[7] HOWELL (James[6]), the son of James[6] and Louisa (Terrell) Howell {3868}, was born in about 1826.
    J. Addison Howell married Mary A. Hammond {3869}.
    On 20 Jly 1870, James A. Howell, 44, working in mill, with personal property worth $400, was enumerated as the head of a family consisting of himself, his wife, Mary A., 40, and their children, Louisa, 18, Almira, 10, Lewis E., 7, and Frank, 6, residing in Moriches in the Town of Brookhaven, Suffolk County, New York, in the Ninth Census of the United States {3870}.
    James Addison and Mary A. (Hammond) Howell were the parents of four children.
    1173. i.   LOUISA[8] HOWELL, born in about 1852.

    1174. ii.   ALMIRA[8] HOWELL, born in about 1860.

    1175. iii.   EDWARD LEWIS[8] HOWELL, born in 1863, married Georgia Howell (#1177), three children, died on 22 Jan 1943, and is buried in the Mount Pleasant Cemetery in Center Moriches {3871}.

    1176. iv.   FRANK L.[8] HOWELL, born in 1870, died on 19 June 1925 {3872}.

743. WILLIAM SANDFORD[7] HOWELL (James[6]), the son of James[6] and Louisa (Terrell) Howell, was born on 1 Jan 1834 at Bald Hill, now Farmington, in the Town of Brookhaven. He was educated in the district schools, and became a farmer cultivating seven acres near Moriches {3873}.
    On 4 Jly 1850, William Sandford Howell married Mary Jane Hulse, who was born on 27 June 1836 {3874}, the daughter of Charles and Martha (Penney) Hulse {3875}.
    On 21 Jly 1870, William S. Howell, 37, farmer, with real property worth $1,000, and personal property worth $400, was enumerated as the head of a family consisting of himself, his wife, Mary, 34, and their children, Georgiana, 14, and

3868. Id., 21.
3869. LONG ISLAND STAR, 29 Jan 1851, from THE REGISTER, SCHS, XVII, #1-4, 19 (Summer 1991-Spring 1992).
3870. U.S. Census, Brookhaven, Suffolk County, NY, 1870, Dwelling House 1096, Family Number 1178, Page 380.
3871. Gravestone, Mount Pleasant Cemetery, Center Moriches.
3872. Suffolk County Estates, File #27691.
3873. PORTRAIT & BIOGRAPHICAL RECORD OF SUFFOLK COUNTY, 293.
3874. Grendler, op. cit., 21.
3875. PORTRAIT & BIOGRAPHICAL RECORD OF SUFFOLK COUNTY, 293.

Phebe, 12, residing in Moriches in the Town of Brookhaven, Suffolk County, New York, in the Ninth Census of the United States {3876}.

Mr. and Mrs. William Howell were both members of the Methodist Episcopal Church. He was a Democrat, and served for many years as School Collector for his district. In 1874, he was a successful candidate for Town Collector, a position which required his posting a bond of $65,000, a sum which he was not able to raise himself, "..but his many friends showed their confidence in his integrity and ability by going his security." {3877}.

William Sandford and Mary Jane (Hulse) Howell were the parents of four children {3878}.

1177. i. GEORGIA[8] HOWELL, born in 1855, married Edward Lewis Howell (#1175), three children, died in 1927, and is buried in the Mount Pleasant Cemetery in Center Moriches {3879}.

1178. ii. PHEBE[8] HOWELL, born on 1 Jan 1858, married (1) George D. Gassett, of Brooklyn, four children, married (2) Joseph Lynch, who was born on 22 June 1869, and died on 17 Nov 1931, while she died 6 Mch 1936 {3880}.

1179. iii. SUSAN EMMA[8] HOWELL, born in 1866, lived with her parents, died on 30 Oct 1932 {3881}.

1180. iv. WILLIAM MANFORD[8] HOWELL, born on 17 Nov 1869, married Laura A. K. Clark, who was born on 15 Feb 1871 at Mount Hope, New York, the daughter of Thomas and Mary Ann Clark, on 31 Oct 1894, one child, died on 17 Nov 1955 {3882}, and is buried in the Oakwood Cemetery in Bay Shore, while she died on 30 Dec 1954 and is buried beside her husband at Bay Shore {3883}.

744. WALTER CARLE[7] HOWELL (James[6]), the son of James[6] and Louisa (Terrell) Howell {3884}, was born in about 1839.

At Setauket on 4 Feb 1863, Walter C. Howell married Mary C. Risley {3885}, who was born in about 1845.

3876. U.S. Census, Brookhaven, Suffolk County, NY, 1870, Dwelling House 1113, Family Number 1195, Page 381.
3877. PORTRAIT & BIOGRAPHICAL RECORD OF SUFFOLK COUNTY, 293-294.
3878. Id., 293.
3879. Gravestone, Mount Pleasant Cemetery, Center Moriches.
3880. Grendler, op. cit., 22.
3881. Suffolk County Estates, File #482 P 1932.
3882. Id., File #26 P 1956.
3883. Grendler, op. cit.
3884. Grendler, op. cit., 23.
3885. THE CORRECTOR, 28 Feb 1863.

On 2 Aug 1870, Walter C. Howell, 31, farm laborer, was enumerated as the head of a family consisting of himself, his wife, Mary, 25, and their children, William C., 4, and Mary J., 2, residing in Setauket in the Town of Brookhaven, Suffolk County, New York, in the Ninth Census of the United States {3886}.

Walter Carle and Mary C. (Risley) Howell were the parents of three children {3887}.

1181. i. WILLIAM C.[8] HOWELL, born in about 1866, married Hattie Bellows, four children, was Postmaster at Setauket.

1182. ii. MARY J., "JENNIE"[8] HOWELL, born in about 1868, married Fletcher Condit.

1183. iii. JESSE[8] HOWELL.

745. SUSAN[7] HOWELL (James[6]) was the daughter of James[6] and Louisa (Terrell) Howell {3888}, was born in about 1841.

Susan Howell married Benjamin Risley {3889}, who was also born in about 1841.

On 2 Aug 1870, Benjamin Risley, 29, corker, was enumerated as the head of a family consisting of himself, his wife, Susan E., 29, and their sons, James W., 6, and Benjamin C., 5, residing in Setauket in the Town of Brookhaven, Suffolk County, New York, in the Ninth Census of the United States {3890}.

Benjamin and Susan (Howell) Risley were the parents of at least two children.

i. JAMES W. RISLEY, born in about 1864.

ii. BENJAMIN C. RISLEY, born in about 1865.

6. Reeves[6], James[5]

750. PHEBE ANN[7] HOWELL (Reeves[6]), the daughter of Reeves[6] and Phebe (Gates) Howell, was born in about 1837.

On 21 Aug 1850, Phebe A. Howell, 13, was enumerated as a member of her father's family in the Seventh Census of the United States {3891}.

3886. U.S. Census, Brookhaven, Suffolk County, NY, 1870, Dwelling House 1503, Family Number 1605, Page 405.
3887. Grendler, op. cit.
3888. Id.
3889. Id.
3890. U.S. Census, Brookhaven, Suffolk County, NY, 1870, Dwelling House 1515, Family 1619, Page 406.
3891. Id., 1850, Dwelling House 589, Family Number 666, Page 228.

Phebe Ann Howell married (1) Charles Bartrum, and (2) John Ingraham
{3892}.

Charles and Phebe Ann (Howell) Bartrum were the parents of two children
{3893}.

     i.   CHARLES F. BARTRUM, born in 1863, married Eliza Hoyt, who was born in 1864, on 9 May 1885, two children, died in 1942, while she died in 1942.

     ii.   JOHN BARTRUM.

7. Daniel Brown [6], James [5]

752. SELAH[7] HOWELL (Daniel Brown[6]), the son of Daniel Brown[6] and Caroline (Hawkins) Howell, was born in about 1830.

"Celah Howell", 20, seaman, was enumerated with the family of his father on 21 Aug 1850 in the Seventh Census of the United States {3894}.

Selah B. Howell married Olive Ann Wicks {3895}.

On 5 Jly 1870, Selah Howell, 39, ship carpenter, with real property worth $1,000, was enumerated as the head of a family consisting of himself, his wife, Olive Ann, 31, and their children, Carman B., 12, and Ada M., 6, and his mother, Caroline, 66, residing in Port Jefferson in the Town of Brookhaven, Suffolk County, New York, in the Ninth Census of the United States {3896}.

Selah B. Howell died in 1880, and is buried in the Cedar Hill Cemetery in Port Jefferson {3897}.

Olive Ann Howell died in 1924, and is buried beside her husband at Port Jefferson {3898}.

Selah B. and Olivan (Wicks) Howell were the parents of three children {3899}.

1184. i.   CARMAN B.[8] HOWELL, born in about 1857, married Sarah W. Hastings on 1 Dec 1885 {3900}, two children, died on 25 Dec 1936 {3901}.

3892. Grendler, op. cit., 24.
3893. Id.
3894. U.S. Census, Brookhaven, Suffolk County, NY, 1850, Dwelling House 630, Family Number 717, Page 231.
3895. Grendler, op. cit., 25.
3896. U.S. Census, Brookhaven, Suffolk County, NY, 1870, Page 344, Dwelling House 508, Family Number 568.
3897. Grendler, op. cit.
3898. Id.
3899. Id.
3900. Gertrude A. Barber, MARRIAGES OF SUFFOLK COUNTY, N.Y.
3901. Suffolk County Estates, File #288 P 1937.

1185. ii.   ADA M.[8] HOWELL, born in about 1864, married (1) Edwin A. Gildersleeve on 30 Jly 1882 {3902}, one child, married (2) Edward Shute {3903}.

1186. iii.   SELAH B.[8] HOWELL, born in about 1873, died in 1947.

754. DANIEL B.[7] HOWELL (Daniel Brown[6], James[5], Reeves[4]), the son of Daniel Brown[6] and Caroline (Hawkins) Howell, was born in about 1835.

    Daniel B. Howell, 15, seaman, was enumerated with the family of his father on 21 Aug 1850 in the Seventh Census of the United States {3904}.

    On 3 Jly 1870, Daniel B. Howell, 35, farmer, with real property worth $1,200, and personal property worth $50, was enumerated as the head of a family consisting of himself, his wife, Josephine, 32, and their children, Quardilla, 12, Anna, 3, and a baby boy, 1, residing at Millers Place in the Town of Brookhaven, Suffolk County, New York, in the Ninth Census of the United States {3905}.

    Daniel Brown and Josephine Howell were the parents of at least three children.

1187. i.   QUARDILLA[8] HOWELL, born in about 1858.

1188. ii.   ANNA[8] HOWELL, born in about 1867.

1189. iii.   SON[8] HOWELL, born in about 1869.

755. MARY MELISSA[7] HOWELL (Daniel Brown[6], James[5], Reeves[4]), the daughter of Daniel Brown[65] and Caroline (Hawkins) Howell, was born on 22 Jan 1838 {3906}.

    On 21 Aug 1850, Mary M. Howell, 13, was enumerated in the household of her father in the Seventh Census of the United States {3907}.

    On 22 Jan 1855, Mary Melissa Howell married Ebenezer Darling, who was born on 22 Jan 1834, the son of Henry and Margaret (Nichols) Darling {3908}.

    Ebenezer Darling died on 5 Apr 1909, and is buried in the Cedar Hill Cemetery at Port Jefferson {3909}.

3902. Gertrude A. Barber, op. cit.
3903. Grendler, op. cit., 26.
3904. U.S. Census, Brookhaven, Suffolk County, NY, 1850, Dwelling House 630, Family Number 717, Page 231.
3905. U.S. Census, Brookhaven, Suffolk County, NY, 1870, Dwelling House 465, Family Number 522, Page 341.
3906. Grendler, op. cit.
3907. U.S. Census, Brookhaven, Suffolk County, NY, 1850, Dwelling House 630, Family Number 717, Page 231.
3908. Grendler, op. cit.
3909. Id.

Mary Melissa Darling died on 14 June 1917, and is buried beside her husband at Port Jefferson {3910}.

Ebenezer and Mary Melissa (Howell) Darling were the parents of twelve children {3911}.

i. HENRY CLAY DARLING, born on 9 May 1856, died at sea in 1871.

ii. CAROLINE DARLING, born on 22 June 1858, married Montraville Hubbs in 1873, one child, died on 29 Aug 1938, and is buried in the Cedar Hill Cemetery, while he died in 1936, and is buried in the Commack Cemetery.

iii. SELAH HOWELL DARLING, born on 16 Aug 1860, married (1) Sarah Smith in 1879, one child, married (2) Agnes Wheeler in 1892, six children, died on 19 Dec 1941, buried beside his wives in the Cedar Hill Cemetery {3912}.

iv. DANIEL BROWN DARLING, born on 13 Feb 1862, never married, died on 6 Mch 1947.

v. TRUMAN NICHOLS DARLING, born on 4 Dec 1864, married Julia Wheeler, who was born on 22 Sep 1868, nine children, died on 17 Jly 1930, while she died on 15 Dec 1933. Both are buried in the Oak Hills Cemetery at Stony Brook {3913}.

vi. EBENEZER DARLING, born on 2 Jan 1867, died in 1867.

vii. AMOS PLATT DARLING, born on 9 Nov 1868, married Harriet Babcock, died on 2 Jan 1919.

viii. LYDIA MAY DARLING, born on 3 Aug 1870, died in 1871.

ix. MARY ELIZA DARLING, born on 27 Jly 1874, never married, died on 29 Oct 1948.

x. ALIDA DARLING, born on 3 Nov 1875, married Andrew Holgerson in 1904, seven children, died on 4 Jly 1953 {3914}.

xi. WINFIELD DARLING, born on 10 Jan 1877, married Lida

3910. Id.
3911. Id.
3912. Id., 27.
3913. Id.
3914. Id., 28.

Underwood in Jly 1917, two children {3915}.

    xii.   OLIVE DARLING, born on 7 Aug 1880, married Arthur Park, who was born on 8 May 1874, one child, died in Dec 1960 {3916}.

8. Edmund Wheeler[6], James[5]

757. ELIAS WILLIS[7] HOWELL (Edmund Wheeler[6]), the son of Edmund Wheeler[6] and Sarah (Vail) Howell, was born on 29 Apr 1837 at Riverhead.

In Feb 1858, Elias Willis Howell married Martha Jane Rigby, who was born on 20 June 1843 at West Jordan, Utah, the daughter of James and Jane Lovinia (Littlewood) Rigby. They were divorced in about 1870, and she later became the wife of (2) John Fowles and, later, of (3) Charles Van Valkenburg. She died on 20 Jly 1878 {3917}.

Elias Willis Howell served as a member of the militia when the Utah Territory was invaded by a Federal army under Albert Sidney Johnston in 1858-1860 {3918}.

On 17 Apr 1871, Elias Willis Howell married Mary Jane Sanderson, who was born on 10 Jan 1853, the daughter of Henry Weeks and Rebecca Ann (Sanders) Sanderson, as his second wife {3919}.

Elias Willis Howell died on 26 May 1909, and was buried at Fairview, Utah, on 29 May 1909 {3920}.

Mary Jane Howell died on 21 Dec 1923 {3921}.

Elias Willis and Martha Jane (Rigby) Howell were the parents of five children {3922}.

  1190. i.   SARAH LOVINIA[8] HOWELL, born on 3 Jan 1859 at Unionfort, Utah, married Otis Lysander Terry, Jr., on 28 Dec 1877, 10 children, died on 10 Oct 1898.

  1191. ii.   MARTHA ANN[8] HOWELL, born on 12 Dec 1861 at Unionfort, Utah, married Peter Christian Jensen on 3 Apr 1878, eleven children.

  1192. iii.   ROSALIE FRANCES[8] HOWELL, born on 7 Aug 1864 at

---

3915. Id., 29.
3916. Id.
3917. Elias Willis Howell Family Records.
3918. Biographical sketch, SARAH (VAIL) HOWELL TERRY.
3919. Elias Willis Howell Family Records.
3920. Id.
3921. Id.
3922. Id.

Fairview, Utah, married Peter Henry Hansen, eight children, died on 19 Jan 1930.

1193. iv.   ELIAS WILLIS[8] HOWELL, born in 1866 at Fairview, died on 16 Jan 1867.

1194. v.   DRUSILLA[8] HOWELL, born on 23 Jan 1868 at Fairview, married Thomas Hackford.

Elias Willis and Mary Jane (Sanderson) Howell were the parents of thirteen children {3923}.

1195. vi.   MARY MARZETTA[8] HOWELL, born on 17 May 1872 at Fairview, Utah, married James C. Allred on 28 Oct 1891 at Manti, Utah, eleven children, died on 29 Mch 1939 at Vernal, Utah.

1196. vii.   WILLIS HENRY[8] HOWELL, born on 1 Jan 1874 at Fairview, married Emma Adelia Miner on 19 Apr 1893 at Manti, twelve children, died on 3 Apr 1952.

1197.viii.   SARAH REBECCA[8] HOWELL, born on 2 May 1876 at Fairview, married Jacob Rasmussen on 20 June 1894 at Manti, twelve children, died on 26 Mch 1956.

1198. ix.   EDMUND SYLVANUS[8] HOWELL, born on 19 Aug 1878 at Fairview, married Hannah Lucinda Hurst on 4 June 1913 at Manti, seven children, died on 20 May 1939.

1199. x.   CHAUNCEY VAIL[8] HOWELL, born on 15 Dec 1880 at Fairview, married Mary Keziah Allred on 16 Dec 1903 at Manti, ten children, died on 31 Aug 1956. (NOTE: *Chauncey Vail Howell was the father of Elden Willis and C. Merrill Howell*).

1200. xi.   ADA SIRILLA[8] HOWELL, born on 17 Apr 1883 at Fairview, married Vern Cox on 19 Oct 1904, one child, died on 17 Dec 1936 at Fairview.

1201. xii.   ARTIMISSIA[8] HOWELL, born on 22 Sep 1885 at Fairview, died on 20 June 1891.

1202.xiii.   CLYDIA AMANDA[8] HOWELL, born on 12 Oct 1887 at Fairview, married James Henry Pearson on 10 Jan 1912 at Salt Lake City, six children.

3923. Id.

1203.xiv.   JUNIUS FRANKLIN[8] HOWELL, born on 8 June 1890 at Fairview, married Verona Fielding on 8 Sep 1930, one child, died on 12 Oct 1957 at Price, Utah.

1204. xv.   DELORA[8] HOWELL, born on 15 Sep 1892 at Fairview, married James Andrew Larsen on 26 Nov 1913 at Salt Lake City, four children.

1205.xvi.   IRA VICTOR[8] HOWELL, born on 4 Oct 1894 at Fairview, married Velora Armeda Allred on 24 Oct 1917 at Manti, four children, died on 20 Sep 1966 at Provo, Utah.

1206.xvii.   BERTHA MARINDA[8] HOWELL, born on 23 Nov 1896 at Fairview, married Ulysses Larsen on 6 Dec 1916, five children, died on 17 May 1970 at Orem, Utah.

1207.xviii. ERNEST LEON[8] HOWELL, born on 14 Aug 1899 at Fairview, married Faughn Madsen on 24 May 1923, died on 8 May 1980.

760. MARY LOVINA[7] HOWELL (Edmund Wheeler[6]), the daughter of Edmund Wheeler[6] and Sarah (Vail) Howell, was born on 27 Nov 1844 at New York {3924}.

On 10 Dec 1861, Mary Lovina Howell married Jordan Brady at Fairview, Utah. He was born on 7 June 1843 at Nauvoo, Illinois {3925}.

Mary Lovina Brady died on 20 Sep 1934 at Fairview, Utah {3926}.

Jordan and Mary Lovina (Howell) Brady were the parents of thirteen children {3927}.

i.   JORDAN HENDRICKSON BRADY, born on 26 Jan 1863, married Lavee Alberta Sanderson, who was born in 1865, on 19 Jan 1882, thirteen children, died on 23 Jly 1951, and is buried at Fairview, Utah.

ii.   KEZIAH LOVINA BRADY, born on 10 Nov 1864, married Peter Wimmer Cheney, who was born in 1863, on 17 Sep 1880, died on 28 Aug 1924, and is buried at Fairview.

iii. LINDSAY EDMUND BRADY, born on 20 Sep 1866, married (1) Dorothea Lorena Christensen, who was born in 1867, on 30 Sep 1885, six children, married (2) Mae Weller, and (3) Minnie Hamilton Cash, died on 9 June 1948.

3924. Edmund Wheeler Howell Family Records.
3925. Id.
3926. Id.
3927. Id., Randy Lee Halliday, Personal communication.

iv.   MARTHA ELIZABETH BRADY, born on 7 Mch 1869, married Andrew Rasmussen, who was born in 1864, on 20 Dec 1885, died on 29 Sep 1960, and is buried at Sanford, Colorado.

v.   MARY EMILY BRADY, born on 12 June 1871, married Paul Heber Cornum, who was born in 1868, on 18 Apr 1888, died on 18 Dec 1966, and is buried at Sanford.

vi.   WILLIS ALPHONSO BRADY, born on 22 Oct 1873, married Mary Eliza Christensen, who was born in 1872, on 30 Jan 1895, six children, died on 30 Sep 1959, and is buried at Fairview.

vii.   SARAH MATILDA BRADY, born on 23 Dec 1875, married Jesse Warren Clement, who was born in 1874, nine children, died on 30 June 1970, and is buried at Fairview.

viii.   RADNA ANN BRADY, born on 1 Apr 1878, married (1) Easton Clements, who was born in 1860, married (2) William Orlando Carlston, who was born in 1876, died on 5 Nov 1972, and is buried at Fairview.

ix.   ADA CELESTIA BRADY, born on 1 Apr 1878, married Nephi Cruser, who was born in 1870, on 21 Oct 1896, died on 27 Oct 1963, and is buried at Fairview.

x.   WARREN ABSALOM BRADY, born on 7 Apr 1881, married Anna Maria Tucker, who was born in 1882, on 10 Sep 1902, nine children, died on 23 June 1968, and is buried at Fairview.

xi.   OPHELIA SOPHIA BRADY, born on 3 Feb 1883, married (1) Israel Ezra Watson, married (2) Horatio Cox, eleven children, died on 24 Nov 1967, and is buried at Buhl, Idaho.

xii.   SAMUEL JOSEPH BRADY, born on 7 June 1885, died on 4 Oct 1885.

xiii.   MILLIE REBECCA BRADY, born on 7 June 1885, married Preston Ray Stewart, who was born in 1880, on 25 Oct 1907, four children, died on 28 Dec 1975, and is buried at Provo, Utah.

763. OPHELIA ANN[7] HOWELL (Edmund Wheeler[6]), the daughter of Edmund

Wheeler[6] and Sarah (Vail) Howell, was born on 16 Jan 1852 at Honey Creek, Iowa {3928}.

On 12 Sep 1867, at Fairview, Utah, Ophelia Ann Howell married Samuel Bills, who was born on 22 Mch 1848 {3929}.

Samuel Bills died on 1 Nov 1930 at Fairview, Utah, and is buried there {3930}.

Ophelia Ann Bills died on 11 Dec 1933 {3931}.

Samuel and Ophelia Ann (Howell) Bills were the parents of twelve children {3932}.

    i.   SARAH ELIZABETH BILLS, born on 5 Aug 1868, married Lewis Peterson, who was born in 1868, on 10 Nov 1886, died on 4 Jan 1954, and is buried at Fairview.

    ii.   SAMUEL DAVID BILLS, born on 22 Oct 1870, married Amelia Henrietta Peterson, who was born in 1870, on 20 Mch 1890, died on 14 Apr 1942, and is buried at Fairview.

    iii.   JOHN EDMUND BILLS, born on 2 Feb 1873, married Lydia Marie Mower ON 1 Mch 1893, died on 24 Sep 1932, and is buried at Fairview.

    iv.   WILLIAM GORDON BILLS, born on 3 Apr 1875, died on 23 Oct 1878.

    v.   MARY EFFIE BILLS, born on 12 June 1877, married Homer Franklin Miner on 21 Oct 1896, died on 26 Jan 1937.

    vi.   CELESTIA OPHELIA BILLS, born on 15 Sep 1879, married Moroni Tucker, who was born in 1880, on 12 Sep 1900, died on 7 Jly 1948, and is buried at Blackfoot, Idaho.

    vii.   JORDAN ELIAS BILLS, born on 27 June 1882, married (1) Selma Rebecca Graham on 24 Nov 1909, married (2) Catherine Fowles, and (3) Margaret Nielson.

    viii.   MARTHA ELLEN BILLS, born on 20 Aug 1884, married Joseph Wilford Fowles on 1 Sep 1903, died on 6 May 1951.

    ix.   CHARLES OTIS BILLS, born on 9 May 1887, married Lena Peterson 29 Jan 1908, died on 13 Feb 1948.

3928. Id.
3929. Id.
3930. Id.
3931. Id.
3932. Id.

x.   HAZEL MARANDA BILLS, born on 16 Apr 1889, died on 14 June 1892.

xi.   ANNIE MINERVA BILLS, born on 15 June 1891, married (1) Jehu Earl Garlick on 18 Nov 1908, married (2) Amsa Tucker, died on 17 Oct 1939.

xii.   JAMES SCOTT BILLS, born on 25 Apr 1894, married Amanda Ramsey on 17 Dec 1919, died on 16 Jly 1951.

9. Richard Oakley [6], James [5]

764. JAMES OLIVER[7] HOWELL (Richard Oakley[6]), the son of Richard Oakley[7] and Rebecca Tuttle (Homan) Howell, was born on 26 Sep 1844 {3933}.

On 19 Jly 1850, James O. Howell, 5, was enumerated with the family of his father in the Seventh Census of the United States {3934}.

James Oliver Howell was a traveling salesman. He married Laura Pierce, of Troy, New York {3935}.

James Oliver Howell died on 19 Nov 1893 {3936}, and is buried in the New Village Cemetery at Centereach {3937}.

James Oliver and Laura (Pierce) Howell were the parents of one child {3938}.

1208.   i.   ELVA[8] HOWELL, born on 23 Nov 1874, graduated from Northfield Academy, received the B. A. from Mount Holyoke College, taught Latin and mathematics in North Carolina and at Bethlehem, Pennsylvania, then was a housemother and teacher at Northfield Academy.

765. ELBERT RICHARD[7] HOWELL (Richard Oakley[6]), the son of Richard Oakley[6] and Rebecca Tuttle (Homan) Howell, was born on 13 Aug 1849 at Lake Grove, New York {3939}.

On 19 Jly 1850, Elbert R. Howell, 9 (sic) months old, was enumerated in the family of his father in the Seventh Census of the United States {3940}.

3933. Grendler, op. cit., 43.
3934. U.S. Census, Brookhaven, Suffolk County, NY, 1850, Dwelling House 82, Family Number 89, Page 151.
3935. Grendler, op. cit.
3936. Id.
3937. Gravestone, New Village Cemetery, Centereach.
3938. Grendler, op. cit.
3939. Id.
3940. U.S. Census, Brookhaven, Suffolk County, NY, 1850, Dwelling House 82, Family Number 89, Page 151.

Elbert Richard Howell was a student at Bryant and Stratton College and at Eastman Business College. He married Ann Judson Holmes, who was born on 9 Sep 1837 at Dorchester, Massachusetts, the daughter of Rev. Otis and Sarah (Preston) Holmes. He became a Credit man for New York and Brooklyn firms for his career. He was a member of the Central Congregational Church in Brooklyn, where he was a Deacon. He also taught singing {3941}.

Elbert R. Howell retired to a farm formerly owned by Rev. Otis Holmes at the corner of Middle Country Road and the Stony Brook-Sayville road, known as Holmes Corner {3942}.

Elbert Richard Howell died on 30 Nov 1920 {3943}, and is buried in the New Village Cemetery at Centereach {3944}.

Ann Judson Howell died on 21 Feb 1921 {3945}, and is buried beside her husband at Centereach {3946}.

Elbert Richard and Ann Judson (Holmes) Howell were the parents of three children {3947}.

1209. i.   ARTHUR HOLMES[8] HOWELL, born on 3 May 1872 at Lake Grove, married Grace Bowen Johnson, the daughter of Jerome Fletcher and Eliza Janet (Woodruff) Johnson, on 20 June 1900, three children, died on 10 Jly 1940, while she died on 17 Oct 1942. He was a biologist with the U. S. Department of Agriculture.

1210. ii.   CAROLINE LOUISE[8] HOWELL, born on 10 Nov 1875 in Brooklyn, received her B. A. from Wellesley in 1898, married Maxwell Grendler, who was born in Germany on 5 Oct 1880, on 26 Aug 1915, one child, compiled a genealogy of the descendants of James[5] Howell (#111), which has been heavily relied on in this compilation.

1211. iii.   WILLIAM EDWARD PRESTON[8] HOWELL, born on 26 Aug 1880, married Maude Louise Parkinson at Oswego, New York, on 16 Aug 1904, two children, was an employee and officer of the Dennison Manufacturing Company until his retirement in 1943, was interested in gardening and landscaping, and kept a herd of Guernsey cattle at his farm near Framingham, died on 7 Apr 1953.

766. WILLIAM EDMUND CORWIN[7] HOWELL (Richard Oakley[6]), the son of

3941. Grendler, op. cit.
3942. Id.
3943. Suffolk County Estates, File #24553.
3944. Gravestone, New Village Cemetery, Centereach.
3945. Grendler, op. cit.
3946. Gravestone, New Village Cemetery, Centereach.
3947. Grendler, op. cit.

Richard Oakley[6] and Rebecca Tuttle (Homan) Howell, was born at New Village on 25 June 1853 {3948}.

William E. C. Howell married Hetty Jagger in 1875. "They lived at New Village, N. Y., and Denver, Colorado, where they went hoping he would recover from consumption. They bought and worked a farm there but returned to New Village in 1883 where he died. His wife Betty Jagger returned to the farm outside Denver, CO, and continued to farm for many years." {3949}.

William E. C. Howell died on 28 Apr 1883, and is buried in the cemetery at the New Village Congregational Church in Centereach {3950}.

William Edmund Corwin and Hetty (Jagger) Howell were the parents of one child {3951}.

1212. i.   CORA[8] HOWELL, born on 7 Nov 1877, died on 21 May 1879, and is buried beside her father at New Village, now Centereach {3952}.

C. Jonathan[4], Jonathan[3], John[2], Richard[1]

1. Jonathan Davis[6], Jonathan[5]

767. THADDEUS P.[7] HOWELL (Jonathan Davis[6]), the son of Jonathan Davis[6] and Louise (Howell) Howell {3953}, was born in about 1826.

Thaddeus Howell, 21, married Martha Penny, 17, on 13 Dec 1847 {3954}.

Thadeus Howell, 23, carman, and his wife, Martha, 20, were enumerated as a family residing in the 13th Ward of New York City, in the same building as his father's family, in the Seventh Census of the United States, as recorded on 26 Jly 1850 {3955}.

On 12 Jly 1870, Thaddeus Howell, 43, carman, with real property worth $3500, and personal property worth $300, was enumerated as the head of a family consisting of himself, his wife, Martha, 40, and their children, Violena, 19, and Alice, 17, residing in the First Ward in the City of Brooklyn, Kings County, New York, in the Ninth Census of the United States {3956}.

3948. Id., 46.
3949. Id.
3950. NYG&BR, XXI, 76 (Apr 1890).
3951. Grendler, op. cit.
3952. NYG&BR, XXI, 76 (Apr 1890).
3953. PORTRAIT & BIOGRAPHICAL RECORD OF SUFFOLK COUNTY, 183.
3954. BROOKHAVEN MARRIAGES, from THE REGISTER, SCHS, XVIII, #2, 43 (Fall 1992).
3955. U.S. Census, 13th Ward, New York NY, 1850, Dwelling House 54, Family Number 183, Page 139.
3956. Id. 21st Ward, Brooklyn, Kings County, NY, 1870, Dwelling House 1036, Family Number 956, Page 517.

At some time, Thaddeus P. Howell was a veterinary surgeon in Brooklyn {3957}.

Thadeus Howell died in 1908, and is buried in the Mount Pleasant Cemetery in Center Moriches {3958}.

Thaddeus P. and Martha (Penny) Howell were the parents of at least three children.

1213. i. THADEUS[8] HOWELL, born in about Nov 1848, died on 16 Aug 1849 at New York City {3959}, and is buried in the Mount Pleasant Cemetery at Center Moriches {3960}.

1214. ii. VIOLENA[8] HOWELL, born in about 1851.

1215. iii. ALICE[8] HOWELL, born in about 1853.

768. CHARLES E.[7] HOWELL (Jonathan Davis[6], Jonathan[5], Jonathan[4]), the son of Jonathan Davis[6] and Louise (Howell) Howell, was born in about 1824.

On 26 Jly 1850, Charles Howell, 26, boat builder, was enumerated with his father's family in the Seventh Census of the United States {3961}.

Charles E. Howell was a boat builder in Booklyn {3962}.

769. JONATHAN D.[7] HOWELL (Jonathan Davis[6], Jonathan[5], Jonathan[4]), the son of Jonathan Davis[6] and Louise (Howell) Howell {3963}, was born in about 1833.

On 26 Jly 1850, Davis Howell, 17, boat builder, was enumerated with his father's family in the Seventh Census of the United States {3964}.

Jonathan D. Howell was engaged in the express business in New York {3965}.

770. DAVID PORTER[7] HOWELL (Jonathan Davis[6], Jonathan[5], Jonathan[4]), the son of Jonathan Davis[6] and Louise (Howell) Howell, was born in about 1835.

On 26 Jly 1850, Porter Howell, 15, clerk, was enumerated with his father's

3957. PORTRAIT & BIO. RECORD OF SUFFOLK COUNTY, 182.
3958. Gravestone, Mount Pleasant Cemetery, Center Moriches.
3959. BROOKHAVEN DEATHS, from THE REGISTER, SCHS, XVIII, #3, 83 (Winter 1992).
3960. Gravestone, Mount Pleasant Cemetery, Center Moriches.
3961. U.S. Census, 13th Ward, New York, NY, 1850, Dwelling House 54, Family Number 184, Page 139.
3962. PORTRAIT & BIO. RECORD OF SUFFOLK COUNTY, 182.
3963. Id., 183.
3964. U.S. Census, 13th Ward, New York, NY, 1850, Dwelling House 54, Family Number 184, Page 139.
3965. PORTRAIT & BIO. RECORD OF SUFFOLK COUNTY, 183.

family in the Seventh Census of the United States {3966}.

David Porter Howell was in the express business in New York {3967}.

771. BENJAMIN F.[7] HOWELL (Jonathan Davis[6], Jonathan[5], Jonathan[4]), the son of Jonathan Davis[6] and Louise[6] (Howell) Howell, was born on 5 Sep 1838 {3968}.

On 26 Jly 1850, Benjamin Howell, 13, was enumerated with his father's family in the Seventh Census of the United States {3969}.

Benjamin F. Howell married (1) Almira J. Fowler at New York {3970}. On 8 Jan 1863, he married (2) Alice V. Corwin {3971}, who was born on 22 Mch 1843, the daughter of Hubbard {3972} and Emeline (Aldrich) Corwin {3973}.

Mr. Howell was educated in New York, and was associated with his father in the coal and wood business. After his father's death, he moved to Riverhead, where he engaged in the same business. "He was four terms member of the Board of Education, Overseer of the Poor for five years, Commissioner of Highways two years, and Postmaster of Riverhead four years.." {3974}.

Politically, Mr. Howell was a Democrat, although he separated himself from William Jennings Bryan in the 1896 election, being a believer in the gold standard {3975}.

Alice V. Howell died on 15 May 1906, and is buried in Plot 154 in the Riverhead Cemetery {3976}.

Benjamin F. Howell died on 20 Aug 1918, and is buried in the family plot at Riverhead {3977}.

Benjamin F. and Almira J. (Fowler) Howell were the parents of two children {3978}.

    1216. i.   ALMIRA J.[8] HOWELL, married Carl S. Duryea, who was associated with the New York Police Department, on 12 Mch 1885 {3979}, four children.

3966. U.S. Census, 13th Ward, New York, NY, Dwelling House 54, Family Number 184, Page 139.

3967. PORTRAIT & BIO. RECORD OF SUFFOLK COUNTY, 183.

3968. Id., 182.

3969. U.S. Census, 13th Ward, New York, NY, 1850, Dwelling House 54, Family NUmber 184, Page 139.

3970. PORTRAIT & BIO. RECORD OF SUFFOLK COUNTY, 182.

3971. Id., 183.

3972. Corwin, op. cit., 7.

3973. Gravestone, Riverhead Cemetery.

3974. PORTRAIT & BIO. RECORD OF SUFFOLK COUNTY, 183.

3975. Obituary, 21 Aug 1918, from the Orville Ackerley scrapbooks at the East Hampton Library.

3976. Gravestone, Riverhead Cemetery.

3977. Id.

3978. PORTRAIT & BIO. RECORD OF SUFFOLK COUNTY, 183.

3979. Gertrude A. Barber, MARRIAGES OF SUFFOLK COUNTY.

1217. ii.   ELLA LOUISE[8] HOWELL, born on 18 Aug 1859, never married, resided with her father at Riverhead, died on 25 Jly 1933, and is buried in the family plot at Riverhead {3980}.

Benjamin F. and Alice V. (Corwin) Howell were the parents of six children {3981}.

1218. iii.   EMILY CORWIN[8] HOWELL, married Franklin C. Cooper, the son of George W. Cooper, on 18 Nov 1890 {3982}. He was in the boot and shoe business in Riverhead.

1219. iv.   HARRY B.[8] HOWELL, born in 1866, was cashier at the Suffolk County National Bank, died on 27 Apr 1947 {3983}, and is buried in Plot 70B at the Riverhead Cemetery {3984}.

1220. v.   MORTIMER[8] HOWELL, born on 17 Sep 1869, married L. Jenny Bradley, who was born on 27 June 1869, the daughter of Ahaz and Lorena N. (Burton) Bradley, was associated with the firm of Howell & Howell in the cigar business in Hempstead, died on 22 June 1909, and is buried in Plot 316 in the Riverhead Cemetery, beside his wife, who died on 30 Apr 1951 {3985}.

1221. vi.   ALICE VIRGINIA[8] HOWELL, born on 21 Jly 1871, never married, died on 5 Aug 1947, and is buried in the family plot at Riverhead {3986}.

1222. vii.   HUBBARD CORWIN[8] HOWELL, born on 6 Sep 1875, died on 14 Apr 1879, at the age of 3 years, 7 months, and 8 days {3987}, and is buried in the family plot at Riverhead {3988}.

1223.viii.   BENJAMIN FRANKLIN[8] HOWELL, born in 1878, was a clerk at the Suffolk County National Bank, became Supervisor, Town of Riverhead, died on 21 Feb 1931 {3989}, and is buried in Plot 70B in the Riverhead Cemetery {3990}.

3980. Gravestone, Riverhead Cemetery.
3981. PORTRAIT & BIO. RECORD OF SUFFOLK COUNTY, 183.
3982. Gertrude A. Barber, MARRIAGES OF SUFFOLK COUNTY.
3983. Suffolk County Estates, File #326 P 1947.
3984. Gravestone, Riverhead Cemetery.
3985. Id.
3986. Id.
3987. REPUBLICAN WATCHMAN, 26 Apr 1879.
3988. Gravestone, Riverhead Cemetery.
3989. Suffolk County Estates, File #97 F 1931.
3990. Gravestone, Riverhead Cemetery.

1224. ix.   MAUD I.[8] HOWELL, born on 13 June 1881, never married, died on 4 Mch 1960, and is buried in the family plot at Riverhead {3991}.

772. GEORGE[7] HOWELL (Jonathan Davis[6], Jonathan[5], Jonathan[4]), the son of Jonathan Davis[6] and Louise (Howell) Howell {3992}, was born in about 1841.

On 26 Jly 1850, George Howell, 9, was enumerated with his father's family in the Seventh Census of the United States {3993}.

George Howell served three years in the Ninth New York and the Fifth Maine Batteries in the Civil War {3994}.

George Howell was in the express business in New York {3995}.

2. John H. [6], Jonathan[5]

775. JOHN EGBERT[7] HOWELL (John H.[6]) the son of John H.[6] and Millicent (Benjamin) Howell, was born in 1830 {3996}.

On 7 Aug 1850, Egbert Howell, 19 was enumerated in the family of his father in the Seventh Census of the United States {3997}.

On 25 Jly 1870, Egbert J. Howell, 39, farmer, with real property worth $1,500, and personal property worth $300, was enumerated as the head of a family consisting of himself, his wife, Susan, 38, and their children, Hiram C., 20, Martha W., 18, Gilson G., 12, and Alice M., 8, residing in East Moriches in the Town of Brookhaven, Suffolk County, New York, in the Ninth Census of the United States {3998}.

Susanna Howell, who was born in 1832, was the wife of John E. Howell. She died on 31 Mch 1896, and is buried in the Mount Pleasant Cemetery in Center Moriches {3999}.

John Egbert Howell died on 16 Sep 1904, and is buried beside his wife at Center Moriches {4000}.

3991. Id.
3992. PORTRAIT & BIO. RECORD OF SUFFOLK COUNTY, 183.
3993. U.S. Census, 13th Ward, New York, NY, 1850, Dwelling House 54, Family Number 184, Page 139.
3994. PORTRAIT & BIO. RECORD OF SUFFOLK COUNTY, 183.
3995. Id.
3996. Wilbur Franklin Howell, op. cit., 214.
3997. U.S. Census, Brookhaven, Suffolk county, NY, Dwelling House 73, Family Number 93, Page 193.
3998. U.S. Census, Brookhaven, Suffolk County, NY, 1870, Dwelling House 1207, Family Number 1292, Page 388.
3999. Gravestone, Mount Pleasant Cemetery, Center Moriches.
4000. Id.

John Egbert and Susan Howell were the parents of at least four children.

1225. i.   HIRAM C.[8] HOWELL, born in about 1850.

1226. ii.   MARTHA W.[8] HOWELL, born in about 1852.

1227. iii. GILSON G.[8] HOWELL, born in about 1858, married Ella Beesby in Sabula, Iowa, on 22 Nov 1882 {4001}.

1228. iv.   ALICE M.[8] HOWELL, born in about 1862, married Ira Reeve on 19 Mch 1879 {4002}.

776. **HIRAM F.[7] HOWELL** (John H.[6]), the son of John H.[6] and Millicent (Benjamin) Howell, was born on 3 Sep 1832 in East Moriches {4003}.

On 7 Aug 1850, Hiram Howell, 17, was enumerated as a member of his father's family in the Seventh Census of the United States {4004}.

Hiram F. Howell married Belinda Raynor, who was born in 1839 {4005}. She died in 1867, and is buried in the Mount Pleasant Cemetery at Center Moriches {4006}.

On 19 Oct 1868, Hiram F. Howell married Eunice Elizabeth Warner, who was born on 17 Feb 1850, the daughter of Daniel and Eleanor (Howell) (#883) Warner. "Eunice, like her older sister Frances, a disciplinarian but kindly, according to a grandson. Her stepson and large family were all treated by her as though they were her own" {4007}.

On 25 Jly 1870, Hiram F. Howell, 36, farm laborer, was enumerated as the head of a family consisting of himself, his wife, Eunice, 20, his son, Francis P., 11, and their daughter, Eleanor, 6 months, residing in the same house as his father in East Moriches in the Town of Brookhaven, Suffolk County, New York, in the Ninth Census of the United States {4008}.

"Hiram F. Howell received the advantages of the district school in his youth, but was permitted to attend during the winter months only, as his services were needed on the farm. Being reared in the country, he very naturally took up farming when starting out for himself, and for some fifteen years was occupied in market gardening, doing a very successful business..His beautiful place is twenty acres in extent, and here he has erected substantial and neat buildings." Both he and

4001. Gertrude A. Barber, MARRIAGES OF SUFFOLK COUNTY, N.Y.
4002. Id.
4003. Wilbur Franklin Howell, op. cit., 214.
4004. U.S. Census, Brookhaven, Suffolk County, NY, 1850, Dwelling House 73, Family Number 83, Page 193.
4005. Edna Howell Yeager, op. cit.
4006. Gravestone, Mount Pleasant Cemetery, Center Moriches.
4007. Justine (Warner) Wells. THE DESCENDANTS OF DANIEL, JR., & ELEANOR H. WARNER, 69.
4008. U.S. Census, Brookhaven, Suffolk County, NY, 1870, Dwelling House 1203, Family Number 1289, Page 388.

his wife were active members of the Presbyterian Church. While he was conservative in local affairs, he generally supported the Democratic candidates in national elections {4009}.

Hiram F. Howell died on 29 Oct 1912 {4010}, and is buried beside his wives at Center Moriches {4011}.

Eunice E. (Warner) Howell died on 31 May 1933 {4012}, and is buried beside her husband at Center Moriches {4013}.

Hiram F. and Belinda (Raynor) Howell were the parents of two children {4014}.

1229. i. FRANCES PORTER[8] HOWELL, born on 17 Aug 1859, married Lydia C. Howell (#1161), who was born on 15 Apr 1861, the daughter of Joel C. (#720) and Phebe (Carter) Howell, on 17 Mch 1880, seven children, died on 9 Sep 1936, and is buried in Plot 97 in the Riverhead Cemetery {4015}, while she died on 5 Feb 1927, and is buried at Riverhead {4016}.

1230. ii. CHARLES WICKHAM[8] HOWELL, born on 16 Sep 1865, died on 28 Aug 1866 {4017}, and is buried in the Mount Pleasant Cemetery at Center Moriches {4018}.

Hiram F. and Eunice E. (Warner) Howell were the parents of five children {4019}.

1231. iii. ELEANOR MAUD[8] HOWELL, born on 29 Jan 1870, married (1) Egbert H. Terry on 22 Apr 1908 as his second wife, no children, she married (2) Josiah C. Raynor on 7 Feb 1931, no children, died on 13 Mch 1944. Egbert H. Terry died on 20 Feb 1920. Josiah C. Raynor was born on 2 Sep 1877 {4020}.

1232. iv. EDWINA BROWN[8] HOWELL, born on 7 Apr 1872, married Oliver R. Hammond on 14 Nov 1901, one child, died in 1974, and is buried in the Mount Pleasant Cemetery in Center Moriches, New York. He was born on 5 Dec 1873, died on 13 Jan 1954, and is buried beside his wife {4021}.

4009. PORTRAIT & BIOGRAPHICAL RECORD OF SUFFOLK COUNTY, 672.

4010. Yeager, op. cit.

4011. Gravestone, Mount Pleasant Cemetery, Center Moriches.

4012. Suffolk County Estates, File #170 A 1933.

4013. Gravestone, Mount Pleasant Cemetery, Center Moriches.

4014. PORTRAIT & BIOGRAPHICAL RECORD OF SUFFOLK COUNTY, 672.

4015. Gravestone, Riverhead Cemetery.

4016. Yeager, op. cit.

4017. Wilbur Franklin Howell, op. cit., 215.

4018. Gravestone, Mount Pleasant Cemetery, Center Moriches.

4019. PORTRAIT & BIOGRAPHICAL RECORD OF SUFFOLK COUNTY, 672.

4020. Justine Warner Wells, op. cit., 69.

4021. Id.

1233. v.   JOHN DEWITT[8] HOWELL, born on 19 Oct 1874, married Marion R. Miller on 16 June 1908, one foster child, Amy Roland, died on 2 Dec 1929, and is buried in the Mount Pleasant Cemetery {4022}. She was born in 1873, died on 27 June 1926, and is buried beside her husband {4023}.

1234. vi.   DANIEL WARNER[8] HOWELL, born on 20 Apr 1877, married Bertha Bechtel on 19 Dec 1900, one adopted child {4024}, died on 18 June 1953 {4025}. She was born on 8 Oct 1883, the daughter of John and Ethlenda (Conklin) Bechtel, and died on 23 Nov 1951 {4026}.

1235. vii.   ARTHUR HUME[8] HOWELL, born on 18 Jan 1885, married Gertrude Morris Rhodes Gibson on 5 Feb 1908, two children, died in 1974. She was born in Dec 1886, the daughter of William Morris and Gertrude (Rhodes) Gibson, died on 8 Dec 1969 {4027}.

777. GEORGE A.[7] HOWELL (John H.[6]), the son of John[6] and Millicent (Benjamin) Howell, was born on 7 Apr 1835.

George Howell, 14, was enumerated as a member of his father's family on 7 Aug 1850 in the Seventh Census of the United States {4028}.

In 1859, George A. Howell married Isabell Robinson {4029}, who was born on 17 Dec 1841 at Moriches, the daughter of Hamilton Gideon and Comfort Ann (Ross) Robinson {4030}.

On 22 Jly 1870, George A. Howell, 32, farmer, with real estate worth worth $1,500, and personal property worth $300, was enumerated as the head of a family consisting of himself, his wife, Isabella, 28, and their children, Mary T., 10, Lilian, 7, and Carrie, 4, residing in Center Moriches in the Town of Brookhaven, Suffolk County, New York, in the Ninth Census of the United States {4031}.

4022. Gravestone, Mount Pleasant Cemetery, from the William F. Howell collection of cemetery markings.
4023. Id.
4024. Wells, op. cit., 69-70.
4025. Suffolk County Estates, File #528 P 1953.
4026. Wells, op. cit., 69.
4027. Id.
4028. U.S. Census, Brookhaven, Suffolk County, NY, 1850, Dwelling House 73, Family Number 83, Page 193.
4029. Personal Communication, Carrie Sammis to Bessie A. Hallock, to Riverhead Town Historian's office. Generously provided by Justine Warner Wells.
4030. Justine Warner Wells, op. cit., 29.
4031. U.S. Census, Brookhaven, Suffolk County, NY, 1870, Dwelling House 1157, Family Number 1232, Page 385.

George A. Howell died on 18 Oct 1870, at the age of 35 years, 6 months, and 11 days, and is buried in the Mount Pleasant Cemetery at Center Moriches {4032}.

Isabell Howell married (2) Allen Monroe Warner, the widower of her husband's sister, on 17 Nov 1876, as her second husband. They had no children. She died on 18 June 1886, and is buried beside her first husband at Center Moriches {4033}.

George A. and Isabell (Robinson) Howell were the parents of three children {4034}.

1236. i.   MARY THERESA[8] HOWELL, born on 6 Dec 1859, married Waldo Daniel Warner, the son of Daniel and Eleanor (Howell) (#890) Warner, on 2 Oct 1877, two children, died on 17 Jan 1930. He was born on 11 Feb 1856, died on 10 May 1940, and is buried beside his wife in the Seaview Cemetery at Mount Sinai, New York {4035}.

1237. ii.   LILIAN[8] HOWELL, born in about 1863, married C.I. Kingsbury {4036}.

1238. iii. CARRIE[8] HOWELL, born on 16 Nov 1865, married Jacob H. Sammis on 5 June 1889. He was born on 23 Jly 1866 {4037}.

778. ACHSA MAY[7] HOWELL (John H.[6]), the daughter of John[6] and Millicent (Benjamin) Howell, was born on 8 Aug 1841 at East Moriches.

Achsa M. Howell, 8, was enumerated as a member of her father's family in the Seventh Census of the United States {4038}.

On 10 Jan 1865, Achsa M. Howell married Allen Monroe Warner, the son of Daniel and Eleanor (Howell) (#890) Warner. She died on 11 June 1876, and is buried in the Baiting Hollow Cemetery {4039}.

On 17 Nov 1876, Allen Monroe Warner married (2) Isabell (Robinson) Howell, the widow of George A. Howell (#777). She was the daughter of Hamilton Gideon and Comfort Ann (Ross) Robinson, was born on 17 Dec 1841, and died on 18 June 1886, and is buried beside her first husband at Center Moriches {4040}.

4032. Gravestone, Mount Pleasant Cemetery, Center Moriches.
4033. Wells, op. cit.
4034. Id.
4035. Id., 96.
4036. Personal communication, Carrie Sammis, op. cit.
4037. Id.
4038. U.S. Census, Brookhaven, Suffolk County, NY, 1850, Dwelling House 73, Family Number 83, Page 193.
4039. Wells, op. cit., 29.
4040. Id.

Allen M. Warner married (3) Katherine (Studley) Fordham on 14 June 1888. She was born on 4 Oct 1850, the daughter of Elbridge and Catherine (Cole) Studley, of Claverack, New York, and was the widow of Jonathan Fordham, of Speonk. She died on 20 Jan 1837 at East Weymouth, Massachusetts, and is buried at the Baiting Hollow Cemetery {4041}.

Allen M. Warner was a farmer and sometime substitute teacher, whose homestead and farm were located east of the Baiting Hollow church. He died on 27 Aug 1927 at Baiting Hollow, and is buried there beside two of his wives {4042}

Allen Monroe and Achsa May (Howell) Warner were the parents of five children {4043}.

    i.   ALFRED MONROE WARNER, born on 17 Feb 1867, died on 28 June 1899 from tuberculosis, and is buried at Baiting Hollow.

    ii.   AUGUSTUS THEODORE DOBSON WARNER, born on 31 Aug 1868, married Jocobine Petternille Johansen on 15 Sep 1910, nine children, died on 31 Oct 1938 at Springfield, Oregon. She was born on 25 May 1885 at Flatoy Island, Norway, the daughter of Ulrik and Kristianna Charlotte (Petersen) Johansen, and died on 30 Dec 1931 following childbirth {4044}.

    iii.   GEORGE HOWELL WARNER, born on 17 Apr 1870, did not marry, became an eye doctor, practicing in Bridgeport, CT, died on 4 Feb 1960, and is buried at Baiting Hollow {4045}.

    iv.   HUBERT ELWOOD WARNER, born on 10 June 1872, married Carrie Elizabeth Brown, two children, died on 9 Jan 1915. She was born on 29 Mch 1878, the daughter of Mr. and Mrs. George W. Brown, married (2) Arthur B. Murray, died on 15 Feb 1950, and is buried at Baltimore, MD {4046}.

    v.   LEROY HOLT WARNER, born on 12 Apr 1874, married (Emily) Veola Young on 3 Dec 1902, five children, died on 24 Sep 1953, and is buried in the Sound Avenue Cemetery at Northville, New York. She was born on 20 Jly 1878, the daughter of George Lester and Mary Ella (Hallock) Young, died on 29 Oct 1959, and is buried beside her husband {4047}.

4041. Id.
4042. Id.
4043. Id.
4044. Id., 30.
4045. Id., 40.
4046. Id.
4047. Id., 42.

Allen Monroe and Kate (Studley) Fordham Warner were the parents of one child {4048}.

vi.   IRVING STUDLEY WARNER, born on 12 Jly 1889, married Irene Albertson Tuthill on 9 Aug 1916, two children, died on 27 Feb 1962, and is buried in the Oak Neck Cemetery at Hyannis, Massachusetts. She was born on 7 Oct 1891, the daughter of Frederick Henry and Ruth (Albertson) Tuthill, died in Jly 1987, and is buried beside her husband {4049}.

3. Albert[6], Jonathan[5]

779. JOHN A.[7] HOWELL (Albert[6]), the son of Albert[6] and Hannah (Aldrich) Howell, was born on 26 Mch 1833 {4050}.

On 12 Jly 1850, John Howell, 17, laborer, was enumerated with his father's family in the Seventh Census of the United States {4051}.

John A. Howell was a member of Company E, in the 170th Regiment of the New York Volunteer Infantry {4052}.

On 28 Jly 1870, John Howell, 30 (sic), farmer, with real property worth $700, was enumerated as a member of his father's household at Cutchogue in the Town of Southold, Suffolk County, New York, in the Ninth Census of the United States {4053}.

John A. Howell was the major heir of his father, and the executor of his will {4054}.

John A. Howell died on 17 May 1897, and is buried at Cutchogue {4055}.

780. BETSEY JANE[7] HOWELL (Albert[6]), the daughter of Albert[6] and Hannah (Aldrich) Howell, was born in about 1835.

Betsey Howell, 15, was enumerated with her father's family in the Seventh Census of the United States on 12 Jly 1850 {4056}.

On 6 May 1872, Betsey Jane Howell married Alonzo Osborn Tuthill, who

4048. Id., 29.
4049. Id., 52-53.
4050. Gravestone, Cutchogue New Yard Cemetery.
4051. U.S. Census, Southold, Suffolk County, NY, 1850, Dwelling House 125, Family Number 130, Page 288.
4052. Gravestone, Cutchogue New Yard Cemetery.
4053. U.S. Census, Southold, Suffolk County, NY, 1870, Dwelling House 957, Family Number 1035, Page 291.
4054. Suffolk County Wills, Liber 28, 152-156, Suffolk County Estates, File #12456.
4055. Gravestone, Cutchogue New Yard Cemetery.
4056. U.S. Census, Southold, Suffolk County, NY, 1850, Dwelling House 125, Family Number 130, Page 288.

was born on 13 Feb 1845, the son of Josh and Martha (Paine) Tuthill {4057}.

Alonzo Osborn Tuthill died on 27 Nov 1897 {4058}.

Alonzo Osborn and Betsey Jane (Howell) Tuthill were the parents of four children {4059}.

    i.   NANCY TUTHILL, born on 23 June 1874, married Mr. Norton.

    ii.   JOHN ALONZO TUTHILL, born on 8 Sep 1875, never married, died on 12 Dec 1897.

    iii.   JOSHUA R. TUTHILL, married Lillian Marie Rice, who was born on 23 June 1874, the daughter of Samuel Rice, three children {4060}.

    iv.   MARTHA J. TUTHILL.

4. Van Rensselaer[6], Jonathan[5]

781. ISAAC T.[7] HOWELL (Van Rensselaer[6]), the son on Van Rensselaer[6] and Mary Ann (Terry) Howell, was born on 12 Oct 1837 {4061}.

Isaac T. Howell, 12, was enumerated as a member of his father's family on 11 Jly 1850 in the Seventh Census of the United States {4062}.

On 21 Dec 1857, Isaac T. Howell married Henrietta D. Penny, who was born on 27 Mch 1838 {4063}, the daughter of Benjamin Lewis and Mehitable Catherine (Willets) Penny {4064}.

On 26 Jly 1870, Isaac Howell, 32, farmer, with real property worth $2000, and personal property worth $400, was enumerated as the head of a family consisting of himself, his wife, Henrietta, 32, and their children, Mary, 11, Sarah, 9, and Riley, 7, residing in East Moriches in the Town of Brookhaven, Suffolk County, New York, in the Ninth Census of the United States {4065}.

Isaac T. Howell died on 5 Sep 1905, and is buried in the Mount Pleasant Cemetery at Center Moriches {4066}.

4057. Tuttle, op. cit., 29.
4058. Id.
4059. Id.
4060. Id., 347.
4061. Gravestone, Mount Pleasant Cemetery, Center Moriches.
4062. U.S. Census, Southold, Suffolk County, NY, 1850, Dwelling House 85, Family Number 88, Page 285.
4063. THE REGISTER, SCHS, XV, 56-57 (Fall 1989).
4064. Id., XIV, 45 (Fall 1988).
4065. U.S. Census, Brookhaven, Suffolk County, NY, Dwelling House 1254, Family Number 1339, Page 391.
4066. Gravestone, Mount Pleasant Cemetery, Center Moriches.

Henrietta D. Howell died on 22 Jan 1937, and is buried beside her husband at Center Moriches {4067}.

Isaac T. and Henrietta D. (Penny) Howell were the parents of four children {4068}.

1239. i.   MARY E.[8] HOWELL, born on 13 Feb 1859, died on 1 Nov 1876, and is buried in the Mount Pleasant Cemetery in Center Moriches {4069}.

1240. ii.   SARAH J.[8] HOWELL, born on 27 Dec 1860, married J. Hand, died in 1949, and is buried in the Mount Pleasant Cemetery {4070}.

1241. iii. RILEY P.[8] HOWELL, born on 1 Mch 1863, married Alida E. Terry, the daughter of George E. and Ruth J. Terry, in 1887, was an educator and a farmer, was elected Assessor for the Town of Brookhaven in 1894 as a Republican. He and his wife were Presbyterians {4071}. He died on 17 Apr 1943 {4072}, and is buried in the Mount Pleasant Cemetery {4073}, while she died on 22 Apr 1959 {4074}, and is buried beside her husband at Center Moriches {4075}.

1242. iv. MABEL E.[8] HOWELL, born on 1 June 1880.

782. GILBERT VAN RENSSELAER[7] HOWELL (Van Rensselaer[6]), the son of Van Rensselaer[6] and Mary Ann (Terry) Howell, was born on 23 Sep 1839 {4076}.

On 11 Jly 1850, Gilbert V. Howell, 10, was enumerated with his father's family in the Seventh Census of the United States {4077}.

On 23 Dec 1863, Gilbert van Rensselaer Howell married Sarah Adelaide Buckingham, the daughter of Daniel and Sarah (Brown) Buckingham {4078}, who was born on 16 Feb 1845 {4079}.

4067. Id.
4068. THE REGISTER, SCHS, XV, 57 (Fall 1989).
4069. Gravestone, Mount Pleasant Cemetery, Center Moriches.
4070. Id.
4071. PORTRAIT & BIOGRAPHICAL RECORD OF SUFFOLK COUNTY, 658.
4072. Suffolk County Estates, File #185 P 1943.
4073. Gravestone, Mount Pleasant Cemetery, Center Moriches.
4074. Suffolk County Estates, File #551 P 1959.
4075. Gravestone, Mount Pleasant Cemetery, Center Moriches.
4076. PORTRAIT & BIOGRAPHICAL RECORD OF SUFFOLK COUNTY, 147.
4077. U.S. Census, Southold, Suffolk County, NY, 1850, Dwelling House 85, Family Number 88, Page 285.
4078. PORTRAIT & BIO. RECORD OF SUFFOLK COUNTY, 147.
4079. Gravestone, Cutchogue New Yard Cemetery.

Gilbert V. R. Howell was educated in the common schools, and worked on the family farm until he had the opportunity to go into business with Mr. Case. They were the proprietors of a merchantile establishment in Southold {4080}.

On 18 June 1870, Gilbert Howell, 30, farmer, was enumerated as a member of the family of Daniel Buckingham, 70, as were his wife, Adelaide, 25, and their daughter, Mary, who was born in Oct 1869, in the Ninth Census of the United States. They were residing at Cutchogue in the Town of Southold, Suffolk County, New York {4081}.

Mr. Howell served a term of one year as a Republican member of the School Board {4082}.

Gilbert van Rensselaer Howell died on 26 June 1900, and is buried at Cutchogue {4083}.

S. Adelaide Howell died on 8 Jan 1921 {4084}, and is buried beside her husband at Cutchogue {4085}.

Gilbert van Rensselaer and Sarah Adelaide (Buckingham) Howell were the parents of two children {4086}.

1243.   i.   MARY A.[8] HOWELL, born on 17 Oct 1869, died on 14 Aug 1870, and is buried in the family plot at Cutchogue {4087}.

1244. ii.   DANIEL[8] HOWELL, married Hettie Boutcher, one child.

783. MARIA J.[7] HOWELL (Van Rensselaer[6]), the daughter of Van Rensselaer[6] and Mary Ann (Terry) Howell, was born on 2 Jan 1843 {4088}.

On 11 Jly 1850, Maria J. Howell, 7, was enumerated in her father's family in the Seventh Census of the United States {4089}.

Maria J. Howell married Barnabas F. Billard, who was born on 18 Jly 1840 {4090} at Cutchogue {4091}.

Barnabas T. and Maria J. (Howell) Billard were the parents of three children {4092}.

   i.   LILLIAN W. BILLARD, born on 23 June 1870.

4080. PORTRAIT & BIO. RECORD OF SUFFOLK COUNTY, 147.
4081. U.S. Census, Southold, Suffolk County, NY, 1870, Dwelling House 353, Family Number 373, Page 254.
4082. PORTRAIT & BIO. RECORD OF SUFFOLK COUNTY.., 147.
4083. Gravestone, Cutchogue New Yard Cemetery.
4084. Suffolk County Estates, File #24683.
4085. Gravestone, Cutchogue New Yard Cemetery.
4086. PORTRAIT & BIO. RECORD OF SUFFOLK COUNTY.., 147.
4087. Gravestone, Cutchogue New Yard Cemetery.
4088. Id.
4089. U.S. Census, Southold, Suffolk County, NY, 1850, Dwelling House 85, Family Number 88, Page 285.
4090. Gravestone, Cutchogue New Yard Cemetery.
4091. SAG HARBOR CORRECTOR, 2 Apr 1864.
4092. Gravestones, Cutchogue New Yard Cemetery.

ii.   M. ADA BILLARD, born on 26 Sep 1874.

iii.   CLAYTON H. BILLARD, born on 17 Oct 1880.

785. GEORGE H.[7] HOWELL (Van Rensselaer[6]) was the son of Van Rensselaer[6] and Mary Ann (Terry) Howell.

On 21 Feb 1878, George H. Howell, of Mattituck, married Mary E. Brown, of the same town {4093}.

George H. and Mary E. (Brown) Howell were the parents of at least two children.

1245.   i.   CHARLES FRANKLIN[8] HOWELL, born in about May 1879, died on 20 Aug 1879, at the age of 3 months, and is buried in the cemetery at the Mattituck Presbyterian Church {4094}.

1246.   ii.   GEORGE K.[8] HOWELL, born on 4 Feb 1884, died on 15 Feb 1884 at the age of 11 days, and is buried at Mattituck {4095}.

5. Edward Young [6], Jonathan [5]

788. EMMA[7] HOWELL (Edward Young[6], Jonathan[5]), the daughter of Edward Young[6] and Sarah Howell, was born on 11 Jly 1839.

On 4 June 1879, Emma Howell married Nelson Bishop {4096}.

Emma E. Bishop, the wife of Nelson Bishop, died on 18 June 1890, at the age of 50 years, 11 months, and 7 days, and is buried in the Cutchogue "New Yard" Cemetery {4097}.

6. Eli Woodhull [6], Jonathan [5]

792. ANNIE WOODHULL[7] HOWELL (Eli Woodhull[6]), the daughter of Eli Woodhull[6] and Julia Ann (Tuthill) Howell, was born on 17 Mch 1862 {4098}.

Annie Woodhull Howell married Gilbert Norton Terry, the son of Hiram

---

4093. N. Hubbard Cleveland, op. cit.
4094. Craven, op. cit., 375.
4095. Id.
4096. Cleveland, op. cit.
4097. Gravestone, Cutchogue New Yard Cemetery.
4098. Wilbur Franklin Howell, op. cit., 420.

and Susan (Norton) Terry {4099}.

Gilbert Terry died on 21 Mch 1929 {4100}.

Annie W. Terry died on 6 Mch 1944 {4101}.

Gilbert Norton and Annie Woodhull (Howell) Terry were the parents of three children {4102}.

    i.   ELINOR HOWELL TERRY, born on 5 Sep 1892, married W.A. Wells, died on 10 Mch 1926.

    ii.   SUSAN HORTON TERRY, born on 3 Sep 1894.

    iii.   RAYMOND WOODHULL TERRY, born on 3 June 1896, married Edith Monsell.

D. Jeremiah[4], Jonathan[3], John[2], Richard[1]

1. John[6], Jeremiah[5]

793. JAMES[7] HOWELL (John[6]), the son of John[6] and Hester Howell, was born in 1826 {4103}.

James Howell married Rebecca Birdsall, who was born in 1833 {4104}.

James Howell died in 1907, and is buried in the Cedar Hill Cemetery at Middlehope, New York {4105}.

Rebecca Howell died in 1918, and is buried beside her husband {4106}.

794. JOHN[7] HOWELL (John[6]), the son of John[6] and Hester Howell, was born in 1831 {4107}.

John Howell married Ann Amelia Tooker, who was born in 1840 {4108}.

John Howell died in 1909, and is buried in the Cedar Hill Cemetery at Middlehope {4109}.

4099. Id.
4100. Id.
4101. Id.
4102. Id.
4103. Gravestone, Cedar Hill Cemetery, Middlehope.
4104. Id.
4105. Id.
4106. Id.
4107. Id.
4108. Id.
4109. Id.

Ann Amelia Howell died in 1935, and is buried beside her husband {4110}.

John and Ann Amelia (Tooker) Howell were the parents of at least one child.

    1247.   i.   DORA[8] HOWELL, born in 1868, died in 1870, and is buried beside her parents {4111}.

795. CATHERINE B.[7] HOWELL (John[6]), the daughter of John[6] and Hester Howell, was born in 1833 {4112}.

On 1 Sep 1850, Catherine Howell, 16, was enumerated with her father's family in the Seventh Census of the United States {4113}.

On 3 Sep 1856, Catherine Howell married Theodore Hanford, who was born on 6 Dec 1823 {4114}.

Theodore Hanford removed from Marlborough to Newburgh at the age of 16. He joined Powell & Son to learn the cabinet making trade, and joined the Reformed Church. He later worked in New York as a cabinet maker until, in 1849, he joined the "gold rush". He spent four successful years in California, and then went to Australia. After two years there, he circled the globe to return to New York in Mch 1856. He then met Catherine Howell. After their marriage, he represented L. Thorn & Co. until he retired in 1875 {4115}.

Theodore Hanford died in Nov 1881 {4116}, and is buried in the Cedar Hill Cemetery at Middlehope {4117}.

Catherine B. Hanford died in 1890, and is buried beside her husband {4118}.

796. MARGARETTA C.[7] HOWELL (John[6]), the daughter of John[6] and Hester Howell, was born in 1835 {4119}.

On 1 Sep 1850, Margaret Howell, 14, was enumerated with her father's family in the Seventh Census of the United States {4120}.

Margaretta C. Howell married William F. Rundle, who was born in 1832,

---

4110. Id.
4111. Id.
4112. Id.
4113. U.S. Census, Newburgh, Orange County, NY, 1850, Dwelling House 356, Family Number 383, Page 26.
4114. Id.
4115. Charles H. Cochrane, THE HISTORY OF THE TOWN OF MARLBOROUGH, ULSTER COUNTY, NEW YORK.., 169-170.
4116. Id.
4117. Gravestone, Cedar Hill Cemetery, Middlehope.
4118. Id.
4119. Id.
4120. U.S. Census, Newburgh, Orange County, NY, 1850, Dwelling House 356, Family Number 383, Page 26.

the son of Lockwood and Ann C. Rundle {4121}.

Margaretta C. Rundell, the wife of William F. Rundell, died on 18 Apr 1863, at the age of 27 years, 7 months, and ? days, and is buried in the Cedar Hill Cemetery at Middlehope {4122}.

William F. Rundle died in 1919, and is buried at Genoa, New York {4123}.

William F. and Margaret C. (Howell) Rundell were the parents of at least two children.

    i.   FRANK L. RUNDELL, born on 10 Dec 1857, died on 29 Apr 1865, at the age of 7 years, 8 months, and 10 days, and is buried beside his mother at Middlehope {4124}.

    ii.   FRED RUNDELL.

797. ADELIA[7] HOWELL (John[6]), the daughter of John[6] and Hester Howell, was born on 21 Sep 1840 {4125}.

Adelia Howell, 9, was enumerated in her father's family in the Seventh Census of the United States {4126}.

On 3 Jly 1860, Adelia Howell married John Bloomer {4127}.

Adelia Bloomer died on 11 June 1872 {4128}.

John and Adelia (Howell) Bloomer were the parents of at least two children {4129}.

    i.   ARMINTA BLOOMER, born 19 Sep 1862, married William W. Russell, died on 24 Apr 1913 {4130}.

    ii.   MARY T. BLOOMER, born on 27 May 1872, married John Bingham, died on 22 Apr 1913 {4131}.

2. Elliot [6], Jeremiah [5]

798. CATHERINE[7] HOWELL (Elliot[6]), the daughter of Elliot[6] and Nancy

---

4121. NYG&BR, LIV, 236 (Jly 1923).
4122. Gravestone, Cedar Hill Cemetery, Middlehope.
4123. NYG&BR, LIV, 236 (Jly 1923).
4124. Gravestone, Cedar Hill Cemetery, Middlehope.
4125. Dorothy G. Tuttle, op. cit.
4126. U.S. Census, Newburgh, Orange County, NY, 1850, Dwelling House 356, Family Number 383, Page 26.
4127. Dorothy G. Tuttle, op. cit.
4128. Id.
4129. Id.
4130. LDS IGI Temple Records, Microfilm #1553485, Batch #F5 107 4622.
4131. Id.

(Bloomer) Howell, was born in June 1833 {4132}.

On 29 Jly 1850, Catherine Howell, 16, was enumerated in her father's family in the Seventh Census of the United States {4133}.

Catherine Howell married Timothy Bridgen, who was born on 1 May 1833 {4134}.

Timothy Brigden died on 16 May 1901, and is buried in the Fleming Hill Cemetery in the Town of Fleming in Cayuga County, New York {4135}.

Catherine Brigden died on 10 Nov 1915, and is buried beside her husband {4136}.

Timothy and Catherine (Howell) Brigden were the parents of at least one child {4137}.

      i.   HOWELL G. BRIGDEN, born in about 1863, died on 9 Apr 1879, and is buried beside his parents.

3. Isaac[6], Jeremiah[5]

802. ELIZABETH[7] HOWELL (Isaac[6]), the daughter of Isaac[6] and Jane Howell, was born in Sep 1849 {4138}.

On 22 Jly 1850, Elizabeth Howell, ten months old, was enumerated in her father's family in the Seventh Census of the United States {4139}.

Elizabeth Howell married Mr. Wood {4140}.

Elizabeth Wood died in 1934, and is buried near her parents in the Lakeview Cemetery {4141}.

803. FRANK[7] HOWELL (Isaac[6]), the son of Isaac[6] Howell, was born in 1851 {4142}.

Frank Howell married Ella Slocum, who was born in 1861 {4143}.

Frank Howell died in 1926, and is buried in the Lakeview Cemetery in Cayuga County, New York {4144}.

4132. Gravestone, Fleming Hill Cemetery.
4133. U.S. Census, Locke, Cayuga County, NY, 1850, Dwelling House 249, Family Number 254, Page 103.
4134. Gravestone, Flemming Hill Cemetery.
4135. Id.
4136. Id.
4137. Id.
4138. Petition, Frank Howell, Cayuga County, NY.
4139. U.S. Census, Scipio, Cayuga County, NY, 1850, Dwelling House 169, Family Number 176, Page 179.
4140. Petition, Frank Howell, Cayuga County, NY.
4141. Gravestone, Lakeview Cemetery.
4142. Petition, Frank Howell, Cayuga County, NY.
4143. Gravestone, Lakeview Cemetery.
4144. Id.

Ella Howell died in 1928, and is buried beside her husband {4145}.

804. JEROME[7] HOWELL (Isaac[6]), the son of Isaac[6] Howell, was born in 1853 {4146}.

On 17 Sep 1879, Jerome Howell married Alice Maude Snyder, who was born in about 1857, the daughter of John and Susan (Miller) Snyder {4147}.

A. Maude Howell died on 1 Jly 1931, and is buried in the Scipio Rural Cemetery in Cayuga County, New York {4148}.

Jerome Howell died on 29 Nov 1931, and is buried beside his wife {4149}.

4. Eliza[6], John[5]

806. GEORGE[7] HOWELL (Eliza[6], John[5]) was born GEORGE LONGBOTTOM, the son of James H. and Eliza[6] (Howell) (#349) Longbottom. He changed his name to GEORGE HOWELL, was married, had three children, and moved to Nebraska {4150}.

George Howell was a residual heir of his grandfather, John[5] Howell (#122) {4151}, and was an executor of the will of his aunt, Lydia[6] Howell (#348) {4152}.

George Howell was the father of three children {4153}.

1248. i. Child[8].

1249. ii. Child[8].

1250. iii. Child[8].

807. CHARLES[7] HOWELL (Eliza[6], John[5]) was born CHARLES LONGBOTTOM, the son of James H. and Eliza[6] (Howell) (#352) Longbottom. He changed his name to CHARLES HOWELL, was married, had three children, and moved to Iowa

4145. Id.
4146. Gravestone, Scipio Rural Cemetery, with added notes, from L.D.S. microfilm #1435221.
4147. Id.
4148. Id.
4149. Id.
4150. Sylvester, op. cit., 136.
4151. Ulster County Wills, Liber P, 537-539.
4152. Id., Liber 2, 601-606.
4153. Sylvester, op. cit.

{4154}. He was a residual heir of his grandfather, John⁵ Howell (#122) {4155}.

    1251. i.   Child⁸.

    1252. ii.   Child⁸.

    1253. iii. Child⁸.

5. John Brainard⁶, John⁵

809. HESTER⁷ HOWELL (John Brainard⁶, John⁵), the daughter of John Brainard⁶ and Phebe J. (Watkins) Howell, was born in Oct 1839 {4156}.

    On 23 Aug 1850, Hester Howell, 10, was enumerated in her father's family in the Seventh Census of the United States {4157}.

    Esther Howell married Nelson Horton in Nov 1868 {4158}.

    Nelson and Esther (Howell) Horton had no children {4159}.

810. BRAINARD⁷ HOWELL (John Brainard⁶, John⁵), the son of John Brainard⁶ and Phebe J. (Watkins) Howell, was born in June 1842 {4160}.

    On 23 Aug 1850, Brainard Howell, 8, was enumerated with his father's family in the Seventh Census of the United States {4161}.

    In Dec 1867, Brainard Howell married Mary C. Hasbrouck, the daughter of Charles B. and Jane Hasbrouck {4162}.

    Brainard and Mary C. (Hasbrouck) Howell were the parents of at least one daughter {4163}.

    1254. i.   MARY BRAINARD⁸ HOWELL, born 27 Mch 1867.

4154. Id.
4155. Ulster County Wills, Liber P, 537-539.
4156. Sylvester, op. cit., 136.
4157. U.S. Census, Lloyd, Ulster County, NY, 1850, Dwelling House 590, Family Number 617, Page 289.
4158. Sylvester, op. cit.
4159. Id.
4160. Id.
4161. U.S. Census, Lloyd, Ulster County, NY, 1850, Dwelling House 590, Family Number 617, Page 289.
4162. Sylvester, op. cit.
4163. Id.

E. John [4], Jonathan [3], John [2], Richard [1]

1. Chauncey Perkins [5], Sylvester [5]

815. MARY AUGUSTA [7] HOWELL (Chauncey Perkins[6], Sylvester[5]), the daughter of Chauncey Perkins[6] and Marietta (Young) Howell, was born on 6 Jan 1875 {4164}.

On 4 Dec 1895, Mary Augusta Howell married Frederick Skillman Downs {4165}.

Frederick S. Downs died on 22 Nov 1932 {4166}.

Mary Augusta Downs died on 10 Mch 1949 {4167}.

Frederick S. and Mary Augusta (Howell) Downs were the parents of four children {4168}.

    i.   ELOISE BROWN DOWNS, born on 25 Oct 1896, died on 3 May 19--.

    ii.   MARIETTA ADELIA DOWNS, born on 5 June 1898, married René Gendron on 30 June 1936, two children.

    iii.   RUTH MIRANDA DOWNS, born on 14 Jan 1901, married Herbert L. Wells on 11 Aug 1923, two children, died on 9 Sep 1967. He was born on 23 Jly 1893, and died on 15 Apr 1969.

    iv.   CHAUNCEY H. DOWNS, born on 10 Feb 1910, married S. Marion Bennett on 28 Dec 1933, four children, died on 28 May 1968.

816. ELIZABETH [7] HOWELL (Chauncey Perkins[6], Sylvester[5]), the daughter of Chauncey Perkins[7] and Marietta (Young) Howell, was born on 22 Sep 1881 {4169}.

Elizabeth Howell never married. She was the last of her surname to reside in the family homestead, the second house built on the farm originally deeded to Richard[1] Howell in 1675 {4170}, and one which contained some of the timbers of the original house {4171}.

4164. Mallmann, op. cit., 236.
4165. Id.
4166. Bessie L. Hallock, op. cit.
4167. Wilbur Franklin Howell, op. cit., 405.
4168. Bessie L. Hallock, op. cit.
4169. Mallmann, op. cit., 236.
4170. STR, Liber A, 160, Liber C, 110; (I, 317-318, II, 222-223).
4171. Mallmann, op. cit.

Elizabeth F. Howell died on 8 Jly 1951 {4172}.

F. Eli⁴, Jonathan³, John², Richard¹

1. Elisha K.⁶, John⁵

817. CHARLES H.⁷ HOWELL (Elisha K.⁶, John⁵), the son of Elisha K. and Rosetta (Keen) Howell, was born on 2 Apr 1842 {4173}.

Charles H. Howell grew up on his parents' farm of 142 acres in Mount Pleasant Township, He took over this farm after he started in life for himself, and made it one of the most desirable farms in the area {4174}.

Charles H. Howell married Sarah Southwick in 1865. She was the daughter of Joshua Southwick {4175}.

Charles H. and Sarah (Southwick) Howell were the parents of four children {4176}.

    1255. i.   BERTHA⁸ HOWELL, married Fred Walker.

    1256. ii.   EVELYN⁸ HOWELL.

    1257. iii. MAUD⁸ HOWELL.

    1258. iv. HARRY⁸ HOWELL.

818. HELEN A.⁷ HOWELL (Elisha K.⁶, John⁵), the daughter of Elisha K.⁶ and Rosetta (Keen) Howell, was born in about 1846.

Helen A. Howell married Isaac Johnson, of Starucca, Pennsylvania {4177}.

820. MARY⁷ HOWELL (Elisha K.⁶, John⁵) was the daughter of Elisha K.⁶ and Rosetta (Keen) Howell.

Mary Howell married George Kent, of Binghamton, New York {4178}.

4172. Suffolk County Estates, File #424 P 1951.
4173. COMM. BIO. RECORD..NORTHEASTERN PENNSYLVANIA, 1458.
4174. Id.
4175. Id., 976.
4176. Id.
4177. Id., 975.
4178. Id.

821. ROSA[7] HOWELL (Elisha K.[6], John[5]) was the daughter of Elisha K.[6] and Rosetta (Keen) Howell.

Rosa Howell married Augustus Jennings, of Broome County, New York {4179}.

2. Seth [6], David [5]

824. CLARA A.[7] HOWELL (Seth[6], David[5]), the daughter of Seth[6] and Mary (Buck) Howell, was born in Nov 1852 {4180}.

In 1880, Clara A. Howell married L.P. Curtis, of Scott Township, Wayne County,Pennsylvania {4181}.

L.P. Curtis died on 18 Sep 1887 {4182}.

On 9 June 1900, Clara Howell, 47, was enumerated in the household of her mother, Mary, as were her children, Mary B., 16, and Frank Curtis, 13, in Scott Township, Wayne County, Pennsylvania, in the Eleventh Census of the United States {4183}.

L.P. and Clara A. (Howell) Curtis were the parents of two children {4184}.

    i.   MAY BELL CURTIS, born on 5 Mch 1884.

    ii.   FRANK A. CURTIS, born on 29 Nov 1886.

825. ADELBERT C.[7] HOWELL (Seth[6], David[5]), the son of Seth[6] and Mary (Buck) Howell, was born on 29 Dec 1856 in Richland County, Wisconsin {4185}.

On 18 Oct 1892, Adelbert Howell married Iola Cole, of Scott Township, Wayne County, Pennsylvania {4186}, who was born in Aug 1872 {4187}.

Adelbert Howell lived "..upon a part of the old homestead..", and was "..engaged in the cultivation of the place" {4188}.

On 9 June 1900, Adelbert Howell, 43, farm laborer, was enumerated as a member of the household of his mother, Mary Howell, 66, farmer, as were his

4179. Id.
4180. COMM. BIO. RECORD..NORTHEASTERN PENNSYLVANIA, 1458.
4181. Id.
4182. Id.
4183. U.S. Census, Scott Township, Wayne County, PA, 1900, Dwelling House 118, Family Number 122, Enumeration District 128, Sheet Number 6.
4184. COMM. BIO. RECORD..NORTHEASTERN PENNSYLVANIA, 1458.
4185. Id.
4186. Id., 1459.
4187. U.S. Census, Scott Township, Wayne County, PA, 1900, Dwelling House 118, Family Number 122, Enumeration District 128, Sheet Number 6.
4188. COMM. BIO. RECORD..NORTHEASTERN PENNSYLVANIA, 1459.

wife, Iola, 27, and their daughter, Liza, 6, in the Eleventh Census of the United States {4189}.

Adelbert C. and Iola (Cole) Howell were the parents of at least two children {4190}.

1259. i. MARIA A.[8] HOWELL, born on 11 Mch 1893, died on 30 Apr 1893.

1260. ii. LIZZIE M.[8] HOWELL, born on 19 May 1894.

826. OLIVER P.[7] HOWELL (Seth[6], David[5]), the son of Seth[6] and Mary (Buck) Howell, was born on 24 Oct 1858 in Richland County, Wisconsin {4191}.

Oliver P. Howell married Myra J. Hines, of Starucca, Pennsylvania, in 1882 {4192}, who was born in May 1862 {4193}.

After his marriage, Oliver P. Howell "..located upon a tract of eighty-two acres of wild land in Scott township, which he purchased. He made some improvements on that place..", but returned to the old homestead, where he and his brother operated the farm {4194}.

Like his father, Oliver P. Howell was a Democrat. As such, he was elected school director in 1888, and re-elected after a three year term {4195}.

On 9 June 1900, Oliver Howell, 41, farmer, was enumerated as the head of a family consisting of himself, his wife, Mira, 38, and their children, Ella M., 17, Jessie, 13, Earl, 8, and Albert, 1, residing in Scott Township, Wayne County, Pennsylvania, in the Eleventh Census of the United States {4196}.

Oliver P. and Myra J. (Hines) Howell were the parents of four children {4197}.

1261. i. ELLA M.[8] HOWELL, born on 28 Mch 1883.

1262. ii. JESSE E.[8] HOWELL, born on 21 Sep 1886.

1263. iii. EARL E.[8] HOWELL, born on 5 Apr 1892.

1264. iv. ALBERT[8] HOWELL, born in Nov 1898 {4198}.

4189. U.S. Census, op. cit.
4190. COMM. BIO. RECORD..NORTHEASTERN PENNSYLVANIA, op. cit.
4191. Id.
4192. Id.
4193. U.S. Census, Scott Township, Wayne County, PA, 1900, Dwelling House 119, Family Number 123, Enumeration District 128, Sheet Number 6.
4194. COMM. BIO. RECORD..NORTHEASTERN PENNSYLVANIA, op. cit.
4195. Id.
4196. U.S. Census, op. cit., Dwelling House 119, Family Number 123, Sheet 6.
4197. COMM. BIO. RECORD..NORTHEASTERN PENNSYLVANIA.., op. cit.
4198. U.S. Census, op. cit.

3. Albert C. [6], David [5]

833. PERRY C., "RENO",[7] HOWELL (Albert C.[6], David[5]), the son of Albert C.[6] and Delilah (Rutledge) Howell, was born on 9 Dec 1878 in Damascus Township, Wayne County, Pennsylvania {4199}.

On 14 Jly 1899, Perry C. Howell married Ruby Nichols, who was born on 20 Apr 1882, the daughter of Richard and Mary (Whitmore) Nichols {4200}.

Perry C., "Reno", Howell, who was foreman at the acetate works in Tanner's Falls, died of appendicitis on 5 Oct 1904, and is buried in Damascus Township {4201}.

Ruby Howell married Mr. O'Conner as her second husband. She died of cancer on 13 Apr 1942, and is also buried in Damascus Township {4202}.

Perry C. and Ruby (Nichols) Howell were the parents of two children {4203}.

    1265. i.   LILLIAN M.[8] HOWELL, born on 30 Apr 1900, died of pneumonia on 17 May 1918.

    1266. ii.   CHESTER RENO[8] HOWELL, born on 8 Mch 1902, married Ruth Irene Brunges on 22 Dec 1928, one child, died on 22 Feb 1965 at Bradenton, Florida. She was born on 1 Feb 1908 at Centermoreland, Pennsylvania, the daughter of Hiram and Eva (Weber) Brunges, died on 2 Aug 1981 at Boca Raton, Florida, and is buried at Johnson City, New York. (NOTE: *Chester Reno Howell was the grandfather of Craig Robert Howell*).

4. Wilbur E. [6], Eli [5]

834. ARGUS[7] HOWELL (Wilbur E.[6], Eli[5]), the son of Wilbur E.[6] and Mary (Gaylord) Howell, was born in Jan 1868.

On 15 June 1900, Argus Howell, clerk, was enumerated as the head of a family consisting of himself, his wife, Maggie, who was born in Nov 1874 in Scotland, and their daughter, Mg, residing in Avoca Borough, Luzerne County, Pennsylvania, in the Twelfth Census of the United States {4204}.

On 15 Apr 1910, Argus Howell, 41, butcher, was enumerated as the head

---

4199. Craig R. Howell, op. cit.
4200. Id.
4201. Id.
4202. Id.
4203. Id.
4204. U.S. Census, Avoca, Luzerne County, PA, 1900, Enumeration District 33, Sheet 12, Line 99, Sheet 13, Line 1.

of a family consisting of himself, his wife, Margaret, 34, and their children, Grace, 15, Glen, 9, and William, 4, residing on McAlpine Street in Avoca, Pennsylvania, in the Thirteenth Census of the United States {4205}.

On 12 Jan 1920, Argus Howell, 54, was residing at 404 South Main Street in Avoca, Pennsylvania, with his family consisting of his wife, Margaret, 42, their children, Grace, 25, Glen, 19, and William, 15, and his father, Webb, 73, widower {4206}.

Argus and Margaret Howell were the parents of three children.

1267.   i.   GRACE[8] HOWELL, born in Nov 1894, was a public school teacher in 1920.

1268.   ii.   GLEN[8] HOWELL, born in about 1901, was a repair man at a coal breaker in 1920.

1269.   iii.   WILLIAM[8] HOWELL, born in about 1905.

II. Descendants of David [2] Howell

A. David [4], David [3], David [2], Richard [1]

1. George [6], David [5]

846. WILLIAM H. HARRISON[7] HOWELL (George[6], David[5]), the son of George[6] and Julia Ann (Mapes) Howell, was born in about 1839.

On 5 Sep 1860, Harrison Howell, 11, was enumerated with the household of his uncle, Abner Howell (#381) {4207}.

847. CHARLES EZRA[7] HOWELL, the son of George and Julia Ann (Mapes) Howell, was born in about 1842.

On 31 Jly 1850, Charles Howell, 8, was enumerated with the household of Julius Mapes, 68, farmer, in the Seventh Census of the United States {4208}.

848. PHOEBE A.[7] HOWELL (George[6], David[5]) was born in about 1844 at Goshen, the daughter of George[6] and Julia Ann (Mapes) Howell {4209}.

4205. Id., 1910, Sheet 1A, House Number 4, Family Number 5.
4206. Id., 1920, Enumeration District 7, Sheet Number 12A, House Number 205, Family Number 246.
4207. U.S. Census, Monroe, Orange County, NY, 1850, Dwelling House 170, Family Number 170, Page 278.
4208. Id., Dwelling House 510 (sic) 501, Family Number 501, Page 300.
4209. PORTRAIT & BIOGRAPHICAL RECORD OF ORANGE COUNTY.., 799.

On 31 Jly 1850, Phebe Howell, 6, was enumerated with the household of Julius Mapes, 68, farmer, in the Seventh Census of the United States {4210}.

On 6 Oct 1868, Phoebe A. Howell married Joseph Henry Earl, who was born on 7 Jan 1847 at Highland Mills, the son of Alexander and Melinda (Thorn) Earl {4211}.

"Prior to the age of eighteen..", Mr. Earl "..was a student in the schools of Highland Mills and Central Valley, though some years before that he had begun to be self-supporting. Beginning for himself when thirteen, he worked on a farm by the day until 1872, after which he engaged in teaming for thirteen years. In 1885 he returned to Highland Mills, where he has since been employed on a farm" {4212}.

"In religious belief Mr. amd Mrs. Earl are identified with the Methodist Episcopal Church. His first ballot was cast for Grant, and from that time to this he has never failed to support the Republican candidate for the Presidency {4213}.

Joseph Henry and Phoebe A. (Howell) Earl were the parents of seven children {4214}.

    i.   GEORGE HENRY EARL.

    ii.   MELINDA ANN EARL.

    iii.   MARY FRANCES EARL.

    iv.   Child, died young.

    v.   Child, died young.

    vi.   Child, died young.

    vii.   Child, died young.

2. Edmund W. [6], Josiah [5]

849. JAMES ALLEN[7] HOWELL (Edmund W.[6], Josiah[5]), the son of Edmund W.[6] and Jane G. (Orcutt) Howell, was born in 1846 {4215}.

On 18 Oct 1850, James A. Howell, 4, was enumerated with his father's

4210. U.S. Census, Monroe, Orange County, NY, 1850, Dwelling House 510 (sic) 501, Family Number 501, Page 300.
4211. PORTRAIT & BIOGRAPHICAL RECORD OF ORANGE COUNTY.., 798.
4212. Id., 799.
4213. Id.
4214: Id.
4215. Gravestone, North Chili Rural Cemetery.

family in the Seventh Census of the United States {4216}.

J. Allen Howell married Valeda A. Hubbard {4217}.

On 8 June 1880, James Howell, 33, farmer, was enumerated as the head of a family consisting of himself, his wife, Lida, 32, and their son, Sawyer, 9, residing at Rochester in the Tenth Census of the United States {4218}.

Valeda A. Howell died in 1924, and is buried in the North Chili Rural Cemetery {4219}.

J. Allen Howell died in 1924, and is buried beside his wife {4220}.

James Allen and Valeda A. (Hubbard) Howell were the parents of at least one child {4221}.

> 1270.   i.   SELWYN F.[8] HOWELL, born in 1871, died in 1927, and is buried in the North Chili Rural Cemetery.

B. George [4], David [3], David [2], Richard [1]

1. Orrin Day [6], Benjamin [5]

853. MARION[7] HOWELL (Orrin Day[6], Benjamin[5]), the daughter of Orrin Day[6] and Cornelia (More) Howell, was born in about Nov 1840.

In 1868 {4222}, Marion Howell married Timothy Nathan Holden {4223}, who was born on 21 Mch 1839 at Charlestown, Sullivan County, New Hampshire, the son of Richard and Sophia (Allen) Holden {4224}.

Timothy N. Holden came west with his family, settling at Rockton, Illinois, on 21 Mch 1853. In 1857, they moved to Aurora. He became engaged with Fuller, Finch & Fuller, druggists, of Chicago, as a clerk from 1858 to 1856, when he became a partner in the firm. He remained with the firm until 1869 {4225}, when he went to Leadville, Colorado, in the silver mine rush {4226}. Returning a year later, he established his own glassware business. He continued in this business until the great Chicago fire of 1871, when his entire stock was destroyed. In 1872, he entered the office of the Chicago, Burlington &

4216. U.S. Census, Chili, Monroe County, NY, 1850, Dwelling House 237, Family Number 237, Page 297.

4217. Gravestone, North Chili Rural Cemetery.

4218. U.S. Census, Rochester, Monroe County, NY, 1880, Enumeration District 89, Page 27, Dwelling House 263, Family Number 289.

4219. Gravestone, North Chili Rural Cemetery.

4220. Id.

4221. Id.

4222. Obituary, AURORA BEACON NEWS, 4 Jan 1929.

4223. BIOGRAPHICAL AND HISTORICAL RECORD OF KANE COUNTY, ILLINOIS.., 327.

4224. Id., 324.

4225. THE PAST AND PRESENT OF KANE COUNTY, ILLINOIS, 767.

4226. Obituary, AURORA BEACON NEWS, 4 Jan 1929.

Quincy Rail Road as bookkeeper in the locomotive department {4227}. On 1 Sep 1880, he became an owner of the hardware business, Kendall & Holden {4228}. He later became a realtor, with his office at 225 in the Coulter Block, while his residence was at 4 South Root Street {4229}.

Timothy N. Holden was a lifelong Republican, and attended the 1860 convention at the Wigwam in Chicago. He was the President of the Aurora East Board of Education for many years, and served as mayor of Aurora in 1898 and 1899. He also served as Aurora township supervisor for 15 years {4230}.

Marion Holden died on 21 Oct 1918, at the age of 77 years and 11 months, and is buried in the family plot at the Spring Lake Cemetery in Aurora {4231}.

Timothy N. Holden died at San Diego on 3 Jan 1929, and is buried beside his wife {4232}.

Timothy Nathan and Marion (Howell) Holden were the parents of two children {4233}.

    i.   FRANK HOWELL HOLDEN, born in about 1870, graduated from the Massachusetts Institute of Technology, became a distinguished architect, married Agnes Johnson, the daughter of Robert Underwood Johnson on 15 May 1902, one child, died in May 1937 {4234}.

    ii.   BENJAMIN E. HOLDEN, became an architect, subsequently became a painter, resided in Paris, France.

854. ANNIE[7] HOWELL (Orrin Day[6], Benjamin[5]), the daughter of Orrin Day[6] and Cornelia (More) Howell, was born on 22 Dec 1842 in Saugerties, New York {4235}.

On 28 June 1866, Annie Howell married Frank M. Annis {4236}. He was born in about 1840, and was a lawyer with an office at #5 in the Eagle Block. They also resided at 4 South Root Street {4237}.

Judge Frank M. Annis died on 1 Aug 1920, and is buried in the family

---

4227. THE PAST & PRESENT OF KANE COUNTY, ILLINOIS, 767.
4228. THE AURORA DIRECTORY 1886.., 138.
4229. AURORA CITY DIRECTORY 1907-1908.., 214.
4230. Obituary, AURORA BEACON NEWS, 4 Jan 1929.
4231. Gravestone, Spring Lake Cemetery, Aurora, IL, from SPRING LAKE CEMETERY, Section II, Surname Index H-P, 36.
4232. Id.
4233. Obituary, AURORA BEACON NEWS, 4 Jan 1929.
4234. Id., 1 June 1937.
4235. Id., 29 June 1924.
4236. MARRIAGE RECORD INDEX, 1836-1866, KANE COUNTY, ILLINOIS, 3.
4237. THE AURORA DIRECTORY, 1886.., 54.

plot in the Spring Lake Cemetery {4238}.

Annie H. Annis died on 28 June 1924, and is buried beside her husband {4239}.

It does not appear that Frank M. and·Annie (Howell) Annis had any children.

855. EDWIN BEN[7] HOWELL (Orrin Day[6], Benjamin[5]), the son of Orrin Day[6] and Cornelia (More) Howell, was born on 17 Sep 1852 at Moresville, New York {4240}.

Edwin B. Howell graduated from the Chicago Medical College on 30 June 1874 {4241}. He also studied at Vienna, Paris, Prague and London. While in Vienna, he was married Etoile Coulter, of Aurora, on 18 Nov 1875 {4242}. For a time, he was a surgeon at Aurora, with an office at 24 Main Street, and a residence at 10 North Fourth Street {4243}. Because of his poor health, he went to California. This did not restore his health, and he died there {4244}, on 6 Feb 1887. He is buried in the Coulter lot at the Spring Lake Cemetery at Aurora {4245}.

It is not known that Edwin Ben and Etoile (Coulter) Howell had any children.

2. Daniel Everts[6], Jeremiah[5]

862. FRED MINIER[7] HOWELL (Daniel Everts[6], Jeremiah[5]), the son of Daniel Everts[6] and Fatima (Minier) Howell, was born on 25 Nov 1860 {4246}.

Fred M. Howell "..lived in the family home on West Hill Street in Elmira and attended the Elmira Schools. After his High School graduation in 1879 he was employed by Fitch & Aldrich, a wood working business.." {4247}.

"From earliest boyhood Fred had attended the Lake Street Presbyterian Church of which his father was a Charter Member, and in 1874 he organized a Bible Class for Men and Boys. This class grew in size to 125 members during the forty years before his death. Every good or ill that happened to the members was

4238. Gravestone, Spring Lake Cemetery, from SPRING LAKE CEMETERY, AURORA, ILLINOIS, Section I, Surname Index A-G, 13.

4239. Id.

4240. BIO. DICTIONARY & PORTRAIT GALLERY..REPRESENTATIVE MEN.., 349.

4241. COMMEMORATIVE BIOGRAPHICAL AND HISTORICAL RECORD OF KANE COUNTY, ILLINOIS, 888.

4242. BIO DICTIONARY & PORTRAIT GALLERY..REPRESENTATIVE MEN.., 349.

4243. HOLLAND'S AURORA CITY DIRECTORY FOR THE YEARS 1880-84, 163.

4244. COMM. BIO. & HISTORICAL RECORD..KANE COUNTY, 888.

4245. SPRING LAKE CEMETERY, AURORA, ILLINOIS, Section II, 45.

4246. Finch, op. cit., 14.

4247. Finch, op. cit., 15a.

felt as keenly by him as by them. He had many other interests but the Class came first in his mind." {4248}.

In 1883, with John E. Aldrich as his partner, Fred M. Howell founded the box and label manufacturing business known as F. M. Howell & Co. "Mr. Aldrich disposed of his share of this concern to John Brand, who in 1919 sold part of his interest to Fred and Chester Howell." {4249}.

Fred M. Howell married Louese Hunter, who was born in 1856 {4250}.

Fred M. Howell was deeply concerned with the 1926 addition to his church. He also was concerned with the YMCA, for which he was President of the Board of Directors for several years. He also worked with the Elmira College Trustees Board, and with the Chemung Valley Savings and Loan Association {4251}.

Fred M. Howell died on 29 Apr 1934 {4252}.

Louese Howell died on 11 Nov 1943 {4253}.

Fred Minier and Louese (Hunter) Howell were the parents of one daughter {4254}.

    1271.   i.   HAZEL HUNTER[8] HOWELL, born on 5 May 1892, married Eugene Quick, one child.

863. SIDNEY LLEWELLYN[7] HOWELL (Daniel Everts[6], Jeremiah[5]), the son of Daniel Everts[6] and Fatima (Minier) Howell, was born on 6 Mch 1866 {4255}.

Sidney L. Howell married Janet Preswick, who was born on 19 Aug 1867, the daughter of Edward and Amelia Jarvis Preswick, of Elmira {4256}.

Sidney L. Howell joined the business of his brother, Fred, where he stayed until 1899, "..when he left Elmira to go into the grocery business with Elmer Wanzer of Ithaca. In 1921 he formed his own business in real estate and insurance..", which became the firm of Howell and Stevens. "For 8 years he was Supervisor from the 4th Ward and was Chairman of the Board of Supervisors at the time of the controversial building of the County Court House. Other activities in Ithaca gained largely from his participation, among them the Business Men's Association, the Chamber of Commerce, Rotary Club and Liberty Loan Drives. He was a founder of the Savings and Loan Association and its President for many years.." {4257}.

4248. Id.
4249. Id.
4250. Id., 14.
4251. Id., 15a.
4252. Id., 14.
4253. Id.
4254. Id.
4255. Id.
4256. Id.
4257. Id., 15a.

Sidney L. Howell was a member of the First Presbyterian Church {4258}.

Janet, "Jennie", Howell died on 14 Sep 1937 {4259}.

Sidney Llewellyn Howell died on 5 Nov 1938 {4260}.

Sidney LLewellyn and Janet (Preswick) Howell were the parents of two children {4261}.

1272. i. SIDNEY PRESWICK[8] HOWELL, born on 11 Jly 1896 at Elmira, married Marcia May McCartney, of Mound City, IL, who was born on 17 Mch 1899, the daughter of Marcus and Ida Huckleberry McCartney, five children. She died on 26 Oct 1958 at Ramsey, New Jersey.

1273. ii. HELEN ILSE[8] HOWELL, born on 14 Sep 1899 at Elmira, married William Tristam Stevens III, of Kent Island, MD, on 24 Aug 1924, two children. He was born on 25 Apr 1898, the son of William Tristam and Kate Elliot Stevens.

864. CHESTER EVERTS[7] HOWELL (Daniel Everts[6], Jeremiah[5]), the son of Daniel Everts[6] and Fatima (Minier) Howell, was born on 12 Aug 1867 {4262} on West Hill Road in Elmira {4263}.

In 1885, Chester E. Howell "..went to the Michigan north woods region for his health. At Manistique he lived an outdoor life, working first on a Great Lakes barge; next as a transit man in the survey for the Minneapolis & Sault Ste. Marie R. R." {4264}.

On 1 Jan 1889, Chester E. Howell married Marion Rachel Elizabeth Connor at Manistique, MI. She was born at Rose Center, MI, on 18 Aug 1862, the daughter of Henry H. and Miriam Connor {4265}.

After his marriage, Chester E. Howell's health improved and "..he returned to Elmira. Here he worked in the box manufacture business established by Fred his brother, after whose death he became its president. During his life he was connected with church & civic affairs; headed several campaigns for raising charity funds; a charter member & trustee of North Presbyterian Church; later trustee and Chairman of the Board, Lake St. Presbyterian Church; director & vice-president of Mechanics Bank; charter member & a president of Rotary; director & president of the Central YMCA; a president of Century Club; a Masonic Shrine member; a president of the Newtown Battlefield Chapter of the Sons of the Revolution; appointed by Gov.

4258. Id.
4259. Id., 14.
4260. Id.
4261. Id.
4262. Id.
4263. Id., 15.
4264. Id.
4265. Id., 14.

Dewey in 1945 Commissioner of the Battlefield." {4266}.

Chester Everts Howell died on 10 Apr 1949 at Elmira {4267}.

Marion Rachel Elizabeth Howell died on 6 May 1951 at Elmira {4268}.

Chester Everts and Marion Rachel Elizabeth (Connor) Howell were the parents of four children {4269}.

1274. i. JESSIE EVERTS[8] HOWELL, born on 12 Sep 1889 at Manistique, married Frank Clifford Finch on 9 Sep 1920, one son, died on 16 Oct 1968 {4270}. Frank Clifford Finch was the son of Cornelius and Alice (Rowley) Finch, of Endicott, N.Y. She was the compiler of a useful genealogy of the ancestry of Chester Everts Howell and some of his relatives, on which we have relied heavily.

1275. ii. EDITH LOUESE[8] HOWELL, born on 12 Oct 1890 at Elmira, married James Edwin Riley on 9 Sep 1920, three children. He was born on Jan 1889, the son of James Edward and Amanda Dinsmore Riley.

1276. iii. EVERTS HOWE[8] HOWELL, born on 11 Mch 1897 at Elmira, married Gladys Mae Shaw, the daughter of Jay W. and Clare Coolbaugh Shaw, one child, joined F. M. Howell & Co. as a young man, became General Manager in 1940, President in 1949 and, later, Chairman of the Board. He founded the Howell Advertising Agency in 1942. He served as President of the Rotary Club and was active at the local and state levels in the Presbyterian Church {4271}.

1277. iv. CHESTER EVERTS[8] HOWELL, JR., born on 16 Jly 1899, married Georgia Isabel Lowman, the daughter of Martin and Lena Long Loman of Wellsburg, N.Y., three children, joined F.M. Howell & Co. as a young man, was factory superintendent in the late 1930s, became General Manager in 1950, and President in 1966. He was a leader of the Lake Street Church and the Elmira Exchange Club {4272}.

4266. Id., 15.
4267. Id., 14.
4268. Id.
4269. Id., 15.
4270. TREE TALKS, 9, 5-6 (1969).
4271. Thomas E. Byrne, CHEMUNG COUNTY | 1890-1975, 314-315.
4272. Id.

3. Robert D. [6], George [5]

865. HELEN E.[7] HOWELL (Robert D.[6], George[5]), the daughter of Robert D.[6] and Elizabeth (Hager) Howell, was born in about 1856 {4273}.

Helen E. Howell married Asa C. Farlin, the grandson of Jemima (Howell)(#158) Farlin {4274}.

Helen E. Farlin died on 31 May 1918 {4275}.

866. HENRY C.[7] HOWELL (Robert D.[6], George[5]), the son of Robert D.[6] and Elizabeth (Hager) Howell, was born on 6 Jly 1858 {4276}.

Henry C. Howell married Sarah Ella Owen, who was born on 20 Apr 1860, the daughter of Jonathan and Elizabeth Neate Owen {4277}.

Henry C. Howell died on 15 Jan 1931 {4278}.

Sarah E. Howell died on 2 June 1942 {4279}.

Henry C. and Sarah Ella (Owen) Howell were the parents of two daughters {4280}.

    1278.   i.   HARRIET[8] HOWELL, born in 1887, married Claude Smith, two children, died on 28 May 1928.

    1279.   ii.   BERTHA E.[8] HOWELL, married (1) George Neale, one child, married (2) John Covert, two children.

867. IDA B.[7] HOWELL (Robert D.[6], George[5]), the daughter of Robert D.[6] and Elizabeth (Hager) Howell, was born on 20 Sep 1861 {4281}.

On 27 Dec 1882, Ida B. Howell married Peter Bishop, of Lodi, N.Y., who was born in 1848 {4282}.

Ida B. Bishop died on 21 Feb 1938 {4283}.

Peter Bishop died in 1942 {4284}.

Peter and Ida B. (Howell) Bishop were the parents of one daughter {4285}.

4273. Finch, op. cit., 11.
4274. Id.
4275. Id.
4276. Id.
4277. Id.
4278. Id.
4279. Id.
4280. Id.
4281. Id.
4282. Id.
4283. Id.
4284. Id.
4285. Id.

i. MARY ELIZABETH BISHOP, born in April 1888, married Peter Murphy on 18 May 1910, one child, died 18 Mch 1914.

868. LUCY[7] HOWELL (Robert D.[6], George[5]), the daughter of Robert D.[6] and Elizabeth (Hager) Howell, was born in 1866 {4286}.

Lucy Howell married Henry J. Burnett {4287}.

Henry J. Burnett died on 4 Dec 1933, at the age of 73 years, 9 months, and 5 days {4288}.

Lucy Burnett died on 26 Jly 1937 in Logan {4289}.

Henry J. and Lucy (Howell) Burnett were the parents of eight children {4290}.

i. CHESTER BURNETT, married Marguerite Coon.

ii. BLANCHE E. BURNETT, married Claude Williams, of Valois.

iii. HELEN BURNETT, of Washington, D.C.

iv. EONA BURNETT, married Willard Gatchell, of Washington, D.C.

v. GLADYS BURNETT, married Luther Clust, of Burdette.

vi. ROBERT BURNETT.

vii. RALPH BURNETT, married Hazel Fitch.

viii. MILDRED BURNETT, married Harold Blanchard, of Logan.

869. OAKLEY DURLAND[7] HOWELL (Robert D.[6], George[5]), the son of Robert D.[6] and Elizabeth (Hager) Howell, was born in about 1869 {4291}.

Oakley D. Howell married (1) Josephine Johnson, (2) Susan ----, and (3) Josephine --- {4292}.

Oakley D. Howell died in about 1954 {4293}.

Oakley Durland and Josephine (Johnson) Howell were the parents of one child {4294}.

4286. Id.
4287. Id.
4288. Id.
4289. Id.
4290. Id.
4291. Id.
4292. Id.
4293. Id.
4294. Id.

1280.   i.   DAUGHTER[8], died young.

870. SARAH[7] HOWELL (Robert D.[6], George[5]), the daughter of Robert D.[6] and Elizabeth (Hager) Howell, was born in 1872 {4295}.

     Sarah Howell married Homer Robinson, of Burdette {4296}.

     Sarah Robinson died on 22 Aug 1934 {4297}.

     Homer and Sarah (Howell) Robinson were the parents of one daughter {4298}.

     i.   MADELYN ROBINSON.

871. GEORGE O.[7] HOWELL (Robert D.[6], George[5]) was the son of Robert D.[6] and Elizabeth (Hager) Howell {4299}.

     George O. Howell married Estelle Murphy, who was a widow living in Binghamton, N.Y., in 1945 {4300}.

4. George Oliver[6], George[5]

872. FRANK E.[7] HOWELL (George Oliver[6], George[5]), the son of George Oliver[6] and Lucy (Rowland) Howell, was born on 16 May 1856 {4301}.

     Frank E. Howell married Harriet Emden, of Utica, N.Y. {4302}.

     Frank E. Howell died on 5 Dec 1939 {4303}.

     Frank E. and Harriet (Emden) Howell had no children {4304}.

874. FRED S.[7] HOWELL (George Oliver[6], George[5]), the son of George Oliver[6] and Lucy (Rowland) Howell, was born on 15 May 1865 {4305}.

     Fred S. Howell married Jane Rickard {4306}.

     Fred S. Howell died in Jan 1944 in New York, N.Y. {4307}.

4295. Id.
4296. Id.
4297. Id.
4298. Id.
4299. Id.
4300. Id.
4301. Id.
4302. Id.
4303. Id.
4304. Id.
4305. Id.
4306. Id.
4307. Id.

Fred S. and Jane (Rickard) Howell were the parents of three children {4308}.

1281.   i.   BERNICE EVELYN[8] HOWELL, born on 20 June 1895.

1282.   ii.   F. SYDNEY[8] HOWELL, born on 24 Jly 1897.

1283.   iii.   GEORGE RICKARD[8] HOWELL, born on 19 May 1899.

875. CORA M.[7] HOWELL (George Oliver[6], George[5]), the son of George Oliver[6] and Lucy (Rowland) Howell, was born on 6 Nov 1867 {4309}.
    Cora M. Howell married Frank E. Hyde {4310}.
    Cora M. Hyde died on 27 Apr 1912 {4311}.
    Frank E. and Cora M. (Howell) Hyde were the parents of one daughter {4312}.
    i.   FREDDA HYDE, married Arthur Cotens.

876. GEORGIA OLIVER[7] HOWELL (George Oliver[6], George[5]), the daughter of George Oliver[6] and Lucy (Rowland) Howell, was born on 4 Nov 1872 {4313}.
    Georgia Oliver Howell married Fred C. Hall {4314}.
    Georgia Oliver Hall died on 12 May 1937 {4315}.
    Fred C. and Georgia Oliver (Howell) Hall were the parents of three children {4316}.
    i.   FRANCES HALL.

    ii.   LILLIAN HALL.

    iii.   SYDNIE HALL.

5. George[6], George W.[5]

878. LEVI L.[7] HOWELL (George[6], George W.[5]), the son of Dr. George[6] and Sarah

---

4308. Id.
4309. Id., 12.
4310. Id.
4311. Id.
4312. Id.
4313. Id.
4314. Id.
4315. Id.
4316. Id.

L. (Skidmore) Howell, was born on 3 Apr 1856 {4317}.

On 5 Jan 1882, Levi L. Howell married Carrie Louise Hill {4318}, who was born on 11 Feb 1858 {4319}.

Levi L. Howell, D. D. S., died on 4 Aug 1902, and is buried in Plot 240 at the Riverhead Cemetery {4320}.

Carrie L. Howell died on 29 June 1932 {4321}, and is buried beside her husband at Riverhead {4322}.

Levi L. and Carrie Louise (Hill) Howell were the parents of three children.

1284. i.   LE GRAND WHIPPLE[8] HOWELL, born on 28 Apr 1887, died on 5 Aug 1944, and is buried in the family plot at the Riverhead Cemetery {4323}.

1285. ii.   MADELINE A.[8] HOWELL, born in 1892, died in 1968, and is buried in the family plot at Riverhead {4324}.

1286. iii. FRANCES E.[8] HOWELL, born in 1894, died on 20 Jly 1964 {4325}, and is buried in the family plot at Riverhead {4326}.

6. Thomas Jackson[6], Cadwallader[5]

881. CARRIE P.[7] HOWELL (Thomas Jackson[6], Cadwallader[5]) was the daughter of Thomas Jackson[6] and Matilda (Post) Howell {4327}.

In 1883, Carrie P. Howell married M.C. Brownlee, of Monmouth, Illinois {4328}.

M.C. and Carrie P. (Howell) Brownlee were the parents of at least one child {4329}.

  i. HOWELL N. BROWNLEE.

4317. Gravestone, Riverhead Cemetery.
4318. Gertrude A. Barber, MARRIAGES IN SUFFOLK COUNTY.
4319. Gravestone, Riverhead Cemetery.
4320. Id.
4321. Suffolk County Estates, File #409 P 1932.
4322. Gravestone, Riverhead Cemetery.
4323. Id.
4324. Id.
4325. Suffolk County Estates, File #935 P 1964.
4326. Gravestone, Riverhead Cemetery.
4327, PORTRAIT & BIO. ALBUM..HENRY COUNTY.., 209.
4328. Id.
4329. Henry County (IL) Wills, Book E., 271-272.

7. Micah [6], Micah [5]

886. SAREPTA[7] HOWELL (Micah[6], Micah[5]), the daughter of Micah[6] and Anna (Youngs) Howell, was born on 12 Apr 1816 {4330}.

On 25 Dec 1834, Sarepta Howell married George Benjamin, who was born on 15 May 1810 at Mattituck, the son of Isaiah and Sarah (Corwin) Benjamin {4331}.

Sarepta Benjamin died on 31 May 1837, at the age of 20 years, 8 months, and 18 days, and is buried in the Baiting Hollow Cemetery {4332}.

George Benjamin married (2) Ann J. Cook, who was born in 1816, the daughter of Calvin and Hannah (Judge) Cook {4333}.

On 31 Jly 1850, George Benjamin, 40, farmer, having real property valued at $3000, was enumerated as the head of a family consisting of himself, his wife, Ann, 33, and his children, John, 14, Sarepta, 10, George, 9, Alice, 7, Sarah, 5, and Sophia, 1, residing in the Town of Southold, Suffolk County, New York, in the Seventh Census of the United States {4334}.

George and Sarepta (Howell) Benjamin were the parents of one son {4335}.

   i.   JOHN HOWELL BENJAMIN, born on 30 Oct 1835, died on 27 Aug 1863 at Washington, D.C., buried at Baiting Hollow.

George and Ann J. (Cook) Benjamin were the parents of seven children {4336}.

   ii.   SAREPTA A. BENJAMIN, born in 1839, died in 1925, and is buried in the Laurel Cemetery.

   iii. GEORGE WASHINGTON BENJAMIN, born on 17 Jan 1841 at Mattituck, married (1) Hannah M. Homan on 1 Dec 1881 at Franklinville, N.Y., one child, died 18 Nov 1918 and is buried in the Laurel Cemetery, where his gravestone indicates that he died at the age of 77 years, 9 months and 10 days. Hannah (Homan) Benjamin was born in 1856, and died on 24 Nov 1889, at the age of 33 years and 1 month, and is buried beside her husband. George W. Benjamin married (2) Susan, the widow of Elbert H. Edwards, at New York on 31 Mch 1898 {4337}.

4330. Wilbur Franklin Howell, op. cit., 11.
4331. Bicha and Brown, op. cit., 735.
4332. Id.
4333. Id.
4334. U.S. Census, Southold, Suffolk County, NY, 1850, Dwelling House 848, Family Number 924, Page 333.
4335. Bicha and Brown, op. cit.
4336. Id.
4337. Id., 805.

iv.   ALICE M. BENJAMIN, born in 1843, died on 21 Jan 1923 at Brooklyn, and is buried in the Laurel Cemetery.

v.   SARAH M. BENJAMIN, born on 9 Aug 1845, died on 6 Nov 1885, and is buried in the Laurel Cemetery.

vi.   SOPHIA M. BENJAMIN, born in about 1848, married Lester Gildersleeve.

vii. ISAIAH TUTHILL BENJAMIN, born 26 June 1851 at Mattituck, married Edith Louise Hallock on 27 Jan 1879, two children, died on 16 May 1887, at the age of 35 years, 10 months and 21 days. Edith (Hallock) Benjamin was born in 1856, and died on 8 Dec 1946, at the age of 90 years, 6 months and 28 days {4338}.

viii. IDA BENJAMIN, born in 1855, died in 1928.

888. POLLY MARIA[7] HOWELL (Micah[6], Micah[5]), the daughter of Micah[6] and Anna (Youngs) Howell, was born on 20 Apr 1827 {4339}.

On 8 Dec 1847, Polly Maria Howell married Austin Benjamin Tuthill at Baiting Hollow. He was the son of Abiel and Harmony (Benjamin) Tuthill, and was born on 13 Sep 1823 {4340}.

On 12 Jly 1850, Austin B. Tuthill, 26, farmer, having real property valued at $1200, and his wife, P. Maria, 23, were enumerated as a family residing in the Town of Southold, suffolk County, New York, in the Seventh Census of the United States {4341}.

Polly Maria Tuthill died on 8 Dec 1907 {4342}.

Austin Benjamin Tuthill died on 17 Sep 1909 {4343}.

Austin Benjamin and Polly Maria (Howell) Tuthill were the parents of one daughter {4344}.

i.   ANNIE SOPHIA TUTHILL, born on 20 June 1851.

889. LUCETTA PRISCILLA[7] HOWELL (Micah[6], Micah[5]), the daughter of Micah[6] and Anna (Youngs) Howell, was born on 10 May 1831 {4345}.

On 17 Sep 1850, Lucetta P. Howell, 19, was enumerated with her father's

4338. Id.
4339. Tuttle, op. cit., 51.
4340. Id.
4341. U.S. Census, Southold, Suffolk County, NY, 1850, Dwelling House 128, Family Number 133, Page 288.
4342. Tuttle, op. cit.
4343. Id.
4344. Id.
4345. Wilbur Franklin Howell, op. cit., 12.

household in the Seventh Census of the United States {4346}.

On 2 Jan 1854, Lucetta Priscilla Howell married Barnabas Wines Hulse, who was born on 11 Nov 1829, the son of Hampton and Eliza Ann (Wines) Hulse {4347}.

On 16 Jly 1870, Barnabas Wines Hulse, 41, farmer, having real property valued at $2000, and personal property valued at $1000, was enumerated as the head of a family consisting of himself, his wife, Lucetta, 39, and their daughters, Bertha M., 14, Eliza S., 12, and Julia B., 6, residing in the Town of Riverhead, Suffolk County, New York, in the Ninth Census of the United States {4348}.

Barnabas Wines Hulse died on 7 Jly 1901 {4349}.
Lucetta Priscilla Hulse died on 18 Jun 1902 {4350}.

Barnabas Wines and Lucetta Priscilla (Howell) Hulse were the parents of four children {4351}.

    i.   BERTHA MARIA HULSE, born on 3 Dec 1856, married Lewis Smith Turner on 18 Dec 1879, five children, died on 29 Sep 1935 {4352}.

    ii.   LIDA SOPHIA HULSE, born on 24 June 1860, married S. W. Luce on 3 Sep 1893.

    iii.   JULIA BENJAMIN HULSE, born on 15 Sep 1864, married Timothy J. Davis on 15 Oct 1885, at least four children. Timothy J. Davis was the son of Daniel W. and Ann Eliza (Davis) Davis, and was born on 5 Nov 1856 {4353}.

    iv.   HOWARD EVERETT HULSE, born on 23 Jly 1870, married S. W. Brown on 25 Mch 1891.

8. Daniel[6], Micah[5]

890. ELEANOR[7] HOWELL (Daniel[6], Micah[5]), the daughter of Daniel[6] and Jemima[6] (Howell) Howell, was born on 15 May 1825 {4354}.

On Tuesday evening, 19 Oct 1841, Eleanor Howell married Daniel

4346. U.S. Census, Riverhead, Suffolk County, NY, 1850, Dwelling House 477, Family Number 523, Page 279.
4347. Wilbur Franklin Howell, op. cit.
4348. U.S. Census, Riverhead, Suffolk County, NY, 1870, Dwelling House 500, Family Number 543, Page 96.
4349. Wilbur Franklin Howell, op. cit.
4350. Id.
4351. Id.
4352. Id., 13.
4353. Mallmann, op. cit., 194.
4354. Id., 226, 234.

Warner, both of Baiting Hollow, before the Rev. Azel Downs {4355}.

On 11 Sep 1850, Daniel Warner, 32, farmer, having real property valued at $2000, was enumerated as the head of a household consisting of himself, his wife, Eleanor, 25, their children, Allen M., 8, Frances M., 5, Martha R., 2, and an unnamed baby girl of four months, and Henrietta Hamilton, 13, a black girl, residing in the Town of Riverhead, Suffolk County, New York, in the Seventh Census of the United States {4356}.

Eleanor Warner died on 7 Mch 1895, and is buried in the Baiting Hollow Cemetery {4357}.

Daniel Warner, who was born on 9 June 1818, died on 15 June 1895, and is buried beside his wife at Baiting Hollow {4358}.

Daniel and Eleanor (Howell) Warner were the parents of thirteen children {4359}.

    i.   ALLEN MONROE WARNER, born on 6 Oct 1842, married (1) Achsa Howell (#778), (2) Isabel Howell, and (3) Kate Fordham {4360}, died on 27 Aug 1927.

    ii.   FRANCES MARIA WARNER, born on 11 Jly 1844, married [Alsoph] Henry Corwin on 10/24 Jan 1864, two children, died on 22 Aug 1934, died at Rutherford, New Jersey, and is buried at Cutchogue. He was born in Jly 1841, the son of Abel and Catherine Elizabeth (Ryder) Corwin, died on 2 May 1900 and is buried beside his wife at Cutchogue {4361}.

    iii.   JOSEPHINE AMELIA WARNER, born on 27 May 1846, died on 17 Oct 1848.

    iv.   MARTHA ROSALIE WARNER, born on 3 Mch 1848, married Daniel M. Goldsmith on 2 Nov 1876, one child, died on 14 Sep 1944, and is buried at Cutchogue. He was born on 10 Jan 1845, the son of Daniel and Frances Maria (Webb) Goldsmith, died on 19 Jan 1918, and is buried beside his wife at Cutchogue {4362}.

    v.   EUNICE ELIZABETH WARNER, born on 19 Feb 1850, married Hiram F. Howell (#776) as his second wife, five children, died

4355. REPUBLICAN WATCHMAN, 30 Oct 1841.
4356. U.S. Census, Riverhead, Suffolk County, NY, 1850, Dwelling House 348, Family Number 382, Page 271.
4357. Justine Warner Wells, op. cit., 26.
4358. Id.
4359. Id.
4360. Mallmann, op. cit., 235.
4361. Justine Warner Wells, op. cit., 56.
4362. Id., 65.

on 31 May 1933 {4363}, and is buried at Center Moriches {4364}.

vi.   MARY AGNES WARNER, born on 16 Dec 1851, married, on 14 Dec 1870, Chauncey Aezel Edwards, who was born on 2 Oct 1847, the son of Sells Hallock and Sarah (Howell) (#584) Edwards, four children, died on 15 Jan 1922, while he died on 6 Oct 1898 {4365}.

vii.   JULIA HOWELL WARNER, born on 14 Dec 1853, died on 10 May 1871.

viii.   WALDO DANIEL WARNER, born on 11 Feb 1856, married Mary Teresa Howell (#1236), two children, died on 10 May 1940, and is buried in the Seaview Cemetery at Mount Sinai {4366}.

ix.   CHARLES HENRY WARNER, born on 11 May 1858, married Ella Etta Terry on 23 Dec 1879, one child, died on 30 Nov 1935, and is buried in the Mount Pleasant Cemetery at Center Moriches. She was born on 19 Dec 1857, the daughter of Samuel and Perilla (Robinson) Terry, died in Apr 1953, and is buried beside her husband {4367}.

x.   ELEANOR BLANCHE WARNER, born on 20 Jly 1860, married John H. Posson (Parsons?) on 16 Nov 1882, no children, died on 7 Aug 1892, and is buried at Baiting Hollow {4368}.

xi.   JOHN BENJAMIN WARNER, born on 12 Aug 1862, married Carrie Eliza Terry on 28 Sep 1885, six children, died on 20 June 1920, and is buried in the Aquebogue Cemetery. She was born on 29 Aug 1862, the daughter of Gilbert and Almeda Vincent (Robinson) Terry, died on 20 June 1910, was buried at Baiting Hollow, and is buried beside her husband at Aquebogue {4369}.

xii.   EUGENE GOLDSMITH WARNER, born on 27 Nov 1864, married, on 17 Dec 1888, (1) Leatta E. Hallock, who was born

4363. Suffolk County Estates, File #170 A 1933.
4364. Gravestone, Mount Pleasant Cemetery, Center Moriches.
4365. Justine Warner Wells, op. cit., 77.
4366. Id., 96.
4367. Id., 106.
4368. Id., 108.
4369. Id., 110.

on 22 Nov 1870, the daughter of Horace and Anice (Brown) Hallock, and who died on 17 Jly 1889 . On 4 June 1891, he married (2) Alice Sophia Hammond, who was born on 16 Nov 1864, the daughter of Austin Roe and Eliza (Poyntz) Hammond, five children. He died on 5 Nov 1952, and is buried in the Baiting Hollow Cemetery, while she died on 25 Apr 1954, and is buried beside her husband {4370}

xiii. FRANKLIN EVERETT WARNER, born on 5 Jan 1868, married Grace E. McKney on 5 Feb 1889, no children, died on 3/4 May 1908, and is buried in the McKney plot at the Fantinekill Cemetery, Ellenville, New York. She was born on 10 Sep 1863, the daughter of James K. and Maria (Blackmon) McKney, died on 4 Apr 1932, and is buried beside her husband at Ellenville {4371}.

891. HANNAH ROSETTA[7] HOWELL (Daniel[6], Micah[5]), the daughter of Daniel[6] and Jemima Luce (Howell) Howell, was born on 28 Sep 1828 {4372}.

On 14 Dec 1849, Hannah Rosetta Howell married Jeremiah Goldsmith Tuthill, who was born on 24 Dec 1826, the son of Ira B. and Elizabeth (Goldsmith) Tuthill {4373}.

Jeremiah G. Tuthill died on 1 Jly 1898 {4374}.

Jeremiah G. and Hannah R. (Howell) Tuthill were the parents of eight children {4375}.

i. ELLA C. TUTHILL, born on 11 Jly 1851, died on 17 Dec 1860.

ii. HARRISON H. TUTHILL, born on 11 Apr 1853, married Rhoda Gildersleeve on 14 June 1877, at least two children.

iii. ELIZABETH H. TUTHILL, born on 13 Mch 1855, married, on 16 Apr 1879, Charles B. Hudson, who was born in Nov 1858, at least two children {4376}.

iv. IRA B. TUTHILL, born on 13 Mch 1855, died on 3 Aug 1855.

v. H. ROSETTA TUTHILL, born on 18 Nov 1857, married Dr. Arthur Terry on 31 May 1883, at least three children.

4370. Id., 129.
4371. Id., 168.
4372. Mallmann, op. cit., 235.
4373. Id.
4374. Id.
4375. Id.
4376. Mallmann, op. cit., 233.

vi.   JEREMIAH G. TUTHILL, born on 19 Jly 1861, married Hattie Hildreth on 10 Dec 1884, at least three children.

vii.   HOWARD G. TUTHILL, born on 14 Nov 1863, married (1) Adaline Ahillict on 13 June 1887, married (2) Irene Conkling on 12 June 1895, at least one child.

viii.   JOHN T. TUTHILL, born on 19 Sep 1867, married Harriet B. Knight on 12 Dec 1892, at least two children.

892. HENRY HARRISON[7] HOWELL (Daniel[6], Micah[5]), the son of Daniel[6] and Jemima Luce (Howell) Howell, was born on 31 Mch 1830 {4377}.

Harrison H. Howell, 20, was enumerated with his father's family on 21 Sep 1850 in the Seventh Census of the United States {4378}.

On 8 Sep 1858, H. Harrison Howell married Catherine Tuthill, who was born on 15 Oct 1836, the daughter of Charles and Phebe (Raynor) Tuthill {4379}.

On 29 Jly 1870, Harrison Howell, 40, farmer, having real property valed at $3000, and personal property valued at $800, was enumerated as the head of a household including himself, his wife, Catharine, 34, their son, Michael, 10, and Wealthy Raynor, 20, domestic servant, residing in the Town of Riverhead, Suffolk County, New York, in the Ninth Census of the United States {4380}.

Catherine Howell died on 7 Aug 1874, and is buried in the Baiting Hollow Cemetery {4381}.

On 29 Dec 1875, H. Harrison Howell married (2) Melinda J. Young, who was born on 18 Sep 1841, the daughter of Samuel and Jane (Cook) Young {4382}.

H. H. Howell was "..for many terms a successful teacher..not a college man; others had undoubtedly taken larger shares of books, but I say, in all candor, my best teacher." {4383}.

H. H. Howell was Postmaster at Aquebogue, lived on the Main Road two houses east of District #8 Schoolhouse, elected Chairman of Church meeting 1897-1900 {4384}.

H. Harrison Howell died on 2 Oct 1915, and is buried in the Baiting

---

4377. Wilbur Franklin Howell, op. cit., 42.
4378. U.S. Census, Riverhead, Suffolk County, NY, 1850, Dwelling House 481, Family Number 527, Page 280.
4379. Mallmann, op. cit., 235.
4380. U.S. Census, Riverhead, Suffolk County, NY, 1870, Dwelling House 601, Family Number 651, Page 104.
4381. Wilbur Franklin Howell, op. cit.
4382. Id.
4383. James Franklin Young, op. cit., VII, #4, 96 (Mch 1982).
4384. Wilbur Franklin Howell, op. cit.

Hollow Cemetery {4385}.

Melinda J. Howell died on 24 Jan 1929, and is buried at Baiting Hollow {4386}.

Henry Harrison and Catherine (Tuthill) Howell were the parents of one son {4387}.

1287. i. HARRY MICAH[8] HOWELL, born on 24 Nov 1859, married Hannah C. Vail on 22 Feb 1889, at least one child. She was born in 1867, the daughter of Daniel and Ada E. Vail, died on 9 May 1944 {4388}, and is buried in Plot 477 in the Riverhead Cemetery {4389}. Harri M. Howell died on 13 Jan 1947 {4390}, and is buried beside his wife at Riverhead {4391}.

893. ELECTA H.[7] HOWELL (Daniel[6], Micah[5]), the daughter of Daniel[6] and Jemima Luce (Howell) Howell, was born on 7 Mch 1834 {4392}.

Electa H. Howell, 16, was enumerated with her father's family on 21 Sep 1850 in the Seventh Census of the United States {4393}.

On 15 Apr 1855, Electa H. Howell married Benjamin R. Griffing, who was born on 25 Nov 1831, the son of Moses and Hettie A. (Moore) Griffing {4394}.

On 15 June 1870, Benjamin Griffin, 38, seaman, having real property valued at $3500, and personal property valued at $3000, was enumerated as the head of a household consisting of himself, his wife, Electa, 36, their children, Hettie, 12, and Daniel, 10, and Martha Warner, 22, seamstress, residing at Cutchogue in the Town of Southold, Suffolk County, New York, in the Ninth Census of the United States {4395}.

Benjamin R. and Electa H. (Howell) Griffing were the parents of three children {4396}.

 i. HETTIE D. GRIFFING, born on 24 Jly 1858, married Dr. H. P. Terry.

4385. Id.
4386. Id.
4387. Mallmann, op. cit.
4388. Suffolk County Estates, File #238 P 1944.
4389. Gravestone, Riverhead Cemetery.
4390. Suffolk County Estates, File #51 A 1947.
4391. Gravestone, Riverhead Cemetery.
4392. Mallmann, op. cit., 235.
4393. U.S. Census, Riverhead, Suffolk County, NY, 1850, Dwelling House 481, Family Number 527, Page 280.
4394. Mallmann, op. cit.
4395. U.S. Census, Southold, Suffolk County, NY, 1870, Dwelling House 268, Family Number 288, Page 249.
4396. Mallmann, op. cit.

ii. DANIEL H. GRIFFING, born on 17 Sep 1860, married Emma Richards, at least one child.

iii. MARIA T. GRIFFING, born on 26 Oct 1872.

894. MARINDA ANN[7] HOWELL (Daniel[6], Micah[5]), the daughter of Daniel[6] and Jemima Luce (Howell) Howell, was born on 21 Feb 1841 {4397}.

Marinda Ann Howell, 9, was enumerated with her father's family on 21 Sep 1850 in the Seventh Census of the United States {4398}.

On 4 Jan 1860, Marinda Ann Howell married H. Beecher Halsey, who was born on 9 Mch 1833, the son of Hiram and Melissa (Tuthill) Halsey {4399}.

H. Beecher and Marinda Ann (Howell) Halsey were the parents of three children {4400}.

i. LIZZIE BEECHER HALSEY, born on 15 Jan 1865, married W. C. Rogers, at least three children {4401}.

ii. BENJAMIN GRIFFING HALSEY, born on 10 Apr 1867, married, on 7 Feb 1889, Josephine M. Jagger, who was born on 22 May 1863, the daughter of Andrew J. and Rachel (Bishop) Jagger, at least four children {4402}.

iii. RUTH AMELIA HALSEY, born on 19 Sep 1876, died on 22 Jan 1877.

9. John Davis [6], Samuel [5]

899. WILLIAM SHEPARD[7] HOWELL (John Davis[6], Samuel[5]), the son of John Davis[6] and Caroline E. Howell, was born in 1850 {4403}.

William S. Howell married Elizabeth Barter Woolston, who was born in about 1866, the daughter of James and Emma L. (Bond) Woolston {4404}.

Elizabeth Howell died in 1916 {4405}.

William Shepard Howell died on 2 Jly 1923 {4406}.

4397. Id.
4398. U.S. Census, Riverhead, Suffolk County, NY, 1850, Dwelling House 481, Family 527, Page 280.
4399. Mallmann, op. cit.
4400. Id.
4401. Id., 238.
4402. Id.
4403. Janice Linda (Howell) Derr, op. cit.
4404. Id.
4405. Id.
4406. Id.

William Shepard and Elizabeth Barter (Woolston) Howell were the parents of three children {4407}.

1288.   i.   WILLIAM FRANCIS[8] HOWELL, born on 13 May 1890, married Marion Reehl on 10 Jly 1914, two children, died on 18 Aug 1960. She was born in Brooklyn on 31 Jly 1896, the daughter of William and Mary (Gathman) Rühl, and died on 18 May 1975. NOTE: *William Francis Howell was the grandfather of Janice (Howell) Derr.*

1289.   ii.   WARREN SHEPARD[8] HOWELL, born on 14 Feb 1897, married Gertrude Liessner on 18 Sep 1918, three children, died on 19 Apr 1953. She was born in 1900 and died in Feb 1971.

1290. iii.   FLORENCE RUTH[8] HOWELL, born on 17 Oct 1898, married John C. Fusi in 1918, six children. He was born on 15 Feb 1893.

10. Harvey Warren [6], Samuel [5]

903. LOTTIE[7] HOWELL (Harvey Warren[6], Samuel[5]) was the daughter of Harvey Warren[6] and Mary (Gould) Howell {4408}.
     Lottie Howell married DeForest Horton {4409}.

11. Michael B. [6], James Brown [5]

908. WILLIAM C.[7] HOWELL (Michael B.[6], James Brown[5]), the son of Michael B.[6] and Lydia (Coomer) Howell, was born in Niagara County, New York, on 20 Jan 1833 {4410}.
     William C. Howell "..began his education under the home roof, and as soon as a log schoolhouse was built in the neighborhood continued his studies therein. He attended the High School at Hillsdale several terms and subsequently went to Hillsdale College one year." He gave much of his time to teaching and was an instructor for thirty terms. His standing in the profession was very creditable and many of his former pupils acknowledged "..with grateful praise his tact in imparting instruction and wisdom in guiding them.." {4411}.
     On 22 Aug 1850, William Howell, 18, farmer, was enumerated with his

---

4407. Id.
4408. Ruth Isabelle Ferris, op. cit.
4409. Id.
4410. PORTRAIT & BIO. ALBUM..BARRY & EATON COUNTIES.., 763.
4411. Id.

father's family in the Seventh Census of the United States {4412}.

Mr. Howell "..remained at home until he was twenty-four years old, then began farming for himself in Hillsdale County. He established a home in 1856..", having married Nancy M. Carter, who was born in New York state {4413}.

William C. Howell enrolled in the Second Michigan Cavalry on 13 Aug 1862. "The first heavy engagement in which he took part was the bloody battle of Perryville, and it was his fortune to fight in other noted fields, among them Chickmauga, Resaca, Lost Mountain, Kenesaw Mountain, Franklin and Nashville. He took part in several other battles and numerous skirmishes, being under fire one hundred times or more. He received no wounds and never entered the hospital, although he suffered some from illness. He was mustered out in June 1865." {4414}.

Mr. Howell was a Republican, and served as Town Clerk and as Treasurer in Roxana Township. He was a member of the Grange, the Grand Army of the Republic, and the Masonic order. He and his wife were faithful members of the Methodist Episcopal Church. In 1891, he owned and operated a farm in Roxana Township, Eaton County, Michigan, near the village of Hoytville {4415}.

William Case Howell died on 4 Sep 1903 in Eaton County, Michigan {4416}.

William C. and Nancy M. (Carter) Howell were the parents of six children {4417}.

    1291.   i.   CHILD[8].

    1292.   ii.   CHILD[8].

    1293.   iii.   CHILD[8].

    1294.   iv.   JESSE A.[8] HOWELL, born on 13 Nov 1858 and died on 8 Mch 1910.

    1295.   v.   INEZ[8] HOWELL.

    1296.   vi.   ARTHUR E.[8] HOWELL, born in 1875, married Vera S. Dilley, one child, died in 1961. Vera Howell was born in 1876 and died in 1931.

911. CHAUNCY L.[7] HOWELL (Michael B.[6], James Brown[5]), the son of Michael

---

4412. U.S. Census, Jefferson, Hillsdale County, MI, 1850, Dwelling House 114, Family Number 117, Page 380.
4413. PORTRAIT & BIO. ALBUM.BARRY & EATON COUNTIES.., 763.
4414. Id., 763-764.
4415. Id., 764.
4416. Ronald Lee Howell, Jr., op. cit., 123.
4417. Id.

B. and Lydia (Coomer) Howell, was born in 1840 in Jefferson Township, Hillsdale County, Michigan {4418}.

On 22 Aug 1850, Chauncy Howell, 9, was enumerated with his father's family in the Seventh Census of the United States {4419}.

Chauncy L. and Della Howell were the parents of at least one daughter {4420}.

   1297.   i.   MINNIE P.[8] HOWELL, born in about 1873.

912. EMELINE[7] HOWELL (Michael B.[6], James Brown[5]), the daughter of Michael B.[6] and Lydia (Coomer) Howell, was born in about 1844 {4421}.

On 22 Aug 1850, Emeline Howell, 6, was enumerated with her father's family in the Seventh Census of the United States {4422}.

Emeline Howell married Horace Ewing on 14 Apr 1868 {4423}.

12. Olser D.[6], James Brown[5]

919. ERASTUS M.[7] HOWELL (Olser D.[6], James Brown[5]), the son of Olser D.[6] and Hannah (Savins) Howell, was born in 1842 in Portland Township, Iona County, Michigan {4424}.

On 3 Sep 1850, Erastus Howell, 8, was enumerated with his father's family in the Seventh Census of the United States {4425}.

Erastus M. Howell, 23, and Elvira Mulford, 17, both of Portland Township, were married on 4 Sep 1865, before the Rev. H. Pettit, a Baptist minister, with Henry O. and Cynthia Ann Howell as witnesses {4426}.

Erastus M. and Elvira (Mulford) Howell were the parents of five children {4427}.

   1298.   i.   SHERMAN[8] HOWELL, born in about 1867.

   1299.   ii.   HANNAH E.[8] HOWELL, born in about 1870.

4418. James W. Howell, op. cit.

4419. U.S. Census, Jefferson, Hillsdale County, MI, 1850, Dwelling House 114, Family Number 117, Page 380.

4420. James W. Howell, op. cit.

4421. Ronald Lee Howell, Jr., op. cit., 123.

4422. U.S. Census, Jefferson, Hillsdale County, MI, 1850, Dwelling House 114, Family Number 117, Page 380.

4423. Ronald Lee Howell, Jr., op. cit.

4424. James W. Howell, op. cit.

4425. U.S. Census, Portland, Ionia County, MI, 1850, Dwelling House 240, Family Number 240, Page 140R.

4426. Ionia County Marriage License Book, 1837-1867.

4427. James W. Howell, op. cit.

1300. iii. LOTTIE M.⁸ HOWELL, born in about 1874.

1301. iv. MARTHA E.⁸ HOWELL, born in about 1876.

1302. v. ELVIRA⁸ HOWELL, born in about 1879.

927. WALTER W.⁷ HOWELL (Olser D.⁶, James Brown⁵), the son of Olser D.⁶ and Hannah (Savins) Howell, was born on 4 Apr 1854 {4428}, in Portland Township, Ionia County, Michigan {4429}.

Louisa Howell, who was born in 1859 {4430}, and was the wife of Walter W. Howell, died on 16 Apr 1886 {4431}.

Walter W. Howell, engineer and widower, of Portland Township, died of cancer on 1 Jan 1903, at the age of 48 years, 8 months, and 26 days {4432}.

Walter W. and Louisa Howell were the parents of at least one child {4433}.

1303. i. ALTON⁸ HOWELL, born in about 1880.

13. James Peter⁶, James Brown⁵

932. ARMILLA⁷ HOWELL (James Peter⁶, James Brown⁵), the daughter of James Peter⁶ and Emily (Perrin) Howell, was born on 26 June 1845 in Pittsford Township, Hillsdale County, Michigan {4434}.

Armilla Howell married Mr. Cooley {4435}.

937. JAMES CLAIR⁷ HOWELL (James Peter⁶, James Brown⁵), the son of James Peter⁶ and Emily (Perrin) Howell, was born on 13 Feb 1855 in Pittsford Township, Hillsdale County, Michigan {4436}.

James C. Howell was enumerated in the household of William M. and Arabella Lowe in Ottawa County, Michigan, the Tenth Census of the United States, 1880 {4437}.

On 21 Dec 1881, in St. Joseph County, Indiana, James C. Howell married Mary Cornelia Adams, who was born on 26 Oct 1856 in Jefferson Township,

---

4428. IONIA COUNTY RECORD OF DEATH, #5739.
4429. James W. Howell, op. cit.
4430. Id.
4431. Marilyn Wedsie (?), Personal communication, in the possession of Ronald L. Howell, 1995.
4432. IONIA COUNTY RECORD OF DEATH, #5739.
4433. James W. Howell, op. cit.
4434. Id.
4435. Id.
4436. Id.
4437. Id.

Elkhart County, Indiana {4438}.

Mary C. Howell died on 27 Apr 1916 in Cass County, Michigan {4439}.

James C. Howell died on 3 Mch 1933, and is buried in the Crane cemetery in Cass County {4440}.

James Clair and Mary Cornelia (Adams) Howell were the parents of six children {4441}.

1304. i. HOWELL[8] HOWELL, born on 20 Nov 1882.

1305. ii. JAMES WILLIAM[8] HOWELL, born on 6 Nov 1883 in Delta Township, Eaton County, Michigan, married Mabel Fosdick on 6 Nov 1903, two children, died on 16 Oct 1950 at Kalamazoo, Michigan, and is buried in the Yorkville Cemetery in Ross Township in Kalamazoo County. Mabel Howell died on 13 Jan 1965 and is buried near her husband. NOTE: *James William Howell was the great-grandfather of James W. Howell.*

1306. iii. PANSY ELIZABETH[8] HOWELL, born on 26 Apr 1886 in Delta Township, married Charles Swank, died on 9 Feb 1935 in Glenwood, and is buried in the Crane Cemetery.

1307. iv. PEARL EMILY[8] HOWELL, born on 24 Oct 1888 in Millets in Eaton County, married Matthias Carpenter Springsteen on 31 Oct 1905, four children, died on 23 Oct 1918 at Yorkville, and is buried in the cemetery there. Matthias Carpenter Springsteen was born on 12 Oct 1881, died on 17 Jly 1936 at Cassopolis, and is buried in the old Van Riper Cemetery in Cass County.

1308. v. ROLAND CLAIR[8] HOWELL, born on 8 Apr 1891 in Millets, married Faye Korn on 1 May 1913, five children, died on 13 Sep 1963 at Kalamazoo, and is buried in the Crane Cemetery. Faye (Korn) Howell was born on 14 Oct 1890 at Rockford, Indiana, died on 5 Jly 1977 at Fletcher, North Carolina, and is buried in the Crane Cemetery.

1309. vi. ARTHUR HERBERT[8] HOWELL, born on 9 Nov 1894 at Mill Creek, Indiana, married Cecil Korn at Battle Creek, Michigan, on 9 Oct 1913, four children, died on 8 Oct 1954 at Onaway, Michigan, and is buried in the Allis Township Cemetery there. Cecil (Korn) Howell was born on 9 Mch 1892 at Barber Mills, Indiana, died on 31 Jly 1960, and is buried near her husband.

4438. Id.
4439. Id.
4440. Id.
4441. Id.

NOTE: *Arthur Herbert Howell was the father of Arthur Herbert Howell, and the father-in-law of Gwendolyn June (Cole) Howell.*

10. William L. ⁶, James Brown ⁵

939. MARY E.⁷ HOWELL (William L.⁶, James Brown⁵), the daughter of William L.⁶ and Belinda S. (Taft) Howell, was born on 1 Aug 1837 {4442}.

Mary E. Howell, 13, was enumerated with her father's family on 15 Nov 1850 in the Seventh Census of the United States {4443}.

On 21 May 1854, Mary E. Howell married David Taylor {4444}.

940. MICHAEL S.⁷ HOWELL (William L.⁶, James Brown⁵), the son of William L.⁶ and Belinda S. (Taft) Howell, was born on 11 Aug 1839 in Jefferson Township, Hillsdale County, Michigan {4445}.

On 15 Nov 1850, Michael S. Howell, 11, was enumerated with his father's family in the Seventh Census of the United States {4446}.

In the Fall of 1861, Michael S. Howell enlisted in the Ninth Michigan Volunteer Infantry, and was in the service of his country for about four years, mostly on detached duty. He was honorably discharged at Nashville, Tenn {4447}.

Michael S. Howell settled on 40 acres of wild land which he bought in Fulton Township, Gratiot County, Michigan. He lived there for two years, and then he traded for 80 acres in North Shade Township. He lived there for eleven years, and bought 80 acres in Section 18, Fulton Township, where the family made its home {4448}.

On 18 Aug 1866, at Maple Rapids, Michigan, Michael S. Howell married (1) Hattie M. Huyck, who was born on 5 May 1884 in Huron County, Ohio, the daughter of Henry and Roxy (Francis) Huyck {4449}.

Michael S. Howell was a member of the Masonic Order, and a supporter of the Democratic Party {4450}.

On 26 Nov 1887, Michael S. Howell became the first Postmaster at

4442. Ronald Lee Howell, Jr., op. cit., 129.
4443. U.S. Census, Adams, Hillsdale County, MI, 1850, Dwelling House 84, Family Number 86, Page 463.
4444. Ronald Lee Howell, Jr., op. cit.
4445. PORTRAIT & BIOGRAPHICAL ALBUM, GRATIOT COUNTY, MICHIGAN, 559.
4446. U.S. Census, Adams, Hillsdale County, MI, 1850, Dwelling House 84, family Number 86, Page 463.
4447. PORTRAIT & BIO. ALBUM, GRATIOT COUNTY, MI., 559.
4448. Id.
4449. Id.
4450. Id.

Middleton, Michigan, which closed about a year later {4451}.

     Hattie M. Howell died on 9 Dec 1910 at Middleton, Michigan, and is buried in the Payne Cemetery in Fulton Township {4452}.

     On 23 Aug 1911, Michael S. Howell married (2) Ellen (Porter) Swigert {4453}.

     Michael S. Howell died in 1920 in Coleman, Michigan {4454}, and is buried beside his wife {4455}.

     Michael S. and Hattie M. (Huyck) Howell were the parents of four children {4456}.

1310.	i.	ARTHUR W.[8] HOWELL, born in 1867, married Jannie Hannah Griffith on 31 Aug 1889, one child, died in 1930. Jannie H. Howell was born in 1870, and died in 1930.
1311.	ii.	MYRTIE B.[8] HOWELL, married Peter B. Stites on 9 Aug 1891.
1312.	iii.	LAURA M.[8] HOWELL, born in about 1870, died on 17 June 1893 in Fulton Township, Gratiot County, Michigan.
1313.	iv.	FLOYD R.[8] HOWELL.

941. JAMES C.[7] HOWELL (William L.[6], James Brown[5], Phineas[4]), the son of William L.[6] and Belinda S. (Taft) Howell, was born on 7 June 1841 in Hillsdale Township, Hillsdale County, Michigan {4457}.

     On 15 Nov 1850, James C. Howell, 9, was enumerated with his father's family in the Seventh Census of the United States {4458}.

     In 1863, James C. Howell married Lucretia Reynolds, who was born in Ohio on 3 Jan 1844, the daughter of Isaac and Samantha Reynolds {4459}.

     On 18 Mch 1864, James C. Howell enlisted in Company B, Twenty-seventh Infantry at Lebanon, Tennessee, for three years. He was wounded in the right thigh while loading his rifle before Petersburg on 17 June 1864, and was hospitalized for about a year following. He was mustered out on 14 Apr 1865, and was transferred to the Veterans Reserve on 1 May 1865. He was awarded a pension as a result of being wounded {4460}.

     The first home of the family of James C. Howell was built from logs in

---

4451. Ronald Lee Howell, op. cit., 148.
4452. Id.
4453. Id., 130.
4454. Id., 129.
4455. Id., 148.
4456. Id., 129.
4457. Ronald Lee Howell, op. cit., 149.
4458. U.S. Census, Adams, Hillsdale County, MI, 1850, Dwelling House 84, Family Number 86, Page 463.
4459. Ronald Lee Howell, Jr., op. cit.
4460. Id.

North Shade Township, on the south side of Route M57, just east of Pingree Road, on land purchased from Robert Spiece. He later bought land from Norhan Church, and from Elizabeth Crismore {4461}.

Lucretia Howell died of paralysis on 8 Apr 1895 in North Shade Township, Gratiot County, Michigan, having suffered a stroke, and is buried in the Payne Cemetery {4462}.

James C. Howell died on 4 Jan 1899 in North Shade Township, and is buried beside his wife {4463}.

James C. and Lucretia (Reynolds) Howell were the parents of six children {4464}.

1314. i.   ALICE UDILLA[8] HOWELL, born on 23 Dec 1863 in Gratiot County, married Robert Spiece on 1 Aug 1881, four children, died on 17 June 1924, and is buried in the Payne Cemetery. Robert Spiece was born in 1863 and died in 1944 {4465}.

1315. ii. LAFAYETTE S.[8] HOWELL, born on 9 Jly 1865 in North Shade Township, married (1) Isadora Hartman, three children, married (2) Dorothy Ella Bowser on 28 Aug 1915, one child, died 21 Sep 1925 in Fulton Township, Gratiot County. Dorothy E. (Bowser) Howell was born on 17 June 1898 in North Shade Township, and died on 9 Nov 1987 at Ithaca, Michigan {4466}. NOTE: *Lafayette S. Howell was the grandfather of Ronald Lee Howell, Jr.*

1316. iii. ELMER E.[8] HOWELL, born in 1866 in Middleton, Michigan, married Ellen E. Howell (#1322) on 29 Jly 1890, eight children, died on 22 Nov 1945. Ellen E. Howell was born on 27 May 1874 in Fulton Township, the daughter of William H. (#944) and Mary E. (Helms) Howell, and died on 3 Oct 1929 {4467}.

1317. iv. IRENE MARY[8] HOWELL, born on 17 Aug 1868 in North Shade Township, married Edwin Greer. She died in 1924, while he died in 1929 {4468}.

1318. v.   JAMES WILLIAM[8] HOWELL, born on 12 Sep 1871 at Middleton, married (1) Clara Mae Shepard in about 1895, eight children, married (2) Cyrena Pearl Samsel, died in 1938. Clara M.

4461. Id.
4462. Id.
4463. Id.
4464. Id.
4465. Id., 130.
4466. Id., 151.
4467. Id., 131-133.
4468. Id., 133.

(Shepard) Howell was born in about 1867, and died on 28 Nov 1915 at St. Louis, Michigan. Cyrena P. (Samsel) Howell died in 1968 {4469}.

1319. vi. ALTA MAY[8] HOWELL, born in 1877, died on 14 Aug 1884 in North Shade Township {4470}.

1320. vii. EDNA PEARL[8] HOWELL, born about 26 June 1881 at Middleton, married Louis William Blair on 30 Nov 1899, one child, died on 3 Mch 1925 at Alma, Michigan. Louis W. Blair was born on 6 Feb 1878, and died on 25 Jly 1946 at Middleton {4471}.

1321. viii. CLAUDE ALTON[8] HOWELL, born on 30 Aug 1887, married Lulu Mae Carr on 7 Nov 1906, three children, died on 11 Nov 1959 at Kissimmee, Florida. Lulu M. (Carr) Howell was born on 1 Mch 1890 in Constantine, Michigan, and died on 23 Jly 1986 in Lakeland, Florida {4472}.

942. WESLEY[7] HOWELL (William L.[6], James Brown[5]), the son of William L.[6] and Belinda S. (Taft) Howell, was born in 1844 in Hillsdale Township, Hillsdale County, Michigan {4473}.

On 15 Nov 1850, Wesley Howell, 6, was enumerated with his father's family in the Seventh Census of the United States {4474}.

Wesley Howell married Nellie E. Hazelton {4475}.

Wesley Howell died in 1895 {4476}.

943. DEWITT[7] HOWELL (William L.[6], James Brown[5]), the son of William L.[6] and Belinda S. (Taft) Howell, was born in 1849 {4477}.

On 15 Nov 1850, DeWitt Howell, 1, was enumerated with his father's family in the Seventh Census of the United States {4478}.

4469. Id., 133-134.
4470. Id., 134.
4471. Id.
4472. Id., 134-136.
4473. Id., 136.
4474. U.S. Census, Adams, Hillsdale County, MI, 1850, Dwelling House 84, Family Number 86, Page 463.
4475. Ronald Lee Howell, Jr., op. cit.
4476. Id.
4477. Id., 131-133.
4478. U.S. Census, Adams, Hillsdale County, MI, 1850, Dwelling House 84, Family Number 86, Page 463.

DeWitt Howell married Cora M. (?) Howell {4479}.
DeWitt Howell died in 1881 {4480}.

944. WILLIAM H.[7] HOWELL (William L.[6], James Brown[5]), the son of William L.[6] and Belinda S. (Taft) Howell, was born in 1852 {4481}.

William H. Howell married (1) Mary Musser {4482}.

On 14 June 1873, William H. Howell married (2) Mary E. Helms, who was born in New York state in 1852 {4483}.

Mary E. Howell died on 1 Dec 1924 {4484}.

William H. Howell died on 13 Jan 1926 {4485}.

William H. and Mary E. (Helms) Howell were the parents of two children {4486}.

   1322. i.   ELLEN E.[8] HOWELL, born on 27 May 1874, married Elmer E. Howell (#1316) on 29 Jly 1890, died on 3 Oct 1929.

   1323. ii. CHILD[8] HOWELL, born in Jly 1877, died on 12 Oct 1877.

945. CORDELIA[7] HOWELL (William L.[6], James Brown[5]), the daughter of William L.[6] and Belinda S. (Taft) Howell, was born in 1854 {4487}.

Cordelia Howell married Joseph Reynolds {4488}.

Cordelia Reynolds died in 1937 {4489}.

946. EMILY[7] HOWELL (William L.[6], James Brown[5]), the daughter of William L.[6] and Belinda S. (Taft) Howell, was born in 1856 in Hillsdale Township, Hillsdale County, Michigan {4490}.

On 22 June 1873, Emily Howell married Proctor J. Shepard, who was born in about 1856 {4491}.

Proctor J. Shepard died on 3 Nov 1892 in Arcadia Township, Gratiot County, Michigan {4492}.

4479. Ronald Lee Howell, Jr., 136.
4480. Id.
4481. Id.
4482. Id.
4483. Id.
4484. Id.
4485. Id.
4486. Id.
4487. Id.
4488. Id.
4489. Id.
4490. Id.
4491. Id.
4492. Id.

Proctor J. and Emily (Howell) Shepard were the parents of two children {4493}.

    i.   LAURIE B. SHEPARD.

   ii.   SUSSIE D. SHEPARD.

11. Walter B. [6], James Brown [5]

947. ELVIRA AMANDA[7] HOWELL (Walter B.[6], James Brown[5], Phineas[4]), the daughter of Walter B.[6] and Elvira (Johnson) Howell, was born on 8 Jly 1852 in Jefferson Township, Hillsdale County, Michigan {4494}.

On 18 June 1871, Elvira Amanda Howell married Elbridge Gerry Peabody, who was born on 20 May 1849 in Lorain County, Ohio {4495}.

Elbridge Gerry Peabody died on 12 Nov 1926 at Barryton in Mecosta County, Michigan {4496}.

Elvira Amanda Peabody died on 14 Sep 1930 at Barryton {4497}.

Elbridge Gerry and Elvira Amanda (Howell) Peabody were the parents of three children {4498}.

    i.   FRANK W. PEABODY, born on 3 June 1873, married Sylvia M. Belding on 28 Aug 1892.

   ii.   MYRTLE M. PEABODY, born on 19 Dec 1878, married Frank Nelson on 6 Jan 1904, died in 1905.

  iii.   FRED DELANO PEABODY, born on 9 Oct 1887, married Dora Ellen Wheeler on 11 Oct 1905, one child, died on 29 Apr 1947 at Barryton. Dora Ellen Peabody was born on 2 Nov 1884 at Breckenridge, Michigan, and died on 14 Aug 1972 at Big Rapids, Michigan {4499}.

12. John [6], Parshall [5]

950. PARSHALL[7] HOWELL (John[6], Parshall[5]), the son of John[6] and Marriet (Decker) Howell, was born in New Jersey on 24 Jan 1836, and moved to

4493. Id.
4494. James W. Howell, op. cit.
4495. Ronald Lee Howell, Jr., 136.
4496. Id.
4497. Id.
4498. Id.
4499. Id., 137.

Stockbridge, Michigan at the age of two {4500}.

"Parson Howell", 14, was enumerated with his father's family on 30 Jly 1850 in the Seventh Census of the United States {4501}.

On 5 Jan 1862, Parshall Howell married Sarah Elizabeth Torrey, who was born on 30 May 1844 {4502}.

Parshall and Sarah E. Howell purchased a 200 acre farm in Sections 35 and 36 of White Oak Township, Ingham County, Michigan {4503}.

Parshall Howell died on 12 Nov 1912, and is buried in Lot 169, Block A, in the Oakland Cemetery at Stockbridge {4504}.

Sarah E. Howell died in 1926, and is buried beside her husband at Stockbridge {4505}.

Parshall and Sarah Elizabeth (Torrey) Howell were the parents of two children {4506}.

1324.   i.   FLOYD PARSHALL[8] HOWELL, born on 16 Feb 1863 in Isoco Township, Livingston County, Michigan, married (1) Lucy Ann Mapes on 20 Mch 1884, four children, married (2) Mrs. Emma King on 27 Sep 1940. Lucy Ann Howell was born on 21 Mch 1862, and died on 13 Aug 1936. NOTE: *Floyd Parshall Howell was the great-grandfather of Kathleen Mary (Pollock) McCurdy.*

1325.   ii.   ALVA JAMES[8] HOWELL, born on 12 May 1878, died in 1939, and is buried beside his parents at Stockbridge.

13. George W. [6], Parshall [5]

958. MARY ELIZABETH[7] HOWELL (George W.[6], Parshall[5]), the daughter of George W.[6] and Hellen Belle (Coleman) Howell, was born on 18 Mch 1844 {4507}.

On 1 Oct 1850, Mary Howell, 7, was enumerated with her father's family in the Seventh Census of the United States {4508}.

Mary Elizabeth Howell married Dr. Palmer Corille {4509}.

Dr. Palmer and Mary Elizabeth (Howell) Corille were the parents of one

---

4500. Mr. & Mrs. Larry A. McCurdy, op. cit.
4501. U.S. Census, Stockbridge, Ingham County, MI, 1850, Dwelling Place 211, Family Number 211, Page 28.
4502. McCurdy, op. cit.
4503. Id.
4504. Id.
4505. Id.
4506. Id.
4507. Gregory A. Inman, op. cit.
4508. U.S. Census, Dexter, Washtenaw County, MI, 1850, Dwelling House 3, Family Number 3, Page 548.
4509. Inman, op. cit.

child {4510}.
     i.   DORIS HELLEN CORILLE.

960. HELLEN AMANDA[7] HOWELL (George W.[6], Parshall[5]), the daughter of George W.[6] and Hellen Belle (Coleman) Howell, was born in Ionia County, Michigan, on 2 Nov 1848 {4511}.

    On 1 Oct 1850, Helen A. Howell, 3, was enumerated with her father's family in the Seventh Census of the United States {4512}.

    On 26 Jly 1868, Hellen Amanda Howell married Charles Packingham at Otisco, Michigan {4513}. She married (2) Marshall T. King at Ionia, Michigan, on 11 Feb 1874 {4514}.

    Helen (Howell) King died of consumption on 13 Apr 1884 at the age of 35 and is buried in the Greenville Cemetery {4515}.

    Charles and Hellen Amanda (Howell) Packingham were the parents of one child {4516}.
     i.   SUSIE HALLIE PACKINGHAM, born on 29 May 1869, died on 9 Nov 1892 at Greenville, Michigan.

Marshall T. and Hellen Amanda (Howell) Packingham King were the parents of one child {4517}.
    ii.   JOHN KING, born on 19 Jan 1877.

961. CATHERINE JANE[7] HOWELL (George W.[6], Parshall[5]), the daughter of George W.[6] and Hellen Belle (Coleman) Howell, was born on 23 Aug 1850 {4518}.

    On 1 Oct 1850, Catherine J. Howell, two months old, was enumerated with her father's family in the Seventh Census of the United States {4519}.

    Catherine Jane Howell married Benjamin Briggs {4520}.

    Benjamin and Catherine Jane (Howell) Briggs were the parents of one child {4521}.

4510. Id.
4511. Id.
4512. U.S. Census, Dexter, Washtenaw County, MI, 1850, Dwelling House 3, Family Number 3, Page 548.
4513. Inman, op. cit.
4514. Betty Spooner, SOME MONTCALM COUNTY, MICHIGAN, CHURCH RECORDS, 107.
4515. Id., 118; Family Bible says 9 Apr 1884 (1485).
4516. Inman, op. cit.
4517. Id.
4518. Id.
4519. U.S. Census, Dexter, Washtenaw County, MI, 1850, Dwelling House 3, Family Number 3, Page 548.
4520. Inman, op. cit.
4521. Id.

i.   GEORGE A. BRIGGS, born on 13 Nov 1875.

962. IDA MARIAN[7] HOWELL (George W.[6], Parshall[5]), the daughter of George W.[6] and Hellen Belle (Coleman) Howell, was born on 5 Dec 1853 in Ionia County, Michigan {4522}.

    Ida Marian Howell married John Thorpe {4523}.

    Ida M. Thorpe died on 12 Jan 1897 at the age of 43 {4524}.

    John and Ida Marian (Howell) Thorpe were the parents of one child {4525}.

    i.   MYRTIE ELIZABETH THORPE, born on 2 Feb 1877.

963. GEORGE DAVID[7] HOWELL (George W.[6], Parshall[5]), the son of George W.[6] and Hellen Belle (Coleman) Howell, was born on 29 May 1855 in Ionia County, Michigan {4526}.

    George David Howell married Paulina Walters {4527}.

    George D. Howell died on 4 Jan 1936, at the age of 80 {4528}.

    George David and Paulina (Walters) Howell were the parents of five children {4529}.

1326. i.   WALTER[8] HOWELL, born in 1884, died in 1884 at the age of 1 months and 16 days {4530}.

1327. ii. LEROY E.[8] HOWELL, born in 1886, died on 11 May 1886 at the age of 3 months {4531}.

1328. iii. JOHN WILLIAM[8] HOWELL, born on 15 Sep 1888, married Lottie ----, died on 16 Oct 1954.

1329. iv. GEORGE P.[8] HOWELL, born on 8 Jly 1891, died on 10 Oct 1891, at the age of 3 months and 2 days {4532}.

1330. v. JOSEPH[8] HOWELL, born on 8 Jly 1891.

4522. Id.
4523. Id.
4524. Id.
4525. Id.
4526. Id.
4527. Id.
4528. Id.
4529. Id.
4530. Gravestone, ST. MARY'S MIRIAM CEMETERY, OTISCO TOWNSHIP, IONIA COUNTY, MICHIGAN).
4531. MONTCALM COUNTY DEATH RECORDS, BOOK A, 202, #1943, Gravestone, St. Mary's Miriam Cemetery.
4532. Gravestone, St. Mary's Miriam Cemetery.

964. WILLIAM BENJAMIN[7] HOWELL (George W.[6], Parshall[5]), the son of George W.[6] and Hellen Belle (Coleman) Howell, was born on 23 Mch 1858 in Ionia County, MIchigan {4533}.

William Benjamin Howell was the father of two children {4534}.

1331.   i.   SAMPSON[8] HOWELL, born in 1872, died in 1904.

1332.   ii.   JOHN WILLIAM[8] HOWELL, died in 1954.

967. FREDERICK JAMES[7] HOWELL (George W.[6], Parshall[5]), the son of George W.[6] and Hellen Belle (Coleman) Howell, was born on 25 June 1869 at Cook's Corner, Michigan {4535}.

Fred James Howell married Grace Lillian Smalley at Greenville, Michigan, in 1890. She was born on 25 Dec 1870 at Onondaga, Michigan, the daughter of Abner and Mary Ann (Davis) Smalley {4536}.

In 1900, Fred Howell, 31, butcher, was enumerated as the head of a family consisting of himself, his wife, Grace, 29, and their children, Belle, 7, and Fred, 3, residing on Grove Street, in the City of Greenville, Montcalm County, Michigan, in the Twelfth Census of the United States {4537}.

Grace Lillian Howell died on 16 Nov 1944 at Greenville, Michigan {4538}, and is buried in the East Montcalm Cemetery {4539}.

Fred J. Howell died on 6 Aug 1958 {4540}, and is buried beside his wife {4541}.

Fred James and Grace Lillian (Smalley) Howell were the parents of four children {4542}.

1333.   i.   LENA BELLE[8] HOWELL, born on 6 June 1891 at Greenville, married (1) Harvey B. Lohr, one child, married (2) Mr. Rich, no children, married (3) Mr. McGregor, no children, died on 8 Jan 1962 at Ionia, buried at the East Montcalm Cemetery.

1334.   ii.   LAURA[8] HOWELL, born in 1893, died in 1893.

1335.   iii.   FRED JAMES, JR.[8], HOWELL, born on 2 Oct 1896 at Greenville, married Leda M. Jensen at Gowen, on 27 Oct 1917, seven children, died on 8 Feb 1960, and is buried at the East

---

4533. Inman, op. cit.
4534. Id.
4535. Id.
4536. Id.
4537. U.S. Census, Greenville, Montcalm County, Michigan, 1900, Dwelling House Number 154, Sheet Number 7, Enumeration District 131.
4538. MONTCALM COUNTY DEATH RECORDS, BOOK 1944, 331.
4539. Inman, op. cit.
4540. MONTCALM COUNTY DEATH RECORDS, BOOK 1958, 269.
4541. Inman, op. cit.
4542. Id.

Montcalm Cemetery.

1336. iv. LYLE PERCY[8] HOWELL, born on 15 Aug 1903 at Greenville, married Violet Elaine Delehanty, at Ionia on 30 Mch 1925, divorced on 26 Feb 1945, three children, died on 18 Jan 1969 at Grand Rapids, buried in East Montcalm Cemetery. Violet E. Delehanty was born on 3 Mch 1908 at Greenville, the daughter of David P. and Mabel Filina (Warren) Delehanty, died on 22 June 1986 at Fort Myers, Florida, and is buried in the Oak Lawn Cemetery at Sturgis, Michigan. NOTE: *Lyle Percy Howell was the grandfather of Gregory A. Inman.*

III. Descendantsof Richard[2] Howell -

A. Richard[4], Richard[3], Richard[2], Richard[1].

1. Josiah[6], Abner[5]

976. CHRISTIANA[7] HOWELL (Josiah[6], Abner[5]), the daughter of Josiah[6] and Amanda (Wells) Howell, was born on 7 Nov 1837 at Riverhead, New York {4543}.

On 17 Sep 1850, Christiana Howell, 12, was enumerated with her father's family in the Seventh Census of the United States {4544}.

Christiana Howell married Joshua Tuthill, who was born at Speonk on 10 Feb 1830, the son of Elisha and Harriet (Rogers) Tuthill {4545}.

On 2 Aug 1870, Joshua Tuthill, 40, farmer, having real property valued at $2000, and personal property valued at $500, was enumerated as the head of a family consisting of himself, his wife, Christianna, 33, and their children, Bertha E., 10, Flora E., 9, Morris J., 6, and Grace A., 1, residing at Sag Harbor in the Town of Southampton, Suffolk County, New York, in the Ninth Census of the United States {4546}.

Christiana Tuthill died on 30 Apr 1912 at West Hampton {4547}.

Joshua Tuthill died in 1915 {4548}.

Joshua and Christiana (Howell) Tuthill were the parents of five children {4549}.

4543. Tuttle, op. cit., 347.
4544. U.S. Census, Riverhead, Suffolk County, NY, 1850, Dwelling House 465, Family Number 510, Page 279.
4545. Tuttle, op. cit.
4546. U.S. Census, Southampton, Suffolk County, NY, 1870, Dwelling House 1166, Family Number 1711, Page 219.
4547. Tuttle, op. cit.
4548. Id.
4549. Id.

i.   BERTHA E. TUTHILL, born on 5 Nov 1859.

ii. LUCY FLORA TUTHILL, born on 25 Apr 1861.

iii. MAURICE J. TUTHILL, born on 30 Mch 1864.

iv. GRACE A. TUTHILL, born on 16 Feb 1869.

v.   JESSE W. TUTHILL, born on 25 May 1878.

977. MARY MEHETABLE[7] HOWELL (Josiah[6], Abner[5]), the daughter of Josiah[6] and Amanda (Wells) Howell, was born on 3 Oct 1841 {4550}.

On 17 Sep 1850, Mary M. Howell, 8, was enumerated with her father's family in the Seventh Census of the United States {4551}.

On 20 Nov 1864, Mary Mehetable Howell married Elias Purdy Tuttle, who was born in New York City on 14 Feb 1836, the son of Daniel Tuttle {4552}.

On 1 Aug 1870, Elias P. Tuthill, 34, carriage maker, having real property valued at $1000, and personal property valued at $500, and his wife, Mary M., 28, were enumerated as a family residing at West Hampton in the Town of Southampton, Suffolk County, New York, in the Ninth Census of the United States {4553}.

Elias P. Tuttle died on 22 Mch 1914 at West Hampton {4554}.

Mary M. Tuttle died on 7 Sep 1917 at Washington, D.C. {4555}.

Elias Purdy and Mary Mehetable (Howell) Tuttle were the parents of two children {4556}.

i.   DANIEL WELLS TUTTLE, born on 2 Sep 1872.

ii. AMY HOWELL TUTTLE, born on 16 May 1875.

979. HENRIETTA[7] HOWELL (Josiah[6], Abner[5]), the daughter of Josiah[6] and Amanda (Wells) Howell, was born in about 1848.

On 17 Sep 1850, Henrietta Howell, 2, was enumerated with her father's

---

4550. Id., 149.
4551. U.S. Census, Riverhead, Suffolk County, NY, 1850, Dwelling House 465, Family Number 510, Page 279.
4552. Tuttle, op. cit.
4553. U.S. Census, Southampton, Suffolk County, NY, 1870, Dwelling House 1152, Family Number 1195, Page 218.
4554. Tuttle, op. cit.
4555. Id.
4556. Id.

family in the Seventh Census of the United States {4557}.

Henrietta Howell, 22, was enumerated with her father's family on 22 Jly 1850 in the Ninth Census of the United States {4558}.

On 14 Dec 1872, Henrietta Howell married Charles M. Corwin, who was born on 2 Aug 1846, the son of Daniel Arden and Mary Frances (Corwin) Corwin {4559}.

Charles M. Corwin died in 1926, and is buried in Plot 241 in the Riverhead Cemetery {4560}.

Henrietta Corwin died in 1932, and is buried beside her husband at Riverhead {4561}.

980. HENRY JOSIAH[7] HOWELL (Josiah[6], Abner[5]), the son of Josiah[6] and Amanda (Wells) Howell, was born in 1851.

On 23 Jly 1870, Henry Howell, 18, who worked on his father's farm, was enumerated with the family in the Ninth Census of the United States {4562}.

Henry J. Howell married Katherine Jane Fanning {4563}.

Katie J. Howell died on 13 Mch 1898 {4564}, and is buried in Plot 45 in the Riverhead Cemetery {4565}.

Henry J. Howell died on 24 Nov 1926 {4566}, and is buried beside his wife at Riverhead {4567}.

Henry Josiah and Katherine Jane (Fanning) Howell were the parents of two children {4568}.

    1337.   i.   ARTHUR J.[8] HOWELL, born on 25 Sep 1884, married Helen P. Skidmore, who was born in 1876, the daughter of Theodore and Charlotte E. (Pettens) Skidmore {4569}, died on 28 Nov 1942 {4570}, and is buried in Plot 380 in the Riverhead Cemetery {4571}. Helen P. Howell died on 2 Apr 1945 {4572}, and is buried beside her husband {4573}.

4557. U.S. Census, Riverhead, Suffolk County, NY, 1850, Dwelling House 465, Family Number 510, Page 279.
4558. Id, 1870, Dwelling House 585, Family Number 636, Page 103.
4559. Mallmann, op. cit., 308.
4560. Gravestone, Riverhead Cemetery.
4561. Id.
4562. U.S. Census, Riverhead, Suffolk County, NY, 1870, Dwelling House 585, Family Number 636, Page 103.
4563. Wilbur Franklin Howell, op. cit., 95.
4564. Id.
4565. Gravestone, Riverhead Cemetery.
4566. Suffolk County Estates, File #29603.
4567. Gravestone, Riverhead Cemetery.
4568. Wilbur Franklin Howell, op. cit.
4569. Skidmore, op. cit., 156.
4570. Id., File #483 P 1942.
4571. Gravestone, Riverhead Cemetery.
4572. Id., File #184 P 1945.

1338. ii. ALICE L.[8] HOWELL, born on 10 Apr 1893.

981. HERBERT WELLS[7] HOWELL (David Wells[6]), the son of David Wells[7] and Sarah A. (Robinson) Howell, was born on 7 Jan 1863 {4574}.

On 29 Jly 1870, Herbert W. Howell, 7, was enumerated with his father's family in the Ninth Census of the United States {4575}.

Herbert Wells Howell married (1) Leah Sargeant and (2) Bertha M. Goff, the daughter of Alvin Edward and Harriet (Dean) Goff {4576}.

Herbert Wells Howell died in Apr 1947, and is buried in the Wonx Springs Cemetery at Plantville, Connecticut {4577}.

Herbert Wells and Leah (Sargeant) Howell were the parents of three children {4578}.

1339. i. ARCHIE WELLS[8] HOWELL, born on 11 Oct 1896 at East Moriches, married (2) Lena Doir on 4 Apr 1920, two children (NOTE: *Archie Wells Howell had three children by his unknown first wife*).

1340. ii. EDITH[8] HOWELL.

1341. iii. ERNEST[8] HOWELL, married Florence Brodie.

Herbert Wells and Bertha M. (Goff) Howell were the parents of six children {4579}.

1342. iv. ALVIN[8] HOWELL, born on 7 Apr 1903 at Coventry, CT, married (1) Gladys ----, one child, two other marriages.

1343. v. MABEL[8] HOWELL, born 23 Mch 1904, married Ernest Miller, the son of Jacob and Henrietta (Frie) Miller, five children, died on 2 Nov 1986.

1344. vi. FRANCES[8] HOWELL, born on 26 Oct 1905 in Bolton, CT, married Henry McFadden, the son of William E. and Alice (Jennings) McFadden, on 26 Nov 1930 at Cleveland, OH, one child, died on 22 June 1998.

1345. vii. LILLIAN[8] HOWELL, born on 6 Mch 1909 at Bolton, CT,

---

4573. Gravestone, Riverhead Cemetery.
4574. Pawson, op. cit.
4575. U.S Census, Brookhaven, Suffolk County, NY, 1870, Dwelling House 1232, Family Number 1317, Page 389.
4576. Pawson, op. cit.
4577. Id.
4578. Id.
4579. Id.

married (1) Lester Andrews, two children, married (2) George McKenna, one child, died on 24 Sep 1995 in Vermont.

1346. viii.　MYRTLE[8] HOWELL, born on 10 Jan 1911 at Bolton, CT, married Lawrence Michael Craven, Jr., the son of Lawrence Michael and Elizabeth (Newberry) Craven on 22 Apr 1939 at Plantville, CT, three children.

1347. ix.　NETTIE MAE[8] HOWELL, born on 13 Aug 1913 at Marion, CT, married Harry Irving Shaffer, the son of Perry Cutler and Flora Berry (Rodgers) Shaffer, at Millerton, N.Y. on 13 Nov 1932, one child, died on 12 Oct 1936 at Hartford, CT, and is buried in the Wonx Springs Cemetery at Plantville, CT (NOTE: *Nettie Mae (Howell) Shaffer was the mother of Lois Anne (Shaffer) Pawson).*

IV. Descendants of Isaac [2] Howell –

A. Isaac [4], Isaac [3], Isaac [2], Richard [1].

1. Samuel [6], Isaac [5]

986. AMANDA B.[7] HOWELL (Samuel[6], Isaac[5]), the daughter of Samuel[6] and Delia (Olmstead) Howell, was born on 23 Aug 1824 {4580}.

On 24 Sep 1845, Amanda Howell married Eri Kent, Jr., of Windsor, New York. He was born on 26 Jan 1826 at Windsor, the son of Useba and Martha (Woodruff) Kent {4581}.

On 20 Sep 1850, Eri Kent, 27, farmer, having real property valued at $1500, was enumerated as the head of a household consisting of himself, his wife, Amanda, 26, their children, Charles, 3, and Alice, 1, as well as Silas Loveland, 17, farmer, and Jay Loveland, residing in the Town of Windsor, Broome County, New York, in the Seventh Census of the United States {4582}.

Eri Kent, Jr., died on 14 Oct 1902 at Windsor, and is buried there {4583}.

Amanda B. Kent died on 19 Feb 1904 at Windsor, and is buried beside her husband {4584}.

4580. Hawkes, op. cit., 19.
4581. Id.
4582. U.S. Census, Windsor, Broome County, NY, 1850, Dwelling House 402, Family Number 414, Page 224.
4583. Hawkes, op. cit.
4584. Id.

Eri and Amanda B. (Howell) Kent were the parents of ten children {4585}.

    i.   CHARLES C. KENT, born on 18 June 1846, died on 2 Apr 1851.

    ii.   GEORGE H. KENT, born on 14 Dec 1847, died on 7 Sep 1848.

    iii.   ALICE DELIA KENT, born on 19 Oct 1849 at Windsor, married Eli Henry Stow on 30 Nov 1867, three children, died on 9 Dec 1897 at Binghamton, New York. Eli Stow was born on 25 Jly 1848 and died on 8 Feb 1918.

    iv.   SARAH JANE KENT, born on 21 Oct 1850, married William Tiffany on 24 Feb 1892, died on 14 Nov 1921 {4586}.

    v.   CHARLES H. KENT, born on 18 May 1852, married (1) Eliza J. Scott on 24 Mch 1873, two children, married (2) Bertha Hawkins, died on 4 Oct 1924, and is buried in the Spring Forest Cemetery at Binghamton. Eliza J. Kent was born on 23 Jly 1847, died on 7 Jly 1915, and is buried beside her husband {4587}.

    vi.   JAMES ERASTUS KENT, born on 10 Nov 1853, on 8 Dec 1875 married Ella L. Woodmansee at Windsor, two children. She was born on 3 Sep 1854 at Lake Como, Pennsylvania {4588}.

    vii.   NELLIE A. KENT, born on 12 Apr 1855 at Windsor, on 12 Oct 1876 married Rev. Orville N. Frink, who was born on 28 Feb 1837 at North Pharsalia, New York, the son of Hiram and Malinda (Barton) Frink, two children. He was a member of Company B, 114th Regiment, N. Y. Volunteers, died on 3 Apr 1910, buried at South Plymouth, New York {4589}. NOTE: *Nellie A. (Kent) Frink was the mother of Amanda N. (Frink) Hawkes.*

    viii.   MARY EMMA KENT, born on 3 Sep 1856 at Windsor, on 24 Mch 1875 married Vernon Charles Blatchly, who was born on 23 Sep 1851, twelve children, died on 3 Jan 1907, while he died on 31 Jan 1925 {4590}.

4585. Id., 18-19.
4586. Id., 21.
4587. Id.
4588. Id.
4589. Id.
4590. Id.

ix.   CLARE ALIDA KENT, born on 15 Apr 1862 at Windsor, married Clarence B. Hewitt, of Wellsville, New York, on 12 Mch 1884 at Windsor, two children {4591}.

x.   MARTHA A. KENT, born on 11 Nov 1863, died on 12 Apr 1871.

987. GEORGE[7] HOWELL (Samuel[6], Isaac[5]), the son of Samuel[6] and Delia (Olmsted) Howell, was born on 30 Oct 1825 {4592}.
George Howell married Jennie Armstrong {4593}.
George Howell died on 19 Jan 1895 {4594}.
George and Jennie (Armstrong) Howell had no children {4595}.

988. DELIA[7] HOWELL (Samuel[6], Isaac[5]), the daughter of Samuel[6] and Delia (Olmsted) Howell, was born on 9 May 1829 {4596}.
Delia Howell married (1) Mr. Smith (2) Mr. Havens, and (3) Dr. Chase {4597}.
Delia (Howell) Smith Havens Chase died on 11 Mch 1910 {4598}.
Delia (Howell) Smith was the mother of one son {4599}.
i.   HOWE SMITH.

Delia (Howell) Smith Havens was the mother of another son {4600}.
ii.   REID HAVENS.

Delia (Howell) Smith Havens Chase was the mother of another son {4601}.
iii.   SAMUEL CHASE.

989. EMMA[7] HOWELL (Samuel[6], Isaac[5]), the daughter of Samuel[6] and Delia (Olmsted) Howell, was born on 7 Dec 1830 {4602}.

4591. Id., 21-22.
4592. James Barnaby Howell, op. cit., 9.
4593. Hawkes, op. cit., 20.
4594. Id.
4595. Id.
4596. James Barnaby Howell, op. cit.
4597. Hawkes, op. cit.
4598. Id.
4599. Id.
4600. Id.
4601. Id.
4602. James Barnaby Howell, op. cit.

Emma Howell married Mr. Stevens {4603}.

Emma Stevens died on 24 Apr 1895 {4604}.

Emma (Howell) Stevens was the mother of two children {4605}.

    i.   ELLA STEVENS, married Kay Stone.

    ii.   DOLLY STEVENS, married Albert Struble.

990. HOLLAND S.[7] HOWELL (Samuel[6], Isaac[5]), the son of Samuel[6] and Delia (Olmsted) Howell, was born on 11 Sep 1832 {4606}.

    Holland S. Howell died on 4 Jly 1877 {4607}.

991. ISAAC N.[7] HOWELL (Samuel[6], Isaac[5]), the son of Samuel[6] and Delia (Olmsted) Howell, was born on 11 Feb 1834 {4608}.

    Isaac N. Howell married Helen Ulshoefer {4609}.

    Isaac N. Howell died on 7 Dec 1862 in the area of Fredericksburg, Virginia, and is buried in the Spring Forest Cemetery at Binghamton, New York {4610}.

    Isaac N. and Helen (Ulshoefer) Howell had no children {4611}.

992. MARY[7] HOWELL (Samuel[6], Isaac[5]), the daughter of Samuel[5] and Delia (Olmsted) Howell, was born on 11 May 1838 at Franklin, New York {4612}.

    Mary Howell married Frank Lovell {4613}.

    Mary Lovell died on 6 June 1920 {4614}.

    Frank and Mary (Howell) Lovell were the parents of two children {4615}.

    i.   EMMA LOVELL.

    ii.   H. F. LOVELL.

4603. Hawkes, op. cit.
4604. Id.
4605. Id.
4606. James Barnaby Howell, op. cit.
4607. Hawkes, op. cit.
4608. James Barnaby Howell, op. cit.
4609. Hawkes, op. cit.
4610. Id.
4611. Id.
4612. Id.
4613. Id.
4614. Id.
4615. Id.

2. Alfred Milton [6], Abraham [5]

1005. ALFRED MILTON[7] HOWELL (Alfred Milton[6], Abraham[5]), the son of Alfred Milton[6] and Patience (Bowen) Howell, was born on 15 Sep 1838 {4616}.

On 3 Oct 1875, Alfred Milton Howell married Louise Eastland, who was born in Apr 1851 {4617}.

Alfred Milton Howell died on 24 Apr 1924, and is buried in the McKinstry Cemetery in Delevan, New York {4618}.

Lois Howell died on 19 Jan 1935, and is buried beside her husband {4619}.

Alfred Milton and Lois (Eastland) Howell were the parents of five children {4620}.

    1348.   i.   HERBERT[8] HOWELL.

    1349.   ii.   MYRTLE[8] HOWELL.

    1350.   iii.   ETHEL A.[8] HOWELL, married Clarence Whitney.

    1351.   iv.   FRANK[8] HOWELL.

    1352.   v.   BERTHA[8] HOWELL.

1008. NATHANIEL MILFORD[7] HOWELL (Alfred Milton[6], Abraham[5]), the son of Alfred Milton[6] and Patience (Bowen) Howell, was born on 24 Oct 1844 {4621}.

On 6 Jan 1878, Nathaniel Milford Howell married Eva Eulie Everts, who was born on 29 Dec 1859, the daughter of Jefferson and Catherine (Low) Everts {4622}.

Nathaniel Milford Howell died on 13 June 1908, and is buried in the McKinstry Cemetery at Delevan {4623}.

Eva Eulie Howell died on 22 Mch 1941, and is buried beside her husband {4624}.

Nathaniel Milford and Eva Eulie (Everts) Howell were the parents of seven

---

4616. Duane A. Howell, per Gordon Adams.
4617. Id.
4618. Id.
4619. Id.
4620. Id.
4621. Duane A. Howell, op. cit.
4622. Id.
4623. Id.
4624. Id.

children {4625}.

1353. i. NELLIE LOUISA[8] HOWELL, born on 25 Feb 1879, married
Wells Rogers on 13 Jan 1897, three children, died on 15 June
1958, and is buried in the Curriers Cemetery.

1354. ii. ALTA MAY[8] HOWELL, born on 11 June 1881, never married,
died in June 1963, and is buried in the McKinstry Cemetery.

1355. iii. EUGENE MILFORD[8] HOWELL, born on 7 Dec 1882, married
Katie M. Wagner on 5 Jan 1905, two children, divorced, died on
11 Mch 1921, and is buried in the McKinstry Cemetery.

1356. iv. ALICE EVA[8] HOWELL, born on 21 Mch 1884, died at the age
of 5 months, and is buried in the McKinstry Cemetery.

1357. v. HENRY LEO[8] HOWELL, born on 27 Oct 1889, married Iva
Genvieve Wilson on 6 Nov 1915, three children, died on 23 Aug
1955, and is buried in the Yorkshire Cemetery. She was born on
4 Mch 1894, died on 17 Jly 1973, and is buried beside her
husband. NOTE: *Henry Leo Howell was the father of Duane
Allen Howell.*

1358. vi. FLORENCE ELIZABETH[8] HOWELL, born on 11 Jan 1893,
married (1) William Himelien, married (2) Roy Brady, died on 13   Oct
1973, and is buried in the Gowanda Cemetery beside her first
husband.

1359. vii. NETTIE LENORA[8] HOWELL, born on 9 June 1896, married
Rev. Cecil Clay Cagwin on 21 June 1916, four children, died on
28 May 1954, and is buried in the Delevan Cemetery. Rev.
Cagwin was born on 28 June 1894, died in 1971, and is buried
beside his wife.

3. Samuel Hawkins[6], Abraham[5]

1024. RALPH MILLARD[7] HOWELL (Samuel Hawkins[6], Abraham[5]), the son of
Samuel Hawkins[6] and Eveline (Meech) Howell, was born on 8 Dec 1856 at
Delevan, New York {4626}.

On 6 Sep 1888, at Arcade, New York, Ralph Millard Howell married
Mary Arabel Emery, who was born in Mch 1861 at Arcade, the daughter of Levi

---

4625. Id.
4626. Nancy Allen (Howell) Ornce.

and Mary Ann (O'Neil) Emery {4627}.

Mary Arabel Howell died on 13 Nov 1912 at Chaffee, New York {4628}.

Ralph Millard Howell died on 4 Dec 1947 at Chaffee, and is buried in the Sardinia Rural Cemetery at Sardinia, New York.{4629}.

Ralph Millard and Mary Arabel (Emery) Howell were the parents of three children {4630}.

1360.   i.   LEIGH HAWKINS[8] HOWELL, born on 16 Sep 1893, married Olga Guenbant on 10 June 1926, one child, died on 7 Dec 1974, and is buried in the Sardinia Rural Cemetery.

1361.   ii.   ALICE EULALIE[8] HOWELL, born on 4 Mch 1892, married Frederick Randall, later divorced, died on 6 Mch 1984, and is buried in the Sardinia Rural Cemetery.

1362.   iii.   EMERY JAMES[8] HOWELL, born on 14 Jan 1896 at Chaffee, married (1) Marian Lucy Allen at Buffalo, New York, on 20 Apr 1920, one child. Marian Allen was born on 4 Nov 1896 at Buffalo, the daughter of Ernest Chauncey and Charlotte Evangeline (Wolfe) Allen, and died on 6 Mch 1941 at Baltimore, Maryland. He married (2) Bernice Mae Marshall on 17 June 1942. He died on 31 Dec 1987 at Chaffee, and is buried in the Sardinia Rural Cemetery. NOTE: *Emery James Howell was the father of Nancy Allen (Howell) Ornce.*

4. Uriah Flynt [6], Abraham [5]

1025. SARAH[7] HOWELL (Uriah Flynt[6], Abraham[5]), the daughter of Uriah Flynt[6] and Nancy (Smith) Howell, was born in 1853 in Indiana {4631}.

Sarah Howell married (1) Mr. Bonnell, from whom she was divorced by 16 June 1880. She later married (2) Nathan B. Sadler {4632}.

On 16 June 1880, Sarah Bonnell, 27, who was divorced, was enumerated as the head of a household consisting of herself, her brothers, Byron Howel, 25, and Walter Howel, 22, both farm laborers, and her sister, Eva L., 9, who had attended school in the previous year, all residing in Alpine Township, Kent County,

---

4627. Id.
4628. Id.
4629. Id.
4630. Id.
4631. Gordon Adams, op. cit.
4632. Id.

Michigan, in the Tenth Census of the United States {4633}.

Sarah Sadler died on 21 Jan 1934 at Georgetown, Michigan {4634}.

1028. WALTER[7] HOWELL (Uriah Flynt[6], Abraham[5]), the son of Uriah Flynt[6] and Nancy (Smith) Howell, was born in New York state on 22 May 1858 {4635}.

On 22 Dec 1938, "Walter Howell, aged 80, passed away Thursday morning at his home, 753 ⅃ Grandville Ave., S.W. Surviving are the widow Esta, one brother George of Georgetown, and one sister, Mrs. George Adams of Grand Rapids. The body was removed to Hildreth Funeral Home where services will be held Saturday afternoon at 2 o'clock. Interment in the Georgetown Cemetery." {4636}.

1029. GEORGE WILLIAM[7] HOWELL (Uriah Flynt[6], Abraham[5]), the son of Uriah Flynt[6] and Nancy (Smith) Howell, was born in 1865 in Indiana {4637}.

At one time, George Howell was the Sexton at his church {4638}.

On 24 Dec 1934, George William Howell married Grace Ewing, who was born in 1875. She died in 1952, and is buried in the Georgetown Cemetery {4639}.

George William Howell died in 1959, and is buried beside his wife {4640}.

1031. EVA LINA[7] HOWELL (Uriah Flynt[6], Abraham[5]), the daughter of Uriah Flynt[6] and Nancy (Smith) Howell, was born on 1 Aug 1871 at Marne, Ottawa County, Michigan {4641}.

Eva Howell was given to her sister, Sarah Sadler, to raise at about the time when her father died. She told her daughters that she did not remember her mother, and never spoke of her father {4642}.

Eva Howell married George Douglas Adams on 24 Dec 1887 at Grandville, Kent County, Michigan {4643}.

Eva Adams died on 14 Sep 1861 at Grand Rapids, Kent County, Michigan,

---

4633. U.S. Census, Alpine Township, Kent County, MI, Dwelling House 126, Family Number 128, Enumeration District 121, Page 13, Line 4ff.
4634. Gordon Adams, op. cit.
4635. Id.
4636. GRAND RAPIDS PRESS, 22 Dec 1938.
4637. Gordon Adams, op. cit.
4638. Id.
4639. Id.
4640. Id.
4641. Id.
4642. Id.
4643. Id.

and is buried beside her husband in the Georgetown Cemetery {4644}.

George Douglas and Eva Lina (Howell) Adams were the parents of five children {4645}.

    i.   GEORGE WORDEN ADAMS, born on 18 Mch 1889 at Wyoming, Michigan, and died on 24 June 1954.

    ii.   LOLA MONTEZ ADAMS, born on 12 May 1893 at Wyoming, married Sidney Wesley Root on 24 Dec 1912 at Cherry Grove, Michigan, and died on 13 May 1973.

    iii.   MARCELLUS WHITE ADAMS, born on 16 Nov 1897 at Cherry Grove, married (1) Myrtle Smith on 5 Apr 1923, (2) Esther L. Davis, and (3) Jane Louise Feeback, died on 1 Mch 1957 at Greenville, Michigan. NOTE: *Marcellus White Adams was the grandfather of Gordon J. Adams.*

    iv.   JOHN QUINCY ADAMS, born on 14 Jly 1903 at Cherry Grove, married Eleanore --- in 1929, died on 2 Mch 1971.

    v.   FANNY ALIDA ADAMS, born on 27 Jly 1907 at Cherry Grove, married Ralph Vibber on 14 Mch 1925, died on 31 Aug 1978 at Grand Rapids, Michigan.

5. James Barnaby [6], Jacob [5]

1032. ELLA ELIZABETH[7] HOWELL (James Barnaby[6], Jacob[5]), the daughter of James Barnaby[6] and Louisa (Dewey) Howell, was born on 6 Mch 1852 {4646}.

Ella Elizabeth Howell preceded her father as Treasurer of the Township school fund in 1882, and held this office until her marriage in 1887 {4647}.

Ella Elizabeth Howell married Mr. Pyle {4648}.

On 1 June 1900, Ella H. Pyle was the wife of Ellis W. Pyle, 43, manager, who was enumerated as the head of a household consisting of them as well as her aunt, Marianne Howell, 83, and Minnie Anderson, 19, servant, residing in the same house as her father in the city of Rockford, in Rockford Township, Winnebago County, Illinois, in the Twelfth Census of the United States {4649}.

4644. Id.
4645. Id.
4646. James Barnaby Howell, op. cit., 16.
4647. Church, op. cit., 274.
4648. Id., op. cit., Title page.
4649. U.S. Census, Rockford, Winnebago County, IL, 1900, Dwelling House 2, Family Number 4, Enumeration District 131, Sheet Number 1.

B. Silas⁴, Daniel³, Isaac², Richard¹

1. Charles Ransom⁶, Daniel⁵

1043. CHARLES HENRY⁷ HOWELL (Charles Ransom⁶, Daniel⁵), the son of Charles Ransom⁶ and Elizabeth (Corwin) Howell, was born on 18 Jly 1832 {4650}.

On 5 Sep 1850, Charles H. Howell, 18, was enumerated with his father's family in the Seventh Census of the United States {4651}.

C. Henry Howell "..remained at home and gave his attention to cultivating the old place until about thirty years of age." {4652}.

On 22 Jan 1861, C. Henry Howell married Susan M. Aldrich {4653}, who was born on 25 Feb 1838 {4654}, and "..began life for himself on part of the old estate." {4655}.

On 20 June 1870, Chas. H. Howell, 38, farm laborer, having real property worth $2000, and personal property worth $500, was enumerated as the head of a family consisting of himself, his wife, Susan M., 32, and their son, Edwin H., 8, residing in the Town of Riverhead, Suffolk County, New York, in the Ninth Census of the United States {4656}.

C. Henry Howell was a "..staunch and substantial citizen..and a man of sterling principles, progressive ideas and generous impulses." He and his wife were members of the Methodist Episcopal Church, and were interested in all good works in their neighborhood. For many years Mr. Howell was associated with the Republican party, and was elected to the office of Assessor of his town and Inspector of Elections. His interest in educational affairs resulted in his being placed on the Board of Education of the village of Riverhead." {4657}.

Susan Howell died on 22 Apr 1903, and is buried in Plot 206 at the Riverhead Cemetery {4658}.

C. Henry Howell died on 3 Apr 1909, and is buried beside his wife at Riverhead {4659}.

C. Henry and Susan (Aldrich) Howell were the parents of one son {4660}.

4650. Charles Ransom Howell Family Bible.

4651. U.S. Census, Riverhead, Suffolk County, NY, 1850, Dwelling House 150, Family Number 170, Page 258.

4652. PORTRAIT & BIOGRAPHICAL RECORD OF SUFFOLK COUNTY.., 489.

4653. Id.

4654. Gravestone, Riverhead Cemetery.

4655. PORTRAIT & BIOGRAPHICAL RECORD OF SUFFOLK COUNTY.., 489.

4656. U.S. Census, Riverhead, Suffolk county, NY, 1879, Dwelling House 189, Family Number 210, Page 74.

4657. PORTRAIT & BIOGRAPHICAL RECORD OF SUFFOLK COUNTY, 489-490.

4658. Gravestone, Riverhead Cemetery.

4659. Id.

4660. PORTRAIT & BIOGRAPHICAL RECORD OF SUFFOLK COUNTY.., 489.

1363.   i.   EDWIN HERBERT[8] HOWELL, born on 14 Nov 1861, married Carrie Delmar Kirk, of Brooklyn on 4 Feb 1885 {4661}, three children, died on 18 May 1921, and is buried at Riverhead {4662}.

1045. SARAH BETHIAH[7] HOWELL (Charles Ransom[6], Daniel[5]), the daughter of Charles Ransom[6] and Elizabeth (Corwin) Howell, was born on 21 Sep 1840 {4663}.

Sarah Howell, 10, was enumerated with her father's family on 5 Sep 1850 in the Seventh Census of the United States {4664}.

On 13 Dec 1865, Sarah B. Howell married James M. Pettie {4665}.

Sarah B. Petty died on 25 Sep 1876 {4666}.

James Minor Petty married (2) Roberta Tuthill as his second wife {4667}.

James M. and Sarah Bethiah (Howell) Petty were the parents of at least one child {4668}.

    i.   CHILD[8], born on 20 June 1869, and died on 10 Sep 1869.

1046. DANIEL HALSEY[7] HOWELL (Charles Ransom[6], Daniel[5]), the son of Charles Ransom[6] and Elizabeth (Corwin) Howell, was born on 9 Mch 1848 {4669}.

On 5 Sep 1850, Daniel H. Howell, 2, was enumerated with his father's family in the Seventh Census of the United States {4670}.

Daniel H. Howell, 22, seaman, was again enumerated with his father's family on 20 June 1870 in the Ninth Census of the United States {4671}.

On 1 Jan 1873, Daniel Halsey Howell married Eunice Fidelia Benjamin {4672}.

Daniel Halsey Howell died on 12 Nov 1879 {4673}, and is buried in Plot 206 in the Riverhead Cemetery {4674}.

4661. Gertrude A. Barber, MARRIAGES OF SUFFOLK COUNTY.
4662. Gravestone, Riverhead Cemetery.
4663. Charles Ransom Howell Family Bible.
4664. U.S. Census, Riverhead, Suffolk County, NY, 1850, Dwelling House 150, Family Number 170, Page 258.
4665. PORTRAIT & BIOGRAPHICAL RECORD OF SUFFOLK COUNTY.., 489.
4666. iD.
4667. Wilbur Franklin Howell, op. cit., 132.
4668. Id.
4669. Charles Ransom Howell Family Bible.
4670. U.S. Census, Riverhead, Suffolk county, NY, 1850, Dwelling House 150, Family Number 170, Page 258.
4671. Id., 1870, Dwelling House 187, Family Number 208, Page 74.
4672. Id.
4673. Charles Ransom Howell Family Bible.
4674. Gravestone, Riverhead Cemetery.

Eunice F. Howell died in 1928, and is buried beside her husband at Riverhead {4675}.

Daniel Halsey and Eunice Fidelia (Benjamin) Howell were the parents of three children {4676}.

1364.   i.   DAUGHTER[8], died on 6 Oct 1873, and is buried at Riverhead.

1365.   ii.   MARTHA LOUISE[8] HOWELL, born on 27 Nov 1874, married Herbert Rackett, one child, died on 22 May 1958 {4677}.

1366.   iii.   CHARLES HALSEY[8] HOWELL, born on 9 Nov 1878, married Jessie Raynor on 24 June 1901 {4678}, six children {4679}, died on 14 May 1950 {4680}.

2. Daniel Griffing[6], Silas Hamilton[5]

1047. CHARLES HAMILTON[7] HOWELL (Daniel Griffing[6], Silas Hamilton[5]), the son of Daniel Griffing[6] and Jemima Amanda (Benjamin) Howell, was born on 9 Apr 1850 at Riverhead {4681}.

On 5 Sep 1850, Chas. H. Howell, two months old, was enumerated with his father's family in the Seventh Census of the United States {4682}.

"Charles H. Howell's youthful days were spent in active employment on his father's farm, and he received his primary education in the public schools. Later he completed his studies at Fort Edward Collegiate Institute, and at Eastman's Business College at Poughkeepsie. Prior to this, when but sixteen years old, he had taught school, and teaching has been his life work. In 1872 he established a commercial institute at Bridgehampton, and there he remained until 1876, when he opened Franklinville Academy, which he purchased two years later. In that institution he remained until the spring of 1880, when he was called to the principalship of the Riverhead school and remained in the same until the year 1888. In that year he was elected by the Republican party to the position of Commissioner of Schools for Suffolk County..The first time he was elected by a majority of three hundred and fourteen, the second time by seven hundred and seventy-seven, and..by a still larger majority. He..made one of the most thorough and faithful Commissioners the county has ever had." {4683}.

4675. Id.
4676. Charles Ransom Howell Family Bible.
4677. Wilbur Franklin Howell, op. cit., 134.
4678. Gertrude A. Barber, MARRIAGES OF SUFFOLK COUNTY.
4679. Wilbur Franklin Howell, op. cir., 136.
4680. Suffolk County Estates, File #264 A 1950.
4681. PORTRAIT & BIOGRAPHICAL RECORD OF SUFFOLK COUNTY.., 548.
4682. U.S. Census, Riverhead, Suffolk county, NY, 1850, Dwelling House 144, Family Number 164, Page 258.
4683. PORTRAIT & BIOGRAPHICAL RECORD OF SUFFOLK COUNTY, 548-549.

On 25 June 1870, Charles H. Howell, 19, fisherman, was again enumerated with his father's family in the Ninth Census of the United States {4684}.

On 24 Nov 1873, Charles H. Howell married Rosie E. Barber, of East Moriches, the daughter of Henry T. Barber {4685}.

"In 1895 Mr. Howell was made vice-president of the State Association of School Commissioners..in every way qualified for that position.." Mr. Howell was a member of the Independent Order of Odd Fellows, and was a grand master in that order. In religion, he was a Methodist, and was vice-president of the Suffolk County Camp Meeting Association. "During his youthful days he was a great lover of the water, and as a boy spent much of his time on the same. In 1868 he was wrecked near Narragansett Bay, being caught in the great cyclone of that time. At another time he was cast off on the banks of the river near Riverhead, and in 1871 he was in the sloop commanded by Capt. Charles M. Reeve, on the way from New York to Shelter Island, and they were run down by a schooner off City Island, the sloop sinking in deep water in about two minutes. To save themselves they jumped on board the schooner and were landed in Oyster Bay. During all these wrecks he was with Capt. Charles M. Reeve..of Patchogue." These experiences did not abate his desire for the water, and he continued to enjoy a sail for the rest of his life {4686}.

Charles Hamilton Howell died in 1915, his funeral being one of the largest ever held in Riverhead up to that time {4687}. He is buried in Plot 321 in the Riverhead Cemetery {4688}.

Rose E. Howell died on 17 Jan 1944, and is buried beside her husband at Riverhead {4689}.

Charles Hamilton and Rosa E. (Barber) Howell were the parents of two children {4690}.

1367.   i.   HERBERT HALSEY[8] HOWELL, born on 26 Oct 1880, married Jennie Hagen, two children {4691}, died on 11 Jly 1955 {4692}.

1368.   ii.   ROBERT R.[8] HOWELL, born in 1888, died on 20 Nov 1976 {4693}, and is buried beside his wife, Clara Wells Howell,

---

4684. U.S. Census, Riverhead, Suffolk County, NY, 1870, Dwelling House 235, Family Number 258, Page 77.
4685. Id., 549.
4686. Id.
4687. Newspaper clipping, 8 May 1915, from Orville B. Ackerley's Obituary Book 5, p. D, in the LONG ISLAND COLLECTION at the East Hmapton Library.
4688. Gravestone, Riverhead Cemetery.
4689. Id.
4690. PORTRAIT & BIOGRAPHICAL RECORD OF SUFFOLK COUNTY.., 549.
4691. Wilbur Franklin Howell, op. cit., 148.
4692. Suffolk County Estates, File #525 P 1955.
4693. Suffolk County Estates, File #2001 P 1976.

in Plot 321 in the Riverhead Cemetery {4694}.

1049. FRANCIS GRIFFING[7] HOWELL (Daniel Griffing[6], Silas Hamilton[5]), the son of Daniel Griffing[6] and Jemima Amanda (Benjamin) Howell, was born on 20 Jan 1855 {4695}.

On 25 June 1870, Francis G. Howell, 14, was enumerated with his father's family in the Ninth Census of the United States {4696}.

Francis Griffing Howell married (1) Anna Webb, who was born in 1856, and died in 1888, and (2) Angie M. Allen {4697}, who was born on 26 Aug 1866 {4698}.

Francis G. Howell, D. D., was educated in the Fort Edward Institute and the Mount Union Theological College, Ohio, and received his degree from that institution. His first charge was at Jamesport, thence to Port Washington, and from there he went to Grace Church, Long Island City, Bethel Church, Long Island City, and thereafter for four years to the old John Street Methodist Episcopal Church in Manhattan before going to Andrews Methodist Episcopal Church in Brooklyn, where he was pastor for the last nineteen years of his life. His residence there was at 95 Richmond Street, next door to the church {4699}.

When he became pastor at Andrews Church, it was heavily in debt, however, he managed to reduce the debt to virtually nothing during his pastorate. It was his intention to round out an even twenty years of service in Andrews Church, and then to retire from the pulpit. For many years, he refused to take a vacation from his church work, although he had acted as superintendent of the Sunday School attached to his church, as well as filling the pulpit. His church and school were among the largest in the New York East Methodist Episcopal Conference, and he marched at its head every year in the Anniversary Parade {4700}.

At the time of his death, on 4 Mch 1915, Dr. Howell was the oldest minister in the Conference, from the point of view of continuous service. At the last Sunday service before his death, he preached a part of the sermon on his feet, and the rest while seated on a chair on the pulpit platform. He had previously been seized with an attack of heart failure while officiating at a funeral, but carried on with his ministrations, knowing that he might collapse at any time. He died suddenly in his bed at home {4701}. He is buried in Plot 321 at the

4694. Gravestone, Riverhead Cemetery.
4695. Id.
4696. U.S. Census, Riverhead, Suffolk County, NY, 1870, Dwelling House 235, Family Number 258, Page 77.
4697. Wilbur Franklin Howell, op. cit., 151.
4698. Id.
4699. Obituary, THE BROOKLYN EAGLE, 5 Mch 1915, from Orville B. Ackerley's Obituary Book 5, p. 2.
4700. Id.
4701. Id.

Riverhead Cemetery {4702}.

Angie M. Howell died on 12 Jly 1946, and is buried beside her husband at Riverhead {4703}.

Francis Griffing and Angie M. (Allen) Howell were the parents of one daughter {4704}.

1369.　i.　ETHEL M.[8] HOWELL, born in 1887, died in 1962, and is buried in the family plot at Riverhead {4705}, was a teacher in the Andrews Methodist Episcopal Sunday School at the time of her father's death.

1050. USHER B.[7] HOWELL (Daniel Griffing[6], Silas Hamilton[5]), the son of Daniel Griffing[6] and Jemima Amanda (Benjamin) Howell, was born on 17 Dec 1858 {4706}.

Usher B. Howell, 9, was enumerated with his father's family on 25 June 1870 in the Ninth Census of the United States {4707}.

"Usher B. Howell received his primary education at the public school and later attended the Bridgehampton Literary Institute. For a period thereafter he read law, and subsequently entered Claverack College, Columbia county, New York.." He accepted an offer to become an assistant teacher at his brother's Franklinville Academy, and became principal the following year. "Deciding to abandon the profession of teaching for a business career, he left the school and took a position as clerk in a drug store, where he remained for four years. Later, he entered a business house in Riverhead and kept books for a number of years. From this position he was called to occupy the place of assistant secretary of the Riverhead Savings Bank." He later became secretary of the institution. Politically, he was a Republican {4708}.

On 3 June 1885, Usher B. Howell married Minnie M. Miller {4709}, who was born in 1863 {4710}, the daughter of Gilbert L. and Charry M. (Benjamin) Miller, of East Moriches {4711}.

Usher B. Howell died on 1 Mch 1932 {4712}, and is buried in Plot 436 at the Riverhead Cemetery {4713}.

4702. Gravestone, Riverhead Cemetery.

4703. Id.

4704. Obituary, BROOKLYN EAGLE, 5 Mch 1915.

4705. Gravestone, Riverhead Cemetery.

4706. William S. Pelletreau, op.cit., 132.

4707. U.S. Census, Riverhead, Suffolk County, NY, 1870, Dwelling House 235, Family Number 258, Page 77.

4708. Id., 132-133.

4709. Gertrude A. Barber, MARRIAGES OF SUFFOLK COUNTY.

4710. Gravestone, Riverhead Cemetery.

4711. Pelletreau, op. cit., 133.

4712. Suffolk County Estates, File #112 P 1932.

4713. Gravestone, Riverhead Cemetery.

Minnie M. Howell died on 31 Oct 1950 {4714}, and is buried beside her husband at Riverhead {4715}.

Usher B. and Minnie M. (Miller) Howell were the parents of four daughters {4716}.

1370. i. GRACE AMANDA[8] HOWELL, born on 24 Sep 1888, died on 15 May 1967 {4717}, and is buried in Plot 436 in the Riverhead Cemetery {4718}.

1371. ii. EDITH MILLER[8] HOWELL, born on 20 Sep 1891, died on 21 Oct 1986 {4719}, and is buried in the family plot at Riverhead {4720}.

1372. iii. HELEN[8] HOWELL, born on 21 Dec 1893, died on 12 Jly 1894 {4721}, and is buried in the family plot at Riverhead {4722}.

1373. iv. MARION[8] HOWELL, born on 17 Aug 1898, died on 30 Mch 1943 {4723}, and is buried in the family plot at Riverhead {4724}.

3. John Franklin[6], George[5]

1055. LYDIA MARIA[7] HOWELL (John Franklin[6], George[5]), the daughter of John Franklin[6] and Lucretia (Jennings) Howell, was born on 19 Nov 1844 {4725}.

Lydia M. Howell, 6, was enumerated with her father's family on 5 Sep 1850 in the Seventh Census of the United States {4726}.

On 19 Nov 1866, Lydia M. Howell married Dr. Webster C. Wood {4727}.

Dr. Webster C. Wood died on 20 Oct 1871 {4728}.

4714. Suffolk County Estates, File #652 P 1950.
4715. Gravestone, Riverhead Cemetery.
4716. Pelletreau, op. cit., 133, Wilbur Franklin Howell, op. cit., 152.
4717. Suffolk County Estates, File #271 A 1967.
4718. Gravestone, Riverhead Cemetery.
4719. Suffolk County Estates, File #2184 P 1986.
4720. Gravestone, Riverhead Cemetery.
4721. Wilbur Franklin Howell, op. cit., 152.
4722. Gravestone, Riverhead Cemetery.
4723. Wilbur Franklin Howell, op. cit.
4724. Gravestone, Riverhead Cemetery.
4725. NYG&BR, LXXXI, 142 (Apr 1950).
4726. U.S. Census, Riverhead, Suffolk County, NY, 1850, Dwelling House 148, Family Number 168, Page 258.
4727. Wilbur Franklin Howell, op. cit., 175.
4728. Id.

Lydia M. Wood died on 30 Apr 1919 {4729}.

1058. WILLIAM HENRY[7] HOWELL (John Franklin[6], George[5]), the son of John Franklin[6] and Lucretia (Jennings) Howell, was born on 6 Apr 1856 {4730}.

On 20 June 1870, "Willie Howell", 14, was enumerated with his father's family in the Ninth Census of the United States {4731}.

On 17 Jan 1888, William Henry Howell married Mary Jane Schirra, who was born on 5 Jly 1867 at Southampton, New York, the daughter of Christian and Elizabeth Dorothea (Lane) Shirra {4732}.

Mary Jane Howell died on 6 June 1944, and is buried in the Aquebogue Cemetery {4733}.

William Henry Howell died on 24 Dec 1944 {4734}, and is buried beside his wife at Aquebogue {4735}.

William Henry and Mary Jane (Shirra) Howell were the parents of three children {4736}.

1374.　i.　WILBUR FRANKLIN[8] HOWELL, born on 27 Oct 1889, married Ruth Weir, who was born on 22 Jan 1886, the daughter of Dr. George Sutton and Sara (Bawtenheimer) Weir, two children {4737} {4738}, died on 21 Apr 1967, and is buried in the Aquebogue Cemetery, as is his wife, who died on 21 Nov 1967 {4739}. NOTE: *Wilbur Franklin Howell prepared the most comprehensive genealogy available of the family of Richard[1] Howell, one which we have relied on extensively in this compilation.*

1375.　ii.　EDITH DOROTHY[8] HOWELL, born on 22 Jan 1902, married Harry Julius Kratoville, who was born on 17 Dec 1896, the son of Charles F. and Mary (Jedlicka) Kratoville, three children {4740}.

1376.　iii.　KRISTINE[8] HOWELL, born on 26 Apr 1906 at Aquebogue, married Raymond L. Young, who was born on 15 Feb 1910, the

4729. NYG&BR, 81, 145 (1950).
4730. NYG&BR, LXXXI, 142 (Apr 1950).
4731. U.S. Census, Riverhead, Suffolk County, NY, 1870, Dwelling House 212, Family Number 234, Page 75.
4732. Wilbur Franklin Howell, op. cit., 176.
4733. Id.
4734. Suffolk County Estates, File #49 P 1945.
4735. Wilbur Franklin Howell, op. cit.
4736. Id.
4737. Wilbur Franklin Howell, op. cit., 177.
4738. Id., 178.
4739. Gravestone, Aquebogue Cemetery, from the William F. Howell collection of cemetery markings.
4740. Id., 179.

son of Addison and Lizzie Young {4741}.

4. Joseph Chauncey⁶, George⁵

1061. GEORGE WILBUR⁷ HOWELL (Joseph Chauncey⁶, George⁵), the son of Joseph Chauncey⁶ and Dency Maria (Youngs) Howell, was born on 26 Dec 1852 {4742}.

On 20 June 1870, George W. Howell, 17, who was a clerk in a store, was enumerated with his father's family in the Ninth census of the United States {4743}.

On 17 Jan 1883 {4744}, George Wilbur Howell married Louisa Corwin {4745}, who was born in 1851, the daughter of Harrison and Betsey A. Corwin.

Louisa A. Howell died in 1924, and is buried in Plot 63 in the Riverhead Cemetery {4746}.

George W. Howell died on 2 Feb 1928 {4747}, and is buried beside his wife at Riverhead {4748}.

George W. and Louisa A. (Corwin) Howell had no children.

1062. ELLEN ADELAIDE⁷ HOWELL (Joseph Chauncey⁶, George⁵), the daughter of Joseph Chauncey⁶ and Dency Maria (Youngs) Howell, was born on 29 Dec 1854 {4749}.

Ellen A. Howell, 15, was enumerated with her father's family in the Ninth Census of the United States {4750}.

On 21 May 1878, Ellen Adelaide Howell married Clifford Burnell Ackerly {4751}, who was born on 26 May 1851 {4752}.

On 19 Feb 1885, Clifford B. and E. Adelaide (Howell) Ackerly adopted Florence Van Dyck, who was born on 9 Sep 1879, the daughter of Clifford B. Ackerly's oldest sister, Marion Lelia {4753}.

4741. Wilbur Franklin Howell, op. cit.
4742. Id., 180.
4743. U.S. Census, Riverhead, Suffolk county, NY, 1870, Dwelling House 186, Family Number 207, Page 74.
4744. Gertrude A. Barber, MARRIAGES OF SUFFOLK COUNTY.
4745. Wilbur Franklin Howell, op. cit.
4746. Gravestone, Riverhead Cemetery.
4747. Suffolk County Estates, File #29919.
4748. Gravestone, Riverhead Cemetery.
4749. Id.
4750. U.S. Census, Riverhead, Suffolk County, NY, 1870, Dwelling House 186, Family Number 207, Page 74.
4751. RIVERHEAD WEEKLY NEWS, May 28, 1878, Wilbur franklin Howell, op. cit., 181.
4752. Gravestone, Riverhead Cemetery.
4753. Wilbur Franklin Howell, op. cit., 181-1.

Clifford B. Ackerly died on 10 Oct 1899, and is buried in Plot 85 in the Riverhead Cemetery {4754}.

E. Adelaide Howell Ackerly died on 20 Nov 1943, and is buried beside her husband at Riverhead {4755}.

Clifford Burnell and Ellen Adelaide (Howell) Ackerly were the parents of one daughter {4756}.

     i.   RUTH ACKERLY, born on 26 June 1882, died on 8 Jan 1965, and is buried in the family plot at Riverhead {4757}.

5. Joshua M. ^{6}, George ^{5}

1063. JOHN D.^{7} HOWELL (Joshua M.^{6}, George^5), the son of Joshua M.^{6} and Selina (Downs) Howell, was born on 20 Feb 1858 {4758}.

On 19 Mch 1879, John D. Howell married Carrie Louise Downs, who was born on 31 May 1860, the daughter of Captain William and Nancy (Overton) Downs {4759}.

John D. Howell was for many years the Suffolk County agent for the Fleischmann Yeast Company {4760}.

John D. Howell died on 21 Apr 1905, and is buried in Plot 171 in the Riverhead Cemetery {4761}.

C. Louise Howell died on 3 Feb 1946, and is buried beside her husband at Riverhead {4762}.

John D. and C. Louise (Downs) Howell were the parents of three children {4763}.

1377. i.   JOHN RAYMOND^8 HOWELL, born on 16 Dec 1880, died of pneumonia on 5 Sep 1888.

1378. ii.   LEONE^8 HOWELL, born on 3 Aug 1882, married L.F. Moore on 9 Nov 1904.

1379. iii.   PERCY^8 HOWELL, born on 20 May 1884, died on 18 Aug 1885.

4754. Gravestone, Riverhead Cemetery.
4755. Id.
4756. Wilbur Franklin Howell, op. cit.
4757. Gravestone, Riverhead Cemetery.
4758. Wilbur Franklin Howell, op. cit., 183.
4759. Id.
4760. Id.
4761. Gravestone, Riverhead Cemetery.
4762. Id.
4763. Wilbur Franklin Howell, op. cit.

C. Joseph [4], Daniel [3], Isaac [2], Richard [1]

1. Joseph Marthers [6], Ebenezer [5]

1065. AZELIE FRANCES[7] HOWELL (Joseph Marthers[6], Ebenezer[5]), the daughter of Joseph Marthers[6] and Marie Rose (Pacaud) Howell, was born on 31 Jan 1844 (or 1845) in New Orleans {4764}.

Azelie F. Howell moved to Texas, thence back to New Orleans with her family, but returned to Corpus Christi to marry Lyman Dwight Brewster on 10 Oct 1867. He was the son of D.W. (probably Dwight William) and Emily C. (Kinney) Brewster, and was born in 1842 in Illinois {4765}.

Lyman D. Brewster served as a Sergeant Major in Company D of the 3rd Texas Infantry. It is said that his brother, Calvin G. Brewster, served in the Grand Army of the Republic, and was captured by Lyman's company in the early part of the Civil War {4766}.

Lyman D. Brewster died on 7 May 1883, and is buried in the old Bayview Cemetery at Corpus Christi {4767}.

"Subsequent to Lyman D. Brewster's death, Azelie married Stanley O. Welch, a native of New Orleans." He had previously been married to Lottie M. Ritchie in Bexar County on 10 Nov 1868, but this marriage was annulled, and she took back her maiden name. He then married the widow, Elizabeth Ada Lovell, on 27 May 1880 in Nueces County. She died on 15 Dec 1883, leaving him with a stepson. He married Azelie F., "Lee", Brewster on 8 Nov 1884 {4768}.

Azelie L. Welch is said to have fallen and hurt herself, and to have subsequently developed a form of cancer. She died on 28 Dec 1895, and is buried beside Lyman Brewster in the Bayview Cemetery {4769}.

On 1 Mch 1896, Stanley O. Welch married Georgie Barnard, whose sister, Lydia, was the wife of Calvin Brewster. Their father, James Barnard, was a pioneer newspaper reporter and publisher, and had been a fellow citizen of Joseph M. Howell. Stanley O. Welch became a Federal District Judge, and was assassinated on 6 Nov 1906 while monitoring elections in Rio Grande City {4770}.

Lyman Dwight and Azelie Frances (Howell) Brewster were the parents of four children {4771}.

     i.   LYMAN HOWELL BREWSTER, born on 25 Mch 1869, married Jane McIntosh Frierson, died on 4 Jan 1946, while she was born on 30 Nov 1876, and died on 10 Oct 1958. Both are buried in the

4764. Michael A. Howell, op. cit.
4765. Id.
4766. Id.
4767. Id.
4768. Id.
4769. Id.
4770. Id.
4771. Id.

Conroe Memorial Park Cemetery.

ii.   DWIGHT CALVIN BREWSTER, born on 5 Nov 1870, married
       Vernon E. Shelbourne on 17 Oct 1907 at Brownsville, Texas, was
       a clothing merchant, died in a car accident near Torreon, Mexico,
       on 12 Feb 1931, while she was born in 1890, and died in 1925.

iii.   JOSEPH WILLIAM BREWSTER, born on 30 Oct 1873, was a
       stenographer, married (1) Frances M. Pinder on 4 Sep 1901. She
       was born on 10 Dec 1880, and died on 20 Mch 1922. He married
       (2) Zena Seal on 8 May 1928, and died on 8 Mch 1938.

iv.   EDWARD BUCKLEY BREWSTER, born on 28 Aug 1879, was
       a railroad clerk, married Georgia Dodd on 6 Oct 1899 at Laredo,
       died on 24 Aug 1924. She was born on 13 Dec 1877 (or 1878),
       and died on 18 June 1931.

Stanley Osborne and Azelie Frances (Howell) Brewster Welch were the parents of
two children {4772}.

v.   AZELIE SARAH WELCH, born on 2 Aug 1885, married Thomas
       Clark Wilson, Jr., on 24 June 1908, six children, died on 12 Jly
       1967. He was born on 17 Oct 1883, and died on 20 Sep 1969.

vi.   ADA WELCH, died of typhoid fever as a child.

1066. MARY ROSALINE[7] HOWELL (Joseph Marthers[6], Ebenezer[5]), the daughter
of Joseph Marthers[6] and Marie Rose (Pacaud) Howell, was born in June 1847 in
New Orleans {4773}.
       On 30 Mch 1875, Mary R. Howell married Joseph Thompson Kendall,
who was born in Sep 1846, the son of Thompson and Louise A. (Greene) Kendall,
of Grandwall, Mississippi {4774}.
       Joseph T. and Mary R. Kendall lived in New Orleans, in fact, they lived
with her mother for some time after her father died. They were living at 740 Third
Street in 1898 {4775}.
       Mary Rose Kendall died on 6 Dec 1906, and is buried in Lafayette
Cemetery #1 in downtown New Orleans {4776}.
       Joseph T. Kendall died on 2 June 1913, and is buried next to his wife
{4777}.

4772. Id.
4773. Id.
4774. Id.
4775. Id.
4776. Id.
4777. Id.

Joseph Thompson and Mary Rosaline (Howell) Kendall were the parents of five children {4778}.

    i.   ROSE ALMIRA KENDALL, born on 3 Oct 1876, never married, was employed by Loyola University, New Orleans, when she died on 13 Sep 1961.

    ii.   JOSEPH HOWELL KENDALL, born on 15 Oct 1878, had no descendants, did much business in north, and died shortly after 1930.

    iii.   AZELIE IRENE KENDALL, born on 14 Sep 1881, married Peter Anthony Bauer on 10 Apr 1901, died on 1 June 1946, while he died on 9 Apr 1961.

    iv.   PERRY DODDRIDGE KENDALL, born on 27 Mch 1884, died on 12 Jan 1885, and is buried near his parents.

    v.   FERDINAND STANLEY KENDALL, born on 28 Jan 1886, died on 24 Oct 1898 as result of being kicked while playing with some other youths in Clay Square. It appears that the kick injured his kidneys, since he died of uremia a few days later.

1067. JOSEPH[7] HOWELL (Joseph Mathers[6], Ebenezer[5]), the son of Joseph Marthers[6] and Marie Rose (Pacaud) Howell, was born in about 1849 in New Orleans {4779}.

    Joseph Howell was living with his parents in 1850 and 1860, with his sister, Azelie Brewster, in 1870, when he was a clerk, and, in 1895, in San Francisco {4780}.

    Joseph Howell may have died abroad as an employee of an American company. It has been reported that he had no family or property {4781}.

1068. FERDINAND COATES[7] HOWELL (Joseph Marthers[6], Ebenezer[5]), the son of Joseph Marthers[6] and Marie Rose (Pacaud) Howell, was born on 9 Dec 1852 at New Orleans {4782}.

    Ferdinand C. Howell returned to Corpus Christi by the end of 1876, having lived with his parents up until then. He was not a very stable young man at that time, having been cited by the Municipal Court in Oct and Dec 1876, and in Apr 1877, for drunk and disorderly conduct. In 1880, he was a cowboy, and

4778. Id.
4779. Id.
4780. Id.
4781. Id.
4782. Id.

probably consorting with some rough characters {4783}.

At Laureles Ranch on 5 Jan 1884, Ferdinand C. Howell married Minnie Thomas, who was born in Dec 1859, the daughter of Aisom (Isom) Hodges and Martha Lee (Simms) Thomas. They lived at first in the vicinity, but homesteaded in what was known as Sunshine, Texas, to the south of Corpus Christi {4784}.

Ferdinand C. Howell died on 10 Sep 1895 of a lingering illness, although his death was a shock {4785}.

On 5 Aug 1896, Minnie Howell married John McManigle, who was born on 31 Dec 1871 {4786}.

Minnie McManigle died on 16 Jan 1908 {4787}.

John McManigle married (2) Geneveva Quintanilla on 12 Mch 1924, and died shortly thereafter on 19 Mch 1924 {4788}.

Ferdinand Coates and Minnie (Thomas) Howell were the parents of seven children {4789}.

1380. i. KEARNEY FERDINAND[8] HOWELL, born on 24 Oct 1884, never married, died on 6 Jan 1910 from complications of being thrown from a horse.

1381. ii. PRICILLA ROSE[8] HOWELL, born on 31 Dec 1885, died on 4 Dec 1886, and is buried in the Holy Cross Cemetery at Corpus Christi, Texas.

1382. iii. NELLIE RACHEL[8] HOWELL, born on 6 Feb 1887, married Charles Luis Lege on 3 Sep 1905, three children, died on 22 Jan 1960, while he was born on 20 June 1880, and died on 8 Aug 1933.

1383. iv. ROBERT HENRY[8] HOWELL, born on 21 Sep 1888, never married, died on 2 Feb 1958.

1384. v. MINNIE JOSEPHINE[8] HOWELL, born on 21 Jan 1890, married Herbert George Hemme on 24 Dec 1907, three children, died on 11 Apr 1970. He was born on 20 Nov 1888, the son of Wilhelm Edward and Catherine Jane (Murray) Hemme, was a driller, and died on 26 Feb 1931 at Yates Center, Kansas.

1385. vi. MATT ARNOLD[8] HOWELL, born on 25 Jan 1892 at Corpus

4783. Id.
4784. Id.
4785. Id.
4786. Id.
4787. Id.
4788. Id.
4789. Id.

Christi, married (1) Stella Lela Westbrook on 14 Mch 1915, three children, died on 19 Jan 1977 at Bay City, Texas. She was born on 26 Nov 1897 at Madisonville, Texas, the daughter of William Scott and Angie (Redding) Westbrook, and died on 19 Oct 1975 at Houston. He married (2) Sarita Florence Brown on 27 Mch 1937. She was born on 23 Mch 1906, and died on 1 Mch 1991. Stella L. (Westbrook) Howell married Jack M. Crozier on 2 Dec 1935. She later married Fred Gloger, who was born on 23 Jan 1910, and died on 20 Mch 1970. NOTE: *Matt Arnold Howell was the grandfather of Michael A. Howell.*

1386. vii.   IRENE ALVERIA[8] HOWELL, born on 28 Oct 1893, married (1) LeRoy Frock on 12 Jly 1912, at least one child, died on 4 Sep 1984, while he died on 23 Sep 1916. She married (2) James Forrest Citty.

John and Minnie (Thomas) Howell McManigle were the parents of one child {4790}.

       viii.   MARGARITA CATHERINE McMANIGLE, born on 22 May 1897, married Robert L. Parry on 8 Oct 1915, died on 3 Jan 1975, while he was born on 23 Apr 1890, and died on 29 Dec 1954.

1070. PAMELIA IRENE[7] HOWELL (Joseph Marthers[6], Ebenezer[5]), the daughter of Joseph Marthers[6] and Marie Rose (Pacaud) Howell, was born on 4 Apr 1854 in New Orleans {4791}.

On 3 Nov 1894 in Orleans Parish, Pamelia Irene Howell married Edgar Haymaker, who was born in June 1860 in Winchester, Virginia, the son of Adam and Elizabeth (Barr) Haymaker {4792}.

Pamelia I. Howell, who often went by the name of Irene P. Howell, was probably the best known member of her family among the Howell relatives, by whom she was usually known as "Aunt Mella" {4793}.

Edgar Haymaker died on 26 Aug 1909, and is buried in the Haymaker plot at the Metairie Cemetery {4794}.

Mella Haymaker died on 21 Sep 1941, and is buried next to her husband at Metairie {4795}.

4790. Id.
4791. Id.
4792. Id.
4793. Id.
4794. Id.
4795. Id.

Edgar and Pamelia Irene (Howell) Haymaker were the parents of one child {4796}.

   i. CLARENCE MENTOR HAYMAKER, born on 3 Jan 1901, died on 6 May 1901, and is buried in the family plot in the Metairie Cemetery.

1071. PHILOMENE PATTERSON[7] HOWELL (Joseph Marthers[6], Ebenezer[5]), the daughter of Joseph Marthers[6] and Marie Rose (Pacaud) Howell was born in about Jan 1858 at Corpus Christi. She was named for a close personal friend of the family, Philomene Patterson, the daughter of George Patterson of New Orleans, and wife of Lucien Myers of Corpus Christi {4797}.

   In the Orleans Parish on 29 Mch 1880, Philomene P. Howell married John A. Cairns, a native of New York, and the son of John and Isabella (Watson) Cairns {4798}.

   John A. Cairns died on 9 Jly 1903, and was buried in Vault #28 in the Cypress Grove Firemen's Cemetery {4799}.

   "Aunt Lolo", Philomene P. Cairns, died on 14 Jan 1933, and was buried beside her husband. They were removed to the Metairie Cemetery in 1953, along with the other family members buried there {4800}.

   John A. and Philomene Patterson (Howell) Cairns were the parents of six children {4801}.

   i. ROBERT LAWRENCE CAIRNS, born on 31 Aug 1885, married Irene Maude Peters, died on 29 Nov 1949, while she died on 14 Jan 1948.

   ii. RALPH WATSON CAIRNS, married Viola Regel.

   iii. VIVIAN C. CAIRNS, married George Hamilton Broussard, who died on 10 Oct 1971.

   iv. ETHEL MARKHAM CAIRNS, married Henry L. Datz.

   v. HOWELL CAIRNS, born on 27 Aug 1896.

   vi. VIOLA MYRTLE CAIRNS, born on 23 May 1901, died on 17 Feb 1904.

4796. Id.
4797. Id.
4798. Id.
4799. Id.
4800. Id.
4801. Id.

1072. GEORGIANA MYER[7] HOWELL (Joseph Marthers[6], Ebenezer[5]), the daughter of Joseph Marthers[6] and Marie Rose (Pacaud) Howell, was born on 12 Aug 1860 at Corpus Christi, Texas {4802}.

On 20 Nov 1877, in Orleans Parish, Georgiana M. Howell married George Vincent Martin, who was born at Staten Island, New York, on 17 Oct 1850, the son of Henry and Mary (Gauthier) Martin. He was a sewing machine salesman {4803}.

George V. Martin died on 25 June 1882 at New Orleans and was buried in the family vault at the Cypress Grove Firemen's Cemetery {4804}.

Georgia M. Martin married Lorenzo Stanley Washburn on 24 Mch 1892. He had been born in Petersboro, New Hampshire, in Nov 1823, the son of Martin and Ora (Stanley) Washburn, and was a photographer. It is said that he was a jealous husband and contributed to the development of Georgie's blindness by not allowing her to see a doctor {4805}.

Lorenzo S. Washburn died on 7 Apr 1907, and was also interred in the family Vault #28 {4806}.

Georgia M. Washburn was living with her sister, Mella, at 6066 Annunciation Street in New Orleans when she died on 26 Aug 1938 {4807}.

George Vincent and Georgia Myer (Howell) Martin were the parents of two children {4808}.

    i.   CLIFTON PACAUD MARTIN, born on 22 Nov 1878 at Baton Rouge, married Rosa Buechler, of Brooklyn, on 11 May 1906, nine children, died on 2 Jly 1938 in Pennsylvania, and is buried in the Philadelphia National Cemetery. At the time of his death, he was a retired quartermaster sergeant from the U.S. Marines, and had seen service in the Spanish-American War, the Boxer Rebellion, the Philipines Incident, and World War I. Rosa Martin was born on 12 Jan 1891, and died at Darby, Pennsylvania, on 15 Feb 1952.

    ii.   GEORGE VINCENT or VINCENT ALBERT MARTIN, born on 8 June 1881 at Baton Rouge, died on 21 Mch 1928, at the residence of his mother at 6066 Annunciation Street, and was buried in the family vault at Cypress Grove.

1073. SUSIE WATERS[7] HOWELL (Joseph Marthers[6], Ebenezer[5]), the daughter of Joseph Marthers[6] and Marie Rose (Pacaud) Howell, was born at Corpus Christi,

---

4802. Id.
4803. Id.
4804. Id.
4805. Id.
4806. Id.
4807. Id.
4808. Id.

Texas, in Mch 1863 {4809}.

In the Orleans Parish on 21 Dec 1881, Susie W. Howell married Horatio Oscar Bertel, who was born in Louisiana in March 1860, the son of August and Josephine (Robertson) Bertel {4810}.

Horatio O. and Susie W. Bertel were living at 2518 Clio Street in New Orleans in 1900. They had moved about considerably, probably in response to then demands of his work {4811}.

Susie W. Bertel died on 23 Feb 1940, and was interred in the family Vault #28 in the Cypress Grove Firemen's Cemetery, but was removed to Plots 37 and 38 in Section 78 of the Metairie Cemetery with the other members of the family who had been interred in Vault #28 on 13 May 1953, by order of her daughter, Mrs. Frank Doar {4812}.

Horatio Oscar Bertel died at New Orleans on 8 May 1948 {4813}.

Horatio Oscar and Susie Waters (Howell) Bertel were the parents of eight children {4814}.

 i. HORATIO OSCAR BERTEL, died on 16 Apr 1883.

 ii. WILLIAM ROBERT BERTEL, born in Louisiana in Sep 1883, died on 20 Oct 1952.

 iii. CORALIE BERTEL, born in Louisiana in Sep 1884, married William Arthur Herbert, at least one child.

 iv. CLEMENCE BERTEL, born in Mississippi in May 1890, married Joseph A. Rey, two children.

 v. ELOISE BERTEL, born in Mississippi in Nov 1893, married Frank Doar, one child, was responsible, with others, for the removal of the family members interred in Vault #28 in the Cypress Grove Firemen's Cemetery to the Howell/Haymaker plots in the Metairie Cemetery on 13 May 1953.

 vi. RICHARD BERTEL, born in Louisiana in Apr 1900, married Rose Sunsere, two children.

 vii. FRANK OSCAR BERTEL.

 viii. YVONNE GLADYS BERTEL, born on 12 Oct 1906, married Charles Fox, two children.

4809. Id.
4810. Id.
4811. Id.
4812. Id.
4813. Id.
4814. Id.

1074. CARRIE LEE[7] HOWELL (Joseph Marthers[6], Ebenezer[5]), the daughter of Joseph Marthers[6] and Marie Rose (Pacaud) Howell, was born in New Orleans in about 1866 {4815}.

On 20 Oct 1891, Carrie Lee Howell married James Brander Vienne before the Rev. Thomas Markham, paster of the Lafayette Presbyterian Church in New Orleans. James B. Vienne was the son of Francois A. and Margie O. (Barkley) Vienne {4816}.

Carrie L. Vienne, who became blind at an early age, died on 4 Sep 1892, with complications from the birth of her only child {4817}.

James B. Vienne married (2) Mary Ann Willis in about 1907 {4818}.

James B. Vienne died on 14 Oct 1938 at New Orleans {4819}.

Mary Ann Vienne died on 8 Sep 1955 {4820}.

James Brander and Carrie Lee (Howell) Vienne were the parents of one child {4821}.

    i.   CARRIE LEE HOWELL VIENNE, born on 1 Sep 1892, married (1) Thomas Campbell Spotts, the son of J.C. Spotts, one child. Thomas C. Spotts died on 23 Oct 1918, having become sick while aboard a ship on the Mississippi River. Carrie L.H. Spotts married (2) J.C. Casey, and died on 18 Nov 1927.

James Brander and Mary Ann (Willis) Vienne were the parents of two children {4822}.

    ii.   MARGUERITE VIENNE, never married.

    iii.   MADELINE VIENNE, never married.

2. Charles[6], Ebenezer[5]

1076. CHARLES E.[7] HOWELL/RIVERS (Charles[6], Ebenezer[5], Joseph[4]), the son of Charles[6] and Maria W. (Philips) Howell, was born on 21 Jan 1859 in New York State {4823}.

Charles E. Howell, like his father, was a dancing teacher. Also, like his father, he went by the name of Charles H. Rivers {4824}.

4815. Id.
4816. Id.
4817. Id.
4818. Id.
4819. Id.
4820. Id.
4821. Id.
4822. Id.
4823. Id.
4824. Id.

Charles E. Howell married Laurel M. Caldwell, who was born in Aug 1876, and was also a dance teacher. They were living on 131st Street in Manhattan when the Twelvth Census of the United States was taken in 1900 {4825}.

Charles E. Howell died on 11 June 1925, and is buried under the name of Charles H. Rivers in the family plot in the Oak Hill Cemetery at Nyack, New York {4826}.

1077. HENRY, "HARRY", F.[7] HOWELL/RIVERS (Charles[6], Ebenezer[5]), the son of Charles[6] and Maria (Philips) Howell, was born in Brooklyn in Jly 1860 {4827}.

Harry Howell/Rivers was a theatrical manager {4828}.

Harry Howell/Rivers was the father of at least five children {4829}.

1387. i.   EVELINE[8] HOWELL/RIVERS, born in Aug 1883.

1388. ii.   GENEVIEVE[8] HOWELL/RIVERS, born in June 1886.

1389. iii. HAROLD[8] HOWELL/RIVERS, born in Dec 1893.

1390. iv.   GRACE[8] HOWELL/RIVERS, born in Mch 1898.

1391. v.   SADIE[8] HOWELL/RIVERS, born in Feb 1899.

1078. WILLIAM P.[7] HOWELL/RIVERS (Charles[6], Ebenezer[5]), the son of Charles[6] and Maria (Philips) Howell, was born in Brooklyn in Feb 1863 {4830}.

William P. Howell/Rivers was employed at the Rivers' Academy of Dancing in 1900 {4831}.

William P. and Mertha Howell/Rivers were the parents of at least two children {4832}.

1392. i.   WILLIAM A.[8] HOWELL/RIVERS, born in Oct 1883.

1393. ii.   ABICKLE[8] HOWELL/RIVERS, born in June 1885.

1079. MARIA ANTOINETTE[7] HOWELL (Charles[6], Ebenezer[5]), the daughter of

4825. U.S. Census, Manhattan, New York County, New York, 1900, Enumeration District 870, Sheet 6B.
4826. Michael A. Howell, op. cit.
4827. Id.
4828. Id.
4829. Id.
4830. Id.
4831. Id.
4832. Id.

Charles[6] and Maria W. (Philips) Howell, was born in Brooklyn in Jly 1864 {4833}.

Maria A. Howell married Marcus A. Downing, who was born on 1 May 1865 {4834}. They were living in Rutherford, New Jersey, on 30 Jan 1911 when her father, who was living with them, died {4835}.

Maria A. Downing died on 17 Feb 1928, and is buried in the Oak Hill Cemetery in Nyack, New York {4836}.

Marcus A. Downing died on 8 Apr 1943, and is buried in the Greenwood Cemetery in Brooklyn {4837}.

Marcus A. and Maria Antoinette (Howell) Downing were the parents of at least one son {4838}.

    i.   MARCUS A. DOWNING, JR., born in 1902, married Ethel E. Jackson, five children. He died in Apr 1994.

1081. MARTIN EUGENE[7] HOWELL/RIVERS (Charles[6], Ebenezer[5]), the son of Charles[6] and Maria (Philips) Howell, was born in Brooklyn in Feb 1869 {4839}.

As Eugene Martin P. Rivers, Martin Eugene Howell was a dance instructor at the Rivers' Academy of Dancing in 1900 {4840}.

Eugene Martin P. and Alice E. Howell/Rivers were the parents of at least one child {4841}.

1394. i.   ALICE[8] HOWELL/RIVERS, born in Aug 1891.

1082. FRANCIS A.L.[7] HOWELL/RIVERS (Charles[6], Ebenezer[5]), the son of Charles[6] and Maria (Philips) Howell, was born in Brooklyn in Jan 1871 {4842}.

Francis A.L. and Hattie Howell/Rivers were the parents of at least two children {4843}.

1395. i.   GERTRUDE LORRAINE[8] HOWELL/RIVERS, born in May 1895.

1396. ii.   AUBREY[8] HOWELL/RIVERS, born in Sep 1898.

4833. Id.
4834. Id.
4835. NYACK JOURNAL, 1 Feb 1911.
4836. Michael A. Howell, op. cit.
4837. Id.
4838. Id.
4839. Id.
4840. Id.
4841. Id.
4842. Id.
4843. Id.

V. Descendants of Jacob[2] Howell -

A. Jacob[4], Jacob[3], Jacob[2], Richard[1]

1. William[6], Jacob[5]

1084. GIDEON[7] HOWELL (William[6], Jacob[5]), the son of William and Cynthia (Sherman) Howell, was born on 9 Sep 1824 {4844}.

On 4 Jly 1847, Gideon Howell married Elvira Sherman, who was probably born on 4 Jly 1824 {4845}.

On 10 Oct 1850, Gideon Howell, 26, engineer, was enumerated as the head of a household consisting of himself, his wife, Alvira, 25, their son, Albert M., 1, and James Sherman, 22, farmer, residing in the Town of Marion, Wayne County, New York, in the Seventh Census of the United States {4846}.

Gideon and Elvira Howell, of Palmyra, New York, were witnesses to the signing of the will of Hannah Howell, dated 26 Jan 1864, and proved on 12 Sep 1864 {4847}.

Gideon Howell died on 29 Nov 1921 at Spokane, Washington {4848}.

Gideon and Elvira (Sherman) Howell were the parents of at least one child {4849}.

   1397.   i.   ALBERT MELVIN[8] HOWELL, born on 21 Oct 1849, married Isabell Bannister, at least one child, died on 27 Aug 1906 at Spokane. Isabell Howell was born on 15 Aug 1863, the daughter of Chester Calvin and Hannah Mariah (Aldrich) Boggs Bannister, and died on 21 Sep 1940 at Hillsboro, Oregon.

1086. ISRAEL[7] HOWELL (William[6], Jacob[5]), the son of William[6] and Cynthia (Sherman) Howell, was born at Palmyra, New York, on 17 Feb 1838 {4850}.

On 10 Oct 1850, Israel Howell, 13, was enumerated with his father's family in the Seventh Census of the United States {4851}.

At the age of 14, Israel Howell was apprenticed to a tinsmith in Rochester,

---

4844. Alice Howell, op. cit.
4845. Id.
4846. U.S. Census, Marion, Wayne County, NY, 1850, Dwelling House 1644, Family Number 1729, Page 234.
4847. Wayne County (NY) Wills, Liber K, 264-266.
4848. Unknown, Personal communication.
4849. Alice Howell, op. cit.
4850. Notes of Historian Lambert from an interview with Israel Howell, from a copy generously provided by Betty (Howell) Huntsman and provided to her by Alice Howell.
4851. U.S. Census, Marion, Wayne County, NY, 1850, Dwelling House 1645, Family Number 1730, Page 234.

New York, where he served as such for four years. After learning his trade, he worked for a time in Buffalo, New York. He also worked in Burlington, Vermont, and for one winter in New Orleans, Louisiana {4852}.

Israel Howell came west in 1855. He came to Peoria, Illinois, where he worked as 2nd Engineer to his brother, the First Engineer, on the steamboat, CITY OF LANCASTER, which ran between Peoria and St. Louis {4853}.

On 6 Aug 1856, Israel Howell married Phebe Matilda Seely, the daughter of Ezra and Phebe Ann (Pierson) Seely {4854}.

Israel Howell served in Company E, of the 17th Regiment, and in Company C, of the 47th Regiment of Illinois Volunteer Infantry, and in the 2nd Illinois Artillery {4855}.

Israel Howell worked at Princeville, Illinois, after the Civil War. In 1875, he took a homestead and timber claim adjoing the present town of Plainview in Pierce County, Nebraska. He opened a hardware store and tin shop in Neligh, Nebraska, in 1877 {4856}.

Israel Howell died on 17 Oct 1914, while Phebe Howell died on 16 Nov 1914 {4857}.

Israel and Phebe Matilda (Seeley) Howell were the parents of eight children {4858}.

1398. i.   FRANK LINCOLN[8] HOWELL, married Josie Butcher, five children, died at Seattle, Washington.

1399. ii.   ADDIE LOUISE[8] HOWELL. NOTE: *Addie Louise Howell was the grandmother of Betty (Howell) Huntsman.*

1400. iii. LYDIA ARILLA[8] HOWELL, born on 27 Aug 1863, married Niels M. Nelson on 24 Dec 1882, seven children, died on 30 Sep 1953. Niels Nelson was born on 18 Mch 1855.

1401. iv. HARRY GRANT[8] HOWELL, born on 31 Oct 1868. NOTE: *Harry Grant Howell was the grand father o f Frank Howell, the husband of Alice Howell.*

1402. v.   JESSIE ADELLA[8] HOWELL, married Nate Souders, three children.

1403. vi. MARY CHRISTIE[8] HOWELL, died young.

4852. Notes of Historian Lambert.
4853. Id.
4854. Alice Howell, Personal communication to Betty (Howell) Huntsman.
4855. Notes of Historian Lambert.
4856. Id.
4857. Alice Howell, op. cit.
4858. Id.

1404. vii.   ALBERT GEORGE[8] HOWELL, married Emma Atkins, three children.

1405. viii.   ELMER LEONARD[8] HOWELL, born on 5 Apr 1883, married Eva Duncan, four children, died in 1955.

2. Samuel[6], Jacob[5]

1106. FANNY J.[7] HOWELL (Samuel[6], Jacob[5]), the daughter of Samuel[6] and Nancy (Scullens) Howell, was born in Sodus, New York, on 9 Apr 1859 {4859}.

On 20 Mch 1878, Fanny J. Howell married William H. Messinger at Afton, New York. He was born on 16 June 1849 at Sodus {4860}.

Fanny J. Messinger died on 23 Dec 1920 at Newark, New York {4861}.

William H. Messinger died on 14 June 1934 at Newark {4862}.

William H. and Fanny J. (Howell) Messinger were the parents of at least one son {4863}.

     i.   CLARENCE DOW MESSINGER, born on 20 Aug 1879, married Nevada Addie Johnson at Dresden, New York on 28 June 1906, at least one child, died on 1 Nov 1942 at Penn Yan, New York. She was born in 1886 at Dresden, and died 3 Feb 1921 at Penn Yan.

1107. SYLVESTER[7] HOWELL (Samuel[6], Jacob[5]), the son of Samuel[6] and Nancy (Scullins) Howell, was born on 15 Aug 1861 at East Williamson, New York {4864}.

On 9 Mch 1887, Sylvester Howell married Ida Sarah Ware at the home of Thomas Austin in Sodus, New York {4865}. She was born on 23 Nov 1861 at Sodus, the daughter of Joseph and Mary Melissa (Atwater) Ware {4866}.

Sylvester Howell died on 24 Jan 1927 at Rochester, New York {4867}.

Ida Sarah Howell died on 29 Aug 1937 at Rochester {4868}.

4859. Diane Howell Friis, op. cit.
4860. Id.
4861. Id.
4862. Id.
4863. Id.
4864. Id.
4865. WAYNE COUNTY ALLIANCE, 16 Mch 1887.
4866. Friis, op. cit.
4867. Id.
4868. Id.

Sylvester and Ida Sarah (Ware) Howell were the parents of three children {4869}.

1406. i.   OLEN JOSEPH[8] HOWELL, born on 11 Feb 1888, married (1) Edna Blair McCormick at Rochester on 30 Sep 1908, married (2) Hildegard R. Chapin, died on 7 Oct 1938 at San Pablo, California. NOTE: *Olin Joseph Howell was the grandfather of Diane (Howell) Friis.*

1407. ii. ROY SYLVESTER[8] HOWELL, born in Apr 1895, married Iva Baker.

1408. iii. RAYMOND WARE[8] HOWELL, born in Dec 1899, married Marion Pauline Brown.

- END OF SEVENTH GENERATION -

4869. Id.

BENNETT, S. Marion 464
BERRY, James 89
BERTEL, Clemence 536 Coralie 536 Eloise 536 Frank Oscar 536 Horatio Oscar 536 Richard 536 Susie Waters (Howell) 536 William Robert 536 Yvonne Gladys 536
BICHA, Gloria Wall, & BROWN, Helen Benjamin, THE BENJAMIN FAMILY IN AMERICA, 34 95 96 116 274 328 329 352 359 360 383 482 483
BIGELOW, Lucinda N. 293
BIGGAR, Mary Ann 148
BIGGER, John 148
BIGGS, Edward 9
BILLARD, Barnabas F. 277 456 Clayton H. 457 Lillian W. 456 Maria J. (Howell) 277 456 M. Ada 456
BILLS, Annie Minerva 441 Celestia Ophelia 440 Charles Otis 440 Hazel Maranda 441 James Scott 441 John Edmund 440 Jordan Elias 440 Mary Effie 440 Ophelia Ann (Howell) 440 Samuel 440 Samuel David 440 Sarah Elizabeth 440 William Gordon 440
BINGHAM, John 460
BIRDSALL, Charlotte (Howell) 286 David 136 286 Mr. 137 286 Rebecca 458
BIRGE, Henry 187 Joseph 187
BISBEE, Elder 267
BISHOP, Elizabeth (Howell) 409 Emma (Howell) 457 George Mitchell 409 Ida (Howell) 477 Mary Elizabeth 478 Nelson 457 Peter 477 Sarah Jane 409 William M. 409
BLACKBURN, Jessie 177 Mrs. 177
BLACKMAN, Dr. Francis B. 307
BLAIR, Louis William 499
BLANCHARD, Betsey (Howell) 187

Harold 478 Seth 323
BLATCHLY, Vernon Charles 511
BLESSED VIRGIN, ii
BLOOMER, Adelia (Howell) 460 . Arminta 281 460 Delia (Howell) 281 Gertrude Deyo 285 Gilbert, Esq. 39 John 460 Mary T. 281 460 Nancy 282
BLYDENBURGH, Thirza J. 266
BOND, Hannah (Howell) 251 258 John C. 251
BONNELL, Mr. 516 Sarah (Howell) 516
BOOTH, Antonia iv Catherine (Griffith) 254 Edith 254 George Lafayette 252-254 Sarah Ann (Howell) 252 William 252 254
BOSTWICK, Abel 221 Elizabeth (Howell) 379 Homer 379 James G. 379 Julia E. 379 Laura 178
BOUTCHER, Hettie 456
BOWEN, Arnold 366 Patience 366
BOWSER, Dorothy Ella 498
BRADING, James 3
BRADLEY, Ahaz 446 Lorena (Burton) 446 L. Jenny 446
BRADY, Ada Celestia 439 Jordan 438 Jordan Hendrickson 438 Keziah Lovina 438 Lindsay Edmund 438 Martha Elizabeth 439 Mary Emily 439 Mary Lovina (Howell) 438 Millie Rebecca 439 Ophelia Sophia 439 Radna Ann 439 Roy 515 Samuel Joseph 439 Sarah Matilda 439 Warren Absalom 439 Willis Alphonso 439
BRAINARD, David 137
BRAND, John 474
BRANDT, Joseph 71
BRATT, Lindley 401
BRENENSTUL, Robert Henry 344
BREWSTER, Azelie Frances (Howell) 529 531 Calvin G. 529 Daniel 9 Dwight Calvin 530 Dwight William 529

546

GARDNER (cont.) -
Frances 153 George 395
Isabella B. (Howell) 175 John
Elmer Smith 153 319 Merit
H.C. 319 Phebe Millicent
(Cash) 319 Virginia 395
GARLICK, Jehu Earl 441
GARRARD, Gilbert 117 122 Zophar
117 122
GASSETT, George D. 431
GATCHELL, Willard 478
GATES, Mary 143 Phebe 261
GAYLORD, Mary 296
GENDRON, Rene 464
GERARD, Hannah M. 272 Sarah M.
272
GIBSON, Estella 315 Gertrude
Morris (Rhodes) 450 William
Morris 450
GILDERSLEEVE, Edwin A. 434
Lester 483 Rhoda 487
GILLET, Charles 161
GILMORE, John 187
GILSON, George 255
GLADWICH, John 246 William 246
GLADWISH, Althea 246 Althea
(Howell) 246 Edward 246
George 246 John 246
GLENN, Capt. Thomas 393
GLOGER, Fred 533
GLOVER, Chas. A. 51
GOBLE, Betsy (Corwin) 155
Elizabeth 155 Milton 155
GOFF, Alvin Edward 509 Bertha M.
509 Harriet (Dean) 509
GOLDSMITH, Benjamin, Jr. 324
Elizabeth (Terry) 324 Hannah
324 John 14 Joseph 21 Rebecca
97
GOODALE, Josiah 47
GOODRICH, Zady 94
GORDON, Jane 359 Samuel 359
Susan 359
GOULD, Mary 337 Samuel 334
GRAHAM, Selma Rebecca 440
GRANT, General 329

GREENE, Rev. Zachariah,
RECORD OF MARRIAGES
PERFORMED BY.., 85 261
262 264
GREEG, Edwin 498
GREGORY, Josiah 310
GRENDLER, Caroline (Howell) iv
Maxwell 442
GRENDLER, Caroline (Howell),
THE RECORD OF JAMES
HOWELL AND SOME OF HIS
DESCENDANTS, 8 23 51 54
124 126 256 258 259 260 261
262 263 264 265 266 267 268
270 426 427 428 429 430 431
433 434 441 442 443
GRIFFEN, Capt. Daniel 83
GRIFFIN, Benjamin 38 489 Captain
Daniel 70 74 Daniel H. 489
Electa (Howell) 489 Mr. 245
Sidney L. 207
GRIFFIN, Augustus, GRIFFIN'S
JOURNAL, ii 26
GRIFFING, Anna 229 Bartlett 229
Benjamin R. 489 Daniel H. 490
Electa H. (Howell) 489 Hettie
D. 489 Jasper 5 Jemima 229
John 14 104 110 229 Maria T.
490 Mary 230 Mary (Albertson)
230 Mehitable (Howell) 229
Moses 489 Nathaniel 230 Polly
230 Prudence (Hallock) 14
Stephen 216
GRIFFITH, Catherine 254 Jannie
Hannah 497
GRUFFEDD, Prince iii
GRUNENDIKE, Mary Ann (Howell)
149 300 301 303 Edward
Howell 302 Eliza E. 301
Elizabeth (Anderson) 300 Frank
Parks 301 302 Fred Alesworth
302 John 300 John Howell 301
Mary Elora 301 Reuben
Alesworth 300 301 Samuel 301
GUENBANT, Olga 516
GWYN, iii

HAMMOND (cont.)
Forest 405 Charles Glover 423 Cyrus Fancher 422 Daniel 405 Deborah (Howell) 405 Edith Cary 422 Edmund 405 Edward R. 405 Eleanor Summerfield 422 Eliza (Poyntz) 487 Elizabeth 189 Ethel Willis 422 Fanny (Howell) 421 Frances Amanda (Howell) 54 421 Frances Octavia 418 421 Frederic H.L. 422 George E. 405 Grace Lillian 422 Grace Mowbray 422 Hallie 422 Herbert F. 422 Jerusha 199 John 405 Joseph Howell 422 Laura (Hallock) 421 Marion Lincoln 422 Mary A. 430 Oliver R. 449 Rev. Mowbray S. 421 Ruth F. 405 Ruth (Mills) 405 Samuel M. 422 Samuel Mowbray 54 420 421
HAMMOND, Frederick S. HISTORY AND GENEALOGIES OF THE HAMMOND FAMILIES IN AMERICA, 405 419 421 422
HAND, J. 455
HANDFORD, Catherine B. (Howell) 281
HANFORD, Catherine B. (Howell) 136 459 Theodore 459
HANNION, Catherine 135 David 135 Elizabeth (Shaw) 135
HANSEN, Peter Henry 437
HARRIS, Elthena 60 Dr. Gale I. iv
HARRIS, Gale I., "HARWOOD OR HARRUD FAMILY OF BOSTON, NEW LONDON, WARWICK, AND SOUTHOLD", 1 2
HARRISON, Samuel 331
HARRUD, Elizabeth 1 Elizabeth (Cooke) 2 George 3 Job 3 John 1 2
HARTMAN, Isadora 498
HARWOOD, John 1 2

HASBROUCK, Charles B. 463 Jane 463 Mary C. 463
HASBROUCK, Kenneth E., DEATH NOTICES | From the Scrapbook of ' | ELMIRAH FREER | Born 1820, 138 287
HASTINGS, Sarah W. 433 Sidney 221
HATCH, Peter Holt 324
HATHORN, Major John 73
HAUGHINS, Hannah (Howell) 5
HAVENS, Betsey (Raynor) 414 Daniel Tuthill 414 Delia (Howell) Smith 512 Mary J. 414 Mr. 512 Reid 512
HAVENS, Barrington S., THE MOORES OF SOUTHOLD, 134
HAWKES, Amanda N. (Frink) 40 511
HAWKES, Amanda N. (Frink), and Ella Elizabeth (Howell) Pyle, Supplement to James Barnaby Howell's HOWELL GENEALOGY, 107 221 361 363 510 512 513
HAWKINGS, Zachary 5
HAWKINS, Angelina 190 Azariah Franklin 259 Benjamin 260 Bertha 511 Caroline 262 Catherine 260 Celia (Blydenburg) 254 Charity (Howell) 190 Clarissa A. 191 Delia 190 Deliverance (Tuthill) 260 Edna C. 191 Eleazer 10 Eleazor 9 Eliza (Hammond) 259 Ernest 115 Gershom 121 Hannah (Brigard) 121 Hannah (Howell) 9 10 Israel 190 James 262 Jane E. 244 Jerusha Ann (Rogers) 244 John Sheperd 191 Jonas 50 Joseph 8 13 Mary 121 Mary (Bayles) 262 Mary (Biggs) 9 Phebe 244 Phebe (Brush) 190 Rachel (Rose) 244 Samuel Atwood 259 Samuel Conklin 244 Selah 244 Silas

HOWELL (cont.) -

Benjamin *(250)* 106 210 212 215 216 217 359 Benjamin *(573)* 205 206 350 351 Benjamin F. *(771)* 274 445 446 Benjamin Franklin *(1121)* 408 409 Benjamin Franklin *(1223)* 446

Bernice Evelyn *(1281)* 480

Bertha *(1255)* 465 Bertha *(1352)* 514 Bertha E. *(1279)* 477 Bertha J. *(Tyler)* 427 Bertha Marinda *(1206)* 438 Bertha M. *(Goff)* 509

Bethia *(97)* 44 109 Bethia *(263)* 112 226 227 Bethia *(326)* 131 132 Bethia *(Howell)* 109 Bethia *(Reeve)* 44 56 108 109 Bethia *(Wines)* 188

Bethiah *(120)* 59 135 Bethiah *(260)* 108 Bethiah *(Downs)* 93 199 Bethiah *(Howell)* 56 130 132 133 Bethiah *(Wines)* 187

Betsey *(108)* 54 55 119 Betsey *(324)* 274 Betsey *(495)* 187 323 Betsey *(583)* 215 356 Betsey *(611)* 220 370 Betsey *(694)* 242 Betsey *(McCall)* 223 224 377 378 379 380 381 Betsey *(Wells)* 242 Betsey Jane *(780)* 276 453 Betsey Urania *(638)* 224 380

Betsy *(324)* 131 132 Betsy *(Corwin)* 382

Boadicea *(143)* 69 70 150

Bon *(485)* 181

Brainard *(810)* 288 463

Brown *(314)* 262 263

Buckley *(606)* 368

Buel *(578)* 215

Burton *(1137)* 414

Byron *(1027)* 373 516

C. Louise *(Downs)* 528

C. Merrill 266 437

Cadwalader *(187)* 82 178 179 320 321 322

Capt. Richard *(21)* 33

Carey J. *(1012)* 367

Carey J. *(1019)* 369

Carman B. *(1184)* 433

Carmelete W. *(1069)* 394

Caroline *(626)* 223 Caroline *(910)* 339 Caroline *(Halsey)* 418 Caroline *(Hawkins)* 263 433 434 Caroline Amanda *(1163)* 425 Caroline E. 334 490 Caroline Louise *(1210)* 442

Carrie *(1163)* 424 Carrie *(1238)* 450 451 Carrie A. *(873)* 314 Carrie Lee *(1074)* 394 537 Carrie Louise *(Hill)* 481 Carrie M. *(1130)* 411 Carrie P. *(881)* 320 429

Catherine *(201)* 84 Catherine *(311)* 126 259 Catherine *(343)* 137 284 Catherine *(740)* 261 429 Catherine *(798)* 282 283 460 461 Catherine *(Hannion)* 135 136 Catherine *(Hennion)* 280 281 282 283 284 285 286 Catherine *(Tuthill)* 488 489 Catherine *(Wood)* 178 179 320 322 Catherine *(Youngs)* 55 125 126 256 258 259 261 262 264 265 266 269 Catherine B. *(795)* 281 459 Catherine Jane *(961)* 348 503

Caty *(Youngs)* 125 127

Cecil *(Korn)* 495

Cecilla M. *(1117)* 408

Celah *(752)* 433

Charity *(?)* 148 214 Charity *(106)* 51 118 Charity *(211)* 86 190 Charity *(232)* 93 102 Charity *(242)* 102 Charity *(292)* 116 Charity *(496)* 187 Charity *(518)* 189 Charity *(Davis)* 197 333 334 335 336 337 Charity *(Mather)* 101 102 204 Charity *(Youngs)* 207 Charity J. *(647)* 231 385

Charles *(293)* 118 240 241 405 406 407 Charles *(385)* 146 Charles

HOWELL (cont.) -
(484) 181 Charles *(565)* 206
Charles *(567)* 205 206 349
Charles *(666)* 235 396 397 537
538 539 Charles *(700)* 242
Charles *(753)* 263 Charles *(768)*
273 Charles *(807)* 287 462 463
Charles *(Longbottom)* 137
Charles B. *(399)* 301 304
Charles C. *(914)* 339 Charles E.
(768) 274 444 Charles E.
(1076) 397 537 538 Charles
Ezra *(847)* 145 299 469 Charles
Franklin *(1245)* 457 Charles H.
(817) 292 465 Charles H.
(1146) 414 415 Halsey *(1366)*
521 Charles Hamilton *(1047)*
384 385 521 522 Charles Henry
257 Charles Henry *(1043)* 382
519 Charles Henry *(1168)* 428
Charles Manley *(700)* 243 414
Charles Ransom *(643)* 227 228
381 382 519 520 Charles Reeve
(690) 241 Charles W. *(1133)*
412 Charles Wickham *(1230)*
449
Charlotte *(296)* 118 Charlotte *(346)*
137 286 Charlotte *(688)* 241
406 407 Charlotte *(1166)* 407
Charlotte A. *(Petty)* 407
Chauncey G. *(170)* 77 171 Chauncey
Vail *(1199)* 437 Chauncey
Perkins *(356)* 140 141 290 291
464
Chauncy *(479)* 178 179 321 Chauncy
(570) 205 206 350 351 Chauncy
L. *(911)* 339 492 493
Chester Everts *(864)* 311 474 475
476 Chester Everts, Jr.
(1277) 476 Chester Reno *(1266)*
468
Christian *(262)* 43
Christiana *(976)* 211 352 353 506
Christianna *(262)* 108 225
Christina C. *(439)* 168
Christine C. *(439)* 315

Clara A. *(824)* 294 466 Clara B. 406
Clara M. *(Shepard)* 499 Clara
Wells 522
Clarisa *(255)* 107 221 Clarisa
(622) 223 375 376 Clarisa
(Kingsley) 369
Clarissa *(334)* 133 280 Clarissa *(640)*
225 Clarissa Agard *(165)* 165
Claude Alton *(1321)* 499
Clinton *(917)* 339
Clydia Amanda *(1202)* 437
Coe 81 Coe *(192)* 82 181 182 Coe
(487) 181 323 Coe Sayer *(180)*
28 79 174 175 176 177 318 319
Cora *(?)* 500 Cora *(1212)* 443 Cora
Bell *(1135)* 413 Cora M. *(875)*
314 480
Cordelia *(945)* 343 500
Cornelia *(?)* 308 309 Cornelia *(462)*
174 Cornelia *(1102)* 403 404
Cornelia *(More)* 307 308 471 472
Cynthia *(119)* 56 130 133 Cynthia
(596) 218 362 Cynthia
(Sherman) 399 540 Cynthia Ann
493
Cyrena P. *(Samsel)* 499
Cyrus Fancher *(710)* 247 248 418
Cyrus Lyman *(1103)* 403 404
Daniel *(36)* 17 18 41 44 45 75 109
112 Daniel *(113)* 52 53 54 55
122 127 128 270 271 Daniel
(118) 43 56 130 132 133 280
Daniel *(169)* 77 170 171 Daniel
(264) 112 227 228 381 382
Daniel *(301)* 124 Daniel *(333)*
133 280 Daniel *(376)* 144 145
Daniel *(504)* 188 326 327 354
484 487 488 489 490 Daniel
(620) 223 375 Daniel *(728)* 255
Daniel B. *(754)* 263 434 Daniel
Brown *(314)* 126 262 263
433 434 Daniel Elias *(728)* 256
426 Daniel Everts *(423)* 165
310 311 473 474 475 Daniel
Griffing *(646)* 231 383 384 385
521 523 524 Daniel Halsey

HOWELL (cont.) -
(1042) 382 383 520 521 Daniel
T. (546) 201 202 Daniel
Warner (1234) 450 Daniel
Youngs (733) 257
Darius (364) 142 143 292 295
David 12 David (4) 4 5 6 7 10 11 12
13 15 16 19 26 27 30 31 33 35
David (17) 11 27 28 29 31 35
66 68 70 72 74 75 77 80 81 82
109 David (52) 29 David (55)
28 29 68 69 145 146 147 148
149 150 201 202 David (89) 35
David (134) 66 142 292 293
295 David (136) 69 145 146
298 299 David (214) 87 88 192
193 194 195 273 331 332 333
David (234) 98 99 200 David
(341) 136 282 283 285 David
(406) 150 David (555) 203
David Porter (527) 192 194
David Porter (770) 274 444 445
David Van Ness (390) 145 146
298 299 300 David Wells (577)
207 211 212 353 509
Davis (290) 116 Davis (364) 292
Davis (689) 241 Davis (769)
273
De Witt (884) 321 De Witt (943) 342
499 500
Deanna (?) 148
Deborah (?) 36 38 39 Deborah (25)
15 35 Deborah (51) 29 Deborah
(67) 28 30 82 Deborah (113) 54
55 128 Deborah (245) 104 208
Deborah (Conkling) 44 Deborah
(Jagger) 210 Deborah
(Ketchum) 363 Deborah (Reeve)
241 405 406 407 Deborah
(Reeve?) 15 37 Deborah
(Satterly) 27 29 66 68 70
Deborah Ann (686) 241 405
Deborah Roe (317) 127 264
Debrah (?) 14
Delia (988) 361 512 Delia
(Olmstead) 510 512 513 Delia

(Olmsted) 361
Delilah (438) 167 168 Delilah
(Brown) 167 315 Delilah
(Rutledge) 295 468
Della (?) 493
Delora (1204) 438
Dency Maria (Youngs) 389 390 527
Desire (229) 93
Dora (1247) 459
Dorothy (9) 4 6 19 20 Dorothy (28)
16 38 Dorothy (283) 113 114
Dorothy Ella (Bowser) 498
Dr. George (447) 481
Dr. O.D. (418) 307 308
Drusilla (1194) 437
Earl E. (1263) 467
Earnest (1162) 424 Earnest Augusta
(271) 112 233
Ebenezer (273) 113 234 235 392 394
395 396 398 Ebenezer (667)
235
Edgar F. (1129) 411
Edith (1340) 509 Edith (Lent) 282
Dorothy (1375) 526 Edith
Louese (1275) 476 Edith Miller
(1371) 525
Edlia (?) 321
Edmund (81) 34 91 92 93 101 197
199 Edmund F. (1120) 408
Edmund H. (691) 241 242 407
Edmund Sylvanus (1198) 437
Edmund W. (396) 149 301 302
470 Edmund Wheeler (318) 55
127 266 267 268 436 438 440
Edna Jane (651) 233 Edna Jane (659)
233 392 Edna Pearl (1320) 499
Edward 12 418 Edward (405) 150
Edward (855) 307 Edward
Lewis (1175) 430 431 Edward
S. (1139) 414 Edward Young
(330) 131 132 278 457
Edwin (595) 218 Edwin (599) 219
363 Edwin (711) 248 Edwin
(993) 363 Edwin Ben (855) 308
473 Edwin Herbert (1363) 519
520

HOWELL (cont.) -
Edwina Brown *(1232)* 449
Egbert J. *(775)* 275 447
Elbert *(190)* 82 180 322 323 Elbert
    Richard *(765)* 269 270 441 442
Elden Willis 51 437
Eleanor *(580)* 215 Eleanor *(890)* 327
    484 Eleanor *(Luce)* 214 215 326
    354 355 356 357 358 Eleanor
    (Webb) 76 172 Ann *(402)* 147
    150 304 Eleanor Ann *(452)* 173
    Eleanor Luetta *(588)* 215
    Eleanor Maude *(1231)* 448 449
Electa Amelia *(698)* 243 413 Electa
    H. *(893)* 327 489
Eli *(50)* 26 27 65 66 141 142 144
    (135) 66 144 145 295 296 297
    Eli John *(366)* 143 Eli
    Woodhull *(332)* 131 132 279
    457
Elias Willis *(757)* 51 55 267 268 436
    437 Elias Willis *(1193)* 437
Elihu McCall *(632)* 224 Elihu Platt
    (736) 257
Elijah *(132)* 65
Eliot *(181)* 79
Elisha *(131)* 65 Elisha *(728)* 255
    Elisha K. *(357)* 141 251 252
    465 466
Eliza *(11)* 4 Eliza *(163)* 74 Eliza
    (315) 126 Eliza *(349)* 138 287
    Eliza *(393)* 149 300 Eliza *(513)*
    189 330 Eliza *(1018)* 369 Eliza
    (Wygant) 329 Eliza Ann *(435)*
    167 Eliza Ann *(564)* 205 346
Elizabeth *(?)* 5 6 Elizabeth *(11)* 6
    Elizabeth *(44)* 26 56 Elizabeth
    (79) 34 90 Elizabeth *(108)* 54
    55 119 Elizabeth *(216)* 89 195
    Elizabeth *(216)* 89 195
    Elizabeth *(240)* 101 203
    Elizabeth *(275)* 113 114
    Elizabeth *(337)* 136 280
    Elizabeth *(368)* 142 143
    Elizabeth *(386)* 146 Elizabeth
    (436) 167 Elizabeth *(481)* 179

322 Elizabeth *(482)* 181 322
Elizabeth *(492)* 184 Elizabeth
(532) 197 333 Elizabeth *(628)*
223 377 Elizabeth *(694)* 243
409 Elizabeth *(784)* 277
Elizabeth *(802)* 285 461
Elizabeth *(816)* 291 464 465
Elizabeth *(Brown)* 59 Elizabeth
(Cooke) Harrud 2 3 6 16
Elizabeth *(Corwin)* 382 519 520
Elizabeth *(Dimon)* 49 113
Elizabeth *(Hager)* 313 477 478
479 Elizabeth *(Hallock)* 131 132
273 274 276 278 279 331
Elizabeth *(Hammond)* 189 330
Elizabeth *(Horton)* 204 344 346
347 349 350 351 Elizabeth
(Hurtin) 126 Elizabeth
(Johnson) 396 398 Elizabeth
(Johnston) 235 Elizabeth *(Jones)*
375 Elizabeth *(Kent)* 419
Elizabeth *(Mapes)* 145 146 298
299 Elizabeth *(Sherrill)* 26 55
57 60 61 63 65 Elizabeth
(Smith) 186 187 323 324
Elizabeth *(Tuthill)* 34 89 90 91
93 95 97 100 101 195 196
Elizabeth *(Wakeman)* 412
Elizabeth *(Wells)* 242 243 408
409 410 411 413 414 415
Elizabeth A. *(358)* 141 142
Elizabeth Barter *(Woolston)* 490
491 Elizabeth C. *(636)* 224 379
Elizabeth Delia *(Olmsted)* 361
Elizabeth J. *(Weeden)* 150 304
305
Ella *(822)* 292 293 Ella *(Slocum)* 462
Ella Elizabeth *(1032)* 378 518
Ella Louise *(1217)* 446 Ella M.
(1261) 467 Ella T. *(845)* 298
299
Ellen *(374)* 142 143 Ellen *(456)* 172
173 Ellen Adelaide *(1062)* 390
527 Ellen E. *(1322)* 498 500
Ellen Florette *(374)* 144 Ellen
L. *(997)*

HOWELL (cont.) -
475 Helen Louisa *(1007)* 366
367 Helen P. *(Skidmore)* 508
Hellen Amanda *(960)* 348 503 Hellen
Belle *(Coleman)* 502 503 504
505
Helotus R. *(998)* 364
Helyn H. (?) *(850)* 302
Henrietta *(979)* 211 352 353 507
Henrietta D. *(Penny)* 454 455
Henrietta M. *(920)* 340
Henry *(172)* 77 172 Henry *(205)* 85
185 Henry *(493)* 185 Henry
(514) 189 Henry *(605)* 219 367
Henry *(639)* 224 381 Henry C.
(866) 313 477 Henry F. *(1077)*
397 538 Henry G. *(885)* 324
Henry G. *(1048)* Henry
Harrison *(892)* 214 326 327 488
489 Henry Josiah *(980)* 352 353
508 Henry Leo *(1357)* 515
Henry O. *(921)* 340 493 Henry
Partridge *(860)* 309 Henry W.
(799) 282 283 Henry W. *(1134)*
412
Hepsebe *(151)* 71
Hepzibah *(151)* 72 159
Herbert *(1348)* 514 Herbert Halsey
(1367) 522 Herbert Wells *(981)*
354 509
Herseba *(1010)* 367
Hester Ann (?) 135 281 458 459 460
Hester *(809)* 288 463
Hetty *(568)* 205 349 350 Hetty
(Jagger) 443 Hetty *(Wines)* 225
Hiram *(410)* 155 156 Hiram
Benjamin *(535)* 197 335 Hiram
C. *(922)* 340 Hiram C. *(1225)*
447 448 Hiram F. *(776)* 275
425 448 449 485
Holland S. *(990)* 361 513
Homer Theron *(1041)* 381
Hopping *(56)* 29
Horace *(171)*77
Howard S. *(1054)* 387
Howell *(1304)* 495

Hubbard *(335)* 133 280 Hubbard
Corwin *(1222)* 446
Huldah *(494)* 187 Huldah *(530)* 194
Huldah *(Albertson)* 410 411
Huldah *(Hallock)* 216 217 359
Huldah Maria *(590)* 217
Hunting *(56)* 29
Huntting *(177)* 79 173 318
Hyleasa *(679)* 238
I.M. *(419)* 309
Ida B. *(867)* 313 477 Ida E. *(1051)*
387 Ida Marion *(962)* 348 504
Ida Sarah *(Ware)* 543
Inez *(1295)* 492
Iola *(Cole)* 294 467
Ira Victor *(1205)* 438
Irael *(75)* 87
Irene Alveria *(1386)* 533 Irene Mary
(1317) 498 Irene P. *(1070)* 533
Irene W. *(1080)* 397
Isaac *(7)* 4 5 6 7 16 17 18 40 41 44
45 106 *(32)* 17 40 106 107
Isaac *(95)* 40 106 107 217 218
219 220 221 222 223 Isaac
(252) 107 218 361 362 363 364
365 Isaac *(299)* 124 Isaac *(344)*
136 137 282 283 285 461 Isaac
(597) 219 363 Isaac *(678)* 238
402 403 Isaac Conklin *(746)*
261 Isaac M. *(419)* 159 160 308
Isaac N. *(991)* 361 513 Isaac
Reeve(s) *(110)* 52 53 54 55 121
122 123 124 245 246 247 248
251 252 255 Isaac Reeve(s)
(304) 123 124 247 415 417 418
419 423 Isaac Reeve(s) *(702)*
247 415 416 419 420 Isaac T.
(781) 277 454 455 Isaac
Westbrook *(957)* 346
Isabel *(Robinson)* 485 Isabel
(Swartwood) 309
Isabell *(Bannister)* 540 Isabell
(Robinson) 451
Isabella *(Robinson)* 450 Isabella
Borland *(469)* 174 175 176 319
Isaiah *(71)* 31 83 183 Isaiah *(672)*

HOWELL (cont.) -
237
Israel *(20)* 11 12 31 32 84 86 88
Israel *(75)* 32 86 87 88 191 192
194 Israel *(522)* 194 195 331
Israel *(1086)* 399 400 540
J. Addison *(741)* 430 J. Merritt *(416)*
155 J. Mitchell *(699)* 243 413
J. Warren *(637)* 380
Jack 11
Jacob *(8)* 4 5 6 7 11 16 18 19 48 49
Jacob *(40)* 19 49 113 Jacob
(102) 49 113 236 237 238 239
Jacob *(230)* 93 Jacob *(258)* 107
223 224 377 378 379 380 381
Jacob *(281)* 113 237 399 400
401 402 403 404 Jacob *(676)*
238 401 Jacob Warren *(637)*
224 379 380
James *(22)* 11 12 35 James *(111)* iv
8 52 54 55 122 124 125 126
127 256 258 259 261 262 264
265 266 269 442 James *(123)*
61 James *(139)* 70 147 148
James *(165)* 77 168 316 James
(241) 102 James *(312)* 126 260
261 429 430 431 432 James
(342) 136 282 283 285 James
(506) 188 James *(725)* 255 256
James *(793)* 136 281 458 James
(968) 350 James Addison *(741)*
261 430 James Allen *(849)* 302
470 471 James B. *(738)* 257
James Barnaby *(633)* 224 377
378 518 James Benjamin *(738)*
257 428 James Bowen *(1000)*
366 James Brown *(238)* 99 203
338 339 340 342 343 James C.
(941) 342 497 498 James Clair
(937) 341 494 495 James
Elwood *(954)* 345 James H.
(401) 150 James Oliver *(764)*
269 270 441 James Peter *(552)*
203 340 341 494 James R.
(918) 340 James R. *(1033)* 380
James W. 495 James William

(1305) 495 James William
(1318) 498
Jane *(?)* 282 461 Jane *(194)* 82 182
Jane *(397)* 149 302 Jane *(624)*
223 376 Jane *(938)* 341 Jane
(Beardsley) 285 Jane *(Chatfield)*
79 173 174 176 177 Jane
(Jennings) 389 Jane *(Moffat)*
159 160 306 308 Jane *(Rickard)*
480 Jane A. *(372)* 143 Jane C.
(184) 79 Jane Dunning *(443)*
170 Jane Elizabeth *(407)* 147
150 305 Jane G. *(Orcutt)* 302
470
Janet *(Preswick)* 475
Jannie *(961)* 348 Jannie H. *(Griffith)*
497
Jason *(236)* 98 99 200 201 202 338
Jefferson *(387)* 146
Jeffree *(147)* 71
Jeffrey *(147)* 72 154 155 156 158
305 Jeffrey *(414)* 155 156
Jemima *(?)* 278 Jemima *(14)* 8 9 23
Jemima *(61)* 28 29 75 109
Jemima *(158)* 74 163 Jemima
(267) 112 229 Jemima *(579)*
215 326 354 Jemima *(Benjamin)*
384 Jemima *(Corwin)* 154 155
156 305 Jemima *(Howell)* 75
111 112 214 226 227 229 230
232 234 484 Jemima *(Jennings)*
140 289 Jemima *(Smith)* 322
323 Jemima Amanda *(Benjamin)*
385 521 523 524 Jemima Luce
(Howell) 327 487 488 489 490
Jennie *(1182)* 432 Jennie *(Armstrong)*
512 Jennie *(Preswick)* 475
Jennie Kirk *(861)* 309 312
Jeremiah *(46)* 26 60 61 135 137
Jeremiah *(121)* 61 135 136 280
281 282 283 284 285 286
Jeremiah *(160)* 74 163 164 165
166 309 310 311 312 Jeremiah
(338) 136
Jerome *(804)* 285 462
Jeromus *(444)* 170

HOWELL (cont.) -

Jesse *(488)* 184 Jesse *(1183)* 432 Jesse A. *(1294)* 492 Jesse E. *(1262)* 467 Jesse H. *(1171)* 429 Jesse L. *(1126)* Jesse S. *(739)* 257 427 428

Jessie *(801)* 283 Jessie Adelia *(1402)* 541 Jessie Everts *(1274)* 476

Joanna *(82)* 34 93 Joanna *(138)* 69 70 147 Joanna *(287)* 114 Joanna *(465)* 176 Joanna *(Warner)* 353 Joanna *(Wells)* 194 273 331 332 333

Job Tuthill *(476)* 177 178 319

Joel Conklin *(720)* 249 250 424 449 Joel Ernest *(1162)* 425

Johannah *(287)* 113 Johannah *(Wells)* 193

John *(?)* 23 John *(0)* iii 99 203 John *(2)* 4 5 6 7 8 13 15 16 18 21 22 23 25 27 35 John *(12)* 8 21 22 23 50 51 John *(41)* 22 50 51 53 55 115 116 118 John *(49)* 26 27 56 63 64 131 138 139 John *(57)* 28 29 70 71 72 151 152 153 154 156 158 159 John *(105)* 51 55 116 117 118 122 240 242 243 244 John *(122)* 61 137 138 286 287 462 463 John *(128)* 65 John *(133)* 66 141 291 John *(149)* 71 72 158 159 John *(168)* 77 170 171 317 John *(176)* 79 173 John *(195)* 82 183 John *(219)* 89 John *(239)* 100 John *(294)* 118 242 243 408 409 410 411 412 413 414 415 John *(339)* 135 136 281 458 459 460 John *(400)* 149 304 John *(561)* 205 344 345 501 John *(786)* 278 John *(794)* 136 281 458 459 John *(909)* 339 John *(1140)* 414 John A. *(779)* 276 453 John Abner *(984)* 354 John B. *(434)* 167 John Brainard *(350)* 137 138 286 287 288 463 John D. *(1063)* 391 528 John Davis *(533)* 197 334 490 John DeWitt *(1233)* 450 John Dickerson *(1170)* 429 John E. *(449)* 171 317 John Egbert *(775)* 275 447 448 John Franklin *(652)* 233 243 388 389 409 410 525 526 John H. *(325)* 131 132 274 275 447 448 450 451 John H. *(661)* 235 394 John L. *(680)* 238 403 John LeRoy *(389)* 1056 John Meritt *(416)* 155 156 John Raymond *(1377)* 528 John Smith *(499)* 187 324 John Wesley *(360)* 141 142 John William *(1328)* 504 John William *(1332)* 505

Jonah *(749)* 262

Jonathan *(5)* 4 5 6 7 8 12 13 14 23 32 Jonathan *(15)* 8 9 25 26 55 57 60 61 63 65 Jonathan *(43)* 26 55 56 63 109 130 131 132 133 Jonathan *(103)* 49 Jonathan *(104)* 51 54 115 116 240 Jonathan *(117)* 56 130 131 132 273 274 276 278 279 331 Jonathan *(274)* 113 114 235 236 237 238 239 Jonathan *(685)* 236 238 Jonathan D. *(769)* 274 444 Jonathan Davis *(323)* 131 132 273 274 331 332 443 444 445 447

Joseph *(100)* 45 110 112 113 234 Joseph *(207)* 86 186 187 188 323 324 Joseph *(272)* 113 Joseph *(1021)* 372 Joseph *(1026)* 373 Joseph *(1067)* 394 531 Joseph *(1330)* 504 Joseph B. *(142)* 69 70 149 179 304 305 Joseph Benjamin *(497)* 187 Joseph Benton *(409)* 150 305 Joseph Chauncey *(653)* 233 389 390 527 Joseph Marthers *(660)* 235 392 393 529 530 531 534 535 537 Joseph N. *(729)* 257 426 427 Joseph Raynor *(703)* 248 417 418

HOWELL (cont.) -
Josephine *(?)* 434 478 Josephine *(Johnson)* 478
Joshua *(220)* 89 Joshua *(282)* 113 236 238 Joshua M. *(655)* 232 233 391 528
Josiah *(140)* 69 70 148 149 300 302 303 304 Josiah *(575)* 207 211 352 353 506 507 508 Josiah *(749)* 262
Judson P. *(1125)* 409
Julia *(?)* 318 Julia *(200)* 84 Julia *(508)* 188 327 328 Julia *(558)* 203 343 Julia *(601)* 219 364 Julia *(936)* 341 Julia Ann *(Mapes)* 299 469 Julia Ann *(Tuthill)* 279 457
Juliaett *(461)* 174
Juliet *(183)* 79 177
Juliette *(471)* 177 178 Juliette *(591)* 217 359 Juliette *(669)* 235
Junius Franklin *(1203)* 438
Justin *(985)* 354
Katherine *(1100)* 403 Katherine Jane *(Fanning)* 508
Katie J. *(Fanning)* 508
Katurah *(231)* 93
Kearney Ferdinand *(1380)* 532
Keziah *(85)* 34 100
Kristine *(1376)* 526
Lafayette S. *(1315)* 498
Laura *(509)* 189 328 Laura *(1153)* 419 Laura *(1334)* 505 Laura *(Pierce)* 441 Laura M. *(1312)* 497
Lavinia *(543)* 201 202
Leah *(Sargent)* 509
Leander P. *(352)* 140 Leander Young *(354)* 141 290
LeGrand Whipple *(1284)* 481
Leigh Hawkins *(1360)*516
Lelia *(?)* 350
Lena Belle *(1333)* 505
Leolin *(1149)* 414 415
Leone *(1378)* 528
LeRòy E. *(1327)* 504

Levi *(460)* 174 Levi L. *(878)* 317 480
Lewis *(415)* 155 156 Lewis A. *(837)* 297 Lewis E. *(1175)* 430
Lida *(Hubbard)* 471
Lilian *(1237)* 450 451
Lillian *(1345)* 509 Lillian M. *(1265)* 468 Lillian May *(1165)* 426
Lillie *(832)* 295 Lillie *(1161)* 424 Lillie E. *(?)* 415
Linsey *(811)* 288
Liza *(1260)* 294
Lizzie *(1260)* 467
Lloyd *(805)* 285
Lois *(137)* 69 146 Lois Maria *(383)* 145 146
Lottie *(?)* 504 Lottie *(903)* 337 491 Lottie M. *(1300)* 494
Louese *(Hunter)* 474
Louisa *(?)* 494 Louisa *(569)* 205 206 349 350 Louisa *(1173)* 430 Louisa *(Dewey)* 378 518 Louisa *(King)* 391 Louisa *(Terrell)* 260 261 429 430 431 432 Louisa A. *(Corwin)* 527
Louise *(523)* 194 273 331 Louise *(Eastland)* 514 Louise *(Howell)* 274 331 443 444 445 447
Lucetta Priscilla *(889)* 325 326 483
Lucia H. *(1104)* 404
Lucinda *(153)* 73 160 Lucinda *(322)* 55 129 273 Lucinda M. *(925)* 340 Lucinda N. *(Bigelow)* 292 293
Lucretia *(174)* 79 177 Lucretia Jane *(Jennings)* 388 389 525 526 Lucretia *(Reynolds)* 498
Lucy *(868)* 313 478 Lucy Ann *(722)* 249 250 Lucy Ann *(Mapes)* 502 Lucy B. *(?)* 283 Lucy Corwin *(812)* 290 Lucy H. *(1104)* 403 Lucy *(Rowland)* 314 479 480
Luiza *(569)* 350
Lulu M. *(Carr)* 499
Luther *(511)* 189 330 Luther Clark *(427)* 165 166 312

HOWELL (cont.) -

Lydia *(?)* 113 Lydia *(65)* 28 30 80 Lydia *(196)* 82 183 Lydia *(279)* 113 114 Lydia *(348)* 137 138 286 462 Lydia *(858)* 308 309 Lydia *(1112)* 406 Lydia *(Allison)* 201 202 338 Lydia *(Case)* 29 72 74 75 78 109 Lydia *(Conklin)* 249 250 424 425 Lydia *(Coomer)* 339 491 493 Lydia *(Howell)* 113 236 237 238 239 Lydia Arilla *(1400)* 541 Lydia C. *(718)* 250 Lydia C. *(1161)* 425 449 Lydia Maria *(1055)* 389 525 Lydia Marie *(657)* 233

Lyle Percy *(1336)* 506

M.L. 144

Mabel *(1343)* 509 Mabel *(Fosdick)* Mabel E. *(1242)* 455

Madeline A. *(1285)* 481

Major John *(168)* 171

Mandana *(433)* 167 315

Mandy *(572)* 205 350

Margaret *(?)* ii 7 324 469 Margaret *(39)* 19 48 Margaret *(47)* 26 61 Margaret *(277)* 113 114 236 Margaret *(450)* 172 173 Margaret *(490)* 184 Margaret *(675)* 237 400 Margaret *(796)* 281 Margaret *(Parshall)* 11 19 48 49 Margaret *(Reeve?)* 21

Margaretta C. *(796)* 459

Maria *(?)* 379 Maria *(327)* 131 132 Maria *(Raynor)* 355 Maria *(Rockwell)* 363 Maria Amelia *(534)* 197 335 Maria A. *(1259)* 467 Maria Antoinette *(1079)* 397 Maria E. *(603)* 219 365 Maria J. *(783)* 277 456 Maria Lovitia *(1001)* 366 Maria W. *(Philips)* 397 537 538 539

Mariah *(563)* 205 346

Marian D. *(?)* 297

Marianne *(635)* 224 379 518

Marie Antoinette *(1079)* 538 539

Marie Rose *(Pacaud)* 393 529 530 531 533 534 535 537

Marietta *(Decker)* 345 Marietta *(Young)* 290 291 464

Marinda Ann *(894)* 327 490

Marion *(683)* 238 Marion *(853)* 308 471 Marion *(1373)* 525 Marion D. *(?)* 297 Marion Rachel Elizabeth *(Connor)* 310 476

Marquis *(880)* 318

Mariet(t) *(Decker)* 345 501

Martha *(544)* 202 Martha *(1014)* 367 Martha *(Ben jamin)* 117 118 240 242 243 244 Martha *(Horton)* 59 135 Martha *(Penny)* 443 444 Martha *(Stephens)* 127 128 270 Martha Ann *(1191)* 436 Martha Bennett *(428)* 166 Martha E. *(1301)* 494 Martha Jane *(Rigby)* 436 Martha Louisa *(408)* 150 305 Martha Louise *(1365)* 521 Martha W. *(1226)* 447 448

Martin *(682)* 238 404 Martin Eugene *(1081)* 539

Mary *(?)* 11 103 104 206 208 213

Mary *(?)* Mulford 223 376 377 Mary *(18)* 12 30 31 Mary *(64)* 28 29 Mary *(76)* 32 Mary *(83)* 34 94 Mary *(116)* 52 54 55 Mary *(141)* 69 70 Mary *(189)* 82 179 Mary *(202)* 84 Mary *(203)* 85 184 Mary *(237)* 99 Mary *(280)* 113 114 Mary *(302)* 124 244 Mary *(336)* 133 280 Mary *(422)* 165 166 309 310 Mary *(453)* 173 Mary *(489)* 184 Mary *(539)* 200 Mary *(668)* 396 Mary *(692)* 242 Mary *(712)* 247 Mary *(820)* 292 465 Mary *(929)* 341 Mary *(930)* 341 Mary *(975)* 351 Mary *(992)* 361 513 Mary *(1016)* 368 Mary *(1088)* 400 Mary *(Ben jamin)* 84 85 184 185 186 188 189 190 191 Mary *(Buck)* 294 466 467 Mary

HOWELL (cont.) -
(Brown) 98 99 200 203 Mary
(Curtice) 40 106 Mary *(Dowd)*
98 200 Mary *(Gates)* 143 Mary
(Gaylord) 296 297 468 Mary
(Gould) 337 491 Mary
(Griffing) 231 383 385 386 387
Mary *(Hawkins)* 123 124 245
246 247 248 251 252 255 Mary
(Herrick) 12 Mary *(Homan)* 257
426 427 428 Mary *(Hulp)* 202
Mary *(Jewell)* 298 Mary
(Luther?) 276 Mary *(Murrow)*
28 29 80 81 82 *(Osborn)* 100
204 Mary *(Tuthill)* 177 178
Mary *(Youngs)* 227 228 381
Mary A. *(556)* 203 Mary A.
(1243) Mary A. *(Halsey)* 410
Mary A. *(Hammond)* 430 Mary
A. *(Terry)* 277 Mary Albertson
(645) 231 Mary Amanda *(375)*
144 145 296 Mary Amna *(1023)*
372 Mary Ann *(?)* 350 Mary
Ann *(369)* 143 Mary Ann *(395)*
149 300 Mary Ann *(411)* 156
305 Mary Ann *(712)* 248 418
Mary Ann *(730)* 257 Mary Ann
(853) 307 Mary Ann *(Biggar)*
148 300 302 304 Mary Ann
(Terry) 454 455 456 457 Mary
Arabel *(Emery)* 516 Mary
Augusta *(351)* 140 288 Mary
Augusta *(815)* 291 464 Mary
Bradner *(Tuthill)* 319 Mary
Brainard *(1254)* 463 Mary C.
(Hasbrouck) 463 Mary C.
(Richardson) 380 Mary C.
(Risley) 432 Mary Christie
(1403) 541 Mary Cornelia
(Adams) 495 Mary E. *(787)* 278
Mary E. *(923)* 340 Mary E.
(939) 342 496 Mary E. *(1017)*
369 Mary E. *(1239)* 454 455
Mary E. *(Brown)* 457 Mary E.
(Helms) 498 500 Mary E.
(Reeve) 387 Mary E. *(Strather)*

381 Mary Eleanor *(1127)* 410
Mary Eliot *(983)* 354 Mary
Elizabeth *(958)* 348 502 Mary
· Elizabeth *(1044)* 382 383 Mary
Emma *(1150)* 416 417 Mary F.
(830) 295 Mary Frances *(Jayne)*
428 Mary J. *(1182)* 432 Mary
J. *(Havens)* 414 Mary Jane
(475) 177 178 Mary Jane
(Hulse) 430 431 Mary Jane
(Sanderson) 436 437 Mary Jane
(Shirra) 526 Mary Lovina *(760)*
267 268 438 Mary Marzetta
(1195) 437 Mary Mehetable
(977) 211 352 353 507 Mary
Melissa *(755)* 263 434 Mary O.
(531) 194 Mary Rosaline *(1066)*
394 530 Mary Sarah *(116)* 129
Mary T. *(844)* 298 Mary Teresa
(1236) 451 451 486 Mary W.
(574) 211 351
Maryette *(1004)* 366
Matilda *(877)* 169 316 Matilda C.
(Post) 320 321 481
Matt Arnold *(1385)* 532
Maud *(1257)* 465 Maud I. *(1224)*
447
Meale *(145)* 71
Mehetable *(60)* 29
Meheteble 33
Mehitabel *(228)* 93 199
Mehitable 55 Mehitable *(60)* 28 74
    Mehitable *(155)* 73 162
    Mehitable *(266)* 112 229
    Mehitable *(568)* 206 349
    Mehitable *(Wines)* 225
    Mehitable C. *(973)* 351
    Mehitable Coleman *(965)* 348
Melinda J. *(Young)* 489
Melissa (sic) *(Benjamin)* 275
Mellicent *(145)* 72
Melton B. *(545)* 202
Merit *(92)* 102 Merrit(t) *(92)* 38 104
    105 106 209 210 212 213 215
    216 Merrit(t) *(249)* 14 106 210
    212 214 215 216 326 354 355

HOWELL (cont.) -
356 357 358 Merrit B. *(586)* 215

Mertha *(?)* 538

Micah *(35)* 17 18 33 41 42 43 44 56 84 86 108 109 Micah *(96)* 43 44 108 109 224 225 Micah *(208)* 86 99 109 188 324 325 326 327 328 329 330 354

Micah *(503)* 188 324 325 326 482 483

Michael *(1287)* 488 Michael A. 533 Michael B. *(550)* 203 338 491 493 Michael S. *(940)* 342 496 497

Millicent *(145)* 151 Millicent *(Benjamin)* 275 447 448 450 451

Milly *(224)* 90

Milo *(835)* 297

Mimi *(Demarest)* 182

Mina Ann *(Demarest)* 181

Minnie *(1036)* 380 Minnie *(Thomas)* 532 Minnie Josephine *(1384)* 532 Minnie M. *(Miller)* 525 Minnie P. *(1297)* 493

Minor S. *(1169)* 429

Miriam *(?)* 77 Miriam Augusta *(714)* 247 248 419

Mitchell *(96)* 108 Mitchell *(297)* 118 244 Mitchell *(699)* 242

Moie *(?)* 307

Mordeca *(441)* 169 316

Mortimer *(1220)* 446

Moses *(197)* 83

Mr. John *(12)* 21

Mrs. Chauncey 109

Mrs. Job T. 319

Myra J. *(Hines)* 467

Myron *(994)* 363 Myron *(1091)* 401 402

Myrtie B. *(1311)* 497

Myrtle *(1346)* 510 Myrtle *(1349)* 514 Myrtle Lena *(966)* 348

N.W. *(696)* 412

Nancy *(215)* 193 195 331 Nancy *(251)* 107 217 Nancy *(289)* 116 240 Nancy *(310)* 55 126 258 Nancy *(607)* 220 368 nancy *(Bloomer)* 282 283 460 Nancy *(Newton)* 337 Nancy *(Scullen(s))* 403 404 542 Nancy *(Smith)* 516 517 Nancy *(Young)* 140 288 289 290 Nancy M. *(Carter)* 492

Nathan *(93)* 17 40 106 Nathan S. *(468)* 174 175 176

Nathaniel Milford *(1008)* 366 367 514 Nathaniel Robinson *(1131)* 411 Nathaniel Wells *(696)* 410 411

Nellie *(1158)* 249 424 Nellie Louisa *(1353)* 515 Nellie Rachel *(1382)* 532

Nelson *(571)* 205 206 350 351 Nelson A. *(576)* 212

Nettie Leonora *(1359)* 515 Nettie May *(1347)* 510

Nilbur (sic) *(378)* 296

Noah Buckley *(606)* 219 368

Noble *(66)* 28 30 81 82 178 179 181 182 183

Norman *(1085)* 400

Norton *(291)* 116

Oakley Durland *(869)* 313 478

Olen Joseph *(1406)* 543

Olivan *(Wicks)* 433

Olive Ann *(Wicks)* 433

Oliver *(916)* 339 Oliver P. *(826)* 294 467

Olser D. *(551)* 203 339 340 493 494

Ophelia Ann *(763)* 268 439 440

Ora Annie *(972)* 351

Orlanda J. *(829)* 295

Orrin Day *(418)* 159 160 306 307 471 472

Orson *(1090)* 402

Pamelia *(629)* 224 377 Pamelia *(1013)* 367 Pamelia Irene *(1070)* 394 533

Pansy Elizabeth *(1306)* 495

Parnal(l) *(225)* 93 197

HOWELL (cont.) -

Parshall *(88)* 34 101 102 204 Parshall *(243)* 102 197 204 205 344 346 347 349 350 351 Parshall *(950)* 345 501 502

Parson *(950)* 502

Patience *(247)* 212 Patience *(284)* 113 114 238 Patience *(Bowen)* 366 514 Patience *(Wells)* 37 102 104

Patty *(544)* 201

Paulina *(Rockwell)* 380 Paulina *(Walters)* 504

Pearl Emily *(1307)* 495

Percy *(1379)* 528

Permelia *(144)* 69 70

Perry C. *(833)* 295 468

Peter *(193)* 82 181 182 Peter Chrysler *(1098)* 403

Phebah *(148)* 71

Phebe *(?)* 17 40 41 44 45 55 84 92 93 172 Phebe *(33)* 17 40 Phebe *(148)* 72 156 157 Phebe *(1178)* 431 Phebe *(Barteau)* 129 273 Phebe *(Case)* 379 Phebe *(Gates)* 261 262 432 Phebe *(Youngs)* 228 Phebe Ann *(483)* 181 322 Phebe Ann *(750)* 261 262 432 Phebe Ann *(848)* 145 299 Phebe Huldah *(Carter)* 424 449 Phebe J. *(Watkins)* 288 463 Phebe Phebe (?) Jane *(Dunning)* 173 Phebe Matilda *(Seely)* 541

Phenis *(84)* 98

Philomene Patterson *(1071)* 394 534

Phineas *(84)* 34 97 98 99 200 203 Phineas *(233)* 98 99 200

Phinehas *(84)* 98 Phinehas *(233)* 200

Phoebe A. *(848)* 469 470 Phoebe G. *(673)* 237 400

Phylinda B. *(529)* 194 333

Polly *(116)* 54 55 Polly *(254)* 107 220 Polly *(302)* 123 Polly *(612)* 220 371 Polly *(619)* 223 374 Polly *(Hawkins)* 122 Polly *(Little)* 366 367 368 369 Polly

B. *(Wells)* 232 233 388 389 390 391 392 Polly Lydia *(269)* 112 Polly Maria *(644)* 228 Polly Maria *(888)* 326 483

Porter *(770)* 273

Preston W. *(173)* 77 172

Pricilla Rose *(1381)* 532

Prudence *(Hallock)* 15

Quardilla *(1187)* 434

Rachel *(37)* 18 45 Rachel *(674)* 237 Rachel *(823)* 292 293 Rachel *(Tuthill)* 93 197 Rachel Adeline *(1075)* 394

Ralph *(608)* 220 369 Ralph Millard *(1024)* 372 515 516

Ransom *(643)* 382

Raymond Ware *(1408)* 543

Rebecca *(?)* 255 Rebecca *(831)* 295 Rebecca *(Birdsall)* 458 Rebecca *(Howell)* 269 Rebecca Ann *(Clausen)* 171 317 Rebecca Tuttle *(Homan)* 270 441 443

Recompence *(45)* 26 57 58 59 135

Reeve(s) *(42)* 22 51 52 53 54 55 119 120 121 122 124 127 128 129 Reeve(s) *(298)* 124 Reeve(s) *(313)* 126 261 262 432

Reno *(833)* 295 468

Retus 44

Reuben *(54)* 29

Rhoda *(370)* 142 143 Rhoda *(Corwin)* 100 Rhoda *(McCall)* 374 375 376 Rhoda *(Ross)* 171 Rhoda E. *(828)* 295

Richard 249 Richard *(1)* ii iii iv 1 2 3 4 5 6 7 9 10 12 13 14 16 17 18 19 23 86 99 464 526 Richard *(6)* 4 5 6 7 13 14 15 23 32 35 36 37 38 39 Richard *(21)* 11 12 33 34 90 91 92 93 94 95 97 98 100 101 Richard *(27)* 15 16 23 36 37 38 39 102 104 Richard *(87)* 34 100 203 Richard *(90)* 37 102 103 104 206 208 210 213 Richard *(244)* 103 206 207 210 216 Richard

HOWELL (cont.) -
    D. *(540)* 200 Richard Oakley
    (319) 127 267 269 270 441 443
    Richard S. *(982)* 354
Riley B. *(1105)* 403 404 Riley P.
    (1241) 454 455
Rinelche Hallock *(1158)* 424
Robert D. *(429)* 167 312 313 477
    478 479 Robert Henry *(1383)*
    532 Robert R. *(1368)* 522
Rody *(Corwin)* 100
Roke *(45)* 57
Roland Clair *(1308)* 495
Ronald Lee, Jr., 99 498
Rosa *(821)* 292 466
Rosabella *(?)* 141 291
Rosalie Frances *(1192)* 436
Rosaline V. *(658)* 233 391
Rose E. *(Barber)* 522
Rosetta *(541)* 201 202 Rosetta *(Keen)*
    292 465 466
Roy Sylvester *(1407)* 543
Ruby *(Nichols)* 468
Ruth *(10)* 4 6 Ruth *(53)* 28 29 66
Sadie *(1391)* 538
Salle *(146)* 71
Sally *(154)* 73 161 Sally *(300)* 124
    Sally *(307)* 123 Sally *(584)* 215
    356 357 Sally *(Daugherty)* 151
    153 Sally *(Durland)* 167 312
    313 314 Sally *(Fisk)* 219 220
    369 370 371 372 373 Sally J.
    (553) 203 342
Sampson *(1331)* 505
Samuel *(77)* 33 88 89 195 196
    Samuel *(164)* 74 167 168
    Samuel *(221)* 89 196 197 333
    334 335 336 337 Samuel *(593)*
    218 361 510 512 513 Samuel
    (681) 238 403 404 542 Samuel
    (883) 321 Samuel B. *(969)* 350
    Samuel H. *(164)* 315 Samuel
    Hawkins *(613)* 219 220 371 372
    515 Samuel M. *(851)* 306
Sarah *(?)* 83 183 278 457 Sarah *(26)*
    16 36 Sarah *(101)* 45 Sarah

(146) 72 153 Sarah *(206)* 85
186 Sarah *(248)* 106 209 213
Sarah *(259)* 109 Sarah *(265)*
112 Sarah *(276)* 113 114 Sarah
(424) 165 311 Sarah *(445)* 170
Sarah *(500)* 187 Sarah *(625)*
223 376 Sarah *(721)* 249 250
Sarah *(870)* 313 479 Sarah
(1020) 369 Sarah *(1025)* 373
516 Sarah *(Dougherty)* 71 72
154 156 158 159 Sarah *(Drake)*
183 Sarah *(Hallock)* 31 83 84
Sarah *(Holmes)* 235 392 394
395 Sarah *(Howell)* 209 211
213 351 352 353 Sarah *(Jewell)*
336 Sarah *(Johnson)* 368 Sarah
(Luce) 106 209 212 213 215
Sarah *(Mather)* 112 113 234
Sarah *(Roe)* 108 224 225 Sarah
(Skidmore) 481 Sarah
(Southwick) 465 Sarah *(Stage)*
203 338 339 340 342 343 Sarah
(Swesey) 45 75 109 112 Sarah
(Vail) 267 268 436 438 440
Sarah *(Webster)* 76 168 170 171
172 Sarah A. *(898)* 330 Sarah
A. *(Robinson)* 354 509 Sarah
Adelaide *(Buckingham)* 456
Sarah Amanda *(978)* 211 352
353 Sarah Ann *(307)* 124 252
Sarah Ann *(616)* 220 373 Sarah
Bethiah *(1045)* 382 383 520
Sarah E. *(379)* 144 145 Sarah
Elizabeth *(762)* 267 268 Sarah
Elizabeth *(1152)* 416 417 Sarah
Elizabeth *(Torrey)* 502 Sarah
Ella *(Owen)* 477 Sarah Emily
(451) 172 173 Sarah Emily
(Arthur) 427 Sarah J. 181 Sarah
J. *(486)* 181 323 Sarah J.
(1240) 454 455 Sarah Jane
(413) 155 156 Sarah Jane *(466)*
176 Sarah Jane *(662)* 235 394
395 Sarah Jane *(1064)* 394
Sarah L. *(735)* 257 Sarah L.
(902) 336 Sarah L. *(Skidmore)*

LYNCH, Joseph 431
MACGREGOR, Esther 264
MACY, Elizabeth 345 Harry 227
Hiram 345
MADDRAH, Ida A., Personal
communication, 86 88 191 192
194 195
MADSEN, Faughn 438
MAIN, Ann Eliza (Howell) 377
Wm. H. 377
MALLMANN, Jacob H.,
HISTORICAL PAPERS ON
SHELTER ISLAND AND ITS
PRESBYTERIAN CHURCH,
101 133 184 204 213 215 248
249 250 280 290 291 326 327
354 355 356 357 358 414 424
425 464 484 485 487 488 489
490 508
MALMESBURY, William of ii
MALTBY, Jennie 315
MANN, Horace 221
MANN, Conklin, THE FAMILY OF
CONCKELYNE, CONKLIN AND
CONKLING IN AMERICA,
THE LINE OF JOHN
CONKLYNE OF SOUTHOLD
AND HUNTINGTON, 11
MAPES, Amy 186 Benjamin 186
Edward 147 Elizabeth 145 Elma
186 Eunice 162 Garret Brink
157 Huldah 186 Jabez 4 Jabish
3 John 162 Jonathan 5 Joseph
21 Joshua D. 298 299 Julia Ann
299 Julius 299 469 Lucy Ann
502 Lydia 186 Mary 3 Mary
(Dains) 145 Mehitable (Howell)
162 Nathan 145 Phebe (Beach)
299 Sarah 186 Sarah (Howell)
186 Silas Howell 186 Tabitha
81 Thomas 3 5 William 3 16 18
31 162
MARADUDD, Prince, iii
MARKHAM, Rev. Thomas 537
MARSHALL, Bernice Mae 516
MARTHER, Charity 101 Sarah 113

MARTIN, Clifton Pacaud 535
George Vincent 535 Georgia
Myer (Howell) 535 Henry 535
. Mary (Gautier) 535 Vincent
Albert 535
MATHER, Ebenezer 48 Nathaniel 17
MATHER, Frederic Gregory, THE
REFUGEES OF 1776 FROM LONG
ISLAND TO CONNECTICUT,
33 40 41 42 47 50 51 56 57 62
63 64 68 85 86 88 90 91 95 97
100 108 110 112 118 119 197
MATTHEWS, Mabel 314 Mr. 428
MCCALL, Betsey 223 Helen E. 374
375 Hiram 374 375 Mary J.
374 375 Polly (Howell) 374 375
Rhoda 222 Samuel 374 375
Simeon 375
MCCAMBLY, David 70 71
MCCANTH, Mr. 246
MCCARTHY, Kate 337
MCCARTNEY, Ida Huckleberry 475
Marcia May 475 Marcus 475
MCCORMICK, Edna Blair 543
MCCORN, Mary Jane 161
MCCURDY, Kathleen Marie
(Pollock) 502
MCCURDY, Mr. Larry A. and Mrs.
Kathleen M., Personal
communication, 102 204 205
345 348 349 502
MCDONALD, Andrew 234
MCDOWELL, Alexander 375 Susan
(Howell) 375
MCFADDEN, Alice (Jennings) 509
Henry 509 William E. 509
MCGAHEY, John 136 Maria 136
MCGARRAH, Elizabeth, "Libbie",
Crane 319
MCGONQUER, Helen 369
MCGREGOR, Mr. 505
MCKALYON, Mary 66
MCKENNA, George 510
MCKINNEY, Anna (Allen) 144
Daniel 144 Fannie E. 144
MCKNEY, Grace E. 487 James K.

SAINT JOHN, Abigail 218 Clarissa 218 E. Howell 218 Esther 306 Elijah 217 218 Fanny 218 Myron 218 Nancy 218 Nancy (Howell) 218 Pamelia 218 Philo 218

SAMMIS, Carrie (Howell) 450 451 Jacob H. 451

SAMSEL, Cyrena Pearl 498

SANDERSON, Henry Weeks 436 Lavee 438 Mary Jane 436 Rebecca Ann (Sanders) 436

SANDFORD, Abigail (Jessup) 62 David 62 Jane 62

SANFORD, Grover Merle, THE SANDFORD/SANFORD FAMILIES OF LONG ISLAND, 62

SANFORD, Theodore M., III, 275

SARGENT, Isaac 76 Leah 509

SATERLY, Deb 27

SATTERLY, John 10

SAVINS, Hannah 339

SAXTON, Daniel 53 Urania, "Rena", 167

SCHELLINGER, Lois 40 107

SCHIRRA, Mary Jane 526

SCOTT, Eliza J. 511 Joseph 67 Mary A. (Mullock) 155 Rev. A.B. 155

SCOTT, Dr. Kenneth, GENEALOGICAL DATA FROM ADMINISTRATION PAPERS.., 349

SCRAFFORD, Hiram 306

SCULLEN, Nancy 403

SCULLINGER, 414

SEAL, Zena 530

SEAMAN, Walter S. 396

SEDERLUND, Marjorie (Mrs. William W.) 83 183

SEELY, Clara 151 Ezra 541 Phebe Ann (Pierson) 541 Phebe Matilda 541

SENIER, William 333

SEXTON, Daniel 122

SHAFFER, Flora Berry (Rogers) 510

Harry Irving 510 Nettie May (Howell) 510 Perry Cutler 510

SHAW, Clare Coolbaugh 476 Gladys Mae 476 Jay W. 476 Osborn 51 243 Thomas 16 18

SHAY, Lydia Mathers 129

SHELBOURNE, Vernon E. 530

SHEPARD, Clara Mae 498 Emily (Howell) 501 Laurie B. 501 Proctor J. 500 501 Sussie D. 501

SHEPHERD, Henry 80 Sarah (Fuller) 80

SHERMAN, Cynthia 399 Elvira 540 James 540

SHERRILL, Margaret (Cady) 25 Recompense 25 Sarah (Parsons) 25

SHERRY, Elizabeth 25

SHERWOOD, Grace Lillian (Hammond), Notes, 54 55 121 123 124 127 128 245 246 247 248 249 251 252 255 273 418 419 420 421

SHIPMAN, Christine (Howell) 315 Harvey D. 315 Mr. 168 Myron 315 Ralph 315 Shalor 315 Walter 315

SHIPMAN, Patricia, Personal communication, 168 315

SHIRRA, Christian 526 Elizabeth Dorothea (Lane) 526

SHOEMAKER, Joseph 67

SHUTE, Edward 434

SIMMONS, Sarah 75

SINGLETERY, Mr. 36

SKIDMORE, Charlotte E. (Pettens) 508 Esther Ann (Whipple) 316 Helen P. 508 Luther 316 Sarah L. 316 Theodore 508

SKIDMORE, Warren, THOMAS SKIDMORE (SCUDAMORE), 1605-1684.., 316 317 508

SLIKER, (Richard) Scott 296

SLIKER, Scott, Personal communication, 66 141 144 145

STEVENS (cont.) -
181 182 Mr. 513 Patty 127
STEWART, Charles iii Elizabeth
(Bradner) 174 Frances Amelia
174 John 174 Preston Ray 439
STEWART, Ronald A., Personal
communication, 176 318 319
STICKNEY, Benjamin M. 157 158
STICKNEY (cont,) -
Charles 158 Charles E. 157 Dr.
James 157 Eliphalet 157
Elizabeth 157 Ellen 157 Erastus
155 157 158 Frances R. 155
Francis 155 Hannah 157 Hattie
155 John 157 Julia Ann 157
Lucy R. (Allen) 157 Mary 158
Mary (Belknap) 157 Phebe
(Howell) 157 W.C. 321
STICKNEY, Charles E., THE
HOWELL FAMILY, 28 29 70 74 75
77 78 79 81 82 98 99 147 149
150 151 153 154 157 158 159
168 169 170 171 172 173 174
175 176 177 178 179 181 182
200 201 202 204 304 305 318
319 322 323 338
A HISTORY OF THE MINISINK
REGION, 70 71 151 152 155
158
OLD SUSSEX COUNTY
FAMILIES, 80 81
STOCUM, Mary 310 Phoebe 310
Susan 310
STONE, Clara J. 230 Kay 513
STOW, Eli Henry 511
STRAHAN, John 151
STRONG, Benjamin 52 Captain
Thomas S. 52 Selah 9
STRUBLE, Albert 513
STUART, Charles iii
STUBBLEFIELD, James Jacob 344
STUDLEY, Catherine (Cole) 452
Elbridge 452
SUNSERE, Rose 536
SWANK, Charles 495
SWARTHOUT, Jacob 69

SWARTWOOD, Isabel 309
SWAZEY, John 14
SWAZY, John 14 John, Senr., 3
SWEEZEY, Amelia (Howell) 243
Annie Augusta 244 Electa Jane
244 Elizabeth Elmore 244 John
251 John Warren 244 Moses
243 Stephen Jarvis 243 Warren
243 William Egbert 243 244
William Jarvis 243
SWESEY, Elizabeth 19 John 8
Margaret (Parshall) 19 Richard
19 Sarah 44
SWEZEY, Ann 128 Christopher 128
Daniel Howell 251 252 Eunice
(Howell) 236 238 239 Gershom
Hawkins 251 252 Hannah
(Howell) 251 252 Isaac Reeves
251 252 258 James 251 252
John 251 252 255 258 Jonathan
Howell 239 Julia Stephens 128
Martha (Stephens) Howell 128
Mary A. 251 252 Richard 128
Sarah (Tuthill) 251 William 53
252 258 William Clark 251 252
SWEZEY, C. Eugene, Personal
communication, 251 258
SWIGERT, Ellen (Porter) 497
SWINGLE, Alton W. 297
SYLVESTER, Nathaniel Bartlett,
HISTORY OF ULSTER COUNTY,
60 61 137 138 286 287 462 463
TAFT, Belinda S. 342
TALMADGE, Isaac 172 305 John
M. 155 156 305 306 Mary
(Hurd) 305 Mary Ann (Howell)
155 306
TAYLOR, David 496 Eliza 283
Elizabeth (Brown) 59 Frances
Anna 344 George 59 Jonathan
39 Mary Ann 254
TELEBALL, Elizabeth 45
TERREL, Mr. 245
TERRELL, George Washington 265
Harriet (Hawkins) 265 Louisa
260 Richard Clinton 265

WING, Rev. Hiram 288
WINTRUP, Mr. 21
WISE, Benjamin 174
WISNER, Cpt. Henry 28
WOOD, Capt. 268 Catherine 178
David K. 346 David M.E. 300
Dr. Webster C. 525 Elizabeth
75 Elizabeth (Howell) 461
Emily 304 Erskine 301 John 28
35 68 70 73 Jonathan 75 Lydia
Maria (Howell) 389 526 Mary
172 Mr. 461 Vincent 148
WOODHULL, Charles Edward 358
David 53 Hannah 185 John 102
Josiah 24 85 86 88 Lillian 387
Rev. John 358 Richard 21
Richard, Esq. 21 Sarah Matilda
264
WOODMANSEE, Ella L. 511
WOODRUFF, Jehiel H. 51 Mary
298
WOODS, Eliza (Howell) 149 300
John 9 Josiah Howell 149 300
WOOLLEY, Richard 21
WOOLSTON, Elizabeth Barter 490
Emma L. (Bond) 490 James 490
WORTHINGTON, Edward 249
WOSEAS, Mr. 38
WRIGHT, Samuel 318
WYGANT, Elizabeth 329
YEAGER, Edna (Howell) 425
YEAGER, Edna (Howell), Personal
communication, 250 416 424
425 448 449
YORK, Asa Clinton 419 Benjamin F.
420 Charles 420 Frank 420
Henry 420 I. Howell 420 Lucy
H. 420 Mary Emily 420 Minnie
420 Miriam (Howell) 420
YOUNG, Abigail (Wells) 359
Addison 527 Ann W. 359
Arletta 226 Arminda 226
Christopher 328 Daniel 130
Emily Veola 452 George Lester
452 James 193 Jane (Cook) 488
John Corwin 360 Joshua 290

Lizzie 527 Luther 359 Marietta
290 Mary 130 227 Mary
(Halsey) 227 Mary Ella
(Hallock) 452 Melinda J. 488
Nancy 139 Phebe 227 Raymond
L. 526 Rev. Christopher 359
Rev. Daniel 227 Samuel 488
Sophronia (Benjamin) 290
Thomas 92 139
YOUNG, James Franklin, BAITING
HOLLOW - PEOPLE AND
PLACES, 24 25 32 43 85 86
325 326 488
YOUNG, Leigh Mark, THE
CONKLING FAMILIES OF THE
FIRST AQUEBOGUE
DIVISION, 43
YOUNGS, Abigail 61 Amy 125
Anna 324 Anna (Wells) 206
Aseph 389 Catherine 124
Catherine (Brown) 124 Charity
206 Charity J. (Howell) 385
386 Christopher 13 206 Daniel
55 61 124 125 Daniel R. 386
Dency 109 Dency Jane (Luce)
386 Dency Maria 389 Drusilla
386 Edna A. 386 Henry Wilson
386 James 97 James W. 384
Jeremiah 325 John 16 Josiah 13
Keziah (Reeve) 385 Leander
Edson 386 Mary (Penny) 61
Mehitable (Wells) 325 Noah
385 Noah Wilson 385 386
Parnell (Corwin) 389 Rev.
Daniel 215 Sarah Keziah 386
Violetta 255
YOUNGS, Selah, Jr., YOUNGS
FAMILY, 124 385 389

www.ingramcontent.com/pod-product-compliance
Lightning Source LLC
Chambersburg PA
CBHW060546280326
41932CB00011B/1409